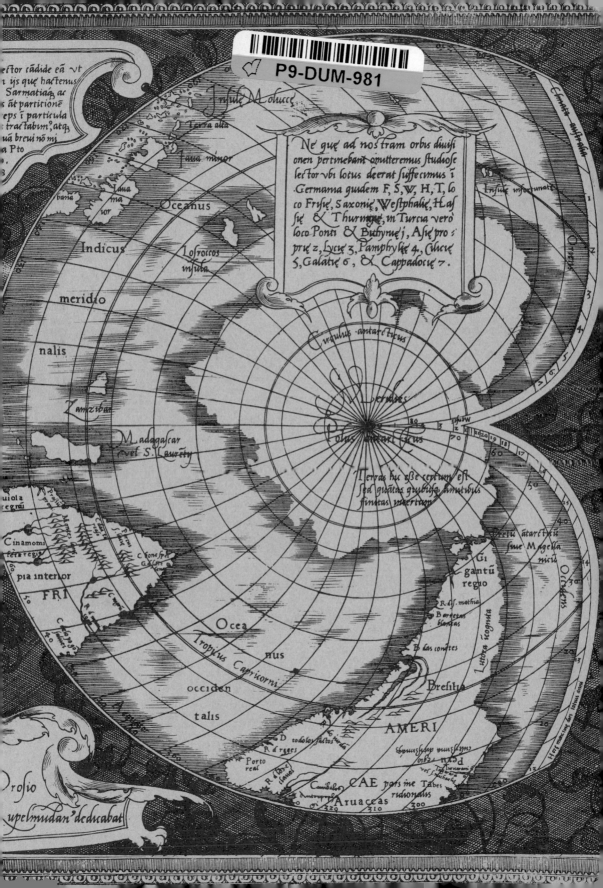

Beverly Gaston
1355 Center St.

THE WORLD SINCE 1500

THE WORLD

P R E N T I C E - H A L L , I N C .

L. S. STAVRIANOS

SINCE 1500

A Global History

Englewood Cliffs, N.J.

THE WORLD SINCE 1500:
A Global History

BY L. S. STAVRIANOS

Library of Congress Catalog Card Number: 66-12093

Printed in the United States of America

96813-C

Current printing (last digit):

10 9 8 7 6 5 4 3 2 1

PRENTICE-HALL INTERNATIONAL, INC., *London*
PRENTICE-HALL OF AUSTRALIA, PTY., LTD., *Sydney*
PRENTICE-HALL OF CANADA, LTD., *Toronto*
PRENTICE-HALL OF INDIA (PRIVATE) LTD., *New Delhi*
PRENTICE-HALL OF JAPAN, INC., *Tokyo*

Acknowledgments

W hile assuming full responsibility for all facts and interpretations in this book, I take pleasure in acknowledging the generous
help of the following scholars who read and criticized individual
chapters: Professors Gray C. Boyce, Richard M. Brace, Carl Condit,
George Daniels, Warren M. Gunderson, Karl de Schweinitz, Jr.,
Robert L. Hess, Jacques Hymans, Richard W. Leopold, John R.
McLane, Alfred J. Rieber, Franklin D. Scott, James E. Sheridan,
and Lacey Baldwin Smith, all of Northwestern University, and also
Helen Liebel of the University of Alberta, Theodore Rabb of Harvard
University, Edward Malefakis and John Meskill of Columbia Uni-
versity, Franklin C. West of Reed College, and, above all, Marshall
G. S. Hodgson of the University of Chicago, whose counsel and
concepts have been invaluable.

I am indebted to the staff of Deering Library at Northwestern
University for responding unfailingly to repeated requests and to the
staffs of the Newberry Library and the Chicago Natural History Museum for assistance in assembling and reproducing the illustrations.

I am also deeply appreciative of the patience and warm interest
in the venture shown by Mr. Edgar P. Thomas, Assistant Vice-
President, Prentice-Hall, Inc., and of the professional skill, percep-
tiveness, and unfailing good humor of my editors, Mrs. Maurine Lewis
and Mr. Cecil Yarbrough.

My wife, in this venture as in previous ones, has rendered invaluable research assistance and has shared in all the labors of authorship, both at home and abroad.

I should like to extend my thanks to the Carnegie Corporation of New York, which has contributed generously to the World History Project at Northwestern University, of which this study is a product.

The following authors and publishers gave permission for quotation of the epigraphs:

Geoffrey Barraclough's words on the page following the Contents are from *History in a Changing World* (Oxford: Basil Blackwell & Mott, Ltd., 1955), p. 18; the Gogol quotation on that page was cited in R. Rozdestvensky, "Nikolai Gogol on the Teaching of World History," *Comparative Education Review*, VII (June, 1963), 81. Étienne Gilson's *Les Metamorphoses de la Cité de Dieu* (Paris: Publications Universitaires de Louvain, 1942) is quoted on page 3. Arnold J. Toynbee's *The World and the West* (London: Oxford University Press, 1953) is quoted on pages 9 and 324; the third quotation from his writings, on page 506, is from *Survey of International Affairs, 1931* (London: Oxford University Press, 1932, under the auspices of the Royal Institute of International Affairs), p. 1. B. H. Sumner's *A Short History of Russia*, p. 1 (New York: Harcourt, Brace & World, Inc., 1943) is quoted on page 142. The quotation of Herbert Butterfield on page 185 is from his *Origins of Modern Science* (London: G. Bell & Sons, Ltd., 1957), p. 179. John U. Nef's words, on page 206, are reprinted by permission of the publishers from *War and Human Progress* (Cambridge, Mass.: Harvard University Press; copyright 1950 by the President and Fellows of Harvard College). Peter Chaadayev's *Apology of a Madman,* quoted on page 279, was cited in H. Kohn's *The Mind of Modern Russia* (New Brunswick, N. J.: Rutgers University Press, 1955), p. 50. H. A. R. Gibb's "Social Change in the Near East," which appears in P. W. Ireland, ed., *The Near East* (Chicago: The University of Chicago Press, 1942), p. 43, is quoted on page 302. J. K. Fairbank's "The Influence of Modern Western Science and Technology on Japan and China," from *Explorations in Entrepreneurial History,* VII, No. 4, is quoted on page 345. K. M. Panikkar's *Asia and Western Dominance,* published in England by George Allen & Unwin, Ltd., in the United States by The John Day Company, Inc., is quoted on page 431 by permission of the publishers; I have also quoted this work within the text, on pages 95 and 100–101. Hajo Holborn's *The Political Collapse of Europe* (New York: Alfred A. Knopf, Inc., 1951), p. x, and F. L. K. Hsu's *Americans and Chinese* (New York: Abelard-Schuman, Limited, 1953), p. 441, are quoted on page 645. The Bertrand Russell quotation on page 655 is from *Human Society in Ethics and Politics* (London: George Allen & Unwin, Ltd., 1954), p. 237.

Toward Freedom: The Autobiography of Jawaharlal Nehru (New York: The John Day Company, Inc., 1941) is quoted within the text, on page 477, by permission of the publisher. The quotation from Charles Merz's *And Then Came Ford* on page 221 (copyright 1929 by Doubleday & Company, Inc.) is reprinted by permission of the publisher.

Preface

All prefaces should be in capsule form; but this one should be a space capsule, a vehicle that will take the reader to the moon, where he can watch the whole planet as its significant events are illuminated in the pages that follow.

A global approach to history is not new. Indeed, it represents a return to the historiographic tradition of the Enlightenment, when the idea of universal history, as it was then called, fitted in with the prevailing views regarding progress. Prior to that period, Western historians had been constrained by the need to fit all known historical events into a rigid biblical context. Their custom was to divide the past into periods corresponding to the four world empires presaged in the book of Daniel: the Assyrian, the Persian, the Greek, and the Roman. But by the late seventeenth century this traditional approach was becoming increasingly inadequate in the face of new historical data concerning China and India. The first clear break with the old pattern came with Voltaire's *Essai sur les moeurs et l'esprit des nations* (1752) and the multivolume *Histoire universelle* (1736–1765), both of which dealt with China, India, and America, as well as with the traditional regions of biblical antiquity.

But interest in global history began to peter out by the end of the eighteenth century. The development of a more scientific attitude toward history set standards of reliable factual information that could not then be met in dealing with civilizations other than those of Greece and Rome. And perhaps a more important reason for a narrowed view was the rise of the militant nation-state, which stimulated national history instead of the earlier universal history. This restricted frame of reference prevailed at least until the First World War and to a large degree until the Second.

The past few decades, however, have witnessed the beginnings of a renewed interest in world history. The accelerating tempo of historical research has vastly enlarged the fund of dependable data, while the impact of the two world wars and of the scientific-technological revolution, with its remarkable advances in communication, has compelled general recognition of the fact of "One World." Symptomatic of the new trend are the *Outline of History* by H. G. Wells (1919), *The Great Cultural Traditions* by Ralph Turner (1941), and *The Rise of the West: A History of the Human Community* by William H. McNeill (1963), as well as the current UNESCO publications *Journal of World History* and *History of Mankind*.

This new interest has had little impact thus far on classroom teaching, apparently because of misgivings regarding the pedagogical viability of world history—doubts that are quite justified if it is assumed, as it too often is, that world history is the sum of the histories of all the countries or civilizations of the world. This assumption, of course, is preposterous. The Modern European History course, after all, does not deal in sequence with the histories of England, France, Germany, Italy, Russia, the Scandinavian countries, and the Balkan and Baltic countries. Rather, it considers the essential internal developments of the principal states, but equally important, it also traces those forces or movements that had a continentwide impact. The objectives of the Modern World History course are of a corresponding nature. Its aims are to analyze the essential characteristics and experiences of the major world regions, but equally important, to consider also those forces or movements that had a worldwide impact. Thus, it is not a matter of a greater number of facts in the World History course, but rather of a different angle of vision— a global rather than a regional or national perspective.

What this different angle of vision means may be illustrated concretely by considering the early modern period between the voyages of Columbus and the outbreak of the French Revolution. In the European History course, the principal topics usually considered for this period include: for the sixteenth century, dynastic conflicts, Protestant revolt, overseas expansion; for the seventeenth century, Thirty Years' War, rise of absolute monarchies, English Revolution; for the eighteenth century, dynastic and colonial wars, Enlightenment, enlightened despots.

Too often, the Modern World History course retains these traditional topics and adds others concerning developments in non-European regions. The net result is an overburdened course that is neither European nor world history. It is essential, therefore, to start afresh and to organize the course on a new and genuinely global basis. When this is done, it becomes apparent at once that the outstanding development of worldwide significance during this early modern period was the emergence of Western Europe. At the end of the fifteenth century, Europe was only one of four Eurasian centers of civilization, and by no means the most prominent. By the end of the eighteenth century,

Western Europe had gained control of the ocean routes, had organized an immensely profitable worldwide commerce, and had conquered vast territories in the Americas and in Siberia. Thus this period stands out in the perspective of world history as a period of transition from the regional isolation of the pre-1492 era to the West European global hegemony of the nineteenth century.

If the early modern period is appraised from this viewpoint, then it becomes apparent immediately that the traditional topics of European history are irrelevant for world history and must be discarded. In their place, accordingly, the following three general topics are emphasized in this study:

1. The roots of European expansion (why Europe, rather than one of the other Eurasian centers of civilization, expanded).

2. The Confucian, Moslem, and non-Eurasian worlds on the eve of Europe's expansion (their basic conditions and institutions, and the manner in which they affected the nature and course of European expansion).

3. The stages of European expansion (Iberian stage 1500–1600; Dutch, French, British stage 1600–1763; Russian stage in Siberia).

This organization makes clear the main trends in world history during these centuries, and in a manner no more difficult to comprehend than the very different organization usually followed in the European History course. Also it should be noted that the role of Western Europe in this early modern period is emphasized, not because of any Western orientation, but because from a global viewpoint Europe at this time was in fact the dynamic source of global change. This is true also of the nineteenth century when the unifying feature of world history was Europe's domination of the globe, and of the twentieth when the non-Western world reacted against Europe's hegemony. The fact is that since 1500 the West has been the region of innovation and decision in global affairs. Consequently, the history of the world in modern times centers on Europe, just as during the millennia before Christ it focuses for the same reason on the Middle East, and during certain centuries of the medieval period on the Mongol and Islamic Empires. This explains why the organization of this book is based essentially on Europe's emergence, dominance, and decline and triumph. But as indicated above and reflected in the chapter titles, focus does not preclude global perspective and coverage. Both are essential for a meaningful and viable World History course.

A word about the notes to the text, and then about the illustrations. Notes are of two kinds: source notes, and references to the readings in *The Epic of Modern Man: A Collection of Readings*. Source notes are numbered by chapter and are printed at the end of the text (pp. 673–85); references to the readings appear at the foot of the text page and are indicated by symbols.

Illustrations have been chosen to emphasize the three main periods of history since 1500; a few examples from each period may demonstrate this point:

The travels of Columbus, da Gama, and their successors altered Western man's vision of marvelous inhabitants of foreign lands ("The Wondrous People to be Found in Guinea," p. 93). Europeans discovered strange new people and customs in the underpopulated (and underdeveloped) Americas ("The Indians of South Carolina," p. 167). In Eurasia, they found much to admire in densely populated ancient empires, where they themselves were often kept at arm's length—at best admitted only as traders ("The Imperial Court of Peking," p. 179).

Scientific, economic, and political developments during the late eighteenth and the nineteenth centuries made Europe the master of the world. During this time, she effectively conquered and exploited entire continents; she sent out millions of emigrants, not only to the west, but also the ancient Eastern lands; she built canals and dams, plants and embassies. Pictures such as "Napoleon in Egypt," p. 263, and "The construction of the Suez Canal," p. 310, illustrate these events. How the colonial peoples reacted to the ubiquitous Europeans is illustrated in the wood carvings reproduced on p. 426.

By the twentieth century, the non-Western world had had enough of being conquered and exploited. All over the globe, the Western empires began to collapse ("The last British troops leave India," p. 601). But if this was the period of the West's decline, it was also that of its triumph, for Western science, technology, and government had been diffused throughout the globe ("Copper mining in Southern Rhodesia," p. 610). Indeed, the camera records substantial evidence that the idea of Western civilization has made the real conquest and has become the triumphant, benevolent dictator.

L. S. STAVRIANOS

This book is for
BERTHA, MARJORIE, and PETER

OTHER BOOKS BY L. S. STAVRIANOS:

The Balkans, 1815–1914

Balkan Federation: A History of the Movement Toward Balkan Unity in Modern Times

The Balkans Since 1453

The Epic of Modern Man: A Collection of Readings, editor

A Global History of Man (with others)

Greece: American Dilemma and Opportunity

The Ottoman Empire: Was It the Sick Man of Europe?

Readings in World History, editor (with others)

Contents

Part
III
WORLD OF WESTERN DOMINANCE, 1763–1914

Part
IV

WORLD OF WESTERN DECLINE AND TRIUMPH, 1914–

MAPS BY VAUGHN GRAY *(opposite listed pages):*

*By universal history I understand that
which is distinct from the combined history of
all countries, which is not a rope
of sand, but a continuous development, and
is not a burden on the memory but an illumination
of the soul. It moves in a succession
to which the nations are subsidiary.
Their story will be told, not for their own
sake, but in reference and subordination to a
higher series, according to the time
and the degree in which they contribute
to the common fortunes of mankind.*

LORD ACTON

*. . . universal history is more than
the sum of its parts; it cannot be divided
and subdivided without being denaturalized, much
as water, separated into its chemical
components, ceases to be water and
becomes hydrogen and oxygen.*

GEOFFREY BARRACLOUGH

*In its true meaning, universal history
is not a collection of separate histories
of all the nations and states without general
connection or common purpose;
nor is it a mass of occurrences in a lifeless
or dry form, in which it is too often
presented. . . . It must assemble in one
all the nations of the world,
separated by time, by accident, or by
mountains and seas, unite them in one
proportionate, harmonious whole and from them
compose one magnificent poem.*

NIKOLAI GOGOL

WORLD OF
ISOLATED REGIONS,
TO 1500

The throes of the contemporary world are those of a birth. And what is being born with such great pain is a universal human society. . . . What characterizes the events we witness, what distinguishes them from all preceding events back to the origins of history is . . . their global character.

ÉTIENNE GILSON

Chapter

1

Introduction: From Regional to Global History

Why should a study of world history begin with the year 1500? Man has existed on this globe for roughly one million years. Why then should this small fraction of one per cent of his total history be selected for special attention?

The answer is that until 1500, man had lived in regional isolation. The various racial groups had been scattered about in a pattern of virtual global segregation. Only about 1500 was there for the first time direct contact amongst them all. Not until approximately that date were they at last all brought together, whether South African Bushmen or cultivated Chinese Mandarins or primitive Patagonians.

The year 1500 represents, therefore, a major turning point in human history. Future historians probably will draw a parallel between Columbus breaking the bonds of regional isolation in landing on San Salvador and the astronaut or cosmonaut of the near future likewise breaking the bonds of planetary isolation in landing on the moon.

Indeed, world history in the strict global sense did not begin until the voyages of Columbus and da Gama and Magellan. Prior to their exploits, there were relatively parallel histories of separate peoples rather than one unified history of mankind. If the monogenetic theory of the origin of man is valid, there was a unity at the beginning. But during the long millennia of the Paleolithic, the human race gradually scattered over most of the earth's land surface. Then the ending of the Ice Age raised the level of the oceans, thereby separating Africa from Europe, the Americas from Northeast Asia, and Australia from Southeast Asia, to mention only the major disseverances.

Henceforth mankind lived in varying degrees of regional isolation. Some were completely cut off, such as the Australian aborigines, who had no contact with the outside world for the 50,000 years between the last migrations from Southeast Asia and the appearance of Captain James Cook. Almost as isolated were the inhabitants of North and South America, where the last crossings from Siberia had occurred some 10,000 years before Columbus. The few Norse expeditions to the northeast coast of North America and possible Polynesian landings in South America had no lasting repercussions on the Indian populations. Sub-Saharan Africa also became isolated to a considerable degree about 6,000 years ago, when the Sahara became dry enough to constitute a major barrier to human movement. Despite this formidable obstacle, the African Negroes did have limited and intermittent contacts with the outside world. Thanks largely to these contacts they enjoyed certain advantages denied to the American Indians and the Australian aborigines. Seafaring peoples from Southeast Asia brought the yam and the banana; Middle Easterners introduced the arts of mining, smelting, and forging iron; while the Arabs spread their civilization as well as their religion from bases in North and East Africa. These and other advances made possible more efficient exploitation of natural resources, greater production of food, a corresponding increase in population, and a general raising of culture levels.

The remaining portion of the globe consists of Europe, Asia, and North Africa, the last mentioned having had, throughout history, closer ties with the lands across the Mediterranean than with those across the Sahara. For purposes of convenience, this landmass, stretching from Morocco to Kamchatka and from Norway to Malaya, may be referred to as Eurasia. It is this Eurasia that constitutes the "heartland" of world history. It spreads over two-fifths of the land area of the globe and includes nine-tenths of the world's people. It is the place of origin of the earliest and most advanced civilizations of mankind. Prior to 1500, world history was essentially the history of Eurasia as here defined. Only in Eurasia was there continuous and substantial interaction of peoples and civilizations. While the Australian aborigines and the American Indians lived for millennia in virtually complete isolation, and the sub-Saharan Africans in semiseclusion, the Eurasians by contrast were exchanging technologies, ideas, institutions, and material goods.

This interaction within Eurasia was much less intensive before 1500 than after, when direct sea contact was established amongst all regions. During the pre-1500 period, interaction varied greatly from era to era. In general, it was most limited in the early millennia, and then gradually increased in scope and tempo. The ancient civilizations that flourished in the Nile, Tigris-Euphrates, Indus, and Yellow River valleys during the pre-Christian millennia were confined mostly to their restricted localities. There was, of course, some give and take; indeed, the very origin of civilization in these various regions is explained by the diffusion of the arts of civilization from Mesopotamia. Yet the fact remains that these early civilizations were tightly circumscribed oases surrounded by vast stretches of barbarism, across which there was relatively little communication.

This pattern changed radically during the centuries of the classical civilizations. By A.D. 100, when the classical age was at its height, the Roman Empire extended around the entire Mediterranean basin, the Parthian Empire stretched across the Middle East, the Kushan Empire covered northwestern India, and the Chinese Han Empire included all the remaining territory eastward to the Pacific Ocean. Thus the political units of the period encompassed entire regions rather than single river valleys, and the civilized world extended in a continuous band from the Scottish highlands to Southeast Asia. As a result, there came to be interregional contacts of a new magnitude and of all varieties. This was the period when religions such as Christianity and Buddhism began to spread over large areas of Eurasia, with far-reaching political and cultural as well as religious repercussions. At this time also the mixed Greek–Middle Eastern culture known as Hellenism spread from the eastern Mediterranean in all directions—to Western Europe, North Africa, India, and to a certain degree to China and Japan. This was also a period of greatly increased interregional trade. Both by land and by sea there was an exchange of linen, copper, tin, and glass from the Roman Empire; cotton textiles, aromatics, and precious stones from India; spices from Southeast Asia; and, above all, silk from China.

Later, in the Middle Ages, there was even more interaction amongst Eurasian peoples, with the establishment for the first time of great interregional empires. Between 632 and 750 the Moslems conquered an empire stretching from the Pyrenees to the Indian Ocean, and from Morocco to the borders of China. In later centuries Islam expanded much further into Central Asia, India, Southeast Asia, and Africa's interior. Even more impressive was the thirteenth century Mongol Empire that included Korea, China, all of Central Asia, Russia, and most of the Middle East.

Indicative of the new horizons opening up were the exploits of famous travelers who now took advantage of the peace and security prevailing in the Moslem and Mongol empires, to journey back and forth across the breadth of Eurasia. Best known in the West is the Venetian Marco Polo (1254–1324) who entered the service of the Mongol ruler, Kublai Khan, functioned as governor of a Chinese city of a million inhabitants, and after twenty-five years returned home to astound his fellow citizens with tales of his adventures. Even more extensive were the travels of the Moslem Ibn Battuta (1304–1378). Starting from his native Morocco, he made the pilgrimage to Mecca and journeyed on through Samarkand to India where he served as judge and also as ambassador to China. Returning later to Morocco, he resumed his travels, crossing north to Spain and then south to Central Africa, where he reached Timbuktu. Less well-known is Rabban Bar Sauma, a Nestorian monk who was born in Peking and who traveled across Eurasia from east to west. In 1287 he reached the Mongol court in Mesopotamia and then went through Constantinople to Naples, Rome, Paris, and London, meeting en route both Philip IV of France and Edward I of England.

This integration and interaction within Eurasia did not proceed uninterruptedly. Empires fell and rose; channels of communication closed and opened. The flourishing silk trade between China and the West dwindled to

6

a trickle with the collapse of the Roman and Han empires. Likewise, European merchants were not able for long to follow in Marco Polo's footsteps because of the early disintegration of the Mongol Empire. Yet the fact remains that during this entire pre-1500 period, Eurasia was a dynamic and self-renewing unit in comparison with the scattered and isolated lands of the non-Eurasian world.

This basic difference in the degree of isolation prevailing within Eurasia compared to the rest of the globe is of primary importance for world history. Its significance is indicated by the following observation of the distinguished anthropologist Franz Boas:

> The history of mankind proves that advances of culture depend upon the opportunities presented to a social group to learn from the experience of their neighbors. The discoveries of the group spread to others and, the more varied the contacts, the greater the opportunities to learn. The tribes of simplest culture are on the whole those that have been isolated for very long periods and hence could not profit from the cultural achievements of their neighbors.[1]

In other words, *if other geographic factors are equal,* the key to human progress is accessibility and interaction. Those people who are the most accessible and who have the most opportunity to interact with other people are the most likely to forge ahead. Those who are isolated and receive no stimulus from the outside are likely to stand still.

If this hypothesis is applied on a global scale, the remote Australian aborigines should have been the most retarded of all major groups; next, the American Indians in the New World; then the Negroes of sub-Saharan Africa; and finally, the least retarded, or the most advanced, the various peoples of Eurasia who were in constant and generally increasing contact with each other. This, of course, is precisely the gradation of culture levels found by the European discoverers after 1500. The Australian aborigines were still at the Paleolithic food-gathering stage; the American Indians varied from the Paleolithic tribes of California to the impressive civilizations of Mexico, Central America, and Peru; the African Negroes presented comparable diversity, though their over-all level of development was higher; and finally, at quite another level, there were the highly advanced and sophisticated civilizations found in Eurasia—the Moslem in the Middle East, the Hindu in South Asia, and the Confucian in East Asia.

If the Boas hypothesis is applied to Eurasia alone, it helps to explain the traditional primacy of the Middle East. Centrally located at the crossroads of three continents, the Middle East was in fact the region that pioneered in human progress during most of history. It was here that agriculture, urban life, and civilization originated, as well as the Christian, Judaistic, and Islamic religions. It is significant also that after civilization got under way in the Middle East about 3700 B.C., it then took root in India about 2500 B.C., and finally, about 1500 B.C., in China on the isolated eastern tip of Eurasia, and in Western Europe on the isolated western tip.

During almost all of the pre-1500 period, Western Europe was what today would be termed an underdeveloped area. Its peoples were on the periphery—

on the outside looking in. That they were quite conscious of being isolated and vulnerable is evident in the following account by the twelfth century English chronicler William of Malmesbury:

7

> The world is not evenly divided. Of its three parts, our enemies hold Asia as their hereditary home—a part of the world which our fore-fathers rightly considered equal to the other two put together. Yet here formerly our Faith put out its branches; here all the Apostles save two met their deaths. But now the Christians of those parts, if there are any left, squeeze a bare subsistence from the soil and pay tribute to their enemies, looking to us with silent longing for the liberty they have lost. Africa, too, the second part of the world, has been held by our enemies by force of arms for two hundred years and more, a danger to Christendom all the greater because it formerly sustained the brightest spirits— men whose works will keep the rust of age from Holy Writ as long as the Latin tongue survives. Thirdly, there is Europe, the remaining region of the world. Of this region we Christians inhabit only a part, for who will give the name of Christians to those barbarians who live in the remote islands and seek their living on the icy ocean as if they were whales? This little portion of the world which is ours is pressed upon by warlike Turks and Saracens: for three hundred years they have held Spain and the Balearic Islands, and they live in hope of devouring the rest.[2]

How different were these fearful medieval Europeans from their confident and aggressive descendents who set out from their beleaguered peninsula, won control of the oceanic routes, became the besiegers rather than the besieged, and thereby determined the main course of world history to the present day! This surprising denouement raises a fundamental question: Why was it the Western Europeans who assumed this fateful role? In view of their previously modest influence on world affairs, why was it they rather than Arabs or the Chinese who brought together the continents of the world and thus began the global phase of world history? *

SUGGESTED READING

The post-World War II period has witnessed renewed interest in world history, the most significant manifestation being W. H. McNeill's *The Rise of the West: A History of the Human Community* (Chicago: Univ. of Chicago, 1963). This justifiably acclaimed work is the most comprehensive, integrated, and globally oriented study of its kind. By contrast, the well-known works of Toynbee and Spengler are not world histories, strictly speaking, but rather interpretations in the comparative study of civilizations. Nevertheless, they present a vast amount of factual data and stimulating hypotheses. Another manifestation of the current in-

* See "World History in Modern Education," Reading No. 1 in *The Epic of Modern Man: A Collection of Readings*, by L. S. Stavrianos (Englewood Cliffs, New Jersey: Prentice-Hall, Inc., 1966). Subsequent footnote references to this volume (distinguished by their symbols from the numbered source notes printed on pages 673–85) will have the following form: See "World History in Modern Education," *EMM*, No. 1.

terest in world history is UNESCO's *Journal of World History* published since 1953, and UNESCO's multivolume *History of Mankind: Cultural and Scientific Development,* of which the first volume has appeared: J. Hawkes and L. Woolley, *Prehistory and the Beginnings of Civilization* (London: Allen, 1963). Finally, stimulating essays on various aspects of world history are to be found in G. Barraclough, *History in a Changing World* (Oxford: Blackwell, 1955); C. Dawson, *Dynamics of World History* (New York: Sheed, 1956); R. Grousset, *The Sum of History* (London: Tower Bridge, 1951); and K. Jaspers, *The Origin and Goal of History* (New Haven: Yale Univ., 1953).

Roots of West European Expansion

In the late Middle Ages, a curious and fateful development occurred in the Eurasian world. On the one hand, Islamic and Confucian empires were becoming increasingly ossified and were withdrawing into themselves. On the other hand, the western tip of Eurasia was experiencing an unprecedented and thoroughgoing transformation. Far-reaching changes were taking place in almost all phases of West European life. One manifestation of this new dynamism was the great expansion overseas.

This expansion vitally affected the future history of the entire globe. It gave the Western Europeans control of the ocean routes. It enabled them to reach, conquer, and populate vast and relatively empty territories in the Americas and Australasia, thus transforming the traditional territorial distribution of the races of the world. Eventually, Western Europe derived such wealth and strength from this expansion that in the nineteenth century she was able to penetrate and to dominate even the old established centers of Eurasian civilization in the Middle East, in India, and in China.

All this was absolutely unprecedented in the history of mankind. Never before had one part of the globe succeeded in dominating the remainder. The repercussions inevitably were profound. The globe attained a new and unique unity. Interregional ties—economic, intellectual, and political—were formed, slowly at first, but steadily and inexorably, until the Eurasian phase of world history ended and the global phase began.

10   The paradoxical feature of these momentous developments is that they were initiated and carried through by the region of Eurasia that hitherto had been the least developed and the least conspicuous. Prior to the late Middle Ages, Western Europe had lagged behind in most fields. She had received more than she had given in cultural matters. Her economy had lagged in certain respects, so that she had eagerly sought the spices of South Asia and the silk of China, while having little to offer in return. And certainly in military matters, the pattern of invasion had been much more from East to West than in the opposite direction.

What, then, is the explanation for this remarkable, unexpected turnabout? Why did Western Europe suddenly become such a dynamic force in world affairs? The explanation is not to be found in any one factor or in any single event, such as Columbus' landing in the New World. The Vikings had stumbled on North America in the eleventh century and for about 100 years had tried to maintain settlements there, but they failed to do so. In contrast, Columbus was followed by people from all countries of Europe in a massive and overwhelming penetration of both North and South America along the Atlantic seaboard. The difference in the reaction between the eleventh and the fifteenth centuries suggests that certain developments had occurred in the intervening half millenium that made Europe able and willing to expand overseas. The nature and the unfolding of these developments is the problem that we shall now consider.

I. Crusading Christendom

The expansion of Europe may be explained in part by the expansionism of European Christianity. This religion, in contrast to the other great religions of Eurasia, was imbued with universalism, proselytizing zeal, and crusading militancy.* From the beginning, Christianity, by its emphasis on the brotherhood of man, asserted itself as a universal religion, and missionary activity has characterized the Christian church from the days of the apostles to the present. Furthermore, there has been no hesitancy to employ force in securing conversion. One element of Christianity is derived from the God of Wrath and Vengeance worshiped by Hebrew nomads. Christian writers have frequently employed military analogies, viewing the terrestrial world as a battlefield between the forces of God and of the Devil. It is not surprising, then, that Christian leaders have not hesitated to employ forceful methods in following the command "Go ye into all the world and preach the Gospel to every creature" (Mark 16:15).

The militancy of Christendom was also a reaction to repeated invasion from the East in earlier periods. As an outlying, backward, and thinly populated protuberance of the Eurasian landmass, Europe had suffered the ravages of heathen and infidel Indo-Europeans, Germans, Huns, Magyars, and Arabs. The medieval European consequently lived on a great frontier where he faced Moslem Arabs in the South and heathen Slavic and Baltic peoples in the East.

* See "Religion and the Expansion of Europe," *EMM*, No. 2.

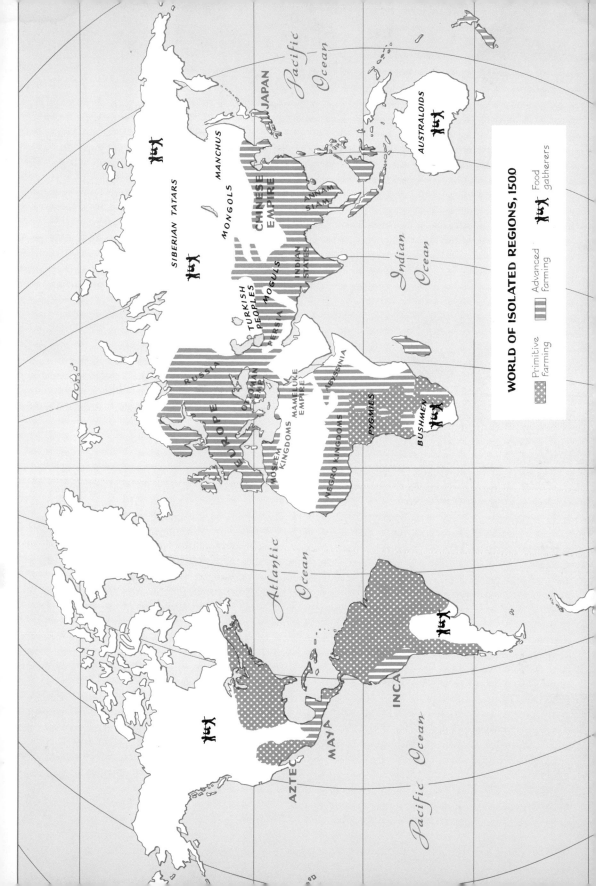

WORLD OF ISOLATED REGIONS, 1500

Primitive farming | Advanced farming | Food gatherers

His response was a long series of crusades, of which those to the Holy Land were the most ambitious and the best known but the least successful. Whereas the Christian toeholds in Syria and Palestine were lost to the Moslems in the thirteenth century, other crusades had more lasting results. The Normans drove the Arabs from Sicily about 1100. The Iberian Christians carried on for two centuries a *reconquista* against the Moslems and by 1250 had won the entire peninsula except Granada in the extreme South. The Teutonic Order in the twelfth and thirteenth centuries carried Christianity at the point of the sword into Prussia and the Baltic lands.

Thus Europe had a long-established crusading tradition, and the expansion overseas represented, in one sense, a continuation of this tradition. The early explorers and their backers were motivated partly by religious considerations. They wanted to reach the great countries of India and China whose existence had been known to Europeans since the thirteenth century travels of Marco Polo. These countries were known not to be Moslem, and so it was hoped that they might join forces with the Christians. Also there was the enduring medieval legend of Prester (or Priest) John, reputed to be a powerful Christian ruler somewhere out in the vague East. For centuries, Christian leaders had dreamed of establishing contact with him and launching a great assault upon the Moslem world from both east and west. The Europeans did not find Prester John, but they did stumble upon strange new peoples in Africa and the Americas—peoples who were barbarians and heathens and, therefore, fit subjects for conquest, conversion, and redemption.

God, along with gold, was perhaps the most compelling of the many motives that led Europeans to begin their overseas enterprises. Vasco da Gama, on arrival at Calicut, explained to the surprised Indians that he had come in search of Christians and spices. Likewise, the conquistador Bernal Díaz wrote in his memoirs that he and his comrades went to the New World "to serve God and His Majesty, to give light to those who were in darkness, and to grow rich, as all men desire to do." [1] Protestants of northern Europe also were motivated by religious considerations in their overseas ventures, though to a lesser degree than the Iberians. Sir Francis Drake, in propagandizing for settlements in America, wrote:

> Their gain shall be the knowledge of our Faith
> and ours such riches as the country hath.[2]

This militancy and proselytizing spirit were noticeably absent amongst the other peoples of Eurasia. The Moslems, it is true, were militant in the sense that they conquered far-flung provinces with the sword. But on the whole, they were indifferent to the religious beliefs of their subjects. Usually they were much more interested in their subjects' paying tribute than in their embracing Islam. The Moslems had little of the Christians' consuming zeal that the souls of the heathen must be saved from perdition. Likewise, the adoption of Buddhism outside India was the result not so much of deliberate missionary enterprise as of a gradual diffusion of Indian culture by peaceful travelers and immigrants. Buddhism spread not by force but by the appeal of its teaching and of its ritual.

The Chinese were perhaps the least dogmatic in matters of religion. The

12

early Christian missionaries to China invariably were impressed by the live-and-let-live attitude that they encountered. They were agreeably surprised by the freedom with which they were allowed to spread the Gospel. In 1326 Bishop Andrew of Perugia wrote, " 'Tis a fact that in this vast empire there are people of every nation under heaven, and of every sect, and all and sundry are allowed to live freely according to their creed. For they hold this opinion, or rather this erroneous view, that everyone can find salvation in his own religion. Howbeit we are at liberty to preach without let or hindrance." [3] Likewise the great Italian Jesuit Matteo Ricci, who lived in China between 1582 and 1610, expressed his astonishment at the religious toleration and lack of militancy and aggressiveness on the part of the Chinese.

> In conclusion to our consideration of the religious sects, at the present time, the most commonly accepted opinion of those who are at all educated among the Chinese is, that these . . . cults really coalesce into one creed and that all of them can and should be believed. In such a judgment, of course, they are leading themselves and others into the very distracting error of believing that the more different ways there are of talking about religious questions, the more beneficial it will be for the public good.
>
> . . . it seems to be quite remarkable when we stop to consider it, that in a kingdom of almost limitless expanse and innumerable population, and abounding in copious supplies of every description, though they have a well-equipped army and navy that could easily conquer the neighboring nations, neither the King nor his people ever think of waging a war of aggression. They are quite content with what they have and are not ambitious of conquest. In this respect they are much different from the people of Europe, who are frequently discontent with their own governments and covetous of what others enjoy. While the nations of the West seem to be entirely consumed with the idea of supreme domination, they cannot even preserve what their ancestors have bequeathed them, as the Chinese have done through a period of some thousands of years.[4]

This difference in degree of proselytizing zeal among the world's religions is apparent to the present day. It is difficult to imagine any but a Christian clergyman adopting the following position enunciated in 1958 by the Methodist Bishop Marvin A. Franklin of Jackson, Mississippi, in the course of a discussion concerning space control.

> Assuming that there are other inhabited planets and stars, we would be compelled to find out how God has revealed himself to these "other sheep" before we could determine what responsibility the Christian church would have for them. It is fascinating to conjecture what their concept of God would be, whether they have fallen short of the glory of God, and have need of the same pattern of salvation which we know. It may be revealed that the Christian church must take to them the experience of the divine-human encounter which we know and introduce them to redemptive processes of the gospel of Christ. Whatever the con-

ditions discovered may call for, the Christian church will be pioneering and daring enough to meet them.[5]

II. NEW INTELLECTUAL HORIZONS

Much less clear than the religious background of West European expansion is its intellectual history. The so-called "Renaissance ferment" involved the growth of individualism and of secularism. The theological and ecclesiastical control of life was challenged and ultimately replaced by new moral and social values arrived at by individual inquiry. A new conception of man himself gradually emerged—a new confidence in his dignity and creativity. Man did not need to be preoccupied with forebodings of divine judgment in afterlife. He had but to develop his innate potentialities and, above all, his power to reason. Erasmus, the Dutch monk and scholar, expressed this triumphant awareness that man is neither a beast nor a savage.

> Now it is the possession of Reason which constitutes a Man. If trees or wild beasts grow, men, believe me, are fashioned. Men in olden time who led their life in forests, driven by the mere needs and desires of their natures, guided by no laws, with no ordering in communities, are to be judged rather as savage beasts than as men.[6]

The new emphasis on man and on what he himself could accomplish obviously was more conducive to overseas expansion than the preceding medieval outlook. On the other hand, this point can easily be exaggerated and needs serious modification. The fact is that Renaissance Europe was not science oriented. The leading figures tended to be more aesthetic and philosophical than objective and skeptical. They retained in various degrees certain medieval patterns of thought. They persisted in admiring and believing the incredible and the fantastic. They continued to seek the philosopher's stone that would convert other metals into gold. They still believed in astrology and confused it with astronomy. Nor did the Reformation modify this antihumanist bias. In the sixteenth century, Luther's and Calvin's view of man as helpless and depraved was just as new as the humanists' glorification of man, and far more influential. Indeed, the Reformation represented an antisecular and antipractical strain that, if anything, became stronger during the sixteenth century.

The Iberian pioneers of overseas expansion definitely were not Renaissance men. Prince Henry the Navigator, for example, was described by his contemporaries as a rigid, pious, and chivalrous ascetic rather than as a humanist. Although a generous patron of sailors and cartographers, he was not interested in learning and the arts. The story of a school of astronomy and mathematics that he allegedly supported at Sagres is a myth. "However Renaissance be defined," states a distinguished historian of European expansion, ". . . the early process of discovery began independently, with medieval motives and assumptions. Prince Henry and his captains were, in the main, men of the Middle Ages. Even Columbus . . . embarked on his famous enterprise with an intellectual equipment which was mainly medieval and traditional." [7]

14

The "new intellectual horizons," then, explain not so much the origins of European expansion before 1500, as its impetus and irresistible power after 1600. The latter, however, is vastly significant in its own right. The fact remains that there was an intellectual ferment in Western Europe and that it had no counterpart in the rest of Eurasia. This is a fundamental difference of enormous import.

In China, Confucianism continued to dominate society. Its esteem for age over youth, for the past over the present, for established authority over innovation made it an unequaled instrument for the preservation of the *status quo* in all its aspects. The resulting atmosphere of conformity and orthodoxy, precluding the possibility of continued intellectual development, helps to explain why China fell behind the West in technology, despite its brilliant initial achievements in developing paper, printing, gunpowder, and the compass. These early inventions were not followed by the formulation of a body of scientific principles.

The situation was basically the same in the other Eurasian lands. In the Ottoman Empire, for example, the Moslem *medressehs* or colleges emphasized theology, jurisprudence, and rhetoric at the expense of astronomy, mathematics and medicine. The graduates of these schools were uninformed about what was being done in the West and quite uninterested in finding out. No Moslem Turk could believe that a Christian infidel could teach him anything of value. Now and then, a rare, far-sighted individual warned of the dangers of this intellectual iron curtain that separated the Ottoman Empire from neighboring Christendom. One of these voices was Katib Chelebi, the famous Turkish bibliographer, encyclopedist, and historian who lived in the first half of the seventeenth century. Coming from a poor family, he was unable to obtain a formal higher education. This proved to be a blessing in disguise. He was spared the superficial, hair-splitting specialization on Moslem sacred studies that characterized Ottoman education at this time. The fact that he was self-taught explains in large part his open-mindedness towards Western learning.

One of Chelebi's works was a short naval handbook that he compiled following a disastrous defeat of the Ottoman fleet in 1656. In the preface of this work, Chelebi emphasized the need for mastering the science of geography and map-making.

> For men who are in charge of affairs of state, the science of geography is a matter of which knowledge is necessary. They may not be familiar with what the entire globe is like, but they ought at least to know the map of the Ottoman State and of those states adjoining it. Then, when they have to send forces on campaign, they can proceed on the basis of knowledge, and so the invasion of the enemy's land and also the protection and defense of the frontiers becomes an easier task. Taking counsel with individuals who are ignorant of that science is no satisfactory substitute, not even when such men are local veterans. Most such veterans are entirely unable to sketch the map of their own home regions.
>
> Sufficient and convincing proof of the necessity for learning this science is the fact that the heathen, by their application to and their

esteem for those branches of learning, have discovered the New World and have over-run the markets of India.[8]

Chelebi grasped the connection between Europe's intellectual advance and her overseas expansion. In his last work before his death in 1657, Chelebi warned his countrymen that if they did not abandon their dogmatism they would soon "be looking at the universe with the eyes of oxen." His prediction proved prophetic. The Turks remained steeped in their religious obscurantism, and like other non-Western peoples, they paid a high price. The Christian infidels with their new learning eventually became the masters not only of the New World but of the ancient empires of Islam and of Confucianism.

III. Expanding Economy

An indisputable and obvious factor in Western Europe's overseas expansion was the marked economic growth of that region during the Middle Ages. The burgeoning economic resources and the dynamism of the area made possible the massive response to Columbus' discovery of the New World, in contrast to the negligible and futile reaction to the Viking expeditions. Europe's economy, it should be noted, did not grow uninterruptedly during the medieval period. There was a steady rise from 900 to 1300, but then came the fourteenth century slump, brought on by a combination of factors: a series of crop failures and famines, especially during 1315 and 1316; the Black Death, which carried off between one-third and two-thirds of the urban populations when it first struck in 1348–1349 and which recurred periodically thereafter for generations; and the Hundred Years' War between England and France, and other conflicts in Germany and Italy. Shortly after 1400, however, a revival set in, and the trend from then on was generally upward.

Apart from the fourteenth century decline, then, Western Europe experienced fairly steady economic growth after the early medieval centuries. One reason for the advance was the cessation of invasions after 1000, with the ending of the Magyar and Viking attacks. This was most significant, for it spared Western Europe the devastation suffered in Eastern Europe from the series of onslaughts that persisted until the defeat of the Turks at the end of the seventeenth century. It is not sufficiently recognized that Eastern Europe functioned as a shock absorber for the West during those centuries and thereby contributed substantially to the latter's progress.

This also explains in part the marked increase of population in Central and Western Europe between the tenth and fourteenth centuries. Population grew then about 50 per cent, a rate of increase that seems insignificant today but that was unmatched at the time in any equivalent world area. This demographic spurt stimulated improvements in agriculture to support the growth of population, and the increased food supply in turn made possible further population increase.

Europe's rising agricultural output was obtained in two ways. One was through intensive development—through improved methods of cultivation.

Outstanding in this respect was the gradual adoption from the eighth century onward of the three-field system of farming, which raised productivity substantially, since only a third of the land was allowed to lie fallow instead of half. Agriculture was aided also by more effective use of horsepower. In antiquity the horse had been of little use on the farm because the yoke then employed strangled the horse if he pulled too hard. Moreover, without nailed shoes, the horse often broke his hoofs and became useless. By the tenth century, however, Europe had developed the horse collar, which rests on the horse's shoulders and does not choke the neck. In addition, the horseshoe was invented, and also the tandem harness, which allows more than one pair of horses to pull a load. The net result was that the horse, fast and efficient compared to the ox, was henceforth an essential source of power in farming operations.

Europe's agricultural output was raised also through extensive development, through opening up areas that had not been farmed before. It is a startling but true fact that in the twelfth century only about half the land of France, a third of the land of Germany, and a fifth of the land of England was under cultivation. The rest was forest, swamp, waste. All around the edges of the small, tilled regions were larger, untilled areas open for colonization. Into these vacant spaces the European peasants streamed, preparing the way for the plow and hoe by clearing forests, burning brushwood, and draining swamps. The peasants not only cultivated the unused lands in their midst but also migrated eastward into the vast underpopulated areas of Eastern and Southern Europe. Just as the United States had its westward movement to the Pacific Ocean, so Europe had its eastward movement to the Russian border. By 1350 in Silesia, for example, there were 1,500 new settlements farmed by 150,000 to 200,000 colonists.

The beckoning frontier loosened the bonds of serfdom. The old restrictions and exactions could not be imposed indefinitely when it became known that cheap land and personal freedom were available to the east. The lords had to modify their demands or else risk the flight of their serfs. It is true that later, in the fifteenth and sixteenth centuries, serfdom was imposed on the hitherto free settlers east of the Elbe. The lords clamped on the bonds in order to be assured of the labor supply necessary to take advantage of the rising prices and the growing market for grain and forest products. But in the meantime the peasants in the West became and remained substantially free, though the final lifting of restrictions had to await the French Revolution at the end of the eighteenth century. This weakening of serfdom was a prerequisite to the expansion of Europe. It created a more fluid society that could accumulate the capital and provide the organization and free manpower needed for the work of exploration, conquest, and settlement. It is not accidental that among the European nations the degree of success in overseas enterprise was in direct ratio to the degree of liberation from the bonds of feudalism.

The growth of population and of agriculture stimulated a corresponding growth of commerce and of cities. From new farm lands, surplus food was shipped back to more densely populated western areas that, in return, provided the tools and the manufactured goods needed by frontier regions. Thus commerce flourished and towns grew up, especially along the Baltic coast. This economic growth is very important. It represents the beginning of the rise of northwestern Europe, a trend that later helped the British and the Dutch to overshadow the Spaniards and the Portuguese throughout the world.

Commerce was growing not only within Europe, but also between Europe and the outside world. Here, again, growth began with the end of the Viking raids, the terror that had dominated European coasts from the Arctic to Sicily in the ninth and tenth centuries. Another impetus was provided by the Crusades, from the eleventh century onward. The tens of thousands of Europeans who had participated in the expeditions returned with an appetite for the strange and luxurious commodities that they had seen and enjoyed. Also, the Crusades enabled the Europeans to snatch the Mediterranean from the hands of the Moslems and to make it once again the great trade route between East and West that it had been in ancient times. A third reason for the growth of international trade was the establishment in the thirteenth century of the Mongol Empire, which imposed an unprecedented unity upon most of the vast Eurasian landmass. European traders, especially the Italians, taking advantage of the peace, security, and well-serviced routes, traded almost directly with the Orient.

This extension and intensification of commercial relations had important repercussions. Europe's economy became geared to international trade to a much greater degree than did the economies of the relatively self-sufficient empires of the East. Both the consumer and the producer in Europe became accustomed to, and dependent upon, foreign commodities and foreign markets. As population increased, the scale of operations also increased. This demographic pressure, together with the spur of competition between nations and city-states, drove merchants to seek new sources, new routes, new markets. Their competitive attitude was very different from that of the contemporary Chinese who voyaged several thousand miles for completely noneconomic reasons (see section VII, this chapter). Being quite uninterested in trade, they brought back to their self-contained homeland curiosities such as giraffes for the pleasure of their emperor. For obvious geographic reasons, Europe was far from being self-contained, having urgent need for spices and other foreign products. This need, together with the burgeoning economic activity and vitality, eventually put European shipping on every ocean and European merchants in every port.*

IV. DEVELOPMENT OF TECHNOLOGY

Closely related to the expanding economy was the developing technology,† a prerequisite for Europe's expansion, since it would have been physically impossible for Europeans to reach India or the Americas without adequate ships and navigation instruments. Their success in effecting technological breakthroughs in these areas is to be explained by the steady, unspectacular, but immensely significant progress made during the medieval period in improving tools and techniques.

A distinguished American historian, Professor Lynn White, has observed

* See "Economic Motive and the Expansion of Europe," *EMM*, No. 4.
† See "Technology and the Expansion of Europe," *EMM*, No. 3.

that "the chief glory of the later Middle Ages was not its cathedrals or its epics or its scholasticism: it was the building for the first time in history of a complex civilization which rested not on the backs of sweating slaves or coolies but primarily on non-human power." [9] Examples of this "non-human" source of power were the watermills and windmills that were developed and used for grinding cereal, cutting wood, and draining swamps and mines. Other useful inventions included the carpenter's plane, the crank, the wheelbarrow, the spinning wheel, and the canal lock. Indeed, the Greeks and the Romans, despite their lofty achievements in philosophy and art, did less in a thousand years to relieve human toil through machine power than the medieval Europeans did in a few centuries. Presumably this is to be explained by the stimulus to invention provided by the relative lack of manpower in Europe together with the labor-demanding tasks of an underdeveloped, frontier-type community. This tendency of the medieval European to shift from a slave or serf economy to a machine-power economy injected a novel and dynamic element into Western culture.

An interesting illustration of the technological progress made by the Western Europeans during the medieval period is to be found in a letter written in 1444 by a Greek scholar, Cardinal Bessarion. This scholar, who had lived many years in Rome, was impressed by the advanced state of handicrafts in Italy. So he wrote to Constantine Palaeologos, then ruler of the autonomous Byzantine province of Morea, suggesting that "four or eight young men" should be sent to Italy surreptitiously to learn Italian craft skills, and to learn Italian "so as to be conversant with what is said." Bessarion was particularly impressed by the water-driven sawmills that eliminated hand labor. He referred to "wood cut by automatic saws, mill-wheels moved as quickly and as neatly as can be." Likewise he had in mind water-driven bellows when he wrote that "in the smelting and separation of metals they have leather bellows which are distended and relaxed untouched by any hand, and separate the metal from the useless and earthy matter that may be present." Bessarion also reported that in Italy "one may easily acquire knowledge of the making of iron, which is so useful and necessary to Man." The significance of this testimony is apparent. The technological advances made by medieval Western Europe had been of such magnitude that for the first time an Easterner was recommending that pupils should be sent to the West to learn the "practical arts." [10]

So far as the expansion of Europe was concerned, the most significant technological advances were those in shipbuilding, in the instruments and techniques of navigation, and in naval armaments. Between 1200 and 1500 the tonnage of the average European ship doubled or trebled. Slender galleys with a burden of 150 to 200 tons gave way to round-hulled sailing ships of 600 to 800 tons. The stern rudder, adopted in the thirteenth century, rapidly displaced the older and less efficient lateral steering devices. Equally important was the adaptation by the Portuguese in the fourteenth century of the Arab lateen rig which enabled vessels to sail more directly into the wind. These advances in the construction and rigging of ships represented a combination of features originally developed in Northern Europe, in the Mediterranean, and in the Middle East. The net result was a ship that was larger, speedier, and more maneuverable. It was also more economical because the elimination of 100 to 200 oarsmen with their food and equipment greatly increased the cargo space.

Hand in hand with these advances in shipbuilding went those in the art of navigation. The most important contributions in this field came from the Mediterranean. The Chinese appear to have possessed a magnetic compass, but it is not certain that the Europeans acquired it from them or from Arab intermediaries. It may have been developed independently by the Europeans in the twelfth century, possibly in the Italian city of Amalfi. In any case, the compass was the most useful single instrument for navigators, but it was supplemented by several others. The astrolabe, a graduated brass circle for estimating the altitude of heavenly bodies, was known before 800 but was first used in Western navigation by the Portuguese about 1485. It was an expensive instrument and was soon replaced by the simpler and cheaper quadrant. The determination of longitude presented more of a problem. A rough estimate could be gained by means of an hour glass but precise reckoning had to await Galileo's discovery of the principles of the pendulum in the seventeenth century.

Navigators were also aided by compilations of nautical information and by maps. The *portolani* of the Mediterranean seamen were the first true maps, furnished with accurate compass bearings and explicit details concerning coastlines and harbors. The art of map-making became fairly well developed by the fourteenth century, the leading centers being at Genoa and Majorca. The *portolani* were refreshingly objective and matter-of-fact compared to the writings of contemporary, learned doctrinaires who debated whether human beings could survive the killing sunbeams and the boiling ocean water at the equator. The following is an example of factual and precise instructions from a fifteenth century *portolano*:

> As you enter the port beware of shoals. Sail close to the middle of the channel, but towards the northeastern shore, where you may anchor. Beware of sailing too close to the shoal recently discovered on the east side. Enter the port, keeping the mainland about two prows' length distant where you have six and six-and-a-half fathoms of water. . . .
>
> From Palamosa to the anchoring-place of Acqua Fredda, 12 miles east-northeast, quarter east. Do not approach nearer the land than one-and-a-half miles by the beacon. The landmark of this bay is a high mountain, bald and cut sheer to the sea, with islands in the distance.[11]

When the Europeans reached the highly developed and militarily powerful countries of South and East Asia, their one decisive advantage was the superiority of their naval armament. This was attained only about the time their overseas expansion began, for naval battles in the Middle Ages had consisted largely of boarding and hand-to-hand fighting on decks. During the fifteenth century, European ships were equipped with guns, but these were of small size, shooting stones weighing ounces rather than pounds. They could kill men, but could not damage ships. Accordingly, they supplemented rather than supplanted the traditional boarding tactics of naval warfare. Large guns

20

were being used at the time on land, as the Turks demonstrated in their successful siege of Constantinople in 1453. But these guns were so heavy that they could not be hoisted on ships, let alone mounted and fired.

In the first two decades of the sixteenth century the metallurgists of Flanders and Germany, and later of England, developed techniques for casting guns that were more manageable but of equal or greater firing power. These new pieces, five to twelve feet long, could shoot round stones—and later cast iron balls—that weighed five to sixty pounds, capable of damaging a hull at a range of 300 yards. Naval tactics now shifted from boarding to broadside gunfire, and warships were redesigned so that they soon were able to carry an average of forty guns.

These developments gave the Europeans a decisive advantage that enabled them to seize and retain control of the oceans of the world. Eastern rulers hastened to arm their own ships, but their vessels were neither designed nor built for mounting guns. Before they could redesign their vessels, European naval armaments developed so rapidly that the disparity increased rather than narrowed. Thus the Westerners remained the unchallenged masters of the seas until the epochal victory of the Japanese over the Russians at Tsushima in 1905.

V. New Business Techniques

The advances in shipbuilding, navigation, and naval armaments were of obvious significance for Europe's overseas expansion. But equally important in the long run was the development of new techniques in the conduct of business affairs. Outstanding in this field was the invention in Italy of double entry bookkeeping. The classic book on this subject was the *Summa de Arithmetica; Geometrica, Proportioni de Proportionalita,* published in 1494 by the Franciscan friar and mathematician, Luca Pacioli. In this work, used as a text throughout Europe, Pacioli urged the merchants to enter all transactions in their ledgers twice, once as credits and once as debits. This system made it possible to determine at any moment the financial state of a business. It also provided a further incentive to European merchants to work harder and to be more money conscious.

Another important business development was the growing use of money and the minting of standard coins that were acceptable anywhere. This occurred partly because of the increase of commerce and partly because the rising output of mines provided more gold and silver for minting. The city of Florence led the way in 1252 with the gold florin, and other cities and states soon followed. Trade benefited immensely from this appearance of currency that was of standard and dependable value.

There was at this time, also, a primitive but significant development of banks and credit instruments. Checks, bills of exchange, and corporations, as we know them today, did not develop until the great expansion of northwestern Europe, between the seventeenth and nineteenth centuries. But the Italians began the long process much earlier. They had evolved simple forms of bills of exchange as early as the twelfth century. By 1408 the Casa di San Giorgi of Genoa was functioning as a bank, circulating accounts and notes.

Gradually, mighty banking families appeared, first in Italy and later in Northern Europe. The trend in the location and amount of wealth may be ascertained by comparing (in 1958 American dollars) the fortunes of the outstanding banking families over three centuries.

1300—the Peruzzi (Florence)	$1,600,000
1440—the Medici (Florence)	15,000,000
1546—the Fuggers (Augsburg)	80,000,000

This spectacular rise of financial activity led inevitably to the abandonment of medieval Christianity's strong condemnation and proscription of interest. Disfavor was understandable and practical in a society where trading was slight and the chance for investing money at a profit correspondingly meager. But these conditions changed in the late Middle Ages, and with the change in conditions came a change in doctrine. For centuries, churchmen had inveighed against interest as constituting usury, "a vice most odious and detestable in the sight of God." But by 1546 the French jurist Charles Dumoulin was pleading for the recognition of "moderate and acceptable usury."

> . . . everyday commercial practice shows that the utility of the use of a considerable sum of money is not slight. . . . Nor does it avail to say that money by itself does not fructify: for even fields do not fructify by themselves, without expense, labor, and the industry of man; money, likewise, even when it has to be returned after a time, yields meanwhile a considerable product through the industry of man. . . . And sometimes it deprives the creditor of as much as it brings to the debtor. . . . Therefore, all . . . hating, condemning, & punishing of usury should be understood as applying to excessive & unreasonable, not to moderate & acceptable, usury.[12]

Finally, European expansion after the initial Iberian phase was greatly strengthened and accelerated by the proliferation of joint stock companies. These new organizations proved most effective instruments for economic mobilization and penetration. The Eastern merchant, however big, traded as an individual or in private partnership. The Europeans, by contrast, organized joint stock companies for trading all over the world. The East India companies (Dutch, English, and French) were followed by many others, including the various Levant companies, the Muscovy Company, and the still extant Hudson's Bay Company.

These institutions were unique because their joint-stock character limited the responsibility of the investor, separated the functions of investing and of management, and also made possible the mobilization of large amounts of capital for specific ventures. Anyone who wished to speculate with a little of his money could do so without risking his whole future. He risked only the amount he invested in company shares, and he could not be held further liable for whatever losses the company might incur. Furthermore, there was no need for the individual investors to know or trust each other, or to concern themselves with the specific conditions of the market and the policies of the company. These details of management were entrusted to directors selected for their responsibility and experience, and these directors in turn could choose dependable individuals to manage company affairs in the field. This arrangement made it attractive for all sorts of scattered individuals—a London wool merchant, a Paris storekeeper, a Harlem herring fisher, an Antwerp banker, or a Yorkshire landowner—to invest their savings in individual ventures. In this manner it was possible to mobilize European capital easily and simply, and vast amounts were invested in various overseas undertakings. No Eastern merchant, limited to his own resources or those of his partners, and choosing his managers from his family or circle of acquaintances, could hope to compete with the powerful and impersonal joint stock company.

VI. RISE OF NATIONAL MONARCHIES

The political trend toward strong national monarchies in the late medieval period contributed substantially to West European expansion by integrating and focusing toward the outside world the forces noted above: the religious militancy, the intellectual ferment, the economic dynamism, and the technological progress.

Europe had entered a period of disintegration and political anarchy following the death of Charlemagne in 814. Several traditions and interests operated at the time at cross purposes. There were feudal kings engaged in continual conflict with their feudal vassals who often held larger fiefs and wielded more power. There were feudal principalities, both lay and clerical, that raised the prickly investiture issue. There were also city-states that sometimes combined in powerful organizations such as the Lombardy and Hanseatic leagues. And in opposition to the particularist interests of the preceeding three groups, there was the striving for a united Latin Christendom headed by the pope in Rome or by a "Roman" emperor as the successor to Charlemagne and his predecessors. This complex of conflicting interests produced an infinite variety of constantly changing alliances and alignments at all levels of political life.

In very broad terms, the political evolution of Western Europe after Charlemagne may be divided into three stages. Between the ninth and eleventh centuries, popes and emperors generally cooperated. The popes helped the emperors against the German secular lords, and in return were supported against the Byzantine opponents to papal authority. In 1073, a period of papal supremacy began with the accession of Pope Gregory VII. The investiture dispute between the papacy and the emperors—the struggle to control the selection of German bishops—was won by Gregory, thereby undermining imperial administration and power. For over two centuries, the papacy was generally recognized as the head of Latin Christendom, particularly because of a succession of pious French and English kings in the mid-thirteenth century. This period of papal supremacy ended in 1296 when Philip IV of France prevailed over Pope Boniface VIII on the issue of taxation of clergy. In that year, the Pope issued a bull asserting that the laity had no authority over the clergy, and threatening to excommunicate anyone who attempted to tax the clergy. Philip rejected the Pope's claims and was able to enforce his policies with complete success. The collapse of papal power was completed when the papacy transferred its seat from Rome to Avignon and collaborated openly with the French monarchy.

Much of the new strength of the French and English monarchs derived from their informal alliance with the rising merchant class. The burghers provided financial support to the monarchs in return for protection against the incessant wars and arbitrary exactions of the feudal lords. As the national monarchs gained in strength and organization, they made a vital contribution in mobilizing human and material resources for overseas enterprise. They ended the crazy-quilt pattern of autonomous local authorities, each with its own customs, laws, weights, and currencies. As late as the end of the fourteenth century there were thirty-five toll stations on the Elbe, over sixty on the Rhine, and so many on the Seine that the cost of shipping grain 200 miles down the river was half its selling price. The monarchs also maintained relatively elaborate courts which supported craftsmen and sometimes whole industries, as in the case of Gobelin tapestry and Sèvres porcelain in France. It was the monarchs, too, who issued charters to joint stock companies and backed them up, if necessary, with their royal navies.

The pioneering Iberian enterprise overseas was the direct result of royal patronage and encouragement. It was the Spanish and Portuguese courts that provided the backing necessary for the achievements of Columbus and da Gama. The British and French courts followed suit somewhat later, though with equal interest and support. In fact, there were closer relations between merchants and monarchs in northwestern Europe than in the Iberian Peninsula. Particularly in Spain, the long struggle against the Moslems had brought together the crown and the feudal lords, while the few large towns tended to oppose both and to demand complete autonomy. In northwestern Europe, by contrast, the merchant class gradually won social prestige and state backing that was unequaled elsewhere in Eurasia.

In China and India, for example, the merchant was looked down upon as inferior and undesirable; in northwestern Europe he had status and, as time passed, growing wealth and political power. In China, the merchants at various times suffered restrictions concerning clothing, carrying of weapons, riding in carts, and owning land. Their function of transporting commodities from place to place was regarded as nonproductive and parasitic, and they were placed at the bottom of the social scale. Likewise in India, the merchant could have no prestige in the face of Hinduism's emphasis on the renunciation of worldly goods. The ideal man in India was not the bustling merchant who made money and built mansions, but the mystic who sat on mats, ate from plantain leaves, and remained unencumbered by material possessions. Consequently, merchants had no opportunity in any of the oriental empires to rise to positions of authority. In China, government was carried on by scholars; in Japan, by soldiers; in the Malay lands and in the Rajput states of India, by the local nobility; but nowhere by merchants.

Nowhere, that is, except in northwestern Europe, where they were steadily gaining in political as well as economic power. There they were becoming lord mayors in London, senators in the German Imperial Free Cities, and grand pensioners in Holland. Such social status and political connections meant more consideration and more consistent state support for mercantile interests and overseas ventures.*

* See "Social Organization and the Expansion of Europe," EMM, No. 5.

VII. Western Europe on the Eve

The significance of this unique West European complex of interests, institutions, and traditions is pointed up by the remarkable history of the famous maritime expeditions sent out from China during the Ming period. Between 1405 and 1433, seven ventures were made under the superintendency of the chief court eunuch, a certain Cheng Ho. The expeditions were startling in their magnitude and in their achievements. The first, composed of 62 ships, carried 28,000 men. The well-known contemporary Moslem traveler, Ibn Battuta, described the Chinese vessels of the period as follows:

> On each ship four decks are constructed; and there are cabins and public rooms for the merchants. Some of the cabins are provided with closets and other conveniences, and they have keys so that their tenants can lock them, and carry with them their wives or their concubines. The crew in some of the cabins have their children, and they sow kitchen herbs, ginger, etc., in wooden buckets.[13]

The average ship had a beam of 150 feet and a length of 370 feet, but the largest were 180 feet wide and 444 feet long. They were veritable floating palaces compared to Columbus' little flagship, the Santa Maria, which was 120 feet long and 25 feet wide. And the Santa Maria was twice as large as Columbus' two other ships, the Pinta and the Niña. The Chinese expeditions were impressive in performance as well as in size. They sailed around Southeast Asia to India; some went on to Aden and the head of the Persian Gulf; while individual ships entered ports on the east coast of Africa. During this time, it should be recalled, the Portuguese were only beginning to feel their way down the coast of Africa, not reaching Cape Verde until 1445.

And yet these remarkable Chinese expeditions were suddenly halted by imperial fiat in 1433. Why they were halted remains as much a mystery as why they were started in the first place. But the significant point here is that such a cessation would have been utterly inconceivable in Europe. There was no European counterpart to the Chinese emperor who could and did issue orders binding on his entire realm. Instead, there were rival national monarchies that were competing in overseas ventures, and there was no imperial authority to prevent them from doing so. The political power and social prestige of the merchants in northwestern Europe, in contrast to the opposite situation in China, assured the impossibility of enforcing any decree banning overseas enterprise. Furthermore, Europe had a tradition of trade with the outside world, and its genuine need and strong demand for foreign products was altogether lacking in China.

There was, in short, an impelling dynamism in Europe—a lust and an opportunity for profit, and a society and an institutional structure that made its realization feasible. Utterly incomprehensible in Europe would have been these Ming voyages, undertaken for unknown but certainly noncommercial reasons, organized and led by a court eunuch rather than a joint-stock company, returning with zebras, ostriches, and giraffes for an imperial court rather than with profit-yielding cargoes for a domestic market, and terminated completely and irrevocably on order from a Celestial Sovereign. Western Europe, then, was unique with its outward-thrusting dynamism—its religious drive, its intellectual ferment, its economic vitality, its technological advances, and its national monarchies that effectively mobilized these human and material resources.

During the late Middle Ages, a combination of developments isolated and fenced in Western Europeans, thereby further stimulating their natural propensity to look overseas. There was the loss of the Crusaders' outposts in the Levant, the breakup of the Mongol Empire, and the expansion of the Ottoman Turks across the Balkan Peninsula and into Central Europe up to the walls of Vienna. European merchants now could no longer penetrate into Central Asia, because disorder reigned where once the Mongols had enforced order. The Black Sea also was closed to Christian merchants when the Turks transformed it into a Moslem preserve. On the other hand, the all-important spice trade was little affected. Italian merchants continued to meet Arab traders in various ports in the Levant and to pick up the commodities demanded by the European public. This arrangement was satisfactory for the Italians and the Arabs who reaped the golden profits of the middleman. But other Europeans were not so happy, and they sought earnestly for some means to reach the Orient directly, in order to share the prize. This explains the numerous plans in late medieval times for breaking through or getting around the Moslem barrier that confined Europeans to the Mediterranean. Europe at this time, as one author has put it, was like a "giant fed through the chinks of a wall." [14] But the giant was growing in strength and in knowledge, and the prison walls were not to contain him for long.*

SUGGESTED READING

No study dealing specifically with the basic question of why Europe expanded exists. General analyses are available in two works concerned with European overseas enterprise: R. L. Reynolds, *Europe Emerges: Transition Toward an Industrial World-wide Society, 600–1750* (Madison: Univ. of Wisconsin, 1961), and J. H. Parry, *The Age of Reconnaissance: Discovery, Exploration and Settlement 1450 to 1650* (New York: World, 1963). Standard general histories of Europe during this period are by E. P. Cheyney, *The Dawn of a New Era, 1250–1453* (New York: Harper, 1952); M. Gilmore, *The Age of Humanism, 1453–1517* (New York: Harper, 1952); and G. Clark, *Early Modern Europe from about 1450 to about 1750* (New York: Oxford Univ., 1960; a Galaxy paperback). These European histories should be read together with works on other regions that emphasize the differences between the development of European society and other societies, for example, J. K. Fairbank, *The United States and China* (Cambridge: Harvard Univ., 1953); G. B. Sansom, *The Western World and Japan* (New York: Knopf, 1950); M. Zinkin, *Asia and the West* (London: Chatto, 1951); and the multivolume work still in progress by J. Needham, *Science and Civilization in China* (Cambridge: Cambridge Univ., 1956 ff.).

* See "Europe's Expansion in Historical Perspective," *EMM,* No. 6.

For the economic and technological background of Europe's expansion there are the first two volumes of the *Cambridge Economic History* (Cambridge: Cambridge Univ., 1941–1952); B. H. S. von Bath, *The Agrarian History of Western Europe, 500–1850 A.D.* (London: Arnold, 1963); R. Ehrenberg, *Capital and Finance in the Age of the Renaissance* (New York: Harcourt, 1928); S. Baldwin, *Business in the Middle Ages* (New York: Holt, 1937); C. Singer *et al.*, *A History of Technology*, Vol. II, *700* B.C. *to* A.D. *1500* (Oxford: Clarendon, 1956); G. Sarton, *Introduction to the History of Science* (Baltimore:Williams, 1927–1947); 3 vols.; and the invaluable study by Lynn White, Jr., *Medieval Technology and Social Change* (New York: Oxford Univ., 1962; a paperback.)

For the intellectual background of Europe's expansion see R. Tawney, *Religion and the Rise of Capitalism* (New York: New Am. Lib., 1947; a Mentor paperback); W. K. Ferguson, *The Renaissance* (New York: Holt, 1940); V. H. H. Green, *Renaissance and Reformation* (London: Arnold, 1952); and G. L. Mosse, *The Reformation* (New York: Holt, 1953).

26

Moslem World at the Time of the West's Expansion

Acombination of forces lay behind Western Europe's dynamism in the fifteenth century, but this dynamism was not the only factor in its unprecedented expansion during the following centuries. In order to understand this expansion fully, it is necessary to consider also the world into which Europe was about to intrude. The state of the overseas societies affected profoundly the course and the results of European expansionism. This chapter, and the two that follow, will deal with these overseas societies—the Moslem world in the Middle East and South Asia, the Confucian world in East Asia, and the non-Eurasian world in sub-Saharan Africa, the Americas, and Australia.

In reflecting on the world of about 1500, the Western mind ordinarily thinks of Columbus, Vasco da Gama, and Magellan. Western Europe appears in retrospect as the dynamic and expansionist part of the globe at that time. Western Europeans, rather than Chinese or Indians or Arabs, were those who then ventured out on fateful voyages of discovery. They were the ones who were then riding the wave of the future—a wave that eventually was to engulf the entire world.

And yet, an observer on Mars, looking at this globe about 1500, would have been more impressed by the Moslem than by the Christian world. In certain respects the Moslems were indeed more advanced than the European Christians. Certainly the world of this period was not dominated by Western Europe, as is so often assumed. This assumption is understandable only in the light of historical retrospect. But if the world of 1500 is regarded through the eyes of contemporaries, an entirely different perspective emerges—in which Christian Europe is overshadowed in many ways by the Moslem and also the Confucian world.

I. Moslem World About 1500

The .mythical observer on Mars would have been impressed first by the extent of the Moslem world and by its unceasing expansion. After their initial explosion in the Middle East in the seventh and eighth centuries, the Moslems enjoyed a second period of expansion between 1000 and 1500. By the latter date they had penetrated westward to Central Europe, northward to Central Asia, eastward to India and Southeast Asia, and southward into the interior of Africa; thus, the Moslem world doubled in size and far surpassed in area the Christian world on the western tip of Eurasia and the Confucian world on the eastern tip.

Not only was the Moslem world the most extensive about 1500 but also it continued to expand vigorously after that date. It was not Western Europe alone that was extending its frontiers at that date, as is commonly assumed. The Moslem world was expanding overland at the same time that the Christian world was reaching overseas. The Portuguese in the early sixteenth century were gaining footholds in India and the East Indies, and the Spaniards were conquering an empire in the New World. But at the same time, the Ottoman Turks were pushing into Central Europe, overrunning Hungary; and in 1529 they besieged the very capital of the Hapsburg Empire—Vienna. Likewise, in India the great Mogul emperors were steadily extending their empire southward until they became the masters of almost the entire peninsula. Elsewhere the Moslem faith continued to spread amongst "primitive" peoples in Africa, in Central Asia, and in Southeast Asia.

This unceasing expansion of Islam was due in part to the forceful conversion of nonbelievers, though compulsion was not employed so commonly by Moslems as by Christians. Yet a fifteenth century Moslem chronicle relates that Mohammed Khan of Turkestan "was a wealthy prince and a good Muslim. He persisted in following the road of justice and equity, and was so unremitting in his efforts, that during his blessed reign most of the tribes of the Mongols became Muslims. It is well-known what severe measures he had recourse to, in bringing the Mongols to be believers in Islam. If, for instance, a Mongol did not wear a turban, a horseshoe nail was driven into his head: and treatment of this kind was common. May God recompense him with good." [1] Likewise the Scotsman Mungo Park, who explored the Niger River in the late eighteenth century, relates that the following message was sent by a Moslem chieftain to his pagan neighbor: "With this knife Abdulkader will condescend to shave the head of Damel, if Damel will embrace the Mohammedan faith; and with this other knife Abdulkader will cut the throat of Damel, if Damel refuses to embrace it; take your choice." [2]

But much more effective than these forceful measures was the quiet missionary work of Moslem traders and preachers, who were particularly successful among the less civilized peoples. Frequently, the trader appeared first, combining proselytism with the sale of his merchandise. His profession gave the trader close and constant contact with those he would convert. Soon after his arrival in a pagan village, he inevitably attracted attention by his regularly recurring times of prayer and prostration, during which he appeared to be conversing with some invisible being. His very assumption of intellectual and moral superiority attracted the respect and confidence of the pagans. Also, there was no color bar, for if the trader were not of the same race as the villagers, he probably would marry a native woman. Such a marriage often led to the adoption of Islam by members of the woman's family. Soon religious instruction was needed for the children, so schools were established and frequented by pagan as well as Moslem children. These children were taught to read the Koran and were instructed in the doctrines and ceremonies of Islam. Some even went on to centers of higher learning and then returned as missionaries among the heathen population of their native land.

This explains why Islam, from the time of its appearance, was far more successful than any other religion in gaining converts. Christianity's present superiority in numbers dates only from the overseas expansion of Europe, which opened up for Christianity the entire non-Eurasian world. Especially in the nineteenth century, Christianity gained great impetus from the unequaled material resources provided by Western technology. Yet even today, Islam is more than holding its own against Christianity in Africa, thanks to its unique adaptability to indigenous cultures as well as to the popular identification of Christianity with the foreign white master.

Apart from this ceaseless extension of frontiers, the Moslem world about 1500 was distinguished by its three great empires—the Ottoman in the Middle East, North Africa, and the Balkans; the Safavid in Persia; and the Mogul in India. These empires had all risen to prominence at this time and now dominated the heartland of Islam.

Why they made their appearance at this particular period is not altogether clear. One important factor seems to have been the invention of gunpowder and its use in firearms and cannon. The Chinese pioneered this field, but the Europeans then took the lead with improvements for military purposes. The new weapons greatly helped the rise of national monarchies in England, France, Spain, and other European countries, since the feudal nobility in their stone castles no longer could defy royal armies equipped with cannon, and only royal treasuries were rich enough to afford the expensive new weapons.

Gunpowder and firearms strengthened central power in the Moslem as well as the Christian world. The Ottoman Turks were able to win in Asia Minor and the Balkans mainly because they were the first Moslems to borrow on a large scale both artillery and artillery experts from the West. In Persia, the great Safavid ruler Shah Abbas I built an artillery force modeled after that of the Turks and was helped by two British adventurers, Anthony and Robert Sherley. And when the Mogul conqueror Babur invaded India in 1523, he followed the example of the Ottoman Turks in placing guns in front of his troops and linking the gun carriages with twisted bullhides to break up cavalry charges.

Firearms, however, were by no means the only factor explaining the rise of the three Moslem empires. Equally significant were the appearance of capable leaders who founded dynasties and the existence of especially advantageous circumstances that enabled these leaders to conquer their empires. Let us consider now the particular combination of factors that made possible the growth of each of the three Moslem empires.

II. RISE OF MODERN MOSLEM EMPIRES

Ottoman Empire

The Ottoman Turks, who founded the empire named after them, were a branch of widely scattered Turkish people who came originally from Central Asia. Over the centuries, successive waves of Turkish tribesmen had penetrated into the rich lands of the Middle East. They had appeared as early as the eighth century and infiltrated into the Islamic Empire where they were employed first as mercenaries. In the tenth century, Mongol pressure from the rear forced more Turkish tribes, including a group known as the Seljuk Turks, to move into the Middle East. These newcomers captured the Moslem capital, Bagdad, in 1055, thereby founding the brilliant, though short-lived, Seljuk Empire.

These Seljuk Turks rejuvenated the moribund Islamic world. They united once more the vast territory from the borders of India, through Persia, to the shores of the Mediterranean. In addition, they successfully repulsed the attacks of the Crusaders in the Holy Land. Above all, they broke the traditional frontier of Asia Minor along the Taurus Mountains—the frontier that had sheltered Rome and Byzantium for 1400 years—by defeating the Byzantine army in the fateful battle of Manzikert in 1071. The victory proved a turning point in the history of Asia Minor. Large numbers of Turkish settlers migrated northward in the wake of their victorious soldiers, and the native Anatolian population accepted Islam and became Turkified. By the thirteenth century, most of Asia Minor had become a part of the Seljuk Empire, leaving only the northwest corner to the Byzantines.

The Seljuk Empire, however, experienced a decline similar to that of the earlier Islamic Caliphate. It disintegrated into a patchwork of independent principalities or sultanates. In the late thirteenth century, the disorder was heightened by new bands of Turkish immigrants, one of which settled down on the extreme northwestern fringe of Seljuk territory, less than fifty miles from the strategic Straits separating Asia from Europe. In 1299 the leader of this band, a certain Uthman, declared his independence from his Seljuk overlord, and from these humble beginnings grew the great Ottoman Empire, named after the obscure Uthman.

The first step in this dazzling success story was the conquest of the remaining Byzantine portion of Asia Minor. Achieved by comparatively primitive Turkish tribesmen, victories against the venerable Byzantine Empire can be attributed, in part, to the important influence of religion. Uthman and his successors owed much of their strength to the steady stream of *ghazis*, or warriors of the faith, who poured in from all parts of the Middle East to battle against the Christian enemies of Islam. And the discontented Christian peasantry, mercilessly exploited by absentee landowners and church officials, accepted—even hailed—the Turks as deliverers from their unbearable lot.

By 1340 all of Asia Minor had fallen to the star and crescent. In 1354 the Turks crossed the Straits and won their first foothold in Europe by building a fortress at Gallipoli. Exactly a century later they were to be the masters of the entire Balkan Peninsula, including the proud imperial capital of Constantinople. After that, they would sweep triumphantly across the plains of Hungary to the very walls of Vienna.

The Ottoman victories over Byzantium were surprising enough. How were a comparative handful of these Turks able to sustain their momentum and drive on to the heart of Europe? The answer is that the whole of Christendom in the fourteenth century was weakened and divided to an unprecedented degree. The terrible plague, the Black Death, had carried off whole sections of the populations of many Christian nations. The ruinous Hundred Years' War immobilized England and France. (The dates of this conflict are significant. It began in 1338, when the Turks were rounding out their conquest of Asia Minor, and it ended in 1453 when they captured Constantinople). The Italian states also could do little against the Turks because of the long feud between Venice and Genoa. And the Balkan Peninsula was hopelessly divided by the religious strife of Catholic and Orthodox Christians and heretic Bogomils, as well as by the rivalries of the Byzantine, Serbian, and Bulgarian empires, all long past their prime. And in the Balkans, as in Asia Minor, the Christian peasants frequently were discontented to the point of little or no resistance to the Turkish onslaught.

The Ottomans hardly could have selected a more propitious moment for their advance into Europe. By 1362 they had the city of Adrianople, whence they spread over the plains of Macedonia. In 1384 they captured Sofia and soon after had control of all Bulgaria. Five years later they destroyed a South Slav army at the historic battle of Kossovo, which spelled the end of the Serbian Empire. These victories left Constantinople surrounded on all sides by Turkish territory. In 1453 the beleaguered capital was taken by assault, ending a thousand years of imperial history.

The Turks next turned southward against the rich Moslem states of Syria and Egypt. In a whirlwind campaign, they overran the first in 1516 and the second the following year. The final phase of Ottoman conquest took place in Central Europe. Under their famous Sultan Suleiman the Magnificent, the Turks crossed the Danube River and in one stroke crushed the Hungarian state in the Mohacs battle in 1526. Three years later, Suleiman laid siege to Vienna but was repulsed, partly because of torrential rains that prevented him from bringing up his heavy artillery. Despite this setback, the Turks continued to make minor gains: Cyprus in 1570, Crete in 1669, and the Polish Ukraine in the following decade.

At its height, the Ottoman Empire was indeed a formidable imperial structure. It sprawled over three continents and comprised some fifty million people, compared to the five million of contemporary England. Little wonder that Christians of the time looked upon the ever-expanding Ottoman Empire with awe and described it as "a daily increasing flame, catching hold of whatsoever comes next, still to proceed further." [3]

Safavid Empire

The second great Moslem Empire of this period was the Safavid in Persia. That country, as noted earlier, had fallen under the Seljuk Turks, as had Asia Minor. But whereas Asia Minor had become Turkified, Persia remained Persian, or Iranian, in race and culture. Probably the explanation for this different outcome is that Persia already had been Moslem, in contrast to Asia Minor, formerly a part of the Christian Byzantine Empire. For this reason, Persia was not swamped by Moslem warriors, as Asia Minor had been, and Persian society was not basically changed by the comparatively small ruling class of Turkish administrators and soldiers.

Persia remained under the Seljuk Turks from approximately A.D. 1000 to the Mongol invasion in 1258. The new Mongol rulers, known as the Il-Khans, were at first Buddhists or Christians, but about 1300 they became Moslems. Persia suffered considerable permanent damage from the Mongols, who destroyed many cities and irrigation systems, but this affliction also passed away when the Il Khan dynasty was replaced by the Safavid in 1500.

Shah Ismail I founded the new dynasty of Safavid monarchs, the first native Persian rulers in several centuries. In the twenty-four years of Ismail's reign, his military abilities and religious policy enabled him to unite the country. By his proclamation, the Shiite sect of Islam became the state religion; and through his ruthlessness, the rival Sunnite sect was crushed. Differences between these two Moslem groups date back to Mohammed's failure to name his successor or caliph. The first three caliphs elected by the community were not related to Mohammed, and it was not until the fourth election that Ali, the cousin and son-in-law of Mohammed, assumed the position. The Shiites recognize only Ali and his successors as the true line of caliphs, maintaining that the selection must be made on the basis of divine right inhering in the family of the Prophet. The Sunnites, on the contrary, regard the caliph simply as "the commander of the community of believers" and accept whoever is chosen by the suffrage of the Moslem community—hence their recognition of the immediate successors of Mohammed. Doctrinal differences also separate the two sects. The Sunnites base their religious authority on the conventional doctrine of the Koran and on the traditions handed down by the respectable divines of the orthodox school. The Shiites reject this as advocating dependence upon the fallible and contradictory opinion of men who lived several generations after the Prophet. On matters not made explicit by the Koran, the Shiites substitute independent personal judgment in place of tradition.

The significance of this doctrinal dispute for Persia at this time is that it provided a basis for the unification of the country and for the development of a certain national sentiment. Persians identified themselves with Shiism, differentiating them from the Turks and other surrounding Moslem peoples who were mostly Sunnites. In fact, Ottomans and Persians, fought a long series of wars caused as much by religious differences as by the inevitable political rivalries between two powerful and neighboring dynasties.

The greatest of the Safavid rulers was Abbas I, the shah from 1587 to 1629. It was he who modernized the Persian army by building up its artillery units.

To accomplish this he hired, among others, two English adventurers, the Sherley brothers. A contemporary writer described the results of this policy.

> The prevailing Persian [Abbas I] hath learned Sherleian arts of war, and he which before knew not the use of ordnance, hath now 500 pieces of brass, and 6000 musketeers. . . . Hence hath the present Abbas won from the Turk seven great Provinces, from Derbent to Bagdat inclusively, and still hath his eyes, mouth, and hands open to search, swallow and acquire more.[4]

Persia, in fact, did become a great power under the Safavids. Evidence of this is the constant stream of envoys from European countries who sought an alliance with Persia against the Ottoman Empire. In fact, both these Moslem states figured prominently in European diplomacy during these years. Francis I of France, for example, cooperated with Suleiman the Magnificent in fighting against the Hapsburg Emperor Charles V. And the Hapsburgs, in turn, cooperated with the Persians against their two common foes. These relationships between Christian and Moslem states were denounced at the time as "impious" and "sacrilegious," but the fact was that the Ottoman and Safavid empires had become world powers that no European diplomat could afford to overlook.

Mogul Empire

Just as two outstanding Safavid rulers founded a "national" dynasty in Persia, so two outstanding Mogul rulers—Babur and Akbar—founded a "national" dynasty in India, a very remarkable achievement for Moslem rulers in a predominantly Hindu country.

The Moslems came to India in three waves, widely separated in time. The first consisted of Arab Moslems who invaded the Sind region near the mouth of the Indus in 712. These Arabs were not able to push far inland, so their influence on India was limited.

The second wave came about A.D. 1000, when Turkish Moslems began raiding India from bases in Afghanistan. These raids continued intermittently for four centuries, with much loss of life and property. The net result was that numerous Moslem kingdoms were established in northern India, while southern India remained a conglomeration of Hindu states. But even in northern India the mass of the people continued to be Indians in race and Hindus in religion. They did not become Islamicized and Turkified, as did the people of Asia Minor. The explanation again is that the Turks who came down from the North were an insignificant minority compared to India's teeming millions. They could fill only the top positions in the government and the armed forces. Their Hindu subjects were the ones who tilled the land, worked in the bazaars, and comprised most of the bureaucracy. In certain regions, it is true, large sections of the population did turn to Islam, especially some depressed castes who sought relief from their exploitation in the new religion. Yet the fact remains that India was an overwhelmingly Hindu country when the third Moslem wave struck in 1500 with the appearance of the Moguls.

34

The newcomers again were Turks, their leader being the colorful Babur, a direct descendent of the great Turkish conqueror, Timur, or Tamerlane. Early in life he had lost the petty principality of Ferghana in Turkestan, which he had inherited from his father. Later he won and lost the magnificent city of Samarkand, formerly Timur's capital. Then followed many adventures, conquests, and flights, until he, himself, admitted that he was tired of wandering about "like a king on a chessboard." In 1504, a stroke of fortune enabled him to seize Kabul in Afghanistan, with 300 ill-clad followers. From Kabul, Babur cast covetous eyes on the rich plains of India to the south. Victory there came some twenty years later, when matchlock muskets and artillery serviced by Ottoman Turks enabled his absurdly small force of 12,000 men to defeat an Indian army of 100,000. After his victory he occupied Delhi, his new capital. Four years later Babur died, but his sons followed in his path, and the empire grew rapidly. It reached its height during the reign of Babur's grandson, the famous Akbar, who ruled from 1556 to 1605.

Akbar was by far the most outstanding of the Mogul emperors. He rounded out his possessions by conquering Rajputan and Gujarat in the West, Bengal in the East, and several small states in the Deccan in the South. Mogul rule now extended from Kabul and Kashmir to the Deccan, and later under Aurangzeb (1658–1707) it extended still further—almost to the southern tip of the peninsula. In addition to his military exploits, Akbar was a remarkable personality of great versatility and wide range of interests. Although illiterate, he had a keen and inquiring mind that won the grudging admiration of Jesuits who knew him well. The astonishing range of his activities is reminiscent of Peter the Great. Like his Russian counterpart, Akbar had a strong mechanical bent, as evidenced in his metallurgical work and in his designs for a gun with increased firepower. He learned to draw, loved music, and played various instruments, the kettledrum being his favorite. He also was an expert polo player and invented a lighted ball for night games.

Above all, Akbar was deeply interested in religion and philosophy, ceaselessly searching for a creed that would satisfy his personal needs and those of his subjects. At first his contemplation was within the framework of Islam; but in 1575, when he was 33, he built his Hall of Worship, within whose walls he discussed theology with learned men from all religions. Akbar was fascinated by the teachings of Hindus, Parsees, Zoroastrians, Jains, and Christians. The Jains caused him to abstain from eating meat and to prohibit the killing of animals. The Portuguese Jesuits induced him to have the Gospel translated into Persian, to wear a medallion of the Virgin around his neck, and to attend the sacrament of mass. At one point the Jesuits believed that Akbar might be converted to their faith, but in the end he evolved an entirely new religion of his own, the *Din Ilahi* or "Divine Faith." It was a vague theism of which he was the sole exponent in his role of vice-regent of God on earth. The new creed was eclectic, with borrowings from many sources, especially from the Parsees, the Jains, and the Hindus.

Akbar's motives were partly to find personal fulfillment, but also to provide a common faith that would unite his Hindu and Moslem subjects and forge a new India. However much the "Divine Faith" may have satisfied his own religious needs, it had little impact on the country. It was too intellectual to appeal to the masses, and even at court there were few converts. But what

Akbar failed to achieve by his synthetic faith, he did by ending discriminatory practices against Hindus and establishing their equality with Moslems. He abolished the pilgrim tax that Hindus had been required to pay when traveling to their sacred shrines. He ended the poll tax on Hindus, a standard levy on nonbelievers in all Moslem countries. Akbar also opened the top state positions to Hindus, who now ceased to look upon the Mogul empire as an enemy organization. A new India was beginning to emerge, as Akbar had dreamt—a national state rather than a divided land of Moslem masters and Hindu subjects.*

It should be emphasized, however, that in contrast to the indubitably Moslem, Persian and Ottoman empires, the Mogul Empire was Moslem in its superstructure but Hindu in its base. The ruling dynasty and court were Moslem. The arts and high culture in general were influenced mostly by Persian models. Persian was the language of the court, of public business, of diplomacy, of literature, and of polite society. Yet beneath this Mogul ruling apparatus and Persian cultural domination, there ran a strong Hindu undercurrent. The mass of the people remained faithful to their inchoate, polytheistic Hinduism that was so different from the austerely monotheistic Islam. Foreigners were aware of the fact that the rural masses were of a faith and a culture quite distinct from those of the ruling groups. "To the ordinary foreigner in 1700," states an authority on this subject, "the Mogul empire seemed as Indian as the Manchu empire appeared to be Chinese to the foreign observer in nineteenth-century China." [5]

III. Splendor of Moslem Empires

Military Strength

All three of the Moslem empires were first-class military powers. Eloquent proof of this is to be found in the appeal sent in December, 1525, by Francis I, King of France, to the Ottoman sultan, Suleiman the Magnificent. The appeal was for a Turkish attack upon the Holy Roman Emperor and head of the House of Hapsburg, Charles V! Suleiman responded in 1526 by crossing the Danube, overrunning Hungary, and easing the pressure on Francis. This was but one of many Ottoman expeditions that not only aided the French (and incidently provided the Turks with additional territories and booty), but also saved the Lutheran heretics by distracting Hapsburg attention from Germany to the threatened Danubian frontier. It is paradoxical that Moslem military power should have contributed substantially to the cause of Protestantism in its critical formative stage. Conversely, the Persians also influenced European developments significantly by cooperating with the Hapsburgs against their common Turkish foe. Persia's second front against the Ottoman Empire prevented it from turning full force upon Europe, an action similar to that of Russia against Germany during the two world wars.

Moslem military forces generally lagged behind those of Europe in artillery equipment. They depended on the Europeans for the most advanced ordnance

* See " 'The Great Mogul,' " EMM, No. 9.

and for the most experienced gunners. The discrepancy, however, was one of degree only. It was not a case of the Moslem empires being defenseless because of lack of artillery. Plenty of equipment was available, though it was not as efficient and as well-manned as in the best contemporary European armies.

On the other hand, European observers were impressed by the vast military manpower of the Moslem world. It is estimated that the permanent regular forces of the whole of India at the time of Akbar totaled well over one million men, or more than double the size of the Indian armies in 1914. Furthermore these huge military establishments were well trained and disciplined when the Moslem empires were at their height. For obvious geographic reasons, Europeans were most familiar with the Ottoman armed forces, with whom they had a good deal of firsthand experience. After this experience the Europeans were very impressed and respectful.* Typical were the reports of Augier Ghislain de Busbecq, Hapsburg ambassador to Constantinople during the reign of Suleiman the Magnificent. After Busbecq inspected an Ottoman army camp in 1555, he wrote home as follows:

> It makes me shudder to think of what the result of a struggle between such different systems [as the Hapsburg and the Ottoman] must be. . . . On their side is the vast wealth of their empire, unimpaired resources, experience and practice in arms, a veteran soldiery, an uninterrupted series of victories, readiness to endure hardships, union, order, discipline, thrift, and watchfulness. On ours are found an empty exchequer, luxurious habits, exhausted resources, broken spirits, a raw and insubordinate soldiery, and greedy generals; there is no regard for discipline, license runs riot, the men indulge in drunkenness and debauchery, and, worst of all, the enemy are accustomed to victory, we, to defeat. Can we doubt what the result must be? The only obstacle is Persia, whose position on his rear forces the invader to take precautions. The fear of Persia gives us a respite, but it is only for a time.[6]

Administrative Efficiency

All emperors of the Moslem states had absolute power over their subjects. Accordingly, the quality of the administration depended upon the quality of the imperial heads. In the sixteenth century, they were men of extraordinary abilities. Certainly Suleiman and Abbas and Akbar were the equals of any monarchs anywhere in the world. In Persia, for example, an English traveler reported that, "this King [Abbas], since his coming to the crown, hath brought this country into such subjection that a man may travel through it with a rod in his hand, having no other weapon, without any hurt. . . ."[7] Likewise in India, Akbar had a well-organized bureaucracy whose ranks were expressed in terms of cavalry commands. Excellent pay and the promise of rapid advance in the Mogul service attracted the best men in India and from abroad. It is estimated that 70 per cent of the bureacracy consisted of foreigners such as Persians and Afghans, the rest being Indian Moslems and

* See "Ottoman Military Strength," *EMM*, No. 7.

Hindus. Upon the death of an official, his wealth was inherited by the emperor, and his rank became vacant. This lessened the evils of corruption and hereditary tenure that plagued Western countries at the time. The tax services were headed by a minister who had the right of direct access to the emperor. This branch of the administration had full autonomy, being independent of the governors of provinces. It was responsible for the assessment and collection of land revenue and also for the collection of customs duties and sales taxes. In order to help agricultural development, officials had the authority to reduce taxes where waste lands had been brought newly under cultivation.

Since Akbar opened his bureaucracy to all his subjects, ability rather than religion became the criterion for appointment and advancement. Busbecq in Constantinople made precisely the same point about the Ottoman administrative system.*

> In making his appointments the Sultan pays no regard to any pretensions on the score of wealth or rank. . . . he considers each case on its own merits, and examines carefully into the character, ability, and disposition of the man whose promotion is in question. It is by merit that men rise in the service, a system which ensures that posts should only be assigned to the competent. . . . Among the Turks, therefore, honours, high posts, and judgeships are the rewards of great ability and good service. If a man be dishonest, or lazy, or careless, he remains at the bottom of the ladder, an object of contempt. . . . These are not our ideas, with us there is no opening left for merit; birth is the standard for everything; the prestige of birth is the sole key to advancement in the public service.[8]

Economic Development

So far as economic standards were concerned, the Moslem states in early modern times were, in current phraseology, developed lands. Certainly they were so regarded by Western Europeans who were ready to face any hardships or perils in order to reach fabled India and the Spice Islands beyond. Closer to home, the Ottoman Empire was an impressive economic unit. Its vast extent and varied climes assured it of virtual self-sufficiency. The fertile plains of Hungary, Wallachia, Asia Minor, and Egypt produced an abundant supply of foodstuffs and raw materials. The skilled artisans of Constantinople, Saloniki, Damascus, Bagdad, Cairo, and other ancient cities turned out a multitude of handicraft products. The empire also possessed large timber resources and important mineral deposits, particularly iron, copper, and lead. All these goods were bought and sold without hindrance in the vast free-trade area provided by the far-flung Ottoman frontiers. The empire's strategic position at the junction of seas and continents also promoted a substantial foreign and transit trade.

The prosperity of the empire was reflected in the substantial surplus left in the treasury. Suleiman's annual revenues during the second quarter of the sixteenth century totaled about six million ducats; his expenditures, about

* See "Ottoman Administrative System," *EMM*, No. 8.

four and one-half million. Another indication of prosperity at this time was the relatively comfortable position of even the Christian peasants under the Ottoman rule. They were required to pay a small head tax, a tithe of approximately one-tenth of the farm produce, and in the case of tenants on feudal fiefs, minor additional obligations to the overlord. These obligations were far from burdensome. Contemporary travelers frequently remarked that the Christian Balkan peasants were less heavily taxed and generally better off than their counterparts in neighboring Christian states. Indeed, Martin Luther observed that "one finds in German lands those who desire the future of the Turks and their government, as well as those who would rather be under the Turks than under the Emperor and the Princes." [9]

For most Europeans, more dazzling than the Ottoman Empire was far-off, exotic India, the weaver of fabulous textiles, especially fine cotton fabrics unequaled anywhere in the world. Here, too, were great stores of spices, for India served as entrepôt for cargoes headed westward from the Spice Islands. It was the country that, since the early days of the Roman Empire, had drained gold and silver away from Europe—a fact that was most impressive for bullion-minded European contemporaries. As one of them observed, "All nations bring Coin, and carry away commodities for the same; and this Coin is buried in India, and goeth not out." [10] It is true that when the Europeans were able to observe at firsthand the Indian countryside, they could not help noticing the wretched condition of the peasant masses that lived virtually at subsistence level. But this did not make as deep an impression as it does today, for Europe then had its own peasantry living close to subsistence. More fascinating for Europeans at that time were the reports of the imperial munificence of the Mogul rulers and of the incredible wealth of the courtiers and top administrators. The reports proved justified, as the English were to demonstrate later when they seized control from the declining Moguls. Within a few years after arrival in India, Robert Clive wrote to his father that he had acquired wealth that

> will enable me to live in my native country much beyond my most sanguine wishes. . . . I have ordered £2000 each to my sisters, and shall take care of my brothers in due time. I would advise the Lasses to marry as soon as possible for they have no time to lose. There is no occasion for your following the Law any more. . . . You may now order the Rector to get every thing ready for the reparation of old Stych [the home of the Clives in Shropshire, which poverty had compelled them to abandon]. . . . If I can get into Parliament, I shall be very glad. . . .[11]

As significant as the wealth of the Moslem empires was the control of South Asian commerce by Moslem merchants. Particularly important was the trade in spices, a term that then covered all manner of oriental products: fragrant spikenard; sandalwood, employed as an astringent and blood purifier; the gum resin galbanum, much appreciated by women; ambergris, camphor, wormwood, and ivory; spices such as cinnamon, mace, nutmeg, cloves, pimento, ginger, and above all, pepper. The spices were eagerly sought after in a world that knew so little of the art of conserving foodstuffs, apart from salting. For centuries these commodities, together with many others such as silk from China and cotton fabrics from India, were transported back and forth along two sets of trade routes—the northern extending from the Far East through Central Asia to ports on the Black Sea and Asia Minor; the southern, from the East Indies and India along the Indian Ocean and up the Persian Gulf or the Red Sea to ports in Syria and Egypt. With the collapse of the Mongol Empire, conditions in Central Asia became so anarchical that the northern routes were virtually closed after 1340. Henceforth, most of the products were funneled along the southern sea routes, which by that time were dominated by Moslem merchants.

This commerce contributed substantially to the prosperity of the Moslem world. It provided not only government revenue in the form of customs duties, but also a source of livelihood for thousands of merchants, clerks, sailors, shipbuilders, camel drivers, and stevedores who were connected directly or indirectly with the trade. The extent of the profits is indicated by the fact that articles from India were sold to Italian middlemen in Alexandria at a mark-up of over 2,000 per cent. Cairo, which profited greatly from this trade, was described by fifteenth century travelers as three times the size of Paris, five times as populous, equipped with a street lighting system, a huge public hospital, and homes for orphans; with schools, colleges, stately mosques, luxurious palaces, and magnificent public buildings.

When the Portuguese broke into the Indian Ocean in 1498, they quickly gained control of much of this lucrative commerce. But they did so because their ships and guns, rather than their goods or business techniques, were superior. In fact, we shall find that the Portuguese at first were embarrassed because they had little to offer in return for the commodities they coveted. They were rescued from this predicament only by the flood of bullion that soon was to pour in from the mines of Mexico and Peru.*

Religious Toleration

In the Christian mind, Islam commonly is equated with religious fanaticism. But in the sixteenth century, fanaticism probably was more widespread in Christendom than in the Moslem world. This was the period of the religious wars when Protestants and Catholics were massacring each other, and both were hounding and pillaging the Jews. It is true that there was no lack of intolerance or savage persecution between the Sunnite and Shiite sects of Islam. Yet the fact remains that the Hindus had far greater liberties under the Moslem Moguls than any subject religious group enjoyed in Christian Europe. Also there is little doubt that both Christians and Jews were better treated in the Moslem world than the Moslems and Jews were treated in the Christian world.

An illustration of this is the well-known fate of the Moslems and Jews in Christian Spain, where they were mercilessly harried and forced to flee. But it is less well known that a good many of the Jewish refugees went to the Ottoman Empire, where they found the toleration denied to them in the West. The Jewish immigrants frequently were people with both means and skills,

* See "Moslem Trade and Prosperity," *EMM*, No. 10.

so that they contributed substantially to their new homeland. Indeed, one Ottoman sultan remarked that he could not understand why the Spanish king foolishly allowed such valuable subjects to leave his realm. "How can you call this Ferdinand 'wise'—he who has impoverished his dominions in order to enrich mine." Also noteworthy is the following description of the position of the Jews in the Ottoman Empire, written in 1717 by Lady Mary Wortley Montagu, wife of the British ambassador in Constantinople:

> I observed most of the rich tradesmen were Jews. That people are an incredible power in this country. They have many privileges above all the natural Turks themselves, and have formed a very considerable common-wealth here, being judged by their own laws, and have drawn the whole trade of the empire into their hands, partly by the firm union among themselves, and prevailing on the idle temper and want of industry of the Turks. Every Pasha has his Jew, who is his homme d'affaires; he is let into all his secrets, and does all his business. No bargain is made, no bribe received, no merchandise disposed of, but what passes through their hands. They are the physicians, the stewards, and interpreters of the great men.[12]

The great majority of non-Moslem subjects in the Ottoman Empire were Christians rather than Jews. These Christians, like those in other Moslem countries, were free to worship as they wished with comparatively minor disabilities. The explanation is to be found largely in the religious law of Islam. The Sacred Law recognized Christians and Jews as being, like Moslems, People of the Book. Both had a scripture—a written word of revelation. Their faith was accepted as true, though incomplete, since Mohammed had superseded Moses and Jesus Christ. Islam therefore tolerated the Christians and Jews. It permitted them to practice their faith with certain restrictions and penalties.

Islam also laid down exact rules for all the concerns of life. It was a civil as well as a religious code. Consequently, in tolerating the religions of the non-Moslems, Islam also permitted their usages and customs. This policy was implemented by permitting non-Moslem subjects to organize into millets, autonomous communities with their own ecclesiastical leaders. Each religious group had its separate millet: the Greek Orthodox, Gregorian Armenian, Roman Catholic, Jewish, and Protestant. Thus, the Turks left their non-Moslem subjects relatively free to govern themselves.

It is true that non-Moslems in the Ottoman Empire did not enjoy full religious equality. They were forbidden to ride horses or to bear arms. They were required to wear a particular costume to distinguish them from the true believers. Their dwellings could not be loftier than those of the Moslems. They could not repair their churches or ring their bells except by special permission, rarely granted. They were required to pay a special poll tax, which Akbar waived in India. Yet with all these discriminations, the position of the religious nonconformist was more favorable under Suleiman than under Charles V or Ferdinand and Isabella. They were free to keep their religion, they could attend their own churches or synagogues, they could have their own clergy, and they administered their communal affairs with little interference by Turkish officials so long as they accepted the rule of the Sultan.*

On Cyprus, Crete, and other islands under Venetian rule, Greeks preferred the earlier reign of the Turks, who had allowed them communal autonomy and religious freedom. The Venetians subjected them to centralized control and to the unceasing proselytism of Catholic priests. When the French traveler Motraye landed at Modon on the west coast of Greece in 1710, he discovered that the townspeople were extremely hostile toward their Venetian overlords, ousters of the Turks some eleven years earlier. One of the local inhabitants complained to Motraye that "their priests come to us to talk against our religion, bothering us incessantly and urging us to embrace theirs, something that the Turks never dreamed of doing. On the contrary, they gave us all the liberty that we could have wished for. . . ."[13]

Cultural Achievements

The Moslem world was as advanced in its cultural achievements as in its religious policies. The culture of the Moslem empires in the sixteenth century was rich, sophisticated, and varied. Its roots went back to the great, flourishing civilizations of the past in the Middle East and South Asia—the civilizations of Byzantium, Egypt, Syria, Mesopotamia, Persia, and India. Centrally located, the Moslem countries benefited from a certain amount of cultural influence from the outside—from Europe and China—stimulating them to cultural attainments of high order, even though perhaps not as fresh and original as those of ancient Greece or of the modern Western world.

In architecture, especially, the Moslems left beautiful creations that hold their own to the present day. Architectural styles varied substantially from one region to another, reflecting local traditions and neighboring influences. Today in Cairo, delicately silhouetted minarets of this period stand in contrast to more solid and square minarets that were built further west in North Africa. In India, the Moguls combined Persian and Indian elements into a distinctive architectural style characterized by the use of the bulbous dome, the cupolas at corners on slender pillars, and lofty vaulted gateways. Among the outstanding monuments of Indo-Islamic architecture were the city of Fathpur Sikri, built by Akbar, with its glorious mosque, tomb, baths, and palace; Shah Jahan's palace at Delhi with its famous Peacock Throne,† and the same emperor's even more famous Taj Mahal.

A particularly pleasant feature of the Persian architecture of this period was the setting of brightly colored buildings in pleasant gardens with pools and streams. Many palaces built by the Safavid monarchs were in such royal gardens. The vigorous state of architecture in the Ottoman Empire is exemplified by the remarkable career of the internationally known Sinan Pasha. Starting out as a military engineer constructing bridges and ferries during campaigns, he was soon engaged exclusively in building mosques and palaces commissioned by the rulers and grandees of the empire. During his ninety-year lifetime, he worked with such energy and distinction that he gained an international reputation as the "Turkish Michelangelo." In every part of the empire, from Bosnia to Mecca, he left the imprint of his genius. Before his

* See "Religious Toleration in the Ottoman Empire," *EMM,* No. 11.
† See "Peacock Throne of the Great Mogul," *EMM,* No. 12.

death in 1679 he had erected no less than 343 buildings, including 81 mosques, 55 schools, 50 chapels, 34 palaces, and 33 baths. Two of his pupils were the designers of the Taj Mahal in India.

History and biography also were very popular in the Moslem lands. The Egyptians were particularly active in compiling encyclopedic works that systematized past information. By far the most outstanding figure in the social sciences was the Tunisian historian ibn-Khaldun (1332–1406). In his great work, *Katib al-Ibar* ("Universal History"), he attempted to treat history as a science and outlined a secular philosophy of history. His study of the growth and decay of the Islamic Empire led him to generalize about the rise and fall of all empires. He emphasized such factors as the *ésprit de corps* of a people, the corrupting influence of luxuries, and the lack of opportunity for dangerous living. In the breadth of his speculations, Khaldun is reminiscent of the Greek historian Thucydides.

Literature was another field of great interest in the Moslem lands. Here the Persians were the acknowledged masters, creating works that were widely admired and imitated. But Moslem prose and poetry seem artificial and excessively ornate for Western taste. Content was subordinated to form of expression. The chief concern was the use of a host of rhetorical embellishments: anagrams, homonyms (words agreeing in sound but different in meaning from another, such as *reed* and *read*), palindromes (verses that could be read either forwards or backwards), adornment (the arrangement of verses in geometrical shapes), quadrilaterals (the arrangement of verses in a rectangle so that they could be read either horizontally or vertically), suppression (the deliberate avoidance of the use of a given letter of the alphabet), and enigmas (in which numerical dates are obtained from the sum total of the assigned numerical value of the letters in certain words). In addition to these elaborate devices, Persian writers faithfully repeated certain traditional phrases and associations. The "moon-face," the "cypress-form," and the "ruby-lip" all appeared with monotonous regularity. And if the "nightingale" was mentioned, the "rose" was never far away. Within this narrow framework, Moslem writers concerned themselves with a few familiar themes, presented again and again with ever-increasing beauty of language and ever subtler ingenuity of phrase.

In addition to these major fields of cultural activity, the Moslems excelled in several others, including miniature painting,* carpet and textile weaving, and porcelain, leather, and jewelry work.

IV. DECLINE OF MOSLEM EMPIRES

The Moslem world of the sixteenth century was most impressive. Suleiman, Akbar, and Abbas ruled empires that were at least the equals of those in other parts of the globe, and yet these empires began to go downhill precipitously during the seventeenth century. By the following century they were far behind Western Europe, and they have remained behind to the present day.†

One explanation is the deterioration of the ruling dynasties. Suleiman the

* See "Persian Miniature Painting," *EMM*, No. 13.
† See "Roots of Moslem Decline," *EMM*, No. 14.

Magnificent was succeeded in 1566 by Selim II, lazy, fat, dissipated, and so addicted to wine that he was known to his subjects as Selim the Sot. Yet he was not so degenerate as many of his disgraceful successors. An Ottoman courtier of this period wrote that when Ibrahim I, became the sultan in 1649, he "fell into the hands of all the favourites and associates of the harem, the dwarfs, the mutes, the eunuchs, the women . . . and together they threw everything into confusion." [14] The same thing happened in Persia, where Abbas' successor, who came to the throne in 1629, also came under harem influences.

In India the decline began with Aurangzeb (1659–1707), a capable general, good administrator, and a conscientious, hard-working ruler, but one with the fatal defect of intolerance toward his Hindu subjects, especially in the second half of his long reign. He regarded Akbar's policy of a national state as the very negation of Islamic ideas. In 1669 he issued orders "to demolish all temples and schools of the infidels." Ten years later, he reimposed the poll tax on Hindus, which Akbar had abolished over a century earlier. Aurangzeb also excluded Hindus as completely as possible from his armed forces and bureaucracy. Such discriminatory measures naturally aroused violent opposition from the Hindu majority. Fighting broke out and dragged on until the death of the inflexible Aurangzeb at the age of 91. He left India in a state of tension and exhaustion, and his successors were sorry specimens who were quite unequal to the problems they faced. The dynasty that had produced the great Babur, Akbar, and the equally great though misguided Aurangzeb now came forth with Bahadur Shah the "Heedless" and Mohammed Shah the "Jolly" or "Pleasure Loving." So India fell to pieces in the eighteenth century, with Moslems fighting against Hindus, Persians and Afghans invading from the northwest, and Europeans seizing footholds along the coasts.

This dynastic degeneration was particularly serious for the Moslem world, where political authority was concentrated in the person of the ruler. "The fish stinks from the head," says the Turkish proverb. Dynastic decline, however, was not the only factor responsible for the blight of the Moslem lands. All the European royal families had their share of incapable and irresponsible rulers, yet their countries did not go down with them.

A more basic explanation for the misfortunes of the Moslem world was that it lacked the dynamism of Europe. It did not experience those far-reaching changes, noted in the preceding chapter, that were revolutionizing European society during these centuries.

In the economic field, for example, there were no basic changes in agriculture, in industry, in financial methods, or in commercial organization. A traveler in the Moslem lands in the seventeenth or eighteenth centuries would have observed essentially the same economic practices and institutions as the Crusaders saw 500 years earlier. In fact, an Englishman who did visit Constantinople at the end of the seventeenth century described very vividly the stagnation and decay.

> Suppose a stranger to arrive from a long journey, in want of clothes
> for his body; furniture for his lodgings; books or maps for his instruction and amusement; paper, pens, ink, cutlery, shoes, hats; in short those

articles which are found in almost every city of the world; he will find few or none of them in Constantinople; except of a quality so inferior as to render them incapable of answering any purpose for which they were intended. The few commodities exposed for sale are either exports from England, unfit for any other market, or, which is worse, German and Dutch imitations of English manufacture. . . . Let a foreigner visit the bazaars . . . he will see nothing but slippers, clumsy boots of bad leather, coarse muslins, pipes, tobacco, coffee, cooks' shops, drugs, flower-roots, second-hand pistols, poignards, and the worst manufactured wares in the world. . . . View the exterior of Constantinople, and it seems the most opulent and flourishing city in Europe; examine its interior, and its miseries and deficiencies are so striking that it must be considered the meanest and poorest metropolis of the world.[15]

The traveler quoted above concluded his remarks with this observation: "Under a wise government, the inhabitants of Constantinople might obtain the riches of all the empires of the earth." This is significant, because there is little doubt that the lack of economic progress was closely related to the deterioration of the Moslem imperial governments. So long as the rulers were strong and enlightened, the autocratic empires functioned smoothly and effectively, as Busbecq reported. But when central authority weakened, then the courtiers, bureaucratic officials, and army officers all combined to fleece the productive classes of society, whether peasants or artisans or merchants. Their uncontrollable extortions stifled private enterprise and incentive. Any subject who showed signs of wealth was fair game for arbitrary confiscation. Consequently, merchants hid their wealth rather than openly investing it in order to expand their operations. This point was made specifically and repeatedly by foreign observers. For example, the French physician, François Bernier, who lived for several years in the mid-seventeenth century in Egypt, Persia, and India, wrote as follows:

There is no one before whom the injured peasant, artisan, or tradesman can pour out his just complaints; no great lords, parliaments, or judges of local courts, exist, as in *France,* to restrain the wickedness of those merciless oppressors [governors, feudal lords and tax collectors]. . . . There can be little encouragement to engage in commercial pursuits, when the success with which they may be attended, instead of adding to the enjoyments of life, provokes the cupidity of a neighboring tyrant possessing both power and inclination to deprive any man of the fruits of his industry. When wealth is acquired . . . the possessor, so far from living with increased comfort and assuming an air of independence, studies the means by which he may appear indigent: his dress, lodging and furniture, continue to be mean, and he is careful, above all things, never to indulge in the pleasures of the table. In the meantime, his gold and silver remain buried at a great depth in the ground. . . .

The peasant cannot avoid asking himself this question: "Why should I toil for a tyrant who may come tomorrow and lay his rapacious hands upon all I possess and value, without leaving me . . . the means to drag on my miserable existence. . . ."

The facts I have mentioned are sufficient to account for the rapid decline of the *Asiatic* states. It is owing to this miserable system of government that most towns in *Hindoustan* are made up of earth, mud, and other wretched materials; that there is no city or town which, if it be not already ruined and deserted, does not bear evident marks of approaching decay.[16]

Foreign observers were not alone in reaching these conclusions. Very revealing is the following lament of a Greek merchant, John Priggos, who had left his Turkish-ruled homeland and made his fortune in Amsterdam. While living in that city he had been impressed by the security and justice with which commercial operations could be conducted.

But all cannot exist under the Turk. He has neither order nor justice. And if the capital is one thousand he multiplies it tenfold so that he may loot and impoverish others, not realizing that the wealth of his subjects is the wealth of his kingdom. . . . he is altogether unjust, and he is not one for creating anything but only for destroying. May the Almighty ruin him so that Greece may become Christian, and justice may prevail, and governments may be created as in Europe where everyone has his own without fear of any injustice. . . . [17]

Another cause and symptom of retrogression was the blindly invincible superiority complex of the Moslems vis-à-vis the West. It never occurred to them at this time that they might conceivably learn anything from *giaours* or nonbelievers. Their attitude stemmed partly from religious prejudice and partly from the spectacular successes of Islam during the preceding centuries. Islam had grown from an obscure desert sect to the world's largest and most rapidly growing religion—which it was in 1500. Consequently, Moslem officials and scholars looked down with contempt and arrogance on anything relating to Christian Europe. As late as 1756, when the French ambassador in Constantinople announced the alliance between France and Austria that marked a turning point in the diplomatic history of Europe, he was curtly informed that the Ottoman government did not concern itself "about the union of one hog with another." [18] This attitude was perhaps understandable in the sixteenth century; in the eighteenth it was grotesque and suicidal.

One of the most damaging results of this self-centeredness was that it let down an intellectual iron curtain between the Moslem world and the West, especially in the increasingly important field of science. Moslem scholars knew virtually nothing of the epoch-making achievements of Paracelsus in medicine, Vesalius and Harvey in anatomy, and Copernicus, Kepler, and Galileo in astronomy. Not only were they ignorant of these scientific advances, but they themselves were doing nothing and had no intention of doing anything in the future.

This ignorance and self-centeredness cannot be attributed to Islam itself. Tradition ascribes to Mohammed the saying "Seek for knowledge, even unto China." Also the brilliant achievements of Moslem science and scholarship in the Middle Ages indicate that Islam cannot be equated with intellectual stagnation. So the failure of the Moslem to keep up with the West is to be

46

explained not by the tenets of Islam but rather by its moribund state in early modern times. Islam by that period had degenerated to the point where it meant little more than a series of rituals to be performed and a Heaven-sent book to be memorized. This in turn had its effect upon education, which regressed to superficial, hair-splitting concentration on Moslem sacred studies.

Particularly valuable in this connection are the observations and conclusions of Bernier, a trained physician who had studied under the noted French scientist, Pierre Gassendi, before spending the years 1656 to 1668 in the Middle East and especially India. Bernier attributed the sterility in education and science partly to the exploitative political system and partly to the lack of any notion or desire for experimental and verifiable scientific research.

> A profound and universal ignorance is the natural consequence of such a state of society as I have endeavoured to describe. Is it possible to establish in *Hindoustan* academies and colleges properly endowed? Where shall we seek for founders? or, should they be found, where are the scholars? Where the individuals whose property is sufficient to support their children at college? or, if such individuals exist, who would venture to display so clear a proof of wealth? . . .
>
> It is not surprising that the *Gentiles* [Hindus] understand nothing of anatomy. They never open the body either of man or of beast, and those in our household always run away, with amazement and horror, whenever I opened a living goat or sheep for the purpose of explaining . . . the circulation of the blood. . . . Yet notwithstanding their professed ignorance of the subject, they affirm that the number of veins in the human body is five thousand, neither more nor less; just as if they had carefully reckoned them. . . .
>
> In geography they are equally uninstructed. They believe that the world is flat and triangular, that it is composed of seven distinct habitations, differing in beauty, perfection, and inhabitants, and that each is surrounded by its own peculiar sea; that one sea is of milk; another of sugar; a third of butter; a fourth of wine; and so on. . . . and finally that the whole of this world is supported on the heads of a number of elephants, whose occasional motion is the cause of earthquakes.[19]

A final factor explaining Moslem decline is that the three great Moslem empires were all land empires. They were built by the Turks, the Persians, and the Moguls, all peoples with no seafaring traditions whose empires therefore faced inwards, with their backs turned to the sea. It is true that they did include certain provinces that for long had carried on oceanic trade. In the Ottoman Empire was Egypt, for centuries a focal point in the trade in spices and other commodities exchanged between South Asia and Europe. Similarly, the Mogul Empire included the state of Gujarat on the west coast of India, which for long had sent out fleets eastward to Southeast Asia and westward to the Middle East. Egypt had been conquered by the Turks in 1517, and Gujarat by the Moguls in 1572. The new rulers were not vitally interested in overseas trade, so that when the Portuguese began seizing all the strategic locations in the Indian Ocean, little was done to check them. The Turks did send some expeditions down the Red Sea, but these were negligible compared to their land expeditions to Persia and Central Europe. Nor did the Mogul emperors effectively aid their Gujarat subjects against the Portuguese interlopers who were seizing control of the Indian Ocean trade routes.

The significance of this situation is that the Europeans were able to become the masters of the world trade routes with little opposition from the Moslems who hitherto had controlled most of the trade between Asia and Europe. The repercussions were far-reaching, for the control of world trade enriched the Europeans tremendously and stimulated further their economic, social, and political development. Thus a vicious circle developed, with worldwide trade making Western Europe increasingly wealthy, productive, dynamic, and expansionist, while the once-formidable Moslem empires, taking little part in the new world economy, remained static and fell further and further to the rear.*

Turning to the Confucian world, the situation there was basically similar, though with local variations—the same general forces at work, and the same decline vis-à-vis the West.

SUGGESTED READING

The spread of Islam from the time of Mohammed to the end of the nineteenth century is well described by T. W. Arnold, *The Preaching of Islam,* rev. ed. (London: Constable, 1913). A general survey of the history of the Moslem world is given in C. Brockelman, *History of the Islamic Peoples* (New York: Putnam, 1947). An invaluable source for many aspects of Islamic history is available in M. G. S. Hodgson, *Introduction to Islamic Civilization: Course Syllabus and Selected Readings* (Chicago: Univ. of Chicago, 1958–1959), 3 vols. Finally, the general trends and characteristics of the Moslem world in early modern times are analyzed perceptively in M. G. S. Hodgson, "The Unity of Later Islamic History," *Journal of World History,* V, No. 4 (1960), 879–914.

For the Ottoman Empire, the most detailed and authoritative study is by H. A. R. Gibb and H. Bowen, *Islamic Society and the West,* Parts I, II (London: Oxford Univ., 1950, 1957). See also S. N. Fisher, *The Middle East* (New York: Knopf, 1959) for the Asiatic provinces of the Ottoman Empire, and L. S. Stavrianos, *The Balkans since 1453* (New York: Holt, 1958) for the European provinces. A short collection of source materials are available in L. S. Stavrianos, *The Ottoman Empire: Was It the Sick Man of Europe?* (New York: Holt, 1957).

A comprehensive history of Persia is given in P. Sykes, *History of Persia* (London: Macmillan, 1930), 2 vols. The Safavid period is treated in the two works by L. Lockhart, *Nadir Shah* (London: Luzac, 1938) and *The Fall of the Safavi Dynasty* (Cambridge: Cambridge Univ., 1958).

An excellent survey of historical literature on India is given in R. I. Crane, *The History of India: Its Study and Interpretation* (Washington: Service Center for Teachers of History, 1958). The standard general histories of India are in this survey. Since its publication has appeared perhaps the best and most readable general history: P. Spear, *India: A Modern History* (Ann Arbor: Univ. of Michigan, 1961). On the Mogul period, there is H. Lamb, *Babur the Tiger* (New York: Doubleday, 1961); M. Prawdin, *The Builders of the Mogul Empire* (London:

* See "Results of Moslem Decline," *EMM,* No. 15.

48

Allen, 1963); W. H. Moreland, *India at the Death of Akbar* (London: Macmillan, 1920); W. H. Moreland, *From Akbar to Aurangzeb* (London: Macmillan, 1923); and P. Spear, *Twilight of the Mughals* (Cambridge: Cambridge Univ., 1951). For foreign reactions to Mogul India, see E. F. Oaten, *European Travellers in India* (London: K. Paul, 1909) and J. C. Locke, ed., *The First Englishmen in India* (London: Routledge, 1930).

Finally, on the decline of the Moslem Empires, see J. J. Saunders, "The Problem of Islamic Decadence," *Journal of World History,* VII (1963), 701–20; T. Stoianovich, "Factors in the Decline of Ottoman Society in the Balkans," *Slavic Review,* XXI (December, 1962), 623–32; and B. Lewis, "Some Reflections on the Decline of the Ottoman Empire," *Studia Islamica,* No. 9 (1959).

*One need not be obsessed with the merits of
the Chinese to recognize that the organization
of their empire is in truth the best that
the world has ever seen.*

VOLTAIRE, *1764*

Chapter
4

Confucian World at the Time of the West's Expansion

Corresponding to the Moslem world in the Middle East and South Asia was the Confucian world in East Asia. Just as the Moslem world was dominated by the Ottoman, Safavid, and Mogul empires, so the Confucian world was dominated by China, with Korea and Japan as peripheral entities. The two worlds were similar in one fundamental respect: they were both agrarian-based and inward-looking societies. Their tempo of change was slow and within the framework inherited from earlier times. On the other hand, the Confucian world differed substantially from the Moslem by virtue of its much greater unity. This was provided by the overpowering pre-eminence of China in all fields—cultural, political, and military. Furthermore, China herself possessed a cohesion that none of the Moslem empires could match. China had no indigestible minority blocs comparable to the various Balkan Christians in the Ottoman Empire, and no religious divisions analagous to Hindus and Moslems in the Mogul Empire. This cohesiveness of China was not a recent phenomenon. It dated back for millennia to the beginnings of Chinese civilization and has persisted to the present day. Indeed, the Chinese civilization is the oldest continuous civilization in the world. This fact is of considerable significance, for it helps to explain the great difference between China's and Japan's response to the intrusion of the West.

50   I. CONTINUITY OF CHINESE CIVILIZATION

One reason why China possesses the oldest continuous civilization in the world is geographic—its unparalleled degree of isolation from the other great civilizations of mankind. China possesses nothing comparable to the Mediterranean which linked together Mesopotamia, Egypt, Greece, and Rome, or comparable to the Indian Ocean which allowed India to interact with the Middle East, Africa, and Southeast Asia. Instead, during most of her history, China was effectively cut off on all sides. To the southwest and west are the highest mountain ranges in the world. To the east is the Pacific Ocean, impassable until very recent times. To the north and northwest are deserts and steppe lands that offer considerable protection, which the Chinese reinforced by building their 1,400-mile Great Wall to keep out the threatening nomads. The significance of this isolation is that it allowed the Chinese to develop their civilization with fewer intrusions from the outside than the peoples of the Middle East or India faced. Consequently, their civilization was both more continuous and also more distinctive—it has more fundamental differences from the other great Eurasian civilizations than they have from one another.

The unique size of China's population has also contributed to the continuity of civilization. From the beginning China has been able to support a huge population because of a favorable combination of soil and climate. The monsoon rains come during the warm months of the year, so that two crops per year are possible, in contrast to the Middle East and Europe. Furthermore, rice produces a much larger yield per acre than the wheat or barley grown in most parts of Eurasia. Thus the census of A.D. 2 showed that Han China had a population of 59.5 million—more than that of the Roman Empire at its greatest extent. By the early sixteenth century when the Portuguese first arrived, China's population was over 100 million, more than that of all Europe. By the mid-nineteenth century when China was being forced open by Western gunboats, her population had spurted upward to over 400 million, partly because of the introduction of such New World food crops as peanuts, maize, and sweet potatoes. The 1953 census revealed a population for mainland China of 583 million, and it has been growing since then at a rate of between 13 and 20 million per year. There are today about 700 million Chinese, comprising one quarter of the entire human race!

Such unparalleled manpower resources made it possible for the Chinese to retain their identity regardless of the course of events. They have been conquered and ruled by the Mongols and Manchus, as well as battered and subverted by the West. But in the end their superiority in numbers together with their superiority in civilization always enabled them to assimilate or expel the intruders, and to adapt selected aspects of foreign cultures to their traditional civilization. Never has wholesale transformation been imposed from the outside, as it was in Europe with the Germanic invasions or in the Middle East and in India with the Moslem ones.

China's agricultural way of life contributed to the continuity of its civilization. Agriculture was the foundation of China's society, and the feasibility of cultivating land set the limits of Chinese civilization. Where agriculture was possible, there developed Chinese civilization; where it was not possible, there was a pastoral way of life, whether Mongol or Manchu or Turkic. In the agricultural zones the typical Chinese peasant with his straw hat was to be found working hard in his wheat field or rice paddy. But in the North and West, where rainfall was insufficient for agriculture, there was instead the non-Chinese nomad, mounted on his horse and tending his flocks. China, like the Moslem world, experienced no commercial and industrial revolution. Instead, the villages remained the foundation on which the Middle Kingdom rested, and the peasants, who always comprised at least four-fifths of the total population, supported on their broad backs the city dwellers and courtiers and soldiers.

Another important factor in China's cohesiveness is the existence of a single written language that goes back several millennia to the earliest Shang dynasty. This written language is of special significance because it is understood by Chinese from all regions, speaking dialects as different from each other as Italian is from Spanish, or Swedish from German. The reason it is understandable to all is that it consists of characters representing ideas or objects. These characters are pronounced in different ways in different parts of China, but the meaning of any character is the same no matter how it is pronounced. It is as if an Italian, a Swede, and an Englishman took the figure 8 and pronounced it in their various tongues; the meaning to each of the three still would be the same. This common written language has been an important force in providing unity and historical continuity to China. In fact, it has done so to all of East Asia, for the Chinese method of writing has been adopted in whole or in part by most of the surrounding peoples, including the Japanese, Koreans, and some of the Southeast Asians.

Related to the common written language is the extraordinary system of public examinations by which for nearly two millennia China staffed her civil service on the basis of merit. "When the right men are available, government flourishes. When the right men are not available, government declines." This maxim from the Doctrine of the Mean, one of the Confucian classics, expresses the fundamental Chinese tenet that problems of state are better met by recruiting men of talent than by the legal and institutional change that is typical of the West. When fully evolved, the system consisted of a series of examinations. The first, in the district and prefectural cities, occurred every two or three years, and the approximately 2 per cent of the candidates who were passed took the prefectural exams a few weeks later. Survivors (about half the candidates) became eligible for appointment to minor posts and for further examinations held every three years in the provincial capitals. Success here entitled one to take the imperial examinations at the capital. Only 6 per cent passed this hurdle and became eligible for appointment to high office; and only a third of these normally passed the climactic palace examination in the presence of the Emperor himself, and were admitted to membership in the most exalted fraternity of Chinese scholarship, the Hanlin Academy, from which were selected the historiographers and other high literary officers.

At first the examinations were fairly comprehensive, emphasizing the Confucian classics but including also subjects like law, mathematics, and political affairs. Gradually, however, they came to concentrate on literary style and Confucian orthodoxy. The net result was a system that theoretically opened

52

offices to all men of talent, but that in practice favored the classes with sufficient wealth to afford the years of study and preparation. This did not mean that a hereditary aristocracy ruled China; rather, it was a hierarchy of the learned, a literocracy, providing China with an efficient and stable administration that won the respect and admiration of Europeans. On the other hand, it was a system that stifled originality and bred conformity. So long as China remained relatively isolated in East Asia, it provided stability and continuity. But with the intrusion of the dynamic West it served instead to prevent effective adjustment and response, until it was finally abolished altogether in 1905.*

But perhaps the most important factor contributing to the cohesiveness of Chinese civilization was the moral code and the literary and intellectual heritage known as Confucianism. This comprised the teachings of Confucius as modified and embellished by later generations. Traditional accounts record that Confucius (551–479 B.C.)—his name is the Latinized form of K'ung-fu-tzu, or "Master Kung"—was a minor official who attracted a number of students because of his reputation as a scholar. He and his disciples wandered for years through China in search of some ruler who would practice his principles of government and give him a post worthy of his talents. Failing in his search Confucius returned to his native state and resumed his teaching until death. In his chosen role as a practical politician, Confucius was a complete failure, but in his incidental occupation as a teacher he had history-making though belated success.

Like most Chinese thinkers, Confucius was concerned primarily with the establishment of a happy and well-organized society in this world. Although he believed in the spirits and Heaven, he was not much interested in metaphysics or in speculation about the afterlife. When asked about the meaning of death, Confucius replied, "We have not yet learned to know life; how can we know death?" This lack of concern for the otherworldly led in time to a strong agnostic strain in Confucian thought, which contrasts sharply with the traditional interest in the divine in India, the Middle East, and the West.

Confucius' first principle was "every man in his place"—"Let the ruler be a ruler and the subject a subject; let the father be a father and the son a son." Confucius defined the proper social relationships between people of different stations of life. If each individual acted in accordance with his station, then the family would be orderly, and when the family was orderly, the state would be peaceful and all would be harmonious under Heaven.

Confucius also provided China with a philosophy of government. His innovation was the concept that government is basically an ethical problem. He made no distinction between politics and ethics, since social harmony depended on virtuous rulers providing for the welfare and happiness of their subjects. Just as the individual should be subordinate to the family, so the family should be subordinate to the emperor. But the emperor in turn should set an example of benevolent fatherhood, and this was to be done by following the ethics of Confucianism rather than a system of law. These teachings represented a radical departure in Chinese thought, which hitherto had been essentially premoral, centering primarily around auguries and sacrifices. Confucius

* See "The Civil Service Examination," *EMM,* No. 17.

thus was the founder of a great ethical tradition in a civilization that, more than any other, came to concentrate on ethical values.

One reason for the extraordinary success of Confucianism is that its moral justification for authority and social inequality appealed to rulers and to the wealthy. Yet at the same time its high ethical principles gave the *status quo* a stronger foundation than mere hereditary right, and served as a constant stimulus to improve government and social relationships. Confucianism triumphed also because of its timeliness. It provided China, and much of East Asia, with both a rationalization and a guide line for its way of life. As a result, it served as the bedrock of Chinese civilization for over two millennia. As late as the mid-twentieth century, Generalissimo Chiang Kai-shek strove to bolster his nationalist regime against the Communists by a return to the ethics of Confucianism! *

All these factors, perhaps, are necessary to explain the continuity of Chinese civilization since its beginnings about 1500 B.C. The history of the Middle East presents a sharp contrast: Alexander's conquests spread the new Hellenistic culture; the Moslem conquests brought radical changes in race, language, and culture, as well as religion. India, likewise, was transformed fundamentally with the Aryan invasions about 1500 B.C. and the Moslem invasions after A.D. 1000. The historical evolution of China was never jarred by such seismic upheavals. There were many invasions, and on two occasions foreign dynasties ruled the entire country, but these intrusions disturbed rather than transformed. Instead of massive breaks and new beginnings, China throughout her history experienced merely the rise and fall of dynasties within the traditional framework.

II. DYNASTIC CYCLES

An observant Westerner, Thomas Meadows, commented in the nineteenth century: "Of all the nations that have attained a certain degree of civilization, the Chinese are the least revolutionary and the most rebellious." He was referring to the rise and fall of dynasties that has characterized Chinese history and that has brought not revolutions but merely changes of ruling families. This cyclical pattern can be explained by certain recurring trends that caused dynastic decline.

Each new dynasty normally began by ruling the country efficiently and ushering in a period of comparative peace and prosperity. It stimulated intellectual and cultural life, and protected the country by sending military expeditions against the nomads and extending the imperial frontiers. But gradually the dynasty was weakened by the personal degeneration of individual rulers and by court struggles between gentry cliques and palace eunuchs. This deterioration and factionalism undermined central authority and promoted corruption in the bureaucracy. The corruption, together with the increasing luxuriousness of court life, meant heavier taxes on the peasantry who ultimately produced the surplus that supported the entire imperial structure. Taxes tended to increase also because of the costly foreign wars and the emperors'

* See "The Confucian Way of Life," *EMM*, No. 16.

practice of granting tax exemption to many of the gentry and to Buddhist temples and monasteries. And as the government became lax, the irrigation systems and other public works essential for agriculture tended to be neglected.

Thus an increasingly impoverished peasantry had to bear the burden of a mounting tax load. When to this was added the inevitable visitation of crop failures and famines, the explosion point came, and revolts broke out against government tax collectors and landlord rent agents. In time these local uprisings broadened into general insurrections, which in turn were an invitation to the nomads to invade, especially since the imperial armies by this stage were poorly maintained. The combination of internal rebellion and external invasion usually heralded the beginning of a new cycle—the approaching end of the old dynasty and the coming of a new one.

The first dynasty, the Shang (1523–1028 B.C.), arose in the north in the Yellow River valley. Already the Chinese had learned to make silk, had devised their distinctive writing system, had mastered the art of creating beautiful earthenware and bronze vessels, and had begun to make a clear distinction between "Chinese" and "barbarians" based on a sense of cultural rather than racial superiority.

The succeeding Chou dynasty (1028–221 B.C.), although long lived, was unable to establish a stable central government. The Chou political structure was somewhat similar to that of medieval Europe, with a large number of warring feudal states disregarding the nominal Chou overlord. But this troubled political scene led to anxious soul-searching among Chinese intellectuals. Their speculations on the nature of man and society culminated in the great philosophical systems and literary classics of Chinese civilization. Both Confucianism and Taoism were now evolved, so that the Chou centuries, spanning a period as long as the entire European Middle Ages, stand out as the era when the cultural foundations of China were laid.

The following Ch'in dynasty (221–206 B.C.), despite its short duration, was responsible for replacing Chou feudalism with a tightly organized imperial structure that lasted until the fall of the last dynasty in 1912. This structure included an all-powerful emperor, an efficient and disciplined bureaucracy, a network of military roads, and the Great Wall in the North, all of which gave China the most stable and lasting government in the world.

The Ch'in dynasty was succeeded by the Han (206 B.C.–A.D. 220), which is noted for its expansion of China's frontiers in all directions—west into Central Asia, north into Manchuria, and south into Indochina. This Han Empire was at least the equal of the contemporary Roman Empire in size, population, wealth, and cultural achievement. Chinese silk was in great demand among the wealthy classes in Rome, the famous Chinese glazed pottery became known abroad as "China," and Chinese paper and printing began their slow penetration westward.

The Han Empire, like the Roman, collapsed because of internal decay and invasions from the north. But in the West the fall of Rome led to several centuries of disorder and convulsion until a radically different type of society emerged. The Europe of A.D. 1000, when the various invasions finally petered out, was very different from the Europe of Roman days. The new Europe was a combination of German and Christian as well as Roman elements. It was a Europe with a new religion, new ethnic strains, new Germanic and Romance languages, and new nation-states arising from the imperial ruins. In China, by contrast, the Han dynasty was followed, after an intervening period of disorder, by the T'ang and Sung dynasties (618–907 and 960–1279), which represented a continuation of the traditional civilization, albeit with certain refinements and modifications, as well as foreign contributions such as Buddhism from India.

The following Yuan dynasty (1279–1368) was unique in that it was Mongol rather than Chinese. In the past, China had been invaded frequently by nomads who occasionally had gained control of individual regions. Now for the first time one of these barbarian invaders succeeded in conquering and ruling the entire country. The Mongols, in fact, had overrun most of Eurasia, so that China was now part of a huge empire extending from the Pacific to the Black Sea. But these Mongol rulers were few in numbers compared to their millions of Chinese subjects, and they failed to win the support of the Chinese gentry and peasants. They ruled as conquerors, making few concessions to Chinese institutions or the Chinese way of life. They used foreigners in administration, favored a degenerate form of Buddhism to Confucianism, and generally exploited the country. When their military power declined, their regime was swept away by rebellious peasants and estranged scholar-bureaucrats.

Following the expulsion of the Mongols, China was ruled by two more dynasties, the Chinese Ming (1368–1644) and the Manchu Ch'ing (1644–1912). Although the Manchus were foreigners like the Mongols, they were successful in ruling China because they gave prestige and opportunity to Chinese scholar-bureaucrats while maintaining administrative control. They respected and utilized Chinese institutions, but created a system of checks to protect their own position. A substantial minority of Chinese were included in the top imperial councils, while local government remained largely in Chinese hands. Consequently, the transition from the Ming to the Ch'ing was relatively easy. There was the inevitable banditry and rebellion associated with dynastic demise, but it was minor compared to the devastation and massacres during the contemporary Thirty Years' War (1618–1648) in Europe.

Consequently, this entire period, from the mid-fourteenth century to the nineteenth when the European intrusion in China began in earnest, is one of the great eras of orderly government and social stability in human history. The traditional institutions and practices continued smoothly and satisfyingly— the agricultural economy, the Confucian way of life, the examination system for the selection of public officials, and the revered rule of the Son of Heaven in Peking.

In ordinary times such order and permanence would be considered a blessing. But these were the centuries that witnessed the rise of a new and dynamic Europe—the centuries of the Renaissance, the Reformation, the Commercial and Industrial Revolutions, the French Revolution, and the rise of powerful national states that quickly extended their domination over the entire globe. In such a period, stability became a curse rather than a blessing. China appeared, and in fact was, relatively speaking, static and backward. The idea of continual change and "progress," which now was taken for granted in the West, remained alien to the Chinese mind. Change was acceptable only within the limits of the traditional order. In a period of revolutionary change on a global scale, the comfortable and satisfied Chinese had their eyes fixed firmly on the past.

III. THE MIDDLE KINGDOM AND THE TRIBUTE SYSTEM

The basic difference between Chinese and European attitudes to the world about them was manifested in the Chinese decision to discontinue the spectacular overseas expeditions of the Ming dynasty (see Chapter 2, section VII). Because the Chinese Empire was agrarian, the Mings and the Manchus, like the Moguls, were uninterested in the possibilities of profit from overseas enterprise, and left the oceans to the Arabs and the Europeans.

The Chinese tribute system regulating relations with foreign states is further evidence of the difference. As early as the Shang period the Chinese regarded foreigners as culturally inferior barbarians. Later they applied Confucian family morality to their relations with other states. The family of nations naturally was to be headed by the Son of Heaven. China, the superior "Middle Kingdom," was surrounded by inferior tribute states which were considered as children. Just as children were expected to obey and revere their parents, so the lesser states were to act likewise toward China. Specifically, this took the form of periodic tribute missions which offered presents to the emperor and paid homage to him, including the kowtow—three kneelings and nine prostrations. The frequency of these missions depended on proximity, varying from yearly visits in the case of Korea to one every ten years for Burma or Laos.

The main purpose of the tribute system was to secure peace and order for China along her vast frontiers, and in practice it was generally successful. The lesser states accepted the system because of the prestige of relations with the Celestial Court, because of the cultural advantages to be gained from the great center of civilization, and because the Chinese made the tributary status economically profitable by giving more valuable presents than they received and by granting certain trade concessions. But again the very success of the Chinese contributed to their undoing. It reinforced their assumption that China was the center of a world system lacking competing states or authority. Tributary relations were the only form of international conduct they recognized. The idea of the legal equality of nations was for them incomprehensible. Thus, the Chinese concept of international relations was in direct conflict with the emerging international law of Europe. There was no common ground on which relations between China and the Western world could be based.

IV. EARLY RELATIONS WITH THE WEST

Relations between China and the West did not become continuous until the expansion of Europe following the voyages of Columbus and the Portuguese navigators. Prior to that time the interaction between the extreme east and west ends of the Eurasian landmass had been sporadic and usually indirect. The earliest was the silk trade with Rome. Carried on through Middle Eastern merchants, this trade reached such proportions that the Roman economy was affected by the resulting drain of gold and silver, since the Chinese were not interested in importing Roman or any other foreign goods. This situation, in fact, was typical of China's economic relations with the outside world until the nineteenth century, and it reflected not Chinese prejudice but rather superior wealth and technology during most of those centuries.

During the T'ang and Sung periods, Persian and Arab merchants established large trading communities in the ports of the South China coast and the lower Yangtze. Some of these foreign trading families remained in China for five generations. They became quite Sinicized, taking local wives and even producing learned men who entered the Chinese bureaucracy through the examination system.

Much greater interaction with the lands to the west occurred during the Mongol period. Thanks to the continentwide Mongol conquests, safe travel between China and Europe became possible for the first time during the century after 1240. A considerable number of Europeans now journeyed eastward, some being churchmen who hoped to convert the Mongols to Christianity, others, like the Polos, being merchants who were attracted by the dazzling new trade opportunities. But with the disintegration of the Mongol Empire, the Moslems once again blocked the routes between East and West, and direct relations ceased (see Chapter 2, section VII).

China began to feel directly the impact of the dynamic new Europe when Portuguese merchants opened trade with Canton in 1514 and established a permanent commercial base at Macao in 1557. The Portuguese purchased Chinese silks, wood carvings, porcelain, lacquerware, and gold, and in return they sold nutmeg, cloves, and mace from the East Indies, sandalwood from Timor, drugs and dyes from Java, and cinnamon, pepper, and ginger from India. No European goods were involved for the simple reason that there was no market for them in China. The Portuguese were functioning as carriers and middlemen for a purely intra-Asian trade.

The Dutch and the British eventually arrived to challenge Portugal's monopoly in the China trade. Representatives of the Dutch East India Company arrived in Canton in 1604, and representatives of the English East India Company in 1637. Neither was given official permission to trade, so that for decades the Dutch and English preyed on Portuguese shipping and conducted an irregular trade along the South China coast. By the mid-eighteenth century the Chinese opened up the trade to all countries, though confining it to Canton and Macao. The English soon won the lion's share of this trade, partly because of their growing commercial and industrial superiority and also because of their unequaled base of operations in India.

Meanwhile the Russians in Siberia had been trying to open trade relations with China, and the Chinese had reacted in the same way by restricting and regulating the commerce closely. The treaties of Nerchinsk (1689) and Kiakhta (1727) allowed the Russians to trade at three border points and to send commercial caravans every three years to Peking. There they were permitted to build a church and maintain a priest and three curates, though their community in the Chinese capital was limited in numbers to 300. Under these terms a few goods were exchanged—Russian furs, leather goods, textiles, cattle, horses, and glassware for Chinese silks, tea, lacquerware, and porcelain (see Chapter 8, section IV).

Cultural interaction between China and the West during these early centuries was confined to the efforts of the Jesuits to propagate their faith. Realizing that the normal means of conversion by preaching among the masses would not be effective in a country with an advanced culture like China, the Jesuits concentrated their efforts on the court and the bureaucracy. In 1582 Matteo Ricci was allowed to reside in Canton, and twenty years later in Peking, where his knowledge of mathematics and astronomy impressed Chinese officials and intellectuals. When at last he ventured to discuss religious matters, he sought to show that Christian doctrine was compatible with Confucianism.* Later Jesuit priests continued with this approach and made themselves useful to Ming and Manchu emperors as technicians, tutors, and diplomatic agents. Jesuit fathers helped the Chinese cast their first cannon and negotiate their first treaty with Russia. These methods did not produce mass conversions, but they did win respect for Western Christianity and science, and by the eighteenth century over 300,000 had been converted to the faith.

Unfortunately for the Christian cause, the Jesuits' accommodation to Confucianism led to controversies with other Catholic orders and to eventual disaster. The main issue was the "rites controversy" concerning the compatibility of Chinese ancestor worship with Christianity. The Jesuits maintained that ancestor worship was only a civil rite, intended to preserve the continuity of family tradition; the Dominicans and Franciscans argued to the contrary that it was a heathen religious ceremony, incompatible with Christianity. When the Pope finally ruled against the Jesuits in 1745, the emperor, already alienated by the long bickering and by the insolence of occasional papal legates to his court, retaliated by banning all Christian missionary activities. From then on Christianity declined rapidly in China.

The net result of centuries of Jesuit enterprise had proven negligible. Indeed, Europe had been much more impressed by China's examination system and Confucian ethics than China had been by Europe's science and mathematics. A European traveler of this period referred to the Chinese as being *Di nostra qualità*—"of our quality." It never would have occurred to the Chinese to return the compliment.†

During the century following the papal decision, there was no intellectual contact between China and the West. The Chinese remained supremely self-confident and self-contained following their first encounter with Europe. They had kept Western merchants confined to a few seaports and frontier trading posts; they had recognized with a few exceptions only tributary relations in their conduct of international affairs; and they had evinced only a passing interest in Jesuit teachings about science and theology that they eventually rejected or forgot. Never in history had a people faced the future with so much self-assurance and with so little justification.

V. Japan Absorbs Chinese Civilization

Japan was even more isolated than China from the rest of Eurasia. Few travelers reached its shores, so that it was the object of much speculation and myth. Marco Polo, for example, despite all his travels and official connections, could only repeat a few rumors concerning Japan. "The people of the great

* See "Jesuit Report on Sixteenth Century China," *EMM*, No. 18.
† See "Failure of Jesuit Mission to China," *EMM*, No. 19.

island of Chipango," he wrote, "were white, civilized, and well-favored; idolaters dependent on nobody and possessed of endless quantities of gold."

Compared to China, Japan obviously was a peripheral country and civilization in the sixteenth century when the Europeans first appeared. This does not mean that the Japanese were primitive; indeed, they had evolved a complex and dynamic society. Their first reaction to the appearance of the Europeans was positive, many of them embracing Christianity. But then, like the Chinese, they reacted against the "insolent barbarians," and severed virtually all ties with them. But the Japanese eventually realized that this policy of withdrawal was not feasible, and proceeded to study the ways of the West and adapt them to their needs. Thanks to their unique historical and cultural background, the Japanese were extraordinarily successful, quickly outdistancing the Chinese who for so long had been their mentors.

The importance of geographic location is particularly apparent in the case of Japanese history. In this respect there is a close parallel with the British Isles at the other end of the Eurasian landmass. The Japanese islands, however, are more isolated than the British, 115 miles separating them from the mainland compared to the 21 miles of the English Channel. Thus before their recent defeat by the United States, the Japanese had only once before been seriously threatened by foreign invasion, and that was in the thirteenth century. The Japanese, therefore, have been close enough to the mainland to benefit from the great Chinese civilization, but distant enough to be able to select and reject as they wished. In fact, the Japanese have been unusually sensitive and alert to what they have imported from abroad. Although popularly regarded as a nation of borrowers, they have independently evolved, because of their isolation, a larger proportion of their own culture than have any other people of comparable numbers and level of development.

The Japanese are basically a Mongoloid people who migrated from Northeast Asia, but the hairy Caucasoid Ainu who originally inhabited the northern islands contributed to their racial composition, and Malayan and Polynesian migrants from the south probably did also. Early Japan was organized in a large number of clans, each ruled by a hereditary priest-chieftain. Toward the end of the first century after Christ, the Yamato clan established a loose political and religious hegemony over the others. Its chief was the emperor, and its clan god was made the national deity.

This clan organization was undermined by the importation of Chinese civilization, which began on a large scale in the sixth century. Buddhism, introduced from Korea, was the medium for cultural change, fulfilling the same function here as Christianity did in Europe among the Germans and Slavs. Students, teachers, craftsmen, and monks crossed over from the mainland, bringing with them a new way of life as well as a new religion. The impetus for change culminated in the Taika Reform, which began in 645 and sought to transform Japan into a centralized state on the model of T'ang dynasty China. In accordance with the Chinese model, the country was divided into provinces and districts ruled by governors and magistrates who derived their power from the emperor and his council of state. Also, all land was nationalized in the name of the emperor and allotted to peasant households. The new owner-cultivators were responsible for paying to the central government a land tax in the form of rice and a labor tax that sometimes involved military service.

These and other changes were designed to strengthen imperial authority, and they did so in comparison with the preceding clan structure. But in practice, the Japanese emperor was far from being the undisputed head of a highly centralized state. The powerful hereditary aristocracy forced certain modifications in this Chinese-type administration that ultimately brought about its downfall. Although officials supposedly were appointed, as in China, on the basis of merit through examination, actually the old aristocracy succeeded in obtaining positions of status and power. Likewise, they retained many of their large landholdings, which were usually tax exempt and became manors outside the governmental administrative system. During this period the Fujiwara family perfected the dyarchy, or dual system of government. They did the actual work of ruling, furnishing the consorts for the emperor and filling the high civil and military posts. Meanwhile, the emperor passed his life in luxurious seclusion, not bothered by affairs of state or degraded by contacts with common men. His prime responsibility was to guarantee unbroken succession for ages eternal. This dyarchical system of government, which had no parallel in China, remained the pattern in Japan until the country was opened up by the Europeans in the nineteenth century.

In cultural matters there was the same adaptation of Chinese models. The Japanese borrowed Chinese ideographs but developed their own system of writing. They borrowed Confucianism but modified its ethics and adjusted its political doctrines to suit their social structure. They accepted Buddhism but adapted it to satisfy their own spiritual needs, while retaining their native Shintoism. They built new imperial capitals, first at Nara and then at Kyoto, that were modeled after the T'ang capital, Ch'ang-an. But there was no mistaking the Japanese quality of the temples, pavilions, shrines, and gardens. The imperial court became the center of highly developed intellectual and artistic activity. Court life is delightfully described in Lady Murasaki's famous eleventh century novel, *The Tale of Genji*. But this novel also reflects a society grown effeminate and devoted almost exclusively to the pursuit of aesthetic and sensual pleasures. This degeneration, which worsened in the next century, contributed to the coming of the new age of feudalism, when political power shifted from the imperial court to virile rural warriors.

VI. JAPANESE FEUDALISM

The Chinese system of imperial organization introduced by the Taika Reform of 645 worked effectively for a long period. By the twelfth century, however, it had been undermined and replaced by a Japanese variety of feudalism. One reason was the tendency of provincial governors, who were too fond of the refinements of Kyoto, to delegate their powers and responsibilities to local subordinates. Another was that powerful local families and Buddhist communities were always hungry for land and often able to seize it by force. They were willing to bring new land under cultivation so long as the incentive of tax exemption was maintained. These trends reduced the amount of tax-paying land, which meant an increased tax load for the peasant owner-cultivators. The latter in turn either fled to the northern frontier areas where the Ainu were being pushed back by force of arms, or else they commended themselves and their lands to lords of manors. This relieved them of taxes and provided them with protection, but at the cost of becoming serfs. The net result of this process was that by the end of the twelfth century, tax-paying land amounted to 10 per cent or less of the total cultivated area, and local power had been taken over by the new rural aristocracy.

At the same time, this aristocracy had become the dominant military force because of the disintegration of the imperial armed forces. The Taika Reform had made all males between the ages of twenty and sixty subject to military service. But the conscripts were required to furnish their own weapons and food and were given no relief from the regular tax burden. This arrangement proved unworkable and was abandoned in 739. Government military posts became sinecures generally filled by effeminate court aristocrats. As a result, the campaigns against the Ainu were conducted by the rural aristocrats. They became mounted warriors and gradually increased their military effectiveness until they completely overshadowed the imperial forces. A feudal relationship now developed between these rural lords and their retainers, or *samurai* (literally "one who serves"). This relationship was based on an idealized ethic, known as *bushido*, or "way of the warrior." The *samurai* enjoyed special legal and ceremonial rights, and in return they were expected to give unquestioning service to their lords.

By the twelfth century, Japan was controlled by competing groups of feudal lords. For some time the Fujiwara were able to maintain a balance of power by throwing what strength they had on one side or another. In the end, one of these lords, Minamoto Yoritomo, emerged victorious. In 1192 the Emperor commissioned him *Seii-Tai-Shogun* (Barbarian-Subduing-Generalissimo), with the right to nominate his own successor. As Shogun, Yoritomo was commander-in-chief of all the military forces and responsible for the internal and external defense of the realm. From his headquarters at Kamakura, Yoritomo controlled the country in the name of the emperor, who continued to remain in seclusion in Kyoto. It was during this Kamakura Shogunate that the Mongols made their two attempts to invade Japan, in 1274 and 1281. On both occasions the Mongols were able to land, were fiercely resisted by the Japanese, and then scattered by great storms that destroyed the expeditionary forces. The Japanese, believing their deliverance due to the intervention of the gods, called these storms "divine winds" or *kamikaze*.

In 1333 the Kamakura Shogunate was brought to an end, largely as a result of intrigues at the imperial court as well as growing disaffection among the warrior class. The Ashikaga family now obtained the title of Shogun, but their authority never extended far beyond the environs of Kyoto. In the rest of Japan, local lords struggled to gain control of as much land as possible. The outcome was the rise of great territorial magnates known as *daimyo* ("great name"). At the beginning of the sixteenth century there were several hundred of these daimyo, each seeking to attain hegemony over all Japan. Toward the end of the century, Oda Nobunaga (1532–1582), after long campaigns against rival daimyo and independent Buddhist communities, had united about half the country under his rule.

Nobunaga was succeeded by his ablest general, Toyotomi Hideyoshi (1536–1598), a farmer's son who had started his career as a common foot soldier. Hideyoshi proved to be one of the greatest military leaders in Japanese history.

Not only did he unite the entire country, but he sent expeditionary forces to the mainland in 1592 and 1597 with the aim of conquering China. His death in 1598 led to the withdrawal of the second expedition. After a short struggle, Hideyoshi was succeeded by Tokugawa Ieyasu, who was made Shogun by the Emperor in 1603. This marked the beginning of the great Tokugawa Shogunate that was to rule the country until the restoration of imperial rule and the beginning of modernization in 1868.

VII. Tokugawa Shogunate

Ieyasu and his immediate successors formulated policies designed to perpetuate their family dominance. The material basis of their power lay in the Shogunal domain, which comprised between a fourth and a third of the total arable land and consisted of estates scattered strategically throughout the country, constituting control points against potentially hostile daimyo. Top government posts were filled by members of the Tokugawa family or personal retainers. The emperor was provided with revenues for his own support as well as that of a small group of court nobles, but he had no political function or authority. The headquarters of the Shogun administration was established at Edo, later Tokyo, where the daimyo were required to reside at regular intervals, and to leave both their wives and heirs as hostages when they returned to their lands. The Tokugawa also limited castle construction and placed restrictions on the number of retainers that each daimyo could retain.

As part of their effort to prevent any change that might undermine their rule, the Tokugawa perpetuated a rigid, hereditary class structure. At the top was the aristocracy, comprising about 6 per cent of the population. This included the court nobles, who had social priority but no power or property, and were therefore dependent on the shogun for support. Much more important was the feudal aristocracy headed by the shogun and including the daimyo as well as the samurai retainers.

The vast majority of Japanese were farmers, the second ranking class, which included landless tenants as well as landholders with plots ranging from an acre and a quarter to as many as 85 acres. Whatever their status, these peasants produced the rice that, in the final analysis, supported the aristocracy. The latter, in fact, measured their income in terms of rice.

The last two classes recognized by the Tokugawa were, in order of rank, the artisans and the merchants. The long period of peace and security during this shogunate allowed these townspeople to grow enormously in numbers and wealth. Money became increasingly the medium of payment, and the rice brokers and money exchangers became the most important merchants. They disposed of the surplus produce of the feudal aristocracy and provided credit at high interest, usually on the security of next year's income. Many of the daimyo, and sometimes the shogun himself, became indebted to these merchant-financiers. One reason was the heavy expense of maintaining at Edo the large establishments required by the hostage system. The rural classes also suffered because the price of rice failed to keep pace with the rising prices of other goods. Thus the wealth of the country flowed increasingly into the coffers of the merchants. In large cities such as Edo and Osaka, they lived on a lavish scale and generated their own cultural forms, such as the Kabuki drama, the woodblock print, and the novel of high life.

The Tokugawa created an ideological basis for their regime by sponsoring the Chu Hsi school of Confucianism, which stressed the virtues of filial piety and of loyalty to one's superior in any social grouping. Paternal power was absolute and unquestioned in the ideal Japanese family, and even more specifically articulated than in China. Particularly appealing to the Tokugawa was the Confucian emphasis on the moral basis of political legitimacy and on all the conservative virtues. Ieyasu himself, in his *Laws for the Military Houses,* prescribed a code of conduct for his samurai that stressed personal loyalty, sobriety, frugality, and the acceptance of class distinctions. One effect of this ideology was that the Japanese family system, especially that of the samurai, was closely integrated into society because of its subordination to the interests of the shogun or the daimyo. This harmony between the family and the state was much stronger than in China, and facilitated the modernization of Japan in the nineteenth century by providing a grassroots basis for national unity and action.

VIII. EARLY RELATIONS WITH THE WEST

The Tokugawa policy of preserving the *status quo* was for a while theatened by the intrusion of Western Europeans. The first to appear were a band of Portuguese sailors who were shipwrecked in 1542, over half a century before the establishment of the Tokugawa Shogunate. It was typical of the Japanese that the local daimyo, much impressed by the Portuguese firearms, learned how to make guns and gunpowder.

This initial contact was followed by regular visits by Portuguese traders who discovered that rich profits could be made in commerce between China and Japan. Because of raids by Japanese pirates, the Ming emperors had banned all trade with Japan. The Portuguese quickly stepped into the void and prospered handsomely, exchanging Chinese gold and silk for Japanese silver and copper. The extent and the profitable nature of this carrying trade are indicated by the meteoric rise of the terminal ports, Macao and Nagasaki. When first visited by the Portuguese in the mid-sixteenth century, they were obscure fishing villages; by the end of the century they had become among the most prosperous ports in Asia.

The Portuguese combined missionary enterprise with their commercial activities. Francis Xavier and other Jesuit fathers landed in 1549 and were allowed to preach among the masses of the people. They were unusually successful, apparently because their revivalist methods of proselytism satisfied the emotional needs of the downtrodden peasantry during this period of endemic civil war. Nobunaga permitted the new faith to prosper, welcoming it as a counterweight to the independent Buddhist communities that were causing him trouble. By 1582, when Hideyoshi succeeded Nobunaga, there were 150,000 converts, mostly in western Japan.

Hideyoshi viewed with concern both the new trade and the new religion. The Portuguese for example, were demanding the right to administer the city of Nagasaki, and threatened a trade boycott if they were refused. Likewise, the militant activities of the foreign missionaries seemed to the new shogun to be subverting the traditional Japanese society. In 1587 Hideyoshi ordered that all missionaries must leave, but his order was not effectively enforced, because of the fear that it would affect the profitable trade.

With the advent of the Tokugawa in 1603, Dutch traders, and a few British, were active in Japan alongside the Portuguese. The intense rivalry among these Europeans gave the Japanese a new freedom of action. They could now move against the missionaries without fear of losing the commerce. Furthermore, the Europeans intrigued against each other in their efforts to curry favor and win concessions. The Dutch, for example, reported to the shogun Portuguese plots to arm disaffected daimyo and overthrow his rule. Accordingly, Ieyasu decreed in 1614 that all missionaries must leave, and their converts, who by now numbered 300,000, must renounce their faith. This order was ruthlessly enforced. As a control measure, converts were forced to belong to a Buddhist temple, and many were executed on refusing.* Missionaries also were martyred, but it often proved difficult to distinguish between commercial and religious activities. The Japanese therefore went a step further and in 1624 banned all Spaniards, since they had been the most aggressive and defiant. In 1637, all Portuguese also were forced to depart, leaving only the Dutch, who had never shown any interest in propagating Christianity. Henceforth only the Dutch, besides the Chinese, were allowed to carry on trade, and this under severely restricted conditions on the Deshima islet in Nagasaki harbor. The isolationist policy was extended in 1636 to Japanese subjects, who were prohibited from going abroad on penalty of death. To reinforce this ban, ship construction was restricted to small vessels for the coastal trade. Thus began over two centuries of seclusion for Japan.†

This policy of excluding all foreign influences and freezing the internal *status quo* was designed to perpetuate the Tokugawa dominance. In practice it proved extraordinarily effective. Japan was reunified and subjected to a centralized political control as thorough and as efficient as in any European state before the French Revolution. But a heavy price was paid for this security and stability. Japan did not experience the transforming and rejuvenating historical movements that Western Europe did during this period. There was no ending of feudalism, no Reformation or Counter-Reformation, no overseas expansion, and no Commercial Revolution. For the Japanese, as for the Chinese, the price for two centuries of comforting seclusion was institutional and technological backwardness. This became apparent, more quickly to the Japanese than to the Chinese, when the Europeans forcibly broke into the hermit world of East Asia in the mid-nineteenth century.

SUGGESTED READING

Useful annotated bibliographies are provided by the Service Center for Teachers of History of the American Historical Association: J. W. Hall, *Japanese History* (Washington: 1961) and C. O. Hucker, *Chinese History* (Washington: 1958). Invaluable source materials on the culture of East Asia are available in W. T.

* See "Christian Martyrdom in Japan," *EMM,* No. 20.
† See "Edict Closing Japan," *EMM,* No. 21.

de Bary *et al., Sources of Chinese Tradition* (New York: Columbia Univ., 1960) and R. Tsunoda *et al., Sources of the Japanese Tradition* (New York: Columbia Univ., 1958).

The most recent and authoritative study of all East Asia is by E. O. Reischauer and J. K. Fairbank, *A History of East Asian Civilization,* Vol. I, *East Asia: The Great Tradition* (Boston: Houghton, 1958), which carries the story to the eve of modernization. Standard general histories of China are by K. S. Latourette, *The Chinese: Their History and Culture,* 3rd ed. (New York: Macmillan, 1946), 2 vols.; L. C. Goodrich, *A Short History of the Chinese People,* 3rd ed. (New York: Harper, 1959); and C. P. Fitzgerald, *China: A Short Cultural History,* rev. ed. (London: Cresset, 1950). Comparable histories of Japan are by G. B. Sansom, *Japan: A Short Cultural History,* rev. ed. (New York: Appleton, 1944) and the same author's definitive three-volume *A History of Japan* (Stanford: Stanford Univ., 1958–1964).

Finally, for the initial contact between East Asia and the West, see G. F. Hudson, *Europe and China: A Study of Their Relations from Earliest Times to 1800* (Boston: Beacon paperback, 1961); C. R. Boxer, *Fidalgos in the Far East, 1550–1770* (The Hague: Martinus Nijhoff, 1948); A. H. Rowbotham, *Missionary and Mandarin: The Jesuits at the Court of China* (Berkeley: Univ. of California, 1942); and C. R. Boxer, *The Christian Century in Japan, 1549–1650* (Berkeley: Univ. of California, 1951).

*To the nations, however, both of the East
and West Indies, all the commercial benefits
which can have resulted from these events
[the expansion of Europe] have been sunk
and lost in the dreadful misfortunes which
they have occasioned.*

ADAM SMITH

Non-Eurasian World at the Time
of the West's Expansion

W hen the Europeans penetrated the Moslem and Confucian worlds by sea, their initial reaction was generally one of respect and admiration. The only clear superiority the Westerners enjoyed was in naval warfare. In virtually all other matters they found the peoples of the Middle East and of South and East Asia to be at least their equals. This explains why three centuries elapsed before the Europeans were able to impose any degree of control over India and China.

In the non-Eurasian world, however, the situation was quite different. The peoples of sub-Saharan Africa, the Americas, and Australia had not attained comparable levels of political organization, economic development, and military effectiveness. Consequently they succumbed relatively early to European domination, though in quite different degrees. This chapter will deal with the conditions and institutions prevailing in the non-Eurasian world at the time of the West's intrusion, with emphasis on why sub-Saharan Africa remained impervious, apart from its coasts, until the nineteenth century, why the Americas were relatively easily penetrated, and why Australia from the beginning was wide open.

I. SUB-SAHARAN AFRICA   67

Geography

Sub-Saharan Africa (hereafter referred to as Africa) presents a curious paradox so far as its relations with Eurasia are concerned. Africa, in contrast to the Americas and Australia, has maintained an unbroken, though at times tenuous, contact with Eurasia. Yet the Europeans were much slower in penetrating into Africa than into either the Americas or Australia. Africa remained the "Dark Continent" centuries after the other newly discovered continents had been opened up and colonized. As late as 1865, when the Civil War was ending in the United States, only the coastal fringe of Africa was known, together with a few isolated sections of the interior. Even by 1900 about a fourth of the interior of Africa remained unexplored. Until relatively recently, cartographers depended heavily on their imaginations in preparing maps of the Dark Continent. As Dean Swift wrote:

> Geographers, in Afric's maps,
> With savage creatures filled the gaps;
> And o'er unhabitable downs
> Placed elephants for want of towns.

What is the explanation for Africa's strange imperviousness to Europe's dynamism despite the fact that the two continents are neighbors in the Eastern Hemisphere and have maintained connections since earliest times? The answer is to be found in part, though by no means entirely, in the operation of certain geographic factors. One of these is the hot, humid climate and, closely associated with it, the many tropical diseases that are particularly prevalent in the low-lying coastal areas. Not all of Africa is unhealthful: along the northern, southern, and eastern fringes of the continent are small but important areas of Mediterranean and subtropical climates where the majority of the European settlers live today. But large portions of the continent have an inhospitable climate, and it was these portions that the Europeans usually first encountered. One of the greatest African explorers observed:

> Africa is the chief stronghold of the real Devil—the reactionary forces of Nature hostile to the rise of Humanity. Here Belzebub, King of the Flies, marshals his vermiform and anthropoid hosts—insects, ticks, and nematode worms—which . . . convey to the skin, veins, intestines, and spinal marrow of men and other vertebrates the microorganisms which cause deadly, disfiguring, or debilitating diseases.[1]

The continent is also extraordinarily inaccessible. One reason is that the coastline, unbroken by bays, gulfs, or inland seas, is even shorter than Europe's, though Africa has thrice the area. And the lack of a Mediterranean, Baltic, or Black Sea means that Africa's interior is not open to the outside world. Africa's inaccessibility was enhanced by a formidable barrier in the north comprising the great Sahara and the Nile marshes. Effective barriers were to be found also in the form of thousand-mile-long sand bars along both the east and west coasts. And if these bars were penetrated, then still another obstacle remained —the rapids and waterfalls created by the rivers tumbling down a succession of escarpments from the interior plateau to the low coastlands.

The early Europeans were further discouraged by the lack of readily available sources of wealth in the interior of Africa, comparable to the gold and silver of the Americas or the spices of the East Indies. We shall see later (Chapter 6, section I) that the Portuguese became pioneers of European overseas exploration in order to tap the profitable gold and slave trade in the interior of Africa, hitherto controlled by Moslem merchants. But after the Portuguese discovered the Cape route to the Spice Islands of the East Indies, and after the Spaniards stumbled upon the treasures of Mexico and Peru, the African trade seemed inconsequential. The Europeans continued to hold their posts on the west coast of Africa in order to obtain slaves for the plantations of the New World. But the coastal footholds sufficed for that purpose, so no serious effort was made by Europeans to penetrate the interior until the establishment of the African Association in London in 1788.

Geography, however, was not the only factor that hindered European penetration. At least as important was the African Negro's general level of social, political and economic organization, which was high enough to offer effective resistance to the Europeans for centuries. But before considering the culture of the Negroes, we shall first examine their ethnic composition.

Peoples

In contrast to what is sometimes assumed, the African peoples are far from ethnically homogeneous. Various strains are to be found south of the Sahara, and have been throughout history. Their origins and diffusion remain in large part a mystery, however, and authorities are far from agreement. The ethnic classification that, for the present, at least, meets with the fewest objections, recognizes four major peoples: (1) Bushmen, who speak the Khoïsan language, (2) Pygmies, whose original language is unknown because they adopted those of their later conquerors, (3) Negroes, who speak the Niger-Congo language, and (4) Caucasoids, known also as Capsians, Cushites, and Hamites, who speak the Afroasiatic language. These four peoples seem to have originated in the region of Lake Victoria, whence the Bushmen migrated south to southern Africa, the Pygmies west to the Congo and the coastal rain forests of West Africa, the Negroes west to West Africa and northwest to the then fertile Sahara region, and the Caucasoids northwest to Egypt and North Africa, as well as northeast to Arabia and West Asia.

These categories and migrations, it should be re-emphasized, are by no means universally accepted. Indeed, one authority has summarized current knowledge, or lack of knowledge, as follows:

> . . . we can say little more than this: if one stands at Suez and looks south and southwest, people tend to get darker the further one goes. One must, even in this generalization, except the Bushmanoids. . . . The fact

of the matter is that, empirically, Egyptians are more or less Mediterranean Caucasoids; that as one goes south and southwest, there is a gradual change; along the Guinea Coast or in the Congo forests, the Negro stereotype is dominant. There is not, however, an undisputed "line" that can be drawn on a map, or distinctions that can be made between tribes (in other than statistical terms) with the claim that one is unequivocally Caucasoid and the other Negroid. In even the most dominantly Negroid tribes, there are to be found individuals with light skin and green eyes. . . .[2]

Cultures

The cultures of Africa were the outcome of a much greater degree of interaction with the outside world than had been possible in the Americas or Australia.* Agriculture, for example, which originated in Mesopotamia and then took root in Egypt in the fifth millennium B.C., may have spread from there to the Sudan. This is the savannah zone between the Sahara and the tropical rain forests, stretching from the Ethiopian highlands to the Atlantic coast. Some authorities, it should be noted, believe that agriculture was invented independently in this zone, along the upper reaches of the Niger River. Whether or not this is so, the fact remains that the great majority of the plants that eventually were cultivated in sub-Saharan Africa were importations. The most important of these were: from Mesopotamia and Egypt via the Nile—barley, wheat, peas, and lentils; from Southeast Asia—bananas, sugar cane, the Asian yam, and new forms of rice; from the New World via the Portuguese and later slave traders—tobacco, corn, lima and string beans, pumpkins, and tomatoes.

As basic for Africa as the introduction of agriculture was that of iron metallurgy. The latter definitely was an importation, with two sources being the most likely. One was Carthage, whence the art probably was spread by regular traders who still were able to cross the small but growing Sahara with horses. Shortly thereafter, when horses no longer could survive in the desert, the Romans solved the problem by introducing camels from Central Asia. The second source was the kingdom of Kush located on the upper Nile, with its capital at Meroë, a little north of Khartum. The Kushites, who were predominantly Negroids, learned ironmaking from the Assyrians. They were able to put their knowledge to good use, for their country, unlike Egypt, had abundant resources of iron ore and fuel. Meroë soon became a great iron-producing center. The huge mounds of slag still to be seen around the ruins of the capital suggest that it had served as the Pittsburgh of Central Africa. Presumably the iron and other products of civilization were traded for traditional African commodities such as slaves, ivory, and ostrich feathers. After more than a thousand years' existence, the Kushan kingdom declined during the third and fourth centuries A.D., but not before ironmaking had spread far to the south and west.

This diffusion of agriculture and iron metallurgy had profound repercussions on Africa. Population increased spectacularly, thanks to the new food plants

* See "The Nature of African History," *EMM,* No. 22.

70

and also to the new iron tools that made possible the extension of agriculture into the rain forest. Another important repercussion was the radical change in the ethnic composition of the continent. It was the accessible Negroes and Caucasoids of the Sudan, rather than the inaccessible Pygmies and Bushmen of the rain forests and the southern regions, who adopted and profited from agriculture and iron metallurgy. Consequently, it was they also who increased disproportionately in number and who were able, with their iron tools and weapons, to push southward at the expense of the Bushmen-Pygmies.

This expansionism was particularly marked in the case of the Bantus, a predominantly Negroid linguistic group. Starting from their original center in the Cameroon Highlands, they infiltrated in the early Christian era into the Congo basin, eliminating or subjugating the sparse Pygmy hunters. From there some pushed southeast to the fertile, open Great Lakes country, between A.D. 600 and 900. Then they continued southward across the savannah at the expense of the Bushmen, who suffered the same fate as the Pygmies. Meanwhile other Bantus were driving directly southward along the Atlantic coast, ultimately encountering a new people, the Hottentots. These are now believed to be simply Bushmen who had learned stockraising earlier, thus improving their diet and becoming larger than other Bushmen, whom they otherwise resemble. These migrations explain why the Negroes were the predominant ethnic group by the time the Europeans arrived, whereas a millennium earlier they had shared the continent fairly evenly with the Caucasoids, Bushmen, and Pygmies.

The development of Africa was affected basically not only by the coming of agriculture and iron, but also by the manifold contributions of Islam. These came partly from the Moslem colonies along the East African coast, but much more from Moslem North Africa. Although the Roman Empire had included all the arable lands along the entire 4,000 mile stretch of Africa's Mediterranean coast, its authority never extended across the desert. Yet it appears that a trans-Saharan trade was conducted from Lixus in present-day Morocco, and from Leptis Magna in present-day Libya, south toward the great bend of the Niger. The Africans provided gold, civet for perfumes, kola nuts for transportable food, slaves, and, after 1300, copper, and in return received cloth, cowrie beads, and, above all, salt, which was in urgent demand throughout the Sudan.

Contacts with North Africa increased greatly when the Moslem Arabs overran that entire region in the seventh century A.D. Later the Moslems also extended their influence down Africa's east coast, first as merchants, and, from the thirteenth century onward, as colonists. Their settlements dominated the coast as far south as Zanzibar, and their influence was felt much beyond to the mouth of the Zambezi.

From their bases on the northern and eastern coasts of the continent, the Moslem Arabs exerted a profound influence on Africa. They used the camel, much more than did the Romans, and correspondingly expanded the trans-Saharan trade. Likewise on the east coast they traded with the Negro interior for ivory, gold, slaves, and, later, iron ore. This ore was shipped to southern India, made into steel, reshipped to Persia and Asia Minor, and worked into the so-called Damascus blades. Among the products imported in return for these African commodities were Chinese and Indian cloth, and Chinese porcelain, remains of which can be found along the entire coast.

These commercial contacts led to Moslem cultural penetration. Islam spread down the east coast as far as Zanzibar, and intermittently beyond. From the Mediterranean coast it spread south across the Sahara into the Sudan. As is usually the case with the diffusion of a new faith, Islam was adopted first by the Negro ruling class and then seeped through to the people. In this manner an important part of Negro Africa was Islamized and became part of the vast Moslem world. Thus Ibn Battuta, the enterprising fourteenth century Arab traveler, included the Sudan in his journeys, which extended as far east as China.

The Islamization of the Sudan had repercussions extending far beyond religious matters. This was evident most obviously in the externals of life— names, dress, household equipment, architectural styles, festivals, and the like. It was evident also in the agricultural and technological progress that came with enlarged contact with the outside world. In East Africa the Arabs introduced rice and sugar cane from India. And it is recorded of Mai Idris alooma of Bornu, roughly a contemporary of Queen Elizabeth of England, that "Among the benefits which God (Most High) of his bounty and beneficence, generosity, and constancy conferred upon the Sultan was the acquisition of Turkish musketeers and numerous household slaves who became skilled in firing muskets." [3]

Islam also greatly stimulated the intellectual life of the Sudan. Literacy was spread with the establishment of Koranic schools. Scholars could pursue higher learning at various Sudanese universities, of which the University of Sankore at Timbuktu was the most outstanding. This institution was modeled after other Moslem universities at Fez, Tunis, and Cairo. It was the custom for scholars to move about freely among these universities and others in the Moslem world, to study at the feet of particular masters. The Moslem traveler Leo Africanus, who visited Timbuktu in 1513, found that the flourishing state of learning was due to the support it received from the ruler, Askia the Great. "Here [in Timbuktu] are great store of doctors, judges, priests, and other learned men, that are bountifully maintained at the kings cost and charges. And hither are brought divers manuscripts or written books out of Barbarie [North Africa], which are sold for more money than any other merchandize." [4]

The adoption of Islam also enhanced the political cohesion of the Sudanic kingdoms. Their rulers traditionally could claim the allegiance only of their own kinship units or clans, and of such other related kinship units as recognized descent from a great founding ancestor. But when the kingdoms were enlarged into great empires, this kinship relationship obviously became inadequate as the basis for imperial organization. The more widely an empire was extended, the more alien its emperor appeared to a large proportion of the subjects. Local chiefs could not be depended upon to serve as faithful vassals; they tended instead to lead their own people in resistance to imperial rule. Islam helped to meet this institutional problem by strengthening the imperial administration. Moslem schools and colleges turned out a class of educated men who could organize an effective imperial bureacracy. These men were not dominated by their kinship alliances; their own interests were tied to imperial authority, and they normally could be counted upon to serve that authority loyally.

It was this combination of agricultural and metallurgical progress, corresponding growth in economic productivity, flourishing interregional trade, and the stimulus from Islam that explains the succession of great Sudanic empires.* The most important were the Ghana (A.D. 300–1076), the Mali (1238–1488), and the Songhai (1488–1591) empires. The Songhai stretched 1,500 miles from the Atlantic into the interior, and in this expanse the rule of law and a common administrative system were given to many diverse subjects. Songhai's outstanding ruler, Askia the Great (1493–1528), was one of the foremost monarchs of his time—the equal of contemporary European kings, and superior to many in humaneness, religious tolerance, and devotion to learning. Moslem writers have depicted Askia as "a brilliant light shining after a great darkness; a saviour who drew the servants of God from idolatry and the country from ruin. The Defender of the Faithful, who scattered joy, gifts, and alms around him." [5]

It should be emphasized that, in contrast to what is often assumed, Islam was not the only, or even the leading, force behind these empires. In fact, the Ghana Empire largely preceded Islamic influence, which did not affect the Sudan until the eleventh century. Furthermore, the Islamic world played a destructive as well as constructive role in Africa. The disintegration of the Sudanic empires was in part the result of devastating Arab invasions across the Sahara. These marauding expeditions decimated the local populations, ruined prosperous agricultural areas, and disrupted lucrative trade patterns. Indeed, there is a striking parallel here between African and European history. Western Europe was able to forge ahead of Eastern Europe in the late Middle Ages because the latter region suffered continual invasions from the East, whereas Western Europe was immune after the tenth century. Likewise the Sudanese empires, which at one point boasted civilizations comparable to those of contemporary Europe, fell far behind in modern times because of the invasions from the north. These corresponded to the Mongol and Turkish invasions of Eastern Europe, and were in fact more cataclysmic in their consequences.

In large part because of the marked compartmentalization of the continent, the level of general development varied strikingly from region to region of sub-Saharan Africa. Uniform growth was impossible because of natural obstacles obstructing communication and movement between savannahs, rain forests, and deserts. By and large, the amount of progress varied with the amount of contact a particular area had had with the Eurasian centers of civilization. Political units thus included individual village communities recognizing only local chieftains, and the great empires of the Sudan. Economically, the range was as great: from the food-gathering Bushmen-Hottentot-Pygmies † to the following complex situation observed in Timbuktu by Leo Africanus in the sixteenth century:

---

* See "Negro Empire in the Sudan," *EMM*, No. 23.
† See "Pygmies of the Belgian Congo," *EMM*, No. 24.

It is a woonder to see what plentie of Merchandize is dayly brought hither, and how costly and sumptuous all things be. Horses bought in Europe for ten ducates, are here sold againe for fortie and sometimes for fiftie ducates a piece. There is not any cloth of Europe so course, which will not here be sold for fower ducates an elle, and if it be anything fine they will give fifteene ducates for an ell: and an ell of the scarlet of Venice or of Turkie-cloath is here worth thirtie ducates . . . but of al other commodities salt is most extremelie deere.[6]

It was with the highly developed peoples of West Africa that the Portuguese pioneers first established contact. They did so very naturally, because here there was enough population density and economic development to make trading profitable. Thanks to the banana and the yam, there was vigorous economic activity not only in the Sudan zone of West Africa, but also in the forested zone to the south, known as Guinea. The flourishing agriculture supported a relatively dense population and a brisk trade. A Dutch merchant was very much impressed by Benin, in present-day Nigeria, when he visited that city in 1602:

The town seemeth to be very great; when you enter it, you go into a great broad street, not paved, which seems to be seven or eight times broader than the Warcrooks . . .; it is thought that the street is a mile long [this is a Dutch mile, equal to about four English miles] besides the suburbs. At the gate where I entered on horseback, I saw a very high bulwark, very thick of earth, with a very deep broad ditch. . . . Without this gate there is a great suburb. When you are in the great street aforesaid, you see many great streets on the sides thereof, which also go right forth. . . . The houses in this town stand in good order, one close and even with the other, as the houses in Holland stand. . . . Their rooms within are four-square, over them having a roof that is not close[d] in the middle, at which place the rain, wind, and light come in, and therein they lie and eat their meat; but they have other places besides, as kitchens and other rooms. . . .

The King's Court is very great, within it having many great four-square plains, which round about them have galleries, wherein there is always watch kept. . . . It seems that the King has many soldiers; he has also many gentlemen, who when they come to court ride upon horses. . . . There are also many men slaves seen in the town, that carry water, yams, and palm wine, which they say is for the King; and many carry grass, which is for their horses; and all this is carried to the Court. . . .[7]

All this meant that the Portuguese were dealing with a people of sophisticated enough background to be able to meet them without fear or wonderment. The trading that arose with the coming of the Portuguese was novel for the West Africans only in its scale. Mercantile activity was not, in itself, something strange, since they for long had maintained trade ties with areas as far removed as Morocco and Egypt. It follows that the West Africans reacted to the Portuguese very differently from the manner in which the American

Indians were reacting to the Spaniards at the same time. It is true that the forest dwellers, who had not had direct contact with the Arabs, were astonished by the white skin of the Europeans, by the loud noise of their firearms, and by the fact that these newcomers came from the sea, which was much revered by the coastal peoples. Yet the fact remains that the arrival of the Portuguese did not produce the demoralization and disintegration in Africa that the Spaniards did in the Americas. Accordingly, the Africans traded with the Europeans on terms that they themselves dictated. For centuries the coastal chieftains refused to allow the Europeans to penetrate inland because they wished to maintain their profitable position as middlemen between the European buyers and the producers in the interior. A British official wrote in 1793 that Africa remained an unknown continent "rather from the jealousy of the inhabitants of the sea coasts, in permitting white men to travel through their country, than from the danger or difficulty attending the penetration." This jealousy he attributed to the middlemen's fear "that the advantages of their trade with Europe should be lessened [and] transferred from them to their neighbours; or that the inland kingdoms by obtaining European arms" would become dangerous rivals.[8]

Adam Smith, writing in 1776, realized this difference between the American Indians and the African Negroes in their capability for resisting European penetration.

> Though the Europeans possess many considerable settlements both upon the coast of Africa and in the East Indies, they have not yet established in either of those countries such numerous and thriving colonies as those in the islands and continent of America. Africa, however, as well as several of the countries comprehended under the general name of the East Indies, are inhabited by barbarous nations. But those nations were by no means so weak and defenceless as the miserable and helpless Americans; and . . . they were besides much more populous. . . . In Africa and the East Indies, therefore, it was more difficult to displace the natives, and to extend the European plantations over the greater part of the lands of the original inhabitants.[9]

II. AMERICAS

Geography

The Europeans were able to penetrate the Americas easily, and to bring the two continents quickly under their control and exploitation. This occurred despite the fact that an ocean separated the Old and the New Worlds, and that there had been no effective contact between the two in historic times until Columbus' voyage. The "miserable and helpless" plight of the Indians, noted by Adam Smith, did indeed prevent them from holding out against the Europeans; but certain geographic considerations also increased their vulnerability.

The Americas, in contrast to Africa, were on the whole easily accessible. No sandbars obstructed the approaches to the coasts. Harbors were much more frequently available along the indented coastline of the Americas than along the unbroken coastline of Africa. Also the Americas had a well-developed pattern of interior waterways that were relatively free of impediments and offered easy access to the interior. There was no counterpart in Africa to the majestic and smooth-flowing Amazon, Mississippi, or St. Lawrence. The explorers soon learned the use of the native birch-bark canoe, and they discovered that with comparatively few portages they could paddle from the Atlantic up the St. Lawrence, along the Great Lakes, and thence south down the Mississippi to the Gulf of Mexico, or north down the Mackenzie to the Arctic Ocean, or west down the Columbia or the Fraser to the Pacific Ocean!

The climate of the Americas, too, is generally more attractive than that of Africa. The Amazon basin, it is true, is hot and humid, and the polar extremities of both continents are bitterly cold, but the British and the French settlers flourished in the lands they colonized north of the Rio Grande, and the Spaniards likewise felt at home in Mexico and Peru, which became their two principal centers. The climate there is not much different from that of Spain, and certainly a welcome contrast to the sweltering Gold and Ivory Coasts.

Peoples

Almost all the native peoples were descendants of immigrants who crossed the Behring Sea from northeastern Siberia. *Almost* all—because small numbers of peoples from the islands of the South Pacific reached the west coast of South America after the arrival of the Behring Sea migrants. It is not known how many times these argonauts of the South Seas discovered South America, but the evidence from domesticated plants alone is sufficient to establish the fact of their transoceanic expeditions. When the same plants, so highly domesticated that they cannot survive without the aid of man, are found on both sides of the Pacific, their distribution can be explained only in terms of man's migrations.

It remains true, however, that at least 99 per cent of the Indians whom the Europeans found in the Americas were descended from the stock that had crossed the Behring Sea. Until recently it was believed that the Indians first began crossing over to the Americas about 10,000 years ago. New archaeological findings, together with the use of carbon-14 dating, have forced drastic revision of this estimate. It is now generally agreed that man certainly was in the New World 20,000 years ago, and probably 10,000 years before that. The last major migration of Indians took place about 3,000 years ago. Then came the Eskimos, who continued to travel back and forth across the Straits until modern political conditions forced them to remain on one side or the other. In any case, the parts of America closest to Asia were by this time sufficiently densely populated to discourage further migration.

The actual crossing to the New World presented little difficulty to the early Indians. The level of the sea was then considerably lower because much of the earth's water was frozen in the ice sheets. Accordingly, the first immigrants crossed over a wide land-bridge connecting Northeast Asia and northwest North America. After the sea level had risen, the crossing of the narrow

Straits could have been easily effected in primitive boats without ever being out of sight of land. Later and more advanced migrants may have traveled by boat from Asia to America and then continued along the northwest coast until they finally landed and settled directly in what is now British Columbia.

Most of those who crossed to Alaska moved on into the heart of North America through a gap in the ice sheet in the central Yukon plateau. They were impelled to press forward by the same forces that led them to migrate to America—the search for new hunting grounds and the continual pressure of tribes from the rear. In this manner both the continents were soon peopled by scattered tribes of hunters.

Regardless of their origin, all Indians may be classified as Mongoloids. They have the characteristic straight black hair, sparse on the face and body; high cheekbones; and the Mongolian spot that appears at the base of the spine in young children. Considerable variation exists, however, among the different tribes: the earliest varieties of American Indian are much less Mongoloid than the later ones, because they left Asia before the Mongoloids, as we know them today, had fully evolved. That the immigrants at once spread out and settled in small, inbred groups in a variety of climates also explains the presence of individual physical types.

The American Indians differed much more in the languages they spoke than in their physical appearance. Indeed, it is quite impossible to generalize about their languages, since practically every kind of phonetic and grammatical structure can be found. This linguistic diversity, like the physiological, developed because the Indians migrated to the Americas in small groups over a long period of time, and continued wandering and splitting up after their arrival. Thus, dialectical variations rapidly became emphasized and developed into separate languages. Closely related languages may be found in widely separated parts of America, reflecting the degree to which tribes moved about. The net result is that some 2,000 distinct Indian languages have been classified. This represents almost as much variation in speech as in the entire Old World, where about 3,000 languages are known to have existed in A.D. 1500.

Cultures

Anthropologists have defined some 22 culture areas in the New World—the Great Plains area, the Eastern Woodlands, the Northwest Coast area, and so forth. A simpler classification, on the basis of how food was obtained, involves three categories: hunting, gathering, and fishing cultures; intermediate farming cultures; and advanced farming cultures. This scheme is not only simpler but is also meaningful from the viewpoint of world history, for it helps to explain the varied responses of the Indians to the European intrusion.

The advanced farming cultures were located in Mesoamerica (central and southern Mexico, Guatemala, and Honduras) and the Andean highland area (Equador, Peru, Bolivia, and northern Chile). The intermediate farming cultures were generally in the adjacent regions, while the food-gathering cultures were in the more remote regions—the southern part of South America, and the western and northern part of North America.

This geographic distribution of culture points up the fact that in contrast to Africa, the most advanced regions in the Americas were not located closest to Eurasia. One reason is that northeast Siberia was not a great center of civilization, as was the Middle East and the Mediterranean basin that contributed so much to the Africans. Also, climatic conditions in Alaska and the Canadian Arctic obviously were not conducive to rapid cultural development as was the case in the Sudan savannah zone. Thus the tempo of advance in the Americas depended not on proximity to Eurasia but rather on suitability for the invention and development of agriculture. It is significant, then, that agriculture was first developed in the Americas in regions that were strikingly similar to the area in Mesopotamia where agriculture originated in Eurasia— that is, highland regions not requiring extensive clearing of forests to prepare the fields for crops, and with enough rainfall to allow the crops to mature.

In the course of the third millennium before Christ, the food-collecting tribes in Mesoamerica and the Andean highland area began to cultivate plants. During the following centuries they were extraordinarily successful in domesticating a host of plants that have become mainstays of human existence throughout the world. The most important was maize, but the Indians also cultivated over 100 other species. Outstanding were beans (the major source of proteins), squashes, tomatoes, and chocolate. In South America the potato was also a staple of great importance. Tobacco was widely grown, and cotton was the most important source of fibers for cloth. In all, about as many plants were domesticated in the Americas as in the entire Old World— a truly extraordinary achievement. That none of the plants grown in America was cultivated in the Old World before the Discoveries proves conclusively the independent development of agriculture in the two hemispheres.

The regions where the Indians originated agriculture were also the regions where they first developed it further, and gradually evolved "advanced farming cultures." This in turn profoundly changed the Indians' way of life. In general, the result was, as in Eurasia, a greatly increased sedentary population and the elaboration of those cultural activities not directly connected with bare subsistence. In other words, it was in these advanced farming cultures that it was possible to develop large empires and sophisticated civilizations comparable in certain respects to those of West Africa. Unfortunately, these indigenous American civilizations were suddenly overwhelmed by the Spaniards and thus left little behind them other than their precious domesticated plants.

The three major American civilizations were the Mayan in present-day Yucatan, Guatemala, and British Honduras, the Aztec in present-day Mexico, and the Inca, stretching for 3,000 miles from mid-Equador to mid-Chile. The Mayan civilization was outstanding for its extraordinary development of the arts and sciences. Its accomplishments included a unique stone architecture, a sculpture that ranks among the great art of all times, an ideographic writing in which characters or signs were used as conventional symbols for ideas, and a knowledge of the movements of heavenly bodies that demonstrated the Mayans were better astronomers than any in contemporary Europe, and as competent mathematicians. The Aztecs were brusque and warlike compared to the artistic and intellectual Mayas—a contrast reminiscent of that between the Romans and the Greeks in the Old World. The Aztecs paid more attention to the army, training all able-bodied men for war and holding them liable for military service. Their state also was better organized, including a well-developed judiciary and arrangements for the care of the needy.*

78

The Incas were even more advanced than the Aztecs in their material accomplishments. Their remarkable roads, fortresses, and temples were built of great blocks of stone so perfectly joined that even now, nearly 500 years later, a knife cannot be inserted between them. An extensive irrigation system, parts of which are still in use, made the Inca Empire a flourishing agricultural area. Above all, the Incas organized the only integrated and dynamic state in the Americas—a state geared for indefinite expansion outside and for regimentation and paternalism inside. The instruments of control included state ownership of land, mineral wealth, and herds, obligatory adherence to the official Sun religion, careful census compilations for tax and military purposes, deposition of local hereditary chieftains, forced population resettlement for the assimilation of conquered peoples, and mass marriages under state auspices. The Inca Empire probably was the most successful totalitarian state the world has ever seen.

Impressive as these attainments are, the fact remains that a comparative handful of Spanish adventurers was able to overthrow and ruthlessly destroy all three of these civilizations. And this despite the fact that Mexico and the Inca Empire each had a population of at least three million (and some estimates are as much as five times that number). The explanation is to be found ultimately in the isolation of the Americas, which left the Indians too far behind the Eurasians, and especially behind the technologically precocious Europeans. By A.D. 1500 the New World had reached the stage of civilization that Western Europe had attained in 1500 B.C. and the Middle East in 3500 B.C.

Precisely what did this mean when the clash occurred with the arrival of the Spaniards? It meant, in the first place, that the Indians found themselves economically and technologically far behind the civilizations represented by the invaders. The highly developed art, science, and religion of the Indians should not be allowed to obscure the fact that they lagged seriously in more material fields. The disparity was most extreme in Mesoamerica, but it also prevailed in the Andean area. In agriculture, the Indians were brilliantly successful in domesticating plants but much less effective in actual production. Their cultivation techniques never advanced beyond the bare minimum necessary for feeding populations that rarely reached the density of those of the Old World. Their tools were made only of stone, wood, or bone. They were incapable of smelting ores, and though they did work with metal, it was almost exclusively for ornamental purposes. The only ships they constructed were canoes and seagoing rafts. For land transportation they made no use of the wheel, which they knew but used only as a toy. Only the human back was available for transportation, with the exception of the llama and the alpaca, which were used in the Andes but which could not carry heavy loads.

The immediate significance of this technological lag should not be exaggerated. The Indians obviously were at a grave disadvantage with their spears and arrows against the Spaniards' horses and guns. But after the initial shock the Indians became accustomed to firearms and cavalry. Furthermore, the

* See "Aztec Civilization of Mexico," *EMM,* No. 25.

Spaniards soon discovered that the Indian weapons were sharp and durable, and they came to prefer the Indian armor of quilted cotton to their own. One of the conquistadors relates that the Aztecs had 79

> two arsenals filled with arms of every description, of which many were ornamented with gold and precious stones. These arms consisted in shields of different sizes, sabres, and a species of broadsword, which is wielded with both hands, the edge furnished with flint stones, so extremely sharp that they cut much better than our Spanish swords: further, lances of greater length than ours, with spikes at their end, full one fathom in length, likewise furnished with several sharp flint stones. The pikes are so very sharp and hard that they will pierce the strongest shield, and cut like a razor; so that the Mexicans even shave themselves with these stones. Then there were excellent bows and arrows, pikes with single and double points, and the proper thongs to throw them with; slings with round stones purposely made for them; also a species of large shield, so ingeniously constructed that it could be rolled up when not wanted; they are only unrolled on the field of battle, and completely cover the whole body from the head to the feet.[10]

This suggests that factors in addition to technological disparity lay behind the Spanish victories. One was the loose political organization of the Indian peoples. Nowhere did they develop beyond the tribal stage, with the exception of the Inca Empire in the century before the Spanish conquest. And the Incas seem to have been weakened by their extreme regimentation, for when Pizarro killed their emperor, they proved lacking in initiative to continue resistance. Furthermore, the Spaniards were able everywhere to take advantage of the dissensions among the Indians and to play one against the other. Cortez, for example, could not have won his victories without the active assistance of discontented native tribes that had been subjugated by the Aztecs.

In Mexico, the Spaniards were aided by the Aztec conception of war as a short-term ritual endeavor. The Aztecs were interested primarily in capturing prisoners whose hearts they offered to their gods in order to ensure victory. This practice led to a gruesome vicious circle. In order to take prisoners, the Indians had to wage war, and in order to win the war they had to provide yet more prisoners to win the favor of the gods. The end result was the orgies of human sacrifice indulged in by the Aztecs shortly before the conquest. To maintain the supply of sacrificial victims, the Indians fought one-battle campaigns or even so-called "wars of flowers," ceremonial contests fought in order that prisoners might be taken for sacrifice without the economic dislocation of formal war. This type of military tradition obviously was a serious handicap. The Spaniards killed to win; the Aztecs tried to take prisoners.

Beyond the Mesoamerica and the Andean highlands were the food-gathering and the intermediate farming culture areas. These economically less productive areas had a correspondingly lower general level of development,* and were more vulnerable to European penetration. In the first place, they

* See "Indians of Virginia," *EMM,* No. 26.

had a scanty population, though estimates vary tremendously in range. Taking the lower and more generally accepted figures, there were, as against the three million in the Inca Empire, only about one million in the rest of South America. Likewise, only another million lived north of the Rio Grande as against the three million to the south. When the Europeans appeared, the American Indians in these less developed regions simply lacked the numbers to hold their ground. Their weakness in this respect was accentuated by the diseases that the first explorers brought with them. The Indians, lacking immunity, were decimated by the epidemics, so that the early colonists often found abandoned fields and deserted village sites that they could take over. Later, when the full flood of immigration from Europe got under way, the Indians were hopelessly overwhelmed. First came the traders who penetrated throughout the Americas with little competition or resistance, for the Americas, unlike Africa, had no rival native merchant class. Then appeared the settlers who, attracted by the combination of salubrious climate and fertile land, came in ever increasing numbers and inundated the hapless Indians. When the latter occasionally took up arms in desperation, they were foredoomed to failure because they lacked both unity and the basic human and material resources. Thus, the unequal contest ended relatively quickly with the victorious white man in possession of the choice lands and the Indians relegated to reservations or to the less desirable regions that did not interest the new masters.

It is apparent that the balance of forces was quite different in America from what it was in Africa. Geography, relatively small population, and a comparatively low level of economic, political, and social organization all worked against the Indian to make it possible for the Europeans to take over the Americas at a time when they were still confined to a few toeholds on the coasts of Africa. Adam Smith was indeed justified in referring to the Indians as "miserable and helpless Americans" in contrast to the Negroes.

III. AUSTRALIA

Australia is the most isolated large landmass in the world, being more extreme in this respect than the southern tips of South America and of Africa. This isolation made it possible for archaic forms of life to survive to modern times, including plants such as the eucalyptus family, and mammals such as the monotremes and the marsupials. In Australia also survived archaic human types that were still in the Paleolithic stage when the first British settlers arrived in the late eighteenth century.* These aborigines were descended from three different ethnic groups that had ferried over to Australia perhaps some 50,000 years ago when narrow straits separated the continent from the Indonesian archipelago. These three strains are discernible in the present-day aboriginal population. The majority are slender, long-limbed people with brown skins, little body hair, and wavy to curly head hair and beards. They have survived in substantial numbers because they live in desert areas that are of little use to the white man. In the cool and fertile southeastern corner

* See "Australian Aborigines," EMM, No. 27.

of the continent are a few survivors of a very different native stock—thick set with light brown skin, heavy body hair, and luxuriant beards. Along the northeastern coast, in the only part of Australia covered with dense tropical rain forest, lives the third ethnic group. Part of the Negroid family, they are small, of slight build, and with woolly hair and black skins.

The culture of these peoples was by no means uniform. The most advanced were those in the southeast, where rainfall was adequate for permanent settlements. But throughout the continent the aborigines, thanks to their complete isolation, had remained Paleolithic food gatherers. Their retardation was particularly evident in their technology and in their political organization. They wore no clothing except for decorative purposes. Their housing consisted, in dry country, of simple, open windbreaks, and, in wet country, of low, domed huts thrown together of any available material. Their principal weapons were spears, spear throwers, and boomerangs, all made of wood. They were ignorant of pottery, their utensils consisting merely of a few twined bags and baskets and occasional bowls of bark or wood. As food gatherers and hunters they were highly skilled and ingenious. They had a wide range of vegetable as well as animal foods, and an intimate knowledge of the varieties, habits, and properties of these foods. They did all in their power to keep up the rate of reproduction of the plants and animals on which they depended. But not being food producers, their method of ensuring an adequate food supply was one of ritual rather than of cultivation. A typical ceremony was the mixing of blood with earth in places where the increase of game or plants was desired.

The poverty of Australian technology was matched by an almost equal poverty of political organization. Like most food-gathering peoples, the aborigines lived in bands, groups of families who normally camped together and roamed over a well-defined territory. They had no real tribes, but only territorial divisions characterized by differences in language and culture. Consequently they did not have chiefs, courts, or other formal agencies of government. Yet these same aborigines had an extraordinarily complex social organization and ceremonial life. The hunter who brought in game or the woman who returned from a day of root digging was required to divide his take with all his kin according to strict regulations. Among the northern Queensland natives, when a man sneezed, all those within hearing slapped themselves on their bodies, the place varying according to their precise relationship to the sneezer.

So involved were these nonmaterial aspects of Australian society that they have been a delight to students of primitive institutions. But precociousness in these matters was of little help to the aborigines when the Europeans appeared in the late eighteenth century. If the American Indians with their flowering civilizations and widespread agricultural communities were unable to stand up to the White Man, the Paleolithic Australians obviously had no chance. They were few in numbers, totaling about 300,000 when the Europeans arrived. They lacked both the arms and the organization necessary for effective resistance. And unlike the American Indians and the African Negroes, they showed little inclination to secure and use the white man's "fire stick." Thus the unfortunate aborigines were brutally decimated by the British immigrants, many of whom were lawless convicts shipped out from overcrowded jails. The combination of disease, alcoholism, outright slaughter, and wholesale land confiscation reduced the native population to 75,000 by 1921, when the first reliable census was taken. The treatment accorded to the Australians is suggested by the following typical observation of a Victorian settler in 1853: "The Australian aboriginal race seems doomed by Providence, like the Mohican and many other well known tribes, to disappear from their native soil before the progress of civilization." [11]

Even more tragic was the fate of the approximately 2,500 Tasmanians who were separated by the Bass Straight from Australia. What the Australian aborigines lacked the Tasmanians lacked too, and still more. They did without spear throwers, boomerangs, nets, and all other implements for fishing. The British sent their most hardened criminals to Tasmania, and when these individuals landed in 1803 they proceeded to hunt the natives as though they were animals. Within a few decades the majority were wiped out. The last male died in 1869 and the last female in 1876. This woman—Truganini—was born in 1803, the opening year of the white invasion, so that her life spanned the entire period of the extermination of her people. She begged that her body not be dissected, but despite her pitiful request her skeleton stands in Hobart Museum—an apt memorial to the fate of a people doomed because they happened to settle in an inaccessible and unstimulating portion of the globe. A Reverend Thomas Atkins, who witnessed the extermination of the natives, was moved to deduce certain conclusions that are relevant not only for Tasmania but for all the portions of the globe where the Europeans encountered peoples retarded in their material arts:

> Indeed, from a large induction of facts, it seems to me to be a universal law in the Divine government, when savage tribes who live by hunting and fishing, and on the wild herbs, roots and fruits of the earth, come into collision with civilized races of men, whose avocations are the depasturing of flocks and herds, agricultural employment and commercial pursuits, the savage tribes disappear before the progress of civilised races. . . .[12]

SUGGESTED READING

On Africa, there is a useful bibliographical essay by R. I. Rotberg, "The Teaching of African History," *American Historical Review*, LXIX (October, 1963), 47–63. An indispensable guide to current knowledge and research is provided by R. A. Lystad, *The African World: A Survey of Social Research* (New York: Praeger, 1965). There are three standard works on African geography: L. Dudley Stamp, *Africa: A Study in Tropical Development* (New York: Wiley, 1953); W. Fitzgerald, *Africa: A Social, Economic, and Political Geography of its Major Regions*, 8th ed. (New York: Dutton, 1957); and Vol. I of G. H. T. Kimble, *Tropical Africa* (New York: Twentieth Century Fund, 1960). The most thorough study of African ethnography is by G. P. Murdock, *Africa: Its Peoples and Their Culture History* (New York, McGraw, 1959). A useful collection of source materials is provided by B. Davidson, *The African Past: Chronicles from Antiquity to Modern Times* (Boston: Little, 1964). The pre-Western history of

Africa is presented, as authoritatively as current knowledge permits, by R. Oliver, ed., *The Dawn of African History* (London: Oxford Univ., 1961); R. Oliver and J. D. Fage, *A Short History of Africa* (Baltimore: Penguin, 1962); and the more popularized account by B. Davidson, *The Lost Cities of Africa* (Boston: Little, 1959). The study by D. L. Wiedner, *A History of Africa South of the Sahara* (New York: Knopf, 1962), concentrates mostly on the period following the appearance of the Europeans. Finally, much valuable data and interpretation of various aspects of Africa's past and present appear in the paperback by P. Bohannan, *Africa and Africans* (New York: Am. Mus. Sci. Books, 1964).

83

On the American Indians as a whole there is the excellent and convenient collection of readings by H. E. Driver, ed., *The Americas on the Eve of Discovery* (Englewood Cliffs, N. J.: Prentice-Hall, 1964; a Spectrum book) and also the short survey by J. Collier, *Indians of the Americas* (New York: New Am. Lib. paperback, 1947). The standard work on the South American Indians is by J. H. Stewart and L. C. Faron, *Native Peoples of South America* (New York: McGraw, 1959), and a more readable, yet reliable, account is provided by C. Beals, *Nomads and Empire Builders: Native Peoples and Cultures of South America* (Philadelphia: Chilton, 1961). The leading comparative study of the Indians from the Arctic to Panama is by H. E. Driver, *Indians of North America* (Chicago: Univ. of Chicago, 1961). V. W. Von Hagen has readable accounts of all three of the leading American civilizations: *The Aztec: Man and Tribe* (New Am. Lib., 1958; a Mentor paperback); *The Incas: People of the Sun* (Cleveland: World, 1961); and *World of the Maya* (New Am. Lib., 1960; a Mentor paperback). Other important studies of these civilizations are by S. G. Morley, *The Ancient Maya* (Stanford: Stanford Univ., 1946); F. A. Peterson, *Ancient Mexico: An Introduction to the Pre-Hispanic Cultures* (New York: Putnam, 1964); L. Baudin, *A Socialist Empire: The Incas of Peru* (Princeton: Van Nostrand, 1961); and J. A. Mason, *The Ancient Civilizations of Peru* (Baltimore: Penguin, 1947). The best general book on the Eskimos is by K. Birket Smith, *The Eskimos* (London: Methuen, 1959).

For the Australian aborigines the standard works are by A. P. Elkin, *The Australian Aborigines,* 3rd ed. (Sidney: Angus, 1954) and W. E. Harney, *Life Among the Aborigines* (London: Hale, 1957). There is also the classic pioneer anthropological study by Baldwin Spencer and F. J. Gillen, *The Native Tribes of Central Australia* (London: Macmillan, 1899). Clive Turnbull's *Black War: The Extermination of the Tasmanian Aborigines* (Melbourne: Cheshire, 1948) is a harrowing documentary account of the decimation of the Tasmanians by the zealous ministrations of well-wishers who tried to Christianize and civilize them, as well as by the greed and lust of the convicts and settlers.

WORLD OF
THE EMERGING WEST,
1500-1763

† The discovery of America, and that of a
passage to the East Indies by the Cape of
Good Hope, are the greatest and most important
events recorded in the history of mankind.

ADAM SMITH

Chapter

6

West European Expansion:
Iberian Phase, 1500-1600

The two countries of the Iberian Peninsula, Spain and Portugal, took the lead in the expansion of Europe in the sixteenth century. This seems paradoxical on first thought. The Iberian Peninsula for centuries had been a Moslem stronghold. A residue of this Moslem rule was ethnic and religious diversity, large numbers of Moors and Jews having been left behind in the country. And it is well-known that after the sixteenth century the Iberian countries declined rapidly, and that throughout modern times they have been quite insignificant. What, then, is the explanation for the short-lived but brilliant expansion of Spain and Portugal during the sixteenth century? This chapter is concerned first with this problem of the origins of Iberian expansionism, then with the process of empire building in the East and in the New World, and finally with the causes and symptoms of Iberian decline at the end of the sixteenth century.

I. ROOTS OF IBERIAN EXPANSIONISM

Religion was an important factor in European overseas expansion, but nowhere was it so important as in the Iberian Peninsula. Both the Spaniards and the Portuguese were impelled by memories of their long anti-Moslem crusade. To other peoples of Europe, Islam was a distant menace, but for the Iberians it represented a traditional and ever present ✓ enemy. Most of the peninsula at one time had been under Moslem rule, and now, in the fifteenth century, Granada in the south still remained a Moslem stronghold. Furthermore, the Moslems were in control of the nearby North African coast, while the growing Turkish seapower was making itself felt throughout the Mediterranean. Other Europeans were crusaders by fits and starts, but for the devout and patriotic Iberian, the struggle against Islam was a stern imperative—a combination of religious duty and patriotic necessity.

Prince Henry the Navigator first won fame in 1415 for his gallant role in the capture of the town and fortress of Ceuta across the Straits of Gibraltar. Likewise Queen Isabella, moved by intense religious conviction, was determined to wipe out Moslem Granada and to carry the war into the enemy's territory in North Africa, as the Portuguese had done at Ceuta. Isabella began her crusade against Granada in 1482, and pressed on, village by village, until final victory in 1492. Immediately thereafter, the Spaniards crossed the Straits and captured the city of Melilla. In this same year, 1492, a royal decree required all Jews in Spain to accept the Catholic faith or leave the realm. Ten years later a similar decree was issued against the Moslems remaining in Castile.

This Iberian crusading impulse extended across the oceans when the Discoveries revealed more Moslems to be exterminated and new heathen to be delivered from idolatry. Thus the Portuguese viceroy Alfonso de Albuquerque spurred his men on during the siege of Malacca by glorifying "the great service which we shall perform to Our Lord in casting the Moors out of this country and quenching the fire of the sect of Mahamede so that it may never burst out again hereafter." [1] Likewise Bernal Díaz, one of the conquistadors who served under Cortes in Mexico, wrote in his memoirs, "After we had abolished idolatry and other abominations from among the Indians, the Almighty blessed our endeavors and we baptized the men, women, and all the children born after the conquest, whose souls would otherwise have gone to the infernal regions." [2]

The Iberians were lured overseas also by four groups of islands—the Canaries, the Madeira, the Azores, and the Cape Verde—stretching westward across the Atlantic and southward down the coast of Africa. These were highly attractive, partly because they were fertile and productive, but also because they provided strategic bases and ports of call. When the Portuguese began settling Madeira in 1420, they first obtained high quality timber; next they produced sugar very profitably, and, when this was undercut by Brazilian sugar, they introduced from Crete the Malvoisie grape, from which the characteristic dessert wines of Madeira are made to the present day.

In contrast to Madeira, which was indisputably Portuguese, the Canaries were claimed by both Spain and Portugal. After appeals to the Pope and savage local fighting, the Portuguese dropped their claim to the Canaries, and the Spaniards conceded the other three island groups to the Portuguese. This settlement forced the Portuguese to sail far out into the Atlantic on their way south, to avoid Spanish privateers based on the Canaries. Their first port of call, therefore, was the Azores, which they explored systematically, until by the mid-fifteenth century they had reached the westernmost islands, about a quarter of the way across the Atlantic.

Throughout the fifteenth century, then, sailors had been discovering islands located far out into the ocean. It was natural that they should assume the existence of more islands awaiting discovery and exploitation. Atlantic charts were peppered with such imaginary islands, providing stepping stones to the East. The agreement that Columbus reached with Isabella in 1492 provided that he should head an expedition "to discover and acquire islands and mainland in the Ocean Sea."

It was Portugal, however, rather than Spain, that took the lead in overseas enterprise during the fifteenth century. Spain moved belatedly, and usually in reaction to Portuguese initiative. There were two reasons for Portugal's head start. One was its small size and its location on the Atlantic coast, surrounded on three sides by Spanish territory. This effectively safeguarded the Portuguese from temptation to squander their resources in European wars. Thanks to the leadership of Prince Henry, they turned instead to oceanic projects. The other was Portugal's superior knowledge of navigation, gained primarily from the Italians. Lisbon was on the route of Genoese and Venetian sea traffic with Flanders through the Straits of Gibraltar; and the Portuguese took advantage of this, by employing Italian captains and pilots in the royal navy. Prince Henry followed up by assembling a galaxy of talented seamen, including Italians, Catalans, and even a Dane. Furthermore, Henry's work was continued by the crown following his death, so that the Portuguese became the most knowledgeable of all Europeans in seamanship and geography. It was this steady and consistent government direction and support that gave the Portuguese a decisive advantage over their Spanish neighbors and rivals.

Portugal's interest in exploration quickened following the capture of Ceuta in 1415. Moslem prisoners divulged information concerning the ancient and profitable trade across the Sahara with the Negro kingdoms of the Sudan (see Chapter 5, section I). For centuries the latter had provided ivory, slaves, and gold in return for various manufactured goods and salt. Since Western Europe in general and Portugal in particular were then suffering from a serious shortage of bullion, Prince Henry was intrigued by the possibility of tapping this gold trade. According to one of his lieutenants, Diego Gomez, Henry learned of "the passage of traders from the coasts of Tunis to Timbuktu and to Cantor on the Gambia." Gomez added that this information "led him [Henry] to seek those lands by way of the sea." [3] In other words, Henry's original objective was confined to Africa and did not extend to the East.

A major step forward in early Portuguese exploration was taken when Prince Henry's captains passed the desert coast in 1445 and found below it a verdant new land "covered with palms and other green and beautiful trees, and it was even so with the plains thereof." [4] By the time of Henry's death, the coast had been explored down to Sierra Leone, and a number of coastal stations had been established which enabled the Portuguese to attract at least a part of the caravan trade that they were after. Later on, in 1487, they established a factory at Wadan, an inland entrepôt, which enabled them to obtain a larger share of the north-south caravan traffic.

Meanwhile, even before Henry's death, Portuguese aspirations had come to encompass India as well as Africa. Because Europe at this time was blocked from access to the East by the Moslem power that controlled all of North Africa and the Middle East, the Mediterranean was for the Europeans a prison rather than a highway (see Chapter 2, section VII). Therefore, with the exception of the Venetians, who profited as middlemen, they eagerly sought a new route "to the Indies where the spices grow." Prince Henry had not thought of India when he first began his operations, but as his ships crept further and further down the African coast, it was natural that his horizon should expand from the African caravan trade to the Indies spice trade. From then on, the discovery and the domination of the spice route was the prime objective of Portuguese policy.* It is significant that when Albuquerque urged his followers before Malacca to "quench the fire of the sect of Mahamede," he also emphasized the prospects for material gain. "I hold it certain that if we take this trade of Malacca away from them (the Moors) Cairo and Mecca will be entirely ruined and Venice receive no spiceries unless her merchants go and buy them in Portugal." [5]

II. COLUMBUS DISCOVERS AMERICA

In view of Portugal's pioneering work in the theory and practice of oceanic navigation, it is paradoxical that the first great discovery—that of the New World—was effected under Spanish auspices. It is even more paradoxical that the reason for this outcome is that the Portuguese were more advanced in their geographical knowledge than the Spaniards and figured correctly that Columbus was wrong in his calculations. It was common knowledge among informed people by the fifteenth century that the world was round. The question was not the shape of the world but its size, and the relationship of the continents to the oceans. By combining Marco Polo's estimate of the east-west extent of Asia, which was an overestimate, the same traveler's report of the distance of Japan from the Asian mainland—1,500 miles—an extreme overestimate, and Ptolemy's estimate of the circumference of the globe, which was an underestimate, Columbus concluded that less than 3,000 miles of ocean separated Europe from Japan. Accordingly, he believed that the shortest and easiest route to Asia was by a short voyage across the Atlantic, and this was the project that he proposed before various courts. The Portuguese, thanks to Prince Henry, had more practical experience and were better informed of the most advanced knowledge of the day. They were convinced that the globe was larger than Columbus held, that the oceans were wider, and that the shortest route to the Orient was around Africa rather than across the Atlantic. For this reason the Portuguese king turned Columbus down when he applied for financial assistance in 1484. Two years later Columbus was at the Spanish court where, after a preliminary rejection, he finally won the support of Queen Isabella.

On August 2, 1492, Columbus set sail from Palos with three small ships manned by reliable crews with capable and seasoned officers. By September 6 the expedition had left the Canary Islands behind and sailed into the open ocean. Luckily there was a fair wind all the way out, but as the days and weeks went by, the men became restless. To calm their apprehension, Columbus gave out false information about the distances covered. Birds were sighted on

* See "Roots of Portuguese Expansion," *EMM*, No. 28.

Columbus departs from Palos.

October 7, but still no land appeared on the horizon. Even Columbus became worried, for he had now sailed so far west that, according to his calculations, he should have sighted Japan. On October 9 he promised to turn back in three days if land were not found. Just before time ran out, the lookout sighted one of the Bahaman Islands, which Columbus named San Salvador. It was an hour fraught with destiny for all of mankind.*

One of the supreme ironies of world history is that Columbus was convinced until the end of his life that he had reached Asia. He was certain that San Salvador was very near to where Japan ought to be, and the next step was to find Japan itself. When he sailed southwest to the mainland of the New World, he believed that he was somewhere near the Malacca Straits. The fact that Columbus persisted in his delusion had momentous consequences: it spurred on further exploration of the Americas until the great prizes in Mexico and Peru were discovered. But if the Spaniards had realized from the outset that they had merely chanced upon a New World far away from the continent of Asia, they might very well have turned away from what appeared at first to be an unattractive and unprofitable wilderness. In that case, the New World might have been ignored for many decades, particularly because Portugal's Vasco da Gama had in the meantime opened the extremely profitable Cape route to India.

The Spanish monarchs loyally supported Columbus and invested large sums in outfitting him for three additional expeditions. But not till 1518 did the Spaniards stumble upon the rich Aztec Empire in Mexico. During the

* See "Columbus Discovers the New World," *EMM*, No. 29.

quarter century between this windfall and Columbus' first expedition, disappointment followed disappointment as the Spaniards explored the innumerable and unpromising islands of the West Indies.

On his first trip Columbus explored Colba (Cuba) and Hispaniola (Haiti) before returning home. In 1493 he left Spain at the head of an impressive armada of seventeen ships. His aim was to establish a colony in Hispaniola and, from that base, to continue his journey to nearby Japan and India. Diligent exploring in the West Indies failed to disclose anything remotely resembling the Oriental kingdoms he was seeking. To make matters worse, Columbus was as poor an administrator as he was an expert navigator. He failed as governor of the new colony of Hispaniola, and when he returned to Spain in 1496 the colony was in an uproar and the natives were in revolt. Two years later he started on his third voyage, during which he discovered the island of Trinidad and the mouth of the Orinoco. But upon a renewed outbreak of trouble in Hispaniola he was superseded as governor, and his successor sent him home in irons. His sovereigns stuck by him, and in 1502 sent him on his fourth and last voyage. He explored a long stretch of mainland coast in Honduras and Costa Rica, but still no sign of Cathay. The Spanish sovereigns not unreasonably refused to back him further, and he died in 1506, an embittered but by no means an impoverished man.

Columbus' great discovery at first appeared to be a grand failure. Several thousand adventurers had flocked to the West Indies and found disappointingly small quantities of gold. But the discovery of the New World did cause an immediate reaction that was of great significance. It prodded the Portuguese to circumnavigate Africa and reach India directly by sea.

III. PORTUGAL IN ASIA

The Portuguese in the meantime had been making considerable profit from their trade along the African Guinea Coast. Coarse pepper, gold, ivory, cotton, sugar, and slaves now entered European commerce through Portugal. The slave trade alone supported fifty to sixty merchants in Lisbon. It is significant that when the conquistador Bernal Díaz observed the sale of slaves in the Aztec capital, he was moved to remark, "This slave market was upon as great a scale as the Portuguese market for negro slaves at Guinea." [6]

Prince Henry's successors continued his work of opening up the West African coast. A breakthrough occurred in 1487 when Bartholomeu Dias, while probing along the coast, was caught by a gale that blew his ships south for thirteen days out of sight of land. When the wind moderated, Dias steered for the West African coast but discovered that he had already passed the Cape without knowing it. He landed at Mossel Bay on the Indian Ocean, and wished to explore further, but his weary and frightened men forced him to return. On the homeward passage he first sighted the great cape, and named it the Cape of Storms. It was the Portuguese king who, upon Dias' return, renamed it the Cape of Good Hope.

In the same year, 1487, the Portuguese sent Pedro da Covilhã, a linguist, soldier, spy, and diplomatist, on an overland mission to India to collect information about that country. Covilhã spoke Arabic and made his way

The credulity of the West regarding unexplored territories is illustrated by this engraving, "The Wondrous People to Be Found in Guinea."

along the traditional trade routes to Cairo and Aden, where he shipped in an Arab dhow to Calicut in India. He made a reconnaissance of the ports of the western or Malabar coast of India and then returned on another Arab ship to East Africa. There he visited a number of Arab towns, made his way back to Cairo, and finally ended up in Abyssinia, where he spent the last thirteen years of his life. But before leaving Cairo he sent a priceless report of his findings to Lisbon.

These expeditions, and several others by both land and sea, made the Portugese the best informed in Europe on global geography and trade routes. But they failed to follow up on Dias' rounding of the Cape because of political and financial complications. The result, as noted, was that Columbus was the first to reach the New World, which he persisted in claiming to be the Orient. The more knowledgeable Portuguese were dubious from the beginning, but they now hastened to open and secure the Cape route to India. On July 8, 1497, Vasco da Gama sailed from Portugal with four ships, and at the end of May, 1498, he entered Calicut harbor.* This was not so great a feat of navigation as that of Columbus. Da Gama had been able to stop at various Portuguese stations on the way south, and he knew from various sources of the Arab cities on the East African coast. He stopped at one of them,

* See "Vasco da Gama reaches India," *EMM*, No. 30.

94

Vasco da Gama.

Milindi, where he picked up a famous Arab pilot, Ahmad-Ibn-Madjid, who guided him across the Indian Ocean. In view of the sequel to this voyage, Ibn-Madjid bitterly regretted what he had done, and his memory is still execrated by his co-religionists.

Da Gama did not receive a warm welcome in Calicut. The resident Arab merchants were naturally alarmed by this threat to their traditional monopoly and did their best to throw obstacles in the way of the European intruders. Furthermore, the Portuguese trade goods—mostly trinkets and woolen cloth— were unsuitable for the Indian market. The fact is that the Portuguese had completely underestimated the level and sophistication of Indian civilization. This is evident in the nature of the presents that da Gama offered to the ruler of Calicut—woolen cloth, hats, strings of coral beads, washbasins, and jars of oil and honey—which definitely did not make a favorable impression. Thus, da Gama had difficulty trading in Calicut not only because of the hostility of the resident Arab traders but also, and more important, because Portugal (and all Europe) produced little at this time that was of interest to the Eastern peoples. European manufactures were generally inferior in quality and higher in price than the goods produced in the East. One of Vasco da Gama's companions relates that "We did not . . . effect these sales at the prices hoped for . . . for a very fine shirt which in Portugal fetches 300 reis, was worth here . . . only 30 reis, for 30 reis in this country is a big sum." [7]

With much effort da Gama collected a cargo of pepper and cinnamon and cleared for home, arriving in September, 1499. The cargo proved to be worth sixty times the cost of the entire expedition. Dazzling horizons opened

Da Gama's flagship, the Sao Gabriel.

up before the delighted Portuguese, and King Manuel assumed the titles "Lord of the Conquest, Navigation, and Commerce of Ethiopia, Arabia, Persia, and India." These titles were taken quite seriously. The Portuguese were determined to monopolize the trade along the new route and to exclude, not only other Europeans, but also the Arabs and other Eastern peoples who had traded in the Indian Ocean for centuries. To enforce their claims, the Portuguese resorted to ruthless terrorism, particularly when they encountered the hated Moslems. Da Gama, on a later voyage, found some unarmed vessels returning from Mecca. He captured the vessels and, in the words of a fellow Portuguese, "after making the ships empty of goods, prohibited anyone from taking out of it any Moor and then ordered them to set fire to it." [8] Another contemporary Portuguese declared,

> It is true that there does exist a common right to all to navigate the seas and in Europe we recognize the rights which others hold against us; but the right does not extend beyond Europe and therefore the Portuguese as Lords of the Sea are justified in confiscating the goods of all those who navigate the seas without their permission.[9]

Such was the nature of the epochal meeting of two Eurasian cultures brought face to face for the first time after millennia of regional isolation. The Europeans were the aggressive intruders. They were the ones who seized the initiative and retained it until gradually, but inexorably, they emerged the masters in every quarter of the globe. This unprecedented domination of the world is at first difficult to understand. Why was Portugal, with a population of approximately two million, able to impose her will on highly civilized Asiatic countries with much greater human and natural resources?

One reason was that the Portuguese had the great good fortune of being able to utilize the vast bullion supply that soon was to start pouring in from the New World. The flood of bullion from the treasures of the Aztec and Inca empires and from the Mexican and Peruvian silver mines came just in time to finance Portugal's trade with the East. Without this providential windfall the Portuguese would have been most seriously restricted, because they had neither natural resources nor manufactured goods that were of interest to the Eastern peoples. The fact that Portuguese-made shirts cost ten times as much as Indian, as da Gama discovered, suggests that the Portuguese would have had difficulty finding something to exchange for the spices they wanted. That something was provided by the New World silver mines. The East was always eager to accept bullion. When da Gama left India, the King of Calicut handed him a note for the King of Portugal which read, "Vasco da Gama, a gentleman of your household, came to my country, whereat I was pleased. My country is rich in cinnamon, cloves, ginger, pepper, and precious stones. That which I ask of you in exchange is gold, silver, corals, and scarlet cloth." [10] America provided the gold and the silver that the King asked for, and thereby made possible the full development of the Cape route trade. Hence the observation that "The voyage of Columbus was an imperative supplement to that of da Gama." [11]

Another reason for the triumph of the Portuguese was the disunity of the Indian subcontinent. When the Portuguese arrived upon the scene, northern Indian was controlled by the new Mogul invaders who were interested in conquest rather than trade, while southern India, and especially the Malabar Coast, was under the control of petty Hindu rulers who were at odds with one another. By contrast, the Portuguese and their European successors had a singleness and continuity of purpose that more than counterbalanced their inferiority in resources. The Europeans obviously were not united; they were riddled with political and religious dissension. But on one point they were all agreed—the need to expand eastward in order to reap profits and to outflank Islam. In pursuit of this objective the Europeans demonstrated a determination to succeed that was stronger than the will of the Asiatic peoples to resist. There was no counterpart in Asia to the sustained drive of the Portuguese throughout the fifteenth century in sending out expedition after expedition at great cost of energy and treasure. And when da Gama returned from his historic voyage, the Portuguese court was prepared to follow up promptly. It had a detailed plan for organized trade, involving the establishment of factories in the Malabar ports and the dispatch of annual fleets under royal charter.

The Portuguese were successful also because of the superiority of their naval power. This was due in part to the ability of the Portuguese to execute squadron maneuvers rather than depending on the individual performance of the ships comprising the squadron. More important was the naval artillery and gunnery of the Portuguese. Western Europeans were developing efficient new naval artillery that enabled them to use ships as floating batteries rather than as transports for boarding parties (see Chapter 2, section IV). The gun, not the foot soldier, was now the main instrument of naval warfare, and the guns were employed against the enemy's ships rather than against his men. It was these new developments that made it possible for the Portuguese to smash Moslem naval power in the Indian Ocean and thus to gain control of the spice trade.

97

It does not follow, of course, that the Portuguese were able to impose their will on land areas beyond the range of their naval guns. In fact, the Indians soon began to employ Italians and other Europeans to strengthen their rudimentary ordnance. After about a dozen years a Portuguese commander observed that "the people with whom we wage war are no longer the same; . . . artillery, arms, and fortresses are according to our usage." [12] This meant that the Portuguese, with their extremely limited manpower, could not hope to conquer a land empire. They realized this at an early date and adjusted their objectives and strategy accordingly.

Their objectives were to monopolize the spice trade and, where possible, to smite the Moslem enemy and propagate the faith. To attain these objectives it was necessary to drive out the Arab middlemen who hitherto had transported the spices from their places of origin to the ports of the Levant. This was not an easy task, because the Arabs had been conducting this trade for centuries and had deep roots, including many colonies, in the entire area from Alexandria to Malacca. Furthermore, the Arabs were peaceful and well-behaved residents. They performed valuable economic services in the areas in which they settled and did not attempt to seize political power so long as they were treated fairly by the local rulers. Thus, a live-and-let-live atmosphere prevailed in most areas, with each alien community being allowed freedom in customs, religion, and trade. A Persian traveler who visited Calicut in 1442, only half a century before the coming of the Portuguese, reported an ideal laissez-faire regime:

> Security and justice are so firmly established that merchants bring thither from maritime countries considerable cargoes, which they unload and unhesitatingly send to the markets and bazaars, without thinking of the necessity of checking the accounts or watching over the goods. . . . Every ship, whatever place it may come from or wheresoever it may be bound, when it puts into this port is treated like other vessels and has no trouble of any kind to put up with." [13]

In the light of this background it is understandable that the Portuguese, with their claims of trade monopoly as "Lords of the Sea," should have been regarded as intolerably barbarous and pretentious. The Portuguese, therefore, had to contend with the hostility of most of the local Hindu rajas as well as of the Arab merchants. Despite this opposition, the Portuguese succeeded in building up a farflung and, for several decades, fabulously profitable, Asiatic empire.

The architect of this empire was the great Alfonso de Albuquerque, governor general from 1509 to 1515. His policy was to smash the Arab trade network by capturing control of the narrow sea passages leading to and from the Indian Ocean. He seized the islands of Socotra and Hormuz, which were the keys to the Red Sea and the Persian Gulf, respectively. In India he failed in an attempt to seize Calicut and took instead the city of Goa located in the middle of the Malabar Coast. He made Goa his main naval base and general headquarters, and it remained a Portuguese possession until 1961. Further to the east he captured Malacca, commanding the strait through which all commerce with the Far East had to pass. Two years later, in 1513, the first Portuguese ship to reach a Chinese port put into Canton. This was the first recorded European visit to China since Marco Polo's day. The Portuguese at first had trouble with the Chinese government because the ruler of Malacca had recognized Chinese suzerainty and had fled to Peking with complaints against the violent and barbarous Europeans. But in due course the Portugese secured the right to establish a warehouse and a settlement at Macao, a little downstream from Canton, and from there they carried on their Far Eastern operations (see Chapter 4, section IV).

The Portuguese Empire in Asia was negligible in its actual extent, comprising only a few islands and coastal posts. But these possessions were so strategically located that they gave the Portuguese command of trade routes spanning half the globe. Each year Portuguese fleets sailed down the African coast, which was dotted with stations for provisioning and refitting the ships. After rounding the Cape, they put in at Mozambique in East Africa, another Portuguese possession. Then they sailed with the monsoon across to Cochin and Ceylon, where they loaded the spices that had been brought in from the surrounding territories. Further east was Malacca, which gave them access to the trade of East Asia, for which they served as middlemen and carriers. Thus, the Portuguese profited from purely Asian trade—between China and Japan and the Philippines, for example—as well as from the trade between Europe and the East.

Arabs and Turks battling the Portuguese.

With this network of trading stations and strong points, Albuquerque realized the goal he had set before his men during the siege of Malacca. He had broken the traditional monopoly of the Arab merchants in the Indian Ocean, and in doing so he was competing with the Venetian merchants for the "spiceries" that they had customarily obtained in the ports of the Levant. The extent of his success may be gauged from the fact that in the four years 1502–1505, the Venetians were able to obtain an average of only 1 million English pounds of spices a year at Alexandria, whereas in the last years of the fifteenth century they had averaged 3.5 million pounds. Conversely, Portuguese spice imports rose from 224,000 pounds in 1501 to an average of 2.3 million pounds in the years 1503–1506.

These statistics explain why the Egyptians, with full Venetian support, sent a naval expedition in 1508 to aid the Indian rajas to drive the Portuguese interlopers out of the Indian Ocean. The effort failed, but the Turks, who conquered Egypt in 1517, continued the campaign against the Portuguese and sent several fleets during the following decades. They were all unsuccessful, and the spices continued to flow around the Cape to Europe. Yet it should not be assumed that the old routes through the Middle East fell into complete disuse. In fact, after the initial dislocation, they regained much of the lost trade.

As it turned out, all the advantages were by no means on the side of the oceanic route. It is true that Portuguese ships could take relatively large cargoes compared to the limited carrying loads of the caravans plying from the Red Sea and Persian Gulf to Mediterranean ports. Furthermore, the Cape route involved only one long haul, in contrast to the numerous and expensive loadings, unloadings, and reloadings from the Spice Islands to India to the Red Sea and Persian Gulf and thence to the Levant ports.

On the other hand, shipwrecks on the long voyage around the Cape were frequent and costly. And, since the Portuguese had no goods to offer for profitable outward freight, they shipped out New World bullion for the spices, and thus had to sell the spices at prices sufficiently high to meet the costs of both the outward and homeward passages. As a result, Portuguese-imported spices often were little cheaper in Western Europe than those brought by land from the Middle East. Furthermore, it was widely believed that spices tended to lose their aroma during the long sea voyage. Perhaps this was a story put out by the Venetians, but it may very well have had some foundation in fact. Portuguese cargoes were carried in bags, in leaky ships, and through latitudes with extreme weather fluctuations.

The Portuguese, besides, were unable to establish a total monopoly on the ocean route, because corrupt Portuguese officials usually were willing, for a consideration, to allow Arab shipping to enter the Red Sea and the Persian Gulf. The net result was that the Arabs and the Venetians, far from being put out of business following da Gama's voyage, competed successfully with the Portuguese throughout the sixteenth century. It was not until the following century, with the appearance in the Indian Ocean of the more efficient and economically powerful Dutch and English, that the old Italian and Arab middlemen were supplanted and that the traditional Middle Eastern trade routes were overshadowed by the oceanic.

IV. DIVISION OF THE WORLD

The discoveries of Columbus and of da Gama raised the question of sovereignty over the newly found areas. Just as international law today has no provisions concerning sovereignty over outer space and over other planets, so international law in the fifteenth century had no provisions concerning the new continents. This problem had never agitated medieval Europe because all the territory with which its rulers had any practical concern was already possessed by states sufficiently alike in sentiment and organization to be capable of entering into mutual relations. When Europe began to expand, there was adopted by tacit mutual agreement the convenient doctrine that Christian states had the right to possess themselves of the lands of the heathen and infidel without regard for the native peoples concerned. Another doctrine that was accepted, at least by Portugal and Spain, was the right of the Pope to allot temporal sovereignty to any lands not possessed by a Christian ruler. As early as 1454, Pope Nicholas V issued a bull granting to the Portuguese title to the territories they were discovering along the African coast toward India. The phrasing of this document is as revealing as its provisions.

> Our joy is immense to know that our dear son, Henry [the Navigator], Prince of Portugal, following the footsteps of his father of illustrious memory, King John, inspired with a zeal for souls like an intrepid soldier of Christ, has carried into the most distant and unknown countries the name of God and has brought into the Catholic fold the perfidious enemies of God and of Christ, such as the Saracens and the Infidels.
>
> After having established Christian families in some of the unoccupied islands of the Ocean and having consecrated churches there for the celebration of Holy Mysteries the Prince, remembering that never within the memory of man had anyone been known to navigate the sea to the distant shores of the Orient, believed that he could give God the best evidence of his submission, if by his effort the Ocean can be made navigable as far as India, which, it is said, is already subject to Christ. If he enters into relations with these people, he will induce them to come to the help of the Christians of the West against the enemies of the faith. At the same time, he will bring under submission, with the King's permission, the pagans of the countries not yet inflicted with the plague of Islam and give them knowledge of the name of Christ. . . .
>
> We, after careful deliberation, and having considered that we have by our apostolic letters conceded to King Affonso, the right, total and absolute, to invade, conquer and subject all the countries which are under the rule of the enemies of Christ, Saracen or Pagan, by our apostolic letter we wish the same King Affonso, the Prince, and all their successors, occupy and possess in exclusive rights the said islands, ports and the seas undermentioned, and all faithful Christians are prohibited without the permission of the said Affonso and his successors to encroach on their sovereignty. Of the conquests already made, or to be made, all the

conquests which extend to Cape Bajador and Cape Non to the coast of
Guinea and all the Orient is perpetually and for the future the sovereignty
of King Affonso.[14]

When Columbus returned from his first voyage with the conviction that he
had reached the Indies, the Spanish court feared Portuguese counterclaims
and therefore pressed Pope Alexander VI for recognition of Spanish sovereignty. On May 4, 1493, Pope Alexander defined a line of demarcation running 100 leagues west of the Azores and Cape Verde Islands, and granted to
Spain all lands to the west of it, and to Portugal all lands to its east. On
June 7, 1494, Spain and Portugal negotiated an agreement, the Treaty of
Tordesillas, moving the line 270 leagues further west. The effect of this
change was to give Portugal a claim to Brazil in the New World. At the time,
the Spaniards thought they had the better of the bargain, believing that the
route to the Indies was westward. Actually the demarcation line left to Portugal the only route to India feasible at the time.

The riches that Portugal reaped from the spice trade following da Gama's
voyage goaded the other European countries to a frantic search for another
route to the Indies. The successive failures of Columbus to find Cathay did
not kill the hope of reaching Asia by sailing west. It might still be possible to
thread a way between the various masses of inhospitable land so far discovered. The hope was encouraged by the chance discovery of a Spanish
adventurer, Vasco Nuñez de Balboa, who, while exploring for gold in the
Isthmus of Darien, came within sight of the Pacific. The new knowledge that
a narrow strip of land separated the two oceans encouraged the explorers
seeking the elusive passage to the East.

Under these circumstances a new class of professional explorer appeared
in the early sixteenth century. Mostly Italians and Portuguese (they being
the best informed and the most experienced explorers at that time), they
were men whose national allegiance sat lightly upon them and who undertook
explorations for any monarch willing to finance them. The Italians included
Amerigo Vespucci who sailed for Portugal and Spain, John Verrazano who
sailed for France, and the two Cabots, father and son, who sailed for England.
The Portuguese included Juan Diaz de Solís, Juan Fernandez, and Ferdinand
Magellan, all of whom sailed for Spain.

Only Magellan found the passage to Asia. Spain sent him out because, with
regular spice cargoes arriving in Lisbon, it realized that it was being beaten in
the race for the Spice Islands. Claiming that the line of demarcation defined
by the Tordesillas Treaty ran right round the globe, Spain dispatched Magellan
west for Asia, hoping that he would find at least some of the Spice Islands on
the Spanish side of the line.

Magellan's expedition is one of the great epics of seafaring. He set out
from Seville on September 10, 1519, with a fleet of five ships, each about
100 tons. In March he reached Patagonia, where a mutiny broke out, possibly
inspired by Portuguese agents, since Portugal was violently opposed to this
challenge to her predominance in the East. Magellan managed to suppress
the rebels and to execute their leaders, and by October he reached the straits
that bear his name. The seas were so rough that it took well over a month

to cross into the Pacific. Meanwhile one ship had been wrecked and another had deserted, so with the remaining three he sailed up the Chilean coast to the fiftieth latitude and then veered to the northwest.

During the next eighty days only two uninhabited islands were sighted. The suffering endured during those months has been graphically related by one of the crew.

> The biscuit we were eating no longer deserved the name of bread; it was nothing but dust, and worms which had consumed the substance; and what is more, it smelled intolerably, being impregnated with the urine of mice. The water we were obliged to drink was equally putrid and offensive. We were even so far reduced, that we might not die of hunger, to eat pieces of the leather with which the main-yard was covered to prevent it from wearing the rope. These pieces of leather, constantly exposed to the water, sun, and wind, were so hard that they required being soaked four or five days in the sea in order to render them supple; after this we boiled them to eat. Frequently indeed we were obliged to subsist on saw-dust, and even mice, a food so disgusting, were sought after with such avidity that they sold for half a ducat a piece.
>
> Nor was this all, our greatest misfortune was being attacked by a malady [scurvy] in which the gums swelled so as to hide the teeth, as well in the upper as the lower jaw, whence those affected thus were incapable of chewing their food. Nineteen of our number died of this complaint. . . . Besides those who died, we had from twenty-five to thirty sailors ill, who suffered dreadful pains in their arms, legs, and other parts of the body. . . .[15]

On March 6 they reached an island, perhaps Guam, where they were able to obtain provisions. On the sixteenth of the same month they arrived at the Philippines, where Magellan and forty of his men were killed in a local war. With the aid of native pilots, the surviving Spaniards sailed to Borneo and thence to their destination, the Moluccas or Spice Islands, which they finally reached in November, 1520. The Portuguese, who were already there, did not hesitate to attack the two remaining Spanish ships (one having been abandoned in the Philippines). Despite all obstacles the Spaniards were able to obtain cargoes of cloves, and then set off on the journey back home by different routes. The one that tried to recross the Pacific was turned back by head winds and captured by the Portuguese. The other successfully negotiated a fantastic voyage through the Macassar Strait, across the Indian Ocean, around the Cape of Good Hope, and up the entire length of Africa. On September 3, 1522, this last surviving ship, the Victoria, leaking badly and with a decimated crew, limped into the harbor of Seville. Yet the single cargo of spices was valuable enough to defray the expense of the entire expedition. The Spaniards sent out another expedition which reached the Spice Islands in 1524. But it proved to be a disastrous failure because the Portuguese were too firmly established to be challenged profitably. Furthermore, the Spanish king was desperately in need of money at this time to finance his war with France. So in 1529 he signed the Treaty of Saragossa with Portugal, by which, in return for 350,000 ducats, he gave up all claims to the Spice Islands and accepted a demarcation line fifteen degrees east of them. This treaty marked the end of a chapter in the history of discovery. The Portuguese held on to the Spice Islands until they lost them to the Dutch in 1605, while the Spaniards continued to show interest in the Philippines and eventually conquered them in 1571, even though the islands were east of the line stipulated by the Saragossa Treaty. Long before this, however, Spain had shifted her attention to the New World, where great treasures had been found equal in value to the spices of the East.

V. Age of Conquistadors

The year 1519, in which Magellan left Seville on his famous voyage around the world, was also the year in which Hernando Cortes left Cuba on his equally famous expedition against the Aztec Empire. In doing so, Cortez heralded what might be termed the age of the conquistadors. The preceding decades, from 1500 to 1520, had been the age of the explorers, when numerous navigators under various flags probed the entire length of the Americas in search of a passageway. In the thirty years that followed, a few thousand Spanish adventurers won the first great European overseas empire.

These adventurers were the product of the Iberian crusading tradition. They had flocked to the New World in the hope of making their fortunes, just as their counterparts who stayed in Europe hired themselves out to foreign rulers or went off to fight against the Moslem Turks or Arabs. Such men did not make ideal settlers in the new Spanish island possessions in the West

Conquistadors introducing Negro slaves to work in the gold and silver mines of Hispaniola.

Indies. They were too proud and too restless for sustained work. Instead they quarreled among themselves, mistreated the Indians, and were ever ready to go off in search of the gold strikes that were constantly being rumored. But these very qualities that made them misfits in settled society enabled them to perform remarkable feats in overrunning two centers of civilization developed by the American Indians.

One of these soldiers of fortune was Hernando Cortes, an unsuccessful law student and the son of a respectable family. In 1504 he arrived in Hispaniola, and five years later he participated in the conquest of Cuba. Distinguishing himself during this campaign, he was selected to head an expedition to Yucatan to investigate reports of civilized city dwellers living in the interior. In March, 1519, Cortes landed on the mainland coast near present-day Veracruz. He had only six hundred men, a few small cannon, thirteen muskets, and sixteen horses. Yet with this insignificant force he was to win fabulous riches and become master of an exotic, highly advanced empire. The reasons for this spectacular success have already been noted—the courage, ruthlessness, and superior weapons of the Spaniards, the impractical fighting tactics of the Indians, and their bitter dissensions that Cortes exploited cleverly and decisively.

Cortes began by scuttling his ships to show his men that they had no hope of returning to Cuba in case of setbacks. Then, after some fighting, he reached agreements with various tribes that were hostile to their Aztec overlords. Without the food, the porters, and the fighting men provided by these tribes, Cortes could not have won the victories he did. By playing upon the superstitions of Montezuma, the Aztec war-chief, Cortes was able to march peacefully into the capital, Tenochtitlan. He was graciously received by Montezuma, whom he treacherously took prisoner and kept as a hostage. This was a brazen bluff that could not be maintained for long. The Indians were vastly superior in numbers, and their priests were stirring them up to rebellion. The Spanish policy of destroying native temples provoked an uprising during which Monte-

Quauhtemoc, the last king of the Aztecs, surrendering to Cortes.

Pizarro's attack on Cuzco.

zuma was killed. Cortes fought his way out of the capital by night, losing a third of his men and most of his baggage in the process. But his Indian allies remained loyal, and he received reinforcements from Cuba. A few months later he returned and laid siege to the capital with a force of 800 Spanish soldiers and at least 25,000 Indians. The fighting was bitter and dragged on for four months. Finally, in August, 1521, the surviving defenders surrendered their city, which was almost entirely reduced to rubble. Today, Mexico City stands in its place, with hardly a trace left of the original Aztec capital.

Even more audacious was the conquest of the Inca Empire by a Spanish expedition comprising 180 men, 27 horses, and 2 cannon.* The leader was Francisco Pizarro, an illiterate and a drifter who was the illegitimate son of a Spanish officer. After preliminary explorations from which he learned the general location of the Inca Empire, he set forth in 1531, with his four brothers, on his great adventure. After a long delay in crossing the Andes, Pizarro reached the deserted city of Cajamarca on November 15, 1532. The following day the Inca ruler, Atahualpa, who was curious about these strange "men with beards," paid a formal visit to Pizarro. In imitation of Cortez, Pizarro captured the unarmed and unsuspecting emperor and massacred many of his followers. The emperor paid an enormous ransom for his free-dom—a room 22 feet by 17 feet piled 7 feet deep with gold and silver articles. Having seized the booty, Pizarro, with customary treachery and bigotry, offered Atahualpa his choice of being burned at the stake as a heathen or bap-tized and strangled as a Christian. The unfortunate emperor selected the latter alternative. The Inca Empire now was left leaderless, and the Indian popu-

* See "Spanish Conquest of the Inca Empire," *EMM*, No. 31.

lation, accustomed to paternaltistic regimentation, offered little resistance. A few weeks later Pizarro entered and looted the capital, Cuzco. The next year, 1535, he left for the coast, where he founded Lima, still the capital of Peru.

The triumphs of Cortes and Pizarro inspired other conquistadors to march through vast areas of both the American continents in search of more booty. They found nothing comparable to the Aztec and Inca treasures, but in the process they did determine the major configuration of all South America and of a large part of North America. By the middle of the sixteenth century they had followed the Amazon from Peru to its mouth. By the end of the century they were familiar with the entire coastline of South America, from the Gulf of California south to Tierra del Fuego and north to the West Indies. Likewise in North America, Francisco de Coronado, in his search for the fabled Seven Cities of Cibola, traversed thousands of miles and discovered the Grand Canyon and the Colorado River. Hernando de Soto, who had been prominent in the conquest of Peru, explored widely in the southeast of what was to become the United States. He landed in Florida in 1539, made his way north to the Carolinas and west to the Mississippi, and followed that river from its junction with the Arkansas River to its mouth. These men, and many others like them, opened up the New World for the Spaniards in the same manner that La Salle and Lewis and Clark opened it for the French- and English-speaking peoples.

VI. EUROPE'S FIRST COLONIAL EMPIRE

By 1550 the conquistadors had completed their work. The way was now clear for the Spaniards to proceed with the development of their overseas possessions. Since the native populations were not so dense or so highly organized as those of Africa and Asia, it was possible for the Iberians to settle in considerable numbers in the New World and to impose their cultures. Thus they built up Europe's first true colonial empire—something quite different from the purely commercial empires in Africa and Asia.

The swashbuckling conquistadors were effective as empire builders but quite ineffective as empire administrators. They could not settle down; they fell to fighting among themselves, decimating their ranks during prolonged feuding and internecine warfare. For example, only one of the five Pizarro brothers who had conquered Peru survived these wars, and he ended his days in a Spanish prison. Had these conquistadors been left to themselves, they probably would have gradually developed scattered and virtually independent feudal communities based on the exploitation of native labor. But the Spanish crown had no intention of allowing such a state of affairs to materialize. It had curbed feudal tendencies within Spain and would not tolerate the emergence of a new feudal aristocracy overseas. Accordingly, the conquistadors were replaced by bureaucrats who imposed royal authority and royal justice.

At the apex of the imperial administrative structure was the Council of the Indies, located in Spain and closely supervised by the crown. It made all important appointments and exercised general jurisdiction over colonial affairs. Supreme authority in the New World was entrusted to two viceroys who sat in Mexico City and Lima, respectively. The official in Mexico City headed the

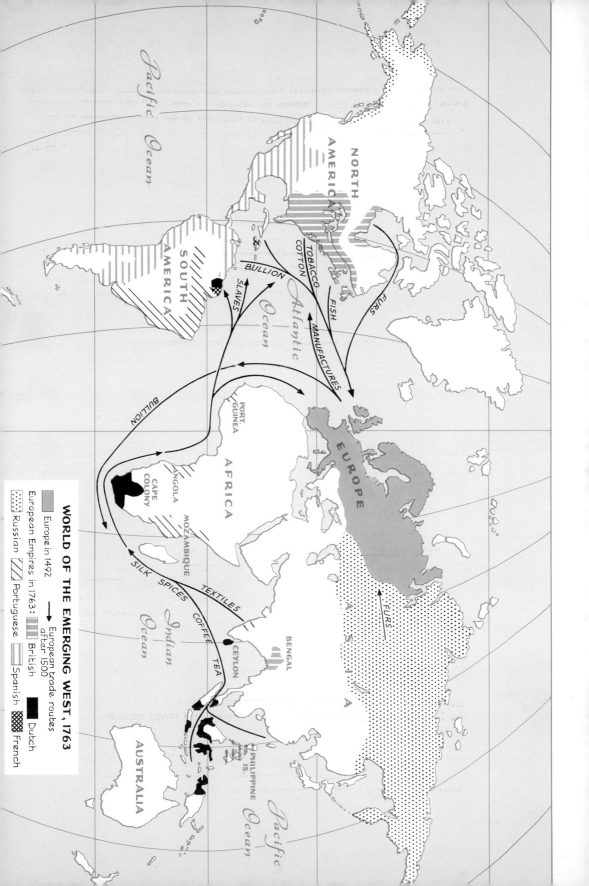

WORLD OF THE EMERGING WEST, 1763

Europe in 1492

European Empires in 1763:

→ European trade routes after 1500

- Russian
- Portuguese
- British
- Spanish
- Dutch
- French

NORTH AMERICA

SOUTH AMERICA

EUROPE

ASIA

AFRICA

AUSTRALIA

Pacific Ocean

Atlantic Ocean

Indian Ocean

Pacific Ocean

BULLION

SLAVES

TOBACCO

COTTON

FISH

FURS

MANUFACTURES

BULLION

PORT. GUINEA

ANGOLA

CAPE COLONY

MOZAMBIQUE

FURS

BENGAL

CEYLON

SILK SPICES TEXTILES COFFEE TEA

PHILIPPINE IS.

viceroyalty of New Spain, which comprised all the Spanish territories in North America together with the West Indies, Venezuela, and the Philippines. The Lima official presided over the viceroyalty of Peru, comprising the remaining Spanish possessions in South America. These two vast viceroyalties were sub-divided into smaller units ruled by *audiencias,* or councils, modeled on bodies that had been established in Spain to administer territories newly liberated from the Moslems. These audiencias were staffed by professional lawyers who usually had no excessive family pride or military ambition and therefore made ideal royal servants. In the sixteenth century there were ten such audiencias in the New World.

A basic problem of Spanish administration in the Americas was the treat-ment of the Indians. The conquistadors and their descendants demanded a free hand in dealing with them. They argued that the natives were shiftless, unreliable, and treacherous, and that the only practical arrangement was un-fettered local lordship based on forced labor. The powerful Catholic Church strongly opposed this position. Its missionaries—especially the famous Do-minican friar Las Casas—maintained that the Indians were subjects of the Crown and enjoyed equal rights with the Spanish settlers. They insisted that Europeans who wished to reside in the New World should live apart from the Indians and support themselves from their own labor. Meanwhile the Indians would live under their own headmen, though subject to the authority of benevolent royal officials and to the ministrations of the missionaries.

The outcome, as is usual in such cases, was a compromise settlement. The crown granted large estates, each containing several Indian villages, to de-serving conquistadors and other colonists. These individuals, who were known as "protectors," or encomenderos, had the right to draw specified tribute from the villages and also to levy forced labor. In return, the encomenderos were required to give military service and to pay the salaries of the parish clergy. The provision for forced labor obviously opened the door to abuse, so it was modified in the mid-sixteenth century. The natives still could be made to work, but the compulsion was provided by public rather than private authority, and official wage rates had to be paid to the laborers so recruited. It is unneces-sary to add that these safeguards were not always enforced. The colonies were too far from Madrid and too isolated from each other. Yet the fact remains that the Spaniards discussed seriously and conscientiously a problem for which there were no precedents, and they enforced a system that was certainly ex-ploitative of the Indians but not as much so as the enemies of Spain have claimed.*

The all-important fact for the economy of the Spanish colonial empire is the great flood of gold and silver. First there were the countless treasure ob-jects that had been wrought by generations of native craftsmen and that the conquistadors promptly melted into ingots. Then the Spaniards discovered rich silver veins in Mexico and Bolivia which they worked with native labor. They were required to register their claims with royal officials and to bring all precious metals to the royal offices to be stamped and taxed at the rate of one-fifth their value, the royal quinto. Between 1503 and 1660 Spain received from America a total of 18,600 registered tons of silver and 200 registered

* See "Spanish Colonial Policy in the New World," *EMM,* No. 32.

tons of gold. Unregistered bullion smuggled into Spain has been variously estimated at from 10 to 50 per cent of the total, the smaller percentage probably
being nearer the truth. Apart from mining, the principal occupations in
Spanish America were stock raising and, in the tropical coastlands where
cattle could not thrive, sugarcane and tobacco growing.

108

All trade with Spanish America was a monopoly of the merchant guild of
Seville, with its subsidiary organization at Cadiz. Through an elaborate series
of fictions, merchant houses all over Spain became members by proxy of the
Seville guild. Even foreign commercial firms—German, English, and Flemish
—resorted to this device, so that genuine members of the guild performed a
vast commission business that eventually surpassed their own legitimate trade.
The American trade was subject also to licensing regulations of the royal
House of Trade, or Casa de Contratación. There were licensing of emigrants,
to prevent the emigration of Jews and of heretics; licensing of ships, to ensure
their seaworthiness; of navigators, to ensure their competence; of exports, to
control the traffic in firearms and slaves.

All this seems unduly restraining, yet it was simply typical of the age; taken
as a whole, Spanish colonial policy was not more illiberal than that of other
countries. There was, it is true, much smuggling and poaching in the Spanish
colonies, but this was not because the trade regulations were more stringent
than elsewhere. It was rather because the flourishing Spanish empire offered
a much greater market for commodities of all sorts than the comparatively
insignificant French and British colonies of North America. And also because
producers in Spain could not, or would not, export in sufficient quantities and
at competitive prices the goods that the New World needed. This latter point
is crucial because it reflects the basic economic weakness of Spain (and of
Portugal) that was to contribute heavily to the decline of the Iberian countries
and to the rise of northwestern Europe.

VII. IBERIAN DECLINE: EUROPEAN BACKGROUND

During the sixteenth century the Iberian countries led Europe in overseas
enterprise and won vast riches from the Eastern spice trade and from the New
World silver mines. But by the end of the century they were rapidly slipping
back from their respective positions of primacy. The French, the Dutch, and
the English were poaching with increasing success in Portugal's Eastern
empire and in Spain's American colonies. In seeking the roots of this Iberian
decline it is necessary to consider briefly the politics and the wars of the states
at this time. For it was the involvement of the Iberian countries in these
European conflicts that explains to a very large degree their exhaustion and
their decline.

A prominent feature of sixteenth century European politics was dynastic
rivalry and conflict. Strong national monarchies had developed in Western
Europe during the fifteenth century; in the sixteenth, the balance amongst
these dynasties was upset by the sensational rise of the Spanish house through
marriage ties. Ferdinand and Isabella married their daughter Joanna to Philip
of Hapsburg. Charles, the offspring of this union, inherited the united Spanish

kingdom together with the Spanish possessions in the New World and in Italy (Sardinia, Sicily, Naples), and also the hereditary Hapsburg lands in Central Europe (the duchies of Austria, Styria, Carinthia, Carniola, and the county of Tirol). In addition, Charles' grandmother, Mary of Burgundy, left him Burgundian territories, Franche-Comté, Luxembourg, and the wealthy Netherlands. And to crown this imposing edifice, Charles was elected in 1519 Holy Roman Emperor over the opposition of the young French and English monarchs, Francis I and Henry VIII, respectively. Thus Charles V, at the age of nineteen, became the ruler of a larger territory than had been collected under one monarch since the break-up of Charlemagne's empire seven centuries earlier.

For a time it appeared that Western Europe would be united once more in a vast international organization. But the other European dynasties, and especially the Valois of France, were determined to prevent Hapsburg hegemony. The result was a long series of Hapsburg-Valois wars, which were fought primarily by the French and the Spaniards. In his desperate search for aid, Francis I allied himself with the sultan of the Moslem Ottoman Empire, Suleiman the Magnificent. This tie shocked contemporary Christians, who denounced it as the "impious alliance" and the "sacrilegious union of the Lily and the Crescent." But the French and the Turks continued to cooperate against the Hapsburgs, thus reflecting the degree to which dynastic interests had superseded the medieval concept of a united Christendom. And it should be kept in mind that in waging these wars Charles expended mostly Spanish blood and Spanish treasure, particularly in Italy.

Europe at this time was torn by religious strife as well as dynastic. It was in 1517 that Martin Luther began his public opposition to certain church practices and thereby generated a movement that was to split Western Christendom permanently into two camps, Catholic and Protestant. When Luther refused to recant, Charles declared him an outlaw in the Empire in 1521. But at the same time the Turks were advancing up the Danube, and in 1529 they actually besieged and almost captured the city of Vienna in the heart of Europe. Charles had to bear the brunt of the Turkish onslaught, and this prevented him from dealing promptly with the Protestant heretics. By the time he was free to turn to them, they had become too strong to be wiped out, in contrast to various other heretical movements during the medieval period. After a prolonged struggle against the Protestants, Charles was forced in 1555 to accept the Religious Peace of Augsburg, which allowed every German prince and town to choose between Catholicism and Lutheranism.

The following year, Charles V abdicated his throne and retired to a monastery, a disappointed man. He had failed to cope with forces that were far too vast to control. He left Austria and its dependencies to his brother Ferdinand, who was also chosen to succeed Charles as Holy Roman Emperor. To his son Philip II, he left the remainder of his empire—Spain, the Italian possessions, the New World colonies, and the Burgundian lands, including the Netherlands. Like his father, Philip was a conscientious and industrious ruler, but he also was doomed to frustration and failure. He inherited from his father the dynastic struggle with France and also the religious struggle with Protestantism. The Augsburg Treaty applied only to Germany, so that when

Protestantism spread to other parts of northern Europe, new tensions and conflicts developed. This was particularly the case in the Netherlands, where Philip attempted to force Catholicism upon all his subjects. The Dutch revolted in 1567, and a bitter struggle ensued that was still raging when Philip died in 1598. Again it is important to note that Philip depended almost entirely on Spanish manpower and treasure to wage this protracted war. Furthermore, it was a war that was fought on sea as well as land, and against the English as well as the Dutch.

In addition to these dynastic and religious forces, Europe in the sixteenth century was profoundly affected by economic rivalries. The whole of Europe was eyeing covetously the spices that were pouring into Portugal and the bullion that was pouring into Spain. The French, the Dutch, and the English all wished to crack the Portuguese monopoly in the East, to trade with the growing Spanish colonies in the New World, and to establish colonies of their own despite Pope Alexander's division of the overseas world between Spain and Portugal. Accordingly, the English argued that "Prescription without possession availeth nothing"—that is, that territorial claims would be respected only where there was effective occupation. Likewise, the French insisted that "In lands which the King of Spain did not possess they [the French] ought not to be disturbed, nor in their navigation of the seas, nor would they consent to be deprived of the sea or the sky." [16]

Economic considerations were prominent in the revolt of the Dutch. Philip had taxed the Netherlands heavily, and had imposed restrictions on Dutch commerce in the interest of that of Spain. Likewise, the English aided the Dutch for economic as well as religious reasons. They calculated that if the Spanish grip on the Netherlands were broken, the Spanish colonies would become even more vulnerable to English sea power. How important this was for the English is indicated by the fact that in 1562, five years before the Dutch began their revolt, John Hawkins made his famous illicit voyage to Hispaniola with a cargo of slaves and returned the wealthiest man in Plymouth. In 1564 he took another cargo to Venezuela and the Isthmus and returned the wealthiest man in England. His third expedition was ambushed by the Spaniards and disastrously defeated. But Hawkins had shown the way, and during the following decades English sea captains raided the Spanish Indies at the same time that they aided the Dutch. Philip retaliated by sending his Invincible Armada to invade England in 1588. Elizabeth's sea dogs destroyed the Armada and with it Philip's hopes for a Catholic Spanish domination over Europe. Ten years later Philip died, a disappointed man like his father before him. Spain never recovered from this century of lavish and futile squandering of manpower and resources.

In retrospect, it is apparent that the rulers of Spain fatally overextended themselves. They attempted to play the leading role on land as well as on sea. This was in striking contrast to the successful strategy pursued later by England of remaining on the periphery of continental affairs and intervening only in case the balance of power was seriously threatened. This strategy enabled the British to concentrate their efforts on the defense and development of their colonies. Instead, Spain, like France, focused on the Continent and was continually involved in its wars. This cost Spain the economic control of her empire, just as later it cost France physical control of hers.

VIII. Iberian Decline: Causes and Symptoms   111

With this background of dynastic, religious, and economic conflict in Europe, we turn now to the circumstances and process of Iberian decline. It should be noted first that Spanish industry was in the beginning greatly stimulated by the demand for manufactured goods in the American colonies. The early settlers were so intent on their search for precious metals that they imported almost everything—even the barest necessities—from the mother country. Their demands were so great that Spanish merchants commonly made a profit of about 150 per cent on their exports to the New World. Spanish industry expanded so rapidly that in some regions an acute shortage of labor developed, and beggars were seized and forced to work in the factories. Industry continued to grow until a high point was reached about 1560. Then a rapid decline set in.

Why was this incipient industrial revolution in Spain so short-lived? Why did it not develop into a full-fledged Industrial Revolution, as occurred in Great Britain two centuries later? This question is particularly intriguing because Spain had solid assets on which she could have based her industrialization. She was secured from foreign aggression by the Pyrenees. She had a steady and mounting supply of precious metals. Her colonies provided a growing market for her manufactured goods. She had rich natural resources at home as well as overseas. She was strategically located, with access to both the Atlantic and the Mediterranean.

One reason for Spain's failure, paradoxically enough, was the great inflow of treasure, which produced a sharp price inflation. Prices began to rise about 1520 and continued upward until, by the century's end, they were five times as high as they had been at its beginning. Other countries in Europe also experienced a price inflation as bullion reached them through the ordinary channels of commerce. But prices did not rise so high in those countries as in Spain. In France the peak was reached by the end of the sixteenth century, but it was only about two-and-a-half times the level at the beginning. In England the climax was reached in the middle of the seventeenth century, when prices were three times as high as at the beginning of the sixteenth century. This price differential between Spain and the rest of Europe hurt Spanish industry badly, because it meant that Spain was a bad market to buy from and a good one to sell to.

Spanish industry was squeezed by a wage differential as well as a price differential. Wages in Spain lagged only slightly behind the soaring prices, while wages in the rest of Europe were kept far down. This also penalized Spanish industry, making its products too expensive to compete in the international market.

More basic than price and wage inflation was the ruinous influence of the Spanish aristocracy on the national economy and on national values. Ferdinand and Isabella had successfully curbed the political power of the aristocrats by replacing them in the royal councils with professional lawyers. But in return they had to recognize the aristocracy's immunity from taxation and its monopoly of land. Consequently this small group, together with the higher ecclesiastics, owned about 95–97 per cent of the land, though constituting less than 2 per cent of the population. It follows that the peasants, about 95 per cent of all Spaniards, were almost all landless. The remaining 3 per cent—clerics, merchants, and professional men, many of whom were Jews—were not a middle class in any economic or social sense. They were completely overshadowed by the nobility, who had social status and prestige. And since the nobility looked down upon careers in commerce or industry as demeaning for any gentleman, this prejudice became the national norm. Nor was this mere empty vanity, for the hidalgo, or noble, had all the advantages—honors, exemption from taxation, and territorial wealth that was more secure than commercial or industrial. Consequently, the ambition of successful merchants was to acquire estates, buy titles which were sold by the impoverished crown, and thus abandon their class and become hidalgos. So widespread was this practice that the Cortes of Castile repeatedly complained that the sale of titles, with their tax exemption privilege, increased the burden on the remaining commoners.

The injurious economic influence of this hidalgo spirit was evident also in the favoritism shown toward sheep raising as against farming. Sheep raising, unlike most other money-making activities, was considered to be in keeping with hidalgo dignity. Furthermore, the crown, with an eye to the revenues from the export of wool, stipulated that "the breeding and preservation of livestock ought to be the principal substance of these kingdoms." [17] Consequently, the all-powerful sheep-raisers' guild, the Mesta, was given many special privileges. As a result more and more farm lands were converted to pasture, to the point where grain shortage became increasingly serious. In 1506 many parts of Spain were close to famine, and from then on wheat had to be imported on a large scale to feed the population.

Equally unenlightened was the persecution of Jews and Moslems, which damaged commerce and industry as much as the favoritism to the Mesta hurt agriculture. Both the clergy and the aristocracy clamored for religious unity and demanded measures against Moors and Jews who refused baptism, and against those converted Moors (moriscos) and converted Jews (conversos) who were suspected of being secret apostates. It should be noted that national security was also involved, for Spain at this time was on the defensive against the encompassing surge of the Ottoman Turks from the Levant and North Africa, and the Moors were feared, not without justification, as potential fifth columnists. Furthermore, there was a popular underlying resentment against the Jews and Moors precisely because of their non-hidalgo qualities of industry and frugality. Very revealing in this connection is the diatribe of a famous and typical Spaniard, Miguel Cervantes, against "the Moorish scum."

> It would be a miracle to find among so many people even one who believes sincerely in the sacred Christian faith. Their sole aim is to coin money and then keep it, and in order to gain they work and do not eat. When a *real* enters into their possession, provided it be not a worthless one, they condemn it to perpetual imprisonment and eternal obscurity; so that always gaining and never spending, they accumulate the greater part of the money that there is in Spain. They are its money-bags, its moth, its magpies, and its weasels. They gather everything, they hide

everything and they swallow everything. . . . There is no chastity among them, and neither men nor women enter the religious life. They all of them marry, they multiply, because sober living augments the causes of generation. War does not consume them, nor any occupation overtask them. They rob us quietly and easily, and with the fruits of our inheritance which they resell to us they wax rich.[18]

Several unsuccessful measures against the moriscos in the sixteenth century finally culminated in their mass expulsion beginning in 1609. The Jews were forced out earlier, in 1492, when 150,000 refused baptism and left the country, together with 120,000 conversos. Several municipalities protested against the serious economic loss resulting from the departure of the Jews with their skills and capital, but the monarchs replied that they favored the religious to the material welfare of the country. Likewise, travelers reported the ruined houses, dried-up gardens, and neglected irrigation works in those parts of Spain formerly occupied by Moslems.

Spain's economic development was blighted also by the crushing burden of taxation necessitated by the continuous wars against the rival French, the infidel Moslem Turks, and the heretic German, Dutch, and English Protestants. When Charles V abdicated in 1556, he left his son Philip II an unfinished war and a heavy burden of debt. In the next year Philip was forced to declare bankruptcy, and two years later, in 1559, he accepted the Treaty of Cateau-Cambrésis with France because he lacked funds to continue the war. The outbreak of the Dutch revolt in 1567 created further financial difficulties and compelled Philip to declare bankruptcy again in 1574. The Cortes complained repeatedly against the excessive taxes and opposed the continuation of the war in the Netherlands. It was ignored, and the final outcome was the loss of the northern Netherlands, which gained its independence in 1609. The southern Netherlands was retained, but only after its flourishing industry was reduced to ashes. And in the meantime Spain had suffered a disastrous naval setback as well as further financial strain with the defeat of the Armada sent against England in 1588.

The combination of injurious economic policies and unceasing financial pressures explains why the vast amounts of treasure from the New World flowed in and out of Spain as through a sieve. The bullion went out to pay for the foreign manufactured goods that, because of the decline of Spanish industry, were capturing not only the Spanish colonial market but even the home market in Spain itself. The Seville merchants, who enjoyed a monopoly of the colonial trade, exported in their own name goods that belonged to foreign firms and were of foreign manufacture. Also, they commonly took foreign merchants and financiers into informal partnership to raise capital for the purchase of ships and goods. Thus Spanish bullion found its way to northwestern Europe, where it was used to finance the expansion of French, Dutch, and English industry, while Spain became increasingly a mere producer of raw materials such as wool.

New World treasure went to northwestern Europe also to pay interest on the debts incurred by the Spanish government. As Madrid's financial difficulties increased, the bankers increased their rates from 12 to 20 and even 40 per cent per annum. Thus there developed a vicious circle of mounting debts and rising interest rates. In the end, the crown was forced to mortgage in advance all its revenues, whether from its private domains, from customs, taxes, and donations, or from the New World gold and silver mines. The proceeds from all these sources ended up in the vaults of the great Antwerp bankers who were the outstanding international financiers of the time. The situation led a Spaniard of the period to complain that "All that the Spaniards bring from the Indies, acquired after long, prolix, and hazardous navigations, and all that they harvest with blood and labour, foreigners carry off to their homelands with ease and comfort." [19]

This complaint was fully justified. The sixteenth century witnessed Spain's rise to greatness, but also the beginning of her decline; and the seventeenth century saw her sink to the level of a second-rate power. The following report of the Venetian ambassador in Madrid at the end of the seventeenth century reveals to what an extent Spain had failed to fulfill the promise of her short-lived industrial prosperity in the first half of the sixteenth century.

> Even in the royal palace a certain amount of economy has been adopted. Yet it avails little in view of the exorbitant expenditure, chiefly on pensions, which are inherited by wives and children and so almost hereditary. Suffice it to say that more than three hundred and fifty ladies live on them. The finances are in such a state that a large part of the revenue is pledged before it comes in and a considerable part of it is absorbed in the payment of interest. Yet the extravagance continues. . . . While the circle of the Crown embraces so many states upon many seas in two hemispheres, with the gifts of nature and with industry and skill the various parts would remedy one another's deficiencies. But as things are, other nations profit by it, owing to the neglect of agriculture, the supineness of the government, and the national indolence of Spaniards, who without stores or organisation have abandoned seamanship. So that only a few ships of Biscay occupy themselves in gathering the produce of the earth. These have almost lost the art of navigating by the stars, and yet their renown was once spread from pole to pole.
>
> The habit of the people has reduced internal trade to little and foreign trade to less still. . . .
>
> The Dutch and English carry away the wool and export it again manufactured into bombazine and fine draperies. . . . The Genovese supply paper and some silk fabrics. Hamburg and France supply a large part of the linen of Westphalia and Brittany and many other kinds of manufactured goods in small consignments through Geneva. . . . The Portuguese furnish tobacco, sugar and other sweet matter. But the French most of all trade with Spain in time of peace and continue to do so in time of war by concealing their identity.
>
> Of the states of the Spanish Crown in Europe the people of Naples and Milan profit by the export to Spain of silken and golden lace, those of Flanders with fine linen, hangings, white lace and other manufactures. All these nations carry back in exchange only raw material and no manufactured goods.
>
> The unfavourable features of this exchange of goods would matter little if they did not extend also to America. The Spaniards send little

thither except wine, from which they derive much profit owing to their care in preventing the planting of vines there. But commodities of every imaginable kind, manufactured goods and raw material alike, are exported to America from foreign countries under pretence of coming from Spain.[20]

The decline of Spain was matched by that of Portugal, and was noticeable in Portuguese Brazil as well as in the Indies. Brazil, which had fallen to Portugal under the terms of the Tordesillas Treaty, had neither the bullion nor the large and submissive population of Mexico and Peru. Consequently, Portugal at first showed little interest in its New World possession, settling it only to provide ports of call for the Indies fleets and to halt Spanish encroachment over the demarcation line. The early settlements remained small and poor during the sixteenth century, their only important export being brazilwood, a somewhat inferior red dye. In the first half of the seventeenth century, however, Brazil reached a peak of prosperity as the world's chief source of sugar. Northeast Brazil offered vast areas suitable for sugarcane cultivation, and the Portuguese posts in West Africa provided the necessary slave labor. When in the second half of the century Brazil began to lose its lead in sugar production (partly because of soil exhaustion in the northeast), a new source of wealth was uncovered with the discovery of gold in the Minas Gerais to the southeast. This precipitated the first great gold rush of modern times. It is significant that a local official expressed concern at the time that the gold would end up in northwestern Europe to pay for imports of manufactured goods, "so that" he wrote, "these countries will have all the profit and we will have all the work." [21] In point of fact, this is pretty much what did happen. Between half and three-quarters of the Brazilian gold that reached Portugal left it again, especially for England, which supplied most of the manufactured imports.

At the same time Portugal's hold over the East Indies also was weakening. Her maritime troubles arose partly from external pressures and partly from internal weaknesses. Portugal was a small nation with limited manpower, the total population being about one million. A constant supply of recruits was needed to man the ships because of the fearfully high mortality rates during the six-month-long voyages to the East. The fleet of 1571 was typical in reaching Goa with only about half of the 4,000 men who had embarked at Lisbon. The shortage was enhanced by the exodus of many Portuguese seamen who were attracted to the New World by the great treasure finds. Under these circumstances the Portuguese captains had to fall back upon Indian seamen and upon the the half-caste sons of the Portuguese settlers and native women. These recruits did not have the training of the native Portuguese, with the result that loss of ships rose rapidly. During the 83 years between Vasco da Gama's first voyage in 1497 and the union of the Spanish and Portuguese crowns in 1580, 93 per cent of the ships that sailed from Portugal reached India safely. During the next 32 years from 1580 to 1612, only 69 per cent found harbor. The losses cannot be attributed solely to the shortcomings of the sailors. The authorities in Portugal had failed to keep up the nautical researches of Prince Henry the Navigator, so that by the end of the sixteenth century Portugal lost its primacy in the art of navigation to England and

Holland. The Dutch, in particular, were outstripping the Portuguese also in the size of their merchant marine and in their naval manpower, for they employed many Germans and Scandinavians.

In 1580 King Philip II of Spain succeeded to the Portuguese throne following the death of the Portuguese ruler in a crusade against the Moors. The other monarchs of Europe were alarmed by this combination of Spanish and Portuguese power under one head. Actually there was little cause for apprehension. Both countries by this time were definitely on the downgrade. Indeed, the union served merely to open up the rich Portuguese Empire to the aggressive and rising powers of northwestern Europe. Spain in the late sixteenth century was engaged in a bitter and losing struggle against Protestant England, against France, and against Philip's rebellious subjects in the Netherlands. With the union of the Spanish and Portuguese crowns, the trade and possessions of Portugal in the East, as well as those of Spain in the New World, became the legitimate prey of the seafaring enemies of Philip.

By this time Iberian naval power had declined too far to be able to cope with the interlopers who were appearing on every sea. Several British and Dutch expeditions reached the East Indies in the 1590's. They were sufficiently profitable to encourage the British and the Dutch to organize their respective East India companies in 1600 and 1602. The formation of these companies represents a great turning point in the history of European expansion. The hegemony of Spain and Portugal that had characterized the sixteenth century was now giving way before the onslaught of the northwestern powers. The Iberian phase of European expansion was ending, and the Dutch, French, and British were taking the stage.

SUGGESTED READING

Over-all surveys of Iberian expansion are provided in the short collection by R. G. Albion, ed., *Exploration and Discovery* (New York: Macmillan, 1965); in the brief account by C. E. Nowell, *The Great Discoveries and the First Colonial Empires* (Ithaca: Cornell Univ., 1954); and in the fuller account by J. H. Parry, *The Age of Reconaissance: Discovery, Exploration and Settlement 1450–1650* (New York: World, 1963). The following interpretation of European expansion is noteworthy from an Indian viewpoint: K. M. Panikkar, *Asia and Western Dominance* (New York: Day, 1954).

The best study of Columbus is the two-volume *Admiral of the Ocean Sea* (Boston: Little, 1942) by S. E. Morison, who retraced Columbus' route as part of his preparation for the book. Morison also has a paperback entitled *Christopher Columbus, Mariner* (New York: New Am. Lib., 1956; a Mentor Book). For Portuguese maritime and colonial enterprise, see B. W. Diffie, *Prelude to Empire: Portugal Overseas Before Henry the Navigator* (Lincoln: Univ. Nebraska, 1963); E. Bradford, *Southward the Caravels: The Story of Henry the Navigator* (London: Hutchinson, 1961); C. R. Boxer, *Four Centuries of Portuguese Expansion, 1415–1825* (Johannesburg: Witwatersrand Univ., 1961); and H. M. Stephens' two-volume *Albuquerque* (Oxford: Clarendon, 1892, 1897). The original African objectives of the Portuguese are made clear in the important works by E. W. Bovill, *Caravans of the Old Sahara* (London: Oxford Univ.,

1933) and *The Golden Trade of the Moors* (London: Oxford Univ., 1958). A useful collection of readings presenting varied interpretations of the conquistadors is provided by J. F. Bannon, *The Spanish Conquistadores: Men or Devils?* (New York: Holt, 1960), which also provides a bibliography. Still worth reading are the classic and picturesque accounts by a famous American historian, W. H. Prescott, *History of the Conquest of Mexico* and *History of the Conquest of Peru,* published originally in 1842 and 1847, respectively, and available now in many editions. The best general analysis of the Spanish colonial system is C. H. Haring, *The Spanish Empire in America* (New York: Oxford Univ., 1947). For the Portuguese efforts in America there are G. Freyre's *Brazil, an Interpretation* (New York: Knopf, 1945) and C. R. Boxer's *The Golden Age of Brazil, 1695–1750: Growing Pains of a Colonial Society* (Berkeley: Univ. California, 1963).

The background political and military developments in Europe are presented in R. Tyler, *Emperor Charles the Fifth* (Fair Lawn, N. J.: Essential Books, 1956); M. Hume, *Philip II of Spain* (London: Macmillan, 1906); and C. Petrie, *Earlier Diplomatic History, 1492–1713* (New York: Macmillan, 1949). Finally, the roots and course of Iberian decline are presented in J. Lynch, *Spain Under the Hapsburgs,* Vol. I, *Empire and Absolutism, 1516–1598* (New York: Oxford Univ., 1964); in the two excellent studies by R. T. Davies, *The Golden Century of Spain, 1501–1621* (London: Macmillan, 1954) and *Spain in Decline, 1621–1700* (London: Macmillan, 1957); and also in the technical but basic study of E. Hamilton, *American Treasure and the Price Revolution in Spain, 1501–1650* (Cambridge: Harvard Univ., 1934).

*I should like to see Adam's will,
wherein he divided the earth between
Spain and Portugal.*

KING FRANCIS I

West European Expansion: Dutch, French, British Phase, 1600-1763

The period between 1600 and 1763 witnessed the overtaking and surpassing of Spain and Portugal by the powers of northwestern Europe—Holland, France, and Britain. This development was of first significance for the entire world. It made northwestern Europe the most influential and dynamic region of the globe. The countries of northwestern Europe were to dominate the world—politically, militarily, economically, and, to a certain degree, culturally—until 1914. Their practices and institutions became the models for peoples everywhere.

The world hegemony of northwestern Europe did not actually materialize until after 1763. But it was during the years between 1600 and 1763 that the basis for this hegemony was laid. These were the years when the British gained their first foothold in India, when the Dutch drove the Portuguese out of the East Indies, when all the northwestern powers set up stations on the coasts of Africa, and when the British and the French became the masters of North America above the Rio Grande, and also controlled much of the commerce of the Iberian possessions south of it.

This chapter will analyze the roots of northwest European primacy, and the struggles of Holland, France, and Britain for leadership, culminating in 1763 with the emergence of Britain as the dominant colonial power of the world.

I. Roots of Northwest European Primacy

Northwestern Europe did not rise from utter obscurity to the leading position in Continental commerce and in overseas enterprise. For centuries the northwestern countries had played an important and vital role in Europe's economy. France boasted a flourishing agriculture and a population that reached sixteen million by 1600, compared to one million for Portugal and eight million for Spain. England traditionally had been a great wool producer, and after the thirteenth century she began to manufacture the wool into cloth instead of exporting it all in raw form. Flanders for long had been the leading center in Europe for the mass production of textiles. Germany experienced a great frontier expansion along the Baltic between the twelfth and fifteenth centuries. This developing frontier stimulated commerce and handicrafts in the settled regions behind, in the same manner that the westward expansion of the United States was to aid the industrial growth of the Atlantic seaboard. Germany early became the outstanding mining center of the Continent, and more than held her own against the rest of Europe. Only with the discovery of silver mines in the Spanish colonies was her production outstripped; between 1545 and 1560, for example, Germany's production of over 50,000 kilograms of silver was but a fourth that imported from the New World, but still more than four times that produced in the rest of Europe.

Northern Europe had in the Baltic Sea a geographical equivalent of the Mediterranean Sea of southern Europe, but there was a political difference that favored the northern countries. By the fifteenth century, commerce in the Mediterranean was being choked by the corsairs of North Africa and by the advancing Turks who closed the Black Sea and prevented the Italian merchants from reaching southern Russia. By contrast, the Hansa cities that dotted the North and the Baltic seas continued to carry on a flourishing trade, exchanging the grain and timber of the eastern lands for the manufacture of the northwest.

Northwestern Europe, then, had a sound economic foundation that enabled it to exploit promptly and effectively the opportunities offered by the opening up of the New World and the Cape route. It also had a social structure and a cultural climate that were particularly sensitive and responsive to business possibilities. The English Parliament and the Dutch States-General never passed legislation like that of the Spanish Cortes forbidding exports of manufactured goods in order to lower their price. Far from regarding business enterprise with disdain, the patriciate of Holland and the nobility of England, and even of France, were always ready to participate in any business venture that promised profit.

The lesser nobility of France generally did regard trade as beneath their dignity. They were the ones who, as the proverb had it, stayed in bed while their breeches were mended. They filled the files of the Paris ministries with appeals for favors—to get their daughters into convents, their sons into seminaries or the army. But it seems that large financial transactions were respectable in France—only juggling with petty sums was considered mercenary. Thus we find the great names of the French aristocracy associated with investments in the mines of Flanders, in the metal works of Franche-Comté, and in the lucrative sugar and coffee trade with San Domingo.

120

Across the Channel, both the country gentry and the high nobility of England invested heavily in all enterprises that promised profit, including real estate, shipping, mining, and government securities. The Duke of Chandos, one of the wealthiest men of the early eighteenth century England, invested his fortune in oyster fisheries, distilleries, soap factories, glass works, coal, copper, and silver mines, and in land ventures in New York. In addition, he was involved in the South Sea Bubble speculative mania which burst in 1720. The Duke had sunk £200,000 in the South Sea Company, a sum equal to the total revenue of Charles I a century earlier.

Both in England and in France there was mobility between classes. Merchants and financiers entered the ranks of the nobility just as gentlemen participated in commerce. Daniel Defoe observed in 1726 that "trade in England makes gentlemen, and has peopled this nation with gentlemen; for the tradesman's children, or at least their grand children, come to be as good gentlemen, statesmen, Parliament men, privy counsellors, judges, bishops, and noblemen, as those of the highest birth and the most ancient families." [1] This peaceful interpenetration of one class by the other produced at least some community of interest which precluded the myopic and self-centered hidalgo attitude of the Iberian ruling class.

The countries of northwestern Europe were stimulated and strengthened also by the price revolution that followed the influx of New World bullion. As noted in the preceding chapter, price inflation was particularly acute in Spain. Nicolas Cleynaerts, a Dutchman traveling in Spain and Portugal in 1536, was so astonished by the high prices that he wrote home about the exorbitant cost of a shave: "Was it not necessary at Salamance, to pay a demireal to get a shave, which will prevent one being astonished at the greater number of bearded men in Spain than in Flanders." [2] Their lower prices gave the countries of northwestern Europe an obvious advantage in the international market.

Furthermore, northwestern Europe was aided by a wage as well as a price differential. Wages in Spain almost kept up with the soaring prices, while wages in the rest of Europe lagged far behind. During the sixteenth and seventeenth centuries, prices rose 256 per cent in England, while wages rose only 145 per cent. The situation was similar in France, where prices rose almost three times as much as wages.

Rents also lagged badly behind prices in northwestern Europe. Although we do not have precise data, we do have scattered evidence, such as the complaint of an English squire in 1549 that landlords were becoming impoverished because "the most part of the landes of this Realme stand yet at the old Rent."

The significance of these economic trends is that, of the three main elements of society—the laborers, landlords, and entrepreneurs—the entrepreneurs were the ones who reaped golden profits during these centuries of inflation. These profits were plowed back into mining ventures, industrial establishments, and commercial enterprises, with the result that the economy of northwestern Europe boomed ahead at an unprecedented rate. The American economist Earl J. Hamilton has summarized them as follows:

In England and France the vast discrepancy between prices and wages, born of the price revolution, deprived labourers of a large part of the incomes they had hitherto enjoyed, and diverted this wealth to the recipients of other distributive shares . . . rents, as well as wages, lagged behind prices, so landlords gained nothing from labour's loss. For a period of almost two hundred years English and French capitalists—and presumably those of other economically advanced countries—must have enjoyed incomes analogous to those American profiteers reaped from a similar divergence between prices and wages from 1916 to 1919. . . . We find, as might be expected, that during the seventeenth and latter part of the sixteenth centuries England, France, and the Low Countries were seething with such genuinely capitalistic phenomena as systematic mechanical invention, company formation, and speculation in the shares of financial and trading concerns.[3]

Likewise, the famous British economist John Maynard Keynes has described the period from 1550 to 1650 as follows: "Never in the annals of the modern world has there existed so prolonged and so rich an opportunity for the business man, the speculator, and the profiteer. In these golden years modern capitalism was born."[4] That it was born in northwestern Europe explains why the northwestern countries forged ahead of Spain and Portugal and attained a predominant position in world affairs, a position they were to retain until the outbreak of World War I.*

II. EARLY NORTHWEST EUROPEAN EXPANSION

The countries of northwestern Europe were naturally envious of the lucrative empires of Spain and Portugal. But for long they refrained from poaching on these imperial preserves, not out of respect for Papal Bulls, but rather for fear of Iberian power. Accordingly, the English and the French turned to the North Atlantic, which was beyond the limits of Iberian activity. Henry VII of England sent out John Cabot in that direction in 1496, the year of Columbus' second return, and Cabot discovered a resource that proved in the long run to be even more valuable than the silver mines of the Spaniards: he found fish. The sea off Newfoundland was teeming with fish—probably the most important article of trade in fifteenth and sixteenth century Europe, the mainstay of the people in the winter, and their diet on fast days throughout the year.

The Portuguese, however, were the first to exploit the Newfoundland Banks, and large quantities of codfish soon were pouring into Portugal. The French and the English soon followed, and by the first decade of the sixteenth century fishermen from Brittany, Normandy, Cornwall, Devon, and Somerset were regularly visiting the Banks. As the number of ships increased, the nature of the trade changed from the immediate sale of "green" fish to the marketing,

* See "American Treasure and the Rise of Northwestern Europe," *EMM*, No. 33.

at longer intervals, of much larger quantities of "dry" fish. The fishermen set up temporary shelters ashore during the summer months in order to dry and repair nets and to smoke and salt the catch. The scale of operations reached such proportions that it affected Europe significantly in at least two respects. The regular supply of immense quantities of cod represented a great windfall for a continent where many people at that time lived near starvation level for part of every year. And the Newfoundland fisheries bred successive generations of mariners who were trained and fitted for ocean navigation. The ships that later probed the Arctic for a northeast or a northwest passage; the expeditions that began the settlement of North America; the English and the Dutch fleets that fought the armadas of Spain and Portugal—all these were largely manned by seamen trained in the hard school of the Banks fisheries.

The maritime states of northwestern Europe were by no means satisfied with cod. They still hankered after spices, but they were not yet prepared to challenge Portugal's mastery of the Cape route. So they began their long and fruitless series of expeditions in search of a northeast or northwest passage to the Orient. They reasoned that since the Tropics had proved passable, contrary to all expectations, the Arctic should be also. In 1553 an expedition of three ships left England with the express intention of sailing to China by way of the northeast. The commander, Sir Hugh Willoughby, carried an open letter from Edward VI, written in Latin, Greek, and several other languages, and stating that discoveries and trade were the sole objects of the expedition. The letter was addressed to "the Kings, Princes, and other Potentates inhabiting the Northeast partes of the worlde toward the mighty Empire of Cathay."

The ships were separated during a gale, and two of them, under Willoughby, reached the Barents Sea. There they were frozen in for the winter, and the crews all perished, probably of scurvy. The following summer, Russian fishermen found the ships, the bodies, and Willoughby's diary. The last entry in the diary is worth noting as a reminder of the sacrifices and tragedies that Europe's expansion entailed.

> Thus remaining in this haven [in Barents Sea] the space of a weeke, seeing the yeare farre spent, & also very evill wether, as frost, snow, and haile, as though it had beene the dupe of winter [it was September], we thought best to winter there. Wherefore we sent out three men South-southwest, to search if they could find people, who went three dayes journey, but could finde none; after that, we sent other three Westward foure daies journey, which also returned without finding any people. Then sent we three men Southeast three dayes journey, who in like sorte returned without finding of people, or any similtude of habitation.[5]

Meanwhile, the remaining ship under Richard Chancellor reached the mouth of the Dvina River in the White Sea. The "habitation" that Willoughby had sought in vain was found here. After long haggling with the local people, Chancellor and some of his officers set off on an astonishing journey in horse-drawn sleighs, in winter, from the White Sea to Moscow. It proved to be a historic trip. Chancellor learned of the power and wealth of the Russian Tsar,

Ivan IV or the Terrible. The latter in turn was delighted to establish for the first time direct communications with a western European country. The Muscovy Company was organized in 1555 to exploit the new trade opportunity.*

Other attempts to discover a northeast passage invariably ended before a wall of ice. Interest therefore shifted to the possibility of a northwest route. The search began here with the three voyages of the Englishman Martin Frobisher, between 1576 and 1578. Frobisher worked hard to organize the voyages because he considered the discovery of a northwest passage to be "the onely thing of the worlde that was left yet undone, whereby a notable mind mighte be made famous and fortunate." [6] He returned from his third voyage loaded down with black stones which he thought were gold-bearing ore. His hopes for fame and wealth evaporated when the stones were discovered to be worthless and were dumped in Dartford harbor.

Frobisher was followed by a long line of explorers, including John Davis (who explored between 1585 and 1587), Henry Hudson (1607–1611), and Robert Bylot and William Baffin (1615–1616). They were all Englishmen, for, alone among the early exploration projects, the search for a northeast passage was a largely English enterprise. None of them was successful in sailing through to the Pacific. Three centuries were to pass before a Norwegian explorer, Roald Amundsen, would cross the ice-filled waters capping the North American continent. However, the work of the early explorers did have one practical result. It disclosed the Hudson Strait and Hudson Bay, which together provided a back entrance to the richest fur-producing region of the New World. This knowledge later enabled the English to compete in a region that otherwise would have been monopolized by the French.

The failure of the northern Europeans to find new routes to the East drove them to encroach on the preserves of the Iberian powers. Since Portugal's eastern possessions were still too strongly guarded, the northerners struck first at the more vulnerable Spanish colonies in the Americas. The French, operating from La Rochelle, had been engaging in piracy and privateering on the Spanish Main since they had begun their intermittent warfare with the Hapsburgs, from the accession of Charles V in 1516 to the Peace of Cateau-Cambrésis in 1559. The depredations of the French raiders were substantial. In 1556, Captain François le Clerc, whom the Spaniards called *Pie de Palo*—"a seafaring man with one leg"—attacked Havana with ten ships, sacked the town, and scuttled all the shipping in the harbor.

The English interlopers who were showing up in Spanish America at this time tried to carry on trade on a peaceful, commercial basis. They wanted not to plunder but to take advantage of the opportunities offered by the inability of the weak Spanish industry to meet the needs of the colonies. Of the two commodities most in demand in the Spanish colonies—cloth and Negro slaves—the English produced the first and could purchase the second in West Africa. Sir John Hawkins' famous voyages have already been mentioned. Hawkins won fame and fortune as the founder of the English slave trade because he was shrewd enough to sense the possibilities of this situation and bold enough

* See "Northeast Passage to Muscovy," *EMM*, No. 34.

124

to act without regard for legal niceties. In 1562 he made his first voyage, picking up slaves in Sierra Leone and exchanging them in Hispaniola (Haiti) for hides and sugar. The profits were so spectacular that Queen Elizabeth and several of her Privy Councilors secretly invested in his second voyage. He followed the same procedure as before and returned with a cargo of silver that made him the richest man in England.

The Spanish ambassador in London made strong protests against this contraband trade. Even though Hawkins had peacefully exchanged slaves for colonial commodities, the fact remained that it was illegal for foreigners to trade with the Spanish colonies. It was not piracy but it definitely was poaching. Elizabeth wished to remain at peace with Spain and forbade Hawkins to go to the West Indies again, but in 1567, Hawkins persuaded her to change her mind and allow one last voyage. This venture proved to be a disaster. Hawkins' ships were trapped in a West Indian harbor because the annual convoy arrived from Spain several weeks earlier than expected. Three of the five ships were sunk or captured, and the other two, one commanded by Hawkins and the other by his cousin Francis Drake, reached England in 1569 in a sinking condition.

The fate of this third voyage marked a turning point in Anglo-Spanish relations—it ended the hopes of peaceful and legal commerce with the Spanish colonies. And if the commerce could not be conducted peacefully and legally, it was bound to be carried on by other means. The opportunities for profit were too great for the English and the other northerners to refrain and forget. During the following decades, the Protestant sea captains visited the Spanish Indies as pirates and privateers rather than as peaceful, though illicit, traders.

Furthermore, other events in Europe at this time were bringing closer a showdown between the Catholic and Protestant powers. While Hawkins had been away on his third voyage, the Netherlands had risen in revolt against Spanish rule and precipitated a bitter war that dragged on for years. In 1570, the Pope excommunicated Queen Elizabeth and absolved her subjects from their allegiance to her. And two years after that, thousands of French Protestants were murdered in Paris and the provinces on Saint Bartholomew's Eve. The Protestant and Catholic camps clearly were drifting to war, and it was only a matter of time before it would break out. When King Philip of Spain sent his Armada against England in 1588, two of its most formidable adversaries were John Hawkins and Francis Drake. The defeat they inflicted on the Armada was, for them, sweet revenge for what they had suffered in the West Indies.

These developments in Europe vitally affected the course of events overseas. Formal war with Spain (which at this time had absorbed Portugal) removed any inhibitions that may have restrained the Protestant powers. They broke boldly and openly into the Iberian imperial preserves—into the Portuguese East as well as into Spanish America. And the more they penetrated, the more they were encouraged to go on by the unexpected weakness that they encountered. The Dutch were the ones who were first able to exploit this opportunity afforded by Iberian decline. The seventeenth century was to be for Holland *Het Gouden Eeuw*—"the Golden Century."

III. HOLLAND'S GOLDEN CENTURY

The remarkable rise of Holland to power and prosperity in the seventeenth century was in part a result of its favorable geographic location. Stretching across the estuaries of great rivers—the Scheldt, Maas, and Rhine—Holland was provided with excellent harbors looking westward to England and the Atlantic. Backed by the great hinterland of Germany, Holland also was strategically located along the ancient trade routes of Europe running north-south from Bergen to Gibraltar, and east-west from the Gulf of Finland to Britain. Along these routes were transported the basic trade commodities: herring and salt from Biscay, wine from the Mediterranean, cloth from Britain and Flanders, copper and iron from Sweden, and cereals, flax, hemp, timber, and wood products from the Baltic.

The Dutch began their rise to greatness by serving as the carriers of these commodities. Their merchant marine owed its start to the local coastal fisheries and, later, when the herring shoals mysteriously migrated from the Baltic to the North Sea, to the lucrative herring fishery. The Dutch exploited the new source of riches to the full. They devised new methods of preserving, salt-ing, and smoking, and exported their catch to all parts of Europe in return for corn, timber, and salt. With the building of the Spanish and Portuguese overseas empires, the Dutch picked up cargoes of the new colonial products in Seville and Lisbon and distributed them through Europe. In return, they supplied the Iberian countries with Baltic grain and naval stores.

Bengali entertainers performing before Euro-
peans, as seen by a Dutch visitor in the seven-
teenth century.

The outbreak of the Netherlands revolt against Spain in 1566 aided the Dutch substantially. Antwerp, prominent in industry and trade and the leading banking center of Europe, was sacked repeatedly by the Spaniards, and thousands of artisans, merchants, and bankers fled north—especially to Amsterdam. Between 1585 and 1622 the population of Amsterdam increased from 30,000 to 105,000; and the Antwerpers who contributed to the increase were also to contribute their money and skills to Holland's overseas expansion.

The Dutch also were greatly assisted in their enterprises by their *fluyt,* or flyboat, an inexpensive general carrier with enormous capacity. Hitherto the typical merchantman had been built with heavy timbering and galleried transom so that it could mount cannon and serve, when necessary, as a man-of-war. The Dutch were the first to take the risk of building a merchant packet deliberately designed to carry only goods and no guns. The *fluyt's* broad beam, flattened bottom, and restricted cabin accommodations gave it maximum hold space and unusual economy of building material. This slow and ugly but cheap and capacious boat was the mainstay of the Dutch merchant marine that came to dominate the seas of the world.

A combination of circumstances at the end of the sixteenth century drove the Dutch to challenge Portugal's hegemony in the East openly. One was Sir Francis Drake's famous voyage around the world (1577–1580), which revealed that the Portuguese, so far from being the masters of the East, were defending immensely long trade routes and widely scattered strongholds against a host of enemies. The Portuguese East Indies no longer seemed so invulnerable. And the union of the Spanish and Portuguese crowns in 1580 led the Protestant nations to regard Portugal with the fear and hatred they had formerly reserved for Spain. Portugal now was seen as an enemy in Europe and overseas, and her empire became fair game for the Protestant powers. Then, too, the Netherlands revolt interfered with the distribution of colonial goods in northern Europe because the Dutch no longer were able to pick up cargos in Iberian ports. The English for some time had been obtaining Oriental products in the ports of the Levant, but this trade also were throttled when Spanish and Portuguese men-of-war blocked the passage through the Straits of Gibraltar. Under these pressures, the Dutch and the English decided that since they could no longer obtain their spices in Lisbon and in Alexandria, they would fetch them directly from the Indies.

The first task was to collect reliable data to guide the navigators around the long Cape route. The Portuguese had taken the greatest precautions to keep such information secret. In 1504 King Manoel I issued a decree forbidding the inclusion in maps of any indication of the route beyond the Congo. Earlier maps that divulged such data were collected and destroyed or altered. Despite this censorship, the navigation secrets of the Portuguese gradually leaked out. The most important source of information for the northerners was the *Itinerario,* a geographical description of the world published in 1595 by the Dutchman Jan Huyghen van Linschoten. He had lived in India for seven years as a servant of the Portuguese archbishop of Goa, so that he was able to include in his book detailed sailing instructions for the Cape route.

Linschoten's work was used the year it was published to guide the first Dutch fleet to the East Indies. The losses were heavy during the two-and-a-half year expedition, only 89 of the original 289 men returning. But the trade was so lucrative that substantial profit remained despite the losses in manpower and equipment. The next expedition was more fortunate and cleared a profit of 400 per cent. The Dutch now swarmed into the Eastern waters, no less than five fleets, comprising twenty-two ships, sailing in the one year 1598. From the beginning they outmatched the Portuguese. They were better sailors, they could transport spices more cheaply in their *fluyten,* and their trade goods were cheaper and better constructed because their home industry was superior to that of the Iberian states. An unexpected complication was the tendency of the Indonesian rulers and traders to take advantage of the Dutch-Portuguese competition to raise prices and harbor dues. The Dutch responded in 1602 by amalgating their various private trading companies into one great national concern, the Dutch East India Company.

Under the terms of the charter that the company received from the States-General, it enjoyed a monopoly of trade, so far as the Dutch were concerned, between the Cape and Magellan's Strait. It was empowered to make war or peace, seize foreign ships, establish colonies, construct forts, and coin money. The company utilized these powers to the full in its dealings with the native potentates and in its successful drive against the faltering Portuguese. The English had organized their own East India Company two years earlier, in 1600, but they proved to be no match for the Dutch. The subscribed capital of the English company was much smaller, and was, moreover, available only periodically, since the English merchant shareholders financed only individual voyages. After each voyage they distributed both capital and profit and wound up their accounts. Furthermore, the English company received little support from the Stuart kings (understandably, since England was still mainly a nation of farmers), while the Dutch had the strong backing of their trade-oriented government.

Despite their advantageous position, the Dutch at first tolerated English competition in the East Indies. They were still fighting for independence from Spain and could not afford to add to their enemies. But when the Dutch concluded the truce of Antwerp with Spain in 1609, they turned against the English. The outcome of the struggle for monopoly was never in doubt. The Dutch had five times as many ships, and they had built a string of forts that gave them control of the key points in the Indonesian Archipelago. Furthermore, the Dutch had the services of a governor-general of genius, Jan Pieterszoon Coen, who did for his country what Albuquerque had done for Portugal. During his term of office (1618–1629) he drove the Portuguese from the East Indies and made it possible for his successors to expel them from Malacca (1641) and from Ceylon (1658). Coen also harassed the English out of the archipelago, compelling them to retreat to their posts in India. Equally important was Coen's cultivation and development of inter-Asiatic trade, much greater in volume than the traffic that rounded the Cape to Europe. The Portuguese had participated in this trade, but Coen went much further, establishing a base on Formosa (Taiwan) and from there controlling the commerce routes to China, Japan, and the Indies.

At first the Dutch East India Company consciously sought to avoid acquisition of territorial possessions. Theorists and politicians in Amsterdam attributed the decline of Portuguese power in the East to the dissipation of energy and capital in territorial conquest, and warned the Dutch company against a similar mistake. But in its efforts to establish a trade monopoly, the company was led step by step to the territorial expansion it wished to avoid. Monopoly could be enforced only by a network of fortified posts. The posts required treaties with local rulers, treaties led to alliances, and alliances to protectorates. By the end of the seventeenth century the Dutch were actually administering only a small area, but numerous states comprising a much greater area had become protectorates. Then during the eighteenth and nineteenth centuries the Dutch annexed these protectorates outright and built up a great territorial empire.

The export of spices to Europe diminished in value after about 1700, but the inter-Asiatic trade that Coen had developed made up for the shrinkage. Moreover, the Dutch developed a new economic resource at about that time by introducing coffee bushes into the East Indies. In 1711 they harvested 100 pounds of coffee, and by 1723 they were marketing 12 million pounds. Thus, as Europe acquired a taste for coffee, the Dutch became the principal suppliers of this exotic beverage. Through these various means the Dutch East India Company averaged annual dividends of 18 per cent throughout the seventeenth and eighteenth centuries.

Dutch overseas activities were not confined to the East Indies, however. In the Arctic waters around Spitzbergen the Dutch virtually monopolized the whaling industry. In Russia they badly outdistanced the English Muscovy Company. They also dominated the rich Baltic trade so that they became the chief provisioners in Western Europe of the all-important naval stores—timber, pitch, tar, hemp for rope, and flax for canvas sailcloth.

Their merchant marine was by far the largest of the world, numbering 10,000 ships as early as 1600. Dutch shipyards were highly mechanized and could produce almost a vessel a day. Furthermore, the ships were economical to build and to operate, so that Dutch shipowners undercut their competitors. Thus, they served as the carriers between Spain, France, England and the Baltic. Not until the eighteenth century were the English able to compete with the Dutch in merchant shipping.

In the New World, the Dutch founded New Amsterdam on Manhattan Island in 1612. This colony never became large, numbering only 1,900 in 1663. But it served as a base and clearing house for a great volume of Dutch shipping that ran a lucrative though illicit carrying trade between Europe and the Spanish, English, and French colonies in America. In fact, the English captured New Amsterdam in 1664 largely in order to plug what had become an intolerable leak in their mercantile system.

Further south in the Americas, the Dutch operated through their Dutch West India Company, established in 1621. Its purpose was to exploit the loosely held riches of the Spanish and Portuguese colonies in the New World. After a decade of intermittent fighting, the Dutch won control of the Brazilian coast all the way from Bahia to the Amazon. But the company was unwilling and unable to shoulder the expense of maintaining adequate garrisons, and the coastal strip was all lost by 1654. The Dutch West India Company also founded colonies at Caracas, Curaçao, and in Guiana in the Caribbean. Here they left a lasting imprint by introducing sugar cane, which soon became a fabulously profitable crop throughout the West Indies.

The Dutch colony that proved to be the most durable of all was the small settlement established in 1652 on the Cape of Good Hope in South Africa. This was not a trading station but a true colony founded to provide fuel, water, and fresh provisions for the ships en route to the East. One of the company officers wished to settle the Cape with Chinese, knowing them to be the cheapest colonists that could be had. It is interesting to speculate how different the future course of events might have been if his proposal had been adopted. But the Dutch officials in the East Indies refused to supply Chinese coolies, and instead a number of Boers, or peasants, were induced to migrate from Holland, along with some French Huguenots. The colony soon proved its value. The fresh meat and vegetables it provided to Dutch and other ships helped keep down scurvy and saved the lives of thousands of seamen. Today the descendants of these Boers comprise two-fifths of the three million Europeans residing in South Africa. They constitute the only overseas nucleus of Dutch language and culture that persists to the present. This is in striking contrast to the great English-speaking nations that today occupy a large portion of the earth's surface. The contrast explains in part the inability of the Dutch to retain the primacy that they enjoyed during their golden seventeenth century.

IV. DECLINE OF HOLLAND

During the eighteenth century Holland fell behind Britain and France in economic development and in overseas activity. One reason for this decline was the persistent efforts of the French and British governments to build up their merchant marines by discriminatory decrees against the Dutch. Examples of this legislation were the several Navigation Acts passed from 1651 onward providing that no goods should be imported into or exported from any English colony except in English ships—that is, ships built, owned, and at least three-quarters manned in England or an English colony. This legislation was followed by a remarkably rapid growth of the English merchant marine. To what extent the passage of the acts and the upsurge of English shipping are related remains an open question. That there was at least some relationship between the two is suggested by the sustained protests of the Dutch and also of the West Indian planters who resented the higher rates charged by English shippers.

The Dutch were weakened also by a series of exhausting wars—with Britain from 1652 to 1674 over mercantile disputes, and with France from 1667 to 1713 over the territorial ambitions of Louis XIV. The Dutch were peculiarly vulnerable to their enemies during these wars. Their merchantmen were slow and virtually unmanned. Their regular navy was usually neglected because of the concentration on the merchant marine. Thus, the English and especially the French privateers reaped a golden harvest preying on the Dutch ships as they came together from all corners of the world and ran the gauntlet through the English Channel to their home ports. Samuel Pepys relates that he found in a captured Dutch Indiaman "the greatest wealth . . . in confusion that a man can see in the world. Pepper scattered through every chink. You trod upon it, and in cloves and nutmegs I walked above the knees, whole rooms full. And silk in bales, and boxes of copperplate, one of which

I saw opened." [7] The depredations reached such proportions that Dutch insurance rates for ships leaving Holland in 1703 were: to the Levant—20 per cent; to Italy—16 to 20 per cent; to Portugal—7 to 14 per cent; to Curaçao and Surinam—10 per cent; and to England—2.5 to 5 per cent.

The Navigation Acts and the wars with Britain and France do not entirely explain Holland's decline. In fact, the volume of Dutch trade reached its peak in the period 1698 to 1715, and during those years the Dutch merchant marine was still twice the size of England's and probably nine times that of France. But at the same time Holland's share of the total trade was falling. What was taking place, therefore, was a relative rather than an absolute decline. The Dutch were not slipping, but the French and English were catching up. And the basic reason for this was that the Dutch lacked the resources to maintain their original rate of expansion. The French had a large population, a flourishing agriculture, and a rich homeland with outlets on both the Atlantic and the Mediterranean. The English also had much greater natural resources than the Dutch and enjoyed the great boon of an insular location, which spared them the cost of periodic invasions. Furthermore, the English had behind them the rapidly growing wealth and strength of their overseas colonies, whereas the Dutch had only the one small and isolated settlement on the tip of South Africa. Thus we find that the value of British exports rose from £8 million in 1720 to £19 million in 1763, and that French exports increased from 120 million livres in 1716 to 500 million in 1789. The Dutch, who had already reached their peak, were simply incapable of matching such growth. In the final analysis, Holland gave way to Britain and France in the eighteenth century for the same reason that Britain and France were to give way to the United States and the Soviet Union in the twentieth.

V. ANGLO-FRENCH RIVALRY

The eighteenth century was marked by a struggle between Britain and France for colonial supremacy. The two countries were in face-to-face rivalry throughout the globe—in North America, in Africa, and in India.

In North America, the British and French possessions had many characteristics in common. They were settled at about the same time. They were located on the Atlantic seaboard and in the West Indian islands. The native populations were relatively sparse and primitive so that the British and the French unlike the Spanish, could not hope to live off native labor, although they did depend on Negro slave labor in the sugar islands. Since the British and French found no precious metals, they had to support themselves by agriculture, fishing, lumbering, commerce, and fur trading.

The English colonies fell roughly into three groups: Virginia and its immediate neighbors, which produced mostly tobacco; New England with its little groups of nonconformist settlements, which engaged in fishing, lumbering, commerce, and the fur trade; and the British West Indies, by far the most highly prized because of their extremely profitable sugar plantations. One characteristic of these English colonies, taken as a whole, was their populousness, which was much greater than that of the French. Their other chief characteristic was their political intractibility. Every colony had a governor, an executive council, and a judiciary, all appointed from England. Nearly every colony also had an elective legislative assembly, and as a rule it was at loggerheads with the appointive officials.

The assembly was a distinguishing feature of the English Empire, for in no other European colonial empire at that time did representative institutions play a significant role. This is understandable, since England, unlike France and the Iberian countries, embarked upon the settlement of colonies in a period when representative government was gaining strength in the mother country. In any case the elective assemblies in the English colonies fiercely defended what they considered to be their inalienable rights. Their most common quarrel with the London government was the insistence of the latter that all colonial products be sent to England in English ships. This seemed to the royal officers a reasonable requirement, since they in turn gave the colonies a monopoly of the home market for their products. But the colonial merchants and planters protested bitterly when they were not allowed to use the cheaper Dutch shipping and to export their products to more profitable non-English markets.* In 1677, a century before the American Revolution, the Massachusetts assembly wrote openly to the Privy Council in London:

> We humbly conceive, according to the usual sayings of the learned in the law, that the laws of England are bounded within the four seas and do not reach America . . . not being represented in Parliament we have not looked at ourselves to be impeded in our trade by them.[8]

The French settlements in North America were outstanding because of their strategic location. The first French posts were established in Acadia, or Nova Scotia, in 1605, in Quebec in 1608, and in Montreal in 1642. Using the St. Lawrence River valley as their main base of colonization, the French took advantage of the incomparable inland water system to push westward to Lake Superior and southward to the Ohio River. In 1682 a French nobleman, La Salle, paddled down the Mississippi and laid claim to the whole basin, which he named Louisiana in honor of Louis XIV. Thus, the French had penetrated in remarkably short time to the heart of the North American continent.

This raised complications, for most of the colonial charters emanating from the English crown in the seventeenth century included clauses granting lands "from sea to sea"—that is, from the Atlantic to the Pacific. It was clear that whenever the English colonists reached and crossed the Appalachian Mountains, the rival French and English claims would be put to the test. At the outset, however, the French had the great advantage of possession. Their explorers had been the first to open up these regions, and then their officials had planted numerous forts along the route from the St. Lawrence to Louisiana. The English colonies along the Atlantic seaboard were effectively encircled by a great arc running from the Gulf of St. Lawrence to the Gulf of Mexico.†

The French not only possessed the commanding positions in North America, but they also had the great advantage of discipline and cohesion. There were

---

* See "Britain's American Colonies and Their Independent Spirit," *EMM*, No. 35.
† See "Anglo-French Rivalry in North America," *EMM*, No. 36.

no obstreperous elective bodies in the French colonies. Paris appointed the governors who were responsible for the defense of each colony, and the intendants who handled financial and economic affairs. This arrangement was quicker and more efficient than the creaking English representative system. The governors of the English colonies could only request and urge their assemblies to take a certain course of action; they could scarcely command, especially since the assemblies voted the funds for their salaries. In the French colonies the governors and intendants gave the orders, and their subordinates carried them out.

The French and English were neighbors also in the West Indies. The chief French possessions in this region were Martinique and Guadeloupe; the English were Jamaica, Barbados, and the Bahamas. These colonies were valuable as stations for trade with the Spanish and Portuguese colonies to the south, but their greatest asset was their tropical produce—sugar, tobacco, and indigo—which supplemented the economies of France and Britain.

In Africa, the French by the beginning of the eighteenth century had established themselves in Madagascar, at Gorée, and at the mouth of the Senegal River, while the English were in Gambia and on the Gold Coast. These footholds on the African coast served as stations for trade in gold, ivory, wax, and—most important, especially after the development of the West Indian sugar colonies increased the demand for a labor force there—slaves. Africa, however, was little affected by the Anglo-French rivalries of the eighteenth century. The real struggle for that continent was not to come until the nineteenth and twentieth centuries.

India, by contrast, was the scene of sharp Anglo-French conflicts, paralleling those in North America. The British had fallen back on the Indian subcontinent when they were driven out of the East Indies by the Dutch in the early seventeenth century. By the end of the century they had four major footholds in India: Calcutta and Madras on the eastern coast, and, on the western, Surat, the earliest British trading post in India, and Bombay, which passed to England as the dowry of the Portuguese princess whom Charles II married in 1662. The French had organized an East India Company of their own in 1604, but it soon became inactive. It was revived in 1664, and by the end of the century the French were ensconced in two major posts—Chandarnagar near Calcutta, and Pondichéry near Madras.

During the seventeenth century all Europeans who resided and traded in India did so on the sufferance of the powerful Mogul emperors. The latter could easily have driven the Europeans into the sea if they did not behave themselves and submit humble petitions for the privilege of carrying on their commercial operations. During the eighteenth century the situation was completely reversed. From barely tolerated alien merchants confined in a few coastal outposts, the Europeans changed to aggressive intruders who gradually won control of entire provinces of India.

The reason for this transformation is the disintegration of the Mogul Empire. After the great and enlightened Emperor Akbar died, in 1605, his successors failed to follow his wise policies of religious toleration and light taxation. This was especially true of Aurangzeb, the last great Mogul emperor, who came to the throne in 1658. A Moslem fanatic whose religious persecution, especially in his later years, alienated his Hindu subjects, Aurangzeb was forced to wage continual warfare, which in turn led to heavier taxes and to further popular disaffection. With his death in 1707 the Mogul Empire began to fall apart. There was no settled rule of succession, so that for two years his sons disputed the throne. Then between 1712 and 1719 five puppet emperors ruled at Delhi. Under these circumstances the provincial governors began to assert their independence and to establish hereditary local dynasties. The Marathas, who represented Hindu nationalism in a vague and incipient sense, expanded from their capital of Satara, about a hundred miles south of Bombay on the west, to within two hundred miles of Calcutta on the east. This disintegration of central authority gave the British and the French East India Companies the opportunity to transform themselves from mere commercial organizations to territorial overlords and tribute collectors. They built forts, maintained soldiers, coined money, and entered into treaties with surrounding Indian potentates, with no central authority in India capable of denying them the exercise of such sovereign rights.

VI. England's Triumph

Such, then, was the line-up of the rival British and French empires in India, Africa, and the Americas. The duel between the two empires during the seventeenth and eighteenth centuries ended in an overwhelming British triumph. One reason was that France was less interested in overseas possessions than in European hegemony. Since the sixteenth century, the French Bourbons had concentrated primarily on gaining ground in Italy and on combating the Hapsburgs in Austria and Spain. One of Louis XIV's ministers, Jean Baptiste Colbert, was genuinely interested in developing France economically and therefore he sought to encourage trade and colonies. But his great rival was the Minister of War François Louvois, who thought only of military campaigns and territorial expansion on the Continent. In the end Louvois won, and in doing so he established a tradition of Continental involvement. When in 1758 the valiant General Montcalm sent an emissary to Paris to explain the desperate military situation in Canada and the need for immediate assistance, he was informed that one does not attempt to save the stables when the house is on fire. It was not until the nineteenth century, after the Bourbon dynasty had been overthrown, that France turned again to overseas enterprise and expansion.

Another reason for Britain's triumph was that many more Englishmen than Frenchmen emigrated to the colonies. By 1688 there were 300,000 English settlers concentrated in the narrow piedmont region of the Atlantic coast compared to a mere 20,000 Frenchmen scattered over the vast areas of Canada and the Mississippi valley. This disparity arose in part from the refusal of Paris to allow the French Protestants, or Huguenots, to emigrate to the colonies, whereas Massachusetts was populated in large part by Nonconformists who left England because they could not abide Anglicanism. Another significant factor was the richness of the French soil compared to that of England. The peasant masses of France were deeply attached to their holdings and were able to earn enough so that they did not have to resort to emigration. In England, on the other hand, large-scale enclosures had been taking place for some time in order to produce more wool for the growing textile industry and more foodstuffs for the burgeoning towns. Both these commodities could be produced more efficiently on consolidated, scientifically operated holdings than on the small, separate field strips inherited from the Middle Ages. Enclosures meant more productivity, but they also meant social dislocation and distress. This was what Sir Thomas More decried when he wrote indignantly,

> That one covetous and insatiable cormorant and very plague of his native country may compass about and enclose many thousand acres of ground within one pale or hedge, the husbandmen be thrust out of their own . . . either by hook or crook they needs must depart away, poor, silly, wretched souls, men, women, husbands, wives, fatherless children, widows, woeful mothers, with their young babes. . . . And when they have wandered abroad till they be spent, what can they else do but steal, and then justly pardie be hanged, or else go about a begging. And yet then also they be cast in prison as vagabonds, because they go about and and work not, whom no man will set a work, though they never so willingly proffer themselves thereto.[9]

It was these dispossessed who provided the mass basis of the emigration from England to the colonies.

Furthermore, a generous sprinkling of English gentry left for the New World. Reduced to difficult straits by the combined effect of rising prices and stationary rents, they sought government employment, but sought it in vain if they happened to be Puritans. In fact, many Puritans lost their offices during the reign of Charles I. Typical was the case of John Winthrop of Suffolk, who was ousted from his post in the Court of Wards. No longer able to maintain his estate, his manor house, his servants, and the standard of living to which he had grown accustomed, he liquidated his holdings and headed a band of Puritan emigrants to Massachusetts, where he rose to the governorship of the colony.

This combination of factors explains the tremendous discrepancy in the volume of emigration from France and from England. The significance of the discrepancy can scarcely be overestimated. At the time of the American Revolution the population of the English colonies amounted to no less than two million, or a third of the total population of the English-speaking world. This mass transplantation explains in large part the victory of Britain over France in 1763, and of the American Republic over Britain two decades later.

The remarkable development of Britain's industry also contributed to her success in overseas competition. Her industrial growth during the century between 1550 and 1650 was to be surpassed only by that during the Industrial Revolution after 1760. In fact, it was during the earlier period that there was laid the foundation for the later development of heavy industry. This initial spurt of English industry occurred partly because of the Thirty Years' War on the Continent (1618–1648), which created a demand for war materials. In responding to the demand, the British expanded their mining, metallurgical, and chemical industries tremendously, aided by many new techniques introduced by the refugees and immigrants from France, Germany, and Flanders.

The manufacture of woolen cloth, which had begun in the Middle Ages, remained the principal English industry and the most valuable source of exports throughout the seventeenth century. Of the new industries, coal mining grew most spectacularly. Coal was now used widely as a fuel and in industries—such as sugar refining—that required intense heat. The output of coal increased from some 200,000 tons in 1550 to 3 million tons in 1700. This expansion involved improvement of mining equipment and of draining machines, which stimulated the later development of the steam engine. Water power also was harnessed more extensively than before, and water-driven hammers were used in forges. Other industries that expanded markedly at this time were those producing cannon, gunpowder, saltpeter, glass, paper, alum, and salt.

French industry was about equal to the English in volume of output. But it should be kept in mind that the population of France was more than three times that of England. And the French tended to manufacture luxuries, in contrast to the cloth and hardware produced in England. Furthermore, technological advance in France was hampered by the guild system, which was very highly organized and powerful in that country. In general, it may be said that commercial and industrial interests did not receive so much encouragement in France as in England because they lacked the political power of their counterparts across the Channel.

England's flourishing economy helped her overseas enterprises in various ways. It made more capital available for colonial development, and this was an important consideration because both the English and the French colonies required heavy initial expenditures. Unlike the Spanish colonies, they yielded no bullion and they afforded no native labor force that could be exploited. The English and the French promoters of colonization were forced therefore to transplant whole communities with a complete labor force of Europeans. They had to provide these people with transportation, tools, seed, and equipment. All this involved a heavy capital outlay, and as a rule it was more likely to be forthcoming from London than from Paris. There was more money per capita in England, and, rather than being invested in a large standing army and an elaborate court, as was the case in France, it was in an available liquid form. England's industries also provided cheaper and more durable goods, which gave English colonists and traders an advantage over their French rivals. In North America, for example, the English fur traders were able to offer the Indians cheaper and better blankets and kettles and firearms in return for their pelts.

English industry, besides, was well equipped for naval construction. This fact, together with the greater awareness in English ruling circles of the importance of sea power, explains in large part the superiority of the British navy during the long series of Anglo-French wars. Certainly there is no parallel in English history to Louis XV's announcement that "There will never be any other navies in France than those of Venet, the artist." [10] England's naval preponderance was a decisive factor, for a British squadron cruising off Brest could, and repeatedly did, cut off the French colonies from their motherland and leave them helpless.

The colonial and commercial rivalry between Britain and France did not

135

lead to blows until the late seventeenth century. Before that time the English had been much more at odds with the Dutch, their points of conflict ranging the globe—fisheries in the North Atlantic, commercial posts in the East, settlements in America, and slave trading in Africa and the West Indies. These issues precipitated a series of three Anglo-Dutch Wars between 1652 and 1674. Then the situation changed as the British realized that the French were replacing the Dutch as their most formidable rivals. Holland had limited resources and had passed its prime; France was a much richer and more populous country, and was stepping up its overseas activities drastically. The Glorious Revolution in Great Britain (1688) also contributed to the estrangement of Britain and France: it ousted the Stuart dynasty, which had looked to Louis XIV for friendly aid in the creation of absolutism and the reinstatement of Catholicism in England. In the place of the Stuarts came William III, Prince of Orange, Stadholder of the Dutch Netherlands, a firm Protestant, and an archenemy of Louis XIV. Thus the accession of William III served to bring together England and Holland against France. In 1689 began a series of four Anglo-French wars that dragged on for almost a century until England's great victory in 1763.

All these wars had two phases, one European and the other overseas. The European revolved about dynastic ambitions, especially those of Louis XIV of France and Frederick the Great of Prussia. The overseas operations were fought over diverse issues—the balance of power in India, conflicting territorial claims in America, terms of trade in the Spanish colonies, and control of the world trade routes. The dichotomy between the European and overseas aspects of these wars was sufficiently marked so that each one was known by one name in Europe and another in America. Hence the wars have come down in history as the War of the League of Augsburg or King William's War (1689–1697), the War of the Spanish Succession or Queen Anne's War (1701–1713), the War of the Austrian Succession or King George's War (1743–1748), and the Seven Years War or the French and Indian War (1756–1763).

The first three wars were not decisive in their overseas aspects. In Europe they did settle important matters: Louis XIV was effectively checkmated, and Frederick the Great successfully seized the province of Silesia and catapulted Prussia into the first rank of European powers. But in America, where most of the overseas engagements were fought, there were only isolated and inconclusive campaigns. The French enjoyed the support of most of the Indian tribes, partly because their missionaries were far more active than the English, and also because the few French settlers did not represent so great a threat to the Indians as the inexorably advancing tide of English settlement that was beginning to spill over the Appalachians. With their Indian allies, the French repeatedly harried and burned the English frontier villages. The English, on the other hand, used their superior manpower and naval strength to attack the French possessions in present-day Nova Scotia and Cape Breton Island that were vulnerable by sea.

The net result of these first three wars was that the British acquired Nova Scotia, Newfoundland, and the Hudson Bay territories. But these conquests left unsettled the basic question of whether the French would retain Canada and the Mississippi Valley, and thereby restrict the English to the Atlantic seaboard. This question was answered conclusively by the fourth war, which also settled the future of India.

This fateful struggle is known as the Seven Years' War because it was waged for seven years—between 1756 and 1763—in Europe. But in America it began two years earlier because of the growing rivalry for the possession of the Ohio Valley. British colonials had already begun to stream westward through the mountains into the valley when in 1749 the British government chartered the Ohio Company, organized by Virginia and London capitalists for the colonization of the valley. But at the same time the French were constructing a line of forts in Western Pennsylvania—Fort Presqu'Isle (Erie), Fort Le Boeuf (Waterford), and Fort Venango (Franklin). The Ohio Company countered the French by building a fort in 1754 at the strategic junction of the Monongahela and Allegheny rivers. The French promptly captured it, enlarged it, and christened it Fort Duquesne in honor of the governor of Canada. A young Virginian, George Washington by name, hurried to the scene to reinforce the English garrison but arrived too late. He was defeated by the French and their Indian allies on July 4, 1754, and forced to retreat back over the mountains.

In the following year the British General Braddock arrived in America with a regular army to retake Fort Duquesne. But he refused to take the advice of his colonial officers on how to wage frontier warfare, and his forces were badly defeated and he himself killed. The British reverses continued through 1756. The French commander was the Marquis de Montcalm, a European-trained general who, however, readily adapted himself to frontier conditions and brilliantly led his French and Indian forces. The turning point of the war came in 1757, largely by reason of the entrance of William Pitt (the Elder) into the British cabinet. Pitt, who later became Earl of Chatham, was a man of wide vision and infectious confidence. "I know that I can save the country," he said, "and I know that no one else can." He concentrated his resources on the navy and the colonies, while subsidizing his ally, Frederick of Prussia, to fight on in Europe. His strategy was, as he put it, to win an empire on the plains of Germany.

His strategy succeeded brilliantly. His reinforced navies swept the French off the seas, while the American colonists, stirred by his leadership, joined the British regulars to form a force of about 50,000 men. This was a huge host by the standards of American warfare, and it overwhelmed one French fort after another. The climax came with the siege of Quebec, the heart of French Canada and a great natural stronghold defended by the redoubtable Montcalm. The sheer cliffs rising from the banks of the St. Lawrence River seemed invulnerable to assault. Sickness weakened the besieging forces and defeat appeared unavoidable. The British commander, thirty-three-year-old General James Wolfe, decided in despair to risk a hazardous operation. Thirty-six hundred of his men were ferried in the dead of night to a point above the city where they disembarked and scrambled through the bushes and over rocks up a precipitous path to a high plateau, the famous Plains of Abraham overlooking the town of Quebec. That morning, September 13, 1759, the decisive battle was fought. Both Wolfe and Montcalm were killed, but the British veterans prevailed.* Quebec surrendered a few days later. The next

* See "England's Triumph in North America," EMM, No. 37.

year Montreal also fell to the advancing British. This was the end of the French colonial empire in America, for Britain's command of the sea precluded any relief from Paris.

In India the success of the English was no less complete. The situation was quite different from what it was in America, in that neither the British nor the French government had territorial ambitions in India. This was true also of the directors of the English and French East India Companies, who insisted that their agents in India attend strictly to business. They were interested only in profits, and they resented every penny or sou spent on noncommercial objectives. But it took a year or more to communicate with the agents in India, and the latter frequently took advantage of this fact to act independently and involve their companies in Indian affairs. They did so because the disintegration of the Mogul Empire that was taking place at this time offered dazzling opportunities for personal financial aggrandizement and for empire building.

The first European to intervene on a large scale in Indian affairs was the French governor Joseph Dupleix. Even he does not seem to have been interested, at the outset at least, in territorial expansion for its own sake. Rather he wished to acquire territory so that, from taxes and other political revenues, he could obtain more capital for commercial operations. Dupleix had limited French forces under his command, but he extended his influence by drilling native Indians along European military lines. These trained Indian troops, or sepoys, enabled him to back claimants to various Indian thrones and to build up a clientele of native rulers under obligation to himself. This procedure was very effective, because a few European troops or sepoys could overcome much larger numbers of purely Indian forces in pitched battle. But Dupleix was recalled to France in 1754 because the company was apprehensive that his aggressive tactics would lead to war with Britain.

War did come to India in 1756 with the outbreak of full-scale hostilities between Britain and France. At the outset the French, thanks to Dupleix' activities, were in the stronger position. They held more territory, they had more than double the fighting force, and they wielded wider political influence among the native princes. But in the end the British won a crushing victory. Again naval superiority was the deciding factor. Britain was able to transport troops, money, and supplies from Europe while preventing France from doing likewise. The British, too, had the inspired leadership of Robert Clive, a company official who had come out years before as a clerk. Clive possessed both outstanding military talents and an ability to comprehend Indian politics. In 1756, on hearing of the war in Europe, he marched on Bengal. With the support of Indian merchants who had waxed wealthy by virtue of the trade with Europe, Clive defeated the pro-French Moslem ruler at the Battle of Plassey in 1757, put his own puppet on the throne, and extorted huge reparations both for himself and for his company. During the rest of the war the British navy enabled Clive to shift his forces at will from one part of India to another, and at the same time severed the communications of the French posts with each other and with France. The end came with the surrender in 1761 of the main French base at Pondichéry.

The overseas phase of the Seven Years' War was decided by the fall of Quebec in America and of Pondichéry in India. But the war dragged on in

Europe until 1763, when the belligerents concluded the Peace of Paris. Of her American possessions, France retained only Guiana in South America, the insignificant islands of St. Pierre and Miquelon on the Newfoundland coast, and a few islands in the West Indies, including Guadeloupe and Martinique. Britain therefore received from France the whole of the St. Lawrence valley and all the territory east of the Mississippi. These were almost empty territories, and were not considered as valuable as the sugar islands, Guadeloupe and Martinique, which were returned to France. In fact, they were returned on the insistence of the British planters in the West Indies, who feared the competition of the French sugar islands if they were included within the British imperial commercial structure.

Spain had entered the war late on the side of France and was, therefore, compelled to cede Florida to Britain. As compensation, France gave her western Louisiana, that is, the territory west of the Mississippi River. In India the French retained possession of their commercial installations—offices, warehouses, and docks—at Pondichéry and other towns. But they were forbidden to erect fortifications or pursue political ambitions among the Indian princes. In other words, the French returned to India as traders and not as empire builders.

When the Treaty of Paris was signed, the British political leader Horace Walpole remarked, "Burn your Greek and Roman books, histories of little people." This far-seeing observation points up the long-range, worldwide implications of the peace settlement. So far as Europe was concerned, the treaty allowed Prussia to keep Silesia and to become Austria's rival for the leadership of the Germanies. But of much more significance for world history were the overseas repercussions of the Paris Treaty. By its terms France suffered even more humiliating and overwhelming defeat than the Netherlands had suffered in the seventeenth century and Spain in the sixteenth. Spain and the Netherlands had been humbled, but each retained substantial colonial possessions— Spain in America and the Philippines, the Netherlands in the East Indies. France, however, was not only humbled but also shorn of almost all her overseas possessions.

It is true that in the nineteenth century France built up a new colonial empire which grew to be second only to that of Britain. But the important fact for world history is that France in the eighteenth century lost North America and India. This meant that America north of the Rio Grande was to develop in the future as a part of the English-speaking world. Bismarck later observed that the fact that the United States and Britain spoke the same language was the most important single element in modern diplomacy. The course of events during the two World Wars has lent support to this view.

France's expulsion from India was also a historical event of global significance, for it meant that the British were to take the place of the Moguls there. Once installed in Delhi, the British were well on their way to world empire and world primacy. It was the incomparable base offered by the vast and populous subcontinent that enabled the British in the nineteenth century to expand into the rest of South Asia and then beyond to East Asia.

A British historian, J. R. Green, has well summarized the global implications of these developments engendered by the 1763 settlement.

The Seven Years' War is a turning point in our national history, as it is a turning point in the history of the world. Till now the relative weight of the European states has been drawn from their possessions within Europe itself. But from the close of the war, it mattered little whether England counted for less or more than the nations around her. She was no longer a mere European power, no longer a mere rival of Germany or Russia or France. Mistress of Northern America, the future mistress of India, claiming as her own the empire of the seas, Britain suddenly towered high above the nations whose position in a single continent doomed them to comparative insignificance in' the after history of the world.[11]

SUGGESTED READING

For works on general European overseas expansion, see the bibliography for Chapter 6. The economic background of northwest European primacy is given in E. Hamilton, *American Treasure and the Price Revolution in Spain, 1501–1650* (Cambridge: Harvard Univ., 1934) and in J. U. Nef, *Industry and Government in France and England, 1540–1640* (Philadelphia: Am. Philosoph. Soc., 1940).

For Holland's overseas activities, see C. M. Parr, *Jan van Linschoten: The Dutch Marco Polo* (New York: Crowell, 1964); D. W. Davies, *A Primer of Dutch Seventeenth Century Overseas Trade* (The Hague: Nijhoff, 1961); A. Hyma, *The Dutch in the Far East: A History of the Dutch Commercial and Colonial Empire* (Ann Arbor: Univ. of Michigan, 1942); B. H. M. Vlekke, *Nusantara: A History of the East Indian Archipelago* (Cambridge: Harvard Univ., 1943); G. Musselman, *The Cradle of Colonialism* (New Haven: Yale Univ., 1963); and W. R. Shepherd, *The Story of New Amsterdam* (New York: Knopf, 1926).

A general survey of French overseas activity is available in H. I. Priestly, *France Overseas Through the Old Regime: A Study of European Expansion* (New York: Appleton, 1939). More specialized studies are the two works by N. M. Crouse, *French Pioneers in the West Indies, 1624–1664* (New York: Columbia Univ., 1940) and *The French Struggle for the West Indies, 1665–1713* (New York: Columbia Univ., 1943); and C. W. Cole, *Colbert and a Century of French Mercantilism* (New York: Columbia Univ., 1943); G. M. Wrong, *The Rise and Fall of New France* (New York: Macmillan, 1928), 2 vols.; P. C. Phillips, *The Fur Trade* (Norman: Univ. of Oklahoma, 1962), 2 vols.; and S. P. Sen, *The French in India* (Calcutta: Mukhopadhyay, 1958).

Two excellent general surveys of Britain overseas are C. E. Carrington's *The British Overseas: Exploits of a Nation of Shopkeepers* (New York: Cambridge Univ., 1950) and W. B. Willcox's *Star of Empire: A Study of Britain as a World Power, 1485–1945* (New York: Knopf, 1950). For the background of English colonization, see W. Notestein, *The English People on the Eve of Colonization, 1603–1630* (New York: Harper, 1954). The emergence of England as a naval power is described by T. Woodrooffe, *Vantage at Sea: England's Emergence as an Oceanic Power* (New York: St. Martins, 1958); D. W. Waters, *The Art of Navigation in England in Elizabethan and Early Stuart Times* (London: Hollis, 1958); and by G. Mattingly, *The Armada* (Boston: Houghton, 1959). Special aspects of English expansion are treated by V. Stefansson, *Northwest to Fortune: The Search of Western Man for a Commercially Practical Route to the Far East* (Des Moines: Meredith, 1958); L. A. Harper, *The English Navigation Laws: A Seventeenth Century Experiment in Social Engineering* (New York: Columbia Univ., 1939); K. G. Davies, *The Royal African Company, 1672–1752* (New York: McKay, 1957); H. V. Wiseman, *A Short History of the British West Indies* (London: Univ. London, 1950); L. W. Labaree, *Royal Government in America* (New Haven: Yale Univ., 1930); J. S. Galbraith, *The Hudson's Bay Company as an Imperial Factor* (Berkeley: Univ. California, 1957); and M. Kraus, *The Atlantic Civilization: Eighteenth Century Origins* (Ithaca: Cornell Univ., 1949).

The colonial wars are described by E. P. Hamilton, *The French and Indian Wars: The Story of Battles and Forts in the Wilderness* (New York: Doubleday, 1962) and are summarized in A. H. Buffington, *The Second Hundred Years' War, 1689–1815* (New York: Holt, 1929). Special aspects of the wars are treated in C. Wilson, *Profit and Power: A Study of England and the Dutch Wars* (London: Longmans, 1957); S. A. Khan, *The East India Trade in the 17th Century in its Political and Economic Aspects* (London: Oxford Univ., 1923), which deals with the Anglo-Dutch struggle in the East Indies; M. L. Lewis, *Montcalm: The Marvelous Marquis* (New York: Random, 1962; a Vintage book); and finally the classic history of the most dramatic phase of the Seven Years' War in America, by F. Parkman, *Montcalm and Wolfe* (Boston, 1884), 2 vols.

Chapter

8

*Throughout Russian history one dominating
theme has been the frontier; the theme of
the struggle for the mastering of the natural
resources of an untamed country, expanded
into a continent by the ever-shifting movement
of the Russian people and their conquest of and
intermingling with other peoples.*

B. H. SUMNER,
A Short History of Russia

Russian Expansion in Asia

At the same time that the Western Europeans were expanding overseas to all corners of the globe, the Russians were expanding overland across the entire length of Eurasia. The mastering of the continental expanses of Siberia is an epic story comparable to the westward expansion of the United States to the Pacific. In fact, the ever advancing frontier has left as indelible a stamp on the Russian character and Russian institutions as it has on the American.

It should not be assumed that the Russians are alone among the European peoples in having been affected by a frontier. During the medieval period, large parts of Central and Eastern Europe were lightly populated (see Chapter 2, section III). For centuries, various European peoples, and particularly the Germans, pressed a line of settlement eastward along the Baltic coast and down the Danube valley. But this internal colonization ceased to be a dominating theme with the end of the Middle Ages. Overseas colonization took its place, and the peoples of Western Europe concentrated their energies on opening and exploring new frontiers in new worlds. The Russian people, by contrast, continued to expand overland into the vast Eurasian plain stretching out from their doorstep. This was a stupendous undertaking which proceeded apace for several centuries until the last of the Moslem khanates in Central Asia had been subdued in 1895. It is not surprising, then, that the frontier has been a major factor throughout the course of Russian history, as it has been throughout American. In this chapter we shall examine the nature and the course of Russian expansion into Siberia and the Ukraine.

I. Geography of Russian Expansion

In order to understand the remarkable Russian expansion across the plains of Eurasia it is necessary to understand the geography of those plains. A glance at the map shows first and foremost their staggering proportions. Indeed, Russia is associated with size—with limitless space. "Russia," relates a peasant proverb, "is not a country; it is a world." This world encompasses a sixth of the land surface of the globe. It is larger than the United States and Canada and Central America combined. When night falls on Leningrad on the Baltic, day is breaking in Vladivostok on the Pacific. The distance between the two cities is five thousand miles, compared to the three thousand miles between New York and San Francisco. This contrast should be kept in mind in considering Russia's eastward, and America's westward, expansion.

Another prominent characteristic of the Russian landmass is its remarkable topographical uniformity. It is in very large part a flat plains area. The Ural Mountains do run across the plains in a north-south direction, and they are commonly thought of as dividing the country into two separate and distinct parts—European Russia and Asiatic Russia. But the fact is that the Urals are a single, narrow, worn-down chain of mountains with an average altitude of only two thousand feet. Furthermore, they do not extend further south than the 51st parallel, leaving a wide gap of flat desert country stretching down to the Caspian Sea. Under these circumstances the whole plain must be looked upon as a single geographic entity—the subcontinent of Eurasia. This topographic uniformity helps to explain why the Russians were able to spread so rapidly through the area and why it has remained to the present day under Moscow's control. If any dividing line is to be drawn across the Eurasian plains, it should be drawn not north and south along the Urals, but east and west, to demarcate Central Asia in the southeast with its desert and semidesert conditions, from Siberia in the north with its forests and frozen tundra.

The Eurasian plains that comprise most of present-day Russia are surrounded by a natural boundary stretching from the Black Sea to the Pacific Ocean. This boundary consists of an uninterrupted chain of mountains, deserts, and inland seas—from the Caucasus Mountains in the west to the Caspian Sea, the Ust Urt Desert, the Aral Sea, the Kizil-Kum Desert, the Hindu Kush, Pamir, and Tian Shan ranges, the Gobi Desert, and the Great Khingan Mountains east to the Pacific Ocean. The ring of mountains surrounding the Eurasian plains keeps out the moisture-laden winds from the Pacific and the warm monsoons from the Indian Ocean, and explains both the desert climate of Central Asia and the cold, dry climate of Siberia. The whole expanse of Siberia, from the Baltic to the Pacific, has essentially the same continental type of climate, with short, hot summers and long, cold winters. The uniformity of climate, like that of topography, facilitated Russia's eastward expansion, for the frontiersman felt equally at home throughout the five-thousand-mile expanse of plains. The Central Asian deserts, on the other hand, he found to be strange and forbidding. He also found that they were held by militarily powerful Moslem khanates in contrast to the weak tribes in Siberia. The result was that the Russians did not master the Central Asian deserts until 250 years after they had reached the Pacific further north.

Russian expansion was affected by river systems as well as by topography and climate. Because of the flat terrain, Russian rivers are generally long, wide, and unencumbered by rapids. Consequently they have proven invaluable as routes and as vehicles for commerce, colonization, and conquest. Furthermore, they are usable in the winter with sleds as well as in the summer with boats. West of the Urals the outstanding rivers are the Western Dvina flowing into the Baltic, the Dniester, the Dnieper, and the Don flowing south to the Black Sea, and the Volga flowing first east and then south to the Caspian. East of the Urals the Siberian plains are watered by four vast river systems, the Ob in the west, the Yenisei in the center, the Lena in the northeast, and the Amur in the southeast. Since the whole of Siberia tilts downward from the massive Tibetan ranges, the first three of these rivers flow northward into the Arctic, while the fourth makes its way eastward to the Pacific. The Arctic outlet of the Ob, the Yenisei, and the Lena has negated in large part their economic usefulness. But the fact remains that these rivers, together with their numerous tributaries, provided a natural network of highways extending all the way to the Pacific. Once the Russians crossed the Urals they were able to make their way, with few portages, from one waterway to another. Thus they advanced in zigzag fashion, ever eastward, in pursuit of the furred animals.

A final geographic factor in the pace and course of Russian expansion is the combination of soil and vegetation prevailing in various parts of the country. Four major soil-vegetation zones run in east-west layers across Russia. In the far north, along the Arctic coast, is the barren tundra, frozen the year round except for a six-to-eight week growing period in the summer. At that time the sun never sets, and it gives a short but riotous life to myriad wild flowers—violets, marguerites, forget-me-nots, yellow daffodils, and blue blossoms.

To the south of the tundra is the taiga, or forest, belt. The largest of the four zones, being 600 to 1,300 miles wide and 4,600 miles long, it includes a fifth of the total forest area of the world. In its northern reaches the forest is predominantly conifer and birch, while further south it is a mixture of elms, aspens, poplars, and maples. In these forests the Russians felt most at home, and they were able to advance across the whole of Eurasia without losing at any time the familiar protective covering. Many Russian writers have described the beauty of their forests and what they have meant to their people. Typical is the following passage from one of Maksim Gorki's novels, *In the World:*

> The woods came to meet us like a dark army, the fir trees spread out their wings like large birds, the birches looked like maidens. The acrid smell of the marshes flowed over the fields. My dog ran beside me with his pink tongue hanging out, often halting and sniffing the air, and shaking his fox-like head as if in perplexity. Grandfather, in Grandmother's

short coat and an old peakless cap, walked, blinking and smiling at something or other, as cautiously as if he were bent on stealing. Grandmother, wearing a blue blouse, a black skirt, and a white handkerchief about her head, waddled comfortably—it was difficult to hurry when walking behind her.

The nearer we got to the forest the more animated Grandfather became. Walking with his nose in the air and muttering, he began to speak, at first disjointedly and inarticulately and afterwards happily and beautifully, almost as if he had been drinking.

"The forests are the Lord's gardens. No one planted them save the wind of God and the holy breath of His mouth. When I was working on the boats in my youth I went to Jegoulya. Oh, Lexei, you will never have the experiences I have had! There are forests along the Oka from Kasimov to Mouron, and there are forests on the Volga too, stretching as far as the Urals. Yes! it is all so boundless and wonderful." [1]

On their southern edges the forests thin out, and the trees grow smaller until they give way completely to the open, treeless steppe. Here is to be found the fertile black earth formed by millennia of decayed grass. Today it is the breadbasket of Russia, but for centuries it was a source of misery and woe. The steppe was the home of the marauding horse nomads of Central Eurasia. When these nomads were sufficiently strong, they struck out along the line of least resistance—sometimes westward into Central Europe or eastward into China. More frequently they attacked the vulnerable Russians in Eastern Europe. A major theme of Russian history is this continued conflict between the Slavic peasant of the forest zone and the Asiatic nomad of the steppe. At first the nomad prevailed, and the result was two centuries of Mongol rule over Russia. But in the end the Slavic woodsman became stronger, and this enabled him not only to win his independence but also to expand over the Eurasian plains.

The fourth zone, the desert, is the smallest in area, starting in China but extending westward only to the Caspian Sea. We have seen that for various reasons—inaccessibility, severe climate, and the military prowess of the native peoples—the desert zone was not engulfed by the Russian tidal wave until the late nineteenth century.

II. EARLY RUSSIAN EXPANSION

The Russians began their advance eastward about 1500 years ago from their place of origin in the upper reaches of the Dniester, Dnieper, Nemen, and Dvina rivers. From there they fanned out in a great arc, the broad plains beckoning them on to the Arctic shores in the north, to the Black Sea in the south, and to the Urals and beyond in the east. Those who migrated to the east or northeast remained within the shelter of the forests. Within this forest zone they encountered little opposition—only scattered and loosely organized Finnish tribes with which they intermarried or easily pushed aside.

These early Russian colonists combined agricultural and forest pursuits. The proportion depended upon the location. In the northern or conifer woods, agriculture was subsidiary because the climate was severe, the soil infertile, and the open spaces infrequent. Consequently, the colonists in this belt spent most of their time trapping, fishing, and collecting wax, honey, pitch, potash, and other forest by-products. Further south, in the mixed forest belt, agriculture was the primary activity. The forest still was depended upon heavily for its various resources, but more time was spent here on cultivation. Rye was the staple crop, but barley, oats, wheat, flax, and hemp were also grown. The prevailing method of cultivation was temporary cropping on the ash of burnt-over forest or scrub, or in the occasional open spaces of wild grassland. The clearings, after a few years of continuous cropping, were either abandoned to revert to waste or kept as rough pasture until their productivity might be restored. This practice, reminiscent of the American frontier, was crude and wasteful, but it mattered little since the forest stretched on without end.

Under these circumstances, scattered homesteads and small hamlets were the general rule—not compact villages or towns. The few towns that did appear grew up as trade centers along main river routes. This was the case with Kiev on the Dnieper River carrying the north-south traffic, and with Novgorod on Lake Ilmen commanding the east-west commerce. It was this long-distance trade that provided the basis for the first Russian state, which developed in the ninth century after Christ. The center was Kiev, but the state remained a loose federation of principalities strung out along the river routes. Kiev itself was extremely vulnerable to invasion because it was located at the point where the forest zone gave way to the steppe. Consequently, it was forced to wage a continual struggle for existence against the nomad horsemen. At times certain strong Kievan rulers were able to assert their authority south to the Black Sea and west to the Danube. But this show of strength was ephemeral; Russian colonists were unable to settle more than 150 miles south and east of Kiev, for the threat of invasion by the nomads hung over their heads like the sword of Damocles.

The sword descended in 1237 when the Mongols swept over the Russian lands as they did over most of Eurasia. Before the invasion, Kiev had been described by contemporary travelers as a magnificent metropolis with sumptuous palaces, eight markets, and four hundred churches, including the great Cathedral of Saint Sophia. But eight years after the invasion, when the Franciscan Joannes de Plano Carpini passed through Kiev on his way to the Mongol capital, he found only 200 houses still standing in the former capital, and the surrounding fields strewn with bones.

The Mongols continued their devastating inroads into Central Europe, to the gates of Italy and France. Then they withdrew voluntarily, retaining only the Russian lands in Europe. Their sprawling empire did not survive long as an entity. It broke up into regional fragments, of which the so-called Golden Horde included the Russian territories. The capital of the Golden Horde, and of Russia also for the next two centuries, was Sarai, near present-day Stalingrad. In this manner the age-old struggle between the forest and the steppe was settled decisively with the victory of the steppe and its nomad peoples.

The Russians now surrendered their small enclaves on the steppe and withdrew into their forest fastnesses. There they were left to their own devices so long as they recognized the suzerainty of the khan and paid him annual tribute. Gradually the Russians recovered their strength and developed a new national center—the principality of Moscow, located deep in the forest zone away from the dangerous steppe. Moscow had advantages other than its relative inaccessibility to the nomads. It was located at the crossroads of two important highways leading from the Dnieper to the northeastern regions. A number of rivers flowing in various directions came closest to each other in the Moscow region, enabling Moscow to profit by an inland water system. And the principality enjoyed the advantage of a line of rulers who were peaceful, frugal, and calculating. These rulers added to their possessions patiently and ruthlessly, until Moscow became the new national nucleus. Whereas at the opening of the fourteenth century the principality comprised some 500 square miles, by the mid-fifteenth century it had grown to 15,000 square miles. And a century later, during the reign of Ivan the Terrible (1533–1584), all the Russian principalities were brought together under Moscow's sway.

This "gathering of the Russian lands" reversed the balance of power between the Russians and the Mongols, or Tatars as they were now more commonly known. Originally the Tatars had triumphed because they had been united, in contrast to the strife-ridden Kievan state, and also because they had been militarily more advanced with their fast-moving cavalry armies. But by the sixteenth century it was the Russians who were united under Moscow, while the Golden Horde had split into the three rival khanates of Kazan, Astrakhan, and the Crimea, besides the khanate of the Siberian Tatars to the east of the Urals. Furthermore, the Russians were pulling ahead also in military techniques, because they were able to profit from the great advances being made in Western Europe, especially in firearms and artillery. When Ivan attacked the Kazan Tatars in 1552, his superiority in artillery, plus the services of a Danish technician who supervised the mining of the walls of the Kazan fortress, proved decisive. Following the explosion of the mines, the Russians successfully stormed the fortress and then overran the whole Kazan khanate. They swept down the Volga valley and in 1556 captured Astrakhan with little difficulty. To consolidate their gains, the Russians built a series of fortified posts along the banks of the Volga to its mouth at Astrakhan. Thus the Russians became the masters of the great Volga basin and reached the Caspian Sea in the south and the Urals in the east.

The way now was open for limitless Russian expansion beyond the Volga and the Urals. Some of the new territories were won by military force, as was the case in Siberia. This type of expansion we shall consider in the following two sections. Other territories were gained by individual transactions with native chiefs after the fashion of the purchasing of Manhattan Island and of broad tracts in the Ohio and other valleys from the American Indians. This form of aggrandizement is vividly described by the distinguished Russian author Sergei Aksakov, in his two books of memoirs, *A Russian Gentleman.*

> . . . you had only to invite a dozen of the native Bashkir chiefs in certain districts to partake of your hospitality: you provided two or three fat sheep, for them to kill and dress in their own fashion; you produced a bucket of whisky, with several buckets of strong fermented Bashkir mead and a barrel of homemade country beer—which proves, by the way, that even in old days the Bashkirs were not strict Mohammedans— and the rest was as simple as A B C. It was said, indeed, that an enter-

tainment of this kind might last a week or even a fortnight: it was impossible for Bashkirs to do business in a hurry, and every day it was necessary to ask the question, "Well, good friend, is it time now to discuss my business?" The guests had been eating and drinking, without exaggeration, all day and all night; but, if they were not completely satisfied with the entertainment, if they had not had enough of their monotonous singing and playing on the pipe, and their singular dances in which they stood up or crouched down on the same spot of ground, then the greatest of the chiefs, clicking his tongue and wagging his head, would answer with much dignity and without looking his questioner in the face: "The time has not come; bring us another sheep!" The sheep was forthcoming, as a matter of course, with fresh supplies of beer and spirits; and the tipsy Bashkirs began again to sing and dance, dropping off to sleep wherever they felt inclined. But everything in the world has an end; and a day came at last when the chief would look his host straight in the face and say: "We are obliged to you, *batyushka,* ever so much obliged! And now, what is it that you want?" The rest of the transaction followed a regular fashion. The customer began with the shrewdness native to your true Russian: he assured the Bashkir that he did not want anything at all; but, having heard that the Bashkirs were exceedingly kind people, he had come to Ufa on purpose to form a friendship with them, and so on. Then the conversation would somehow come round to the vast extent of the Bashkir territory and the unsatisfactory ways of the present tenants, who might pay their rent for a year or two and then pay no more and yet continue to live on the land, as if they were its rightful owners; it was rash to evict them, and a lawsuit became unavoidable. These remarks, which were true enough to the facts, were followed up by an obliging offer to relieve the kind Bashkirs of some part of the land which was such a burden to them; and in the end whole districts were bought and sold for a mere song. The bargain was clinched by a legal document, but the amount of land was never stated in it, and could not be, as it had never been surveyed. As a rule, the boundaries were settled by landmarks of this kind: "from the mouth of such and such a stream as far as the dead beech-tree on the wolf-track, and from the dead beech-tree in a bee-line to the watershed, and from the watershed to the fox-earths, and from the fox-earths to the hollow tree at Soltamratka," and so on. So precise and permanent were boundaries enclosing ten or twenty or thirty thousand desyatinas of land! And the price of all this might be about one hundred roubles and presents worth another hundred, not including the cost of the entertainments.[2]

III. Crossing of the Urals

The Russian victories had eliminated the Kazan and Astrakhan khanates. But the Tatars in the Crimea and across the Urals remained independent and continued to harass the Russian colonists with continual raids. For various reasons, discussed later in this chapter, the Russians had to suffer the depredations of the Crimean Tatars until the late eighteenth century. But they were able to destroy the Siberian khanate with little difficulty, and in doing so they unwittingly began their epic march to the Pacific.

The crossing of the Urals and the conquest of Siberia were largely the work of the rough-and-ready frontiersmen known as the Cossacks. These men resembled in many respects the frontiersmen of the American West. Most of them were former peasants who had fled from Russia or Poland to escape the bonds of serfdom. Their refuge was the wild steppe country to the south, where they became hunters, fishers, and pastoralists. Just as their counterparts in America became half-Indian, so they became half-Tatar. They were a liberty-loving and equalitarian, but unruly and marauding, element, ever ready to turn bandit-freebooters if it seemed profitable to do so. The famous Russian novelist Nikolai Gogol has left the following picture of the Cossack way of life:

149

> There was no trade which the Cossack did not know: he could distil brandy, make a *telega* (peasant's wagon), make powder, do blacksmith's and locksmith's work, in addition to committing wild excesses, drinking and carousing as only a Russian can,—all this he was equal to. Besides the registered Cossacks, who considered themselves bound to appear in time of war, it was possible to collect at any time, in case of dire need, a whole army of volunteers. All that was required was for the osaul [captain] to traverse all the market-places and squares of the villages and

The type of Russian horseman who conquered Russia's eastern lands.

Yermak's conquest of Siberia.

hamlets, and shout at the top of his voice, standing in his telega, "Hey, ye distillers and beer-brewers! ye have brewed enough beer, and lolled on your ovens, and fed your fat bodies with flour, long enough! Rise, win glory and knightly honor! Ye ploughmen, reapers of buckwheat, tenders of sheep, danglers after women, enough of following the plough, and dirtying your yellow shoes in the earth, and courting women, and wasting your knightly strength! The hour has come to win glory for the Cossacks!" and these words were like sparks falling on dry wood. The husbandman broke his plough; the brewers and distillers threw away their casks, and destroyed their barrels; the mechanic and merchant sent their trade and their shop to the devil, broke the pots and every thing else in their houses, and mounted their horses.[3]

A typical product of this frontier environment was Yermak Timofeevich, the blue-eyed, red-bearded son of a Don Cossack and a Danish slave woman. At the age of twenty-one he was condemned to death for stealing horses, so he fled to the Volga where he became the leader of a band of river pirates. He preyed indiscriminately on Russian shipping and Persian caravans until government troops began to close in. Then he fled with his band up the Volga valley to the Kama tributary, where a wealthy merchant, Grigori Stroganov, had been given vast land concessions. Stroganov's efforts to colonize his domain were being frustrated by nomad raids from across the Urals. The organizer of these raids was the militant Moslem leader of the Siberian Tatars, the blind Khan Kuchum. Faced with this predicament, Stroganov welcomed Yermak and his men, and hired them to guard the settlements.

Yermak the robber now demonstrated that he had in him the stuff of a great empire builder. He did for Russia in Siberia what Pizarro and Cortez had done for Spain in America. With the audacity of the conquistador, Yermak decided that the best defense was the offense. On September 1, 1581, he set out at the head of 840 men to attack Khan Kuchum on his own territory. Yermak, like his Spanish counterparts, had the great advantage of superior weapons. He was well equipped with firearms and cannon, which inspired terror in the natives. Kuchum received intelligence that the invader commanded thunder and lightning that pierced the strongest coats of mail. Nevertheless he fought desperately to save his capital, Sibir. He gathered a force about thirty times that of Yermak's, and appointed his son, Mahmetkul, to head the defense. Fighting doggedly behind felled trees, the Tatars rained arrows upon the advancing Russians and appeared to be gaining the upper hand. But at a critical juncture Mahmetkul was wounded and the Tatar army left leaderless. Blind Kuchum fled south in despair, and Yermak occupied his capital. The Russians now gave the name of the city to the entire trans-Ural area, which became known as Sibir, or, in its Anglicized form, Siberia.

Yermak informed Stroganov of the outcome of the expedition and also wrote directly to Tsar Ivan the Terrible requesting pardon for his past misdeeds. The Tsar was so pleased with Yermak's achievement that he revoked all sentences against him and his men, and also, as a sign of special favor, sent him gifts consisting of a costly fur from his own shoulders, two richly adorned suits of armor, a goblet, and a considerable sum of money. Yermak now showed the vision of an empire builder in seeking to establish commercial relations with Central Asia. The missions that he sent out reached as far as the ancient city of Bukhara. But Yermak was not destined to live to carry out his ambitious plans. Old Kuchum in the south was stirring up the fierce nomads against the Russians. One of his raiding parties fell upon Yermak and his companions on the night of August 5, 1584, while they slept on the banks of the Irtysh. Yermak fought desperately for his life and tried to escape by swimming across the river. Legend has it that he drowned under the weight of the armor given him by the Tsar.

Despite their victory, the Tatars were fighting a losing battle. Their enemy was too strong to be pushed back over the Urals. Even Kuchum finally sensed the futility of further resistance and offered his submission. With his surrender, the first phase of the Russian advance into Siberia was concluded. The road to the Pacific lay open.

The impression that Yermak made upon the popular mind with his exploits is reflected in a folk song recounting his adventures. The following passages give Yermak's exhortation to his Cossacks before the expedition, and also tell of his relations with the Tsar.

> "Ha, brothers, my brave Hetmans!
> Make for yourselves boats,
> Make the rowlocks of fir,
> Make the oars of pine!
> By the help of God we will go, brothers;

152

Let us pass the steep mountains,
Let us reach the infidel kingdom,
Let us conquer the Siberian kingdom,
That will please our Tsar, our master.
I will go to the White Tsar,
I shall put on a sable cloak,
I shall make my submission to the White Tsar."
"Oh! thou art our hope, orthodox Tsar;
Do not order me to be executed, but bid me say my say,
Since I am Yermak, the son of Timofey!

I am the robber Hetman of the Don;
'Twas I went over the blue sea,
Over the blue sea, the Caspian;
And I it was who destroyed the ships;
And now, our hope, our orthodox Tsar,
I bring you my traitorous head,
And with it I bring the empire of Siberia."
And the orthodox Tsar spoke;
He spoke—the terrible Ivan Vasilevich:
"Ha! thou art Yermak the son of Timofey,

Siberian tribesmen, traveling by reindeer and skis. In the background is a Russian fort.

Thou art the Hetman of the warriors of the Don.
I pardon you and your band,
I pardon you and your trusty service,
And I give you the glorious gentle Don as an inheritance." [4]

IV. CONQUEST OF SIBERIA

The Russian conquest of Siberia was a remarkable achievement.* Like the Spaniards in America, so the Russians in Siberia won a great empire in a few years with incredibly small forces. Kuchum's khanate in the Irtysh basin proved to be but a thin crust without solid substance below. Once the crust was pierced, no serious opposition was encountered for thousands of miles. The pace of the Russian advance was staggering. Yermak campaigned between 1581 and 1584. At the same time, in 1584, Sir Walter Raleigh landed on Roanoke Island in North Carolina. Within half a century, by 1637, the Russians reached Okhotsk on the Pacific Ocean, covering a distance half as much again as that between the Atlantic and the Pacific coasts of the United States. During that same period the English colonists had not crossed to the other side of the Allegheny Mountains.

Various factors explain the rapidity of the Russian advance. The climate, the terrain, the vegetation, and the river systems, were, as we have seen, all favorable to the invaders. The native peoples were handicapped by paucity of numbers, inferiority of armaments, and lack of unity and organization. Account should be taken also of the stamina and courage of the Cossacks who, like the *coureurs des bois* of French Canada, endured fantastic hardships and dangers in the wilderness. And the reason they did so may be summed up with one word—"fur." The sable lured them ever eastward, from river to portage and on to new rivers.

As the Cossacks advanced, they secured their communications by building fortified posts or *ostrogs*, which were like the blockhouses of the American frontier. The first ostrog in Siberia was at Tobolsk, near Sibir, at the junction of the Tobol and the Irtysh. Discovering both these rivers to be tributaries of the Ob, the Russians paddled down that river and found themselves within portage distance of the next great waterway, the Yenisei. By 1610 they were in the Yenisei valley in force and had built the Krasnoyarsk ostrog. At this point they encountered the Buriat, a warlike people who offered the first serious resistance since the struggle with Kuchum. The Russians avoided the Buriats by veering to the northeast where they discovered the Lena River. There they built the Yakutsk ostrog in 1632 and conducted a highly profitable trade with the natives, the mild Yakuts. But the Buriats continually attacked their communication lines, so the Russians waged a ferocious war of extermination. Finally the Russians prevailed and pushed on to Lake Baikal where they established the Irkutsk ostrog in 1651.

Meanwhile exploration parties had been going out from Yakutsk in all directions. In 1645 a band of Russians reached the Arctic coast. Two years later another group was on the shores of the Pacific where they built Okhotsk. The following year, 1648, the Cossack explorer, Semion Dezhnev, started out

* See "Russian Conquest and Exploitation of Siberia," *EMM*, No. 38.

from Yakutsk on an extraordinary journey. He sailed down the Lena which he found to be at certain points so broad that he could see neither bank. The delta was filled with debris of a watershed of continental proportions. After passing the delta, Dezhnev sailed eastward along the Arctic coast until he reached the very tip of Asia. Then he sailed down a waterway to be known later as Bering Strait. After losing two boats in a storm he reached the Anadyr River, where he established the ostrog Anadyrsk, no less than 7,000 miles from Moscow! Dezhnev sent a report of his journey to the governor in Yakutsk who filed it away and forgot it. It was not recovered until after the official expedition by Vitus Bering, which was sent out in 1725 to determine whether America and Asia were joined—something that Dezhnev had brilliantly settled 77 years earlier.

Up to this point the Russians had not encountered any power capable of stopping them. But when they pushed down from Irkutsk into the Amur valley they more than met their match, for they came up against the outposts of the mighty Chinese Empire, then at the height of its strength (see Chapter 4, section II).

It was hunger that drove the Russians to the Amur basin. The frozen north yielded furs but no food. And the granaries of European Russia might as well have been on another planet. So the Russians hopefully turned southward to the Amur valley, which, according to native lore, was a fabulous country with fertile soil and golden grain. The Cossack Vasili Poyarkov was entrusted with the task of cutting a trail from the Lena to the Amur. His remarkable expedition stands out in the annals of Siberian exploration together with Dezhnev's journey along the Arctic shores.

Poyarkov started out from Yakutsk on June 15, 1643, with 132 men. He went up the Lena and its tributaries, at one place going through forty-two rapids and losing a boat. After wintering on the way, he sailed down the Amur the following year. When he reached the Sungari, Poyarkov detached twenty-five men to explore this tributary. The whole of this group, with the exception of two men, was ambushed and killed a day later. The main party reached the mouth of the Amur where they spent the winter, suffering terrible privations from the cold and the lack of food. The following spring they sailed boldly out into the open sea in their small craft. Following the coast northward, they reached Okhotsk, and thence returned overland to Yakutsk. Eighty members, nearly two-thirds of the original expedition, had perished during the three-year four-thousand-mile journey. Poyarkov brought back with him 480 sables, and he also wrote a report in which he declared that the conquest of the Amur was feasible.

A series of adventurers followed Poyarkov into the Amur valley. They captured the town of Albazin, built a string of ostrogs, and killed and pillaged in typical Cossack fashion. The Chinese emperor finally was sufficiently exasperated by these outrages on the fringe of his empire to send an expedition northward in 1658. The Chinese recaptured Albazin and cleared the Russians out of the whole Amur basin. But as soon as they withdrew, the Russian adventurers flocked back. Another Chinese force was sent to the Amur, and at the same time the two governments opened negotiations for the settlement of the frontier question. After much wrangling, the Treaty of Nerchinsk was signed on August 27, 1689.

Apart from its extremely important provisions, this treaty is of special interest on two counts: it is the first pact with a European power signed by China, and it was drawn up in Latin, thanks to the presence of Jesuits as interpreters for the Chinese delegation. The frontier was fixed along the Stanovoi mountain range north of the Amur River, so that the Russians were forced to withdraw completely from the valley in dispute. In return, the Russians were given commercial privileges by Article IV, which provided that the subjects of both empires be free to travel freely across the frontier and to buy and sell without hindrance. The trade that grew up in the following years was carried on by caravan, and consisted of gold and furs, which the Russians exchanged for tea. It was from the Chinese that the Russians obtained what was to become their national drink. The Russians soon became greater tea drinkers than even the English.

With the signing of the Nerchinsk Treaty the first stage of the Russian expansion in Asia came to a halt. For the next 170 years the Russians observed the stipulations of the treaty and stayed out of the Amur basin. They did not resume their advance southward until the mid-nineteenth century, when they were much stronger than in the days of Vasili Poyarkov, and the Chinese relatively weaker.

V. Administration and Development of Siberia

Since Siberia was acquired within a short period in one continuous wave of expansion, it was natural that the Russian government should regard it as a unit and administer it as such. The office in charge of Siberian affairs was the *Sibirskii prikaz* or Siberian bureau, located first in Moscow and then in St. Petersburg, after Peter the Great transferred the capital there in 1703. The administrative center was at Tobolsk, and, with one brief interruption, it remained there until 1763. On that date Catherine the Great divided Siberia into two districts with centers in Tobolsk and Irkutsk. This move was necessitated by the fact that western Siberia, adjoining the homeland, was developing faster than the distant eastern regions.

The fur trade dominated Siberia throughout the seventeenth century to an even greater extent than it did French Canada. The government was the chief fur trader; indeed, fur was one of its most important sources of revenue. The government acquired furs by various means: it collected tribute, or tax, from the natives in furs and a 10 per cent tax in the best furs from the Russian trappers and traders; in addition, it reserved the right to buy the best furs obtained by both the natives and the Russians. By 1586, the state treasury was receiving from these various sources 200,000 sables, 10,000 black foxes, and 500,000 squirrels, besides beavers and ermines. Furthermore, the government exercised a lucrative monopoly of the foreign trade in furs. Estimates of the revenue derived from Siberian furs in the mid-seventeenth century vary form 7 to 30 per cent of the total income of the state, the lower figure probably being closer to the truth. A leading student of this subject has concluded that "The government paid the administrative expenses in Siberia out of the fur trade, retained a large surplus, and added an immense region to the state." [5]

The impact of the Russian expansion on the Siberian tribes was as disastrous as the effect of the American expansion on the Red Indians. On the one hand, the Moscow government repeatedly instructed its officials to treat the natives with "clemency and kindness." On the other hand it ordered the same officials to "seek profit for the sovereign with zeal." [6] Since promotion was affected by the number of furs collected, it is understandable that the welfare of the natives did not receive primary consideration. One effect of this fur tribute system was that it checked the missionary activities of the Russian Orthodox Church. Since converts were not required to pay tribute, missionary work was for long discontinued as a luxury that the state treasury could not afford. As a result, Islam spread widely among the Tatar peoples on the southern fringes of the forest zone, and Buddhist Lamaism did likewise among the Mongol Buriat. Thus we see that a basic difference between the Russian expansion in Siberia and the Spanish in the Americas was the great discrepancy in the intensity of Catholic and Orthodox proselytizing zeal. It is inconceivable that the Catholic Church ever would have allowed another creed to be propagated amongst its New World charges.

In the eighteenth century, the traders and trappers began to give way to permanent colonists in the area west of the Yenisei. Some colonists were prisoners shipped off to Siberia in the same manner that prisoners from the Western European countries were shipped to America, Australia, and the French West Indies. Most of these prisoners were hardened criminals, but a considerable proportion were political offenders who comprised the most enlightened and cultivated strata of society. Other colonists were forced to go by official summons. Each region of European Russia was required to provide a certain number of peasants each year for the colonization of Siberia. These people were granted certain exemptions and state assistance to enable them to get started in their new surroundings.

Most of the permanent settlers in Siberia were neither prisoners nor compulsory colonists, but rather peasants who emigrated voluntarily in order to escape creditors, military service, religious persecution, and, above all else, the bonds of serfdom. It is of the utmost importance that serfdom, which developed and spread through European Russia in the sixteenth and seventeenth centuries, did not take root in Siberia at any time. The explanation seems to be that serfdom grew primarily to satisfy the needs of the nobility who were essential for the functioning of the state. But the nobles did not migrate to Siberia, which offered no attractions comparable to those of Moscow and of St. Petersburg. Consequently, Siberia escaped the nobility, and thus also escaped serfdom. Government decrees did stipulate that runaway serfs should be sent back to their owners. But local authorities in Siberia, impressed more by the need for obtaining settlers than for enforcing the law, often provided refuge to the fugitives.

The growth of population in Siberia to 1763 is given in the following figures: [7]

	Natives	Russians and Foreigners	Total
1622	173,000	23,000	196,000
1662	288,000	105,000	393,000
1709	200,000	229,227	429,227
1763	260,000	420,000	680,000

The sable, whose pelt spurred on traders and explorers in Siberia.

It is significant that whereas only 420,000 Russians were living in Siberia by 1763, the population of the Thirteen Colonies had risen by the same date to between 1½ and 2 million, or about four times as many. In other words, the Russians, who had been much faster in exploring and conquering, were now much slower in colonizing. One reason was that Siberia could draw only upon Russia for immigrants, whereas the American colonies were receiving immigrants from several European countries. Even more important was the greater attractiveness of America for would-be colonists. One may visualize the drawbacks of the Siberian environment by imagining a lofty chain of mountains along the Gulf coast of the United States cutting off the warm, moisture-laden southerly winds. The resulting cold and aridity is what the emigrants to Siberia had to face. If, instead, they had found a climate comparable to that of the Atlantic or midwestern states, then Siberia undoubtedly would have attracted many more immigrants from Russia and probably even from countries further west. The fact is that climatic conditions in Siberia were more akin to those prevailing in Canada. It is not accidental that the populations of the two countries by 1914 were about the same—8 million for Canada and 9 million for Siberia. And the United States, smaller in area than either Canada or Siberia, had grown in population by 1914 to 100 million.

VI. Conquest of the Ukraine

We noted earlier that Ivan the Terrible's conquest of Kazan and Astrakhan in the mid-sixteenth century left two independent khanates—that of the Crimean Tatars in the south, and of Kuchum's Tatars across the Urals. The latter were subdued in a few years by Yermak and his successors, but the Crimean Tatars held out until the end of the eighteenth century. One reason for their survival is that they enjoyed the powerful support of the Ottoman Empire. The khan at Bakhchi-sarai, the capital of the Crimean Horde, recognized the suzereignty of the Ottoman sultan in Constantinople, and supplied him with cavalry forces in time of war. In return the sultan went to the assistance of the khan whenever he was threatened by the Christian infidels. Furthermore, the khan usually could play off against each other the various infidels who had conflicting claims to the Ukrainian steppes—that is, the Russians, the Poles, and the Cossacks.

Finally, the khan was greatly aided by the inaccessibility of his domain. The Perekop Isthmus guarding the approaches to the Crimean Peninsula was 700 miles direct from Moscow, and far more in actual riding miles. The last 300 miles were across a particularly arid type of steppe country in which it was extremely difficult to find water and provisions for an invading army. Thus, the Russians were not able to undertake serious campaigning against the Crimean Tatars until their line of settlement had advanced sufficiently far south to provide them with a base for striking across the steppes. Even then, Peter the Great failed to cope successfully with the supply problems that arose during his campaigns against the Tatars and the Turks in 1687 and 1689.

These various factors explain why the Crimean khanate survived until the time of Catherine the Great in the late eighteenth century. The 250 years between Ivan the Terrible and Catherine the Great were years of bloodshed and anarchy on the Ukrainian steppes north of the Black Sea. The Ukraine was a wild no man's land in which Russians, Poles, Cossacks, and Tatars fought intermittently and in constantly changing combinations. Particularly devastating were the incessant Tatar raids that were, in effect, slave-hunting expeditions. Riding up their three main trails crouched "like monkeys on greyhounds," the Tatars raided deep into the heart of Moscow in search of ablebodied men, women, and children. Sir Bernard Pares, a British authority on Russia, has vividly described the nature of this Tatar scourge.

> Every year the Tatars issued from their fastness in the Crimea, through the four-mile-wide Isthmus of Perekop to raid and ravish Russia. They had 30,000 picked cavalry, and their infantry, which accumulated reinforcements from all the other territory populated by Tatars eastward, numbered as many as 120,000 and sometimes rose to 200,000. . . . The Tatars, while on campaign, lived on mares' milk and on dried bread. They carried on their horses baskets in which to kidnap Russian children, particularly girls. They took with them leather thongs, with which to drag away with them Russian men-prisoners. These they sold in the market of Caffa to all parts of Asia Minor, to Africa, and even to some parts of Europe. These slaves were numbered by hundreds of thousands. In one of the Tatar raids on Moscow in the reign of John the Dread 130,000 prisoners were carried away. A Jewish merchant who sat at the entrance of Perekop had seen so many pass through that he asked whether there were any more people left in Russia.[8]

In 1571 the Tatars burned Moscow itself. But after 1591 they never succeeded in crossing the Oka River in front of Moscow, and gradually their raids penetrated less and less far northward. Nevertheless, small bands of a few hundred men continued to harass the Russian peasantry, slipping through where they perceived an opportunity and retiring swiftly with their human booty.

Finally Catherine the Great was able to remove the Tatar thorn from the side of Russia. She succeeded where so many of her predecessors had failed because several factors were operating in her favor. One was the rapid decline of both Poland and Turkey, the two powers that hitherto had contested Russia's claims to the Ukraine. Russia, by contrast, was growing steadily stronger, partly because of her spectacular territorial expansion and also because of her strongly centralized government. Russia's power was particularly effective during Catherine's reign because the empress was a superb diplomat and skillfully took advantage of every opportunity afforded by the international situation. She concluded agreements with Joseph II of Austria and Frederick the Great of Prussia that enabled her to wage war against Turkey without becoming embroiled with any major European power. Furthermore, Catherine had the gift of selecting first-class advisers and generals. The most outstanding was General Aleksandr Suvorov, a military genius comparable to Napoleon, and a matchless instrument for Catherine's policies. Moreover, in the eighty years since Peter the Great's campaigns, the Russian peasantry had been unobtrusively and patiently advancing its line of settlement southward, so that Suvorov had a stronger base for operations than Peter had had.

Catherine fought two wars against the Tatars and the Turks. The first, between 1768 and 1774, gave Russia effective control of the Crimean Peninsula. The Treaty of Kuchuk-Kainarji in 1774 severed the ties between Bakhchi-sarai and Constantinople, and gave Russia several strategic strongholds in the Crimea. The second war, from 1787 to 1792, was marked, like the first, by spectacular victories won by Suvorov. In fact, the magnitude of his triumphs created difficulties, because both Prussia and Austria became alarmed at the sweeping Russian advances toward the Mediterranean. Catherine, however, shrewdly took advantage of the outbreak of the French Revolution by pointing out to the Austrian and Prussian rulers that the revolutionary movement in Paris represented a far greater peril than Russian expansion in the Near East. Thus Catherine was able to press her war against the Turks until in 1792, they accepted the Treaty of Jassy. This settlement gave to Russia the entire north shore of the Black Sea from the Kuban River in the east to the Dniester River in the west.

The whole of the Ukraine now was under Russian rule. The forest at length had triumphed over the steppe. The desert zone of Central Asia still held out, but it also was destined to fall under Moscovy's sway during the following century.

SUGGESTED READING

The best general surveys of the Russian expansion into Siberia are by F. A. Golder, *Russian Expansion on the Pacific, 1641–1850* (Glendale, Calif.: Clark, 1914); R. J. Kerner, *The Urge to the Sea: The Course of Russian History* (Berkeley: Univ. California, 1942); the volume of readings by G. A. Lensen, ed., *Russia's Eastward Expansion* (Englewood Cliffs, N. J.: Prentice-Hall, 1964; a Spectrum book); and the two works by A. Lobanov—Rostovsky, *Russia and Asia* (New York: Macmillan, 1933) and "Russian Expansion in the Light of the Turner Hypothesis," in W. D. Wyman and C. B. Kroeber, eds., *The Frontier in Perspective* (Madison: Univ. Wisconsin, 1957), pp. 79–94. Popular accounts are provided by E. Lessner, *Cradle of Conquerors: Siberia* (New York: Doubleday, 1955); Y. Semyonov, *Siberia: Its Conquest and Development* (London: Hollis, 1963); and E. Lengyel, *Siberia* (New York: Random, 1943). Special phases of Siberian history are treated in D. W. Treadgold, *The Great Siberian Migration* (Princeton: Princeton Univ., 1957); R. H. Fisher, *The Russian Fur Trade, 1550–1700* (Berkeley: Univ. California, 1943); and G. V. Lantzeff, *Siberia in the Seventeenth Century* (Berkeley: Univ. California, 1943).

160

. . . within the memorie of man within these foure-score years, there hath beene more newe countries and regions discovered than in five thousande yeares before; yea, more than halfe the worlde hath beene discovered by men that are yet (or might very well for their age be) alive.

GEORGE BESTE,
a member of Martin Frobisher's expeditions

Chapter
9

Significance of the
Period for World History

The early modern period from 1500 to 1763 is one of the more critical periods in the history of mankind. It was at this time that the great discoveries disclosed the existence of new continents and thereby heralded the global phase of world history. It was during this period also that the Europeans began their rise to world primacy by virtue of their leadership in overseas activities. Certain global interrelationships developed during these centuries naturally became stronger with the passage of time. In 1763 they were much more significant than they had been a century or two earlier, and infinitely less significant than they were to become by 1914. In other words, the years from 1500 to 1763 constitute a period of transition from the regional isolationism of the pre-1500 era to the European global hegemony of the nineteenth century. The purpose of this chapter is to analyze the precise nature and extent of the global ties that developed in various fields.

I. NEW GLOBAL HORIZONS

The first and most obvious result of Europe's expansion overseas and overland was an unprecedented widening of man's horizons. No longer was geographic knowledge limited to one region or continent or hemisphere. For the first time, the configuration of the globe as a whole was determined and charted. This was largely the work of the Western Europeans who had taken the lead in transoceanic exploration. Before the Portuguese began feeling their way down the coast of Africa in the early fifteenth century, Europeans had accurate information only of North Africa and the Middle East. Their knowledge concerning India was vague; it was still vaguer regarding Central Asia, East Asia, and sub-Saharan Africa. The very existence of the Americas and of Australia—let alone Antarctica—was, of course, unsuspected.

By 1763 the picture was altogether different. The main coastline of most of the world had become known in varying degrees of detail, including the Atlantic coasts of the Americas, the Pacific coast of South America, the whole outline of Africa, and the coasts of South and East Asia. In certain areas European knowledge went beyond the coastlines. The Russians were reasonably familiar with Siberia, and the Spaniards and Portuguese with Mexico, Central America, and parts of South America. North of the Rio Grande the Spaniards had explored considerable areas in futile search for gold and fabled cities, while the French and English ranged widely further north, using the canoes and the river-lake routes known to the Indians.

On the other hand, the Pacific coast of North America was largely unknown, while Australia, though sighted on its west coast by Dutch navigators, was almost wholly uncharted. Likewise, the interior of sub-Saharan Africa remained largely a blank, as was the case also with Central Asia, about which the main source of information still was the thirteenth century account of Marco Polo. In general, then, the Europeans had gained knowledge of most of the coastlines of the world during this period to 1763. In the following period they were to penetrate into the interior of continents and also explore the polar regions.

II. GLOBAL DIFFUSION OF MAN, ANIMALS, AND PLANTS

The European discoveries led not only to new global horizons but also to a new global distribution of races.* Prior to 1500 there existed, in effect, worldwide racial segregation. The Negroids were concentrated in sub-Saharan Africa and a few Pacific islands, the Mongoloids in Central Asia, Siberia, East Asia, and the Americas, and the Caucasoids in Europe, North Africa, the Middle East, and India. By 1763 this pattern had been fundamentally altered. In Asia, the Russians were beginning their slow migration across the Urals into Siberia. In Africa the Dutch had established a permanent settlement at the Cape, where the climate was favorable and the natives were too primitive to offer effective resistance. By 1763, 111 years after their landing at Capetown, the Dutch had pushed a considerable distance northward and were beginning to cross the Orange River.

By far the greatest change in racial composition occurred in the Americas. Estimates of the Indian population before 1492 vary tremendously, from 8 million to as high as 100 million. Whatever the figure may have been, there

* See "Demographic Impact of European Expansion," *EMM*, No. 39.

is no disagreement about the catastrophic effect of the European intrusion. Everywhere the Indians were decimated, by varying combinations of physical losses during the process of conquest, disruption of cultural patterns, psychological trauma of subjugation, imposition of forced labor, and introduction of alcohol and of new diseases. Within a century the total indigenous population appears to have declined by 90 to 95 per cent. Most badly hit were the Indians of the Caribbean islands and of the tropical coasts, where they disappeared completely within a generation. More resilient were the natives of the upland tropical regions and of lowland tropical areas such as those of Brazil and Paraguay. Although sustaining very heavy losses, they were able to recover and to constitute the stock from which most of the present-day American Indian population is derived. Only in the twentieth century has this population approached its original numbers in tropical America, while elsewhere it still lags far behind.

The disappearing Indians were replaced by waves of immigrants from Europe and Africa. The resulting settlements were of three varieties. One consisted of the Spanish and Portuguese colonies in which Iberian settlers constituted a permanent resident aristocracy among subjugated Indians in the highlands and imported Negro slaves in the lowlands. Since there were many more men than women among the European immigrants, they commonly took Indian wives or concubines. A mestizo population grew up, which in many parts of the Americas came to outnumber both Europeans and Indians.

A second type of settlement developed in the West Indies, where the Europeans—English and French as well as Spanish—again comprised a resident aristocracy, though with an exclusively Negro imported labor force. At first the planters employed indentured servants from Europe to work their tobacco, indigo, and cotton plantations. But with the shift to sugar in the mid-seventeenth century, much more labor was needed, and slaves were

A depiction of the inhabitants of the Andaman Islands, based on a report given Marco Polo that these people had heads, eyes, and teeth "like those of dogs."

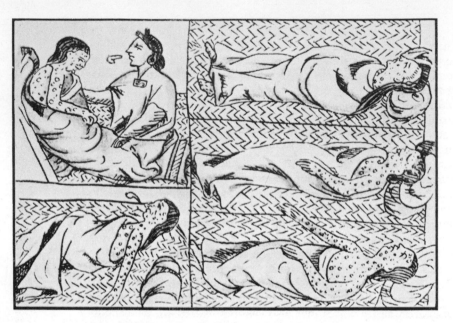

Disease among the Indians. (American Museum of Natural History)

brought over from Africa. In the British Barbados, for example, there were only a few hundred Negroes in 1640, but by 1685 they numbered 46,000 as against 20,000 whites. The French islands, likewise, had 44,000 Negroes and 18,000 whites by 1700.

The third type of settlement in the Americas was to be found along the Atlantic seaboard. There the native Indians were too sparse or too intractable to serve as an adequate labor supply, and, apart from the southern colonies, the crops did not warrant importing Negro labor. Under these circumstances the English and French settlers cleared the land themselves, lived by their own labors as farmers, fishermen, or traders, and developed communities that were exclusively European in composition.

In conclusion, the mass migrations from Europe and Africa changed the Americas from purely Mongoloid continents to the most racially mixed regions of the globe. Negro immigration continued to the mid-nineteenth century, reaching a total of about fifteen million slaves, while European immigration steadily increased, reaching a high point at the beginning of the twentieth century when nearly one million arrived each year. The net result is that the New World today is peopled by a majority of whites, with substantial minorities of Negroes, Indians, mestizos, and mulattoes, in that order (see Chapter 18, section I).

The new global racial pattern that resulted from these depopulations and migrations has become so familiar that it is now taken for granted, and its extraordinary significance generally overlooked. What happened in this period to 1763 is that the Europeans staked out claims to vast new regions, and in the following century they peopled those territories—not only the Americas, but also Siberia and Australia. The meaning of this fundamental redrawing of the racial map of the world may be gauged if it be imagined that the

Chinese rather than the Europeans had first reached and settled the under-populated continents. In that case the proportion of Chinese to the total world population now would probably be closer to three out of four rather than the present one out of four.

165

The intermixture of human races was accompanied inevitably by a corresponding intermixture of plants and animals. With a few insignificant exceptions, all plants and animals being utilized today were domesticated by prehistoric man in various parts of the world. Their diffusion from their respective locales had proceeded slowly until 1500, when globe-spanning man began transplanting them back and forth amongst continents. An important contribution of the Old World was the various stockyard animals, especially horses, cattle, and sheep. The New World had nothing comparable, the llama and alpaca being of relatively little value. Old World grains also were important, especially wheat, rye, oats, and barley. The Spaniards, being lovers of orchards, brought with them a large variety of fruits, as well as the olive and the European vine. Few missions and large houses in early Latin America lacked a walled orchard where these European imports were tended.

The American Indians in return contributed their remarkable store of food plants, particularly corn and potatoes, but also cassava, tomatoes, avocadoes, sweet potatoes, peanuts, and certain varieties of beans, pumpkins, and squashes. Cacao is another native American plant, from which the Aztecs and Mayas made the *chocolatl* that delighted the conquistadors. So important are these Indian plants that today they are responsible for at least a third of the world's total plant food production.

In addition to these food plants, the American Indians were responsible for two major cash crops: tobacco and cotton. Tobacco had been used by the Indians in all the forms known today—in pipes, in cigars, in cigarettes rolled in corn husks, and as snuff. From the New World, tobacco quickly spread all over the world, and in the process new varieties were developed,

Russian trading settlement on Norfolk Sound. The fort is on a hill, with the Russian flag flying over it. Outside the fort are baths and craftsmen's living quarters.

166

such as the so-called Turkish tobacco of the eastern Mediterranean, which are now imported back to the New World. Various species of cotton were known in both the Old and New Worlds prior to 1500, but commercial cotton today is derived largely from varieties domesticated by the Indians. Noteworthy also are several native American drugs that are prominent in modern pharmacology, especially coca in cocaine and novocaine, curare used in anesthetics, cinchona bark as the source of quinine, datura in pain relievers, and cascara in laxatives.

This interchange of animals and plants was not, of course, confined to Eurasia and the Americas. The entire globe was involved, as is illustrated strikingly in the case of Australia, now a leading world exporter of primary products such as wool, mutton, beef, and wheat, all commodities derived from transplanted species. The same is true of Indonesia with its great rubber, coffee, tea, and tobacco production, and of Hawaii with its sugar and pineapples.

III. GLOBAL ECONOMIC RELATIONS

By the latter part of the eighteenth century intercontinental trade of substantial proportions had developed for the first time in history. Before 1500, Arab and Italian merchants had transported certain commodities from one part of Eurasia to another. But now a greater variety of goods were being exchanged in larger quantities among all the continents except Australia.

The Indian village of Secota (North Carolina) in the late sixteenth century.

The Indians of South Carolina were said to kill alligators by driving a long stick down their gullet, turning them over, shooting them with arrows, and then beating them to death.

The chief articles of trade were cotton textiles from India, tea and silks from China, coffee and spices from the East Indies, sugar from the West Indies, and slaves from Africa. The center of this new worldwide trade was Western Europe, since it was the Western Europeans who made the discoveries, who dominated the world trade routes, and who served as the middlemen of the new global trade as the Arabs and the Italians had of the Eurasian trade.

Contrary to general opinion, Europe traded more with the Americas than with Asia. The main reason for this was the tremendous demand by the Europeans for West Indian sugar, and the corresponding demand of the growing number of settlers in the New World for European manufactured goods. Sugar had long been known in Asia, and during the Middle Ages small quantities of it had reached Europe, where it sold at astronomical prices. Then about 1640 the sugar cane was introduced in the West Indies by the Europeans. From the beginning it proved to be a fabulously profitable crop. A Barbados plantation that had sold for £400 in 1640 was worth £14,000 by 1648. Throughout the eighteenth century the West Indian planters reaped a golden harvest by supplying the inexhaustible European market. During the eighty years between 1713 and 1792 Great Britain imported from her own islands alone a total of £162,000,000 worth of goods, almost all sugar. The other country that profited most from this commodity was France, which owned the richest single sugar island, San Domingo, now called Haiti. By the middle of the eighteenth century more than a sixth of the entire foreign commerce of France consisted of West Indian sugar.

The plantation owners made the fortunes they did because they were able to use the labor of Negro slaves from Africa. The first slaves were shipped over to work on the sugar plantations in Portuguese Brazil and in the Spanish colonies. This slave trade was made a government monopoly by the

Iberian states, but it was so lucrative that numerous interlopers, such as John Hawkins, appeared. With the great expansion of the West Indian sugar plantations, Negro slaves were imported on a mass scale. By the eighteenth century the British controlled most of the slave trade, as the Dutch had in the seventeenth century and the Portuguese in the sixteenth. About 610,000 Negroes were landed on the island of Jamaica alone between 1700 and 1800. These slaves in the New World were employed not only in the sugar plantations but also in the cultivation of tobacco, rice, and, at a later date, cotton.

Europe's trade with Asia did not equal the trade with the Americas for two principal reasons. One was the opposition of the long-established European textile industries to the importation of cotton goods from various Asiatic countries. The names by which these cotton fabrics are known in English and other European languages reflect their places of origin. "Gingham" comes from a Malay word meaning "striped," and "chintz" from a Hindustani word meaning "spotted," while "calico" is derived from "Calicut" and "muslin" from "Mosul." These foreign cotton goods were immensely popular in Europe, being light, bright, inexpensive, and, above all, washable. They began to be imported in large quantities, whereupon objections were raised by native textile interests and by those who feared that national security was endangered by the loss of the bullion that was drained away to pay for them. English pamphleteers branded these imports as "light commodities for light women." But their concern for the modesty and morals of English womanhood was as transparent as the fabrics against which they inveighed. Nevertheless the European textile interests brought sufficient pressure to bear upon their respective governments to secure the passage of laws forbidding the importation of Indian cottons. These laws were by no means universally observed, yet they did serve to cut down appreciably the volume of trade with Asia.

The other factor limiting European commerce with Asia was the difficulty of finding something that could sell in the Asiatic market. This problem dated back to classical times when the Roman Empire was drained of its gold to pay for Chinese silk and Indian textiles. So it was in the sixteenth, seventeenth, and eighteenth centuries, when Asia remained uninterested in European goods, while Europe was reluctant to send bullion to pay for the Asiatic produce she desired. Western merchants sometimes went to desperate lengths in their efforts to find a way out of the impasse. The Amsterdam Company exported to Thailand "thousands of Dutch engravings to be sold in the market place of Patani. Among the engravings were Madonnas (to be sold to Buddhists and Mohammedans by order of Calvinist merchants) and biblical scenes; there were, for classically minded Siamese, prints recording the stories of Livy, and finally, prints with a more general human appeal, a collection of nudes and less decent illustrations." [1] The fact is that Europe did not solve this problem of trade with Asia until she developed power machinery at the end of the eighteenth century. Then the situation was reversed, for it was Europe that was able to flood Asia with cheap, machine-made textiles. But until that time, East-West trade was hampered by the fact that Asia was willing to receive from Europe bullion and little else. This situation explains the following revealing observation by Voltaire in the second half of the eighteenth century:

People ask what becomes of all the gold and silver which is continually flowing into Spain from Peru and Mexico. It goes into the pockets of Frenchmen and Englishmen and Dutchmen, who carry on trade in Cadiz, and in return send the products of their industries to America. A large part of this money goes to the East Indies and pays for silk, spices, saltpetre, sugar-candy, tea, textiles, diamonds, and curios.[2]

What was the significance of the new worldwide economic ties? Undoubtedly they had less impact on Asia than on the other continents involved. Most of Asia was quite unaware of, and unaffected by, the persistent and annoying European merchants who were appearing in the coastal regions. Only a few coastal areas in India, and some of the islands in the East Indies, felt significantly the impact of Europe's economic expansion. So far as Asia as a whole was concerned, its attitude was best expressed by the Emperor of China, Ch'ien lung, when he sent the following message in 1793 to the King of Britain, George III:

You, O King, live beyond the confines of many seas, nevertheless, impelled by your humble desire to partake of the benefits of our civilization, you have despatched a mission respectfully bearing your memorial. . . . I have perused your memorial: the earnest terms in which it is couched reveal a respectful humility on your part, which is highly praiseworthy.

In consideration of the fact that your Ambassador and his deputy have come a long way with your memorial and tribute, I have shown them high favour and have allowed them to be introduced into my presence. To manifest my indulgence, I have entertained them at a banquet and made them numerous gifts. . . .

As to your entreaty to send one of your nationals to be accredited to my Celestial Court and to be in control of your country's trade with China, this request is contrary to all usage of my dynasty and cannot possibly be entertained. . . . If you assert that your reverence for Our Celestial dynasty fills you with a desire to acquire our civilization, our ceremonies and code of laws differ so completely from your own that, even if your Envoy were able to acquire the rudiments of our civilization, you could not possibly transplant our manners and customs to your alien soil. Therefore, however adept the Envoy might become, nothing would be gained thereby.

Swaying the wide world, I have but one aim in view, namely, to maintain a perfect governance and to fulfil the duties of the State: strange and costly objects do not interest me. If I have commanded that the tribute offerings sent by you, O King, are to be accepted, this was solely in consideration for the spirit which prompted you to despatch them from afar. Our dynasty's majestic virtue has penetrated into every country under Heaven, and Kings of all nations have offered their costly tribute by land and sea. As your Ambassador can see for himself, we possess all things. I set no value on objects strange or ingenious, and have no use for your country's manufactures.[3]

170

The Americas were much more affected by the new global economy. It led to the development on a large scale of the plantation system of agriculture. A plantation is a considerable tract of land devoted to the production of a staple for export purposes. The plantations in the Americas grew sugar, tobacco, rice, and later, cotton. As Europe's economic tentacles later spread throughout the world, plantations were developed in the East Indies for the production of coffee, rubber, and spices; in Brazil for rubber; in China and Ceylon for tea; and in India for tea and jute. A prerequisite for the successful functioning of the plantation system is a plentiful supply of cheap labor. The native peoples of India, China, and the East Indies were sufficiently numerous and poverty stricken to meet this need. But in the Americas it could be satisfied only by the importation of Negro slaves, which explains the introduction of a substantial Negroid element into the New World ethnic make-up. Today the Negroes are most numerous precisely in those regions that had been devoted to plantation agriculture—northern Brazil, southern United States, and the West Indies.

Africa also was vitally affected, positively as well as negatively, by the new global economy. The slave trade was responsible for the loss of some forty to fifty million Africans who were abducted for transportation to the Americas. Only about fifteen million actually reached their destination, the remainder perishing in transit, either in Africa or on shipboard. The effect of the slave trade varied greatly from region to region. Angola and East Africa suffered severely because their populations were relatively sparse to begin with, and their economies often close to the subsistence level, so that even a small population loss was devastating. By contrast, West Africa was more advanced economically and hence more populous, so that the depredations of the slavers were not so ruinous. Considering the continent as a whole, the demographic repercussion was relatively slight because the slaves were taken over a period stretching from 1500 to 1850, and from a total sub-Saharan population estimated at seventy to eighty million. Nevertheless, the slave trade had a corrosive and unsettling effect on the entire African coast from Senegal to Angola, and for four to five hundred miles inland. The appearance of the European slavers with their cargoes of rum, guns, and hardware set off a chain reaction of slave-hunting raids into the interior, and of wars among assorted groups for control of the lucrative and militarily decisive trade. With some rising to ascendancy, such as the Ashanti Confederacy and the Dahomey Kingdom, and with others declining, such as the Yoruba and Benin civilizations and the Congo kingdom, the over-all effect was definitely disruptive.

And yet the slave trade did involve trade as well as slavery. In return for their fellow countrymen whom the Africans themselves sold to the Europeans, they received not only alcohol and firearms, but also certain useful and economically productive commodities, including textiles, tools, and raw materials for local smithies and workshops. A more important positive influence in the long run was the introduction of new food plants from the Americas. Corn, cassava, sweet potatoes, peppers, pineapples, and tobacco were brought in by the Portuguese and spread very rapidly from tribe to tribe. The substantially larger number of people that could be supported with these new foods far outweighed the manpower lost to the slave trade.

Europe also was vitally affected by the development of intercontinental

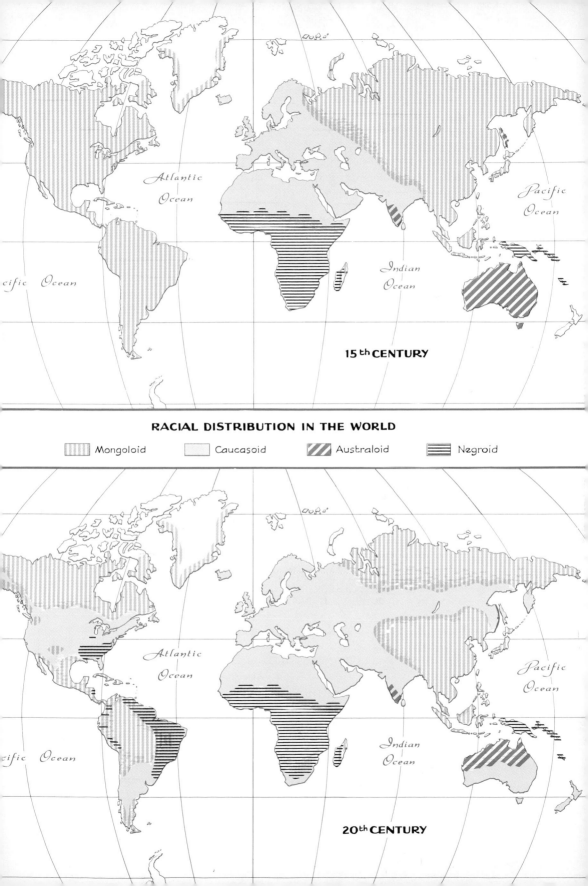

RACIAL DISTRIBUTION IN THE WORLD

Mongoloid   Caucasoid   Australoid   Negroid

15th CENTURY

20th CENTURY

trade in early modern times. And the effect upon Europe was all positive, for the Europeans now were the middlemen of world trade. They had opened the new trade routes. They had supplied the capital and the shipping and the technical skills needed for global commerce. So it was natural that they should have benefited most from the worldwide exchange of commodities. The greater part of the profits made from the slave trade, from the sugar plantations, and from the eastern commerce, flowed first to the Iberian states, and then to Britain, France, and Holland.* Some of the benefits trickled down to the European masses, as is indicated by the fact that tea cost about £10 a pound when introduced in England about 1650, but had become an article of common consumption one hundred years later. More important than the effect on living standards was the stimulating impact of the new global commerce upon Europe's economy. As will be noted later, the Industrial Revolution that got under way in the late eighteenth century owed much to the capital accumulated from overseas enterprises and to the growing demand for European manufactures in overseas markets.

IV. GLOBAL POLITICAL RELATIONS

Global political relations changed as fundamentally during this period to 1763 as did the economic. The Western Europeans no longer were fenced in on the western tip of Eurasia by an expanding Islam. Instead, they had outflanked the Moslem world in the south by winning control of the Indian Ocean, while the Russians had outflanked it in the north by their conquest of Siberia. At the same time, the Western Europeans by their discovery of the New World, had opened vast territories for economic exploitation and colonization. In doing so, they acquired a tremendous reservoir of resources and power that further strengthened their position vis-à-vis Islam, and that was to prove increasingly decisive during the forthcoming century.

All this represented a basic and fateful change in the global balance of power—a change comparable to that which had occurred in the demographic

* See "Adam Smith on the Expansion of Europe," *EMM*, No. 40.

The Hottentots the Natural Inhabitants of the Cape of Good Hope

balance. Hitherto the Moslem world had been the center of initiative, probing and pushing in all directions—into Southeast Europe, into sub-Saharan Africa, into Central and Southeast Asia. Now a new center had arisen which was able to operate on a global, rather than merely Eurasian, scale. From this new center, first in the Iberian Peninsula and later in Northwest Europe, the routes of trade and of political influence radiated outward to envelop the entire world—westward to the Americas, south around Africa, and east to India and around Southeast Asia.

This did not mean actual control of all these territories by 1763. It did mean the effective domination of the underpopulated lands—the Americas, Siberia, and later Australia—even though their actual peopling on a continental scale had to wait till the nineteenth century. But in Africa and Asia the Western Europeans obtained only coastal footholds during this period, with the exception of the Dutch penetration of the Cape and of the East Indies. Elsewhere the native peoples were too strong and highly organized to allow a repetition of what happened in the Americas and in Siberia.

In West Africa, for example, the Europeans were prevented from penetrating inland by climatic difficulties and by the opposition of the coastal chiefs who jealously guarded their profitable position as middlemen between the interior tribes and the Europeans. Consequently, the latter had to content themselves with coastal stations from which they carried on their trade in slaves and in any other commodities that might yield profit.

In India the Europeans were kept at arm's length for 250 years following the arrival of Vasco de Gama in 1498. During those centuries they were allowed to trade in a few ports, but clearly and explicitly on the sufferance of the native rulers. In 1712, for example, John Russell, governor of Fort William and grandson of Oliver Cromwell, prefaced a petition to the Mogul emperor with the following obeisance: "The request of the smallest particle of sand, John Russell, President for the English East India Company, with his forehead at command rub'd on the Ground, and reverence due from a Slave. . . ."[4] It was not until the end of the eighteenth century that the British were strong enough to take advantage of the disintegration of the Mogul Empire to begin their territorial conquests in India.

In China and Japan there was no question whatsoever of European territorial encroachment, as the Russians discovered when they entered the Amur valley. Even trade with the Far East was quite precarious, being subject to unchallengeable arbitrary decrees. In 1763, more than two centuries after the arrival of the Portuguese in the Far East, Western merchants were allowed to trade only in Canton and Nagasaki. Even the Ottoman Empire had lost only its outlying provinces beyond the Danube River. And this despite the fact that it was in a moribund state and was vulnerable to aggression by both the land and naval powers of Europe.

We may conclude that in the political field, as in the economic, Europe in 1763 was at a halfway point. It was no longer a relatively isolated and unimportant peninsula of the Eurasian landmass. It had expanded overseas and overland, establishing its control over the relatively empty and militarily weak Americas and Siberia. But in Africa, the Middle East, and South and East Asia, the Europeans had to wait until the nineteenth century to assert their dominance. To underscore the transitional nature of these centuries, it should be emphasized that while the Western Europeans were executing their

Australian aborigines' war dance.

global flanking movement by sea, the Moslems still had sufficient impetus on land to continue their advances into Central Europe, where they besieged Vienna in 1683, and into sub-Saharan Africa and Southeast Asia, where they were winning new converts.

V. GLOBAL CULTURAL RELATIONS

The imposition of European culture, like that of European political rule, depended on the state of the indigenous societies. The English and the French, for example, were able to transport bodily their respective cultures to the

Abduction of wives in southern Australia.

Americas because the native peoples were either wiped out or pushed aside. Yet even in this case the Indians had an appreciable effect upon the white man's civilization north of the Rio Grande. At the time of the first contacts between the Anglo-French settlers and the Indians, the latter felt secure in their own values and considered their own culture to be at least equal to that of the intruding white man. This is indicated by the reaction of the Iroquois when it was suggested at a conference in 1744 that they send some of their boys to Williamsburg for a European-type education. They countered with the proposition that "if the English Gentlemen would send a dozen or two of their children to Onondago, the great council would take care of their Education, bring them up in really what was the best Manner and make men of them." [5] This sturdy independence of the Indians prompted Benjamin Franklin in 1784 to write: "Savages we call them, because their manners differ from ours, which we think the Perfection of Civility: they think the same of theirs." [6] The white man, it is true, had the numbers, the organization, and the power to dispossess the Indian and to take over the entire continent. Yet in the end he discovered that he had unconsciously adopted many features of the native Indian culture in his vocabulary, his literature, his clothing, his drugs, and in the crops that he grew and consumed.*

* See "Indian Influence on American Civilization," *EMM*, No. 41.

Western ship arriving at Tientsin.

Janissaries of the Ottoman Empire. The scourge of Europe, they twice besieged Vienna.

Indian influence on the Latin American civilization that developed south of the Rio Grande was also substantial. Unfortunately it has not been adequately examined, most studies being focused on the reverse process—the effect of Iberian culture upon the Indians. Yet even the casual traveler in Latin America cannot fail to notice evidence of Indian cultural survivals. There is, for example, the use of adobe for building purposes, and of un-milled pine logs as beams, or vigas. Likewise the blanket, or serape, that is draped over the shoulders is of Indian orgin, as is also the poncho, consisting of two blankets sewn together with a slit left open for the head. The Roman Catholicism currently practiced in much of Latin America is a blend of Christian and Indian beliefs and practices. Although the names of native gods have been dropped, the Indians assign the attributes of these gods to the Virgin Mary and the Saints, expecting the images of the Catholic pantheon to cure disease, control the weather, and keep them from harm, as they believed their gods had done. Perhaps the most conspicuous evidence of Indian influence is to be found in the Latin American cuisine. Tamales, tortillas, and the various chili dishes are based on the two great Indian staples, beans and corn.

European influence upon the indigenous cultures of Africa and Eurasia was negligible in the period prior to 1763, apart from the diffusion of new food plants, which, as noted, was of first importance. In West Africa the native chiefs confined the European traders largely to their coastal posts.

175

The attitude of these chiefs is strikingly revealed in the following speech by Kwame Ansa, a Gold Coast chief, on January 20, 1482. It was delivered in reply to a Portuguese dignitary who had arrived with an impressive retinue and requested permission to build a fort.

> I am not insensible to the high honour which your great master the Chief of Portugal has this day conferred upon me. His friendship I have always endeavoured to merit by the strictness of my dealings with the Portuguese, and by my constant exertions to procure an immediate lading for the vessels. But never until this day did I observe such a difference in the appearance of his subjects: they have hitherto been only meanly attired, were easily contented with the commodities they received; and so far from wishing to continue in this country, were never happy until they could complete their lading, and return. Now I remark a strange difference. A great number richly dressed are anxious to be allowed to build houses, and to continue among us. Men of such eminence, conducted by a commander who from his own account seems to have descended from the God who made day and night, can never bring themselves to endure the hardships of this climate; nor would they here be able to procure any of the luxuries that abound in their own country. The passions that are common to us all men will therefore inevitably bring on disputes; and it is far preferable that both our nations should continue on the same footing they have hitherto done, allowing your ships to come and go as usual; the desire of seeing each other occasionally will preserve peace between us. The Sea and Land being always neighbors are continually at variance and contending who shall give way; the Sea with great violence attempting to subdue the Land and the Land with equal obstinacy resolving to oppose the Sea.[7]

In the old Middle Eastern, Indian, and Chinese centers of civilization, the native peoples, as might be expected, were not at all impressed by the culture of the European intruders. The Moslem Turks, who had the closest ties with the Christian Europeans, looked down upon them with the utmost contempt. Even in the seventeenth and eighteenth centuries, when the Turks were themselves on the downgrade, they did not hesitate to express their disdain for the Christian infidels. "Do I not know you," broke out the grand vizier to the French ambassador in 1666, "that you are a Giaour [nonbeliever], that you are a hogge, a dogge, a turde eater?" [8]

This contemptuous arrogance toward Europe and the Europeans may be explained in large part by the age-old feud between Christianity and Islam. The reaction to the Europeans in the rest of Eurasia was less contumelious, but at the same time there was no indication of respect, much less of awe. When the Portuguese arrived in Ceylon, the native official at Colombo sent the following objective appraisal of the newcomers to his king at Kandy: "There is in our harbour of Colombo a race of people with fair skins, but sufficiently comely; they wear hats of iron and jackets of iron; they rest not a minute in one place; they walk up and down all the time; they eat hunks of stone [ship biscuit] and drink blood [good Madeira, with luck]; they give two or three pieces of gold or silver for one fish or one lime. . . ." The Colombo official, being a perspicacious man, added "their guns are very good." [9] This latter observation is particularly revealing, because where the Europeans made an impression, it invariably was because of their technological accomplishments.

On the mainland of India, the native peoples reacted very negatively when the Portuguese, who were ensconced at Goa, introduced the Inquisition in 1560. Between 1600 and 1773, seventy-three victims were consigned to the flames because of their heretical views. The Indian population could not fail to note the incongruity of a religion that imprisoned, tortured, and condemned to the flames those whose only crime was unorthodoxy, while at the same time it prevented widows being burnt of their own free will as an act of sublime virtue. Furthermore, the lawless and boisterous behavior of European adventurers in India further lowered the opinion that the Indian people held for the Western Christians. An English clergyman, Mr. Terry, was told in 1616: "Christian religion devil religion; Christian much drink; Christian much do wrong; Christian much beat; Christian much abuse others." [10]

The Chinese reaction to the Europeans was relatively favorable at the outset (as noted in Chapter 4, section IV) because of the exceptional ability and intellectual attainments of the Jesuit missionaries. The Jesuits succeeded in winning some converts, including a few scholars and some members of the imperial family. But even the capable Jesuits, with their knowledge of astronomy and mathematics and geography, did not unduly impress the Chinese. One of the most favorable comments was by a writer who praised the Europeans because their Christianity was close to Confucianism and because, to his surprise, some Europeans were "real gentlemen."

> The T'ien-chu kno [the Lord-of-Heaven country, i.e., the Catholic state, presumably Italy], lies further to the west from the Buddhist state [India]. Their people understand literature and are as scholarly and elegant as the Chinese. There is a certain Li-ma-tou [Matteo Ricci] who came from the said state, and after four years reached the boundary of Kwangtung by way of India. Their religion worships T'ien-chu ["the Lord of Heaven," the Catholic term for God], just as the Confucianists worship Confucius and the Buddhists, Buddha. Among his books there is one entitled T'ien-chu shih-i (The true meaning of Christianity) which frequently explains the truth by comparison with Confucianism but sharply criticizes the theories of nothingness and emptiness of Buddhism and Taoism. . . . I am very much delighted with his ideas, which are close to Confucianism but more earnest in exhorting society not to resemble the Buddhists, who always like to use obscure, incoherent words to fool and frighten the populace. . . . He is very polite when he talks to people and his arguments, if challenged, can be inexhaustible. Thus in foreign countries there are also real gentlemen. [11]

This tribute was exceptional. Most Chinese scholars rejected both Western science and Western religion. When in March, 1715, Pope Clement XI issued his bull *Ex illa die,* forbidding Christians from participating in ceremonies of ancestor worship or of reverence to Confucius, the Chinese emperor, K'ang-hsi, scornfully remarked, "After reading this document all I can say is: How could the Occidentals, stupid men as they are, dispute the great teachings of China? Not one of them thoroughly understands Chinese writings, and when they speak, most of them are ludicrous. The bull, which I have now seen, resembles the superstitions of Buddhists and Taoists, but there is nothing so full of blunders as this." [12] So far as the popular Chinese attitude to the Europeans at that time is concerned, it probably was reflected accurately in the proverb that they, the Chinese, alone possessed two eyes, the Europeans were one-eyed, and all the other inhabitants of the earth were blind. Given this atmosphere, it is understandable that, with the exception of certain specialized fields of learning such as astronomy, European influence on Chinese civilization prior to 1763 was negligible.

Although the Chinese, the Indians, and the Turks were unimpressed by the culture of the Europeans during this period, the Europeans, by contrast, were very much impressed by what they observed in Constantinople, in Delhi, and in Peking. They became familiar first with the Ottoman Empire, and their reaction was one of respect, admiration, and apprehension. As late as 1634, after the decline of the empire had set in, a thoughtful English traveler concluded that the Turks were "the only modern people great in action," and that "he who would behold these times in their greatest glory, could not find a better scene than Turkey." [13] Similar tribute was paid at an earlier date by Augier Ghislain de Busbecq, the judicious and observant Hapsburg ambassador in Constantinople during the reign of Suleiman the Magnificent. In a letter to a friend in 1555, Busbecq compared Suleiman to a thunderbolt—

In Goa, the Portuguese adopted Eastern dress.

The Imperial Court of Peking receiving Pieter van Hoorn's Dutch Trade Delegation (1668).

"he smites, shatters, and destroys whatever stands in his way." Busbecq was impressed not only by the strength of the Ottoman Empire but also by the efficiency of the Ottoman bureaucracy, which was based on a strict merit system.

During the seventeenth century the Ottoman Empire lost prestige among Europeans. Numerous symptoms of decay were becoming apparent, including dynastic degeneration, administrative corruption, and military impotence. But at the same time European intellectuals were being fascinated by numerous detailed accounts of the fabulous civilization of far-off Cathay. These accounts, based on the reports of the Jesuit missionaries, generated a tremendous enthusiasm for China and for things Chinese. Indeed, the influence of China on Europe in the seventeenth and early eighteenth centuries was considerably greater than Europe's influence on China. The Westerners were entranced as they learned of China's history, art, philosophy, and government. China came to be held up as a model civilization because of its Confucian system of morals, its examination system for government service, its respect for learning rather than for military prowess, and its exquisite handicrafts, including porcelain, silk, and lacquer work. Voltaire (1694–1778), for example, adorned the wall of his library with a portrait of Confucius, while the German philosopher Leibniz (1646–1716) extolled the Chinese emperor K'ang-hsi as "the monarch . . . who almost exceeds human heights of greatness, being a godlike mortal, ruling all by a nod of his head, who, however, is educated to virtue and wisdom . . . thereby earning the right to rule." [14]

In the late eighteenth century European admiration for China began to

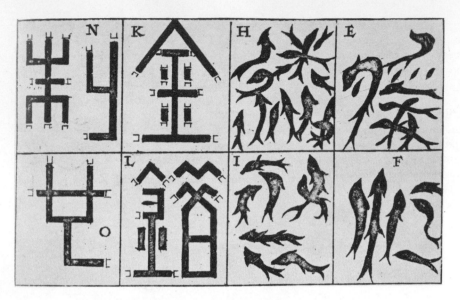

A Jesuit attempt to reproduce ancient Chinese characters.

wane, partly because the Catholic missionaries now were being persecuted, and also because the Europeans were beginning to be more interested in China's natural resources than in her culture. This shift of attitude is reflected in the sixteen volumes of the *Memoirs on the History, Sciences, Arts, etc., of the Chinese,* published in Paris between 1776 and 1814. The eleventh volume, which appeared in 1786, contained little but reports on resources that might interest traders—borax, lignite, quicksilver, ammoniac, horses, bamboo, and wool-bearing animals.

Just as European interest had shifted in the seventeenth century from the Ottoman Empire to China, so now in the late eighteenth century it shifted to Greece and, to a lesser extent, India. The classical Greeks became the great favorites among educated Europeans. "How can you believe," wrote a German scholar in 1778, "that uncultivated Oriental peoples produced annals and poetry and possessed a complete religion and morality, before the Greeks, who were the teachers of Europe, were able to read?" [15] Yet a few European intellectuals did become engrossed in Indian culture. The general European public had long before this time been aware of India, and had been thrilled by the reports of the riches and magnificence of the "Grand Mogul" of Delhi. One can imagine the reaction to the following description of the famous Peacock Throne written by the French physician François Bernier, who attended the imperial family in Delhi between 1658 and 1667.

> The GREAT MOGUL has seven magnificent thrones, one wholly covered with diamonds, the others with rubies, emeralds, or pearls. . . . But that which in my opinion is the most costly thing about this magnificent throne is, that the twelve columns supporting the canopy are surrounded with beautiful rows of pearls, which are round and of fine water, and weigh from 6 to 10 carats each. At 4 feet distance from the throne there

180

are fixed, on either side, two umbrellas, the sticks of which for 7 or 8 feet in height are covered with diamonds, rubies and pearls. The umbrellas are of red velvet, and are embroidered and fringed all round with pearls.[16]

181

This superficial concept of India and her civilization began to deepen as the Europeans gradually became aware of the ancient literature of the Hindus. The Hindu pandits were unwilling to impart their sacred lore to foreigners, but a few Europeans, mostly Jesuit fathers, acquired a knowledge of Sanskrit language, literature, and philosophy. The German philosopher Schopenhauer (1788–1860) fell as much under the spell of Hindu philosophy as Leibniz had under the Chinese. An English scholar, Sir William Jones, proclaimed before the Asiatic Society of Bengal in 1786 that "The *Sanskrit* Language, whatever be its antiquity, is of wonderful structure; more perfect than the Greek, more copious than the Latin, and more exquisitely refined than either." [17]

VI. EARLY MODERN PERIOD IN HISTORICAL PERSPECTIVE

The early modern period from 1500 to 1763 represents a halfway point between the regional isolationism of the preceding ages and the European world hegemony of the nineteenth century. Economically, it was a time when the Europeans extended their trading operations to virtually all corners of the globe, though they were not yet able to exploit the interiors of the great landmasses. Intercontinental trade reached unprecedented proportions, but it was still far below the volume it was to attain in the following centuries.

Politically, the world was still far from being a single unit. The great Seven Years' War which convulsed Europe did not affect the Americas west of the Mississippi, the interior of Africa, most of the Middle East, and the whole of East Asia. The Europeans had secured a firm grip on Siberia, South America, and the eastern portion of North America, but they had as yet only a few territorial enclaves in Africa, India, and the East Indies, while in the Far East they could venture only as merchants. And even in that capacity they had to submit to the most restrictive and arbitrary regulations.

Culturally, it was a period of widening horizons. Throughout the globe peoples were becoming aware of other peoples and other cultures. By and large, the Europeans were more impressed and affected by the ancient civilizations of Eurasia than was the case in reverse. They felt a sense of wide-eyed wonder as they discovered new oceans and continents and civilizations. They exhibited a certain humility at the same time that they were scrambling greedily for booty and for trade. They even underwent on occasion an anxious searching of conscience, as in the case of the treatment of the Indians in Spanish America. But before this period had passed, Europe's attitude toward the rest of the world was noticeably changing.* It was becoming coarser and harder and more intolerant. In the mid-nineteenth century the French sinologist Guillaume Pauthier complained that the Chinese civilization, which in

---

* See "Early Europeans in India," *EMM*, No. 42.

the time of Leibniz had keenly interested European intellectuals, "now scarcely attracted the attention of a select few. . . . These people, whom we daily treat as barbarians, and who, nevertheless, had attained to a very high state of culture several centuries before our ancestors inhabited the forests of Gaul and Germany, now inspire in us only a deep contempt." [18] Part 3 of this book will be concerned with why the Europeans came to feel themselves superior to the "lesser breeds," and how they were able to impose their rule upon them.

SUGGESTED READING

The general effect of Europe's expansion during the early modern period is analyzed by J. H. Parry, *The Age of Reconaissance: Discovery, Exploration and Settlement 1450 to 1650* (New York: World, 1963); A. G. Price, *The Western Invasions of the Pacific and Its Continents: A Study of Moving Frontiers and Changing Landscapes, 1513–1958* (Oxford, Clarendon Press, 1963); E. F. Frazier, *Race and Culture Contacts in the Modern World* (New York: Knopf, 1957); and W. P. Webb, *The Great Frontier* (Boston: Houghton, 1952). The opposite process—the impact of Asia on Europe—is the subject of an exhaustive projected six-volume study by D. F. Lach, *Asia in the Making of Europe,* of which Vol. I, Books 1 and 2, *The Century of Discovery* (Chicago: Univ. Chicago, 1965), which deals with the sixteenth century, has been completed. More specialized studies are J. E. Gillespie, *The Influence of Overseas Expansion on England to 1700* (Vol. 91 in Columbia Univ. Studies in History, Economics and Public Law, 1920); A. I. Hallowell, "The Backwash of the Frontier: The Impact of the Indian on American Culture," in W. D. Wyman and C. B. Kroeber, eds. *The Frontier in Perspective* (Madison: Univ. Wisconsin, 1957), pp. 229–58; A. I. Hallowell, "The Impact of the American Indian on American Culture," *American Anthropologist,* LIX (1957), 201–17; L. S. S. O'Malley, ed., *Modern India and the West* (London: Oxford Univ., 1941); A. Reichwein, *China and Europe: Intellectual and Artistic Contacts in the Eighteenth Century* (New York: Knopf, 1925); and B. Guy, *The French Image of China Before and After Voltaire* (Geneva: Institut et Musée Voltaire, 1964).

WORLD OF
WESTERN DOMINANCE, 1763-1914

The century and a half between 1763 and 1914 stands out in the course of world history as the period of European hegemony over a large part of the globe. In 1763 Europe was still far from being the master of the world, having only coastal footholds in Africa and in Asia. But by 1914 the European powers had annexed the whole of Africa and had effectively established their control over Asia, either directly, as in India and Southeast Asia, or indirectly, as in the Chinese and Ottoman empires. This unprecedented expansion of Europe was made possible by three great revolutions—scientific, industrial, and political—which gave Europe irresistible dynamism and power.

Two features of these revolutions might be noted at this point. One is that they were well under way before 1763. The English Civil War, a major phase of the political revolution, occurred in the 1640's. The scientific revolution took place primarily during the century and a half between the publication of Copernicus' De revolutionibus orbium coelestium (1543) and of Newton's Principia (1687). Likewise, the roots of the Industrial Revolution are to be found in the sixteenth and seventeenth centuries, when the countries of northwestern Europe "were seething with such genuinely capitalistic phenomena as systematic mechanical invention, company formation, and speculation in the shares of financial and trading concerns." [1] But the worldwide impact of none of these revolutions was fully felt until the nineteenth century. That is the principal reason for considering them here rather than earlier in this book.

The other point to note about these revolutions is that they did not run in parallel or independent lines. They were interdependent and reacted continuously one upon the other. Both Newton's discovery of the laws governing the movements of heavenly bodies and Darwin's theories of biological evolution had a profound effect on political ideas. Likewise, modern nationalism is quite unthinkable without technological innovations such as printing and the telegraph. And contrariwise, politics affected science, as in the case of the French Revolution, which provided a powerful stimulus to scientific advance. Politics also affected economics, as was made clear by the English manufacturer John Wilkinson, who stated bluntly, "Manufacture and Commerce will always flourish most where Church and King interfere least." [2]

After analyzing the nature and the unfolding of these three European revolutions, we shall then, in the following chapters of Part III of this volume, trace their effect on various parts of the globe. We shall see how they made possible the Europeanization of the Americas and of Australia, the partitioning of Africa, and the domination over Asia.

[1] E. J. Hamilton, "American Treasure and the Rise of Capitalism (1500–1700)," Economica (November, 1929), p. 356.
[2] Cited by C. E. Robinson, "The English Philosophes and the French Revolution," History Today, VI (February, 1956), 121.

The so-called scientific revolution . . . outshines everything since the rise of Christianity and reduces the Renaissance and Reformation to the rank of mere episodes, mere internal displacements within the system of medieval Christendom. . . . It looms so large as the real origin both of the modern world and of the modern mentality that our customary periodisation of European history has become an anachronism and an encumbrance.

HERBERT BUTTERFIELD

Chapter

10

The Scientific Revolution

Less than four hundred years, or about six average life spans, separate the work of Copernicus from that of Einstein. Yet in that short space of time science has grown from an esoteric avocation of a handful of devotees to what may be properly termed the dominant force of modern civilization. And the central characteristic of science today is its constantly accelerating rate of development. In 1899, the famous British naturalist Alfred Russell Wallace published a book entitled *The Wonderful Century*. He was referring to his own nineteenth century, which, in his opinion, had witnessed more scientific progress than all the preceding centuries of mankind. Yet today we can again boast that more scientific work has been done in the first half of the twentieth century than in the whole of previous history.

In the light of retrospect, it appears that this scientific revolution is of even greater significance than the agricultural revolution of Neolithic times. The agricultural revolution made civilization possible, but once this great step forward was taken, agriculture had no further contribution to make. Science, on the other hand, is by its very methodology cumulative. It contains within itself the possibilities of indefinite advance. If we bear in mind the achievements of science in the past few centuries and its present accelerating pace of development, we may appreciate, if not comprehend, its staggering potentiality and significance. Science, furthermore, is universal; being based

186

on an objective methodology, it has secured general assent to its propositions. It is the one product of Western civilization that non-Western peoples generally respect and seek. In fact, it was science and its related technology that made possible Europe's domination of the world in the nineteenth century. And today the formerly subject peoples are striving to redress the balance by learning the mysteries of the West's great and unique contribution to mankind.

That is why the scientific revolution is of basic significance for the study of world history. This chapter will trace the unfolding of this fateful scientific revolution from its beginnings in early modern times until World War I.

I. Roots of the Scientific Revolution

The roots of science may be traced back to ancient Mesopotamia and Egypt, to classical Greece, and to the medieval Moslem world. Yet the scientific revolution is a unique product of Western civilization. The reason seems to be that only in the West did science become part and parcel of general society. Or, to put it another way, only in the West did the philosopher-scientist and the artisan effect a union and stimulate each other. And it was this union of science and society, of scientist and artisan, that contributed greatly to the unprecedented blossoming of science in the Western world.

In all human societies the artisans developed certain skills in hunting, fishing, farming, and in working with wood, stone, metal, grasses, fibers, roots, and hides. Through their observations and experiments they gradually improved their techniques, sometimes reaching very high levels, as in the case of the Eskimos. Yet the degree of progress achieved by all premodern societies was sharply restricted. The reason was that the artisans were interested only in making pots or building houses or constructing boats, and did not bother with underlying chemical or mechanical principles. They did not inquire regarding the relationship between antecedent and consequent phenomena. In short, the artisans by definition concerned themselves with technological know-how rather than with scientific know-why.

The significance of this is suggested by James Bryant Conant's definition of science as "an interconnected series of concepts and conceptual schemes that have developed as a result of experimentation and observation and are fruitful of further experimentation and observations." [1] It is apparent that artisans lacked the "conceptual schemes" that, according to Conant's definition, constitute the basis of science. Instead, such schemes traditionally have been the concern of philosophers, as intellectuals were generally termed in premodern times. But these philosophers were notoriously ignorant and impractical about questions of everyday life. They deemed themselves to be above mundane matters, and spent their time pondering the eternal verities or trying to reduce an incoherent universe into something comprehensible to the human mind. The philosophers and the artisans undoubtedly did work together at certain times to produce the elaborate calendars, the navigation aids, and the everyday rituals of antiquity. But the fact remains that until recent times the tendency was toward compartmentalization—toward the isolation of the thinker from the worker.

The great achievement of the West was to bring the two together. This fusion of know-how and know-why gave science the grounding and the impulse that was to make it the dominant force that it is today.

Why did this epochal development take place in the West? One reason was 187 the humanistic scholarship of the Renaissance. Scholars and artists set themselves in opposition to the whole pattern of medieval life and strove to create a new pattern as similar as possible to that of classical antiquity. They no longer wished to see the ancients through the distorting spectacles of the Moslems and the schoolmen. Instead they went directly to the sources, digging up the statues and reading the original texts for themselves. They gained access not only to Plato and Aristotle but also to Euclid and Archimedes, who stimulated the study of physics and mathematics. More important was the inspiration received in the biological sciences. Medical men studied the complete works of Hippocrates and Galen, and naturalists those of Aristotle, Dioscorides, and Theophrastus. On the other hand it should be emphasized that there was another side to the Renaissance that was antiscientific, as evidenced in the revival of magic and demonology (see Chapter 2, section II).

These fruits of human scholarship could not by themselves have engendered the scientific revolution without a favorable social atmosphere in Western Europe, which narrowed the gulf between the artisans and the scholars. Artisans were not so despised during the Renaissance as they had been in classical and medieval times. Respect was given to the practical arts of spinning, weaving, ceramics, glass making, and, most of all, to the increasingly important mining and metallurgy. All these crafts in Renaissance Europe were in the hands of freemen rather than of slaves as in classical times. And these freemen were not so far removed, socially and economically, from the ruling circles as had been the artisans of the Middle Ages. The enhancement of the status of the Renaissance craftsman made it possible to strengthen the tie between him and the scholar that had been so tenuous since the beginning of civilization. Each had an important contribution to make. The craftsman had the old techniques of antiquity, to which he added the new devices evolved during the Middle Ages. The scholar likewise provided the facts, speculations, and procedures of rediscovered antiquity and of medieval science. The two approaches fused slowly, but in the end they produced an explosive combination.

Closely connected with this bringing together of the craftsman and scholar was the corresponding bringing together of labor and thought by individual scholars or scientists. A strong prejudice existed in ancient times against combining creative learning and manual work. This prejudice, which presumably arose out of the ancient association of manual labor with slavery, persisted in medieval Europe even after slavery had almost disappeared. Medieval scholastic philosophers drew a distinction between the "liberal" and the "servile" arts, between work done with the mind alone and work that involved a change in matter. Poets, logicians, and mathematicians, for example, belonged to the first category, and sculptors, glaziers, and ironworkers to the second. The deleterious influence of this dichotomy is clearly evident in the field of medicine. The work of a physician did not change matter so it was regarded as "liberal," while that of a surgeon, by the same criterion, was considered "servile." Accordingly, experimentation was looked down upon, and vivisection was deemed illegal and repulsive.

When William Harvey (1578–1657) made his great discovery concerning the movements of the heart and blood, he did so because he resolutely turned his back on this scorn for manual work. Instead, for decades he carried on painstaking experimentation of all types. He cut the arteries and veins of living things, from large animals to tiny insects, observing and recording with care and patience the flow of the blood and the motions of the heart. He also utilized the new magnifying glass to observe wasps, hornets, and flies. Today this procedure seems sensible and obvious, but in Harvey's time it definitely was neither. According to Richard Hooker, the outstanding theologian of the period, *reason,* not experimentation, is the means by which "man attaineth a knowledge of things that are and are not sensible." [2] That Hooker's statement is difficult for us to comprehend demonstrates how fundamental and all-pervasive has been the impact of the scientific revolution on our way of thinking and way of life. But for Harvey, working in the early seventeenth century, adherence to the experimental method was a trying intellectual ordeal that required courage and devotion.

Science was stimulated also by the Discoveries and the opening up of overseas lands. New plants, new animals, new stars, even new human beings and new human societies were found, and all these challenged traditional ideas and assumptions. It is significant that in the writings of a great English exponent of science, Francis Bacon (1561–1626), much of the imagery is borrowed from the voyages of exploration. Bacon expressed himself as aspiring to be the Columbus of a new intellectual world, to sail through the Pillars of Hercules (symbol of the old knowledge) into the Atlantic Ocean in search of new and more useful knowledge. In fact, he explicitly stated that "by the distant voyages and travels which have become frequent in our times, many things in nature have been laid open and discovered which may let in new light upon philosophy." [3]

The scientific revolution in Europe owed much to the concurrent economic revolution. In early modern times Western Europe experienced rapid growth in both commerce and industry. Trade grew enormously, both among European countries and with new overseas markets in the Far East, the East Indies, Africa, and the Americas. Industry also made notable gains, especially in England, where the developments in coal mining and iron manufacturing laid the basis for the later Industrial Revolution. These economic advances led to technological advances, and the latter in turn stimulated, and were stimulated by, science. Oceanic commerce created an enormous demand for shipbuilding and navigation. A new class of intelligent, mathematically trained craftsmen appeared for compass, map, and instrument making. Navigation schools were founded in Portugal, Spain, Holland, and France, and astronomy was studied seriously because of its obvious utilitarian value. Likewise, the needs of the mining industry engendered advances in power transmission and pumps. This proved to be the starting point of a new interest in mechanical and hydraulic principles. In the same manner, metallurgy was responsible for notable progress in chemistry. The expanding mining operations brought to light new ores and even new metals, like bismuth, zinc, and cobalt. Techniques for separating and handling these had to be found by analogy and corrected by painful experience. But in doing so, a general theory of chemistry began to take form, involving oxidations and reductions, distillations and amalgamations.

These achievements gave the scientists, or philosophers, a self-assurance and a confidence that they were the harbingers of a new age. As early as 1530 Jean Fernel, physician to the king of France, wrote:

But what if our elders, and those who preceded them, had followed simply the same path as did those before them? . . . Nay, on the contrary, it seems good for philosophers to move to fresh ways and systems; good for them to allow neither the voice of the detractor, nor the weight of ancient culture, nor the fullness of authority, to deter those who would declare their own views. In that way each age produces its own crop of new authors and new arts. This age of ours sees art and science gloriously re-risen, after twelve centuries of swoon. Art and science now equal their ancient splendour, or surpass it. This age need not, in any respect, despise itself and sigh for the knowledge of the Ancients. . . . Our age today is doing things of which antiquity did not dream. . . . Ocean has been crossed by the prowess of our navigators, and new islands found. The far recesses of India lie revealed. The continent of the West, the so-called New World, unknown to our forefathers, has in great part become known. In all this, and in what pertains to astronomy, Plato, Aristotle, and the old philosophers made progress, and Ptolemy added a great deal more. Yet, were one of them to return today, he would find geography changed past recognition. A new globe has been given us by the navigators of our time.[4]

A century later this confidence had grown to the point where man's future achievements were being anticipated with perception and excitement. Joseph Glanvill, writing in 1661, referred to "those illustrious Heroes"—Descartes, Galileo, Harvey, and others—and then launched into a prophetic paean of the new world they were creating.

Should those Heroes go on as they have happily begun; they'll fill the world with wonders. And I doubt not but posterity will find many things that are now but Rumors, verified into practical Realities. It may be some Ages hence, a voyage to the Southern unknown tracts, yea possibly to the Moon, will not be more strange than one to America. To them that come after us it may be as ordinary to buy a pair of wings, to fly into remotest Regions; as now a pair of Boots to ride a journey. And to confer at the distance of the Indies by Sympathetic conveyances, may be as usual to future times, as to us in a literary correspondence. And the turning of the now comparatively desert world into a Paradise may not improbably be expected from late Agriculture.[5]

In 1662 Charles II of England granted a charter for the establishment of "The Royal Society of London for Promoting Natural Knowledge." Its members, sensing the advantage of cooperation between technicians and scientists, encouraged and coordinated efforts in every occupation throughout the country to gather data that might advance scientific knowledge. "All Places and Corners are now busy and warm about this Work: and we find many noble Rarities to be every Day given in [to the Society] not only by the Hands of

190

learned and professed Philosophers; but from the Shops of *Mechanicks;* from the Voyages of *Merchants;* from the Ploughs of *Husbandmen;* from The Sports, The Fishponds, The Parks, The Gardens of Gentlemen. . . ." [6]

At first, science received much more from the mine and the workshop than they received from science. During this early period science was not an integral part of economic life and was utilized sparingly and sporadically. This was true even in the early phases of the Industrial Revolution in the late eighteenth and early nineteenth centuries. But by the end of the nineteenth century the situation changed basically. Science no longer was in a subsidiary, consultative position: it had begun to transform old industries and even to create entirely new ones.

II. Seventeenth Century New Cosmos

It is understandable that the first major advance of modern science occurred in the field of astronomy which was closely related to geography and to navigation. It is also understandable that Italy was the scene of this advance, since Italy in the fifteenth century was the most advanced country of Europe, economically and culturally. Thus we find that the great Mikolaj Kopernik (1473–1543), who became famous under his Latinized name of Copernicus, left his native Poland to enter the university at Bologna. After six years of studies, he returned to Poland and began an active career in the church. But he continued to work on the problems of astronomy that he had been engaged in in Italy, particularly because there was a general interest at the time in devising a more accurate calendar. He took up the idea of some ancient philosophers that the sun rather than the earth was the center of the universe, and then demonstrated that this provided a simpler explanation of the movements of the heavenly bodies than did the traditional Ptolemaic system.

> First and above all lies the sphere of the fixed stars, containing itself and all things, for that very reason immovable; in truth the frame of the Universe, to which the motion and position of all other stars are referred. Though some men think it to move in some way, we assign another reason why it appears to do so in our theory of the movement of the Earth. Of the moving bodies first comes Saturn, who completes his circuit in XXX years. After him, Jupiter, moving in a twelve year revolution. Then Mars, who revolves biennially. Fourth in order an annual cycle takes place, in which we have said is contained the Earth, with the lunar orbit as an epicycle. In the fifth place Venus is carried round in nine months. Then Mercury holds the sixth place, circulating in the space of eighty days. In the middle of all dwells the Sun. Who indeed in this most beautiful temple would place the torch in any other or better place than one whence it can illuminate the whole at the same time? Not ineptly, some call it the lamp of the universe, others its Electra, the contemplation of all things. And thus rightly in as much as the Sun, sitting on a royal throne, governs the circumambient family of stars. . . . We find, therefore, under this orderly arrangement, a wonderful symmetry in the

universe, and a definite relation of harmony in the motion and magnitude of the orbs, of a kind it is not possible to obtain in any other way.[7]

Copernicus printed a short abstract of his work in 1530, and the complete book, *De revolutionibus orbium coelestium,* was published in 1543, the year of his death. Although Copernicus was a mathematician and astronomer of repute, his hypothesis at first was disregarded. In stating that the earth rotated diurnally on its axis and annually around the sun, he was uttering heresy, for according to scripture Joshua had caused the sun to stand still in the heavens. Furthermore, his hypothesis was repugnant to common sense. If the earth revolved, would not its motion produce a mighty wind? And would not objects thrown upward lag behind the surface of the whirling globe? Copernicus' new astronomy made necessary a new physics. The need was met by a well-to-do Florentine, Galileo Galilei (1564–1642).*

Galileo's approach was strictly empirical. Against the traditional dicta of Aristotle and the schoolmen, he pitted experimental and verifiable facts. He was primarily a physicist interested in solving problems of military and civil engineering by working out laws of terrestrial motion. He conducted further experiments in dynamics, in which he devised more refined means for measuring small intervals of time, found means of estimating air resistance, friction, and other impediments occurring in nature, and conceived of pure or absolute motion, and of force and velocity, in abstract mathematical terms.

Galileo's work in astronomy made a greater impression at the time, though it was not as original or basic. He made use of the telescope that had just been invented in Holland as a by-product of the manufacturing of spectacles. Legend has it that about 1600 a child in a Dutch shop first looked through one lens at another in the window and noticed that it made things outside seem nearer. In any case, Galileo, who already was a convinced Copernican, eagerly used the new instrument to see what actually was in the heavens. Even in these days of fabulous scientific discoveries, one can sense the melodrama of Galileo discovering a whole new world and appreciating the significance of what he observed.

> That which will excite the greatest astonishment by far, and which indeed especially moved me to call the attention of all astronomers and philosophers is this, namely, that I have discovered four planets, neither known nor observed by any one of the astronomers before my time. . . . By the aid of a telescope anyone may behold this in a manner which so distinctly appeals to the senses that all the disputes which have tormented philosophers through so many ages are exploded at once by the irrefragable evidence of our eyes, and we are freed from wordy disputes upon this subject, for the Galaxy is nothing else but a mass of innumerable stars planted together in clusters. Upon whatever part of it you direct the telescope straightway a vast crowd of stars presents itself to view; many of them are tolerably large and extremely bright, but the number of small ones is quite beyond determination.[8]

* See "Galileo Galilei," *EMM,* No. 43.

Galileo was particularly impressed by the discovery that Jupiter had satellites, moons moving around it like the moon around the earth. All this evidence reassured him of the validity of the Copernican theory. It suggested that the heavenly bodies might be of the same substance as the earth, masses of matter moving in space. The traditional distinction between the earth and the heavens was becoming dubious. This struck a shattering and frightening blow at philosophy and theology. Galileo was condemned by the Inquisition and forced to an ostensible recantation. But the impact of his findings on thoughtful minds was overwhelming. Poets repeatedly compared him to Columbus and other discoverers.

> Yield, Vespucci, and let Columbus yield. Each of these
> Holds, it is true, his way through the unknown sea. . . .
> But you, Galileo, alone gave to the human race the sequence of stars,
> New constellations of heaven.[9]

John Donne expressed the unsettling and disturbing effect of the new astronomy when he wrote " 'Tis all in peeces, all cohaerence gone." [10] Two intellectual leaders of this period, however, were not upset by the seeming anarchy. They were René Descartes (1596–1650) and Francis Bacon, scientific thinkers who pointed out the potentialities of science and raised it to a status in polite circles comparable to that of literature. They were essentially prophets and publicists—men who had seen a vision of the possibilities of the new discipline and who made it their business to inform the world.

Descartes and Bacon approached problems in quite different fashions. Descartes was a great mathematician, the inventor of analytic geometry. In a sense it may be said that he unified the geometry received from the Greeks with the algebra learned from the Moslems. Henceforth it was possible to explain geometry algebraically and to develop new types of mathematics. Descartes was so carried away by the possibilities of the mathematical method that he made it the basis of his entire philosophy. He insisted that the only true way of knowing was by mathematical reasoning and abstraction. Experimentation was for him a mere auxiliary to deductive thought. Clear thinking, he believed, could discover anything that was rationally knowable.

By the end of the century Descartes' disciples had multiplied till their numbers were legion. In the words of one historian: "The universities were Cartesian, the marquis, the scientific amateurs, Colbert, the king were Cartesian. France conjugated the verb 'to cartesianate' and Europe followed suit enthusiastically." [11] The significance of this popularity is that rational inquiry and judgment was extended to all fields. All tradition and all authority had to stand the scrutiny of reason.

Bacon, by contrast, employed the inductive method, which begins with facts and then proceeds to general principles. To arrive at the underlying causes, said Bacon, we must study the natural history of the phenomena, collect and tabulate all observations that bear on them, notice which phenomena are related in such a way as to vary together, and then, by a merely mechanical process of exclusion, discover the cause of a given phenomenon. As a corrective to medieval scholastic methods, Bacon's work was of the greatest value in the history of thought. It should be noted, however, that scientific discovery is seldom or never made by the pure Baconian method. Too many phenomena exist for any subject to be studied successfully without the aid of hypothesis conceived by scientific imagination. Facts are collected to prove or disprove the consequences deduced from the hypothesis, and thus the number of facts to be examined becomes manageable.

Bacon also was outstanding in stressing the utilitarian value of science.

> The true and lawful goal of the sciences is simply this, that human life be enriched by new discoveries and powers. . . . The good effects wrought by founders of cities, law-givers, fathers of the people, extirpers of tyrants, and heroes of that class, extend but over narrow spaces and last but for short times; whereas the work of the Inventor, though a thing of less pomp and show, is felt everywhere and lasts for ever.[12]

To derive maximum benefit from science, Bacon urged the founding of institutes to further scientific research. In fact, as early as 1560 there had been formed in Naples the *Accademia Secretorum Naturae*. In 1603 the *Accademia dei Lincei* appeared in Rome, and in 1661 the *Accademia del Cimento* in Florence. Meanwhile in England a scientific society that had been meeting sporadically under the name Philosophical or Invisible College was incorporated in 1662 as the Royal Society. In France a corresponding *Académie des Sciences* was founded by Louis XIV in 1666, and similar institutions followed in other lands. These bodies facilitated the growth of science, especially since most of them soon issued periodic publications which superseded the older method of correspondence between individuals.*

By far the most outstanding figure of this early stage of science was Sir Isaac Newton (1642–1727), who was born the year Galileo died. Of English yeoman stock, Newton worked his way through Cambridge, where he excelled in mathematics. During his long and busy life, he served as mathematics professor at Cambridge, master of the mint, and president of the Royal Society. Newton's contributions mark him as one of the very greatest figures in science, comparable to Euclid and Einstein.†

In mathematics Newton invented the infinitestimal calculus, established the binominal theorem, developed much of the theory of equations, and introduced literal indices. In mathematical physics he calculated tables by which the future position of the moon among the stars could be predicted—an achievement of the utmost value in navigation. He created hydrodynamics, including the theory of the propagation of waves, and made many improvements in hydrostatics. In optics he made important contributions toward the understanding of light beams, refraction of light, and the phenomenon of color. But it was in the field of physics that Newton did his most significant research. Here he built on Galileo, putting the grand copestone on the latter's work. Galileo had concerned himself largely with terrestrial motion; Newton discovered the laws pertaining to the universe itself.

Galileo's finding that moving bodies move uniformly in a straight line unless deflected by a definite force made it necessary to explain why the planets,

---

* See "The Royal Society," *EMM,* No. 44.
† See "Newton, the Man," *EMM,* No. 45.

194

instead of flying off in straight lines, tend to fall toward the sun—the result being their elliptical orbits—and why the moon similarly tends to fall toward the earth. One of Newton's friends has related how the great scientist perceived a clue to this puzzle while watching an apple fall in an orchard.

> After dinner, the weather being warm, we went into the garden and drank tea, under the shade of some apple trees, only he and myself. Amidst other discourse, he told me, he was just in the same situation, as when formerly, the notion of gravitation came into his mind. It was occasion'd by the fall of an apple, as he sat in a contemplative mood. Why should that apple always descend perpendicularly to the ground, thought he to himself. Why should it not go sideways or upwards, but constantly to the earths centre? Assuredly, the reason is, that the earth draws it. There must be a drawing power in matter: and the sum of the drawing power must be in the earths centre, not in any side of the earth. Therefore does this apple fall perpendicularly, or towards the centre. If matter thus draws matter, it must be in proportion of its quantity. Therefore the apple draws the earth, as well as the earth draws the apple. That there is a power, like that we here call gravity, which extends itself thro the universe.[13]

Newton developed this idea into the law of gravitation, which he presented with a wealth of mathematical evidence in his famous book, *Mathematical Principles of Natural Philosophy* (1687), commonly called, after its Latin title, the *Principia*. According to this law, "every particle of matter in the universe attracts every other particle with a force varying inversely as the square of the distance between them and directly proportional to the product of their masses."

Here was a sensational and revolutionary explanation that tore the veils from the heavens. Newton had discovered a fundamental, cosmic law, susceptible of mathematical proof and applicable to the minutest object as to the universe at large. Nature indeed appeared to be a gigantic mechanical contrivance, operating according to certain natural laws that could be ascertained by observation, experiment, measurement, and calculation. All branches of human knowledge seemed to be reducible to a few, simple, uniform laws that rational man could discover. Thus the analytical method of Newtonian physics now began to be applied to the entire field of thought and knowledge, to human society as well as to the physical universe. As Voltaire put it, "It would be very singular that all nature, all the planets, should obey eternal laws, and that there should be a little animal, five feet high, who, in contempt of these laws, could act as he pleased, solely according to his caprice." [14] The search for these eternal laws determining human affairs is the essence of the so-called Enlightenment that preceded the French Revolution.

III. Early Eighteenth Century Calm

No scientific discoveries comparable to those of the seventeenth century were made in the early eighteenth, the main interest being in the formulation of the social, political, and economic theories that comprised the Enlightenment. But noteworthy results were obtained in certain fields of science by the application of the new methodology of empirical research.

Experimentation was carried on, for example, with static electricity, and in 1746 two professors of the University of Leyden invented the so-called Leyden jar for the storage and sudden discharge of electric energy. Benjamin Franklin sensed the analogy between the electric spark in the jar and the lightning in the sky, and proved it with his kite experiment. In his typically practical manner Franklin in 1753 evolved the lightning conductor to prevent lightning strikes, which were particularly heavy and costly in the New World. He went further and evolved the first comprehensive theory of electricity, still used in practical circuitry today.

The early eighteenth century also witnessed a tremendous popular interest in nature, or, as it was called, natural history. Nature was regarded almost as a diety, as something of unlimited interest that could be forever studied and forever yield moral and factual instruction. Visible evidence of the natural history mania was to be found in the natural history cabinets that were assembled by all who could afford the investment of time and money. Minerals, insects, fossils, and other objects were assiduously collected and cataloged. The overseas lands with their exotic specimens stimulated interest in this field. Some collections reached magnificent proportions, like that of the wealthy Sir Hans Sloane (1660–1753), which served as the nucleus of the British Museum.

This collecting and cataloging led to the more basic formulations of systematic botany and zoology. A pioneer in these fields was John Ray (1627–1705), author of a *History of Plants,* a *History of Insects,* and *Synopses* of animals, birds, reptiles, and fishes. As regards plants, for example, Ray used all characteristics—fruit, flower, leaf, etc.—in order to group them according to their real natural affinities. In all his work Ray rejected magic, witchcraft, and all superstitious explanations of occurrences, holding to natural causes as revealed by observation. In his book *The Wisdom of God in the Works of Creation,* Ray abandoned the view, continually recurring from Augustine to Luther, that nature is irrelevant, if not hostile, to religion, its beauty a temptation, and its study a waste of time. "There is no occupation," wrote Ray, "more worthy and delightful than to contemplate the beauteous works of nature and honour the infinite wisdom and goodness of God." [15]

In systematic botany Ray was followed by the Swedish professor Linnaeus (Carl von Linné, 1707–1778), who worked out the first acceptable method of classifying plants and who also divided animals into such classes as mammals, birds, fish, and insects. After Linnaeus it became possible to study plants and animals systematically, and to develop methods of comparing structures and functions. Without such preliminary clarification the further development of biology would have proven impossible.

Another outstanding figure in natural history was the French nobleman Georges Louis Le Clerc, Comte de Buffon (1707–1788). In 1739 he was made keeper of the Jardin du Roi, now Jardin des Plantes, and he turned it into a great research institute where many of the famous scientists of France received their inspiration and training. He also wrote the monumental thirty-six-volume *Histoire Naturelle,* in which he sought to codify all available information on the natural sciences. Rejecting the ancient view that the earth is about 5,000 years old, Buffon saw it as beginning a molten mass, gradually cooling, and developing a crust on which plants and animals eventually appeared. His estimate that the process took some 100,000 years is a good bit lower than the 3 to 5 billion years set by modern science, but at least Buffon had set out on the right track. The French naturalist could not help noticing the striking zoological resemblances between man and the lower animals, and he ventured the remark, which he afterwards withdrew, that, were it not for the express statements of the Bible, one might be tempted to seek a common origin for the horse and the ass, the monkey and the man.

About this time also, great strides forward were being made in geography. The globe began to be explored and studied in a systematic fashion. In 1672 the French government sent Jean Richer to French Guiana "to make astronomical observations of utility to navigation." In 1698 the British Admiralty commissioned William Dampier to explore "New Holland," or Australia. Dampier not only recorded accurate observations on physical geography, flora, and fauna, but he also increased existing knowledge of hydrography, meteorology, and terrestrial magnetism. Interest in exploration steadily increased, and at the instance of the Royal Society, James Cook was sent out in 1768 to observe a transit of Venus at Tahiti in the South Pacific. Cook's later voyages, undertaken to find an antarctic continent, failed in the object, but gave other information of scientific value, as well as new knowledge of the coasts of Australia, New Zealand, and the Pacific Ocean. It might be noted that in his first voyage Captain Cook lost over a third of his men to disease, mostly scurvy. By the time of his later voyages medical knowledge had advanced, so that citrus fruits were added to the sailors' diet and the dread scourge ended.

IV. REVOLUTION IN CHEMISTRY, 1770–1850

The Industrial Revolution, which got under way in the last quarter of the eighteenth century, had a profound effect upon the economy of Britain, Europe, and, ultimately, the world. The Industrial Revolution also affected, and in return was affected by, the scientific revolution. It should be emphasized, however, that throughout the eighteenth century and in much of the nineteenth, the influence was pretty much in one direction only—from industry to science. Many of the inventions in the textile industry were made by illiterate mechanics who found an outlet for their native talents because of the favorable economic circumstances. During these early years science served industry in an auxiliary capacity. For example, when the increased production of cloth outstripped the available supply of natural vegetation dye, science was called upon to provide an artificial substitute. Likewise, when the transition from home to large-scale brewing led to disastrous failures, an appeal was made to science to find the cause and cure. This type of demand upon science contributed a good deal to its development. Proof of the intimate relationship between industry and science is to be found in the fact that most of the scientific advances in the late eighteenth and early nineteenth centuries came, not from Oxford, Cambridge, and London, as in the seventeenth century, but from Leeds, Glasgow, Edinburgh, Manchester, and especially Birmingham.

The one important exception is the case of the steam engine. Utilizing a combination of technical ingenuity and scientific knowledge, James Watt developed the engine to a reasonable level of efficiency when, in 1769, he used a separate condensing cylinder kept always cold, and soon after converted linear into rotary motion by a crankshaft. Had the relatively unlimited power of the steam engine not been available, the Industrial Revolution might well have petered out as a mere speed-up in textile manufacturing, as happened in China, where analogous technical advances were made centuries earlier.

The science that made the most progress during the first half of the nineteenth century was chemistry—partly because of its close association with the textile industry, which experienced such rapid growth during those decades. Chemistry dates back to the earliest stages of human civilization, to the rise of the arts of cooking and metal working, the collection of medicinal plants and extraction of drugs. From the beginning it was sidetracked by the search for means to transmute cheap metals into gold and to discover an *elixir vitae* that would cure all human ills. If these attempts were doomed to failure, they nonetheless disclosed many chemical substances and reactions. These were handed down to the Western Europeans, chiefly from China and the Moslem world.

The Greeks had contributed a theoretical system that conceived of four basic elements—earth, fire, air, and water—which could change one into another in circular fashion. During the eighteenth century most attention was concentrated on the problem of combustion—what happened to materials when they burned? Since they disappeared in smoke and flame and left ash, it was concluded that in every case something escaped during the process of burning. This something, for long called sulphur, was given the name of phlogiston, or the principle of fire. This concept dominated chemical thought until the study of gases revealed that air was a much more complex substance than hitherto imagined. Scientists were attracted to this problem by the "inflammable airs" of mines and marshes that could be collected in bladders and burned. As early as 1755, Joseph Black of Edinburgh succeeded in isolating carbon dioxide by heating limestone. Then in 1781 Henry Cavendish demonstrated that water is composed of two parts hydrogen to one part oxygen. Important advances were next made by Joseph Priestly (1733–1804), who isolated oxygen and demonstrated that it was this element that was used up in burning and breathing. He further showed that in sunlight green plants produced oxygen from the carbon dioxide that they absorbed. Thus he solved the problem of the carbon cycle created by the balance of oxygen-producing plants and carbon dioxide–producing animals.

The full implications of this work with gases were brought out by the great chemist, Antoine Laurent Lavoisier (1743–1794), who fell victim to the guillotine during the French Revolution. Lavoisier's classic experiment with oxidation is very simple. He heated mercury in a sealed jar with air, and found that he obtained mercuric oxide, and that the volume of the air had been reduced by a fifth, that is, by its oxygen component. Lavoisier then heated the mercuric oxide, and obtained once again mercury plus oxygen. Having weighed all his substances most carefully, he found that the weight lost or gained after each step was the addition or subtraction of oxygen in the burning process. Thus he was able to discard the traditional phlogiston theory and to replace it with his famous principle of balance.

> We may lay it down as an incontestable axiom, that, in all the operations of art and nature, nothing is created; an equal quantity of matter exists both before and after the experiment; the quality and quantity of the elements remain precisely the same; and nothing takes place beyond changes and modifications in the combination of these elements.[16]

Lavoisier thus reduced all the previously chaotic phenomena of chemistry to a law of combination of elements. His textbook, *Elementary Treatise on Chemistry,* which appeared in 1789, presented a totally new terminology that is still used. Lavoisier placed chemistry on a solid scientific footing, so that his successors knew what they were doing and where they were heading.

Outstanding among Lavoisier's successors were John Dalton (1766–1844), who formulated the atomic theory of matter (atoms of oxygen combine with atoms of hydrogen to form water), and Jons Jacob Berzelius (1779–1848), a Swedish chemist who isolated many new elements by applying electrical currents to compounds and dividing them electrically (metals tend toward the negative pole, nonmetals toward the positive). Berzelius also introduced the modern notation system into chemistry, thereby facilitating its work tremendously. He used the first letter or the first two letters of the Latin name for elements to serve as the symbol for them.

Another important advance in the nineteenth century was the advent of organic chemistry. Originally chemists believed that organic compounds—the hydrocarbons produced by living organisms—were somehow controlled by a "vital force." But this notion was dropped as chemists discovered that organic compounds could be synthesized. One of the first successes was achieved in 1828 by Friedrich Wöhler, who produced the organic substance urea found in urine. He did this from inorganic compounds by ordinary chemical processes and without the means of a kidney. His friend Justus von Liebig (1803–1873) did invaluable work in showing that the food that plants draw from the ground consists of nitrogen, phosphates, and salts. Thus he was able to prepare chemical compounds with which he enriched a waste patch and made it into a fertile garden. The way was clear for the growth of the great fertilizer industry.

Another major contribution to industry was made by the English chemist W. H. Perkin (1838–1907). While seeking a substitute for quinine, he accidentally discovered in 1856 the first artificial aniline dye, magenta. His discovery was neglected in Britain, where chemistry was still the pursuit of only a few amateurs and the chemical industry boasted of being "practical." But the more scientifically minded directors of German industry saw that Perkin's discovery could provide a valuable outlet for the hitherto waste products of coal tar from the gas industry. The research they subsidized led to the preparation of numerous synthetic dyes, which yielded enormous profits. By the time of World War I the Germans had the most advanced chemical industry in the world and a virtual monopoly of synthetic dyes.

Equally significant for industry was the work of the great French chemist Louis Pasteur (1822–1895). While at the University of Lille, he was called upon to help local distillers who were having trouble extracting alcohol from beets—the pulp sometimes unaccountably spoiled. Finding no chemical explanation, Pasteur examined the mash with a microscope and found it swarming with strange, elongated growths in contrast to the spherical globules in un-spoiled mash. By laboratory demonstration he showed how these harmful growths could be controlled and prevented from interfering with fermentation. This experience led Pasteur to further experiments that enabled him to dis-prove the traditional theory of spontaneous generation of life. In its place he propounded the now accepted doctrine of biogenesis—that life can come only from life. To demonstrate this he showed that by excluding the invisible microbes of the air, it is possible to keep animal and vegetable substances from putrefying. This later became the basis of the great canning industry.

In 1865 Pasteur was called to a more difficult task. The flourishing silk industry of France was threatened with extinction by a mysterious disease of the silkworms. When Pasteur began his investigations he did not know what a silkworm was, or that an ugly caterpillar later turned into a beautiful moth. But after a season's intensive research he found that the disease was caused by an organism that lived and grew inside the caterpillar itself. He speedily discovered a cure, and the silk industry was saved. Pasteur went on to pre-pare serums for anthrax in cattle and, most spectacularly, for rabies in man. Furthermore, his popularization of the germ theory of disease led to the adoption of sanitary precautions that made possible the control of age-old scourges—typhoid, diphtheria, cholera, the plague, and malaria. These medi-cal advances had profound repercussions, leading to a rapid increase of popu-lation, first in Europe and then throughout the world.

V. REVOLUTION IN BIOLOGY, 1850–1914

As Isaac Newton dominated seventeenth century science with his discovery of the laws governing the bodies of the universe, so Charles Darwin (1809–1882) dominated nineteenth, for he discovered the laws governing the evolution of man himself.*

The concept of evolution, however, was by no means new with Darwin: it had been propounded and applied in various fields of science. Jean de Lamarck (1744–1829) had earlier challenged the traditional notion of the immutable fixity of species created at one time and existing ever since. In-stead he envisioned a comprehensive evolution from worm to man, and sought to explain the process of evolution with the theory of acquired characteristics. Horses acquired their speedy legs from the need to run fast, giraffes their long necks from the need to feed on tall branches. And any such body changes are handed on by hereditary processes to be the starting point for the next generation.

Then came Charles Lyell with his classic three-volume *Principles of Geology* (1830–1833), which popularized the "uniformitarian" or evolu-tionary theory of the formation of the earth's surface. Hitherto it had been believed that the surface had been formed by past catastrophes such as volcanoes, earthquakes, and floods. The existence of seashells in high moun-tainous regions was conveniently attributed to Noah's flood. Lyell, by contrast, held that the present surface of the earth is the product of the operation during

* See "Darwin on Evolution," *EMM,* No. 46.

countless millennia of geologic forces such as glaciation, wind and water erosion, and freezing and thawing.

200 The concept of evolution was prominent at this time in the social sciences as well as the physical. From the 1840's, Karl Marx was writing that all social institutions were in constant process of change. Since the beginning of human history one type of society had given way to another—primitive tribalism to ancient slavery to feudal serfdom, to modern capitalism and, as he confidently predicted, to the socialism of the future. Much more influential was the all-embracing doctrine of evolution propounded by Herbert Spencer (1820–1903). He applied his doctrine to all things, material, biological, cultural, and social. In his *Progress, its Law and Cause,* published in 1857, Spencer wrote, "Whether it be in the development of Society, of Government, of Manufactures, of Commerce, of Language, Literature, Science, Art, this same evolution of the simple into the complex, through successive differentiations, holds throughout." [17]

This was the atmosphere in which Darwin worked out his epoch-making theories. Darwin came from a family in which scientific ability had already appeared in two generations (and has since appeared in two more). He attended Cambridge University where he spent less time on his studies than on collecting and studying animals and insects. A professor who recognized his potentialities recommended him for an unsalaried post as naturalist on the government ship *Beagle,* which was starting on a scientific expedition around the world. During this voyage, which lasted from 1831 to 1836, Darwin was impressed by the numerous variations that he observed in individual species. On the isolated Galapagos Islands, for example, he found species that obviously had come from ancestors on the mainland but had somehow grown different. This eliminated the old theory of the fixity of species, but left unanswered the question of how and why variation occurred.

Two years after his return from the expedition, he derived a clue from the book by Thomas Malthus propounding the theory that the human race tends to outrun its means of subsistence unless the redundant individuals are eliminated.

> In October 1838 I happened to read for amusement Malthus on Population, and being well prepared to appreciate the struggle for existence which everywhere goes on from long continued observation of the habits of animals and plants, it at once struck me that under these circumstances favourable variations would tend to be preserved, and unfavourable ones to be destroyed. The result of this would be the formation of new species. Here then I had a theory by which to work.[18]

Darwin developed this theory with his customary caution and painstaking care. In 1839 he began a draft; three years later it was still only a 35-page abstract in pencil. By 1844 he had expanded it to a 230-page study. In that year he wrote to a friend,

> . . . I have read heaps of agricultural and horticultural books and have never ceased collecting facts. At last gleams of light have come, and I am almost convinced (quite contrary to the opinion I started with)

that species are not (it is like confessing a murder) immutable. Heaven
forfend me from Lamarck nonsense of a "tendency to progression,"
"adaptations from the slow willing of animals." But the conclusions I am
led to are not widely different from his; though the means of change
are wholly so. I think I have found out (here's presumption!) the simple
way by which species become exquisitely adapted to various ends.[19]

But still Darwin could not bring himself to publish his findings. He continued
to gather further evidence until 1858, when he received a staggering letter
from another naturalist, Alfred Russell Wallace (1823–1913). Wallace had
spent many years in Brazil and in the Dutch East Indies, where he had absorbed a vast store of zoological knowledge. In February, 1858, as he lay
suffering from malaria at Ternate in the Moluccas, his mind turned to Malthus
whom he also had read, and suddenly there flashed upon him the idea of
the survival of the fittest as the mechanism by which evolution was effected.
Being of an entirely different temperament from Darwin, he immediately put
his thoughts to paper. The same evening, while still racked with fever, he
drafted his new theory. On two succeeding evenings he elaborated upon it,
and then he sent it to Darwin, with whom he had frequently corresponded.

Darwin received the manuscript in June, 1858, and was stupefied to read
a summary of what he already had written. "I never saw a more striking
coincidence," he wrote to Charles Lyell; "if Wallace had my manuscript
sketch written out in 1842, he could not have made a better short abstract!
Even his terms now stand as heads of my chapters." [20] Darwin no longer
hesitated to make public his researches. He read his own essay and that of
Wallace before a learned society in London on July 1, 1858, and the so-called
Darwinian hypothesis of evolution was launched. Darwin set forth his ideas
at greater length in his chief book, *On the Origin of Species by Means of
Natural Selection, or the Preservation of Favoured Races in the Struggle
for Life,* published in 1859.

Darwin's central thesis—his doctrine of evolution—was that animal and
vegetable species in their present diverse forms are not immutably fixed as
results of separate special acts of creation but are different and changing
natural outcomes of a common original source. Darwin believed that the
chief manner in which variation took place was by "natural selection." He
defined this process as follows:

> As many more individuals of each species are born than can possibly
> survive, and as, consequently, there is a frequently recurring struggle for
> existence, it follows that any being, if it vary however slightly in any
> manner profitable to itself, under the complex and sometimes varying
> conditions of life, will have a better chance of surviving, and thus be
> *naturally selected*. From the strong principle of inheritance, any selected
> variety will tend to propagate its new and modified form.[21]

It may be hard to conceive of all the variety in nature as being the product
of what appears to be such an inordinately slow process of change as that
afforded by "natural selection." Yet statistical calculations show that even
if a mutation resulted in only a one per cent better chance of survival, it

202

would establish itself in half the individuals of a species in a hundred generations. In other words, if a hundred and one individuals with this mutation
survived for every hundred without it, it would spread through the species in
what is, biologically speaking, a short time. A specific example of how
"natural selection" operates is provided by a small moth which appears in
light and dark colorations. It has been noticed that the light variety is about
six times more common in light birch forests than the *dark* variety, and,
conversely, that the dark variety is sixteen times commoner in dark pine
forests than the light variety. Evidence of the functioning of "natural selection"
has been found in the coloration of the moth wings left by the birds in the
two types of forests.

Darwin's theories have been modified in details on the basis of later research, but virtually all scientists now accept the essentials of the doctrine.
On July 1, 1958, during the centennial celebration of Darwin's publication
of his essay, a distinguished British scientist, Sir Gavin de Beer, paid the
following tribute: "The fact of evolution is now universally accepted by all
competent to express an opinion, and its mechanism has been in principle,
explained. So soundly was the theory of natural selection grounded that
modern work does nothing but confirm it, even if new formulations are
required as knowledge increases." [22]

Darwin's theory was far from generally accepted during his lifetime, however. It was reinforced, it is true, by the researches and writings of several
distinguished scientists of the period. The geologist, Charles Lyell, accepted
Darwinism in his *Antiquity of Man,* published in 1863. Two leading botanists
also became "Darwinians"—Sir Joseph Hooker, director of the Kew Gardens
in England, and Asa Gray, professor at Harvard University. And among the
most enthusiastic champions of Darwinism were two famous biologists, the
German Ernst Haeckel, and the Englishman Thomas Huxley, who referred
to himself as "Darwin's bulldog."

On the other hand, there was bitter opposition in certain quarters, particularly amongst the churchmen. This was understandable, because just as
the Copernican system of astronomy had deposed the earth from its central
place in the universe, so Darwinism seemed to dethrone man from his
central place in the history of the earth. Such was the natural conclusion of
the churchmen when Darwin published another book, *The Descent of Man,*
in 1871. In this work he marshaled the evidence that man is related to all
animal life, and concluded that "He who is not content to look, like a savage,
at the phenomena of nature as disconnected, cannot any longer believe that
man is the work of a separate act of creation." [23] Darwin, in other words,
was denying the act of divine creation. He was denounced, with less than fair-
ness, for undermining human dignity, morality, and religion, and for saying
that men came from monkeys. Benjamin Disraeli solemnly declared that if it
were a choice between apes and angels, he was on the side of the angels.

Despite this hostile reception in religious and other circles, Darwinism had
profound repercussions upon Western society. The basic reason is that its
emphasis on survival of the fittest and struggle for survival fitted in admirably
with the temper of the times. In politics, for example, this was the period
when Bismarck was unifying Germany by blood and iron. His nationalistic
admirers in all countries believed that Darwinism offered them support and

WESTERN MAN'S KNOWLEDGE OF THE GLOBE, A.D.1 to 1800

justification. They held that in politics, as in nature, the strongest are victorious, and that warlike qualities decide who will win in the international "struggle for survival." In economic life this was the period of free enterprise and rugged individualism. The upper and middle classes, comfortable and contented, stoutly opposed any state intervention for the promotion of greater social equality. They argued that they deserved their blessings and prosperity because they had proven themselves "fitter" than the shiftless poor, and, furthermore, the absorption of smaller concerns by big business was a part of the "struggle for survival." The late nineteenth century was also the golden age of colonial expansion, and Darwinism was used to justify imperialism. It was argued that colonies were necessary for the prosperity and survival of a Great Power, and also that native peoples, judged in terms of worldly success, were weak, inferior, and in need of the protection and guidance of the superior and stronger Europeans.

This application of Darwin's theories to the social scene is known as Social Darwinism.* Darwin himself had never dreamt, let alone intended, that his findings would be exploited in this fashion. But the fact remains that they were, and the reason is that they seemed to offer scientific buttressing to the materialism, or *Realpolitik,* that came over Europe at this time from other causes. Darwinism, in short, fitted in conveniently with Kipling's dictum

> That they should take who have the power
> And they should keep who can.

Another English writer, Hilaire Belloc, expressed the same sentiment in reference to the position of the Europeans in Africa:

> Whatever happens we have got
> The Maxim gun, and they have not.

VI. CONCLUSION

As the nineteenth century passed, science became an increasingly important part of Western society. At the beginning of the century science still was on the periphery of economic and social life. But by the end it was making basic contributions to the old-established industries, it was creating entirely new industries, and it was affecting profoundly the way of thinking as well as the way of living of Western man. Furthermore, this metamorphosis wrought by the scientific revolution affected the entire world in myriad ways, direct and indirect. It made Europe's hegemony over the globe technologically possible, and it determined to a large extent the nature and effects of this hegemony. Also it provided the basis for the West's intellectual predominance in the nineteenth century. European art or religion or philosophy did not greatly affect non-Western peoples because they had made comparable contributions in these fields. But there was no such parity in science and technology. Only the West had mastered the secrets of nature and had exploited them for the material advancement of mankind. This was an undeniable and persuasive fact. Non-Westerners no longer looked down upon

---

* See "Social Darwinism," *EMM,* No. 47.

204

Europeans as uncouth barbarians who happened to have a certain superiority in sailing ships and firearms. Reluctantly they recognized the significance of Europe's scientific revolution.* And today the primary aim of former colonial peoples is to experience for themselves this unique revolution which they missed because of fortuitous historical circumstances. Even before 1914 a native nationalist leader in far-off Uzbekistan exhorted his people to turn to science as the only means for regaining their freedom.

> Science is the cause of the flourishing of a government. Science is the cause of the progress of a people. Science is that very potent means, the existence of which led the savage Americans to their present high status and power and whose . . . absence brought the Persians to their present lowly state and humiliation. Science is the means which made the British masters of India, Egypt, Baluchistan and parts of Arabia, and the Russians the rulers of the Tatar, Kirghiz, Turkestan and Caucausian Moslems. Finally, science is the means, which gave over the broad Turkish dominions into the hands of the foreigners and unfurled the three-colored flag of France over the faithful in Fez. . . .
>
> If you study contemporary science, you will be in a position to construct telegraphs, build railroads, transport hundreds of thousands of troops from one end of the earth to the other in twenty days, . . . to comprehend the secret meaning of the Koran, to prepare rifles and cannon for the defense of Islam, to liberate the fatherland from the hands of the foreigners . . . to free our nation from the yoke of the infidel and to restore Islam to its earlier heights.[24]

The distinguished British historian Herbert Butterfield has summarized this global significance of the scientific revolution as follows:

> There does not seem to be any sign that the ancient world, before its heritage had been dispersed, was moving towards anything like the scientific revolution, or that the Byzantine Empire, in spite of the continuity of its classical tradition, would ever have taken hold of ancient thought and so remoulded it by a great transforming power. The scientific revolution, we must regard, therefore, as a creative product of the West—depending on a complicated set of conditions which existed only in western Europe, depending partly also perhaps on a certain dynamic quality in the life and the history of this half of the continent. And not only was a new factor introduced into history at this time amongst other factors, but it proved to be so capable of growth, and so many-sided in its operations, that it consciously assumed a directing role from the very first, and, so to speak, began to take control of the other factors—just as Christianity in the middle ages had come to preside over everything else, percolating into every corner of life and thought. And when we speak of Western civilization being carried to an oriental country like Japan in recent generations, we do not mean Graeco-Roman philosophy and humanist ideals, we do not mean the Christianising of Japan, we mean the science, the modes of thought and all that apparatus of civilisation which

* See "Western Science and Technology in the Near East," EMM, No. 48.

were beginning to change the face of the West in the latter half of the seventeenth century.[25]

SUGGESTED READING

An excellent and useful bibliography is provided by M. Boas, *History of Science* (Washington: Service Center for Teachers of History, 1958), No. 13. Excellent paperback surveys of the entire history of science are now available, especially W. C. Dampier, *A Shorter History of Science* (New York: Harcourt, 1957; a Meridian Book); A. R. and M. B. Hall, *A Brief History of Science* (New York: New Am. Lib., 1964; a Signet Science Library Book); and F. S. Taylor, *A Short History of Science and Scientific Thought* (New York: Norton, 1949; paperback ed., 1963).

For the modern period, there is H. T. Pledge, *Science Since 1500* (New York: Philosophical Library, 1947). See also the useful collection by W. C. Dampier Whetham and M. Dampier, *Cambridge Readings in the Literature of Science* (London: Cambridge Univ., 1928). The Marxist scientist J. D. Bernal has written a comprehensive survey *Science in History* (London: Watts, 1954), which is valuable for its stress on the relationships between scientific and other developments. Two excellent books analyze the critical phase of the scientific revolution prior to the nineteenth century: H. Butterfield, *The Origins of Modern Science, 1300–1800* (London: Bell, 1957) and A. R. Hall, *The Scientific Revolution, 1500–1800* (Boston: Beacon, 1954). The literary impact of science is described by M. Nicolson, *Science and Imagination* (Ithaca: Cornell Univ., 1956).

Numerous excellent biographies of outstanding scientists are available, among the best being Angus Armitage, *Copernicus: The Father of Modern Astronomy* (New York: Yoseloff, 1957); F. Sherwood Taylor, *Galileo and the Freedom of Thought* (London: Watts 1938); B. Farrington, *Francis Bacon: Philosopher of Industrial Science* (New York: Abelard, 1949); E. S. Haldane, *Descartes: His Life and Times* (New York: Dutton, 1905); E. N. da C. Andrade, *Sir Isaac Newton* (London: Collins, 1954); P. B. Sears, *Charles Darwin* (New York: Scribner, 1950); and Loren Eiseley, *Darwin's Century* (New York: Doubleday, 1958).

Chapter 11

*We find ourselves in a world of swift movement and jerky
retirement; a world thronged as never before with
people hustling by each other on the sidewalks of huge
cities, people brooding or daydreaming in uneasy
seclusion in the cells of high apartment buildings; a
world of streamlined automobiles, railway cars, and
airplanes; sprayed by a din from microphones, bombarded by newspaper headlines and changing scenes of
motion pictures and of television. This world is part of
an economic regime unique in history—the regime of
industrial civilization—now shared by Russians, Americans, and Japanese, even to some extent by Chinese and
Indians, as well as by the peoples of Western Europe.*

JOHN U. NEF

The Industrial Revolution

The material culture of mankind has changed more in the
past two hundred years than it did in the preceding five thousand. In
the eighteenth century man was living in essentially the same manner
as the ancient Egyptians and Mesopotamians. He was still using the
same materials to erect his buildings, the same animals to transport
himself and his belongings, the same sails and oars to propel his
ships, the same textiles to fashion his clothes, and the same candles
and torches to provide light. But today metals and plastics supplement stone and wood; the railroad, the automobile, and the airplane
have replaced the oxen, the horse, and the donkey; steam, diesel,
and atom power drive ships in place of wind and manpower; a host of
synthetic fabrics compete with the traditional cottons, woolens, and
linens; and electricity has eclipsed the candle and has become a source
of power available for a multitude of duties at the flick of a switch.

The origins of this epochal transformation are to be found
partly in the scientific revolution noted in the preceding chapter, and
partly in the so-called Industrial Revolution. The reason for the
qualifying "so-called" is that there has been much uneasiness over
the use of the term *Industrial Revolution*.* It has been pointed out
that, in certain respects, the Industrial Revolution had gotten under

* See "The Industrial Revolution Reconsidered," *EMM*, No. 49.

way before the eighteenth century, and that, for all practical purposes, it has continued to the present day. Obviously, then, this was not a revolution in the sense of a spectacular change that began and ended suddenly.

Yet the fact remains that during the 1780's a breakthrough did occur in productivity, or, as economists now put it, there was "a take-off into self-sustained growth." More specifically, there was created a mechanized factory system that produced goods in such vast quantities and at such rapidly diminishing cost as to be no longer dependent on existing demand but to create its own demand. An example of this now common, but hitherto un-precedented, phenomenon, is the automobile industry. It was not the demand for automobiles existing at the turn of the century that created the giant automobile industry of today, but rather the capacity to build the cheap model T Ford which stimulated the modern mass demand for them.

This Industrial Revolution is of prime importance for world history because it provided the economic and military basis for Europe's world hegemony in the nineteenth century, as well as the main goal for the underdeveloped world in the twentieth century. The aim of every new country today, having successfully "taken off" in the sense of independent political existence, is likewise to "take off" into a corresponding independent economic existence.

I. WHY THE INDUSTRIAL REVOLUTION BEGAN WHEN IT DID

The first question that arises in considering the Industrial Revolution has to do with its timing. Why did it occur in the late eighteenth century rather than a hundred or a thousand years earlier? The answer is to be found in large part in the remarkable economic growth of Europe following the great expansion overseas. This growth, which we noted earlier, was so pronounced that it is commonly referred to as the Commercial Revolution.

The Commercial Revolution was characterized in the first place by a change in the articles of world trade. Before the sixteenth century the most important items were spices from East to West, and bullion in the opposite direction. But gradually new overseas products became staples of consumption in Europe and grew in commercial importance. These included new beverages (cocoa, tea, and coffee), new dyes (indigo, cochineal, and brazilwood), new flavors (allspice and vanilla), and new foodstuffs (guinea fowl and turkeys, and a greatly increased supply of Newfoundland cod). The other main feature of the Commercial Revolution was the marked increase in the volume of trade. Between 1715 and 1787 French imports from overseas territories increased tenfold, and exports increased between seven- and eightfold. England's trade grew almost as spectacularly—in the period from 1698 to 1775 both imports and exports rose between 500 and 600 per cent. Europe's general trade was growing, but colonial trade was accounting for a larger and larger portion of it. In 1698, for example, about 15 per cent of England's seaborne trade was with her colonies, but by 1775 this figure had risen to 33 per cent. Furthermore, the re-export of colonial goods was responsible for much of the increase of France's and England's trade with other European countries.

This Commercial Revolution contributed to the Industrial Revolution in several important respects. First, it provided large and expanding markets for

European industries, particularly those producing textiles, firearms, hardware, ships, and ships accessories, including lumber, rope, sails, anchors, pulleys, and nautical instruments. The great English industrial center of Birmingham rose to prominence by providing a variety of products for the colonies: "axes for India and tomahawks for the natives of North America; and to Cuba and the Brazils chains, handcuffs, and iron collars for the poor slaves. . . . In the primeval forests of America the Birmingham axe struck down the old trees; the cattle pastures of Australia rang with the sound of Birmingham bells; in East India and the West they tended the fields of sugar cane with Birmingham hoes." [1]

To meet the demands of these new markets, industries had to improve their organization and technology. A good example is afforded by the nail industry of the English Midlands. In response to the mounting need for nails in the colonies, it developed rolling and slitting mills that mechanized and increased output. The industry also evolved a putting-out system in which nail ironmongers, or ironmasters, sent out bundles of nailrod to be worked up by nailers in their homes and returned for sale. By 1775, the industry was using 10,000 tons of iron annually, and employing some 10,000 people. A contemporary observer remarked that anyone "who knew the quantity of nails required in America would be surprised unless he saw the immense number of houses built of wood in that country, and then he would rather be surprised where the nails were made that were necessary for the erection of so many wooden houses." [2]

The steps by which the nail industry adapted itself to the New World markets are quite significant. In the first place it made technological advances that, together with those by other industries, provided a solid mechanical basis for the Industrial Revolution. Thus, the pioneers of the Industrial Revolution started off with the assistance of numerous recently developed mechanical contraptions, including printing presses, hand looms, spinning wheels, silk-throwing machinery, mining equipment, smelting furnaces, an automatic ribbon loom, and the stocking frame. The putting-out system employed by the nail industry, as well as other industries, was fundamentally different from the traditional craft guild arrangement in which the same man produced a commodity and sold it to the consumer at a fixed profit. Now a middleman— the capitalist entrepreneur—intervened between the producer and the consumer. He employed his capital to buy raw material which he "put out" to be processed on a piece-rate basis by artisans who were not guild members. Then he picked up the finished product and sold it to the consumer for as much profit as possible. Producers and consumers were now separated by the new entrepreneur, whose objective—in contrast to the fixed prices and profits of the guilds—was to buy cheap, sell dear, and make the maximum profit. It might be added that the putting-out system is also sometimes referred to as the domestic system, the reason being that the artisans normally did the piece work in their own homes, in contrast to the guildsmen who worked in the master's shop.

In any case, the significance of this putting-out system is that it was not bound by the innumerable guild restrictions and thus made possible a great increase in industrial output. Some of the entrepreneurs found it convenient and profitable to bring their craftsmen together under one roof and provide them with tools as well as raw materials. A poem tells of Jack of Newbury who in the early sixteenth century set up his own building, installed over two hundred looms, and employed some six hundred men, women, and children to work them.

> Within one room being large and long
> There stood two hundred looms full strong:
> Two hundred men the truth is so
> Wrought in these looms all in a row.
> By every one a pretty boy
> Sate making quills with mickle joy.
> And in another place hard by,
> A hundred women merrily
> Were carding hard with joyful cheer
> Who singing sate with voices clear.
> And in a chamber close beside,
> Two hundred maidens did abide,
> In petticoats of Stammell red,
> And milk-white kerchers on their head. . . .
> Those pretty maids did never lin
> But in that place all day did spin. . . .
> Then in another room came they
> Where children were in poor array:
> And everyone sate picking wool,
> The finest from the coarse to cull. . . .
> Within another place likewise
> Full fifty proper men he spies,
> And these were shearmen every one. . . .
> And hard by them there did remain
> Full fourscore rowers taking pain.
> A dye-house likewise had he then,
> Wherein he kept full forty men:
> And likewise in his fulling mill
> Full twenty persons kept he still.[3]

Jack and his fellow entrepreneurs in other industries developed both the putting-out system and the factory system. Only labor-saving power machinery was needed to launch the Industrial Revolution.

The Commercial Revolution also contributed the large amounts of capital necessary to finance the construction of factories and machines for the Industrial Revolution. The capital, in the form of profits, poured into Europe from all parts of the world. In Siberia, the Russians sold iron pots to the natives in return for enough pelts to fill the pots. In North America, the price the Hudson's Bay Company traders charged the Indians for a rifle was a pile of beaver skins its height. In Mexico and Peru, the Spaniards used native labor to dig out vast stores of silver. On one of his privateering expeditions against the Spaniards, Drake made a profit of 4,700 per cent on his investment. Queen Elizabeth, who was given shares in return for providing some ships, netted some £250,000. Some of this money she invested in the

Levant Company, whose profits in turn were used for the establishment of the East India Company which won the Indian Empire for Britain. "Indeed," states John Maynard Keynes, "the booty brought back by Drake in the *Golden Hind* may fairly be considered the fountain and origin of British Foreign Investment." [4] Africa also yielded great profits for European adventurers in the form of the hundreds of thousands of slaves seized for labor in New World plantations. Indeed, Bristol was the second city of England during the first three-quarters of the eighteenth century because it was the center of the slave and sugar trades. "There is not," wrote a local analyst, "a brick in the city but what is cemented with the blood of a slave. Sumptuous mansions, luxurious living, liveried menials, were the produce of the wealth made from the sufferings and groans of the slaves bought and sold by the Bristol merchants." [5] More profitable than the slave trade itself were the sugar plantations worked by slave labor. The West Indian sugar planters were the tycoons of the period, rivaled only by the "nabobs" who had made their fortunes in India. These individuals were spectacular in their lavish expenditures, but more significant in the long run were the lucrative earnings of the several East India Companies, West India Companies, Levant Companies, Africa Companies, and assorted others, including the Muscovy Company, the Hudson's Bay Company, and the various land settlement companies in the Americas.

It was this same Commercial Revolution that produced the dynamic and expansive type of society known as capitalism, where "the desire for profits is the driving motive and . . . large accumulations of capital are employed to make profits by various elaborate and often indirect methods." [6] During the Middle Ages it had been considered wrong for a man to try to earn more money than was necessary to keep him comfortably in the station of life to which he was born. But with the coming of the Commercial Revolution, the acquisitive spirit manifested itself in all fields of economic enterprise. In commerce the merchant guilds with their fixed prices and fixed profits were replaced by the joint stock companies seeking to make the highest profit possible for their shareholders. In industry the craft guilds with their numerous regulations concerning quality and mode of production and profits were swept away by the entrepreneurs with their putting-out system. In finance the injunctions of the medieval church against usury were ignored by large banking houses which loaned money, sold bills of exchange, and offered numerous other financial services.

All these manifestations were nascent in the late Middle Ages, but the Commercial Revolution stimulated them immensely. After 1500 the institutions and spirit of capitalism developed rapidly. Capitalism in those centuries was, of course, quite different from the capitalism of today. Because commercial enterprise was organized to a greater degree along capitalist lines than either industry or agriculture, the earlier form is commonly known as commercial capitalism. But whatever name is given to the economic system prevailing in Europe between the sixteenth and eighteenth centuries, the important point is that it was dynamic and expansive. The capitalist, in his unceasing drive for profits, extended his operations to the four corners of the globe. In doing so he contributed in many ways to the coming of the Industrial

Revolution and also to the establishment of European economic hegemony over the world.

II. WHY THE INDUSTRIAL REVOLUTION BEGAN WHERE IT DID

The Industrial Revolution got under way first in England. This is a historical fact of the utmost significance, for it explains in large part England's primary role in world affairs in the nineteenth century. Consequently, the question of why the Industrial Revolution began where it did is of much more than academic interest.*

The problem may be simplified by eliminating those countries that could not, for one reason or another, have generated the Industrial Revolution. Italy at one time had been an economic leader but had dropped behind with the Discoveries and the shift of the main trade routes from the Mediterranean to the Atlantic. Spain had been economically predominant in the sixteenth century but had then lost out to the northwestern states for various reasons already noted. Holland had enjoyed her Golden Age in the seventeenth century, but she lacked the raw materials, labor resources, and water power necessary for machine production. The various countries of Central and Eastern Europe had been little affected by the Commerical Revolution and hence did not develop the technical skills, the trade markets, and the capital reserves needed for industrialization.

This leaves only France and Britain as possible leaders, and of the two, England had certain advantages that enabled her to forge far ahead of her rival. In commerce, for example, the two countries were about equal in 1763, or, if anything, France was somewhat in the lead. But France had a population three times that of England. France also lost ground in foreign trade when she was driven out of Canada and India in 1763. Furthermore, the blockade of the British fleet during the Revolutionary and Napoleonic Wars reduced French commerce to about half its 1788 value, and the loss was not restored until 1825.

Another important advantage enjoyed by Britain is that she had taken an early lead in the basic coal and iron industries. Because her forest reserves were being depleted, Britain early began using coal for fuel and for smelting iron. By the time of the French Revolution in 1789, Britain was producing about 10 million tons of coal per year, while France was producing 700,000 tons. A contemporary poet sensed the significance of this unlimited source of power for English industry when he wrote,

> England's a perfect World! has Indies too!
> Correct your Maps! New-castle is Peru.[7]

England also pioneered in the development of the blast furnace which, in contrast to the old forges, could mass-produce iron. In 1780 Britain's iron output had been a third that of France; by 1840, it was three times more. All this meant that Britain was pushing ahead in the production of goods of mass

---

* See "England's Leadership in Industrialization," EMM, No. 50.

consumption for which there was a large and steady demand, whereas France specialized more in luxury commodities of limited and fluctuating demand. Perhaps Voltaire had this in mind when he wrote in 1735, "In truth we are the whipped cream of Europe." [8]

England also had more fluid capital available for the financing of the Industrial Revolution. More profits from commerce poured into England than into any other country. English court and military expenditures were less than French, so that English taxation was lighter and English government finances were in better condition. Furthermore, banking developed earlier and more efficiently in England, providing pooled funds for individual and corporate enterprise. By the end of the seventeenth century, London was competing with Amsterdam as the money-lending center of the world, while the London stock exchange which was founded in 1698 did not have its official counterpart in Paris until 1724.

Noteworthy also is the impressive concentration of entrepreneurial talent in England. This is to be explained in part by the outstanding contributions of Nonconformists like the Darbys in the iron industry, Cookworthy in pottery, the Brights in cotton milling and in politics, and Dalton and Eddington in science. Freedom from convention and stress on personal responsibility produced a disproportionate quota of experimenters and inventers among the Nonconformists, while their frugality led them to plow profits back into business rather than to squander for luxurious living. The influence of the Nonconformists in England was enhanced by the influx of coreligionists from the continent. With the revocation of the Edict of Nantes in 1685, for example, France lost considerable entrepreneurial talent to England, especially in the textile industry.

Britain also had the advantage of a mobile and plentiful supply of labor made available by the earlier disintegration of the guilds and by the enclosing of the traditional strips of farmland. The passing of the guilds, with their manifold restrictions, made it easier to introduce both the putting-out system and the factories with power machinery. The land enclosures began in the sixteenth century and continued for three centuries, reaching their height in the late eighteenth and early nineteenth centuries. The yeomen frequently were forced to sell out, because the enclosing of common and of waste lands left them no land for grazing and for fuel. The earlier enclosures were impelled by the rising price of wool, so that the land was used mostly for grazing. In the later period the need to grow foodstuffs for the burgeoning cities was more important, so the enclosed land was cultivated according to the most up-to-date and efficient methods. These included crop rotation in place of the wasteful old system of allowing fields to lie fallow, development of superior seeds, improvement of cattle by scientific breeding, and development of some agricultural machinery, including a horse-driven hoeing machine and an automatic drill for planting seeds.

These innovations could not have been effected under the strip system of farming inherited from the Middle Ages. Now, with the enclosures, it was possible to implement them, and it was very profitable to do so. The market for agricultural products was expanding, and the new techniques made it possible to increase output remarkably. Viscount Townshend, known as Turnip Townshend because of his devotion to turnips for crop rotation purposes, increased the yield of wheat on his estates from 10 to 24 bushels per acre. Robert Bakewell's methods of scientific breeding made it possible, between 1710 and 1795, to increase the average weight of calves from 50 to 148 pounds, of beeves from 370 to 800, of sheep from 28 to 80, and of lambs from 18 to 50. Thus it is apparent that from the economic viewpoint, the enclosures made possible a long step forward.

But from the social viewpoint the story was quite different. Between 1714 and 1820, over 6 million acres of land were enclosed in England. This meant serious dislocation and distress. The poor peasants lost part or all of their land, and were forced to become tenants or day laborers, or else to seek employment in the cities. Socially minded individuals were appalled by this wholesale uprooting of England's yeomanry and spoke up against it. The process of enclosing the land was unsettling and unpleasant, but so far as the Industrial Revolution was concerned it fulfilled two essential functions—it provided labor for the factories and food for the cities. For this reason the enclosures may be considered a prerequisite to England's industrial supremacy in the nineteenth century. Enclosures did occur in certain other European countries, but to a much lesser extent. In France, for example, the French Revolution provided the peasants with more land, and thereby increased their attachment to their birthplaces and their unwillingness to pack up and move.

III. INDUSTRIAL REVOLUTION: FIRST STAGE, 1770–1870

The Industrial Revolution cannot be attributed merely to the genius of a small group of inventors. Genius doubtless played a part, but more significant was the combination of favorable forces operating in late eighteenth century England. Inventors seldom invent except under the stimulus of strong demand. Many of the principles on which the new inventions were based were known centuries before the Industrial Revolution, but they were not applied to industry because the incentive was lacking. This was the case, for example, with steam power. It was known, and even applied, in Hellenistic Egypt, but merely to open and close temple doors. In England, however, a new source of power was urgently needed to pump water out of mines and to turn the wheels of the new machinery. The result was a series of inventions and improvements until finally a commercially feasible steam engine was developed.

This pattern of demand leading to invention is plainly evident in the development of the cotton industry.* It was the first to be mechanized because cotton goods, which were originally imported from India, had become exceedingly popular with the British public. In fact, they were used so widely that the old and powerful woolen interests secured the passage of a law in 1700 prohibiting the importation of cotton cloth or goods. The law, however, did not ban the manufacture of cotton cloth. This created a unique opportunity for local industry, and enterprising middlemen soon were exploiting it to the hilt. The problem was how to speed up the spinning and weaving sufficiently to meet the demand of the large and protected home market. The tools in use at that time were basically the same as those employed by the Romans.

* See "Mechanization of the English Cotton Industry," *EMM,* No. 51.

The spinning jenny.

The only exception was John Kay's "flying shuttle" patented in 1733—a simple spring device that speeded up the carrying of the weft back and forth across the warp. But this was insufficient, so a deliberate and coordinated campaign was undertaken to encourage inventions that speeded production. In 1754 there was founded in London the Society for the Encouragement of Arts, Manufacture and Commerce, and this society gave money, medals, and other rewards for specified achievements. In 1760, for example, it offered a prize for a spinning machine, explaining that "manufacturers of woolen, linen, and cotton find it extremely difficult in the summer season, when the spinners are at harvest work, to procure a sufficient number of hands." [9]

These favorable circumstances induced a series of inventions that made possible the complete mechanization of the cotton industry by 1830. Outstanding were Richard Arkwright's water frame (1769), which spun fine strong yarn between rollers, James Hargreaves' spinning jenny (1770), on which one person could spin eight, then sixteen, and finally over a hundred threads of yarn at once, and Samuel Crompton's spinning mule (1779), so called because it combined features of the water frame and of the jenny. All these new spinning machines soon were producing far more thread than could be handled by the weavers. A clergyman, Edmund Cartwright, sought to redress the balance by patenting in 1785 a power loom operated first by horses and after 1789 by steam.* The contraption was clumsy and proved commercially unprofitable. But after two decades of improvement the most serious defects were remedied. By the 1820's the power loom had largely supplanted the handweavers in the cotton industry.

* See "Invention of the Power Loom," *EMM*, No. 52.

214

Just as inventions in spinning led to balancing inventions in weaving, so inventions in one industry stimulated balancing inventions in others. The new cotton machines created a demand for more plentiful and reliable power than that provided by the traditional waterwheels and horses. A primitive steam engine had been built by Thomas Newcomen about 1702, and was widely used to pump water out of coal mines. But it consumed so much fuel in proportion to power delivered that it was economically feasible only in the coal fields themselves. In 1763 James Watt, a technician at the University of Glasgow, began to make improvements on Newcomen's engine. He formed a business partnership with a manufacturer, Matthew Boulton, who financed the rather costly experiments and preliminary models. The enterprise proved eminently successful, and by 1800, when Watt's basic patent expired, some 500 Boulton and Watt engines were in service. Thirty-eight per cent were engaged in pumping water, and the remainder in supplying rotary power for textile mills, iron furnaces, flour mills, and other industries.

The historical significance of the steam engine can scarcely be exaggerated. It provided a means for harnessing and utilizing heat energy to furnish driving power for machines. Thus, it ended man's age-old dependance on animal, wind, and water power. A vast new source of energy now was available, and before long man was also to tap the other fossil fuels locked up in the earth —namely, oil and gas. In this manner began the trend that has led to the present situation in which Western Europe has 11.5, and North America has 29, times as much energy available per capita as Asia. The meaning of these figures is apparent in a world in which economic and military strength is dependent directly upon the energy resources available. Indeed, it may be said that Europe's domination of the globe in the nineteenth century is based more upon the steam engine than upon any other single device or force.

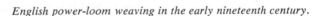

English power-loom weaving in the early nineteenth century.

Cotton weaving in India in the early nineteenth century.

The new cotton machines and steam engines required an increased supply of iron, steel, and coal—the need was met by a series of improvements in mining and metallurgy. Originally, iron ore had been processed in small furnaces filled with charcoal. The depletion of the forests compelled the manufacturers to turn to coal, and it was at this point—in 1709—that Abraham Darby discovered that coal could be reduced to coke just as wood had been to charcoal. Coke proved to be as effective as charcoal and was much cheaper. Darby's son developed a huge bellows driven by a water wheel, thus producing the first mechanically operated blast furnace and greatly reducing the cost of iron. A further improvement was made in 1760 when John Smeaton discarded the leather-and-wood bellows used by Darby and substituted a pump composed of four metal cylinders provided with pistons and valves and operated by a water wheel. More important was the development by Henry Cort in 1784 of the "puddling" process for removing impurities in the smelted iron. Cort placed the smelted iron in a reverberatory furnace, stirred or "puddled" it, and thus decarbonized the molten mass by means of the oxygen in the air circulating through it. This removal of carbon and other impurities produced wrought iron that was more malleable than the original brittle smelted iron or pig iron. Meanwhile, coal-mining methods also had been improved in order to keep up with the rising demands of the iron industry. Most important was the use of the steam engine to pump water out of mines, and the invention in 1815 of Sir Humphry Davy's safety lamp, which greatly reduced mining hazards.

As a result of these various developments Britain was producing by 1800 more coal and iron than the rest of the world together. More specifically, Britain's coal output rose from 6 million tons in 1770 to 12 million tons in

1800 to 57 million tons in 1861. Likewise, her iron output increased from 50,000 tons in 1770 to 130,000 tons in 1800 to 3,800,000 tons in 1861. Iron had become sufficiently plentiful and cheap to be used for general construction purposes, and man had entered the Age of Iron as well as the Age of Steam.

The expansion of the textile, mining, and metallurgical industries created a need for improved transportation facilities to move the bulky shipments of coal and ore. The first significant step in this direction was taken in 1761, when the Duke of Bridgewater built a seven-mile canal between Manchester and the coal mines at Worsley. The price of coal in Manchester fell by half, and the duke extended his canal to the Mersey, offering rates one-sixth those charged by land carriers. These spectacular results generated a canal-building fever that endowed England with 2,500 miles of canals by 1830.

The canal era was paralleled by a great period of road building. Roads were so primitive that people traveled on foot or on horseback, and wagons loaded with merchandise could scarcely be drawn over them during the rainy seasons. After 1750 a group of road engineers—John Metcalf, Thomas Telford, and John McAdam—evolved methods of building hard-surfaced roads that would bear traffic all through the year. Travel by coach increased from four miles an hour to six, eight, or even ten. Travel by night also became possible, so that the journey from Edinburgh to London, which had once taken fourteen days, now required only forty-four hours.

After 1830 both roads and waterways were challenged by the railroad. The new mode of transportation came in two installments. First was the plate or rail track, in common use by the mid-eighteenth century for moving coal from the pit head to some waterway or to the place where it was to be burned. It was claimed that on a track, a woman or a child could pull a cart laden with three quarters of a ton, and that one horse could do as much work as twenty-two horses did on an ordinary road. The second stage was the installation of the steam engine to the cart. The chief figure here was a mining engineer, George Stephenson, who first used an engine to pull coal trucks from a mine to the River Tyne. In 1830 his *Rocket* pulled a train thirty-one miles from Liverpool to Manchester at an average speed of fourteen miles per hour. Within a few years the railroad dominated long-distance traffic, being able to move passengers and freight faster and cheaper than was possible on roads or canals. By 1838 Britain had 500 miles of railroad; by 1850, 6,600; and by 1870, 15,500.

The steam engine was applied also to water transportation. From 1770 onward, inventors in Scotland, France, and the United States experimented with engines afloat. The first commercially successful steamship was built by an American, Robert Fulton, who went to England to study painting but turned to engineering after meeting James Watt. In 1807 he launched his *Clermont* on the Hudson River. Equipped with a Watt engine that operated paddle wheels, it steamed 150 miles up the river to Albany. Other inventors followed Fulton's example, notably Henry Bell of Glasgow, who laid the foundations of Scottish shipbuilding industry on the banks of the river Clyde. The early steamships were used only for river and coastal runs, but in 1833 the *Royal William* steamed from Nova Scotia to England. Five years later the *Sirius* and the *Great Western* crossed the Atlantic in the opposite direction,

THE WONDER of the AGE !!
INSTANTANEOUS COMMUNICATION.

Under the special Patronage of Her Majesty & H.R.H. Prince Albert.

THE GALVANIC AND ELECTRO-MAGNETIC
TELEGRAPHS,
ON THE
GT. WESTERN RAILWAY.

May be seen in constant operation, daily, (Sundays excepted) from 9 till 8, at the
TELEGRAPH OFFICE, LONDON TERMINUS, PADDINGTON
AND TELEGRAPH COTTAGE, SLOUGH STATION.

An Exhibition admitted by its numerous Visitors to be the most interesting and ATTRACTIVE of any in this great Metropolis. In the list of visitors are the illustrious names of several of the Crowned Heads of Europe, and nearly the whole of the Nobility of England.

"This Exhibition, which has so much excited Public attention of late, is well worthy a visit from all who love to see the wonders of science."—MORNING POST.

The Electric Telegraph is unlimited in the nature and extent of its communications; by its extraordinary agency a person in London could converse with another at New York, or at any other place however distant, as easily and nearly as rapidly as if both parties were in the same room. Questions proposed by Visitors will be asked by means of this Apparatus, and answers thereto will instantaneously be returned by a person 20 Miles off, who will also, at their request, ring a bell or fire a cannon, in an incredibly short space of time, after the signal for his doing so has been given.

The Electric Fluid travels at the rate of 280,000 Miles per Second.

By its powerful agency Murderers have been apprehended, (as in the late case of Tawell,)—Thieves detected; and lastly, which is of no little importance, the timely assistance of Medical aid has been procured in cases which otherwise would have proved fatal.

The great national importance of this wonderful invention is so well known that any further allusion here to its merits would be superfluous.

N.B. Despatches sent to and fro with the most confiding secrecy. Messengers in constant attendance, so that communications received by Telegraph, would be forwarded, if required, to any part of London, Windsor, Eton, &c.

ADMISSION ONE SHILLING.
T HOME, *Licensee.*

Norton, Printer, 48, Church St. Portman Market.

An English handbill, 1845.

taking 16½ and 13½ days respectively, or about half the time required by the fastest sailships. In 1840 Samuel Cunard established a regular transatlantic service, announcing beforehand dates of arrival and departure. Cunard advertised his enterprise as an "ocean railway" which had replaced the "maddening irregularity inseparable from the days of sail." [10] By 1850 the steamship had bested the sailship in carrying passengers and mails, and was beginning to compete successfully for freight traffic.

The Industrial Revolution produced a revolution in communication as well as transportation. Hitherto a message could be sent to a distant place only by wagon, postrider, or boat. But in the middle of the nineteenth century the electric telegraph was invented, the work chiefly of an Englishman, Charles Wheatstone, and of two Americans, Samuel F. B. Morse and Alfred Vail. In 1866 a transatlantic cable was laid, establishing instant communication between the Old and New Worlds.

Man thus conquered both time and space. Since time immemorial he had defined distances between places as involving so many hours travel by wagon, by horse, or by sailboat. But now he strode over the earth in seven-league boots. He could cross oceans and continents by steamship and railroad, and he could communicate with fellow-beings all over the world by telegraph. These achievements, and the others that enabled man to harness the energy in coal, to produce iron cheaply, and to spin one hundred threads of yarn at one time—all suggest the impact and significance of this first stage of the Industrial Revolution. It united the globe to an infinitely greater degree than it had been united in the times of the Romans or the Mongols, and it made possible the European domination of the globe that was to last until the Industrial Revolution had diffused to other regions.

IV. INDUSTRIAL REVOLUTION: SECOND STAGE, 1870–1914

The Industrial Revolution which got under way in the late eighteenth century has continued steadily and relentlessly to the present day. Hence it is essentially artificial to divide its evolution into various periods. Yet a case can be made for considering 1870 as a transition date. It was about that time that two important developments occurred—science began to affect industry significantly, and mass-production techniques were perfected and applied.

We noted in the preceding chapter that science, at the outset, had little effect upon industry. Very few of the inventions that we have noted thus far in the textile, mining, metallurgical, and transportation industries were the work of scientists. Rather they were effected mostly by talented mechanics who responded to extraordinary economic incentives. After 1870, however, science began to play a more important role. Gradually it became an integral part of the operations of all large industries. The laboratories of industrial research, equipped with expensive apparatus and staffed by trained scientists who carried on systematic research on designated problems, supplanted the garrets or workshops of lone inventors. Whereas inventions previously were the result of individual response to opportunity, now they were planned and virtually made to order. Walter Lippmann has aptly described the new situation as follows:

There have been machines invented since the earliest days, incalculably important, like the wheel, like sailing ships, like the windmill and the watermill. But in modern times men have invented a method of inventing, they have discovered a method of discovery. Mechanical progress has ceased to be casual and accidental and has become systematic and cumulative. We know, as no other people ever knew before, that we shall make more and more perfect machines.[11]

The impact of science was felt by all industries after 1870. In metallurgy, for example, a number of processes were developed (Bessemer, Siemens–Martin and Gilchrist–Thomas) that made possible the mass production of high-grade steel from low-grade iron ore. The power industry was revolutionized by the harnessing of electricity and by the invention of the internal combustion engine which uses chiefly oil and gasoline. Communications also were transformed by the invention of the wireless, or radio. In 1896, Guglielmo Marconi devised a machine for sending and receiving messages without wires, but his work was based on the researches of the Scottish physicist James Clerk Maxwell, and the German physicist Heinrich Hertz. The oil industry developed rapidly as a result of the work of geologists who located oilfields with remarkable accuracy, and of chemists who devised ways to refine crude oil into naphtha, gas, kerosene, and both light and heavy lubricating oils. One of the most spectacular examples of the effect of science on industry may be seen in the case of the coal derivatives. In addition to yielding coke and a valuable gas that was used for illumination, coal also gave a liquid, or coal tar. Chemists discovered in this substance a veritable treasure trove, the derivatives including hundreds of dyes and a host of other by-products such as aspirin, wintergreen, saccharin, disinfectants, laxatives, perfumes, photographic chemicals, high explosives, and essence of orange blossom.

The second stage of the Industrial Revolution was also characterized by the development of mass-production techniques. The United States led in this field as Germany did in the scientific. Certain obvious advantages explain U.S. primacy in mass production: the great storehouse of raw materials; the abundant supply of capital, both native and European; the constant influx of cheap immigrant labor; and the vast home market of continental proportions and with a rapidly growing population and a rising standard of living.

Two principal methods of mass production were developed in the United States. One was the making of standard interchangeable parts, and the assembling of these parts into the completed unit with a minimum of handicraft labor. The American inventor Eli Whitney employed this system * at the very beginning of the nineteenth century in manufacturing muskets for the government. His factory, based on this novel principle, attracted wide attention and was visited by many travelers. One of these described well the basic feature of Whitney's revolutionary technique: "For every part of the musket he has a mould; and there is said to be so much exactitude in the finishing, that every part of any musket may be adapted to all the parts of any other." [12] During the decades following Whitney, machines were made more and more

* See "Mass Production by Eli Whitney," EMM, No. 53.

accurate, so that it became possible to produce parts that were not nearly alike but exactly alike. The next step, early in the twentieth century, was the working out of the assembly line. Henry Ford gained fame and fortune by devising the endless conveyor belt that carried car parts to the place where they were needed by the assembly workmen. The evolution of this conveyor-belt system has been graphically described as follows:

> The idea of the belt was borrowed from the Chicago packers, who used an overhead trolley to swing carcasses of beef down a line of butchers. Ford tried the idea first in assembling a small unit in his motor, the fly-wheel magneto, then in assembling the motor itself, and then in assembling the chassis.
>
> A chassis was attached to a rope one day, and six workmen, picking up parts along the way and bolting them in place, travelled with it on an historic journey down a line two hundred and fifty feet in length as a windlass dragged it through the factory. The experiment worked, but developed one difficulty. God had not made men as accurately as Ford made piston rings. The line was too high for the short men and too low for the tall men, with a resultant waste in effort.
>
> More experiments were tried. The line was raised; then lowered; then two lines were tried, to suit squads of different heights; the speed of the lines was increased; then lessened; various tests were made to determine how many men to put on one assembly line, how far to subdivide operations, whether to let one man who set a bolt in place put on the nut and the man who put on the nut to take time to tighten it. In the end, the time allotted for assembly on a chasis was cut from twelve hours and twenty-eight minutes to one hour and thirty-three minutes, the world was promised Model T's in new abundance, and mass production entered a new phase as men were made still more efficient cogs of their machines. . . .[13]

Next was perfected the manipulation of large masses of material by means of advanced mechanical devices. The prime example of this method of mass production—also perfected in the United States—is the iron and steel industry. The following description of the manufacturing of steel rail for railroads illustrates this method:

> The . . . continuous operation . . . was worked out on a gigantic geographical scale by the iron and steel industry. Follow the raw iron from the Mesabi range. A steam shovel scoops it into railroad cars; the cars, hauled to Duluth or Superior, run onto the docks over pockets into which the contents of the car are discharged when its bottom folds outward; chutes lead the ore from the pockets into the hold of an ore vessel. At a Lake Erie port the vessel is unloaded by automatic machinery and the ore placed again in railroad cars; at Pittsburgh these cars are unloaded by dumpers which turn the car on its side and cascade the ore into bins; from these, skip cars carry the ore, as well as the coke and limestone, to the top of the blast furnace and dump them in. The blast then

goes into operation. From the furnace the pig iron is transferred, still hot, by ladle cars to a mixer and then to the open-hearth furnaces. Savings in fuel are thus accomplished. Then the open-hearth is tapped, the liquid steel is run into a gigantic ladle and thence poured into molds on flat cars, an engine pushes the cars to pits in which the steel ingots, left bare when the mold is stripped away, are kept warm until they are rolled. Conveyors carry the ingot to the rolls, and automatic platforms, rising and lowering, shoot the fashioning shape back and forth between the rolling apparatus. The resulting rail is so perfectly shaped that variations of a small fraction of an inch insure its rejection. Electric cranes, ladles, conveyors, dumpers, unloaders, chargers make the production of iron from mine to rail a thing uncannily automatic, vibrantly alive.[14]

What mass production on this scale meant in terms of dollars and cents is evident in the justifiable boast of the steel magnate Andrew Carnegie:

Two pounds of ironstone mined upon Lake Superior and transported nine-hundred miles to Pittsburgh; one pound and one-half of coal, mined and manufactured into coke, and transported to Pittsburgh; one-half pound of lime, mined and transported to Pittsburgh; a small amount of manganese ore mined in Virginia and brought to Pittsburgh—and these four pounds of materials manufactured into one pound of steel, for which the consumer pays one cent.[15]

Science and mass-production methods affected agriculture as well as industry. Again it was Germany that led in the application of science, and the United States in mass production. German chemists discovered that to maintain the fertility of the soil it was necessary to replace the nitrogen, potassium, and phosphorus that was taken out by plants. At first guano was used for this purpose, but toward the end of the nineteenth century it gave way to purer forms of the necessary minerals. As a result, world production of the minerals increased between 1850 and 1913 from insignificant amounts to 899,800 net tons of nitrate (three-fourths of which was used for fertilizer), 1,348,000 metric tons of potash, and 16,251,213 tons of superphosphates.

In the United States the large size of the farms and the lack of sufficient rural labor stimulated the invention of agricultural machinery. The tractor which replaced the horse could pull a rotary plow that plowed as much as fifty acres a day. The combine could automatically cut, gather, thresh, and clean the grain, and even bundle it in sacks ready for the market. As important as these new machines were the grain elevators, the canning factories, the refrigerated cars and ships, and the rapid transportation facilities, which resulted in a world market for agricultural as well as for industrial products. The wheat of Canada, the mutton of Australia, the beef of Argentina, and the fruits of California were to be found in markets throughout the world. Thus, the farmer was as much affected by the agricultural revolution as the artisan had been by the Industrial. Agriculture, which traditionally had offered a means of independent livelihood, was becoming a large-scale business enterprise geared to production for national and international markets.

V. Diffusion of the Industrial Revolution

During the nineteenth century the Industrial Revolution spread gradually from England to the Continent of Europe, and even to the non-European portions of the globe. At first there were various obstacles in the way of diffusion. A British law forbade the exportation of machinery, and conditions on the Continent were not conducive to industrialization, particularly because of the strength of the guilds and the disturbances connected with the Revolutionary and Napoleonic Wars. But the wars ended in 1815, and the British law was repealed in 1825. Soon the railway-building fever, which got under way in England in the 1830's, was affecting the Continent. Furthermore, British industrialists by this time were accumulating surplus capital and were on the look-out for investment opportunities on the continent. By 1830, fifteen to twenty thousand British workers were employed in France alone to man the new machines.

Once the Industrial Revolution began to spread, certain factors determined the pattern of diffusion. Most important were an adequate supply of natural resources, particularly iron and steel, and a free and mobile working population, unencumbered by either guild restrictions or feudal obligations. Belgium met both these requirements and hence was the first country on the Continent to be industrialized. The process began before 1830, and proceeded so rapidly that by 1870 the majority of Belgians lived in cities and were directly dependent upon industry or trade. As early as 1830 Belgium was producing 6 million tons of coal per year, and by 1913 the figure had risen to 23 million tons. Other branches of industry grew so fast, however, that from 1840 onward Belgium had to import coal from England.

France followed after Belgium, though—for several reasons—at a much more leisurely pace. French coal and iron resources were located some distance from each other, and the cession of iron-rich Alsace-Lorraine to Germany in 1871 further weakened her position. French industry traditionally had specialized in luxury products that were not so suitable to mechanization and mass production. And the labor supply was limited because of the strength of the guilds and the unwillingness of the peasants to leave the soil, especially after the distribution of land during the revolution. Nevertheless, industrialization did gradually affect France, especially in the north of the country—in Alsace-Lorraine and in the regions about Lille, Rouen, and Paris. The number of steam engines increased from 15 in 1815 to 625 in 1830, 26,146 in 1871, and 82,238 in 1910. The most rapid tempo of industrialization came after 1870, when the value of manufactured products rose from 5 billion francs in that year to 15 billion in 1897. Yet the fact remains that by 1914 France was not so thoroughly industrialized as Belgium, England, or Germany.

The pattern of industrialization in Germany was very different from that in France. Because of the political disunity, the poor transportation facilities, the strong guilds, and other considerations, Germany started very slowly. But after 1871 German industry advanced in such giant strides that all the other economies of Europe, including that of Britain, were left behind. The formation of the German Empire in 1871 contributed to this remarkable progress. The acquisition of Alsace-Lorraine at the same time added valuable iron reserves to Germany's plentiful natural resources. Germany also had the advantage of starting off with new and up-to-date machinery which was more efficient than Britain's older equipment. And the German government aided substantially by building a network of canals and railroads, providing tariff protection and subsidies when they were needed, and establishing an efficient educational system which turned out a stream of well-trained scientists and technicians. These factors enabled Germany by 1914 to surpass all other European states in the iron, steel, chemical, and electrical industries, and to follow after Britain in coal and textiles. In 1914 the number of workers in German industry had risen to two-fifths of the total labor force, and that in agriculture had fallen to one-third.

Several other European countries had developed substantial industries by 1914, the most important being Russia, Austria-Hungary, and Italy. Among the overseas countries, the United States had advanced at a phenomenal rate, while Japan, Canada, and Australia had made appreciable progress. The United States, especially, with its unique advantages previously noted, by the beginning of the twentieth century had become the first industrial power in the world. In steel production, for example, the United States in 1910 was producing 26,512,000 metric tons as against 13,698,000 by Germany, her closest competitor, and in coal her output was 617 million metric tons as against 292 million tons by Great Britain, who was in second place.

We may conclude that by 1914 the Industrial Revolution had spread significantly from its original center in the British Isles. In fact, the diffusion reached such proportions that Britain now not only faced formidable competition, but had been surpassed by two other countries, Germany and the United States. Table 1, listing the powers in the order of their industrial production, demonstrates the changes that had occurred in the world's industrial balance.

TABLE 1.

1860	1870	1880	1890	1900
Great Britain	Great Britain	United States	United States	United States
France	United States	Great Britain	Great Britain	Germany
United States	France	Germany	Germany	Great Britain
Germany	Germany	France	France	France

Source: F. Sternberg, *Capitalism and Socialism on Trial* (New York: Day, 1951), p. 22.

VI. EFFECT OF THE INDUSTRIAL REVOLUTION ON EUROPE

Rise of Industrial Capitalism

One effect of the Industrial Revolution on Europe was to alter the nature of capitalism. We noted earlier that the commercial revolution created commercial capitalism, so called because commerce was more affected by the capitalistic form of organization than agriculture or industry. In the same manner, the Industrial Revolution during its first stage between 1770 and 1870 created industrial capitalism. By this is meant that industry was organized increasingly upon a capitalistic base and was gradually dominating the economic life. After 1870, during the second stage of the Industrial Revolution, still another change occurred in the prevailing form of economic organization, this time to finance capitalism. The distinguishing feature of the new form was the investment banker, who came to be the controlling figure in economic enterprise. This occurred because industrial operations were reaching such huge proportions that the firms were unable to raise the necessary funds. Large orders in most cases required credit for the purchase of raw material and the payment of wages. Likewise, the expansion or modernization of plants frequently could not be carried out unless loans were made available. It was these financial needs that the banks now met by providing capital drawn together from the resources of large numbers of depositors and investors. In doing so they were able to get control of many firms and to maintain their control by a small investment in voting stock. Thus the financier came to replace the industrialist in the supreme control of economic life. Or, to put it another way, finance capitalism took the place of industrial capitalism.

To illustrate this change in economic organization, the Ford Motor Company may be taken as an example of industrial capitalism. Actually this company was an anomaly in the early twentieth century because it flourished in a period when finance capitalism was predominant. But the important point is that Henry Ford was able to secure the capital he required from his exceptionally large and consistent profits, and thus did not need to depend upon banks. In contrast to the independent existence of the Ford Motor Company, the giant United States Steel Corporation, organized in 1901, was as much the creation of the banker J. P. Morgan as of the steel industrialist Andrew Carnegie.

Increase of Population

Another effect of the Industrial Revolution on Europe was to make possible an unprecedented increase in population. In spite of the emigration overseas of millions of Europeans during the nineteenth century, the population of the Continent in 1914 was well over three times that of 1750. The reasons for this population explosion are economic and medical. The great increase of productivity in both agriculture and industry meant increased means of subsistence in terms of food, clothing, shelter, and other necessities of life. Famine in most parts of Europe west of Russia became a memory of the past. Even if crops failed, the new transportation facilities ensured adequate supply from outside. The population increase was due also to the advances of medical science and to the adoption of numerous public health measures. There was little or no increase in the birth rate, but the death rate was sharply reduced by preventing or curing disease. Vaccination, segregation of infected persons, safeguarding of water supplies, knowledge of antiseptics—all these reduced the death rate in northwestern Europe from at least 30 per 1,000 persons in 1800 to about 15 in 1914. Thus Europe's population climbed steeply from 140 million in 1750 to 188 million in 1800, 266 million in 1850, 401 million in 1900, and 463 million in 1914. This rate of increase in Europe was so much higher than in the other regions of the world that it altered the global population balance (see Table 2).

226

TABLE 2.   Estimated Population of the World *

	1650	1750	1850	1900	1950
Millions					
Europe	100	140	266	401	593
United States and Canada	1	1	26	81	168
Latin America	12	11	33	63	163
Oceania	2	2	2	6	13
Africa	100	95	95	120	199
Asia	330	479	749	937	1,379
TOTAL	545	728	1,171	1,608	2,515
Percentages					
Europe	18.3	19.2	22.7	24.9	24.0
United States and Canada	.2	.1	2.3	5.1	6.7
Latin America	2.2	1.5	2.8	3.9	6.5
Oceania	.4	.3	.2	.4	.5
Africa	18.3	13.1	8.1	7.4	7.9
Asia	60.6	65.8	63.9	58.3	55.4
TOTAL	100.0	100.0	100.0	100.0	100.0

* These figures show that Europe's percentage of the total world population rose from 18.3 in 1650 to 24.0 in 1950. But by the latter date, most of the population of the United States, Canada, and Oceania was of European origin, and at least half of the population of Latin America was also. Accordingly, it is more meaningful to say that by 1950 the percentage of Europeans and people of European origin had risen to about one-third of the world total. Adapted from A. M. Carr-Saunders, *World Population* (Oxford: Clarendon, 1936), p. 42; and *United Nations Demographic Yearbook*, 1957, p. 123.

Urbanization

The Industrial Revolution led also to an unprecedented urbanization of world society. Cities date back to the Neolithic period when the invention of agriculture produced a food surplus that could support urban centers. During the following millennia the size of cities depended on the amount of food that the surrounding land could produce. Thus the most populous cities were to be found in the valleys and flood plains, like the Nile, the Fertile Crescent, the Indus, and the Hwang Ho. With the development of large-scale river and sea transport, cities were able to specialize in trade and industry and thus to expand their populations beyond the limits of their agricultural hinterlands.

Far more significant, however, is the modern worldwide urbanization produced by the Industrial Revolution. The replacement of the putting-out system by the factory system led to a mass influx into the new centers of industry. The large new urban populations could be fed because food supplies now were available from all parts of the world. Technological and medical advances made it possible to eliminate the plagues that previously had decimated cities, and even to make city living relatively endurable and pleasant. The more important of these advances include ample provision of pure water, perfection of centralized sewerage and waste disposal systems, insurance of an adequate food supply, and prevention and control of contagious diseases. Thus cities all over the world grew at such a rate that by 1930 they included 415 million people or one-fifth of the human race. This represents one of the great social transformations in human history, for city-dwelling meant an entirely new way of life. Many Western countries, such as Britain, Belgium, Germany, and the United States, had by 1914 a substantial majority of their people living in cities. The pace and scope of urbanization during the nineteenth century is reflected in the figures presented in Table 3.

TABLE 3.   Population of Selected Cities (in thousands)

	1800	1850	1880	1900	1950 (city)	1950 (metro.)
New York	64	696	1,912	3,437	7,900	13,300
London	959 *	2,681 *	4,767 *	6,581 *	8,325 *	10,200
Tokyo	800	—	1,050	1,600	5,425	8,200
Moscow	250	365	612	1,000	4,700	6,500
Shanghai	300	250	300	600	5,500	5,500
Buenos Aires	40	76	236	821	3,290	5,300
Bombay	200	500	773	776	2,810	3,050
Sydney	8	60	225 †	482 †	1,775 †	1,800
Capetown	20	20	35	77	440	575

Source: R. R. Palmer, ed., *Atlas of World History* (Chicago: Rand McNally, 1957), pp. 194–95.

* Greater London.   † Greater Sydney.

Increase of Wealth

The Industrial Revolution, with its efficient exploitation of human and natural resources on a worldwide scale, made possible an increase in productivity that is without precedent in all history. Great Britain, who first was affected in this respect, increased her capital from 500 million pounds sterling in 1750 to 1,500 million pounds in 1800, to 2,500 million pounds in 1833, and to 6,000 million in 1865. In the latter part of the nineteenth century the entire world felt the impact of the increasing productivity. The wool of New Zealand, the wheat of Canada, the rice of Burma, the rubber of Malaya, the jute of Bengal, and the humming factories of Western Europe and eastern United States—all these resources were enmeshed in a dynamic and constantly expanding global economy. The figures in Table 4 indicate the rate at which industrial production rose in the second half of the nineteenth century in Europe and throughout the world.

TABLE 4.   Rise of Industrial Production (1913 = 100)

	1860	1870	1880	1890	1900	1910	1913
Germany	14	18	25	40	65	89	100
Great Britain	34	44	53	62	79	85	100
France	26	34	43	56	66	89	100
Russia	8	13	17	27	61	84	100
Italy	—	17	23	40	56	99	100
U. S. A.	8	11	17	39	54	89	100
World	14	19	26	43	60	88	100

Source: F. Sternberg, *Capitalism and Socialism on Trial* (New York: Day, 1951), p. 21.

Distribution of Wealth

There has been much difference of opinion among authorities in recent years concerning the distribution of the wealth created during the Industrial Revolution. One group holds that all classes benefited to a greater or lesser extent, while the other maintains that a few made huge fortunes while the many were ruthlessly exploited and suffered declining standards of living.*

There is no doubt that there was much exploitation and social disruption in the early days of industrialization. The tenant farmers were dispossessed, and the weavers and other handicraftsmen were wiped out by the irresistible competition of the new machine-made goods. These people, and others like them, faced the strain of moving to the city, finding employment, and adjusting to an unfamiliar environment and to strange ways of living and of working. They were completely dependent on their employers, having no land, no cottage, no tools, and no capital. In short, they had become mere wage earners, having nothing to offer but their labor.

When they found employment, they discovered that the hours were long, a sixteen-hour day being by no means rare. When two twelve-hour shifts were finally won, the workers looked upon the change as a blessing. The long hours alone would have been tolerable, since they were no worse than the hours worked at home under the putting-out system. But the real hardship came in getting used to the discipline and monotony of tending machines in a factory. The workers came and went at the sound of the factory whistle. They had to keep pace with the movements of the machine, always under the strict super-

* See "The Industrial Revolution Reconsidered," *EMM*, No. 49.

Cotton factories in Manchester.

vision of an ever-present overseer. The work was monotonous—pulling a lever, brushing away dirt, mending broken threads. Employers naturally regarded their wage bill as an expense that should be kept as low as possible. Consequently, many of them, particularly in the textile industries, preferred to employ women and children, who were willing to accept smaller wages and were more amenable to orders. Exploitation of woman and child labor reached such proportions that a number of parliamentary committees conducted investigations and found shocking conditions. An eight-year-old girl named Sarah Gooder gave the following testimony before Lord Ashley's Mine Commission in 1842.

> I'm a trapper in the Gawber pit. It does not tire me, but I have to trap without a light, and I'm scared. I go at four and sometimes half past three in the morning, and come out at five and half past. I never go to sleep. Sometimes I sing when I've light, but not in the dark; I dare not sing then. I don't like being in the pit. I am very sleepy when I go sometimes in the morning. I go to Sunday-school and read "Reading made Easy." (*She knows her letters and can read little words.*) They teach me to pray. (She repeated the Lord's prayer, not very perfectly, and ran on with the following addition: "God bless my father and mother, and sister and brother, uncles and aunts and cousins, and everybody else, and God bless me and make me a good servant. Amen.") I have heard tell of Jesus many a time. I don't know why he came on earth, I'm sure, and I don't know why he died, but he had stones for his head to rest on. I would like to be at school far better than in the pit.[16]

It was conditions such as these that moved Percy Bysshe Shelley to write his revolutionary poem "To the Men of England."

> Men of England, wherefore plough,
> For the lords who lay ye low?
> Wherefore weave with toil and care
> The rich robes your tyrants wear?
>
> .   .   .
>
> The seed ye sow, another reaps;
> The wealth ye find, another keeps;
> The robes ye weave, another wears;
> The arms ye forge, another bears.
> Sow seed—but let no tyrant reap;
> Find wealth—but let no imposter heap;
> Weave robes—let not the idle wear;
> Forge arms—in your defence to bear.

There is, however, another side to this question of the effect of the Industrial Revolution on the working class. In the first place, the parliamentary committees investigated only those industries, such as mining and textiles, where conditions were worst. The shocking testimony of the witnesses who appeared before the committees was based on facts, but those facts were by no means applicable to English industry as a whole. Furthermore, the plight of the worker in early nineteenth century England must be viewed in the light of contemporary rather than present-day standards. The fact is that the villages from which these workers came were in many respects as squalid and stultifying as the cities. Rats and vermin infested the straw bedding, and the wind whistled through the thinly thatched roof and the poorly plastered walls. Day laborers in the countryside were so poorly paid that they kept crowding into the new industrial cities. Thousands of Irish also crossed over to fill the jobs opening up in the new factories. Furthermore, the population of England soared during these early days of the Industrial Revolution, a fact that does not jibe with the usual picture of unrelieved and debilitating misery. It is quite possible that most of the workers in these early factories enjoyed higher *real* incomes than their forebears. An English authority, writing in 1955, concluded that "honest observers could differ whether things were getting better or worse for labour at the time." [17]

Although we cannot be sure of the effect of the Industrial Revolution on working-class living standards in the late eighteenth and early nineteenth centuries, we are quite certain that the standards rose substantially in the second half of the nineteenth century. The great increases in productivity together with the profits made from the huge overseas investments gradually benefited even the lower classes in Western Europe. After the "Hungry Forties," when there was much suffering from unemployment, the workers of Western Europe enjoyed general prosperity and rising living standards until World War I. The figures in Table 5 show that between 1850 and 1913, *real* wages in Britain and France almost doubled.

TABLE 5.   Rise in Real Wages, 1850–1913
(1913 = 100)

	Great Britain	France
1850	57	59.5
1860	64	63
1870	70	69
1880	81	74.5
1890	90	89.5
1900	100	100

Source: F. Sternberg, *Capitalism and Socialism on Trial* (New York: Day, 1951), p. 27.

This marked rise in national income did not mean, of course, that all classes benefited equally. The proceeds of the general prosperity did trickle down somewhat, but they were mostly absorbed at the top. In Great Britain, for example, 4.93 per cent of the persons over 25 years of age possessed over 60 per cent of the wealth in 1911–1913. Likewise, in Prussia in 1911, 3,425 individuals had an average wealth of 5,321,400 marks, whereas 1,608,050 individuals had an average of 23,295 marks. This discrepancy meant a corresponding discrepancy in manner of living. The poor no longer starved, but they did live in crowded tenements, they subsisted on monotonous diets, and they were restricted for their pleasure or relaxation to the churches or the drinking establishments. By contrast, the middle classes could afford better living quarters and food, attend the theater and concert, and educate their children adequately. At the top, the wealthy with their town and country houses, their art collections, and their well-advertised sports activities and foreign travels, lived in a style that was all but incomprehensible to the masses at the bottom. How differently and separately these classes lived was stressed by the future British prime minister Benjamin Disraeli in his novel, *Sybil*.

> Two nations; between whom there is no intercourse and no sympathy; who are as ignorant of each other's habits, thoughts, and feelings, as if they were dwellers in different zones, or inhabitants of different planets; who are formed by a different breeding, are fed by a different food, are ordered by different manners, and are not governed by the same laws . . . THE RICH AND THE POOR.[18]

This class differentiation based upon money influenced to a great degree the pattern of European politics. In the following chapter we shall consider the details of these politics, but it should be noted here that economic or class considerations explain why the wealthy, by and large, preferred to maintain the status quo, why the middle classes wanted only enough political reform so that they could participate in political life, and why the working classes wanted thoroughgoing political and social reform in order to secure a more equitable distribution of the fruits of the Industrial Revolution. To put it more specifically, the wealthy tended to be conservative; the middle classes, liberal; and the politically conscious workers, socialist. This working-class socialism, it should be added, was predominantly of the peaceful or revisionist variety: although the workers resented the class inequalities, they also appreciated the rising standard of living.

VII. EFFECT OF INDUSTRIAL REVOLUTION ON THE NON-EUROPEAN WORLD

Europeanization of the Earlier Empires

In the period before 1763 the European powers had only a few footholds in Asia and Africa, their major holdings being in the Americas. After 1763 they established their political control over large parts of Asia and almost all of Africa. In the Americas, however, they were able to do much more than this. Taking advantage of the relatively sparse population in the New World, they literally Europeanized North and South America. This could not be done in Asia and Africa, where the indigenous populations were too numerous and highly developed. But in the Americas, and even more in Australia, the Europeans bodily transplanted their civilization in all its aspects—ethnic, economic, and cultural.

The Industrial Revolution was in large degree responsible for this Europeanization. We have seen that increased productivity together with the advances of medical science had led to a sharp increase in Europe's population in the nineteenth century. This created a population pressure that found an outlet in overseas migration. Railways and steamships were available to transport masses of people across oceans and continents, and persecution of one sort or another further stimulated emigration, the chief example of this being the flight of 1½ million Jews from Russia to the United States in the fifteen years preceding World War I. These various factors combined to produce a mass migration unequaled in human history. With every decade the tide of population movement increased in volume. In the 1820's a total of 145,000 left Europe, in the 1850's about 2,600,000, and between 1900 and 1910 the crest was reached with 9 million emigrants, or almost 1 million per year. Tables 6 and 7 show the sources and destinations of the European emigrants.

TABLE 6. Principal Sources of European Emigration, 1846–1932

Great Britain and Ireland	18,000,000
Russia	14,250,000 *
Italy	10,100,000
Austria-Hungary	5,200,000
Germany	4,900,000
Spain	4,700,000
Portugal	1,800,000
Sweden	1,200,000
Norway	850,000
Poland	640,000 †
France	520,000
Denmark	390,000
Finland	370,000
Switzerland	330,000
Holland	220,000
Belgium	190,000
TOTAL	63,660,000

Source: A. M. Carr-Saunders, *World Population* (Oxford: Clarendon, 1936), pp. 49, 56; and W. S. and E. S. Woytinsky, *World Population and Production* (New York, Twentieth Century Fund, 1953), pp. 69, 93.

* Consists of 2,250,000 who went overseas, 7,000,000 who migrated to Asiatic Russia by 1914, 3,000,000 who migrated to the Urals, Siberia, and the Far East from 1927 to 1939 and 2,000,000 who migrated to Central Asia from 1927 to 1939. Since 1939, Russian emigration, free and forced, into the trans-Ural areas, has been the greatest single population movement in the world.
† 1920–1932 only.

TABLE 7. Principal Destinations of European Emigration

Destination	Period Covered	Total
United States	1821–1932	34,200,000
Asiatic Russia	1800–1939	12,000,000
Argentina	1856–1932	6,400,000
Canada	1821–1932	5,200,000
Brazil	1821–1932	4,400,000
Australia	1861–1932	2,900,000
British West Indies	1836–1932	1,600,000
Cuba	1901–1932	900,000
South Africa	1881–1932	900,000
Uruguay	1836–1932	700,000
New Zealand	1851–1932	600,000

Source: A. M. Carr-Saunders, *World Population* (Oxford: Clarendon, 1936), p. 49.

Before 1885 most of the emigrants came from northern and western Europe; after that date the majority were from southern and eastern Europe. By and large, the British emigrants went to the Dominions and to the United States, the Italians to the United States and Latin America, the Spaniards and Portuguese to Latin America, and the Germans to the United States and, in smaller numbers, to Argentina and Brazil. From the perspective of world history, the significance of this extraordinary migration is that it was all directed to the New World and Oceania, with the exception of the large flow to Asiatic Russia and the trickle to South Africa. The result has been the almost complete ethnic Europeanization of North America and Australia. The Indian population in South America managed to survive but was left a minority. In other words, the colonial offshoots of the pre-1763 period now, during the course of the nineteenth century, became new Europes alongside the old.

The Americas and Australia were Europeanized economically as well as ethnically. Before 1763 the European settlements in these continents were confined largely to the coasts. But during the following century the interiors of the continents were traversed. The Industrial Revolution made this overland penetration possible by providing the necessary machines and techniques. The wilderness could not have been tamed without the roads leading inward from the coast, the canals connecting riverways, the railroads and telegraphs spanning continents, the steamers plying rivers and coastal waterways, the agricultural machines capable of cutting the prairie sod, and the repeating rifle that subdued the native peoples. These mechanical aids for the conquest of continental expanses were as essential to Latin Americans and Australians as to American frontiersmen. For example, an Argentinian writing in 1878 observed that "the military power of the [Indian] barbarians is wholly destroyed, because the Remington has taught them that an army battalion can cross the whole pampa, leaving the land strewn with the bodies of those who dared to oppose it." [19]

The peopling and economic development of the new continents led automatically to the transplanting of European culture as well. It is true that the culture changed in transit. It was adapted as well as adopted. Canada and Australia and the United States today are not identical to Great Britain, nor is Latin America an exact reproduction of the Iberian Peninsula. But the fact remains that the languages are essentially the same, even though Englishmen are intrigued by American slang and Frenchmen by the archaic French-Canadian patois. The religions also are the same, despite the campfire revival meetings and the Mormons. The literatures, the schools, the newspapers, the forms of government—all have roots extending back to England and Spain and France and other European countries.

There are, of course, certain cultural strains in the Americas and in Australia that are not European. The Negro element in the New World has retained a certain residue of its African background. The surviving native peoples, especially the Indians in Latin America, are responsible for a hybrid culture. Nor should one forget the impact of the wilderness, leaving its indelible imprint on the European immigrants and on their institutions. All these forces explain why New York, Melbourne, and Toronto are very different from London, and why Buenos Aires, Brazilia, and Mexico City differ from Madrid. Yet from a global viewpoint the similarities loom larger than the differ-

234

ences. The Arab peoples, in the course of their expansion from their homeland in the Middle East, spread westward across North Africa to the Atlantic Ocean. Today the culture of Morocco is far more different from that of the Arabian Peninsula than the culture of the United States is from that of Britain, or the culture of Brazil from that of Portugal. Yet Morocco is considered, and certainly considers itself, to be a part of the Arab world. In the same sense, the Americas and Australia today are a part of the European world.

New Imperialism Conquers New Empires

The Industrial Revolution was largely responsible not only for the Europeanization of the New World and Australia, but also for the creation of huge European colonial structures in Asia and Africa. This empire building went on steadily during the decades following the great colonial settlement in 1763. It is true that there was much anti-imperialist sentiment in certain French and English circles in the early nineteenth century. The champions of free trade agreed that colonies were of little, if any, economic value, and their theories seemed to be supported by England's experience with the Thirteen Colonies. Yet the fact remains that both Britain and France continued to acquire possessions during those decades. Britain, for example, obtained the Cape Colony and Ceylon in 1815, New Zealand in 1840, Hong Kong in 1842, and Natal in 1843. France likewise conquered Algeria between 1830 and 1847, Cochin China between 1858 and 1867, and attempted unsuccessfully to get a foothold in Mexico in 1862. These acquisitions, however, were insignificant compared to the great wave of empire building after 1870, when the "New Imperialism" made a large part of the earth's surface into an appendage of a few European powers.*

The close relationship between the New Imperialism and the Industrial Revolution may be seen in the growing desire to obtain colonies that might serve as markets for the rising volume of manufactured goods. The several European and overseas countries that became industrialized during the nineteenth century were soon competing with each other for markets, and in the process they raised tariffs to keep out each other's products. Soon it was being argued that each industrialized country must have colonies to provide "sheltered markets" for its manufactures. A typical expression of this attitude was made in 1898 by the Republican Senator Albert J. Beveridge before a group of Boston businessmen:

> American factories are making more than the American people can use; American soil is producing more than they can consume. Fate has written our policy for us; the trade of the world must and shall be ours. And we will get it as our mother (England) had told us how. We will establish trading posts throughout the world as distributing points for American products. We will cover the ocean with our merchant marine. We will build a navy to the measure of our greatness. Great colonies governing themselves, flying our flag and trading with us, will grow about our posts of trade.[20]

* See "Dynamics of Modern Imperialism," *EMM,* No. 54.

The Industrial Revolution also produced surplus capital, which again led the Great Powers to seek colonies as investment outlets. The more capital piled up at home, the lower the returns fell and the greater the need was for more profitable investment markets abroad. Vast amounts of capital were, in fact, invested in foreign countries, especially by Britain, France, and Germany. Britain, for example, by 1914 had invested £4 billion abroad, a sum amounting to one fourth of her total national wealth. By the same date France had invested 45 billion francs, or one-sixth of her national wealth. Germany, a latecomer who was using most of her capital for domestic industrial expansion, had invested overseas between 22 and 25 billion marks or one fifteenth of her national wealth. Thus Europe by 1914 had become the banker of the world. In the first half of the nineteenth century most of these overseas investments were made in the Americas and Australia—in the white man's world. But in the second half of the century they were made mostly in the nonwhite and relatively unstable countries of Asia and Africa. Ten thousands of small private savers and the large banking combinations that provided the capital naturally were anxious about its safety. They preferred "civilized" administration, preferably by their own respective governments, in the regions in which their investments were situated. In this manner the need to invest surplus capital promoted the New Imperialism.

The Industrial Revolution also created a demand for raw materials to feed the machines. Many of these materials—jute, rubber, petroleum, and various metals—came from the "uncivilized" portions of the globe. In most cases heavy capital outlays were needed to secure adequate production of these commodities. Such investments, as we have seen, usually led to the imposition of political control.

The New Imperialism was not entirely economic in its origins; it was not related exclusively to the Industrial Revolution. A variety of other factors also were operative at this time. One was the desire to strengthen national security by strategic naval bases such as at Malta and Singapore. Another was the need to secure additional sources of manpower, as the French did in North Africa. Still another was the influence of the missionaries, who were particularly active during the nineteenth century. Sometimes these missionaries were maltreated, or even killed, by the natives they were seeking to convert. The missionaries themselves might be willing to tolerate such risks as acceptable for the sake of their cause, but public opinion frequently demanded action. And it was not unknown for governments to use such incidents as pretexts for military intervention. Finally, the vogue of Social Darwinism, with its doctrines of struggle for existence and survival of the fittest, led naturally to ideas of racial superiority and of the white man's "burden" of ruling over the "inferior" colored peoples of the earth. The great empire builder Cecil Rhodes was quite outspoken on this matter. "I contend that we are the first race in the world, and that the more of the world we inhabit the better it is for the human race . . . If there be a God, I think what He would like me to do is to paint as much of the map of Africa British red as possible." [21]

The net result of these economic, political, and intellectual-psychological factors was the greatest land-grab in the history of the world, unequaled even by the conquests of Genghis Khan. In the generation between 1871 and 1900 Britain added 4¼ million square miles and 66 million people to her Empire;

France added 3½ million square miles and 26 million people; Russia in Asia added half a million square miles and 6½ million people, and Germany one million square miles and 13 million people. Even little Belgium managed to acquire 900,000 square miles and 8½ million inhabitants. These conquests, added to the existing colonial possessions, produced a fantastic and unprecedented situation in which one small portion of the globe dominated the remainder. The extent of this domination in 1914 is revealed by the figures in Table 8.

TABLE 8. Overseas Colonial Empires in 1914 *

Countries having colonies	Number of colonies	Area (square miles)		Population	
		Mother country	Colonies	Mother country	Colonies
United Kingdom	55	120,953	12,043,806	46,052,741	391,582.528
France	29	207,076	4,110,409	39,602,258	62,350,000
Germany	10	208,830	1,230,989	64,925,993	13,074,950
Belgium	1	11,373	910,000	7,571,387	15,000,000
Portugal	8	35,500	804,440	5,960,056	9,680,000
Netherlands	8	12,761	762,863	6,102,399	37,410,000
Italy	4	110,623	591,250	35,238,997	1,396,176
TOTAL	115	707,116	20,453,757	205,453,831	530,493,654

* Including colonies and other noncontiguous territories.

The industrialized European powers not only owned outright these vast colonial territories, but they also dominated those economically and militarily weak areas that, for one reason or another, were not actually annexed. Examples are China, the Ottoman Empire, and Persia, all of which were nominally independent, but which, in fact, were constantly harried, humiliated, and controlled in various direct and indirect ways. Latin America also was an economic appendage of the Great Powers, though in this region military action by Europe was discouraged by the Monroe Doctrine. The latter, however, did not preclude repeated armed intervention by the United States Marine Corps to "restore law and order." The great Russian Empire also was dominated economically to a very large extent by Western Europe, though in this case the military strength of the Tsarist regime was great enough to prevent foreign economic influence from extending into other fields.

Thus we see that Europe's control extended not only over her farflung empires but also over the equally extensive dependent regions. In fact, more European capital was invested in the dependent countries than in the colonies. These investments were safeguarded through various devices and pressures such as military missions that trained the local armed forces, financial missions that supervised and usually controlled local finances, and extraterritorial and capitulatory arrangements that gave special privileges to Europeans residing or doing business in these areas. If necessary as a last resort, there were always the Marines in the New World or the gunboats in the Old.

The details of these relationships between the Great Powers and the various colonial and dependent areas will be considered in later chapters. The purpose here is to present only the general pattern of the relationships.

This pattern shows clearly that by 1914 most of the earth's surface and most of the world's population had come under the direct or indirect domination of a few European countries, including Russia and the United States. This was a development without precedence in the history of man. Today, in the mid-twentieth century, much of the global turmoil represents the inevitable reaction to this European hegemony.

Impact of the New Imperialism

Why should the great European expansion of the late nineteenth century be labeled the New Imperialism? Imperialism, after all, was not something new. If it be defined as "the rule or control, political or economic, direct or indirect, of one state, nation or people over other similar groups. . . . ,"[22] then imperialism is as old as human civilization. Certainly the Romans were imperialistic, having conquered, and for centuries ruled, large parts of Europe and the Near East. And many other empires, both before and after the Romans, were conquered in all parts of the globe by all types of peoples.

Yet the term "New Imperialism" is justified, because this late nineteenth century European expansion was quite unprecedented in its impact upon the colonial and dependent territories. Rome exploited its possessions simply and directly by plundering and by collecting tribute, chiefly in the form of foodstuffs, but its exploitation did not particularly affect the economic life and structure of the colonies. They continued to produce pretty much the same foodstuffs and handicrafts in the same ways as in the past. To compare this imperialism with the later version that overran and remade entire continents is like comparing a spade to a steam shovel. The traditional imperialism involved exploitation but no basic economic and social change. The tribute merely went to one ruling clique rather than another. The New Imperialism, by contrast, forced a thorough transformation of the conquered countries. This was not so much deliberate policy as it was the inevitable impact of the dynamic industrialism of Western Europe upon the static, self-contained agrarian regimes of Africa and Asia. In other words, Europe's industrial capitalism was far too complex and expansionist for a simple tribute relationship with the colonies.

At the outset, the European conquerors certainly did not hesitate to plunder and to levy tribute. The British did so in India, as the Spaniards had earlier in Mexico and in Peru. But after this initial phase, Europe's dynamic economy began in various ways to enfold and refashion the colonial economic and social structures. This happened because, as we have seen, industrialized Europe needed sources of raw materials and markets for its surplus capital and manufactures. England, for example, shipped to India vast quantities of textiles and capital, the latter principally for building railways. By 1890, approximately 17,000 miles of railroads had been built in India, which was about equal to the English railway system. But from 1890 to 1911 the Indian network was approximately doubled to 33,000 miles, while in the same period the increase in England was only a little over 300 miles.

It should be noted that the railways, and other large projects such as irrigation works and harbor installations, were paid for by British capital. In other words, India did not have to develop her economy and increase her exports until she accumulated sufficient capital. Thus India's economic development at this early stage was stimulated by the tie with Britain. But the important point is that it was not only stimulated but also revamped, and at a later stage, stultified. The British textiles, which were so cheap, and which now could be distributed throughout the country by the railroad system, ruined the native artisans as inexorably as they had the British artisans a century earlier. But there was one vital difference between the two situations. The British artisans went to work in the factories that were mushrooming in the cities; the Indian artisans had nowhere to go because no factories appeared in their cities. The British, not unnaturally, did not wish to build a rival industrial structure in India. They preferred that the Indian economy supplement rather than compete with their own. Thus, India supplied Britian with raw materials, and in return received manufactured goods and capital for construction projects.

This was a natural and understandable arrangement, but it affected the people of India in a profound fashion. They had earned their livelihood traditionally through agriculture and handicrafts. Now the artisans were undercut and had no alternative source of livelihood. Nor did the peasants escape untouched, for many of them became involved in producing jute and other commodities for the British factories. This meant that they no longer merely fed themselves and the people of nearby towns. Now they were part and parcel of the world economy, subject to its fluctuations and crises. Europe also affected India basically by introducing medical science and sanitary measures that resulted in a sharp population increase. This had occurred also in Europe, but Europe's millions went to the cities or overseas, while the Indians could do neither. The net result, therefore, was growing population and arrested economic development.

This, then, was the nature of the impact of the New Imperialism on the colonial and dependent areas. India has been used as an illustration of the impact, but the general pattern was the same in other areas, though naturally with local variations. This pattern should be kept in mind, because it explains why the globe today is divided into developed and underdeveloped worlds, why such a shocking discrepancy prevails in the living standards of the two worlds, and why the primary aim of the people of the underdeveloped world, after they have gained political independence, is to become developed—to reach Western economic levels as rapidly as possible.

New Imperialism in Retrospect

It should not be concluded that the New Imperialism was an unmitigated evil for the world, or even for the subject colonial peoples. In the light of historical perspective it undoubtedly will be viewed as a great step forward for the world, as the Industrial Revolution was a step forward for the Europeans. In fact, the historic role of the New Imperialism was to carry the Industrial Revolution to its logical conclusion—to enable the industrial nations, or industrial capitalism, to operate on a worldwide scale. This resulted in a much more extensive, coordinated, and efficient utilization of the material and human resources of the globe. Certainly world productivity rose immeasurably when European capital and skills were combined with the raw materials and labor power of the underdeveloped regions to produce, for the first time, an integrated global economy. In fact, world industrial production increased three times between 1860 and 1890, and seven times between 1860 and 1913. The value of world trade grew from 641 million pounds in 1851, to 3,024 million pounds in 1880, to 4,025 million pounds in 1900, and 7,840 million pounds in 1913.

There is no disagreement over the advantage of this increase in the size of the cake. The dispute rather centers on how the cake is sliced. The colonial peoples have felt that in the past they have received less than their due share. The total amount that they have received obviously has increased, otherwise their rising populations could not have been supported. For example, a British economist has shown that in 1949 European companies engaged in mining in mineral-rich Northern Rhodesia sold their output for a total of £36.7 million. Of this, they spent only £12.5 million in Northern Rhodesia, which meant that two-thirds of the money was transferred abroad. Moreover, of the £12.5 spent in Northern Rhodesia £4.1 million was paid to Europeans living and working there. Only £2 million out of the £36.7 million went to the Africans working in the mines. And yet these workers were receiving an average of £41 a year compared to an average income of £27 a year per adult African male in the colony.[23]

Under these circumstances it is understandable that colonial peoples are not so impressed by increased productivity or by the wages paid by foreign companies. They are more impressed by the wretched level at which they subsist, especially in comparison with Western levels. They resent also their consignment to the role of hewers of wood and drawers of water, even in regions where human and material resources exist for industrial development.

There is apparent here a parallel between the reaction of Western workers to industrial capitalism and of colonial peoples to the New Imperialism. Both have been dissatisfied with their lot, and both have supported movements designed to bring about radical change. But a basic difference is that the colonial peoples are ranged not against employers of their own nationality but rather against foreign rulers. Accordingly their movement of protest, at least in the first stage, was not socialism, but rather a range of Western political doctrines —liberalism, democracy, and, above all, nationalism.

We turn now to consider these isms, which comprise Europe's political revolution. An understanding of this revolution is as essential for world history as an understanding of the Industrial Revolution. The world, as we shall see, was affected by Western ideas and slogans and political institutions as well as by Western cottons and railways and banks.

SUGGESTED READING

For the historical setting of the Industrial Revolution, consult one of the several available economic histories of Europe. The one most suitably organized for students of history is S. B. Clough and C. W. Cole, *Economic History of Europe* (Boston: Heath, 1952). An excellent and convenient analysis of the interpretations and literature of the Industrial Revolution is provided by E. E. Lampard, *Industrial Revolution: Interpretations and Perspectives* (Washington: Service Center for Teachers of History, 1957), No. 4. A useful collection of readings from the outstanding authorities is available in P. A. M. Taylor, ed., *The Industrial Revolution in Britain: Triumph or Disaster?* (Boston: Heath, 1958). For the diffusion of the Industrial Revolution from England, see W. D. Henderson, *The Industrial Revolution on the Continent* (London: Cass, 1961) and the September, 1963, issue of *Scientific American,* which contains authoritative and stimulating articles on this and other aspects of the Industrial Revolution. The relationships between the industrial and scientific revolutions are brought out by J. G. Crowther, *Scientists of the Industrial Revolution* (London: Cresset, 1962). For the social and political repercussions of the Industrial Revolution, see the important studies by E. J. Hobsbaum, *The Age of Revolution: Europe, 1789–1848* (London: Weidenfeld, 1962) and E. P. Thompson, *The Making of the English Working Class* (London: Gollancz, 1963). Population growth and movements connected with the Industrial Revolution are described by F. D. Scott, *Emigration and Immigration* (Washington: Service Center for Teachers of History, 1963), No. 51; by D. H. Wrong, *Population* (New York: Random paperback, 1956); and by C. Cipolla, *The Economic History of World Population* (Baltimore: Penguin, 1962; a Pelican Book). Readings from the works of the principal theoreticians of imperialism are provided by H. M. Wright, ed., *The "New Imperialism": Analysis of Late Nineteenth-Century Expansion* (Bosworld are available in L. L. Snyder, ed., *The Imperialism Reader: Documents* ton: Heath, 1961). Materials describing imperialism in action throughout the *and Readings on Modern Expansionism* (Princeton: Van Nostrand, 1962). Finally, an invaluable source for statistical data on matters related to industrialization is W. S. and E. S. Woytinsky, *World Population and Production* (New York: Twentieth Century Fund, 1953).

*When individuals and nations have once got
in their heads the abstract concept of full-blown
liberty, there is nothing like it in its uncontrollable strength.*

G. W. F. HEGEL

Chapter

12

The Political Revolution

Europe's domination of the world in the nineteenth century was based not only on its industrial and scientific revolutions, but also on its political revolution, the essence of which was the ending of the concept of a divinely ordained division of humanity into rulers and ruled. No longer was government regarded as something above the people, and the people as something below the government. The political revolution involved for the first time in history, on a scale larger than the city-state, the identification of government and people —the awakening and activization of the masses so that they not only participated in government but also considered it their inherent right to do so. In this chapter we shall consider the general pattern of this political revolution, its origins in the English, American, and French Revolutions, and its varied manifestations and worldwide impact during the nineteenth century.

I. PATTERN OF THE POLITICAL REVOLUTION

The political revolution, like the economic, developed in several stages. We noted that the economic revolution began in England, then spread to the Continent and to the United States, and later to other parts of the globe. Likewise, the political revolution got under way with the English Revolution in the seventeenth century, developed much further with the American and French Revolutions that followed, and then affected the whole of Europe during the nineteenth century and the entire globe during the twentieth.

This parallelism in the diffusion of the two revolutions was not accidental; indeed, the two were intimately related. The economic revolution was in large degree responsible for the political, because it created new classes with new interests and new ideologies that rationalized their interests. This will become clear if we trace briefly the general course of the economic and political revolutions.

During the early medieval period, three well-defined social groups were to be found in Western Europe: the nobility who constituted a military aristocracy, the clergy who formed an ecclesiastical and intellectual elite, and the peasants who labored to support the two upper classes. With the development of commerce, this profile of the medieval social order began to be changed by the appearance of a new element, the urban bourgeoisie. As this class grew in wealth and numbers, it became increasingly discontented with the special privileges of the feudal orders and with the numerous restrictions that hampered the development of a free market economy. Accordingly, the bourgeoisie made a mutually beneficial alliance with the national monarchies. The kings obtained financial support from the bourgeoisie and thereby were able to assert their authority over the feudal orders, and the bourgeoisie in return profited from the establishment of law and order throughout the royal domains. This alliance lasted until it became irksome for the constantly growing middle class, which turned against the kings to free itself from royal restrictions on commerce, from a growing burden of taxation, and from restraints on religious freedom. These objectives were important factors in the English, the American, and the French Revolutions. The success of these revolutions meant also the success of liberalism—the new ideology that provided a rationalization for bourgeois interests and objectives. In this sense liberalism may be defined as the particular program by which the growing middle class proposed to secure for itself those benefits and that control at which it aimed.

The middle class, with its creed of liberalism, was challenged in turn by the urban workers, or proletariat. With the Industrial Revolution of the late eighteenth century, the workers in the crowded cities became increasingly class conscious. More and more they felt that their interests were not identical with those of their employers, and that their situation could be improved only by combined action on their part. Consequently the workers, or rather the intellectuals who led them, developed a new ideology, socialism. It directly challenged the liberalism of the bourgeoisie, calling for social and economic change as well as for political reform. We shall see that socialism was to become a major force in European affairs in the late nineteenth century, and in world affairs in the twentieth.

Europe's political revolution was powered not only by the dynamic creeds of liberalism and socialism, but also by nationalism—an ideology that cut across classes and activated great masses of people. Traditionally the first allegiance of these people had been to region or to church. In early modern times it had extended to the new national monarchs. But beginning with the English Revolution, and particularly during the French Revolution, increasing numbers of Europeans subordinated their loyalty to the the new cause of the nation. The rise of national churches, national dynasties, national armies, and national educational systems, all combined to transform former ducal subjects and feudal serfs and town burghers into the all-inclusive nation. The new national ideology spread during the nineteenth century from Western Europe, where it originated, to all parts of the Continent, and today, in the twentieth century, it is the driving force behind the awakening of formerly subject colonial peoples throughout the world.

243

These three creeds—liberalism, socialism, and nationalism—are the principal components of Europe's political revolution. Together they galvanized into action broader and broader strata of the peoples of Europe, giving them a dynamism and a cohesiveness unequaled in any other portion of the globe. In this manner the political revolution, like the scientific and the economic, contributed vitally to Europe's world hegemony. When the Europeans began to expand overseas, they encountered societies in which there was little rapport between rulers and ruled. The apathy of the masses—their lack of identification with their governments—explains why in region after region the Europeans were able to establish and to maintain their rule with little difficulty. India is perhaps the leading example of the vulnerability to European expansionism of societies that had remained disparate congeries of peoples, religions, and conflicting provincial loyalties. For over a century and a half, this great Indian subcontinent, with its teeming millions, its splendid civilization, and its ancient historical traditions, was ruled with little difficulty by a comparative handful of British officers and officials. When the mutiny against British rule broke out in 1857, it was put down not only by British troops but also Indian. The correspondent of the London *Times* reported this fact with astonishment. "I looked with ever-growing wonder on the vast tributary of the tide of war which was running around and before me. All these men, women and children, with high delight were pouring towards Lucknow to aid the Feringhee [Europeans] to overcome their brethren." [1]

But European political and economic domination inevitably meant the diffusion of European political ideas. Just as the entire globe felt the impact of Stephenson's locomotive, of Fulton's steamship, and Gatling's machine gun, so it felt the impact of the Declaration of Independence, of the Declaration of the Rights of Man and Citizen, and the Communist Manifesto. The worldwide convulsions that are the hallmark of our present age are the direct outcome of these heady documents.

II. ENGLISH REVOLUTION

The first phase of Europe's political revolution was the English Revolution of the seventeenth century. The roots of the upheaval in England are to be found in the conflict between Parliament and the Stuart dynasty, which degenerated to an open civil war from which Parliament emerged victorious. This outcome was by no means unprecedented. Other representative bodies also had humbled monarchs, as in the case of Poland. But the great difference between the two cases is that the victorious English Parliament represented essentially middle-class interests, whereas the representative body in Poland

244

represented the feudal nobility. Consequently, the outcome of Parliament's triumph in England was the establishment of representative constitutional government—England's greatest political contribution to Europe and to the world. By contrast, the victory of the noble-dominated assembly in Poland led to a feudal anarchy that was to culminate in the complete extinction of the state.

The Tudor dynasty which preceded the Stuart was generally popular, particularly with the middle class and the gentry. It brought the warring noble families under central control. It severed the ecclesiastical ties with Rome by establishing a national Anglican church, and in the process distributed extensive lands and other properties that had belonged to the Catholic institution. It also built up the navy and pursued an anti-Catholic foreign policy that met with popular approval.

The first Stuart king, James I (1603–1625), and his son and successor Charles I (1625–1649), soon dissipated this fund of goodwill. They sought to impose the doctrines and ritual of the Anglican church on all the people, thereby alienating their Nonconformist, or Puritan, subjects. They also tried to rule without Parliament, but encountered difficulties because Parliament controlled the national purse. They attempted to get around this obstacle by selling monopolies in the export and import trades, in domestic commerce, and in many fields of manufacturing. This produced considerable revenue, but it also antagonized the bourgeoisie, which demanded that "all free subjects be inheritable to the free exercise of their industry." [2]

The crisis came when the Scots rose in rebellion against Charles's attempt to impose Anglicanism upon them. In order to obtain funds to put down the uprising, Charles was forced to summon Parliament. And this Long Parliament, which met in 1640, ignored his requests for money and instead made a number of far-reaching demands, including the execution of the chief royal advisers and the complete reorganization of the Anglican church. Charles refused to submit, and in 1642 fighting broke out between the royalist Cavaliers and the Puritan Roundheads.

England was not to settle down again for almost half a century, until the so-called Glorious Revolution of 1688. The stirring events of those decades comprise the English Revolution. The details of the revolution do not concern us except insofar as they throw light on the manner and extent to which the revolution contributed to the creeds of liberalism, nationalism, and socialism. It suffices, therefore, to note at this point that the English Revolution went through five stages. The first, from 1642 to 1645, was the civil war, during which the royalists were routed by the famous New Model Army organized by Oliver Cromwell. During the second stage, from 1645 to 1649, a situation developed that was to be repeated with certain variations during the French Revolution in 1792 and the Russian Revolution in 1917. A split occurred between the moderate and radical elements among the victorious Puritans. The moderates, led by Cromwell, prevailed over the radicals, led by John Lilburne. When Charles was executed in 1649, Cromwell emerged as the head of an English republic known as the Commonwealth.

Cromwell and his Puritan followers ruled England with much efficiency and Godliness during the third stage from 1649 to 1660. This was the time when the various feudal rights were suppressed and the religious question settled.

Cromwell died in 1658 and was succeeded as Lord Protector of the Commonwealth by his son Richard. The latter was a nonentity, and furthermore the country was weary of the restricted and austere life under the Puritans. Accordingly, the Stuarts were placed back on the throne, so that the fourth stage, from 1660 to 1688, is known as the Restoration.

The Stuart kings, Charles II (1660–1685) and James II (1685–1688), did not and could not undo the reforms of the republic. But they did try to revive personal rule, and this, together with their subservience to the French crown and their encouragement of Catholicism, made them increasingly unpopular. Finally James II was overthrown with the Glorious Revolution of 1688, which marks the fifth and last stage of the English Revolution. The new ruler was William of Orange, son-in-law of James I. In 1689 William accepted a Bill of Rights which enunciated the essential principles of parliamentary supremacy. The bill stipulated that no law could be suspended by the king, no taxes raised or army maintained except by Parliament's consent, and no subject arrested and detained without legal process. These provisions did not mean that England had become a democracy. Not until the establishment of universal suffrage in the late nineteenth century was this goal attained. But the settlement in 1689 did establish once and for all the supreme authority of Parliament, and in doing so it concluded the English Revolution that had begun almost half a century earlier.

From the viewpoint of world history, the major significance of the English Revolution is that it defined and implemented the principles of liberalism. This was to be expected, because the English Revolution was essentially a middle-class ideology. The merchants and the lesser gentry who supported Parliament had two principal objectives in view—religious toleration and security of person and of property. But there was no unanimity of opinion on the Puritan side concerning these matters. Many conflicting views were expounded and passionately debated. In the case of religion, for example, a veritable torrent of heterodox opinion gushed forth, and numerous new sects appeared, including the Congregationalists, the Baptists, and the Quakers. At the same time, the Presbyterians strove to establish their church as a national organization exercising its discipline upon all citizens. These religious differences obviously had to be reconciled or else Parliament's victory would be undone and the state itself might founder. It was under these circumstances that the basic liberal doctrine of religious toleration was worked out and established. On grounds of principle as well as expedience it came to be generally agreed that it was both immoral and ineffective to attempt to coerce men into belief. It is true that the Anglican Church remained the official, state-supported church, and that its members were favored in the filling of government posts and in other respects. But, by and large, the principle was established that liberty of conscience should be granted to all Christians who did not threaten public order or interfere with other men's worship.

The question of the rights of person and of property also aroused fierce controversy. This question divided the right- and left-wing elements among the Puritans even more sharply than did the religious issue. The split occurred gradually, as the common soldiers of the New Model Army came to feel that their interests were being ignored by their officers and by Parliament. These soldiers, after four years of successful campaigning, had acquired new

246

ideas and a new outlook. They had defeated their betters in battle and, as conquerors, had strode into some of the stateliest mansions in England. This led them to question the authority of the great and to believe in their own capacity. As one authority has observed, "It was one of the great, though accidental, achievements of the English Civil War that it gave the Common Man a chance, briefly, to taste the possibility of power and to speak his mind." [3]

And how the Common Man did speak his mind! In a multitude of voices he demanded a democratic republic and redress of economic grievances as well as complete liberty of conscience. Most articulate in this respect were the Levellers, a name of opprobrium given to a mass movement drawn chiefly from the urban lower-middle class and from agricultural tenants. The leader of the Levellers was John Lilburne or "Freeborn John," whose tempestuous life reflects the trials and aspirations of his followers.

In the 1630's, before the Civil War, he was in trouble with the King's Star Chamber for distributing unlicensed literature; released by the Long Parliament, he enlisted, was taken prisoner at Brentford, tried for high treason and narrowly escaped hanging at the King's hands; subsequently he was exchanged; distinguished himself in the fighting; was wounded; withdrew from the Parliamentary army because he would not take the [Presbyterian] Covenant which was imposed after the alliance with the Scots; next he was in trouble for unlicensed printing (he was concerned with a whole series of clandestine printing presses during the Civil War); for libelling the Speaker, for libelling the Earl of Manchester and others; he was constantly in and out of the Tower; trying to reform the government of the City of London, trying to break down the monopoly of the Merchant Adventurers in the wool trade; organizing the outcry in the New Model Army against Parliament; then the mouthpiece of the Leveller movement; constantly up against Cromwell, who he believed had betrayed the cause of liberty for which the war had been fought; twice acquitted to loud popular acclamation; sent into exile, he returned and was shut up by an exasperated government, and in 1655 became a Quaker only a year or two before his death.[4]

The Levellers furnished the leadership for radical disaffection and produced the written programs out of which were formulated the demands of the rank and file of the Model Army. In this manner was prepared a manifesto, *An Agreement of the People,* which, presented to Parliament in 1649, has been described as "the first written constitution in European history." [5] It sets forth clearly certain basic tenets of liberalism: first, that the individual derives from nature certain inalienable or natural rights which neither state nor church can abridge, and second, the principle of popular sovereignty, that all the powers of government are derived by delegation from the people alone. On the basis of these principles the Army's spokesmen demanded numerous specific reforms, which today are accepted as the foundation of a democratic constitutional state. These included freedom of religion, a written constitution, universal manhood suffrage, biennial parliaments, greater diffusion of property and civil rights, and termination of capital punishment, imprisonment for debt, primogeniture, and all feudal tenures.

Parliament never was compelled to act on *An Agreement of the People.*   247
Cromwell had sufficient strength to imprison Lilburne and to suppress the disaffected groups in the army. This does not mean that the Levellers had no
influence on their contemporaries. The legislation passed by the House of
Commons for the establishment of the Commonwealth included basic
Leveller doctrine: "The People are, under God, the Original of all just Power,"
and the Commons "being chosen by, and representing the People, have the
supreme Power in this Nation." [6]

If Parliament was thus willing to accept the principle of the sovereignty
of the people, then what was the issue dividing Parliament and the Levellers?
The answer is to be found in the definition of the word "people." Cromwell
and his followers held that the "people" who should participate in the election
of the Commons were those with a "real or permanent interest in the kingdom"
—that is, property owners—whereas the Levellers maintained that "any man
that is born in England ought . . . to have his voice in election of burgesses
[members of Parliament]." [7] Thus, the issue was between constitutional parliamentary government and democratic government. Many of those who favored
democratic government did so with the intention of using their votes to bring
about social reform, and fear of such reform motivated Cromwell and his
followers in their resolute opposition to the Levellers.

The fact is that there were two revolutions under way in seventeenth century
England.* The first was the political revolution of the lesser gentry and the
bourgeoisie, who were interested in winning the civil and religious freedom
necessary to make their way in the world. The second was the social revolution of the lower-middle class and the tenant farmers, who had a vision of a
community of small-property owners, with complete religious and political
equality, and with generous provisions for the poor. The social revolution
failed in England in the seventeenth century, as it was to fail in France in
the eighteenth. In both cases the protagonists lacked the numbers, the organization, and the maturity necessary for victory. Their time was to come in the late
nineteenth century, by which time the Industrial Revolution had spawned a
sufficiently large and class-conscious urban proletariat. And this proletariat
was to evolve its own ideology—socialism—distinct from, and in opposition
to, the liberalism of the bourgeoisie.

III. ENLIGHTENMENT

The next stage in Europe's political revolution, following the upheaval in
seventeenth century England, was the so-called Enlightenment that manifested itself during the century before the French Revolution of 1789. The
term *Enlightenment* owes its origin to the fact that the leaders of this movement were convinced that they lived in an enlightened age. They regarded the
past as a time of superstition and ignorance, and believed that only in their

---

* See "Significance of the English Revolution," *EMM*, No. 55.

day was mankind at last emerging from darkness into sunlight. Thus, one basic characteristic of this age of Enlightenment was the idea of progress, an idea that was to persist into the twentieth century. With the Enlightenment, it began to be generally assumed that the condition of man would steadily improve, so that each generation would be better off than that which came before.

How was this unceasing progress to be maintained? The answer was simple and confident: by the use of man's reasoning powers. This faith in reason was the other basic feature of the Enlightenment. Indeed, the two key concepts were progress and reason. And the exponents of these concepts were a highly articulate group known as the philosophes. Not to be confused with formal philosophers, the philosophes were not profound or systematic thinkers in any particular field. They were mostly literary men or popularizers—more journalists than philosophers. They were closer to H. G. Wells and G. B. Shaw than to G. E. Moore and A. N. Whitehead. Like Wells and Shaw, the philosophes were generally opposed to the existing order, and they wrote plays, novels, essays, and histories to popularize their ideas and to show the need for change.

Much influenced by the law of gravitation, the philosophes believed in the existence of natural laws that regulated not only the physical universe, as Newton had demonstrated, but also human society. Acting upon this assumption, they proceeded to apply reason to all fields in order to discover the operating natural laws. They subjected everything—all persons, all institutions, all traditions—to the test of reason. This would be a rigorous ordeal for any society in any period, but it was particularly rigorous for France's *ancien régime,* past its prime and creaking in many joints. Thus the philosophes subjected the old regime in France, and throughout Europe, to a barrage of devastating criticism. More important, they evolved a set of revolutionary principles by which they proposed to effect a wholesale reorganization of society. Of particular interest to us are their specific proposals in three areas —economics, religion, and government.

Their key slogan in economics was laissez faire—let the people do what they will, let nature take its course. This opposition to government intervention was a reaction to the comprehensive and rigid regulation of economic life generally known as mercantilism. In the early period of state building, mercantilism had been accepted as necessary for national security. But by the eighteenth century it seemed superfluous, and even pernicious. Merchants who were hindered by monopolies, internal tolls, or excessive tariffs and taxes, enthusiastically took up the cry of laissez faire. We noted that this was the case with the English merchants who attacked the monopolies sold by the Stuart kings. But mercantilism was even more restrictive in France, so the philosophes naturally turned their attention to it. They sought the natural laws underlying economic behavior, and came forth with the general principle of laissez faire—no state interference with the free play of natural economic forces.

The classic formulation of laissez faire was made by the Scotsman Adam Smith in his famous work, *An Inquiry into the Nature and Causes of the Wealth of Nations* (1776). He argued that individuals are motivated by self-interest so far as their economic activities are concerned; that the national welfare is simply the sum of the individual interests operating in a nation; and that each man knows his own interest better than does any statesman. In Smith's own words:

> Every man, as long as he does not violate the laws of justice, is left perfectly free to pursue his own interest his own way, and to bring both his industry and capital into competition with those of any other man, or order of men. The sovereign is completely discharged from a duty; in the attempting to perform which he must always be exposed to innumerable delusions, and for the performance of which no human wisdom or knowledge could ever be sufficient—the duty of superintending the industry of private people, and of directing it towards the employments most suitable to the interest of society.[8]

In religion the key slogan was "Ecrasez l'infâme!"—crush the infamous thing, or stamp out religious fanaticism and intolerance. This violent opposition to intolerance arose from two considerations. One was the conviction that intolerance stood in the way of scientific discussion and arrival at truth. The other was that intolerance appeared to endanger political unity and stability. Thus Voltaire, the outstanding champion of religious toleration, observed that "If one religion only were allowed in England, the government would very possibly become arbitrary: if there were but two, the people would cut one another's throats; but, as there is such a multitude, they all live happy, and in peace."

More specifically, the philosophes rejected the traditional belief that God controls the universe and determines arbitrarily the fate of man. Instead, they sought a natural religion that was in conformity with the dictates of reason. The outcome was a variety of radical departures from religious orthodoxy. Some became outright atheists, denying the existence of God and denouncing religion as a tool of priests and politicians. Others became agnostics, who neither affirmed nor denied the existence of God. The majority were deists, willing to go along with the proposition that God existed and had created the universe, but insisting that, after the act of creation, God allowed the universe to function according to certain natural laws and refrained from intervention. Thus the deists were able to have their cake and eat it too. They could accept God and the teachings of Christianity, and at the same time reject supernatural features such as the virgin birth, the resurrection, the divinity of Christ, and the divine inspiration of the Bible. The important point to note is that all these new dogmas—atheism, agnosticism, deism—reflected the unprecedented growth of rationalistic skepticism of "revealed" or "supernatural" religion. For the first time since the triumph of Christianity in Europe, a definite break had occurred with the Christian tradition.

In government, also, the philosophes had a key phrase—the "social contract." The contract theory of government was not new: the English political theorist John Locke had formulated it in his *Essay on Civil Government* in 1690. Locke stated in that work that if rulers misgoverned their subjects, "by this breach of trust they forfeit the power the people had put into their hands for quite contrary ends, and it devolves to the people, who have a right to resume their original liberty. . . ." In other words Locke viewed government as a political contract betwen rulers and ruled. But the French philosopher Jean-Jacques Rousseau transformed it into a social rather than a political contract. For him it involved an agreement amongst the people themselves. In his major political work, *The Social Contract* (1762), Rousseau stated that all citizens, in forming a government, fused their individual wills into a combined general will, and agreed to accept the findings of this general will as final. Rousseau's concept of the general will was abstruse and susceptible of various interpretations. Twentieth century dictators were to use this doctrine to justify their totalitarian regimes. But from the viewpoint of Europe's political revolution, the important consideration is Rousseau's emphasis on the sovereignty of the people. He viewed government as simply a "commission," and thus justified revolution as a restoration to the sovereign people of its rightful power. "The depositaries of the executive power are not the people's masters, but its officers; it [the people] can set them up and pull them down when it likes; for them there is no question of contract, but of obedience. . . ."

This brief survey suggests the significance of the Enlightenment for Europe's political revolution. The slogans "écrasez l'infâme," "laissez faire," and "social contract" were subversive of traditional institutions and practices. Furthermore, they represented a challenge to the status quo not only in France, but throughout Europe, and even in overseas lands. In fact, the philosophes thought of themselves, not as Frenchmen or Europeans, but as members of the human race. It is significant that Voltaire criticized Bishop Bossuet's *Discourse on Universal History* on the grounds that it was primarily a history of Jews and Christians and ignored the story of pagan antiquity and other cultures. This criticism is typical of the conscious attempt by the philosophes to think and act in global rather than Western terms. They sought to discover laws of universal applicability, corresponding to Newton's laws of the physical world.

If the philosophes did not discover immutable laws governing the whole of mankind, their writings did influence thinking people in many parts of the world. Their greatest immediate success was in persuading a number of European monarchs to accept at least some of their doctrines. These monarchs still held to the theory that they ruled by divine right, but they changed their ideas about the purpose of their rule. Governmental authority was still to be the prerogative of the kings, but now it was to be used for the benefit of the people. Hence these rulers were known as benevolent despots.

The best known of these benevolent despots were Frederick the Great of Prussia (1740–1786), Catherine the Great of Russia (1762–1796), and Joseph II of the Hapsburg Empire (1765–1790). Catherine was perhaps the most articulate, frequently mouthing typical slogans of the Enlightenment, such as "All citizens ought to be equal before the law," "Sovereigns are made to serve their people," and "It is dangerous for a country to be divided into a few large estates." But Catherine and her fellow sovereigns did not merely talk about reform. Catherine improved the administrative and educational systems of her country substantially; Frederick did much to advance agriculture in Prussia; while Joseph II, the most sincere and conscientious of the enlightened despots, wore himself out during his reign trying to remold his Empire in accord with the new principles. Yet in spite of their royal authority, these rulers had very modest success. Their successors frequently undid their work, while the clergy and the aristocrats fought unrelentingly the reforms that menaced their vested interests.

The doctrines of the Enlightenment inspired not only a small number of monarchs but also some of their subjects. In Russia, for example, a nobleman, Aleksandr Radishchev, published in 1790 a volume entitled *Journey from St. Petersburg to Moscow*. Radishchev was an ardent disciple of the philosophes, and in his book he bitterly denounced the basic institutions of his country—the bureaucracy, the absolutist monarchy, and the system of serfdom. In the Hapsburg Empire, also, were to be found many devoted followers of the philosophes. One of these, a nobleman named György Bessenyei, was generally known as the Hungarian Voltaire. A certain Countess Julia Csáky possessed at the end of the eighteenth century a library of 5,160 volumes, of which over 3,600 were French, including the complete first editions of the works of Voltaire and Rousseau. Even in the Moslem Ottoman Empire, Sultan Selim III was an enthusiastic supporter of the doctrines of the Enlightenment, which he appears to have imbibed from French merchants and diplomats in Constantinople. He did his best to put his ideas into practice, but the opposition of the vested interests was too strong and he was murdered in 1807 after eighteen years of rule. The Sultan's subjects also were affected by Enlightenment, particularly the Balkan Christians who had some contact with Western Europe. Outstanding in this respect was a footloose Serbian monk, Dimitrije Obradović, who traveled widely in England, France, and Germany. In the course of his travels he became an outspoken disciple of the Enlightenment, as is evident in the following selection from his writings:

> I had two primary purposes: first, to show the uselessness of monasteries for society; and second, to show the great need for sound learning, as the most effective method of freeing men from superstition and of guiding them to a true reverence for God, to rational piety, and to enlightened virtue, whereby a man gifted with reason enters on the true path of his temporal and eternal welfare. . . . I shall pay no heed whatever to what religion and faith any man belongs, nor is that a matter for consideration in the present enlightened age.[9]

In the Americas, also, the Enlightenment had a direct and very significant influence. In Latin America the new doctrines were disseminated by a steady stream of officials, merchants, and immigrants. One historian, after analyzing the extensive circulation of the writings of the philosophes in Latin American universities and private libraries, concluded that "The Enlightenment clearly influenced . . . the whole of the generation that came to maturity about 1808 and led the struggle for independence."[10] As for England's Thirteen Colonies, we shall consider them in detail in the following section on the American Revolution. Suffice it to note here that Thomas Paine and Benjamin Franklin and Thomas Jefferson were fully as much philosophes as Voltaire and Rousseau and Montesquieu. It was Jefferson, after all, who declared that every man had two homelands, "his own and France."

The influence of the doctrines of the Enlightenment did not end with the eighteenth century or even the nineteenth. To this day the writings of Voltaire and Tom Paine inspire people living in countries where conditions and institutions prevail that are similar to those against which the philosophes had fought. For example, Professor K. M. Khalid of al-Azhar University in Cairo published in 1950 a book entitled *From Here We Start,* presenting a program for the rejuvenation of the Moslem world. Khalid, sprinkling his book heavily with quotations from Voltaire, Rousseau, and Paine, quotes from Rousseau to make clear his motives in writing the book. "Our conscience is perfectly at ease," he writes in his Preface, "as to the nobility of motives behind this study. Perhaps Rousseau's words come closest to describing them: 'It is our belief in God and faith in humanity which stir within us a will to mould the stupid, servile animal into an enlightened, human person.' " [11]

IV. AMERICAN REVOLUTION

The effectiveness of the benevolent despots in implementing the doctrines of the Enlightenment should not be exaggerated. The Enlightenment did not affect the masses of the people in Europe substantially until the outbreak of the French Revolution in 1789. But before that date a revolution had broken out in England's Thirteen Colonies, and this revolution was to offer a laboratory demonstration of the new doctrines in action.

We noted earlier that a leading characteristic of the Thirteen Colonies was their political intractability, their elective assemblies being continually at loggerheads with the governors and the other officials sent out from London. We also noted that Britain decisively defeated France in the Seven Years' War and, by the Treaty of Paris of 1763, acquired France's colonies north to the Arctic and west to the Mississippi. Both the British and the Americans felt considerable pride in the magnitude of their joint victory. But the victory created new problems at the same time that it settled old ones. One new problem was the growing spirit of independence in the Thirteen Colonies now that the danger of a French attack had been removed. Another was the decision of the British government, following its acquisition of vast new colonial territories, to tighten its imperial organization. This tightening might have been feasible at an earlier date, but now, after a long period of "salutary neglect," and after the elimination of the French danger, the colonists were convinced that they were able to take care of themselves and had every right to do so. Thus the American Revolution arose basically out of the conflicting claims of imperial authority and colonial self-government. Francis Bernard, Governor of Massachusetts, made this point very clearly in a letter that he sent to his superiors in London on November 23, 1765:

> All the political evils in America arise from the want of ascertaining the relation between Great Britain and the American colonies. Hence it is that ideas of that relation are found in Britain and America, so very repugnant and contradictory to each other. In Britain the American governments are considered as corporations empowered to make by-laws, existing only during the pleasure of Parliament, who . . . hath at any time a power to dissolve them. In America they claim . . . to be perfect states, not otherwise dependent upon Great Britain than by having the same King; which having compleat legislatures within themselves,

are no ways subject to that of Great Britain. . . . In a difference so very wide who shall determine? [12]

The answer to that crucial question proved to be armed force. Not all, or even most, of the American colonists favored a recourse to violence. In fact, they were split into two antagonistic camps. The conservatives wished merely to return to the loose relations between the mother country and the colonies that prevailed before 1763. The radicals, on the other hand, wanted a change in imperial relations that would give the colonies complete control of their own affairs, and they also wanted a shift of political power inside the colonies in favor of the common people. On this latter point the conservatives were violently opposed. They had no desire to usher in democracy; rather they wished to retain upper-class leadership after the fashion of the Glorious Revolution of 1688 in England. In the end the radicals had their way, thanks to the blunders of inept officials in Britain.

The steps leading to the Revolution are well-known and need not be related in detail. First there was the Proclamation of 1763 prohibiting settlement west of a line drawn along the crests of the Appalachians. This was intended as a temporary measure to preserve peace until an orderly land policy could be worked out, but the prospective settlers and speculators assumed that they were to be perpetually excluded for the benefit of a few British fur traders. Then there was a series of financial measures—the Sugar Act, Quartering Act, Stamp Act, and Townshend Duties—designed to shift a part of Britain's heavy tax load to the American colonists. These levies seemed reasonable to the British, especially in view of the expenditures incurred in defeating the French in the recent war, and the estimated expenditures necessary to protect the American frontiers in the future. But the colonists, being all affected by these imposts, unanimously opposed them. They called an intercontinental congress which organized a boycott of British goods until the financial measures were repealed. But then another series of ill-considered measures by the British government aroused a fresh storm that was to lead to revolution.

The sequence of the dramatic events is familiar—the East India Company's tea monopoly, the Boston Tea Party, and the Coercive, or Intolerable, Acts intended as punishment for the vandalism in Boston harbor. At the same time, in 1774, Parliament enacted the Quebec Act, providing a governmental system for the conquered French Canadians and drawing the boundaries of Quebec to include all the territories north of the Ohio River—that is, the present states of Wisconsin, Michigan, Illinois, Indiana, and Ohio. Much can be said in defense of the Quebec Act, but the American colonists denounced it as another Intolerable Act that blocked their westward expansion for the benefit of the Catholic French Canadians. The First Continental Congress met in Philadelphia in September, 1774, and organized another boycott on British goods. Fighting began the next year when British troops set out from Boston to seize unauthorized stores of weapons at Concord. It was during this operation that someone fired at Lexington Green the "shot heard round the world." The outcome was that the British troops found themselves besieged in Boston. When the Second Continental Congress met the following month, in May, 1775, it had a full-fledged war on its hands and proceeded to raise an American army.

254

Congress was still reluctant to make the final break with the mother country. But sentiment for independence grew with the spread of the fighting. In January, 1776, Thomas Paine published his incendiary pamphlet, *Common Sense*. Paine, who had come from England only two years earlier, detested English society for its social injustices. Now, in his pamphlet, he passionately exhorted the colonists to cast off the tyranny of the Old World.

> There is something absurd in supposing a Continent to be perpetually governed by an island. In no instance hath nature made the satellite larger than its primary planet; and as England and America, with respect to each other, reverse the common order of nature, it is evident that they belong to different systems. England to Europe; America to itself.
>
> O ye that love mankind! Ye that dare oppose not only the tyrany but the tyrant, stand forth! Every spot of the old world is overrun with oppression. Freedom hath been hunted round the globe. Asia and Africa have long expelled her, Europe regards her like a stranger, and England hath given her warning to depart. O! receive the fugitive, and prepare an asylum for mankind!
>
> Let each of us hold out to his neighbor the hearty hand of friendship . . . let the names of Whig and Tory be extinct; and let none other be heard among us than those of a good citizen; an open and resolute friend; and a virtuous supporter of the RIGHTS OF MANKIND and of the FREE AND INDEPENDENT STATES OF AMERICA.[13]

Common Sense was read everywhere in the colonies, and it contributed substantially to Congress' decision on July 4, 1776, to adopt the Declaration of Independence. Once military operations got fully under way, the decisive factor proved to be France's aid to the revolutionaries. During the first two years of the war France was not officially involved, yet she poured munitions into the colonies. Nine-tenths of the arms used by the Americans in the crucial battle of Saratoga in 1777 were of French origin. The following year France signed an alliance with the insurgents and declared war on Britain. Holland and Spain joined France, while most of the other European powers formed an Armed Neutrality to protect their commerce from Britain's naval power. The help of the French navy and of a French expeditionary force of 6,000 men contributed substantially to the victories of George Washington's forces and to the final British surrender at Yorktown in 1781. The peace treaty signed at Paris in 1783 recognized the independence of the American republic, whose frontiers were to extend west to the Mississippi. But Canada remained British, and received an influx of 60,000 American Tories who remained loyal to Britain and who now balanced the original French population in the St. Lawrence Valley.

From the viewpoint of world history the American Revolution is significant not because it created an independent state but because it created a new and different type of state. The Declaration of Independence had declared, "We hold these truths to be self-evident: that all men are created equal." Now the American people, both during and after the Revolution, passed laws aimed at making this declaration true in life as well as on paper.

These laws, in the first place, abolished the Old World system of entail and primogeniture. Land that was entailed could not be sold outside the family, while the law of primogeniture required that lands be turned over to the eldest son. These were devices designed to maintain large estates intact under their traditional owners. But ten years after the Declaration of Independence every state but two had given up entails, and fifteen years after the Declaration, every single state had given up primogeniture. In other words, the new American Republic was to be based on small holdings worked by the farmer himself, rather than on large estates in the hands of a few. This process was furthered also by the seizure and distribution of the extensive estates owned by the Tories, such as that of the Fairfax family in Virginia, which covered six million acres. These estates were seized and sold in small lots, thus changing appreciably the landholding system in the new republic.

The American Revolution led also to a considerable extension of the franchise, though manhood suffrage was not attained until fifty years later. The Revolution also stimulated an antislavery movement. One state government after another passed laws forbidding the importation of slaves—Rhode Island and Connecticut in 1774, Delaware in 1776, Virginia in 1778, and Maryland in 1783. By 1784 laws had been passed in Pennsylvania, Massachusetts, Connecticut, and Rhode Island providing for the gradual and complete abolition of slavery. Even in the slaveholding center of Virginia, laws passed in 1782 made it easier to free Negroes, and within eight years over ten thousand slaves were freed in that state.

Greater religious freedom was another result. Previously there had been state churches in nine of the thirteen colonies. This meant that Congregationalists living in Maryland had to help support that state's Episcopal church; Epicopalians living in Massachusetts had to do the same for the local Congregationalist church; and even those with no church affiliations at all saw some of their tax money used to support a state church. But immediately after the Revolution began, the established churches in five states were abolished, thus beginning the freedom of religion that characterizes present-day United States.

Constitutionalism was also advanced by the Revolution. All thirteen of the states adopted constitutions based upon the principles of the Declaration of Independence. These constitutions were not fully democratic, giving special privileges to owners of property. But they limited government by a separation of governmental powers, and they appended Bills of Rights, which defined the natural rights of the citizens and the things that no government might justly do.

The Northwest Ordinance of 1787 ensured that western lands would share the hard-won benefits of the Revolution: it provided that new states, identical in all legal respects with the old, but excluding slavery, should be formed in the territories north of the Ohio River. Western lands were not to be subjected to a system of colonial subordination or of competitive expansion on the part of the original states. Instead, as they became eligible for statehood, by the principle of an elastic federalism they were to enjoy the rights and liberties won in war and revolution by the original thirteen states.

These changes were not so far-reaching and fundamental as those that were to be effected by the French and Russian Revolutions. These later revolutions, and particularly the Russian, involved much more social and economic reorganization. Nevertheless the American Revolution had a profound impact in its time. The establishment of an independent republic in the New World was widely interpreted in Europe as meaning that the ideas of the Enlightenment were practicable—that it was possible for a people to establish a state and to formulate a workable system of government based on the rights of the individual.

The constitutions adopted by the various American states particularly impressed contemporary Europeans. They acclaimed the Bills of Rights listing the inalienable rights of man—freedom of religion, freedom of assembly, freedom of the press, freedom from arbitrary arrest. It is not accidental that a high point of the French Revolution, as we shall see, was the Declaration of the Rights of Man and Citizen. The committee that drafted this Declaration acknowledged that "this noble idea" was conceived in the New World. "We have cooperated in the events which have established liberty in North America; she shows us on what principles we should base the conservation of our own. . . ." [14] The United States was to serve as a model again when the Norwegians drew up their constitution in 1814, and the Belgians theirs in 1830.

The important point is that America became a symbol of freedom and of opportunity.* It was envied as a new land, free from the burdens and encrustations of past millennia. For example, the German musician and poet Christian Schubert declared that in America thirteen "golden gates are open to the victims of intolerance and despotism." [15] Likewise Jefferson's Italian friend Philip Mazzei wrote that the great majority of Italians were admirers of America—they "have called it aloud the *cause of mankind,* although they live under despotick governments." [16] In Ireland, the nationalist leader Henry Grattan, was inspired by the success of the American revolutionaries and he told his fellow countrymen, "Before you decide on the practicability of being slaves forever look to America." And then in a warning to England he said, "When America sends forth her ambassadors . . . to Europe and manifests to the world her independency and power, do you imagine you will persuade Ireland to be satisfied with an English parliament making laws for her?" [17]

Even today, in the mid-twentieth century, when great changes have transformed American society, and when new and more radical revolutionary movements have gripped large portions of the globe, the United States, for countless millions, still stands out as the utopia of the common man. The contemporary English stateman Edmund Burke sensed the significance of the American Revolution when he declared:

> A great revolution has happened—a revolution made, not by chopping and changing of power in any of the existing states, but by the appearance of a new state, of a new species, in a new part of the globe. It has made as great a change in all the relations, and balances, and gravitations of power, as the appearance of a new planet would in the system of the solar world.[18]

* See "Significance of the American Revolution," *EMM,* No. 56.

Roots of Revolution

The French Revolution looms much larger on the stage of world history than the English or the American Revolutions. It brought about more economic and social change, and influenced a larger portion of the globe, than did the earlier upheavals. The French Revolution marked not only the triumph of the bourgeoisie but also the full awakening of the hitherto dormant masses. Middle-class liberalism came to the fore, but so did nationalism with its appeal to people of all ranks. And these people, so long in the wings, now strode out to the front of the stage, and have remained there ever since. It was in France, in other words, that the world first felt strongly and unmistakably the earthquake that is still rumbling under our feet.

Why did this great transformation take place in France? The basic reason is to be found in the fact that France, the home of the Enlightenment, was not ruled by an enlightened despot until the advent of Napoleon. Consequently, France was a country of such gross inefficiency and inequity that the machinery of government creaked to a standstill. It was this breakdown that gave the ambitious and dissatisfied bourgeoisie a chance to make its successful bid for power.

This pattern is clearly evident in the financial crisis that was the immediate cause for the outbreak of the revolution. In 1789 the French government debt stood at almost four billion livres, which roughly approximated in volume a similar number of United States dollars after World War II. This was a heavy load, but by no means unprecedented or out of line with contemporary national debts. It was, for example, only half as great as the national debt of Great Britain, and less than a fifth as heavy per capita. Yet France could not carry this debt load because its two privileged classes, the clergy and the nobles, were largely exempt from taxation.

The old regime in France was aristocratic in its organization. All Frenchmen belonged legally to an "estate," or order of society, and this membership determined their legal rights and privileges. The First Estate comprised the clergy, who numbered about 100,000 out of a total population of 24.5 million. The Second Estate consisted of the nobility, who totaled about 400,000. The Third Estate included everyone else—over 20 million peasants, and about 4 million urban merchants and artisans. Thus, the first two estates comprised only about 2 per cent of the total population. Yet they owned about 35 per cent of the land and enjoyed most of the benefits of government patronage. And despite these disproportionate advantages they were exempted from almost all taxes, which, indeed, they deemed to be beneath their station.

The burden of taxation consequently fell upon the Third Estate, and especially upon the peasants. The latter comprised over 80 per cent of the population but owned only 30 per cent of the land. Furthermore, the peasants were required to pay to the church the tithe, to the nobles an assortment of feudal dues, and to the state a land tax, an income tax, a poll tax, and various other imposts. This tax load was particularly onerous because the general price level had risen 65 per cent between 1720 and 1789, while the prices of farm goods lagged far behind.

The artisans in the cities also were discontented, because their wages had risen only 22 per cent during those same decades. The bourgeoisie, by contrast, were not so badly off in the matter of taxes because they were better able to protect themselves than the artisans and the peasants. Furthermore, most businessmen profited from the rising prices and from the fivefold increase in French trade between 1713 and 1789. Yet the bourgeoisie were thoroughly dissatisfied with the old regime. They resented being snubbed by the nobility, treated as second-class subjects by the crown, and excluded from the higher posts in the bureaucracy, church, and army. In short, the bourgeoisie wanted political power and social prestige to match their growing economic importance.

Aristocratic Revolution

Such was the nature of the old regime in France when the great upheaval began. This French Revolution, like others before and after, started moderately and became progressively more radical. In fact, it began, not in 1789 as a bourgeois revolution, but in 1787 as an aristocratic revolution. Then it moved to the left through bourgeois and mass phases until a reaction occurred that brought Napoleon to power.

The aristocrats began the revolution because they wished to regain the political power they had lost to the crown during the sixteenth and seventeenth centuries. The king's intendants had replaced the noble governors, and the king's bureaucracy controlled all levels of government throughout the country. The power of the monarchs was reflected in the fact that they had not bothered to call the Estates-General, or national parliament, since 1614. It is understandable then, that when Louis XVI found himself in financial straits after the heavy expenses incurred in supporting the American Revolution, the nobles attempted to exploit the opportunity in order to regain power.

The nobility and the clergy forced the issue in 1787 when Louis attempted to levy a uniform tax on all landed property without regard to the social status of the holder. The privileged orders branded the new tax illegal and asserted that only the nation as a whole assembled in the Estates-General could institute so sweeping a change. The pinch for money became so acute that the king finally gave way and summoned the Estates-General to meet in the spring of 1789. The nobility assumed that they would be able to control this body and thereby regain a dominant position in government. But their calculations proved completely erroneous. The meeting of the Estates-General led, not to the triumph of the nobility, but rather to the loosing of an elemental revolutionary wave that was to sweep away established institutions and ruling classes in France and in much of Europe.

Bourgeois Revolution

The Estates-General that met in Versailles on May 5, 1789, did not represent the people of France; it rather represented the three estates into which they traditionally had been divided. From the beginning the Third Estate proved to be the most dynamic and decisive. It had the advantage of numbers, there being 600 representatives in the Third Estate as against 300 each in the other two. Actually, the Third Estate outnumbered the other two combined, because a certain number of clergy were ready to throw in their lots with the lower orders, as were also a few liberal-minded noblemen, like the Marquis de Lafayette, who already had fought for the revolutionary cause in America. The middle-class representatives also had the advantage of possessing ideas. They knew that they wanted to change the old regime, and, from their reading in the works of the philosophes, they had at least a general idea of how the change should be effected. They also had the ready cash that the government needed so desperately, and they did not hesitate to use this potent weapon to extract the concessions they desired.

The commoners won their first victory in transforming the Estates-General into a National Assembly. This was a vital change because so long as decisions were made on the basis of estates, the Third Estate would be in a perpetual minority of one amongst three. But as soon as the representatives of all three estates combined to form a National Assembly, the commoners, with their allies in the other two camps, would possess a majority. King Louis, who was a rather stupid and unimaginative man, at first vacillated on this critical issue, then insisted that the traditional estates be preserved. But when the commoners boldly defied him and proclaimed themselves the National Assembly, Louis capitulated, on June 23, and instructed the three estates to merge.

The king's concession did not represent a change of heart. He continued to heed the counsels of the so-called "Queen's party"—the reactionary advisers of Marie Antoinette. Indicative of the king's real intentions was his dismissal on July 11 of Jacques Necker, the minister who was regarded as most favorable to reform. At the same time several regiments of loyal troops were quietly transferred to Versailles. The rumor spread that the king was preparing to dissolve the Assembly by force. Furthermore, it seemed that nothing could prevent him from doing so. He had the bayonets, while the commoners had only words and resolutions. But at this critical point the commoners in the National Assembly were saved by an uprising of the common people in Paris. The masses intervened decisively, initiating the third, or mass, phase of the revolution.

Mass Revolution

The masses that now saved the revolution in France were not the riffraff of the streets. In fact, they were the lesser bourgeoisie, comprising shopkeepers and heads of workshops. They were the ones who circulated news and organized demonstrations, while their illiterate journeymen and clerks followed their leadership. The revolutionary outburst occurred following the dismissal of Necker. Mobs roamed the streets, demanding cheaper bread and parading busts of Necker draped in mourning. On July 14, they stormed and razed the Bastille, an ancient royal castle in Paris used as a prison. The event was of little practical significance, since the Bastille by this time was little used. It contained only seven inmates, of which two were mental cases, four forgerers, and the seventh an abnormal young man kept in custody by his family, who paid his expenses. Nevertheless, the Bastille stood in the eyes of the populace as a symbol of oppression, and now this symbol was destroyed. That is why Bastille Day continues to be celebrated in France as Independence Day is in the United States.

The fall of the Bastille marks the appearance of the masses on the historical stage. Their intervention had saved the bourgeoisie, and the latter were forced henceforth to rely on the street mobs to supply a "dose of revolution" at crucial moments. There were to be a good many such moments in the years to come, as the bourgeoisie waged its struggle for power against the king, against the privileged orders, and, eventually, against the old order in all Europe.

The mass revolution manifested itself in the countryside as well as in Paris. The peasants took up arms, incited by their long-standing grievances and by the stirring news of the storming of the Bastille. In many parts of the countryside they tore down fences, seized lands, and burned manor houses. Faced with this revolutionary situation, the nobles and the clergy in the National Assembly made a virtue of necessity and voted with the commoners to abolish feudalism. During the famous "August Days" of 1789, legislation was passed ending all feudal dues, the privilege of tax exemption, the right of the church to collect tithes, and the exclusive right of the nobility to hold office. Outstanding among the numerous other important measures decreed by the Assembly were the confiscation of church lands, the reorganization of the judicial and administrative systems, and the adoption of the Declaration of the Rights of Man and Citizen.

The Declaration set forth certain fundamental principles concerning liberty, property, and security—"Men are born, and always continue, free and equal, in respect of their rights. . . . The Nation is essentially the source of all sovereignty . . . law is an expression of the will of the community . . . lib-

Storming the Bastille. (Copyright Radio Times Hulton Picture Library)

erty consists in the power of doing whatever does not injure another. . . ."
The final clause showed that the bourgeoisie had not lost control of the direction of the revolution: "The right to property being inviolable and sacred, no one ought to be deprived of it, except in cases of evident public necessity, legally ascertained, and on condition of a previous just indemnity." * This Declaration was the essential message of the revolution. In the words of a French historian, it represents the death certificate of the old regime. Printed in thousands of leaflets, pamphlets, and books, and translated into other languages, the Declaration carried the revolutionary slogan of "Liberty, Equality, Fraternity" throughout Europe, and eventually the world.

King Louis was by no means willing to accept either the sweeping reforms of the Fourth of August or the revolutionary principles of the Declaration. "I will never consent," he told an archbishop, "to the spoliation of my clergy or of my nobility. I will not sanction decrees by which they are despoiled." [19] Once more it was the Paris mob that overcame the royal opposition. The populace was agitated not only by the king's hostility but also by the shortage of food supplies in Paris. Early in October a hungry crowd, composed chiefly of women, raided bread stores in Paris and then marched on the royal palace in Versailles. Under the pressure of this mob, Louis agreed to move the court to Paris. The rioters jubilantly marched back, boasting that they were bringing "the baker, the baker's wife, and the baker's boy." The royal family took up residence in the Tuileries (a palace in Paris), where they became virtual prisoners, and the National Assembly settled down in a nearby riding school. These turbulent October days assured the ratification of the decrees of August. They also increased tremendously the influence of the Paris mob, with both the royal family and the Assembly now being vulnerable to mass action.

War and Terror

Although the king in Paris was virtually powerless, many of the clergy and nobles were determined to regain their lost estates and privileges. Some of them fled abroad, where they worked to embroil foreign powers against the revolutionary regime in France. They were successful, although it should be noted that the radical, or Girondist, group in the Assembly also favored war in the belief that thereby a republic could be established in France and revolutionary doctrines disseminated throughout Europe. War began in April, 1792, with Austria and Prussia ranged against France. At first the poorly prepared French were routed, but thousands of volunteers flocked to the colors in a wave of national patriotism. At the same time the Paris mob swung into action against the unpopular Louis and his hated Austrian queen, Marie Antoinette. Under pressure from the mob, the Assembly suspended the king on August 10 and called for the election of a National Convention.

The Convention, elected by universal franchise, met on September 21, 1792, and was brilliantly successful in meeting its most pressing problem—the defense of the country against the Austra-Prussian invaders. The combination of revolutionary élan and popular support proved irresistible, and the Prussians and the Austrians were driven back across the frontier. In 1793 Britain, Hol-

* See "Significance of the French Revolution," *EMM,* No. 57.

land, and Spain joined the coalition against France. The revolutionaries responded with their famous *levée en masse.* "Let everyone," harangued one orator, "assume his post in the national and military effort that is preparing. The young will fight, the married will forge arms . . . provide subsistence, the women will make soldiers' clothing . . . become nurses in hospitals for the wounded, the children will make lint out of the old linen, and the old men will . . . be carried to the public squares to inflame the courage of the young warriors and preach the hatred of kings and the unity of the Republic." [20] The people rose to the defense of their *patrie.* Fourteen armies were put into the field, under the command of young generals who had risen from the ranks. Inspired by the revolutionary slogan "Liberty, Equality, Fraternity," the French citizen armies swept everything before them. By 1795 the enemy coalition had been smashed.

Meanwhile, the Convention was shifting increasingly to the left, partly because it had been elected by universal franchise, and also because of the revolutionary fervor engendered by the war effort. By June, 1793, the Girondists had been displaced by the more radical Jacobins. The dominant organ of government now was the Committee of Public Safety. With revolutionary zeal and passionate patriotism, this Committee appointed and discharged generals, spurred the masses to heroic action, conducted foreign policy, legislated on countless matters, and crushed the opposition by means of a ruthless Reign of Terror. Thousands were charged with treason, or merely with insufficient patriotism, and were subjected to the "national razor," as the guillotine was called.

But the Terror got out of control, and the revolution began "devouring its own children." In the unceasing struggle for power, one after another of the revolutionary leaders followed Louis and Marie Antoinette to the guillotine. Equally disturbing for the bourgeoisie was the growing social radicalism of the revolution. The *sans-culottes* (literally, those who lacked the knee-breeches of genteel society) were pressing hard for a more egalitarian state. They corresponded to the Levellers of the English Revolution, and they demanded a more equitable division of the land, government regulation of prices and wages, and a social security system. Such measures were quite beyond the plans of the French bourgeoisie. So, like their counterparts in England, they worked to halt the leftward course of the revolution. In England, the outcome was the defeat of the Levellers and rule by Cromwell. In France, the *sans-culottes* were brought under control, first by a Directory of five in 1795, and then by Napoleon Bonaparte in 1799.

Napoleon

Napoleon, having won fame as a brilliantly successful general in Italy, used his reputation and popularity to overthrow the Directory. He governed France as First Consul from 1799 to 1804, and as Emperor from 1804 to 1814. Two features of his fifteen-year rule of France are noteworthy for our purposes: his domestic reforms, which consolidated the gains of the revolution, and his military campaigns, which provoked a nationalist reaction in neighboring countries and eventually brought about his downfall.

So far as domestic policies are concerned, Napoleon may be compared to the enlightened despots. He was interested in technical efficiency rather than abstract ideology. He ruled the country autocratically, but he ruled it efficiently. He codified the laws, centralized the administration, organized a system of national education, established the Bank of France, and reached an agreement with the Papacy concerning church-state relations in France. These solid achievements of Napoleon made him generally popular. There were irreconcilables who hankered for the restoration of the old regime or who thought that Napoleon had betrayed the revolution. But the majority hailed him for ending the turbulence and instituting an honest and energetic government.

Napoleon squandered this goodwill by waging war unceasingly. Being a military genius, he was fabulously successful. By 1810 he reached the height of his fortunes, having extended France's frontiers across the Rhine to Lübeck and across the Alps to Rome. The rest of Europe consisted of dependent satellites or allies. Britain alone remained independent and implacably hostile.

In all his conquered territories Napoleon implemented some of the basic principles of the French Revolution. He abolished feudalism and serfdom, recognized the equality of all citizens, and instituted his famous law codes. These innovations represented progress, or at least modernization. If disturbed vested interests everywhere objected to these changes, there was also widespread support for them in many quarters. The bourgeoisie and many intellectuals responded favorably to them outside France as well as in the countries they occupied. French rule was progressive, but the fact remains that it was foreign rule and that, where necessary, it was imposed by force. On December 15, 1792, the Convention had passed a decree stipulating that, "The French nation declares that it will treat as enemies the people who, refusing liberty and equality, or renouncing them, may wish to preserve, recall, or treat with the prince and the privileged castes. . . ." [21] This was highhanded, but Napoleon

Napoleon in Egypt: The Battle of the Pyramids, 1798.

was even more overbearing and demanding. His non-French subjects eventually grew tired of the requisitioning, the taxes, the conscription, and the wars and rumors of wars. French rule usually meant a raising of the quality of administration, but the time came when people were impressed more by the Frenchness of the administration than by its quality.

In other words, these people had become nationalistic, and their nationalism had developed as a movement of resistance against Napoleon's domination. This explains the unrest in Italy, the armed resistance in Spain, and the growing national unity in Germany. It explains also the soul-searching of an Italian patriot who wrote in 1814, "It is painful for me to say it, for no one feels more than I the gratitude which we owe Napoleon; no one appreciates better than I the value of each drop of that generous French blood which watered the Italian soil and redeemed it; but I must be permitted to say it, for it is the truth: to see the French depart was an immense, an ineffable joy." [22]

Most vital for Napoleon was the bitter resistance of Russians of all classes when he invaded their country in 1812. This resistance, as much as the ice and the snow, was responsible for the catastrophic destruction of his Grand Army. From the frozen plains of Russia, the course of Napoleon's career ended precipitously and inevitably on the island of Elba. Thus the ideology of the French Revolution boomeranged against its originators. The people Napoleon had "offended" were people who had first been awakened and enthused by the slogan "Liberty, Equality, Fraternity" and who then had turned against their teachers when they betrayed their own principles.

Vienna Settlement

The Congress of Vienna, which met in 1815 to redraw the map of Europe after Napoleon's downfall, was guided by three principles—legitimacy, containment, and compensation. By the principle of legitimacy, the monarchs of France, Spain, Holland, and the Italian states were restored to their thrones. By the principle of containment, the states bordering France were made as strong as possible. Holland was given Belgium; Austria received Lombardy and Venetia; and Prussia received lands along the Rhine as well as part of Saxony. The victorious allies compensated themselves with various territories —Norway to Sweden; Malta, Ceylon, and the Cape of Good Hope to Britain; Finland, Bessarabia, and most of Poland to Russia; and Dalmatia and Galicia (as well as Lombardy and Venetia) to Austria. In anticipation of later events it should be noted that Germany and Italy remained disunited: Germany as the loose Germanic Confederation of thirty-nine states, and Italy as a "geographic expression" comprising nine states, all of them dominated by Austria because of her commanding position in Lombardy and Venetia.

VI. Nationalism

What is the significance for world history of the three great revolutions we have studied—the English, the American, and the French? The best answer to this question was given by an illiterate Greek guerrilla chieftain who led his countrymen in revolt against the Turkish overlord in 1821. "According to my judgement," he declared, "the French Revolution and the doings of Napoleon opened the eyes of the world. The nations knew nothing before, and the people thought that kings were gods upon the earth and that they were bound to say that whatever they did was well done. Through this present change it is more difficult to rule the people." [23]

In this simple language the guerrilla leader summarized the essence of the English and the American, as well as the French Revolutions. We have seen how the eyes of the world were opened by Lilburne and Paine and Robespierre; by the Levellers and the Minutemen and the *sans-culottes*. This opening of eyes represented a profound political revolution. It marked the beginning for the first time in history of active and institutionalized mass participation in government. This revolution expressed itself in numerous isms which flourished during the nineteenth century. In the remainder of this chapter we shall concern ourselves with three of them—nationalism, liberalism, and socialism—which have since exerted the most influence on the course of European and of world history.

Nationalism is a phenomenon of modern European history. It was not to be found in recognizable form in the Middle Ages. At that time the universalism of the Roman Empire persisted in the Catholic Church, to which all Western Christians belonged, in the Latin language, which all educated people used, and in the Holy Roman Empire, ramshackle structure though it was. Consequently, mass allegiance to a nation was, during those centuries, unknown. Instead, most men considered themselves to be first of all Christians, second, residents of a certain region such as Burgundy or Cornwall, and only last, if at all, Frenchmen or Englishmen.

Three developments gradually modified this scale of allegiances. One was the rise of vernacular languages and the use of these languages for literary expression. Another was the break-off from the Catholic Church of several national churches. Finally, the western European dynasties built and consolidated several large, homogeneous, independent states—England, France, Spain, Portugal, and Denmark. These developments laid the basis for the rise of nationalism, though it should be noted that until the late eighteenth century the nation was identified with the person of the sovereign. Luther, for example, regarded "the bishops and princes" as constituting Germany, while Louis XIV stated that the French nation "resided wholly in the person of the king."

Nationalism did not assume its modern form until the eighteenth century, when the western European bourgeoisie came to share or obtain full power. They did so in the name of the nation, so that the nation no longer was the king, his territory, and his subjects. Rather it was now composed of citizens (only propertied citizens until the late nineteenth century) "who inhabited a common territory, possessed a voice in their common government, and were conscious of their common (imagined or real) heritage and their common interests." [24]

This modern form of nationalism received its greatest impetus during the French Revolutionary and Napoleonic period. In order to survive the onslaught of the *anciens régimes* of Europe, the revolutionary leaders were forced to mobilize national armies—armies of politically conscious citizens ready and eager to fight for *la patrie*. The French Revolution contributed to the development of nationalism in several other ways. It required all French citizens to speak French—"the central or national language"—in place of the numerous regional dialects. It established a network of public elementary schools for the purpose of teaching French and inculcating love of country. The French Revolution also stimulated the publication of newspapers, pamphlets, and periodicals that were cheap and popularly written, and therefore effective in leaving their imprint upon the whole nation. And it inaugurated such nationalist rites and symbols as the national flag, the national anthem, and national holidays.

All these developments enabled nationalism to overcome the traditional commitments to religion and to region. The nature and the intensity of this new loyalty to the nation is reflected in the following letter written in 1793 by a young Jacobin soldier to his mother:

> When *la patrie* calls us for her defense, we should rush to her as I would rush to a good meal. Our life, and our talents do not belong to us. It is to the nation, to *la patrie,* that everything belongs. I know indeed that you and some other inhabitants of our village do not share these sentiments. You and they are insensible to the cries of this outraged fatherland. But as for me, who have been reared in the liberty of conscience and thought, who have always been a republican in my soul, though obliged to live under a monarch, the principles of love for *la patrie,* for liberty, for the republic are not only engraved on my heart, but they are absorbed in it and they will remain in it so long as that Supreme Being who governs the universe may be pleased to maintain within me the breath of life.[25]

We noted earlier that this passionate identification with the nation spread from France to neighboring countries. It did so by the natural diffusion of nationalist ideology, and also as a reaction to French aggression and domination. Nationalism was further stimulated by the Industrial Revolution which, with its new media for mass communication, made possible a more effective and all-embracing indoctrination of citizens. Thus nationalism became a prime factor in European history in the nineteenth century, and in world history in the twentieth. But nationalism changed in character as the nineteenth century passed. It began as a humane and tolerant creed, based on the concept of the brotherhood rather than the rivalry of the various nationalist movements. But in the latter part of the century it became increasingly chauvinistic and militaristic because of the influence of Social Darwinism and the success of Bismarck in uniting Germany by Machiavellian diplomacy and war, or, as he put it, by "blood and iron." *

Nationalism manifested itself strongly immediately after 1815 because the territorial settlement of that year left millions of peoples either disunited or under foreign rule. This was the case with the Germans, the Italians, the Belgians, the Norwegians, and the numerous nationalities of the Hapsburg and Ottoman empires. The inevitable result was a series of nationalist revolts that broke out in all parts of Europe after 1815. The Greeks revolted successfully in 1821, winning their independence from Turkish rule. The Belgians did likewise in 1830, breaking away from Dutch domination. The Italians, after

* See "Evolution of Nationalism," *EMM,* No. 58.

futile uprisings in 1820, 1830, and 1848, established an independent and united state between 1859 and 1871. The Germans, under the leadership of Prussia, built their German Empire after defeating Austria in 1866 and France in 1870–1871.

The principle of nationalism had triumphed in western Europe by 1871. But in central and eastern Europe the Hapsburg, Tsarist, and Ottoman empires remained "prisons of nationalities." The inmates of these prisons, however, were becoming increasingly ungovernable as nationalist movements succeeded all around them. The rulers of the three empires were aware of the consequences of nationalism for their multinational states, and tried to check it by various restrictive measures and by deliberately playing one subject nationality against another. These measures were successful at first but could not prevail indefinitely. The first breaches in the imperial structures were made by the Balkan subjects of the Turks. By 1878 the Serbs, the Rumanians, and the Montenegrins had gained their independence, and in 1908 the Bulgarians did likewise. Much more significant was the assassination in June, 1914, of the Hapsburg Archduke Francis Ferdinand by a young Serbian patriot, Gavrilo Princip. This was the fateful event that precipitated World War I, whose outcome was the destruction of all the empires of central and eastern Europe—the German, Austro-Hungarian, Russian, and Turkish. The peace treaties that terminated the war (discussed in Chapter 20, section VII) were generally based on the principle of nationalism, so that several new states appeared—Poland, Czechoslovakia, Yugoslavia, and Albania—that embodied the independent existence of hitherto subject peoples. For better or for worse, nationalism had triumphed throughout Europe with the conclusion of World War I.

During and after World War I the idea of nationalism began to awaken and spur to action the hundreds of millions of subject peoples in Europe's overseas possessions. The details of this awakening will be considered in later chapters. Suffice it to note here that until the twentieth century the peoples in the colonial territories had retained the same religious and regional allegiances that the western Europeans had held until the eighteenth century. Only then did they also become nationally conscious, partly as a reaction against Western domination, partly because of the diffusion of European nationalist ideology, and also because of the rise of native middle classes that were particularly susceptible to this ideology. In any case, nationalism manifested itself successively in the Middle East, in South Asia, in the Far East, and in Africa. The irresistible power of this spreading ideology is reflected in the fact that in the two decades following World War II, over fifty countries won their independence. As one historian has concluded, "The twentieth century is the first period in history, in which the whole of mankind has accepted one and the same political attitude, that of nationalism." [26]

VII. Liberalism

Liberalism, whose central feature is the emancipation of the individual from class or corporate or governmental restraint, was the second great European doctrine to affect the globe. Its rise was intimately related to the rise of the bourgeoisie, although in central and eastern Europe, where the bourgeoisie was weak, liberalism was espoused by enlightened members of the nobility. Yet the fact remains that liberalism developed in its classic form in western Europe, and has remained essentially a middle-class movement in both tenets and source of support.

Liberal doctrines were first clearly formulated and implemented during the English Revolution. These doctrines were, at that time, primarily religious toleration and security of person and of property against the arbitrariness of the crown. More specifically, this involved parliamentary control of government, the existence of independent political parties, and the recognition of the need for, and the rights of, opposition parties. On the other hand, the franchise was limited by property qualifications, so that the lower-middle class and the workers, who comprised the great majority of the population, were left voteless. Thus, liberalism in seventeenth century England safeguarded and advanced bourgeois interests. Cromwell, for example, ignoring the Leveller slogan "one vote, one value," secured representation in proportion to taxes paid.

Liberalism was further defined and applied with the American Revolution, when substantial advances were made in restricting slavery, extending religious toleration, broadening the franchise, and establishing constitutional government. The federal constitution adopted in 1791 was based on the principle of the separation of powers in order to prevent tyranny—by having the executive, legislative, and judicial powers check and balance each other. The Bill of Rights guaranteed freedom of religion, speech, press, and assembly. And the American constitution, like the English settlement, carefully safeguarded the interests of the propertied classes: by limiting the franchise and by providing for the indirect election of the president and the senators, and for the election of the various branches of the government for different periods of time. These arrangements were designed to prevent a radical popular movement from obtaining control of the entire government at any one time and introducing dangerous changes.

Even more advanced in its liberal tenets than the American Revolution was the French. Its Declaration of the Rights of Man and Citizen is the classic statement of eighteenth century liberalism, proclaiming in ringing phrases the liberties of the individual. But French liberalism, too, was primarily a bourgeois movement. The Declaration, like all of the several constitutions adopted by the French revolutionaries, stressed the rights of property as "inviolable and sacred." And Napoleon's famous codes, which proved to be the most durable and influential, specifically forbade the organization of trade unions and the waging of strikes. The philosophy behind such provisions was summarized by one of the French lawmakers as follows:

> We ought to be governed by the best men; and these are they who are most instructed, and most interested in the maintenance of the law. Now, with very few exceptions, such men will only be found among the owners of property who thereby are attached to their country, to the laws which protect their property, and the social peace which preserves it. . . .[27]

We may conclude that the liberalism that emerged from the English, American, and French Revolutions took the institutional form of constitutional parliamentary government, and was concerned about equal civil rights, though not equal political and social rights. Even in this restricted sense liberalism was on the defensive during the years following the Congress of Vienna. This was a period of reaction against the excesses of the revolutionary years, and restored monarchs, with the assistance of the aristocracy and the clergy, sought to turn the clock back to 1789. In most cases the monarchs ruled autocratically with no constitutional checks. Where constitutions did operate, the franchise was so severely limited that most of the middle class, not to mention the workers, were left voteless. Consequently, the period after 1815 was one of liberal as well as nationalist agitation.

Where the ruling power was foreign, the revolutionary movements were nationalist in character, as in Greece against Turkey, in Poland against Russia, in Belgium against Holland, and in Hungary against Austria. Where the governments were native but unrepresentative, the revolutionary movements were liberal in character. One example is to be found in France, where the restored Bourbon dynasty was overthrown in 1830 and replaced by the self-styled "bourgeois king" Louis Philippe. Another example is the British Reform Bill of 1832, which extended the franchise somewhat, though so modestly that the number of voters increased only from about half a million to about 813,000.

As the nineteenth century passed, liberalism, like other historical movements, changed appreciably in character. It could not continue to concern itself primarily with bourgeois interests at a time when the masses were becoming more assertive as a result of increasing education and trade-union organization. Consequently, there was a shift from the early, classical liberalism to a more democratic variety. Equality before the law was supplemented by equality before the ballot box. By the end of the nineteenth century manhood suffrage was operative in most of the western European countries. Even the hallowed principle of laissez faire was gradually modified. Hitherto intervention by the government in economic and social matters had been regarded as mischievous and futile meddling with the operation of natural laws. This theoretical proposition, however, did not jibe with the facts of life so far as the workers were concerned. Civil liberties and the right to vote did not relieve them from poverty and insecurity produced by unemployment, sickness, disability, and old age. So they used their voting power and union organization to press for social reforms. Under this pressure a new democratic liberalism developed * which recognized the responsibility of the state for the welfare of all its citizens. Thus the western European countries, led by Germany, adopted social reform programs, including old age pensions, minimum wage laws, sickness, accident, and unemployment insurance, and regulation of hours and conditions of work. These reforms of democratic liberalism were the prelude to the welfare state that has become the hallmark of our own age.

Despite this adjustment to a changing world, liberalism has steadily lost ground since the end of the nineteenth century. The chief reason seems to be that it has failed to win the support of the emerging working class. By and large, the workers have turned to various brands of socialism, either of the

---

* See "Evolution of Liberalism," *EMM*, No. 59.

Marxist or the Christian variety. Thus the liberals in country after country have been squeezed between the conservatives on the right and the socialists on the left. This is true not only of Europe, but even more of the former colonial territories, where the overwhelming majority of those who are politically conscious are attracted by nationalism, as a reaction to foreign domination, and to socialism, as a reaction to poverty and backwardness and the lack of native capital and of a native middle class.

VIII. SOCIALISM

In most respects socialism is the antithesis of the classical liberalism of the eighteenth and early nineteenth centuries, for socialism advocates community control or ownership of the means of production for the benefit of society as a whole. Liberalism emphasizes the individual and his rights, socialism the community and its collective welfare. Liberalism represents society as the product of natural laws and denies the possibility of advancing human welfare artificially by legislation. Socialism, by contrast, holds that man, by rational thought and action, can determine his own social system and social relationships. Furthermore, it maintains that human nature is primarily the product of social environment, and that, accordingly, contemporary evils may be eliminated by establishing a society specifically designed to promote collective well-being rather than individual profit, and cooperative social attitudes and patterns of behavior rather than competitive. In short, socialism stresses society and planned social change rather than the individual and laissez faire.

Plans for the reorganization of society are by no means peculiar to our modern age. Ever since the rise of civilization, political and economic power has been concentrated in the hands of a few. This has led prophets and reformers of all periods to advocate plans promoting social justice and equality. In the classical world, for example, Plato in his *Republic* called for an aristocratic communism, a dictatorship of communist philosophers. In the medieval period the English peasant leader John Ball declared to his followers, "My good people,—things cannot go well in England, nor ever will, until all goods are held in common, and until there will be neither serfs nor gentlemen, and we shall all be equal." [28] And in the early modern period Sir Thomas More, in his *Utopia,* depicted an ideal commonwealth whose citizens were honored not for their wealth or ancestry but for their service to the state.

The turmoil and the passions of the English and French Revolutions naturally stimulated more schemes for the promotion of the common welfare. We have seen that Lilburne and his Levellers strove for social as well as political reform in seventeenth century England. Lilburne's counterpart in the French Revolution was "Gracchus" Babeuf, who organized his "Conspiracy of Equals" in 1795. Babeuf viewed the French Revolution as "but the forerunner of another revolution far more grand, far more solemn, and which shall be the last. . . ." To achieve this final revolution Babeuf declared it was necessary to take the following drastic measures: "place all the existing wealth of the country in the hands of the Republic . . . make all the citizens work . . . effect an equal distribution of productions and enjoyments. . . ." [29]

Babeuf's advocacy of the abolition of private property had no chance of acceptance in the France of his day. Even the urban workers were not ready for such radical measures, while the peasants, who comprised the great majority of the population, violently opposed a program that would deprive them of their recently acquired and cherished land. The Directory consequently had no difficulty in arresting and executing Babeuf and in dispersing his followers. Thus in France, as in England, it was not socialism that prevailed but rather a liberalism based on the sanctity of private property.

271

This does not mean that social protest and agitation ended with the triumph of Cromwell and Napoleon. In fact, a vigorous new school of social reformers —the Utopian Socialists—appeared in the early nineteenth century. The reason is that the French Revolution had aroused popular expectations but failed to satisfy them all. There still were the rich and the poor, the exploiters and the exploited. Indeed, the advent of the Industrial Revolution, with its urban slums and its recurring unemployment, seemed to make even wider the chasm between the haves and the have-nots. The Utopian Socialists reacted to these conditions by setting out to emancipate humanity from exploitive capitalism, as their fathers had emancipated it from repressive feudalism.

The outstanding Utopian Socialists were the two Frenchmen, Henri de Saint-Simon (1760–1825) and Charles Fourier (1772–1837), and the English industrialist Robert Owen (1771–1858). These men are remembered for an assortment of theories and projects that they propounded. Saint-Simon urged that the state should lend capital to cooperative societies which should function on the principle of "from each according to his capacities, to each according to his services." Fourier advocated the reorganization of society into small cooperative communities or phalanxes, each with about 1,600 people and 5,000 acres of land. Robert Owen won wide attention by transforming New Lanark, in which his factory was located, into a model community, and by founding the short-lived communistic colony of New Harmony in Indiana.

All these Utopian Socialists had one basic characteristic in common. They concentrated their attention on the principles and on the precise workings of their projected model communities. But the problem of how these were to supplant the existing society they never seriously faced. They had vague expectations of assistance from wealthy or influential sponsors. Saint-Simon, for example, tried to enlist the support of the Pope and of Louis XVIII. Fourier sat in his room at noon every day for twelve years waiting in vain for responses to his newspaper appeals for support. In other words, the Utopian Socialists were not revolutionaries. They had schemes for social change, but they did not expect or plan to effect this change by a workers' uprising. They definitely did not think in terms of revolution or of class warfare. In fact, they scarcely thought at all about how their elaborate blueprints might be implemented. It is for this reason that they are known as Utopian Socialists.

Karl Marx (1818–1883), the father of modern socialism, differed fundamentally from the Utopian Socialists in almost every respect.* He was as materialistic in his outlook as they were idealistic. He spent most of his life studying the historical evolution and the precise functioning of the existing capitalistic society while they prepared blueprints of model communities.

* See "Evolution of Socialism," *EMM*, No. 60.

He was firmly convinced from his study of history that class struggle offered the only means of social change, while they looked for the support of wealthy benefactors.

Marx was a brilliant German Jew who became the editor of a radical newspaper at the age of twenty-four. Hounded from country to country by the police, he finally settled in London, where, for thirty years, he worked in the British Museum collecting data for his epoch-making work, *Das Kapital* (1867). This book was to exert an influence on future history at least equal to that of Rousseau's *Social Contract* or Darwin's *Origin of the Species.* The three basic doctrines in Marx's writings are the materialist, or economic, interpretation of history, the doctrine of class struggle, and the concept of surplus value.

Marx summarized the materialist interpretation of history as follows in the Preface of his earlier work, the *Communist Manifesto,* which he wrote in 1848 with his lifelong friend and benefactor, Friedrich Engels: "In every historical epoch, the prevailing mode of economic production and exchange, and the social organization necessarily following from it, form the basis upon which is built up . . . the political and intellectual history of that epoch." [30] The slave economy of the classical world, for example, explains its political conditions—democracy for the freemen and bondage for the slaves. It also explains the cultural attainments of the classical world—slave labor allowed a few to live in leisure and to devote themselves to cultural pursuits.

The doctrine of class struggle also is best summarized in the *Communist Manifesto.* "The history of all hitherto existing society is the history of class struggles. Freeman and slave, patrician and plebeian, lord and serf, guild-master and journeyman, in a world, oppressor and oppressed, . . . carried on an uninterrupted . . . fight that each time ended, either in a revolutionary re-constitution of society at large, or in the common ruin of the contending classes." [31] The idea of classes with conflicting interests was by no means new with Marx. But what *was* new, and immensely significant, was the proposition that it is through class struggle that mankind has passed from one type of social organization to another. Marxists state, for example, that the transition from feudalism to capitalism was made possible by the appearance of a middle class whose interests were antithetical to those of the feudal lords and who, therefore, led the revolutionary movement that eventually overthrew feudalism.

The materialist interpretation of history and the doctrine of class struggle form the basis of Marx's interpretation of past history. So far as the future was concerned, he was certain that capitalism would give way to socialism, and his conviction was based on his third major doctrine, the theory of surplus value. According to this theory, the value of a commodity depends on the amount of labor necessary to produce it. A forest of trees, for example, is valueless, but if the trees are chopped down, transported to mills, sawed into lumber and made into furniture, then this final product has a value derived from the expended labor. But the price at which the furniture is sold is higher than the value based on the labor because it also includes the profit exacted by the capitalist. This means that the workingman who provides the labor receives in the form of wages substantially less than the price charged the consumer. Marx argued that this represents the Achilles' heel of capitalism, because the workers as a class cannot purchase with their wages what they produce. In the long run this will lead to overproduction, or, as the Marxists put it, to underconsumption due to inadequate purchasing power because of inadequate wages. Thus, the result is the closing of factories, unemployment, a further decline of purchasing power, and at length, a full-scale depression. Furthermore, Marx believed that these depressions would become increasingly frequent and severe until finally the unemployed proletariat would be driven in desperation to revolution. In this way capitalism would be superseded by socialism as feudalism earlier had been by capitalism. And the new socialist society would be depression-proof because, with government ownership of the means of production, there could be no private employers, no profits, and hence no lack of purchasing power.

The course of events since the mid-nineteenth century when Marx wrote his books has not followed the precise pattern that he forecast. The poor have not become poorer and the rich have not become richer. The United States (although far from being capitalistic today in practices or institutions) has attained not only a fantastic increase in national productivity, but also a more equitable division of national income. In 1929, for example, a third of all personal income in the United States went to 5 per cent of the population. By 1946 the share of the richest 5 per cent had dropped to 18 per cent. This combination of increased productivity and more equitable distribution of income has resulted in an unprecedented rise in the living standards of American workers. An automobile in 1914 cost 2,753 hours of work at average pay, while in 1948 it cost only 953 hours. A pound of rib roast cost 48 minutes of work in 1914 but less than 30 minutes in 1948. Likewise, a man's suit required the earnings of 64 hours in 1914 compared to 24 hours in 1948.

Despite these facts, Marx's doctrines have exerted tremendous influence throughout the world, and today represent one of the most vital forces shaping the course of history. The reason is to be found in the nature and the appeal of his doctrines. In the first place they gave the workers everywhere a feeling of self-confidence, a conviction that time was on their side. For did not the theory of surplus value prove the inevitable collapse of capitalism? Marxism also made the workers active and militant, because the theory of class struggle demonstrated that the socialist millennium was to be won not by the assistance of philanthropic benefactors but rather by the efforts of the workers themselves. Finally, Marxism gave workers throughout the world a sense of brotherhood and cohesion by stressing international class ties rather than national allegiance. The last sentence of the Communist Manifesto reads "Workers of the world, unite!"

Marx was not only a theorist and a writer but also an agitator and an organizer. He played an important role in the establishment in 1864 of the International Workingmen's Association, or, as it is commonly called, the First International. This body was committed to Marx's program of the seizure of power by the workers for the purpose or reorganizing society along socialist lines. It attracted considerable attention with its propaganda and its participation in various strikes. But it disintegrated in 1873, largely because its membership comprised an undisciplined and constantly feuding assortment of romanticists, nationalists, and anarchists, as well as socialists.

In 1884 the Socialist, or Second, International was established in Paris. This was a loosely knit organization to which were affiliated the numerous Socialist parties that had appeared by this time in various countries. The Second International grew rapidly, so that by 1914 it comprised the Socialist parties of twenty-seven countries with a total membership of twelve million workers. It is important to note, however, that this Second International was much more moderate in its doctrines and its actions than the First. It was fundamentally a revisionist, rather than revolutionary, organization.

The reason for this shift in emphasis is that the major constituent parties were themselves turning away from simon-pure Marxism to what was termed Revisionism. A number of factors explain this shift in emphasis. One was the gradual extension of the franchise in the western European countries, which meant that the workers could use ballots rather than bullets to attain their objectives. Another was the steady rise after 1850 in European living standards, which tended to make workers more willing to accept the *status quo*. The German revisionist leader Eduard Bernstein expressed the new viewpoint when he declared that socialists should "work less for the better future and more for the better present." The new strategy, in other words, was to attain immediate gains by gradualist reform measures rather than to strive for a socialist society by revolution. The catchwords of the Second International were not class struggle and revolution, but "Agitate! Educate! Organize!"

Not all socialists were willing to go along with this revisionism. Some of them remained true to what they considered to be the teachings of Marx, so that most Socialist parties split into "orthodox" and "revisionist" factions. The revisionists, however, were more in tune with the temper of the times, and usually controlled their respective parties. Indeed, they were able to organize powerful trade-union movements and to win millions of votes in electoral contests. In fact, the German, the French, and the Italian Socialist parties had by 1914 a larger number of seats in their respective national assemblies than any other political parties. Furthermore, Socialist parties of greater or lesser strength were to be found literally throughout the world—in Central Europe, Russia, the Balkans, the Ottoman Empire, the United States, Canada, Latin America, Australia, New Zealand, South Africa, China, and Japan.

When World War I began in 1914, the Second International paid the price for its revisionism: the majority of its members proved to be nationalists first and socialists second. They responded to the exhortations of their respective national governments, with the result that millions of workers died fighting on both sides of the trenches. Thus the Second International was torn asunder, and although it was revived after the war, it never attained its former strength and prestige.

Socialism, however, did not peter out with the disintegration of the Second International. In fact, it was during World War I that the Russian socialists, or Bolsheviks, as they were called, succeeded in seizing power and establishing the first proletarian government in history. Furthermore, the Bolsheviks organized the Third, or Communist, International to challenge the Second, or Socialist, International. We shall consider later the nature and the activities of the Communist regime in Russia and of the international Communist movement. Suffice it to note here that millions of people today live in avowedly socialist states, that many more millions live in communist states, and that the vast propaganda apparatuses of the communist states proclaim day in and day out that Marx's prophecies will soon be fulfilled—that the days of capitalism are numbered. Thus it is apparent that Marxism, in its socialist and communist varieties, is today a central force in world affairs, rivaling nationalism in its dynamism and in its universal appeal.

SUGGESTED READING

For a comparison and interpretation of the English, French, and Russian Revolutions and for conclusions concerning revolutions in general, see C. Brinton, *The Anatomy of Revolution* (New York: Random, 1958; a Vintage book). This work should be supplemented by the superb collection of readings with meaningful introductions by R. W. Postgate, *Revolution from 1789 to 1906* (New York: Harper, 1962; a Torchbook).

On the English Revolution there are the brief, though up-to-date, survey in M. Ashley, *England in the Seventeenth Century* (Baltimore: Penguin, 1952) and the more specialized study by P. Zagorin, *A History of Political Thought in the English Revolution* (London: Routledge, 1954). Noteworthy also is the outstanding study by H. N. Brailsford, *The Levellers and the English Revolution* (Stanford: Stanford Univ., 1961). For the Enlightenment, see the excellent surveys by R. B. Mowat, *The Age of Reason* (Boston: Houghton, 1934) and E. Cassirer, *The Philosophy of the Enlightenment* (Princeton: Princeton Univ., 1951; also Boston: Beacon Paperback) and also the fine documentary collection in *The Portable Age of Reason Reader,* edited and with an introduction by C. Brinton (New York: Viking, 1956). Also noteworthy is the brief study by G. Bruun, *The Enlightened Despots* (New York: Holt, 1929; Berkshire Study). The most recent studies of the American Revolution are by L. H. Gipson, *The Coming of the Revolution, 1763–1775* and J. R. Alden, *The American Revolution, 1775–1783,* both in the "New American Nation" series (New York: Harper, 1954). For the impact of the American Revolution on Europe, see H. Koht, *The American Spirit in Europe* (Philadelphia: Univ. of Pennsylvania, 1948) and M. Kraus, *The North Atlantic Civilization* (Princeton: Van Nostrand, 1957; Anvil Books). Of the thousands of books on the French Revolution, noteworthy are the fine textbooks by L. Gershoy, *The French Revolution and Napoleon* (New York: Appleton, 1933); the classic study of the origins and early history of the revolution by the French master, G. Lefebvre, *The Coming of the French Revolution* (New York: Random, 1957; Vintage); and the collection of readings by J. H. Stewart, *A Documentary Survey of the French Revolution* (New York: Macmillan, 1951). Of particular significance for the analysis of the revolutionary movement in the Western world between 1760 and 1800 are the two volumes by R. R. Palmer, *The Age of the Democratic Revolution: A Political History of Europe and America, 1760–1800* (Princeton: Princeton Univ., 1959, 1964).

A voluminous literature on nationalism now exists, the most recent comprehensive survey being by B. C. Shafer, *Nationalism: Myth and Reality* (New York: Harcourt, 1955). A substantial collection of readings on the various aspects of nationalism is by L. L. Snyder, ed., *The Dynamics of Nationalism* (Princeton: Van Nostrand, 1964). A briefer treatment, with appended documents, is by H. Kohn, *Nationalism: Its Meaning and History* (Princeton: Van Nostrand, 1955; an Anvil Book). The bibliography on liberalism also is tremendous, though there are few comprehensive studies. Outstanding among these are H. J. Laski, *The Rise of Liberalism* (New York: Harper, 1936); J. R. Pennock, *Liberal Democracy: Its Merits and Prospects* (New York: Holt, 1950); and the brief survey, with appended readings, in J. S. Schapiro, *Liberalism: Its Meaning and History* (Princeton: Van Nostrand, 1958; an Anvil Book). Noteworthy also is the interpretation of liberalism by the Indian historian K. M. Panikkar, *In Defence of Liberalism* (Bombay: Asia Publishing House, 1962). Finally, on socialism, there is almost no end of literature, most of it controversial. The careful and monumental study by G. D. H. Cole, *A History of Socialist Thought* (London: Macmillan, 1955–1958), 5 vols., should be noted. More convenient is the brief survey, with appended readings, by S. Hook, *Marx and the Marxists* (Princeton: Van Nostrand, 1955; an Anvil Book); and also the paperback collection of relevant readings in Marxism, with stimulating comments by C. Wright Mills, in *The Marxists* (New York: Dell, 1962; a Laurel edition).

Finally, there is reliable factual and bibliographical information available in the following publications of the Service Center for Teachers of History, Washington, D. C.: S. Elkins and E. McKitrick, *The Founding Fathers: Young Men of the Revolution* (No. 44); C. Brinton, *European Intellectual History* (No. 57); S. J. Idzerda, *The Background of the French Revolution* (No. 21); B. C. Shafer, *Nationalism: Interpreters and Interpretations* (No. 20); and A. G. Meyer, *Marxism Since the Communist Manifesto* (No. 41).

WORLD OF
WESTERN DOMINANCE, 1763-1914

Having considered the three revolutions that made possible Europe's domination of the globe in the nineteenth century, we turn now to the domination process itself. We shall examine precisely how this domination manifested itself in the various parts of the world. Considering first the Eurasian lands, there is evident a certain pattern in both the timing and the unfolding of Europe's impact.

The timing was determined by three principal factors. The first was geographic location, which explains why Russia, for example, felt Europe's dynamism long before China or Japan. The second was the attitude of the local population, and particularly the local ruling class, toward what the West had to offer. Peter the Great's ardent westernism, for example, ensured the early penetration of Western thought and technology into Russia, while the rigid seclusion policies of China and Japan contributed to the exclusion of Western influence from those countries until the second half of the nineteenth century. The third factor was the strength and cohesion of the local societies. Where there was weakness and disunity, Western penetration and control came early, as in the case of India; where there was strength and unity, the West was for long kept at arm's length, as in the case of China.

As regards the nature of the actual impact itself, it is reminiscent of a pebble falling in a pool and stimulating a series of ever expanding circles.

Western intrusion was at first usually confined to some single specific area, but invariably it had repercussions in other fields, which in turn induced further impulses until the entire society was affected. Precisely this point has been made by Sir Henry Maine, the English jurist and historian who served in India between 1862 and 1869:

> It is by indirect and for the most part unintended influence that the British power [in India] metamorphoses and dissolves the ideas and social forms underneath it, nor is there any expedient by which it can escape the duty of rebuilding upon its own principles that which it unwillingly destroyed . . . we do not innovate or destroy in mere arrogance. We rather change because we cannot help it. Whatever be the nature and value of that bundle of influences which we call Progress, nothing can be more certain than that, when a society is once touched by it, it spreads like a contagion.[1]

More specifically, the contagion from the West usually began in the military field. Non-Europeans were most impressed and alarmed by the West's superior military technology, and strove to learn the secrets of this technology as soon as possible. This happened in region after region—in Russia, in the Middle East, in China, and in Japan. But Western arms required the development of certain industries, so that the original military objectives led to new objectives in the economic field. We shall see that for various reasons there was substantial industrialization in the nineteenth century in Russia and Japan, but comparatively little in the Middle East, in India, and in China. Modernization in tools led inevitably to modernization in ideas and values. Arms and factories required schools and science, as one Western borrowing continued inexorably to necessitate another. Military and economic change produced intellectual change, and also social and political. A new merchant and industrial class appeared which challenged the traditional society and ruling groups, and eventually also challenged Western domination. This explains the intellectual ferment and the revolutionary movements that opposed Tsardom in Russia, British control in India, and Manchu rule in China.

This general pattern overlooks innumerable nuances and exceptions—the virtual absence of a native Moslem middle class amongst the Turks, the fateful disparity in the Japanese and Chinese responses to the West, the significance of total European political domination in India, compared to the semi-control in China, and the relative lack of political control in Russia and Japan. The details of these individual developments we shall now analyze in the following chapters on each of the regions of Eurasia. Succeeding chapters will analyze the even greater influence that the West had beyond Eurasia—in sub-Saharan Africa and the Americas.

[1] H. S. Maine, Village-Communities in the East and West (New York, Henry Holt, 1880), pp. 237, 238.

For three hundred years Russia has aspired to consort with Occidental Europe; for three hundred years she has taken her most serious ideas, her most fruitful teachings, and her most vivid delights from there.

PETER Y. CHAADAYEV

Chapter

13

Russia

It is paradoxical to be considering Europe's impact upon Russia, for Russia, after all, is a part of Europe, and the Russian people are a European people. But Russia lies on the fringe of Europe and comprises a great buffer zone between that continent and Asia. Because of this location the historical experience of the Russian people has been quite different from that of other Europeans, and the culture they have developed is correspondingly different. As a result, Russian thinkers have tormented themselves generation after generation with the basic issue of national orientation and national goals.

Russia's relationship with the West has generally been that of passive recipient. Only in the past century and a half has Russia been able to repay the West, at first with the creations of her great writers and composers, and later with the economic planning techniques and the social stimuli generated by the Bolshevik Revolution. But until the twentieth century, Europe's impact on Russia was much greater than the reverse, and this influence has been a central factor in the development of the country.

I. RUSSIA AND EUROPE TO 1856

The first Russian state developed about the principality of Kiev in the ninth century after Christ (see Chapter 8, section II). This early Russian state had numerous ties with the rest of Europe. It conducted a very considerable trade across the Black Sea with Byzantium, and across the Baltic with northwest Europe. And it is significant that Prince Yaroslav in the eleventh century had marriage connections with the leading dynasties of Europe, his sister being married to Casimir I of Poland, his son to a princess of Byzantium, and his two daughters to Henry I of France and to Harald III of Norway.

During the following centuries two crucial developments combined to isolate Russia rather effectively. One was Prince Vladimir's decision about A.D. 990 to adopt the Byzantine Orthodox form of Christianity rather than the Roman Catholic. The differences between the two religions were not very substantial at the time. But the development during the following decades of the doctrine and practice of papal supremacy led to the schism between the two churches in 1054. Russia inevitably became involved in the resulting feud between the Catholic and Orthodox worlds. This was particularly the case after the fall of Constantinople to the Turks (1453), which left Russia the only independent citadel of Orthodoxy. These events made the Russians self-satisfied, self-righteous, and self-isolated. The greatest conceivable good was the Russian Orthodox way of life, and the greatest conceivable evil was the Latinism of the West. Ignoring and scorning the great changes that were transforming the rest of Europe, Russia under Orthodoxy had but one aim —to remain uncontaminated by the heretical Latins.

The other development that cut off Russia from the West was the Mongol invasion in 1237 (see Chapter 8, section II). The Mongols did not interfere with the affairs of their Russian subjects so long as the latter accepted the suzerainty of the khan and paid him annual tribute. Nevertheless, Mongol domination severed most of the remaining ties between Russia and the rest of Europe. This rupture, which persisted during the two centuries of Mongol rule, came at a time when the West was experiencing the Renaissance, the Reformation, the overseas expansion, and the commercial revolution. But inviolate Russia remained largely unaffected by these profound economic and cultural movements. The Orthodox East had no counterpart to Erasmus or da Vinci, to the Fuggers or the Medici, to Lisbon or Antwerp. Furthermore, the Mongols left their own imprint upon Russian society. Their ideas and administrative usages paved the way for the establishment of the semi-Oriental absolutism of the later Muscovite tsars. It is also not without significance that approximately 17 per cent of the Moscow upperclass at the end of the seventeenth century was of non-Russian or Eastern origin.

When the Russians rid themselves of the Mongols in the fifteenth century, the Muscovite civilization that came to light was quite different from anything in Western Europe. It was a homogeneous civilization in the sense that Orthodoxy shaped and colored men's outlook and actions. But it was also a civilization largely devoid of the commerce, the industry, and the science that had made the West so dynamic and expansionist. The more emancipated and far-seeing Russian leaders soon perceived that their economic and technological backwardness represented an intolerable threat to their national security. Thus it was that the Russians in the sixteenth century, like the Turks and the Japanese and the Chinese in later centuries, began to borrow from the West as a measure of self-defense. And what they were primarily interested in borrowing was military technology.

There was nothing academic or abstract about this policy. Rather, it was a matter of life or death, for Russia was surrounded by the powerful Swedes, Lithuanians, and Poles in the west, and by the Turks and Crimean Tatars in the south. It is significant that when Tsar Ivan IV (1533–1584) proposed to Queen Elizabeth of England a military and even a marriage alliance, the King of Poland hastily wrote to Elizabeth begging her to reject the proposition. "Up to now," he wrote, "we could conquer him [the Russian] only because he was a stranger to education and did not know the arts." [1] And when Ivan fought his way to Narva on the Baltic Sea in 1563, the Polish king complained to Elizabeth that English technical aid was responsible for the growing might of Muscovy.

> The Muscovite, enemy to all liberty under the heavens, daily grows mightier by the increase of such things as be brought to him. Thither are brought not only merchandise but also weapons heretofore unknown to him. Even the artists, makers [of such weapons] are brought him, by whose means he maketh himself strong to vanquish all others. Your Majesty knoweth not the strength of this enemy, nor the authority he has over those who serve him. [2]

Thus the neighbors of Russia were deliberately seeking to prevent that country from acquiring Western arms and techniques. The Russians, on their part, naturally sought to break the isolating encirclement, and they did so with increasing success. During the seventeenth century they employed many foreign officers to train and lead their armed forces. Scottish soldiers of fortune were particularly prominent among these recruits. Most of them served in Russia for only a short time, but some settled permanently and became Russified. For example, a certain Captain Learmont, who left the Polish service for the Russian in the seventeenth century, was the ancestor of the famous nineteenth century Russian poet Lermontov. Likewise Barclay of Towy, in Aberdeenshire, settled in Riga, and one of his descendants was General Barclay de Tolly, who led the Russian forces against Napoleon's Grand Army.

Tsar Peter the Great (1682–1725) accelerated tremendously this process of westernization. With his iron will and herculean energy he issued over 3,000 decrees, many in his own hand, and almost all inspired by him. He reorganized his administration and armed forces along Western lines, established industries to support his armies, imported thousands of foreign experts of various types, sent droves of young Russians to study abroad, and set up a number of schools, all of them utilitarian in character: schools of mathematics and navigation, admiralty schools, war department schools, ciphering schools, and, at the summit, the Academy of Sciences. Peter also shattered all precedent by traveling through Western Europe to study foreign institutions and practices at first hand. He showed no interest in French culture or in English parliamentary institutions, but he did work like an ordinary laborer in English and Dutch shipyards in order to learn what seemed to him to be most useful for his country.

By all these means Peter realized in large part his expressed aim of opening a "window to the West." Furthermore, he opened this window in a literal sense by defeating Sweden and acquiring frontage on the Baltic Sea, where he built his new capital of St. Petersburg—the symbol of the new Russia, as Moscow was of the old. These changes, however, were not brought about without bitter opposition from wide segments of the population. Peter's father, Tsar Alexis, had been forced by such traditionalist elements to abandon his efforts at creating a permanent theater and relaxing the prohibitions against foreign dress. Peter, likewise, throughout his reign had to fight against the overt and covert opposition of conservative boyars and churchmen, as well as against the apathy and suspicions of the masses. Even the changes that he did introduce were limited in two important respects: they were largely military, economic, and technical in character, and they affected only the sympathetic members of the thin upper crust of the population.

Peter's work was continued by the gifted and colorful Catherine the Great (1762–1796). Catherine regarded herself and her court as media for the Europeanization of Russia. Being much more intellectual than the pragmatic Peter, she energetically patronized literature, art, the theater, and the press. She was not an original thinker, but she readily absorbed the ideas of others, especially of the philosophes. In fact, she prided herself on being an Enlightened Despot, and often quoted the maxims of the Enlightenment. During her reign the higher Russian nobility became Europeanized to the point of deracination. The nobles who had worn beards and flowing Oriental robes during Peter's reign now aped the court of Versailles in their speech, clothes, dwellings, and social functions. This was the time when the children of the nobility, brought up by French governesses, learned French as their mother tongue, and then picked up only enough Russian to manage the servants. Thus the Europeanization of Russia no longer was confined to technical matters, though it continued to be limited to the upper class. Indeed, the gulf between the Europeanized upper crust and the peasant masses who were bound to the estates as serfs was becoming wider and more provocative. This division is reflected in the following description of the sybaritic ruling class that was supported by the labor of the serfs:

> It must be remembered that in those days a rich Russian nobleman kept his own tailors, shoemakers, saddlers, carpenters, grooms, stable boys, dairymaids, apothecaries, musicians, actors and actresses, poets, architects, painters, and a whole army of more personal servants such as cooks, bakers, pastry makers, dishwashers, laundresses, footmen, butlers, carvers, coffee servers, maids, valets *et hoc genus omne*. Usually there were several people for each of these jobs, with assistants and under-assistants supporting them. Moreover, as most of the wealthier noblemen possessed not only a number of large town houses, but also innumerable estates in the country, each residence was richly endowed with a staff of its own.

In the antechamber of one gentleman seventeen footmen had to sit day and night, of whom one was to fetch the master's pipe, another a glass of water, the third a book, and so forth. The established ritual in the house of another, who kept 300 servants, included a daily dinner of forty courses. Each was brought in by a separate chef wearing a white apron and a tall cap, who had to put his dish on the table, raise his cap, and retire after a deep bow, while twelve butlers and carvers in red uniforms and powdered wigs attended at the table. The same gentleman, by the way, also had seven cats, which were tied for the night to a table with seven legs, and, if one of them happened to break loose, the special staff of maids who were in charge of these cats were severely punished.

Each "Grand Seigneur" took a snobbish pride in inventing for his guests some new form of entertainment or offering them some special new dish. . . . Turning a field into a lake or a mountain practically overnight, putting up a pavilion, or a tower, or triumphal arch, or some other architectural adornment, almost within a few hours, was a popular pastime. One gentleman was famous for his "Island of Love," where the loveliest girls from the village were placed at his guests' disposal; another provided the best artistic and musical entertainments.[3]

This blatant inequity in Russian society scarcely jibed with the principles of the Enlightenment that Catherine ostentatiously propounded. But Catherine was too much a realist to be unduly concerned about the discrepancy between theory and reality. Knowing that she was dependent upon the nobles for her position, she never seriously challenged their interests and privileges. On the contrary, she turned violently against the teachings of the philosophes when the French Revolution broke out. She denounced the revolution as "an irreligious, immoral, anarchical, abominable, and diabolical plague, the enemy of God and of Thrones." "The National Assembly," she added, "should burn all the best French authors, and all that has carried their language over Europe, for all that declares against the abominable mess that they have made. . . . As for the people and its opinion, that is of no great consequence."[4]

Catherine could afford to dismiss so lightly the views of "the people," but it was to be different with her successors. This was especially true after the great Russian victory over Napoleon's Grand Army. Between 1815 and 1818 a Russian army of occupation was stationed in France. These events naturally made a deep impression on public opinion in Russia. The majority were reinforced in their feelings of superiority and condescension toward the West, but many of the officers of the occupation army were much impressed by the relatively free Western society in which they had lived for four years. They absorbed the liberal and radical ideas in contemporary France and were profoundly influenced by them. When they returned to Russia in 1818, they found the Tsarist autocracy to be intolerable. One of the veterans described as follows his reactions upon his return to his homeland:

From France we returned to Russia by sea. The First Division of the Guard landed at Oranienbaum and listened to the Te Deum performed by the Archpriest Derzhavin. During the prayer the police were mercilessly beating the people who attempted to draw nearer to the lined-up troops. This made upon us the first unfavorable impression when we returned to our homeland. . . . Finally the Emperor [Alexander I] appeared, accompanied by the Guard, on a fine sorrel horse, with an unsheathed sword, which he was ready to lower before the Empress. We looked with delight at him. But at that very moment, almost under his horse, a peasant crossed the street. The Emperor spurred his horse and rushed with the unsheathed sword toward the running peasant. The police attacked him with their clubs. We did not believe our own eyes and turned away, ashamed for our beloved Tsar. That was my first disappointment in him; involuntarily I recalled a cat, transformed into a Beauty, who, however, was unable to see a mouse without leaping upon it.

In 1814 life for youth in Petersburg was tiresome. During the two years events had passed before our eyes which had determined the fate of nations and to some degree we had been participants of them. Now it was unbearable to look at the empty life in Petersburg and listen to the babbling of the old men who praised the past and reproached every progressive move. We were away from them a hundred years.[5]

It was sentiments such as these that explain the so-called Decembrist Revolt that broke out in December, 1825, upon the death of Alexander I. The leaders were mostly army officers who wished to westernize Russia by abolishing serfdom and the autocracy. The revolt failed miserably because there was no mass support. The Russians at this time lived under conditions so utterly different from those prevailing in Western Europe that they simply were not ready for western political ideas and institutions. More specifically, Russia lacked the commerce, the industry, and the middle class that had played so decisive a role in the political evolution of the West. Instead, there were at the bottom the bound and inert serf masses—the "dark people," as they were called—and at the top the nobility and the court. Consequently, there was no mass support for the reforms and for the Western type of society desired by the Decembrists.

The meaning of these basic differences between Russia and the West divided Russian thinkers into two groups, the Westerners and the Slavophils.* The Westerners deplored the differences, interpreting them as a product of Russia's slower rate of development. Accordingly, their hero was Peter the Great, and they urged that other rulers match Peter's heroic efforts to goad Russia to catch up with the West. The Slavophils, on the other hand, rejected the Westerners' basic assumption of the unity of human civilization. They maintained that every state embodies and expresses the peculiar national spirit of its people, and that if an attempt is made to model one state after another, the inevitable result will be contradiction and discord. They held the differences between Russia and the West to be fundamental and inherent, reflecting profound dissimilarities in national spirit rather than degrees of advance. Accordingly these Slavophils idealized the homogeneous Muscovite

* See "Russia and the West," EMM, No. 61.

society of the pre-Petrine period, and regarded Peter as the archenemy of Russian civilization and national unity. Far from considering Western society as superior, they rejected it as being materialistic, faithless, and torn by dissension and revolution.

"In contrast to Russian strength, unity, and harmony," wrote one of those Slavophils, "there is nothing but quarrel, division, and weakness, against which our greatness stands out still more—as light against shadow. . . ." [6] And on the other side a Westerner retorted, "That civilization over there [in Western Europe] is the fruit of so much labor; the sciences and the arts have cost so much sweat to so many generations! All that can be yours if you cast away your superstitions, if you repudiate your prejudices, if you are not jealous of your barbaric past, if you do not boast of your centuries of ignorance, if you direct your ambition to appropriating the works of all the peoples and the riches acquired by the human spirit in all latitudes of the globe." [7]

II. Russia and Europe, 1856–1905

The issue between the Slavophils and the Westerners was settled not by persuasion of one side by the other, but rather by the irresistible pressure of the rapidly developing and expanding Western society. This pressure was dramatically illustrated by the Crimean War (1854–1856) between Russia and a number of Western powers, of which the most important were Britain and France. The war was fought on Russian soil—in the Crimean Peninsula—and yet Russia was defeated and forced to accept the humiliating Treaty of Paris. This treaty required Russia to scrap her naval units in the Black Sea and her fortifications along the Black Sea coast, and also forced her to surrender certain small but strategic territories along the Danube.

The Crimean defeat was a severe shock for the Russian nationalists and Slavophils. They had confidently predicted that the superiority of Russia's autocratic institutions would lead to a victory comparable to that of 1812 over Napoleon. "The West," declared one of these Slavophils, "will learn that her boasted liberty and liberal institutions are of little service in the hour of danger, and the Russians who admire such institutions will be constrained to admit that a strong, all directing autocracy is the only means of preserving national greatness." The Westerners did not share this optimism concerning the outcome of the war. In fact, they predicted disastrous defeat, and precisely because Russia had failed to keep up with Europe.

> What preparations have we made for the struggle with civilization, which now sends its forces against us? With all our vast territory and countless population we are incapable of coping with it. When we talk of the glorious campaigns against Napoleon, we forget that since that time Europe has been steadily advancing on the road of progress while we have been standing still. We march not to victory, but to defeat, and the only grain of consolation which we have is that Russia will learn by experience a lesson that will be of use to her in the future.[8]

This prediction of the Westerners proved to be correct in every respect. Russia was defeated, and the defeat served to unveil the corruption and backwardness of the old regime.* Russia's soldiers had fought as gallantly in 1855 as in 1812. But the odds were hopelessly against them: They had rifles that shot only a third as far as those of the Western armies. They had only sailing ships to use against the steamships of the British and the French. They had no medical or commissariat services that were worthy of the name. And the lack of railways in the Crimean Peninsula forced them to haul military supplies in carts, and to march on foot for hundreds of miles before reaching the front. In short, the war was lost because, as the Westerners had perceived, "Europe has been steadily advancing on the road of progress while we have been standing still."

The revelation of the bankruptcy of the old regime led to its modification. The first change was the emancipation of the serfs, who had been intensely restless even before the war. In fact, over 500 peasant disturbances had broken out during the three decades of Nicholas I's reign between 1825 and 1855. With the disaster in the Crimea, the mounting pressure of the serfs became irresistible, and Nicholas' successor, Alexander II, accepted emancipation as the only alternative to revolution. Alexander's decision was encouraged also by many nobles, who favored emancipation in order to take advantage of the growing demand for grain in a Europe that was becoming increasingly industrialized and urbanized. They discovered that they could not produce a substantial surplus for export so long as all the land was divided among the serfs, who grew only enough for their own needs, and a little extra for the noble proprietors. So the more forward-looking nobles were all in favor of freeing the serfs from the bonds that hitherto had bound them to their plots. In this way the nobles planned to consolidate the small plots, introduce efficient, large-scale agricultural techniques, and employ as day laborers only those former serfs whose labor they actually needed, instead of being required to support the whole of a rapidly growing serf population. In other words, the progressive-minded Russian nobles favored emancipation for the same reason that the English gentry had supported and effected the enclosures during the preceding three centuries.

These circumstances combined to make possible the Emancipation Decree issued on March 1, 1861. By its terms all serfs were declared free, and the land that they tilled was divided between themselves and the noble proprietors. The latter were paid with government treasury bonds for the land that was distributed among the peasants. In return, the peasants were required to compensate the government by paying redemption dues for forty-nine years. This was a great turning point in Russian history, even greater than the 1863 Emancipation Proclamation in American history. Emancipation in the United States concerned only the Negro minority, whereas in Russia it involved the overwhelming majority of the population. So far-reaching were the repercussions of the freeing of the serfs that a series of other reforms proved unavoidable, including the reorganization of the judiciary and of the local government.

During the decades following the Crimean War, Western Europe further

---

* See "Crimean War: Repercussions in Russia," *EMM*, No. 62.

undermined the old regime in Russia by contributing decisively to the industrialization of the country. The number of factory workers rose from 381,000 in 1865 to 1,620,000 in 1890, and to 3,000,000 in 1898. By 1913, Russia was producing as much iron and three-fourths as much coal as France. This rapid growth of industrialization during the half century before World War I was not due exclusively to the assistance of the West. The Tsarist regime adopted various measures to speed up industrialization, including subsidies and protective tariffs. But the significance of the West's contribution is evident in the fact that of the total of £500 million invested in Russian industry in 1917, just over one-third comprised foreign investments. Foreign capital controlled 50 per cent of coal and oil output, 60 per cent of copper and iron ore, and 80 per cent of coke.

These developments meant that the Russia of 1914 was much more similar to Europe than had been the Russia of the Decembrists of 1825. But the growing similarity generated, as the Slavophils had warned, certain divisions and conflicts within Russian society. One of these was the growing unrest and political consciousness of the peasant masses. They had been far from satisfied with the terms of the Emancipation Decree which, they felt, had left too large a proportion of the land to the nobles. During the following decades, as the peasants grew rapidly in numbers, their land hunger grew correspondingly, and they became increasingly dissatisfied with the *status quo*. Another source of grievance for the peasants was the intolerably heavy tax load. They paid not only the redemption dues for the land they had received in 1861 but also an assortment of local taxes. In addition, they bore much of the cost of Russia's industrialization, because the high protective tariffs forced up the cost of the manufactured goods they bought. The extent and the intensity of peasant discontent became apparent with the increasing frequency of violent peasant outbreaks against landlords and unpopular government officials. The incident described in the following selection occurred in 1917,* but thousands of others of a similar nature took place in the late nineteenth and early twentieth centuries.

> One September day in the fateful year 1917, by a roadside in the South Central Steppe, a man climbed a telephone pole and cut the minute thread of communication which joined a manor-house on the northern horizon with the towns, the police stations and the barracks along the railway line to the southward. In one sense the manor-house now stood quite alone, but not really so, for within sight of its groves there were several peasant villages. Thus, the two elements—peasant and proprietorial—were left momentarily to react upon each other in isolation. And within a few hours the estate had been looted, the mansion was in flames, and somewhere within the fiery circle the master of the house lay dead.[9]

This peasant disaffection found political expression in the Socialist Revolutionary party which was organized in 1898. Since no political parties were allowed in Russia prior to the 1905 Revolution, the Socialist Revolutionaries

* See "Peasant Unrest after Emancipation," *EMM*, No. 63.

had to operate as an illegal underground group. The main plank of their platform was the distribution of state and noble lands amongst the peasantry. In two important respects they differed from the various types of Marxist socialists. In the first place, they regarded the peasantry rather than the urban proletariat as the main revolutionary force in Russia. In the second place, they advocated and practiced individual acts of terrorism, rather than relying on mass organization and pressure.* Within the Socialist Revolutionary party was the highly secret Fighting Organization which directed the terroristic activities. Its success may be gauged from its long list of illustrious victims, including governors of provinces, ministers of state, and even the Tsar's uncle, Grand Duke Sergei. After each successful operation, the Fighting Organization issued a statement explaining and glorifying the deed. After the assassination of the Minister of Interior, D. S. Sipiagin, it proclaimed: "The crack of the bullet is the only possible means of talking with our ministers, until they learn to understand human speech and listen to the voice of the country. We do not need to explain why Sipiagin was executed. His crimes were too notorious, his life was too generally cursed and his death too generally greeted." [10]

The unrest of the peasants was matched by that of the urban proletariat who had appeared with the growth of industry. The early days of industrialization in Russia, as elsewhere in Europe, involved gross exploitation of labor: sixteen-hour working days, low wages, child labor, and abominable working and living conditions. According to a report on working-class housing in Moscow in 1895, "These places can only be compared, without exaggeration, to places where cattle are kept. Even in summer, when the doors and windows are open, the air is stifling; along the walls and on the sleeping benches traces of mould are to be seen. The floor is invisible because it is covered with dirt." [11]

Under these conditions the Russian workers, like those of Central and Western Europe, came under the influence of Marxist doctrines. Thus a Social Democratic party was organized in 1898 as similar socialist parties had been established elsewhere in Europe. And like the other socialist parties, that of Russia split into revisionist and orthodox factions, or, as they were called in this instance, the Mensheviks and the Bolsheviks.

The split occurred during the second party congress held in London in 1903. The issues concerned party membership and party discipline. Nikolai Lenin, the leader of the orthodox faction, maintained that because of the repressive Tsarist autocracy, the Social Democratic party had to operate very differently from other socialist parties. Membership should be open not to any sympathizer who paid his dues, but only to a small group of full-time professional revolutionaries. And this select membership was to function according to the principle of "democratic centralism." Any major issue facing the party was to be discussed freely by the members until a decision was reached democratically by a vote. But then the "centralism" part of the principle became operative. Every party member, regardless of his personal inclinations, was required on pain of expulsion to support undeviatingly what was now the "party line."

Only with such rigid discipline, Lenin maintained, could Russian socialists carry on effectively their underground operations. Lenin won the support of

* See "Terrorist Strategy of the Socialist Revolutionaries," *EMM*, No. 64.

most of the delegates to the 1903 congress, so that his followers henceforth were known as Bolsheviks, after the Russian word for "majority," and his opponents as Mensheviks, or "minority." It should be noted, however, that the Bolsheviks remained an infinitesimally small group until the outbreak of World War I. Then the chaos and misery produced by the defeats at the front gave the Bolsheviks the opportunity to use their superior organization to mobilize and lead the disaffected masses.*

In addition to the peasants and the urban workers, there was in Russia at the turn of the century a middle class that also was becoming increasingly discontented with the Tsarist regime. The political organization reflecting the views of this group was the Constitutional Democratic party, commonly known under the abbreviated title of Cadets. The program of this party, founded in 1905, resembled that of the English Liberals: a constitutional monarchy balanced by a parliamentary body similar to Britain's House of Commons. The Cadets included many of Russia's outstanding intellectuals and businessmen. When the Tsar was forced to accept an elected assembly (Duma) following the 1905 Revolution, the Cadets played a leading role in its deliberations because of their articulateness and their knowledge of parliamentary procedures. And yet the Cadets never won a mass following comparable to that of the Social Democrats or the Socialist Revolutionaries. One reason was that the middle class was relatively small in Russia, thanks to the retarded development of commerce and industry. The middle class was further weakened because so much of the national economy was controlled by foreign interests. And the Cadets were peculiarly vulnerable to the pressures of the Tsarist autocracy, because, with their middle-class background, they were less willing to meet force with force.† A contemporary English observer analyzed the weakness of their position as follows: "The Cadets, who deserved their reputation of being the best organized party in the Empire, had not a firm hold on the nation, because they were not of it, they could not place themselves at its angle of vision, were incapable of appreciating its world-philosophy, were not rooted in the people. Hence they did not enlist the peasant and the workingman in their party and stood only for themselves." [12]

Such, then, was the West's impact upon Russia by the turn of the century. The intrusion of the West had undermined a distinctive and homogeneous society; and the repercussions of the resulting stresses and dissensions were to culminate in the great revolutions of 1905 and 1917. Before considering these upheavals, we shall survey Russian policies in Asia to the Russo-Japanese War, which set the stage for the 1905 revolution.

III. Russia and Asia to 1905

Just as the relations between Russia and Europe were determined largely by the economic and technological superiority of Europe, so the relations between Russia and Asia were determined by the superiority of Russia. This

* See "Lenin's Strategy for Revolution," *EMM,* No. 65.
† See "Constitutional Democrats and the Russian People," *EMM,* No. 66.

superiority had enabled Russia between the sixteenth and the eighteenth centuries to overcome the tribespeople of Siberia and to expand eastward to the Pacific. But in the southeast the Russians had been halted by the strong and populous Chinese Empire and forced to accept the Nerchinsk Treaty (1689) confining them to the territory north of the Amur Valley.

During the eighteenth and nineteenth centuries the Russians resumed their advance to the east and the south, rounding out their empire by acquiring Alaska, the Amur Valley, and Central Asia. The addition of Alaska involved simply a continuation of the earlier trans-Siberian push into relatively empty territories. But in the Amur Valley the Russians prevailed over the Chinese Empire, and in Central Asia they imposed their rule upon ancient Moselm khanates. These successes were made possible by Russia's steady technological progress. Inadequate vis-à-vis the West—indeed, it was derived from the West —it was nonetheless sufficient to give the Russians a decisive advantage in their relations with the Chinese in East Asia and with the Moslems in Central Asia. Thus, the Russians continued to extend their imperial frontiers until stopped by powers that were technologically equal or superior—that is, by the Americans in Alaska, by the British in India and Persia, and by the Japanese in Manchuria.

Alaska

The Russian advance to Alaska got under way during the reign of Peter the Great. The westernizing tsar was as much interested in the Far East as in Europe, so he selected Captain Vitus Bering, a naval officer of Danish extraction, to lead an expedition to the American continent. Peter's instructions were characteristically terse and to the point.

> To build in Kamchatka or in some other place one or two decked boats. To sail on these boats along the shore which runs to the north and which, since its limits are unknown, seems to be a part of the American coast. To determine where it joins with America. To sail to some settlement under European jurisdiction and if a European ship should be met with to learn from her the name of the coast and take it down in writing, make a landing, obtain detailed information, draw a chart and bring it here.[13]

Bering conducted two expeditions, in 1728 and 1740. He did not settle the question of the junction of Siberia and America, because he sailed eastward across the Bering Sea before reaching the strait that also bears his name and that separates the two continents. But Bering and his associates did explore the Aleutian Islands and also landed on the coast of Alaska. Russian merchants followed on the heels of the explorers, attracted by the profitable trade in sea-otter skins. The merchants first exploited the Aleutian Islanders and then established posts along the Alaskan coast. In 1799 the various private trading companies combined to form the Russo-American Company. The outstanding Russian leader in Alaska was Alexander Baranov, who directed operations energetically and autocratically for a generation. His chief problem was transporting supplies from Siberia across one of the world's

A Russian church in Kodiak, Alaska. (Courtesy Division of Tourism and Economic Development, Juneau, Alaska)

stormiest and foggiest seas. Accordingly, Baranov sent expeditions down the American coast to establish settlements where fresh supplies could be grown for the Alaskan posts. In November, 1811, Fort Ross was established on the Russian River north of San Francisco, and by 1819 the Russians had a chain of nineteen settlements on the American coast.

This expansion led to friction with Spain and with the United States. In fact, the presence of the Russians in the northwest Pacific contributed appreciably to the enunciation of the Monroe Doctrine in 1823. In the end, the Russians decided to give up their American holdings. The decline in the fur trade had brought the Russo-American Company to the point of bankruptcy. And the Russians feared that Alaska was too distant to be defended against American expansionism. Anticipating that they would lose the territory sooner or later, they sold it to the United States in 1867 for $7 million, or less than two cents per acre.

Amur Valley

Meanwhile, this Russian activity in North America had reawakened Russian interest in the Amur Valley. The Russians needed an outlet on the Pacific Ocean to serve as a base for supplying their American settlements. They did have the port of Okhotsk, but this was altogether inadequate, being frozen every year until June, and almost continually fogbound. Furthermore, the port was located on a shallow river with dangerous sandbars blocking its mouth. Consequently, the Russians once more looked longingly toward the broad and navigable Amur River from which they had been ousted by the Nerchinsk Treaty in 1689.

Russian interest was further whetted by the so-called Opium War of 1839–1842 between Britain and China (see Chapter 16, section I). As a result of the war, Britain annexed Hong Kong and acquired a predominant influence in the Yangtze Valley. The Russians now resolved to establish themselves in the Amur Valley lest the British next gain control of the mouth of the river and thus block their natural outlet to the Pacific. In little more than a decade, the Russians gained all their objectives in this vital region. One reason for their success was the ambition and energy of young Count Nikolai Muraviëv, who was appointed governor general of Eastern Siberia in 1847 at the age of 38. Another reason was the weakness of China, by that time a hollow shell compared to the powerful empire that had expelled the Russians from the Amur Valley in the seventeenth century.

Count Muraviëv was given extensive viceregal powers, but he exceeded them in sending out exploratory expeditions that planted the Russian flag on foreign soil. One of his officers, Captain (later Admiral) Nevelskoi, established the fortress of Petropavlovsk on the Kamchatka Peninsula, explored and occupied Sakhalin Island after ousting Japanese settlers, launched steamships on the Amur River, encouraged Russian colonists to settle in the Amur Valley, and founded a number of posts along the coast between the mouth of the Amur and the Korean frontier. The remarkable feature of this penetration of an enormous territory was the small number of men employed. Nevelskoi had only the crew of his ship at his disposal, so he garrisoned one post with six men, another with seven, and two others with eight men apiece. Such shoestring operations were feasible because the entire region was a no man's land over which the Chinese had only a vague suzerainty and no control whatsoever. In fact, the Chinese court was quite unaware of the Russian measures, and it was the Russian government itself which, in May, 1851, informed the Chinese of what had taken place.

Five years later, in 1856, hostilities broke out once more between China and Britain. The Chinese again were badly beaten and forced by the Tientsin Treaties (1858) to open more ports to Western merchants and to make other concessions. Muraviëv seized the opportunity to warn the Chinese of the danger of British control of the Amur and to propose joint Russo-Chinese defense of the region. The outcome was the Aigun Treaty (1858) by which Russia obtained the left bank of the Amur to the Ussuri River, beyond which Russia and China were to exercise joint sovereignty over both banks of the river to the ocean.

Muraviëv now explored carefully the newly won territories and discovered that the formation of ice on the lower Amur was such that control of both banks was essential for navigation purposes. He also found a magnificent harbor on the coast near the Korean frontier. Despite the provisions of the Aigun Treaty, he founded there a city (1860) which he significantly named Vladivostok, or Queen of the East. Meanwhile, China had become embroiled in further trouble with the Western powers, and in 1860 Peking was occupied by an Anglo-French force. The Russian minister in Peking, Count Nikolai Ignatiev, offered his services as an intermediary and succeeded in getting the allies to evacuate the capital under not too onerous conditions. In return for this service the Chinese government willingly negotiated the Treaty of Peking (1860) giving Russia both banks of the Amur from the Ussuri to the sea, and also the entire coastal area from the mouth of the Amur to the Korean border. With the winning of these new farflung frontiers (which exist to the present day), Russian expansion in the Far East came to a halt. It was not resumed again until the beginning of the twentieth century, when Tsar Nicholas II attempted to penetrate south into Korea and Manchuria, and thereby precipitated a disastrous war with Japan.

Central Asia

In the meantime, the Russians had been penetrating also into Central Asia, although their advance in this region did not begin until the second quarter of the nineteenth century. The delay was due in part to the absence of economic incentives comparable to the profitable fur trade in the north. But there were other reasons: The climate and vegetation of Central Asia were quite different to what the Russians were accustomed. Immediately to the south of Siberia was the steppe country in which lived the Kazakh nomads. Still further south began the great desert, dotted with rich oases that supported the ancient Moslem khanates of Bukhara, Khiva, and Kokand. Much stronger militarily than the scattered Siberian tribes, these khanates were able to keep the Russians at arm's length until the late nineteenth century. In fact, the Russians had been forced to build fortifications from Orenburg to Omsk during the eighteenth century in order to ward off nomadic raids on their Siberian settlements.

During the three decades between 1824 and 1854 the Russians made their first advance into Central Asia by conquering the Kazakh steppes to the Syr Darya River. They hoped that the river would serve as a permanent natural frontier, but this did not prove to be the case. The ambition of local commanders, remote from the capital and eager for glory and promotion, frequently forced the hand of the government by presenting it with a *fait accompli*. The constant harassment of marauding bands also led the Russians to press further in spite of misgivings in St. Petersburg and protests from Britain.* Even the British statesman Lord Curzon conceded that, "in the absence of any physical obstacle, and in the presence of an enemy whose rule of life was depredation, and who understood no diplomatic logic but defeat, Russia was as much compelled to go forward as the earth is to go round the sun." [14]

One after another, the legendary centers of Central Asian Moslem civilization fell to the advancing Russians—Tashkent in 1865, Bukhara in 1868, Khiva in 1873, Geok-Tepe in 1881, and Merv in 1884. These thrusts greatly alarmed the British in India, and there were recurring crises and rumors of war. But the century passed without open conflict, primarily because the distances were so immense and the means of transport so limited. Instead of a test of arms, the Anglo-Russian struggle was fought over the control of intervening states, particularly Persia and Afghanistan.

Russian rule changed Central Asia significantly, though not so much as

* See "Russian Expansion in Central Asia," *EMM*, No. 67.

British rule changed India. On the positive side the Russians abolished the widespread slavery and slave trade, freeing 10,000 slaves in Samarkand and its environs alone. The Russians also built railways—notably the Orenburg-Tashkent line—which helped them both for subjugating and modernizing. Thanks to the cheap transportation and the growing demands of the Russian textile industry, cotton cultivation increased spectacularly. In 1884, 300 desiatinas (1 desiatina = 2.7 acres) were planted to cotton on Russian initiative; by 1899, cotton acreage had jumped to 90,000 desiatinas. The Russians also introduced certain agrarian reforms, including a reduction of peasant tax and labor obligations to the state and to landlords.

On the other hand, the Russians' systematic expropriation of Kazakh grazing lands led to a decrease in the size of herds and to widespread famine. The Russians did nothing for the education of the natives, leaving this almost entirely to the Moslem mullahs. In other areas, such as the judiciary and local government, they were less active than the British were in India. The net result was that prior to the Bolshevik Revolution, which brought as many changes to Central Asia as to other regions of the Tsarist empire, the mass of Kazakhs, Kirghizes, Turkomans, Uzbeks, and Tajik were little affected by the coming of the Russians. Despite the railway building and the spreading cotton cultivation, conquerors and conquered lived in different worlds, separated by barriers of language, religion, and customs.

Manchuria

In the 1890's Russian interest was shifting from Central Asia to the Far East. The Trans-Siberian railway, which was slowly nearing completion, presented new opportunities for Russian economic and political expansion. Count Sergei Witte, the newly appointed Minister of Finance, presented a report to Tsar Alexander III (November 6, 1892) in which he stated that the Trans-Siberian line would supersede the Suez Canal as the principal trade route to China. He foresaw Russia in the position of arbiter between Asia and the Western world, and advocated a Russo-Chinese alliance as the best means for attaining that position.

The outbreak of the Sino-Japanese War in 1895 (see Chapter 16, section I) paved the way for the alliance that Witte favored. China again was easily defeated, and repeatedly requested Britain and the United States to mediate. Their refusal forced China to accept the Treaty of Shimonoseki (April 17, 1895), by which she ceded to Japan the Formosa and Pescadores Islands, and the Liaotung Peninsula. But Russia, together with Germany and France, now intervened and compelled the Japanese to restore the peninsula.

This assistance impressed the Chinese who, in the following year, willingly signed a secret treaty with Russia. It provided for mutual assistance in case of Japanese aggression, and it also granted a joint Russo-Chinese Bank a concession for the construction of the Chinese Eastern Railway across Manchuria to Vladivostok. The bank, nominally a private concern, was actually owned and operated by the Russian government. By the outbreak of the Russo-Japanese War in 1904, it had built a total of 1,596 miles of railway in Manchuria.

Russia's next advance in the Far East was in 1898, with the negotiation of a twenty-five year lease of the Liaotung Peninsula, including strategic Port Arthur. And two years later the Russians took advantage of the disturbances attendant upon the Boxer Rebellion to occupy the entire province of Manchuria. This steady encroachment of Russia alarmed the Japanese, who had ambitions of their own on the mainland of Asia. Being in no position to stop the Russians singlehanded, they decided to strengthen themselves by securing an ally. On January 30, 1902, they concluded a military alliance with Britain (details in Chapter 16, section VIII) and, fortified with this backing, they resolved to settle accounts with Russia. In July, 1903, the Japanese proposed that Russia should recognize their "preponderant interests" in Korea, and in return they would recognize Russia's "special interests in railway enterprises in Manchuria."

The Russians were divided concerning this Japanese offer. The finance minister, Count Witte, favored acceptance because he was interested in economic penetration rather than in political annexation with its dangers of war. But influential Russian adventurers with vast timber concessions in northern Korea wished to involve their government to advance their personal fortunes. Russian military circles wanted to obtain a base along the Korean coast because of the great distance between their existing bases at Port Arthur and Vladivostok. And certain Russian politicians, concerned by the mounting revolutionary wave in the country, favored a "little victorious war" that would serve as a lightning rod for the popular unrest. There was no doubt in their minds, or in those of the military, that Russia would prevail in a war with Japan. In fact, they referred contemptuously to the Japanese as *makaki,* or "little monkeys," and they seriously debated whether one Russian soldier was worth one and a half, or two, Japanese soldiers.

This group of adventurers, militarists, and politicians had their way, securing the dismissal of Witte and the virtual rejection of the Japanese offer. Assured by their British alliance and apprehensive about the near-completion of the Trans-Siberian railway, the Japanese struck promptly and decisively. On February 5, 1904, they terminated the negotiations, and three days later they attacked the Russian fleet at Port Arthur without a formal declaration of war.

Russo-Japanese War

In the campaigns that followed, the Japanese David consistently defeated the Russian Goliath. The single-track Trans-Siberian railway proved quite inadequate to meet the supply needs of Russian armies fighting several thousand miles distant from their industrial centers in European Russia. In the first stage of the war, the Japanese surrounded Port Arthur and, after a siege of 148 days, captured the fortress on December 19, 1904. The second stage consisted of a series of battle on the plains of Manchuria. The Japanese were victorious here also, driving the Russians north of Mukden. These campaigns, however, were not decisive, because the Russian armies remained intact, and were reinforced and strengthened as communications improved. But on the sea the Japanese won an overwhelming triumph that led to the beginning of peace negotiations. With incredible shortsightedness the Russians dispatched their hastily refitted Baltic fleet to sail down the entire length of

Europe and Africa, around the Cape of Good Hope, and then across the Indian Ocean and north along the East Asia coast to Japan—a distance equivalent to more than two-thirds the circumference of the globe. On May 27, 1905, the Russian fleet finally arrived at the Tsushima Straits between Japan and Korea. At once it was attacked by a Japanese fleet superior in both numbers and efficiency. Within a few hours virtually all the Russian units had been sunk or captured, while the Japanese lost merely a few destroyers.*

With this debacle the Russians were ready to discuss peace, especially since the war was very unpopular at home and the 1905 Revolution had started. The Japanese also wanted peace negotiations because, although they had won the victories, their still-meager resources had been strained by the burden of the war. On September 5, 1905, the Treaty of Portsmouth was signed, by which Russia acknowledged Japan's "paramount political, military, and economic interests" in Korea, surrendered all preferential or exclusive concessions in Manchuria, and ceded to Japan the southern half of Sakhalin Island and the lease of the Liaotung Peninsula.

In this manner the Japanese halted Russia's expansion in the Far East. Not until four decades later, when the Japanese were disastrously defeated in World War II, was Russia able to recover the territories lost at Portsmouth. Nevertheless, Russia had yielded in 1905 only a few square miles of her periphery. She still remained, as she does today, a great Asiatic power, with territories stretching across the expanses of Siberia and across the deserts of Central Asia. Thus, Russia alone, of all the European powers, today possesses a frontier running across the heart of Asia—from Korea on the Yellow Sea to Turkey on the Black Sea. Russia alone, of the European powers, is today inside Asia looking out, rather than, as in the case of the Western powers, being left only with imperial remnants such as Macao and Hong Kong. This is the significance, for our own age, of this overland expansion of Russia during the three centuries between Yermak's crossing of the Urals and the Russo-Japanese battles on the plains of Manchuria.

IV. First Russian Revolution and Aftermath, 1905–1914

While the Russo-Japanese War was being fought in the Far East, revolution was spreading behind the lines within Russia. The roots of the revolution are to be found in the chronic disaffection of the peasants, the urban workers, and the middle class. This disaffection was aggravated by the war with Japan, which was unpopular to begin with and became increasingly so after the string of defeats. Finally there occurred the so-called "Bloody Sunday" of January 22, 1905—an episode that provided the spark that set off the First Russian Revolution.

On that fateful Sunday a crowd of several thousand persons marched peacefully toward the Winter Palace in St. Petersburg. It was a unique demonstration, virtually a religious procession, with a priest, Father Georgi Gapon, at the head, followed by unarmed men, women, and children bearing ikons and chanting Russian hymns. Their petition included respectful requests for re-

---

* See "Russia Defeated by Japan," *EMM,* No. 68.

A peasant revolt in Russia.

forms such as a representative assembly, free education, eight-hour working day, increased wages, and better working conditions.* Had the Tsar or his representative received the petition and promised to give it careful consideration, the crowd very probably would have dispersed peacefully. Instead, the Tsar's uncle inexplicably ordered the Imperial Guard to fire on the gathered masses. Between 75 and 1000 were killed, and 200 to 2000 wounded. The discrepancy in the figures is due to the fact that some eyewitnesses reported only the Sunday casualties, whereas the disturbance continued in the capital another two days.

The unprovoked massacre aroused a violent reaction throughout the country. Typical was the outburst of the hitherto peaceful Father Gapon, who declared in a speech on the evening of Bloody Sunday

> Dear blood brethren, the bullets of the Imperial soldiers have killed our faith in the Tsar. Let's take vengeance on him and on his entire family. Vengeance on all his ministers and on all the exploiters of Russian soil. Go, pillage the Imperial palaces! All the soldiers and officers who killed our innocent wives and children, all the tyrants, all the oppressors of the Russian people, I herewith smite with my priestly curse.[15]

Bloody Sunday irreparably smashed the benevolent "Little Father" image of the Tsar that so many Russians had traditionally cherished. Citizens

* See "Petition to the Tsar," *EMM*, No. 69.

throughout the Empire turned against the regime, precipitating the great Russian Revolution of 1905. This elemental upheaval passed through three stages before the imperial government was able to reassert its authority. The first, between January and October, 1905, was the rising wave of revolution. All classes and interests came out against the autocracy: the subject nationalities demanded autonomy, peasants pillaged manor houses and seized estates, city workers organized councils, or soviets, for revolutionary action, university students everywhere walked out of their classrooms, and the sailors of the Black Sea fleet mutinied and seized their ships. The world witnessed the extraordinary spectacle of an entire nation on strike.* The Tsar had no alternative but to yield, so he issued his famous October Manifesto (October 30). This read like a confession of sin by the government. It promised freedom of speech, press, and assembly, and also granted Russia a constitution and an elective national assembly, or Duma.

During the second stage of the revolution, between October, 1905, and January, 1906, the uprising continued at high pitch, but the revolutionaries no longer were united. The moderates, consisting mostly of middle-class elements, accepted the October Manifesto, while the radicals, including the Social Democrats and the Socialist Revolutionaries, demanded that a constituent assembly rather than the Tsar's ministers prepare the new constitution. In order to gain their ends the radicals sought to prolong the revolution by organizing more strikes and disturbances. By this time, however, the government was getting stronger and was able to hit back. The signing of the Portsmouth Treaty with Japan on September 5, 1905, freed many troops that were sent home to restore order; and a timely loan of $400 million from Paris and London greatly strengthened the faltering Tsarist government. Consequently, it was able to crush a dangerous workers' revolt that raged in Moscow between December 22 and January 1. Meanwhile, the moderates, alienated by the prolonged violence, were swinging over to the government's side. Thus by the beginning of 1906 the crest of the revolutionary wave had passed.

The third stage of the revolution, from January to July 21, 1906, was that of Tsarist consolidation of power. Government forces hunted down radicals and rebellious peasants, in some cases burning whole villages. On May 6 the government issued the so-called Fundamental Laws by which the Tsar was proclaimed autocrat and retained complete control over the executive, the armed forces, and foreign policy. The elective Duma was to share legislative power with an upper chamber, while its budgetary power was closely restricted. When the Duma did meet on May 10, it refused to accept the Fundamental Laws and criticized the government violently. A deadlock ensued, and the Tsar dissolved the Duma on July 21. The liberal Duma members retaliated by calling on the country to refuse to pay taxes, but the response was feeble. The fact is that by this time the revolutionary tide had ebbed and the First Russian Revolution had run its course.

Although the Revolution failed, it left its imprint on the course of Russia's history. Russia now had a constitutional regime, even though the Duma was emasculated. A second Duma was elected in February, 1907, but it proved

* See "The 1905 Revolution," *EMM,* No. 70.

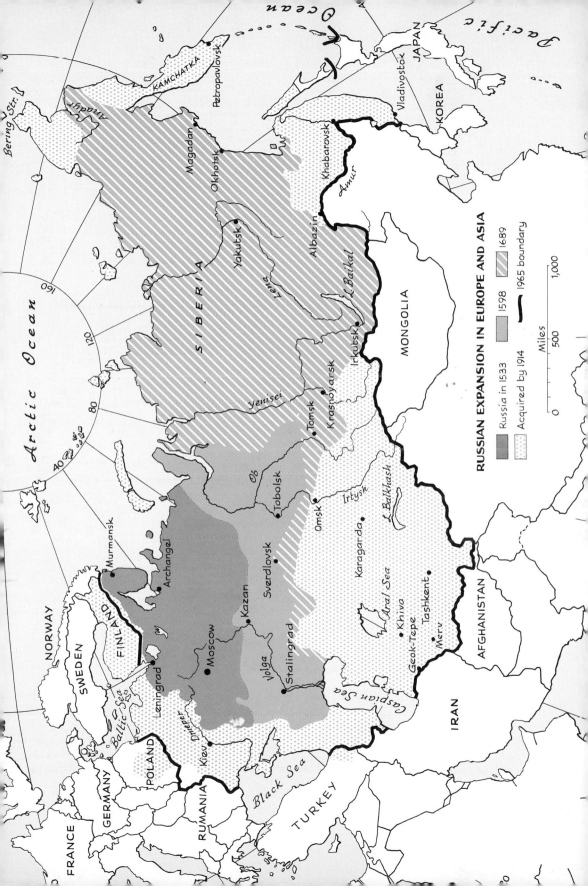

RUSSIAN EXPANSION IN EUROPE AND ASIA

Russia in 1533

Acquired by 1914

1598

1689

1965 boundary

Miles

0   500   1,000

Arctic Ocean

Bering Str.

Ocean

Pacific

JAPAN

KOREA

Vladivostok

Khabarovsk

Amur

Albazin

L. Baikal

Irkutsk

MONGOLIA

Krasnoyarsk

Yenisei

Tomsk

Toboisk

Ob

Irtysh

Omsk

L. Balkhash

Karagarda

Aral Sea

Khiva

Tashkent

Merv

Geok-Tepe

AFGHANISTAN

IRAN

Caspian Sea

TURKEY

Black Sea

RUMANIA

POLAND

GERMANY

FRANCE

SWEDEN

NORWAY

FINLAND

Baltic Sea

Leningrad

Dnieper

Kiev

Moscow

Kazan

Volga

Stalingrad

Sverdlovsk

Murmansk

Archangel

SIBERIA

Yakutsk

Lena

Okhotsk

Magadan

KAMCHATKA

Anadyr

Petropavlovsk

to be even more defiant than the first. The government then reduced the franchise so drastically that the third and fourth Dumas elected in 1907 and 1912 were acceptably conservative and subservient. Nevertheless, the absolutist Tsarist autocracy did end with the October Manifesto, and, after World War I began, the Duma came increasingly into its own until it was swept away with the Bolshevik Revolution.

The events of 1905 are important also because of their contribution to Russian revolutionary experience and tradition. The "Little Father" concept of the Tsar was forever gone, and the political climate was correspondingly affected. Soviets had been organized in the cities and had proven their value as organs for revolutionary action. It is true that after 1906 a lull seemed to set in, but it proved to be a brief respite. For example, the number of workers on strike declined from 1,000,000 in 1905 to 90,000 in 1908 and to 4,000 in 1910. But by 1912, the number had risen again to 1,000,000, and remained at that level during the next two years. Then all discord ceased abruptly with the outbreak of World War I. But with the catastrophic defeats at the front, new storm clouds gathered, and the Tsarist regime entered a new time of troubles from which it never emerged. Thus, the Russian Revolution of 1905 stands out as a dress rehearsal for the world-shaking revolutions of 1917.*

V. Conclusion

Nineteenth century Russia presents the tragic spectacle of an underdeveloped country attempting to modernize itself, but with inadequate results and disruptive repercussions. The great apostle of modernization was Count Sergei Witte, Minister of Finance between 1892 and 1903. In a report to the Tsar in February, 1900, he warned of the need for rapid industrialization in words strikingly similar to those Stalin would speak a quarter century later:

> International competition does not wait. If we do not take energetic and decisive measures so that in the course of the next decades our industry will be able to satisfy the needs of Russia and of the Asiatic countries which are—or should be—under our influence, then the rapidly growing foreign industries will break through our tariff barriers and establish themselves in our fatherland and in the Asiatic countries mentioned above and drive their roots into the depths of our economy. . . . Our economic backwardness may lead to political and cultural backwardness as well.[16]

Witte tried desperately to attain the desired industrialization. He introduced the gold standard, granted subsidies to certain industries, gave concessions to foreign capitalists, floated substantial loans abroad, and erected high protective tariffs. Russian industry did forge ahead under these stimuli, but the country as a whole remained patently and painfully backward in comparison with the West. The census of January, 1897, revealed all the familiar symptoms of underdevelopment—high rates of illiteracy and of infant mor-

* See "Russia and the West: Unresolved Issue ," *EMM*, No. 71.

tality, low per capita mileage of roads and railways, and equally low agricultural and industrial productivity.

Not only was Russia backward, but she was falling further behind the countries of the West. Her rate of economic growth, despite the spurt at the turn of the century, was not equal, for example, to that of Germany. The more Russia tried to catch up, the more she fell behind. Equally alarming was the basic opposition of most elements of Russian society to Witte's program of industrialization. This was true not only of disaffected workers, but also of the peasants who bore much of the cost of industrialization, and of the landed aristocrats who instinctively wished to preserve their traditional agrarian institutions and loathed the rising capitalists, whether native or foreign.

Witte consequently became a political liability for the Tsar and was dismissed in August, 1903. His dismissal pointed up the fatal dilemma of Tsarist Russia—on the one hand the craving for the material attainments of the industrialized West, and on the other the grassroots preference for native agrarian traditions. The outcome of this contradiction was depicted in a memorandum prepared by a high-ranking official in February, 1914, on the implications of war with Germany. He emphasized the "embryonic condition" of Russian industry, the country's "far too great dependence on foreign industry," the "technical backwardness," and the "insufficient network of strategic railroads." War, he concluded, would bring defeat as in 1905, and defeat in turn might bring revolution by the aroused masses.

> The legislative institutions and the intellectual opposition parties, lacking real authority in the eyes of the people, will be powerless to stem the popular tide aroused by themselves, and Russia will be flung into hopeless anarchy, the issue of which cannot be foreseen.[17]

SUGGESTED READING

Aspects of the relations between Russia and the West are treated by W. Weidlé, *Russia: Absent and Present* (New York: Day, 1952); M. M. Laserson, *The American Impact on Russia, 1784–1917* (New York: Crowell-Collier, 1962; a Collier Books paperback); H. Kohn, *Pan-Slavism: Its History and Ideology* (Notre Dame, Ind.: Univ. of Notre Dame, 1953); H. Kohn, *The Mind of Modern Russia* (New Brunswick, N. J., Rutgers Univ., 1955); T. H. Von Laue, *Sergei Witte and the Industrialization of Russia* (New York: Columbia Univ., 1963); M. Raeff, *Peter the Great: Reformer or Revolutionary?* (Boston: Heath, 1963); A. Toynbee, *A Study of History* (New York: Oxford Univ., 1954), VIII, 126–49; M. Malia, *Russia Under Western Eyes: From Peter the Great to Khrushchev* (New York: Wiley, 1964); H. Rogger, *National Consciousness in Eighteenth-Century Russia* (Cambridge: Harvard Univ., 1963); and the stimulating essays by B. H. Sumner, "Russia and Europe," *Oxford Slavonic Papers,* II (1951) and by G. Barraclough, *History in a Changing World* (Oxford: Blackwell, 1955), Chap. 8

For Russian expansion in Central Asia, see A. Lobanov-Rostovsky, *Russia and Asia* (New York: Macmillan, 1933); M. Holdsworth, *Turkestan in the Nine-*

teenth Century: A Brief History of the Khanates of Bukhara, Kokand and Khiva (London: Central Asian Research Center, 1959); R. A. Pierce, *Russian Central Asia, 1867–1917: A Study in Colonial Rule* (Berkeley: Univ. California, 1960); and G. Wint, *The British in Asia* (New York: Institute of Pacific Relations, 1954), Part 2.

*It is not open to question that all social changes
in the Near East during the past century or so
have arisen, directly or indirectly, from the
impact of our Western society and the penetration
of Western techniques and ideas.*

H. A. R. GIBB

The Middle East

The West's influence on the Middle East was quite different
from its influence on Russia, and the response of the Middle Eastern
peoples was as dissimilar. Different peoples, religions, and cultures
were involved, to be sure, but there was also a different political and
social organization. The Ottoman Empire, which embraced most of
the Middle East during the nineteenth century, remained a congeries
of peoples and religions and conflicting loyalties. We noted in Chapter
3 that the empire was organized as a theocracy on the basis of
ecclesiastical communities rather than ethnic groups. These communities, the most important being the Greek Orthodox, Roman Catholic,
and Jewish, were allowed full autonomy under their respective
ecclesiastical leaders. Thus for centuries the various Moslem peoples
(e.g., Turks, Arabs, Albanians, and Kurds) and the various Christian
peoples (e.g., Serbs, Greeks, Bulgars, and Rumanians) lived side by
side in autonomous and self-sufficient communities. Each community
was allowed its own church, language, schools, and local government,
so long as it accepted the sultan's authority and paid taxes to the
imperial treasury.

The significance of this flaccid imperial organization is that
Western ideas and pressures encountered a variety of cultures and
conditions. Consequently, the West did not have a uniform impact on
the Ottoman lands. In analyzing the nature of that impact it is there-

fore essential to take into account the marked variations in regional conditions and responses. For this reason we shall now consider not the Ottoman Empire as a whole, but rather its three main regions in turn—the Balkan Peninsula with its predominantly Christian population, Asia Minor with its ruling Moslem Turkish population, and the provinces south of Asia Minor with their Moslem Arab peoples. Finally we shall consider also certain significant developments in the Persian kingdom, which comprised an important element in the Near East, though not a part of the Ottoman Empire.

I. Balkan Christians

The Balkan peoples were under Turkish rule for four centuries or more. It is often assumed that these were centuries of unrelieved tyranny, and that the oppressed Christians yearned for freedom and waited impatiently for an opportunity to revolt. This interpretation fails to explain the actual course of events. The various Balkan peoples greatly outnumbered the few Turks living in their midst. They lived in compact groups and retained their languages and religions. If they had been eager to revolt, they would have caused more trouble for the Turks than they actually did. Yet, during the early centuries, the Turks had no more trouble ruling their Christian subjects in the Balkans than their Moslem subjects in Asia.

The explanation is that the Turkish conquerors were efficient and benevolent compared to the Byzantine emperors, Frankish nobles, Venetian signors, and Bulgarian and Serbian princes who formerly had ruled the Balkan lands. Ottoman administration was stern but just, taxation was light, and the non-Moslems enjoyed a degree of toleration unparalleled in Christian Europe. During the eighteenth and nineteenth centuries, however, this situation changed drastically. The decline in Ottoman power and efficiency during this period led to widespread corruption and extortion, which in turn drove the now oppressed and embittered Balkan Christians to take up arms in self-defense. At the same time the Balkan peoples, for various reasons, were being affected and aroused by a variety of influences from the West.

The Balkan peoples were affected earlier and more profoundly by the West than any of the other ethnic groups of the Ottoman Empire.* Mostly Christians, they were more receptive to the Christian West than were the Moslem Turks and Arabs. The territorial contiguity of the Balkan lands to the rest of Europe made it easier for persons and goods and ideas to converge upon the Balkan Peninsula from across the Danube and the Adriatic, Mediterranean, and Black Seas. And with the growth of commerce, of industry, and of a middle class during the eighteenth and nineteenth centuries, the growing demand for food imports in Western Europe stimulated agriculture in the Balkans, especially the cultivation of the new colonial products, cotton and maize. The export of these commodities in turn contributed to the growth of a class of native Balkan merchants and mariners. The expansion of trade also stimulated the demand and output of handicraft products. Important manufacturing centers appeared in various parts of the peninsula, frequently in

* See "Dimitrije Obradović: Balkan Disciple of the West's Enlightenment," *EMM,* No. 72.

isolated mountain areas where the artisans could practice their crafts with a minimum of Turkish interference. And the rise of commerce and industry had still another effect: it promoted the growth of a merchant marine along the Dalmatian, Albanian, and Epirote coasts, and amongst the Aegean Islands. The new Balkan marine exported products such as cotton, maize, dyeing materials, wine, oil, and fruits, and brought back mostly colonial products and manufactured goods—spices, sugar, woolens, glass, watches, guns, and gunpowder.

The significance of this economic renaissance is that it created a middle class of merchants, artisans, shipowners, and mariners that was particularly susceptible and sympathetic to Western ideas and institutions. These people, by their very nature, were dissatisfied with Ottoman rule, which by this time had become ineffective and corrupt. Merchants and seamen who journeyed to foreign lands, and frequently resided there, could not help contrasting the security and enlightenment they witnessed abroad with the deplorable conditions at home. Very naturally they would conclude that their own future, and that of their fellow countrymen, depended upon the earliest possible removal of the Turkish incubus. Typical of this attitude was the following lament of a Greek merchant, John Priggos, who had made his fortune in Amsterdam. While living in that city he had been impressed by the security and justice with which commercial operations could be conducted.

> But all this cannot exist under the Turk. He has neither order nor justice. And if the capital is one thousand he multiplies it tenfold so that he may loot and impoverish others, not realizing that the wealth of his subjects is the wealth of his kingdom . . . he is altogether unjust, and he is not one for creating anything but only for destroying. May the Almighty ruin him so that Greece may become Christian, and justice may prevail, and governments may be created as in Europe where everyone has his own without fear of any injustice. . . .[1]

Merchants like Priggos made important contributions to Balkan national development, not only because of their political activities, but also because of their role as intermediaries between their native countries and the outside world. The Serbian merchants in southern Hungary, the Bulgarian merchants in southern Russia, and the Greek merchants scattered widely in the main cities of Europe, all contributed to the intellectual awakening of their fellow countrymen. They did so by publishing books and newspapers in their native languages, by establishing schools and libraries in their home towns and villages, and by financing the education of young men of their race in foreign universities. All this meant not only more education but a new type of education. It was no longer primarily religious. Instead, it was profoundly influenced by the current Enlightenment in Western Europe. A contemporary Protestant missionary complained: "The educated portion of Greece, the elite of her gifted sons, are in the habit of sipping the poison of Voltaire and of Rousseau, whose writings have been put into modern Greek. I have met Greeks who have keenly defended the chilly theory of deism, and to meet their sophistries requires talent." [2]

Western influence in the Balkans became more directly political and inflammatory during the French Revolutionary and Napoleonic era. Politically conscious elements were much impressed by the uprisings in Paris, by the slogan "Liberty, Equality, Fraternity," and by the spectacle of Napoleon toppling over one dynasty after another. A contemporary Greek revolutionary testified: "The French Revolution in general awakened the minds of all men. . . . All the Christians of the Near East prayed to God that France should wage war against the Turks, and they believed that they would be freed. . . . But when Napoleon made no move, they began to take measures for freeing themselves." [3]

The tempo of national awakening varied greatly from one Balkan people to another. The Greeks came first because of certain favorable circumstances: their numerous contacts with the West, their glorious classical and Byzantine heritage which stimulated national pride, and their Greek Orthodox Church which embodied and preserved national consciousness. After the Greeks came the Serbs, who enjoyed a high degree of local self-government as well as the stimulating influence of the large Serbian settlements in southern Hungary. These advantages of the Greeks and the Serbs suggest the reasons for the slower rate of national revival among the other Balkan peoples. The Bulgars had no direct ties with the West and were located near the Ottoman capital and the solid Turkish settlements in Thrace and eastern Macedonia. The Rumanians suffered from a sharp social stratification which was unique in the Balkans and which produced a cultivated upper class and an inert peasant mass. The Albanians were the worst off, with their primitive tribal organization and their division among three creeds, Orthodoxy, Catholicism, and Islam.

These factors explain why in place of a common Balkan revolution against Ottoman rule, there occurred separate uprisings ranging from the early nineteenth century to the early twentieth. The Greeks won complete independence from the Turks following a protracted War of Independence between 1821 and 1829. The Serbs had revolted earlier in 1804, but only gained an autonomous status within the Ottoman Empire in 1815. It was not until 1878 that the Serbian Principality gained full independence and became the Kingdom of Serbia. The Rumanians came next, winning autonomy in 1859 and full independence in 1878. The Bulgarians followed later, gaining autonomy in 1878 and independence in 1908. Three of these Balkan peoples, the Serbs, Greeks, and Bulgarians, combined forces in 1912 to drive the Turks completely out of the peninsula. They were successful on the battlefield, and, despite a fratricidal war amongst the victors, the Turks were compelled in 1913 to surrender all their remaining territories in the Balkans with the exception of an enclave stretching around the Straits from Constantinople to Adrianople.

In this manner the imperial Ottoman frontiers shrank from the walls of Vienna in 1683 to the Danube in 1815, to the mid-Balkans in 1878, and to the environs of Constantinople in 1913. As the empire receded, independent Balkan states took its place—Greece, Serbia, Rumania, Bulgaria, and, in 1912, Albania. The West contributed decisively to this resurgence of the Balkan peoples by providing a revolutionary nationalist ideology, by stimulating the

Russian officers lowering the Ottoman flag from a Turkish gunboat sunk in Rumania, 1877.

growth of a middle class that was ready to act on the basis of that ideology, and by sporadically helping the Balkan revolutionaries in their struggle against Turkish rule.*

II. TURKS

The West affected the Turks much less and much later than it did the Balkan Christians. Various factors explain this difference, of which the most important probably were the Moslem religion of the Turks, and their lack of a native middle class.

If the Christian faith of the Balkan peoples constituted a bond with the West, the Moslem faith of the Turks was a barrier. And it was a most formidable barrier because of the long history of antagonism and conflict between Christianity and Islam. Not only was there this tradition of mutual hostility, but there was also a self-defeating superiority complex on the part of the Turks because of their faith. For centuries they had bested the Christian powers of Europe and had triumphantly carried their star and crescent across the Danube to the walls of Vienna. True, they had suffered reverses in the late seventeenth and eighteenth centuries at the hands of the Austrians and Russians. But until the late nineteenth century they continued to rule most of the Balkan Peninsula with millions of Christian subjects. Thus there was no question in the mind of the average Turk, whatever his station

* See "The Greek Awakening and the West," *EMM*, No. 73.

might be, of the superiority of himself, of his faith, and of his way of life. And this superiority was simply assumed as a natural attribute of the fact of being a Moslem and a Turk. The condescension and contempt of the Turks for all non-Moslems is reflected in the epithets they commonly used to refer to various European peoples. The Albanians they labeled "gut-sellers"; the Bulgarians, "vagabonds"; the Dutch, "cheese mongers"; the English, "atheists"; the French, "mad infidels"; and the Rumanians, "gypsies." [4] This attitude, needless to say, was not conducive to interaction between the Ottoman Empire and the West.

The Turks also were little affected by the West because they never developed their own middle class. They had no interest in, or respect for, commercial pursuits, so that the Ottoman bourgeoisie was largely Greek, Armenian, and Jewish. By contrast, the Turks were either peasants (who were generally apathetic), or teachers and judges in the Moslem ecclesiastical organization (which almost always meant that they were bitterly anti-Western), or else they were officeholders in the imperial bureaucracy (in which case they usually were interested only in retaining their posts and advancing in rank). The significance of this situation is apparent in view of the vital role played by Greek, Serbian, and Bulgarian merchants in their respective countries. It was they who established contact with the West, propagated Western ideas, and undertook political activity. But no group existed among the Turks to perform similar functions. Consequently, the rare advocates of reform who did appear among the Turks found themselves without any following. They found themselves, in other words, in the same plight as did the Decembrists in Russia in 1825, and for the same reason.

This lack of mass support for reform was strikingly illustrated by the fate of Sultan Selim III. Selim ascended the Ottoman throne in 1789—a symbolically appropriate year, given the revolutionary nature of his ideas and aspirations. Selim was not the first sultan to recognize the need for reform in the empire, but he was the first to realize that the reform measures must look forward rather than backward. He was the first to consider reform in terms of borrowing from the West rather than returning to the days of Suleiman the Magnificent. His plans included the reorganization of administration, the revamping of education, and the complete transformation of the janissary corps.

The janissaries, who had once been the elite of the Ottoman infantry, by this time had degenerated to a worthless and insubordinate Praetorian Guard. This became apparent during the wars with Russia at the end of the eighteenth century, when regiments showed up at the front with a total of five or six men. At the sight of the enemy the janissaries were likely to break and run, pausing only to plunder their own camp. Several sultans had attempted in the past to curb or destroy this pernicious body. They all failed because the heads of law and religion, known collectively as the ulema, had sided with the janissaries. Important economic interests also supported the *status quo,* because of the revenue derived from speculation in janissary pay tickets. Each janissary had a sealed pay ticket that served as a passbook to receive pay. In 1740 permission was granted to buy and sell these pay tickets. They quickly became a type of stock certificate, eagerly bought up by officials and speculators in no way connected with the janissary corps. The scramble for tickets led inevitably to wholesale padding of the rolls. The names of dead janissaries were kept on the rolls, and their tickets were bought and sold. This powerful combination of military, religious, and economic vested interests explains why earlier sultans had failed to reform the janissary corps, and why Selim also was destined to fail, and to forfeit his throne and his life. At the outset Selim was able to make some headway because of the popular revulsion against the scandalous showing of the janissaries against the Russians. He began with various peripheral measures designed to improve the imperial defenses, and then, in 1793, he took the decisive step of establishing a new military force known as the New Regulations Army. This was to be a Western-type army with common uniforms, specified enlistment and recruitment procedures, European methods of training, and modern armaments, including the latest types of artillery, and the bayonet in place of the traditional scimitar. The plans called for an initial recruitment of 1,600 men and a gradual increase to 12,000.

The New Army demonstrated its worth in several engagements, but this only intensified the apprehension and opposition of the janissaries and their allies. They countered with a carefully organized campaign designed to exploit the fears, prejudices, and fanaticism of the Moslem population. They spread rumors that the New Army was an invention of the Christian infidels and that Selim sponsored it precisely because he no longer was the true defender of the Faith. Sufficient unrest was formented to enable the janissaries to force Selim to abdicate in May, 1808. Two months later he was strangled when his supporters attempted to rescue him from his palace quarters where he was held captive.

In retrospect it is clear that Selim had tried to do what Peter the Great of Russia had accomplished a century earlier. He failed partly because he was not so forceful or decisive a personality as the Russian Tsar. But his failure was due even more to the fact that the janissaries, together with their allies in the ulema and the bureaucracy and the court, comprised a much more powerful opposition bloc than any that Peter had faced. And Selim had no middle class, no mass party or movement, to fall back upon. Thus, the Ottoman Empire seemed at the end of 1808 to be as unchanging and as unchangeable as ever.*

Yet during the course of the nineteenth century the Ottoman Empire, like the Russian, was penetrated and influenced and controlled by the West in numerous direct and indirect ways. Of the several channels of penetration, the earliest, and in some respects the most effective, was the military, The Turks, like the Russians, found it necessary to adopt European military techniques for self-preservation. During the latter half of the nineteenth century the Western powers actively encouraged the Turks to modernize their military forces in order to block Russian expansion into the Middle East. But military westernization involved more than visits by foreign military missions. To support a modern army it proved necessary to teach European languages, mathematics, and sciences, as well as military subjects. It was necessary to establish medical schools, hospitals, engineering workshops, foundries for heavy arms, naval arsenals, and shipbuilding yards. And of the considerable number of young men who were sent abroad to study in foreign military academies, some inevitably imbibed Western ideologies as well as Western

---

* See "Early Nineteenth Century Turkey," *EMM,* No. 74.

military techniques. Thus, of all Ottoman institutions, the army became the most westernized in outlook as well as in organization. It is not surprising that when the old regime was finally overthrown in the Ottoman Empire in 1908, the coup was executed not by a political party or a mass movement, but by an army clique.

In the field of religion, also, the West impinged upon the Moslem Middle East. Missionaries were preaching and founding schools throughout the empire. By 1875 the American missionaries alone had 240 schools with 8,000 pupils. Most of the latter were Armenians and other Christians, since proselytism amongst Moslems was forbidden. But a fair number of Turkish students were to be found in the foreign colleges scattered throughout the empire, such as the American-operated Constantinople Women's College and Robert College (also in Constantinople), and the French Jesuit University of St. Joseph at Beirut. The Turks themselves by this time had established several institutions of higher learning, including the School of Medicine (1867), the Imperial Lycée (1868), the University of Constantinople (1869), the School of Law (1870), and the School of Political Science (1878). The Turkish press, too, was developing rapidly during these years. In 1859 there was only one official and one semiofficial weekly in the empire. By 1872 there were three daily papers and several weeklies. In addition, six French dailies appeared in cities such as Constantinople, Smyrna, and Alexandria, and were read by educated Turks.*

At least as significant as this cultural impact was the West's economic penetration of the Ottoman Empire. In 1869 the Suez Canal was opened after ten years of construction by a European syndicate headed by a French diplomat and promoter, Ferdinand de Lesseps. The effect of the canal was to place the Ottoman Empire once more on the main trade route between Europe and Asia. At the same time the Ottoman government was falling hopelessly into debt to European governments and to private financiers. They contracted their first loan in 1854, and by 1875 their debts totaled £200 million sterling. Some £12 million sterling a year was required to meet annuities, interest, and sinking fund, a sum that amounted to a little more than half the total revenues of the empire. The load proved too heavy, and some of the interest payments were defaulted, whereupon the European powers imposed in 1881 the Ottoman Public Debt Administration. This body consisted mostly of foreign representatives and was entrusted with the revenues from various monopolies and customs duties for the service of the imperial debts.

In addition to this hold over Ottoman public finances, foreign interests had control over the Turkish banking and railway systems, irrigation works, mining enterprises, and municipal public utilities. The empire, besides, was still subject to the capitulations, or extraterritorial privileges, that foreigners had enjoyed in the Ottoman Empire since the fifteenth century. These privileges included exemption from the jurisdiction of Ottoman courts and from certain taxes, including personal imposts and customs tariffs. The latter were set at a very low level and could not be raised by the Ottoman government without the consent of the European powers, which, needless to say, was not forthcoming. Thus we may conclude that the Ottoman Empire, even more than the Russian, was in a semicolonial economic relationship with Europe.

* See "Westernized Education in Turkey," *EMM*, No. 75.

The effect of all these Western pressures and controls cannot be measured precisely. But there can be no doubt that they gradually cracked the hitherto impregnable and monolithic Islamic structure. Canals, railways, banks, missionaries, schools, and newspapers constitute the background and also the explanation for a literary and intellectual awakening that occurred amongst the Turks in the latter half of the nineteenth century.

The best-known leaders of this awakening were Ibrahim Shinassi, Namik Kemal, and Abdul Hamid Ziya. These men did not agree on all issues, but they did have certain common experiences and they did share certain fundamental principles. They all had lived in Western Europe, and they all had been tremendously impressed by the thought and literature as well as the material achievements of the West. They returned to Constantinople determined to sweep away what they now considered to be the tyranny of Persian classicism which for so long had dominated the Ottoman language and literature. They dropped the Persian and Arabic words and turns of speech in favor of the purer and simpler Turkish. They translated foreign works, particularly those by French authors such as Racine, La Fontaine, Rousseau, Montesquieu, and Condorcet. They founded the first independent Turkish newspapers which, although of limited circulation, reached wide circles in the coffeehouses and bazaars where they were read.

These early reformers did not organize a political party. The only real parties in the Ottoman Empire at this time were the "ins" and the "outs" gathered about individual political leaders. But by 1865 a fairly well-defined group of young Western-minded writers had formed about the newspaper *Mushbir,* or *Herald of Glad Tidings.* The paper championed, among other things, the introduction of some form of constitutional representative government. This was too much for the imperial regime, which suppressed the paper

The construction of the Suez Canal. (Copyright Radio Times Hulton Picture Library)

in 1867. The editor and his colleagues now found themselves in the same position as Selim III in the beginning of the century. Lacking mass support, they were forced to flee to Paris and London, where they continued their journalistic attacks on the imperial regime.

Meanwhile, a few Turkish statesmen had realized that a comprehensive reform program along Western lines was essential for the survival of the empire. Outstanding were Reshid Pasha (1802–1858) and Midhat Pasha (1822–1884), both of whom served as grand vizirs and issued numerous reform decrees.* In May, 1876, Midhat took advantage of a financial crisis at home and a revolution in the Balkan provinces to force Sultan Abdul Aziz to abdicate. He then prepared a constitution providing for an elected parliament, a bill of rights, and an independent judiciary. The new sultan, Abdul Hamid II, was forced to accept the constitution, but he had no intention of abiding by it. In January, 1877, he dismissed Midhat from office and banished him from Constantinople. The only signs of protest were a few placards on walls. Turkish reformers still were faced with a mass inertia comparable to that which had doomed the Russian Decembrists in 1825. Consequently, Abdul Hamid was able to rule as the unchallenged master of his empire for the rest of the century.

During those decades Abdul Hamid kept himself in power by relentlessly combatting the disruptive forces of nationalism and constitutionalism. To this end he discouraged travel and study abroad, maintained a great host of informers, and enforced a strict censorship of the press. Periodically his agents flushed out small groups of disaffected elements, mostly intellectuals and office-holders, who usually fled to Paris for refuge. There they published periodicals and pamphlets criticizing the Hamidian autocracy, and thus became popularly known in Western Europe as the Young Turks. These Turkish exiles were joined by revolutionary leaders of the various subject peoples under Abdul Hamid, including Arabs, Greeks, Armenians, Albanians, Kurds, and Jews. Representatives of all these nationalities held a congress in Paris in February, 1902, with the aim of organizing a common front against the autocracy. But they quickly discovered that they agreed on nothing except that they all disliked the sultan. One group wanted Turkish predominance and centralized rule, while another favored a decentralized empire with full autonomy for the subject peoples.

While the exiled intellectuals were quarreling in Paris, reform-minded Turkish army leaders were taking decisive measures to break the Sultan's grip on the empire. Most of them had studied in the West or had contact with Western military missions within the empire, so that they had come to realize that the Sultan's rigid *status quo* policy was obsolete and dangerous. They organized the Ottoman Society of Liberty with headquarters in Saloniki. Army officers were the backbone of this body, though they were greatly aided by other groups, and particularly by the Jews who were the most numerous and wealthy element in Saloniki. The Society of Liberty was organized into cells of five, so that no one knew more than four fellow members. A new recruit had to be sponsored by a regular member and was observed closely during a probationary period. For the purpose of communication each cell

* See "Turkish Attempts at Westernization," *EMM*, No. 76.

312

contained a "guide" who received the orders of the top central committee from the "guide" of another cell, and who was required to pass on the orders without delay. The activities of the Society have been described as follows:

> To meet the expenses each member was compelled to contribute a fixed percentage of his income to the Committee chest, while rich members, in addition to this tax, made generous donations when funds were required. Arms and ammunition were secretly purchased. A considerable sum was set apart annually to provide for the families of members who lost life or liberty while working for the cause. Their several duties were apportioned to the members. There were the messengers who, disguised in various ways, went to and fro over the Empire carrying verbal reports and instructions. . . . There were the men who had to assassinate those whom the Committee had condemned to death—Government officials who were working against the movement with a dangerous zeal, and Palace spies who were getting on the scent. Other members were sent out to act as spies in the interest of the cause, and the *contre espionage* became at last so thorough that it baffled the espionage of the Palace. . . . The first and most important task . . . was, of course, that of bringing round to the cause the Macedonian garrison—the Third Army Corps. . . . By degrees a number of the young officers were affiliated and received instructions to win over the rank and file. . . . At last the whole Macedonian army was won over to the cause of the Young Turks.[5]

These conspirators openly revolted in July, 1908, being forced to action by two developments. One was the threat of foreign intervention. The British foreign minister, Sir Edward Grey, proposed in March, 1908, an autonomous regime for Macedonia. By this time all Turks, both Young and Old, knew that autonomy was the prelude to independence. A little later it was announced that the British and Russian monarchs would meet at Reval on June 10 to discuss reforms for Macedonia. The Committee of Union and Progress, as the Saloniki organization was now called, feared that the Reval meeting would end with Ottoman partition, so it decided to act at once.

The Committee telegraphed an ultimatum to the sultan, threatening to march upon Constantinople unless the 1876 constitution was restored within twenty-four hours. Abdul Hamid was advised by his State Council to comply to the ultimatum. And the Sheik-ul-Islam, the highest religious and legal authority of the Empire, refused to issue a *fetva* authorizing suppression of the rebels. So on July 24, Abdul Hamid proclaimed the restoration of the constitution. Making the best of the situation, he added that he had always favored constitutional government but had been misled by evil councillors. "I thought," the British Ambassador reported, "that the Sultan, the greatest of living Comedians, was unique when he posed before the crowds as the simple and loving father of his people who for 40 years had been deceived by his advisers as to their real wishes." [6]

The news of the Sultan's capitulation was greeted with wild rejoicing. Christians and Turks embraced one another in the streets. The Young Turk leader Enver Pasha exclaimed, "There are no longer Bulgars, Greeks, Romans,

Jews, Mussulmans. We are all brothers beneath the same blue sky. We are all equal, we glory in being Ottoman." [7] This euphoric atmosphere did not last long. The issue of centralization versus decentralization that had divided the exiles in Paris now had to be faced as an urgent matter of policy rather than of theory. There were also conservative elements who distrusted all Young Turks, as the new leaders were generally called. The dissension came to a head on April 12, 1909, when the conservatives staged a counterrevolution in Constantinople and seized control of the capital. The Young Turks gathered their forces in Macedonia, marched on Constantinople, captured the city after a few hours' fighting, and then compelled Abdul Hamid to abdicate, although his complicity in the coup was not proven. The new sultan, Mohammed V, according to his own account had not read a newspaper in ten years. Accordingly, he served as a compliant figurehead for the Young Turks who now were the undisputed masters in Constantinople.

During the few years before the outbreak of World War I they tried to strengthen and modernize their empire, but with little success. They attempted a policy of centralization and Turkification, but the more they persisted the more opposition they aroused. It was too late to deny the inexorable awakening of Albanians, Arabs, Greeks, Bulgarians, and other subject peoples. Thus the result was a vicious circle of repression and revolt. The Albanians took up arms in 1910, and two years later the Balkan states formed a league and turned upon the Turks. Meanwhile, Italy also had invaded the African province of Tripolitania in 1911. The Young Turks thus found themselves almost continually at war until 1914, when they decided to throw in their lot with that of the Central Powers.

It is apparent, then, that the efforts of the Turks to adjust to the West had proven singularly ineffective. Because of religious and historical traditions they had been more impervious to the West than the Russians, and for that very reason ended up much more vulnerable to the West. They did not develop their own industry, so that their armed forces remained dependent on Western arms as well as Western instructors. Indeed, the Ottoman Empire survived to World War I because of the conflicting interests and policies of the Great Powers rather than because of its own strength. Its survival should not obscure the fact that the empire existed only on sufferance, and that it remained hopelessly inferior to the West in political cohesion, in economic development, and in military strength.*

III. ARABS

Like the Balkan Christians, the Arab peoples were under Ottoman rule for four centuries. Even less than the Balkan Christians did they regard this rule as an onerous foreign yoke. In the first place, Ottoman administration in the early period was efficient and generally acceptable. The Arabs, who as Moslems thought in theocratic rather than secular, Western terms, regarded the Turks more as fellow Moslems than as foreigners, and consequently felt a genuine affinity with the Moslem Ottoman Empire of which they were a

* See "Failure of Turkish Westernization," *EMM,* No. 77.

part. In modern times this feeling was enhanced as a result of the aggressiveness of the Europeans who conquered ancient Moslem kingdoms in North Africa and Central and South Asia. Faced with such a formidable threat, the Arabs very naturally regarded the Turks as protectors who, though becoming increasingly corrupt and oppressive in the later period, nevertheless were still much preferable to the infidels. These considerations explain why the Arabs lagged far behind the Balkan Christians in receptivity to Western influences and in development of nationalist aspirations.

The West's impact upon the modern Arab world may be said to have begun on that day in 1798 when Napoleon landed in Egypt with his army of invasion. Napoleon's real objective was to strike at Britain's position in the East, but after Admiral Nelson destroyed his fleet near Alexandria, Napoleon gave up his objective and returned home. Yet his expedition had a lasting effect on Egypt, for it was more than a military affair.* It was also a cultural incursion by the West into the heart of the Arab world. Napoleon brought with him the first printing press to reach Egypt, as well as scientists who deciphered the ancient hieroglyphic writing, and engineers who prepared plans for joining the Mediterranean and Red Seas. The effect of the French scientists is reflected in the following expression of wonderment by an Arab scholar who visited a laboratory that had been set up by the newcomers:

> Among the strangest things I saw in that place was that one of the people in charge took one of the bottles containing distilled water, and from it poured a little in a test-tube, upon which water he poured a little from another bottle. The two liquids rose, and a coloured cloud ascended therefrom, until it disappeared. The contents of the tube dried up, and became a yellow stone . . . a dry stone which we handled and examined. This he did again using different waters, then produced a blue stone. Repeating the experiment a third time with other waters, he produced a ruby-red stone. Further, he took a pinch of white powder, put it on an anvil and struck it gently with a hammer, then a terrific sound ensued, a sound similar to that of a gun, which gave us a shock. So they laughed at us.[8]

Napoleon also smashed the power of the established ruling class in Egypt during his brief campaigning in that country. This paved the way for the rise to power of an Albanian adventurer of genius, Mehemet Ali. The historical significance of Mehemet Ali is that he was the first Middle Eastern potentate who sensed the significance of Western technology and utilized it efficiently to serve his purposes. His achievements were numerous and revolutionary. He started the modern system of irrigation; introduced the cultivation of cotton, which quickly became the country's greatest resource; reopened the harbor of Alexandria; encouraged foreign trade; sent students to study abroad; opened schools of all varieties, though he himself was illiterate; and established a School of Translation which translated into Arabic about two thousand European books between 1835 and 1848. Mehemet Ali also engaged foreign experts who helped him build the first modern army and navy in the Middle East. He even tried valiantly to build a modern industrial structure in Egypt,

* See "Napoleon and the Arab World," *EMM*, No. 78.

and did erect a considerable number of factories in Cairo and Alexandria. These enterprises, however, eventually failed because of domestic deficiencies and the opposition of the European powers.*

These accomplishments transformed Egypt into a formidable power. With little difficulty Mehemet overran Arabia, the Sudan, the island of Crete, and the entire Levant coast comprising present-day Palestine, Lebanon, and Syria. These conquests raised the question of his relations with Sultan Mahmud, his nominal overlord in Constantinople. Mahmud had attempted to prevent Mehemet from expanding up the Levant coast but had been trounced quickly and decisively. In fact, it was only foreign intervention that prevented the Egyptian armies from entering Constantinople and putting an end to the five-hundred-year-old Ottoman dynasty. It was foreign intervention, also, that prevented Mehemet from realizing an alternate scheme that he seemed to have in mind. This was a plan for creating an Arab Empire out of the Ottoman provinces south of Asia Minor. Mehemet already was well on the way, since he controlled most of the Arab lands, including the Holy Cities. But a strong Arab Empire in command of the routes to India was contrary to British imperial interests. On March 21, 1833, Lord Palmerston commented as follows concerning Mehemet's ambitions:

> His real design is to establish an Arabian kingdom including all the countries in which Arabic is the language. There might be no harm in such a thing in itself; but as it would imply the dismemberment of Turkey, we could not agree to it. Besides Turkey is as good an occupier of the road to India as an active Arabian sovereign would be.[9]

This meant the end of any possibility for an Arab kingdom. Mehemet was forcefully compelled to surrender all his possessions except Egypt, where he remained the hereditary and autonomous ruler. Great Power interests had postponed the realization of Arab unity and independence for over a century. It should be noted, however, that even if Mehemet Ali had been permitted to put his plans into effect, he would have established a personal empire rather than a united Arab nation-state. It could not have been otherwise, for a sense of national consciousness was lacking among the Arab peoples in the early nineteenth century.

Thanks to Napoleon's expedition and to Mehemet Ali's herculean efforts, Egypt became by far the most significant bridgehead for Westernism in the Arab world. After 1870 Syria, which included the entire Levant coast at that time, rivaled Egypt as a center of Western influence. One reason was the flourishing commerce between Syria and Europe, and the large number of Syrian merchants who engaged in business activities abroad and then exerted the same catalytic effect upon their countrymen at home, as the Balkan merchants had done in earlier decades. Another reason was the extensive missionary-educational activity carried on mostly by the French Jesuits and the American Presbyterians. By 1865 the Americans had established the Syrian Protestant College, later to become famous throughout the Middle East as the American University of Beirut. A few years later the Jesuits

---

* See "Mehemet Ali Attempts to Industrialize Egypt," *EMM,* No. 79.

founded, in the same city, their University of St. Joseph. English, Scottish, German, and Russian schools were to follow, though on a more modest scale. These institutions not only trained Arab students, but also printed and distributed Arab books. In this manner the Syrian Arabs were helped to rediscover their past and to learn about Western literature, ideology, and technology.

This stimulus from the outside was responsible for the earliest manifestations of Arab nationalism. The leaders at the outset were mostly Christian Arabs, since the Moslems did not enroll in the missionary schools until a later date. In 1860 Butros el Bustani, a convert to Protestantism, began publication of his newspaper, *Nafir Suriya* (*Syrian Trumpet*). Ten years later he founded a political, literary, and scientific journal, *El Jenan* (*The Shield*). Its motto was "Love of our country is an article of faith"—a sentiment hitherto unknown in the Arab world.

Bustani and the other pioneer nationalists could not carry on political agitation openly because of the repressive measures of the Ottoman authorities. Consequently, the first avowedly political activity was the organization of a secret revolutionary society in 1875 by five students at the Protestant College. They drew up a national program which included demands for self-government, freedom of the press, and the adoption of Arabic as an official language. Turkish officials conducted an investigation and attempted to unearth the secret society's leadership. The latter became alarmed and dissolved their society in 1878. Then they made their way to Egypt, where the imperial agents had little control and where conditions were more promising for modern-minded Arabs.

Khedive Ismail, who ruled Egypt from 1863 to 1879, was as ambitious as Mehemet Ali. During his reign railroads were built, the port of Alexandria enlarged, the Suez Canal opened, modern banks established, and currency stabilized. Indicative of the new economic opportunities was the increase in the number of resident foreigners from 3,000 in 1836 to 68,000 by 1878. Equally important was the great expansion in educational facilities. By 1875 there were 4,685 religious elementary schools with 111,896 pupils, three religious higher schools with 15,335 students, and thirty-six civilian schools with 4,778 students, while the venerable University of al-Azhar in Cairo was attended by 15,000 students from all parts of the Moslem world.

This activity attracted to Egypt Syrian merchants and Western-educated Syrian intellectuals. The latter published newspapers and magazines which acquainted Egyptians with liberal and scientific French and British currents of thought. At the same time the deciphering of the hieroglyphs, the establishment of museums, and the development of Egyptology stimulated an awareness of Egypt's ancient history and a pride in her achievements. This embryonic nationalism was further aroused by the growing Western domination of the country. This domination was imposed because Ismail's heavy borrowings on the European money markets had led to bankruptcy and ultimately to foreign military intervention and rule. During the sixteen years of Ismail's reign the funded debt rose from £3 million to £68 million. Much of this money was spent on constructive projects, but at the same time the country was being ruthlessly robbed by what have been aptly termed "the jackals of finance." The Egyptians, like the Turks, were unaccustomed to the wiles of unscrupulous international financiers and were mercilessly fleeced. In constructing the harbor works of Alexandria, for example, British contractors overcharged about 80 per cent. Loans that normally brought 6 or 7 per cent were made to the Egyptians at anywhere between 12 and 27 per cent.

By 1876 Ismail was bankrupt and was forced to accept an international Public Debt Commission. This body saw to it that all obligations were promptly met, but the country was bled white in the process. The total revenue in 1877 amounted to £9,543,000, of which £7,473,000 had to be paid out for the service of the debt, and other amounts for fixed obligations such as the annual tribute to the Sultan. Only a little over £1 million was left for the administration of the country, a sum that was patently inadequate.*

Under these circumstances a nationalist revolt broke out in 1882 under the leadership of an Egyptian army officer, Ahmed Arabi. It was directed partly against foreign intervention in Egyptian affairs and partly against the khedive and the Turkish oligarchy that monopolized all the senior posts in both the army and the bureaucracy. After some rioting and loss of life in Alexandria, Britain invited first France and then Italy to intervene jointly against the revolt. The intervention ostensibly was designed to support the khedive against the rebels. When her proposal was turned down, Britain proceeded to act alone. A British fleet bombarded the fortifications of Alexandria in July, 1882, and two months later an expeditionary force landed in Egypt and defeated Arabi.

Prime Minister Gladstone declared at the time that an indefinite occupation "would be absolutely at variance with all the principles and views of Her Majesty's government." But Her Majesty, Queen Victoria, herself, held a different opinion. "The Queen," she wrote a few months later, "feels very anxious that nothing should be said to fetter or hamper our action in Egypt; we *must* have a firm hold on her *once for all*." [10] It was this viewpoint that was to prevail. The expeditionary force remained to become an army of occupation. Egypt was still nominally a Turkish province, but Britain now controlled the country in every respect—economically, politically, and militarily.

These events naturally provoked strong xenophobic sentiments in Egypt, but they were directed more against the Westerners than against the Turks. Only a handful of Christian Arab leaders wished at this time to break away from Constantinople. The Moslem masses were still largely apathetic, while the small minority of politically conscious Moslems wanted nothing more than autonomy within the Ottoman imperial structure.

With the Young Turk revolt of 1908 it appeared that this desire would be satisfied. The Arabs, like the other peoples of the empire, welcomed the revolt with unrestrained enthusiasm. A missionary in Syria reported the popular rejoicing as follows: "The universal voice of the Moslem was, 'Now we are brethren and we can live in peace. We shall henceforth know each other only as Ottomans. Long live liberty! Long live the army! Long live the Sultan!' It seemed too good to be true, and for weeks we here, foreigners and Syrians alike, seemed to be living in a dream. The Golden Age seemed to be dawning." [11]

* See "Western Economic Imperialism in Egypt," *EMM,* No. 80.

The dawn proved false. The Young Turk leaders soon were resorting to severe Turkification measures in a desperate attempt to hold the empire together against foreign military aggression and internal nationalist subversion. The Arabs resented this repression, as did the Balkan Christians. A Beirut newspaper commented bitterly in 1908 that

> There was only one Hamid a few days ago,
> But now of Abdul there's a thousand or so.

Yet the great majority of Arabs still aspired to autonomy rather than independence. For example, Moslem Arab students in Paris founded on November 14, 1909, a secret body, the Young Arab Society, better known as *al-Fatat* (Youth), which played a leading role in the Arab nationalist movement. Its goal was Arab autonomy within the framework of a biracial Turko-Arab Ottoman Empire organized along the lines of the Austro-Hungarian Empire. In October, 1913, another secret Arab society, the Covenant, was organized in Istanbul. Its members were mostly Arab officers in the Ottoman army and its program was almost identical to that of the Paris group.

Such were the sentiments of the great majority of Arabs until the outbreak of World War I. Then the decision of the Young Turk leaders to throw in their lot with the Central Powers changed the situation overnight and precipitated a chain reaction of events that culminated in the great Arab Revolt of 1916 against the centuries-old Turkish imperium.

It should be noted that the North African lands to the west of Egypt had by World War I fallen under direct European rule. Back in the sixteenth century the Turks had extended their domination over these territories, with the exception of distant Morocco. It is interesting to observe, in the light of popular Western usages such as "Middle East" and "Far East," that the Moslems referred to Morocco as "al-Maghrib al-Aqsa" or "the Far West," in contrast to "al-Maghrib," or "the West," for the remaining North African territories—Tripolitania, Tunisia, and Algeria. For about a century the Turks ruled these three provinces directly, sending out governors from Constantinople. Then, as Ottoman power waned, these distant provinces became fully autonomous with hereditary dynasties, although they continued to recognize the suzerainty of the Turkish sultan and to contribute naval forces when needed.

The golden period of these North African regencies was in the sixteenth and seventeenth centuries, when they preyed on Christian shipping in the Mediterranean. But by the eighteenth century the Moslem corsairs were increasingly hampered by the growing technical superiority of the European fleets. The population of the formerly flourishing city of Algiers declined drastically, while the number of its Christian captives dropped from a high point of 30,000 to a mere 100 at the time of the French invasion in 1830.

The main purpose of the invasion was to bolster the tottering throne of Charles X by a military victory. The weak Turkish forces were easily scattered, though the French monarch was nevertheless dethroned shortly thereafter. After much vacillation his successor, Louis Philippe, decided to retain the newly acquired North African possession. This necessitated a prolonged and brutal pacification campaign against the native Algerians, who resisted a good deal more stoutly than the small Turkish garrison. Once the French were ensconced in Algeria, it was only a matter of time before they extended their control to the countries on either side. In 1881 they took over Tunisia and in 1912 Morocco. In each case the process involved more diplomacy than military force, in contrast to the earlier and cruder procedure in Algeria. The newly acquired states enjoyed the technical status of protectorates rather than conquered territories, which meant that French control was indirect, though not less decisive. Finally Europe's onslaught upon Arab North Africa was completed in 1911 with Italy's invasion of Tripolitania. As in Algeria, the Turkish garrison was easily defeated, but a protracted struggle against native resistance forces was required before Italian rule was firmly established.

IV. PERSIANS

While these events were taking place in the Arab world, equally significant developments were occurring in neighboring Persia. We have seen in Chapter 3 that Persia reached a pinnacle of greatness under Shah Abbas I, in the early seventeenth century, comparable to that of the Ottoman Empire under Suleiman the Magnificent. Then Persia suffered a decline, again similar to that of the Turks, sinking into a state of impotence and obscurity. Nor did she have a Napoleonic expedition or wide-ranging Syrian merchants or large numbers of foreign missionaries to allow outside influences to freshen the stagnant atmosphere. Thus a British scholar who spent the year 1887–1888 in Persia discovered there a world of the type that had disappeared in the West centuries earlier.

> . . . the atmosphere was mediaeval: politics and progress were hardly mentioned, and the talk turned mostly on mysticism, metaphysics and religion; the most burning political questions were those connected with the successors of the Prophet Muhammad in the seventh century of our era; only a languid interest in external affairs was aroused by the occasional appearance of the official journals . . . ; while at Kirman one post a week maintained a communication with the outer world.[12]

Yet it was about this time in the late nineteenth century that the impact of the ubiquitous West was beginning to be felt appreciably in Persia. The roots and nature of the impact were generally similar to those amongst the Turks. There was first an attempt to borrow Western military techniques, which in turn required greater centralization and a new bureaucracy. The traditional Moslem religious schools, or *madaris,* obviously were not capable of providing graduates to staff the new bureaucracy, let alone the new army. Accordingly, students were sent abroad, while a variety of new Western-type schools were established within the country. Gradually a group of intellectuals appeared who were impressed by the material advances of the West and who wished to introduce Western institutions and practices in their homeland.

In the late nineteenth century this small group of intellectuals was able to arouse considerable mass support in the cities because of growing economic intrusion and exploitation by the West. As early as 1828, the Russians had obtained capitulatory rights similar to the extraterritoriality imposed later upon China. Most European powers quickly followed Russia in securing special rights for their nationals. The process was facilitated by the readiness of the shahs to grant monopoly concessions to foreigners in order to raise funds to pay for their extravagant excesses. One of the ablest rulers of Persia's Kajar dynasty was Nasr al-Din Shah, who was on the throne from 1848 to 1896. Yet even he found it necessary to finance his expensive travels abroad by granting foreigners permission to open banks, issue bank notes, build railways, and enjoy monopoly rights in the sale of tobacco and other commodities. The intensity of the feeling against these practices was demonstrated by the assassination of the Shah in 1896. This solved nothing, the succeeding rulers being less competent and equally extravagant and ready to sell their country to the highest bidders.

Such were the conditions in Persia when news arrived in 1905 of the Russian defeats in Manchuria, and then of the great revolutionary upsurge within Russia itself. These dramatic developments had important repercussions in Persia because of the considerable number of Persian students in Russian universities and the much larger number of Persian workers employed in the oil fields and factories of the Transcaucasus. The Persian consul in St. Petersburg estimated in 1910 that no less than 200,000 migratory workers were crossing over into Russia each year. These laborers inevitably were affected by the revolutionary movements convulsing the Russian working class of the period. Consequently, the stirring events of 1905 aroused a response in Persia among many workers and intellectuals, as well as among religious leaders alarmed by Western encroachment.

A wave of strikes and riots swept the country until the Shah agreed in July, 1906, to dismiss his unpopular prime minister and to convoke a national assembly or *majlis*. The first majlis met at Teheran in October, 1906, and drew up a liberal constitution which the Shah signed two months later, just before he died. The new ruler, reactionary Mohammed Ali Shah, was determined to suppress the constitution, but he had an aroused populace on his hands. For the first time in the modern period, Persia was being shaken by a reform movement with genuine mass following. This movement was strongly nationalistic and anti-Western because of the humiliation and exploitation suffered at the hands of foreigners. An informed British observer described the motivation and objectives of the Persian reformers as follows:

> It was when they became convinced that their country was despised abroad, that their interests were betrayed for a vile price, and that their religion and their independent existence as a nation were alike threatened with destruction, that they began to demand a share in the government of the country. Many European journalists and other writers have made merry over the idea of a Persian Parliament, repeating like so many parrots the expression "comic opera" on almost every page. . . . Yet the Persians have consciously been fighting for their very existence as a Nation, and in this sense the popular or constitutional party may very properly be termed "Nationalists." . . . it is essentially the patriotic

party, which stands for progress, freedom, tolerance, and above all for national independence and "Persia for the Persians." [13]

Thus the reformers were resorting to Western political tactics and slogans in a desperate effort to withstand Western aggression. But their efforts were doomed to failure bacause the *status-quo* forces were too powerful during this pre–World War I period. Tsarist Russia was adamantly opposed to the reformers for obvious reasons, and strongly supported the Shah against the majlis. Britain was ambivalent, being favorably disposed toward the moderate reformers but frowning upon revolutionary or antidynastic activities. If the two powers had neutralized each other, the reformers might have had a fighting chance. But this faint possibility evaporated when Russia and Britain concluded their 1907 entente. One of its provisions designated northern and central Persia as a Russian sphere of influence, southeastern Persia as a British sphere, and the intervening territory as a neutral buffer zone (see Chapter 21, section I). Needless to say, the Persians were not consulted about these arrangements. Their reactions were well represented by a cartoon published in the October 2, 1907, issue of *Punch*. The British lion and the Russian bear are depicted as mauling between them an unhappy Persian cat, and the lion is saying, "You can play with his head, and I can play with his tail, and we can both stroke the small of his back," while the poor cat moans, "I don't remember having been consulted about this."

Punch, October 2, 1907.

THE HARMLESS NECESSARY CAT.

The cat did put up a plucky fight, but to no avail. The chief military force in Persia at this time was the Cossack brigade, trained and officered by Russians. In June, 1908, this body, on the Shah's orders, dispersed the majlis and routed its supporters in Teheran. But the following year Bakhtiari tribesmen marched on Teheran, captured the capital, and deposed the Shah, who was succeeded by his twelve-year-old son. The majlis, now the real ruler of the country, invited an American financial adviser, W. Morgan Shuster, to help repair the economic ravages. Shuster organized a treasury gendarmerie to collect taxes and planned a series of comprehensive reforms, but he aroused the antagonism of influential Persian elements and of the Russians. The latter demanded his ouster, and after a show of force, compelled the majlis in November, 1911, to dismiss him. The following month the majlis was suddenly disbanded, and from then until the outbreak of World War I, Persia was pretty much dominated by Russia.*

SUGGESTED READING

An excellent bibliographical guide is available in R. H. Davison, *The Near and Middle East: An Introduction to History and Bibliography* (Washington: Service Center for Teachers of History, 1959). A valuable, full-length study of the historiography of the Middle East is provided by B. Lewis and P. M. Holt, *Historians of the Middle East* (New York: Oxford Univ., 1962).

The latest and most detailed study of the Balkans is by L. S. Stavrianos, *The Balkans Since 1453* (New York: Holt, 1958). General histories of the Near East included S. N. Fisher, *The Middle East* (New York: Knopf, 1959); P. K. Hitti, *The Near East in History* (Princeton: Van Nostrand, 1961); G. E. Kirk, *A Short History of the Middle East* (Washington: Public Affairs Press, 1949); E. A. Speiser, *The United States and the Near East* (Cambridge: Harvard Univ., 1947); and L. V. Thomas and R. N. Frye, *The United States and Turkey and Iran* (Cambridge: Harvard Univ. 1952). For the West's cultural impact on the Middle East, see H. Kohn, *Nationalism and Imperialism in the Hither East* (New York: Harcourt, 1932); T. C. Young, ed., *Near Eastern Culture and Society* (Princeton: Princeton Univ., 1951); R. N. Frye, ed., *Islam and the West* (The Hague: Mouton, 1957); D. Lerner, *The Passing of Traditional Society: Modernizing the Middle East* (New York: Free Press of Glencoe, 1958); B. Lewis, *The Middle East and the West* (Bloomington: Univ. of Indiana, 1964), and G. E. Von Grunebaum, *Modern Islam: The Search for Cultural Identity* (Berkeley: Univ. of California, 1962). For the West's economic impact on the Middle East, see A. Bonné, *State and Economics in the Middle East* (London: Routledge, 1946); H. A. B. Rivlin, *Agricultural Policy of Muhammad Ali in Egypt* (Cambridge: Harvard Univ., 1961); and H. Feis, *Europe, The World's Banker, 1870–1914* (New Haven: Yale Univ., 1930), Chaps. 12–17.

On Western influence on the Turks in particular, see B. Lewis, *The Emergence of Modern Turkey* (New York: Oxford Univ., 1961); R. H. Davison, *Reform in the Ottoman Empire, 1856–1876* (Princeton: Princeton Univ., 1964); and the translated essays of a pioneer Turkish nationalist: N. Berkes, ed., *Turkish Nationalism and Western Civilization: Selected Essays of Ziya Gökalp* (London:

* See "Reform and Reaction in Persia," *EMM,* No. 81.

G. Allen, 1959); as well as the study of this leader's doctrines by U. Heyd, *Foundations of Turkish Nationalism: The Life and Teachings of Ziya Gökalp* (London: Harvill, 1950). For the Arab world in particular, see E. Atiyah, *The Arabs* (Baltimore: Penguin, 1955); P. K. Hitti, *The Arabs: A Short History* (Chicago: Regnery, 1943; Gateway Editions); B. Lewis, *The Arabs in History* (London: Hutchinson's University Library, 1950); G. Antonius, *The Arab Awakening* (Philadelphia: Lippincott, 1939); H. Saab, *The Arab Federalists of the Ottoman Empire* (Amsterdam: Djambatan, 1958); and the penetrating analyses in N. Safran, *Egypt in Search of Political Community* (Cambridge: Harvard Univ., 1961); J. M. Ahmed, *Intellectual Origins of Egyptian Nationalism* (New York: Oxford Univ., 1960); and A. Hourani, *Arabic Thought in the Liberal Age, 1798–1839* (New York: Oxford Univ., 1962).

Finally, for the revolutions in Turkey and Persia, see I. Spector, *The First Russian Revolution: Its Impact on Asia* (Englewood Cliffs: Prentice-Hall, 1962; a Spectrum book); E. E. Ramsaur, Jr., *The Young Turks: Prelude to the Revolution of 1908* (Princeton Univ., 1957); E. G. Browne, *The Persian Revolution of 1905–1909* (London: Cambridge Univ., 1910); A. K. S. Lambton, "The Impact of the West on Persia," *International Affairs,* XXXIII (January, 1957), 15–19; and J. M. Upton, *The History of Modern Iran: An Interpretation* (Cambridge: Harvard Univ., 1960).

Chapter 15

*India is the one great non-Western society that
has been, not merely attacked and hit, but overrun
and conquered outright by Western arms, and
not merely conquered by Western arms but ruled,
after that, by Western administrators. . . . India's
experience of the West has thus been more painful
and more humiliating than China's or Turkey's,
and much more so than Russia's or Japan's; but,
just for this reason, it has been also much more
intimate . . . our Western iron has probably
entered deeper into India's soul.*

ARNOLD J. TOYNBEE

India

Prior to the appearance of the British, India had been invaded time and time again—by the Aryans, Greeks, Scythians, Turks,
and Moguls. Each of these invaders left its mark on the great subcontinent, contributing in varying degrees to the evolution of India's
traditional society. The historical role of the British was to disrupt
and remold this traditional society. The other invaders wrought
changes mostly at the top, but the British impact was felt down
to the level of the village. The reason for this difference between
the British and their predecessors is to be found in the dynamic
and expansive nature of British society, which consequently undermined the comparatively static and self-sufficient society of India.
To understand this process of penetration and transformation it is
necessary first to study the character of the traditional Indian society.
Then we shall consider the nature of the British impact and the Indian
reaction to it.

I. INDIA'S TRADITIONAL SOCIETY

The basic unit of traditional Indian society was the village, as
it was in most of the rest of the world, including Europe, in the pre-
industrial period.* Within the village it was not the individual that

* See "India's Traditional Society," *EMM*, No. 82.

mattered, but rather the joint family and the caste. This group form of organization was a source of social stability but also of national weakness. Loyalty to the family, to the caste, and to the village was the primary consideration, and this prevented the formation of a national spirit.

The land was regarded by immemorial custom as the property of the sovereign, who was entitled to a share of the gross produce or its equivalent. This constituted the land tax that was the main source of state revenue and the main burden of the cultivator. The share paid to the state varied from period to period from a sixth to a third or even half. Usually the responsibility for making this payment, whether in produce or in money, was collective, resting upon the village as a unit. In some parts of India a rough equality was maintained by a periodic redistribution of the land on the basis of the number of workers in each family. Apart from this practice, the peasant had hereditary right to the use of the land so long as he paid his share of the taxes.

Transportation and communication facilities were primitive, so the villages tended to become economically and socially self-sufficient. Each village had its potter, who turned out on his wheel the simple utensils needed by the peasants; its carpenter, who constructed and repaired the buildings and ploughs; its blacksmith, who made axes and other necessary tools; its clerk, who attended to legal documents and wrote out correspondence between people of different villages; its town herdsman, who looked after the cattle and returned them at night to their various owners; its priest and its teacher, who frequently were combined in the same person; and its everpresent astrologer, who indicated the auspicious time for planting, for harvesting, for marriages, and other important events. These artisans and professional men served their villages on something akin to a barter basis. They were paid for their services by receiving grain from the cultivating households or by receiving tax-free village land for their own use. These hereditary and traditional divisions of occupation and function were given the stamp of obligation by the caste system.

The political structure of the village consisted of an annually elected council of five or more, known to this day as the Panchayat ("Pancha" meaning "five"). The Panchayat, which normally consisted of caste leaders and village elders, met periodically to dispense local justice, to collect taxes, to keep in repair the village wells, roads, and irrigation systems, to see that the craftsmen and other professionals were provided for, and to extend hospitality to travelers passing through the village and furnish them with guides. The village had little contact with the outside world apart from the payment of the land tax and the irregular demand for forced labor. The combination of agriculture and hand industry made each village largely independent of the rest of the country except for a few indispensables like salt and iron. Consequently, the towns that existed in traditional India were not industrial in character. Rather, they were religious centers such as Benares, Puri, and Allahabad, political centers such as Poona, Tanjore, and Delhi, or commercial centers such as Mirzapur on the trade route from Central India to Bengal.

Indian writers have tended to romanticize this traditional society, painting an idyllic picture of village life, continuing peacefully generation after generation in its slow and satisfying rhythm. It is true that the existence of group organizations such as the joint family, the caste, and the village council provided the peasants with both psychological and economic security. Each individual had recognized duties, rights, and status in his native village. If the central government was sufficiently strong to maintain order and to keep the land tax down to the customary sixth of the harvest, then the peasant masses did lead a peaceful and contented existence. But as often as not the central government was too weak to keep order, and the villagers were mercilessly fleeced by rapacious tax collectors and by robber bands. This was the case in the seventeenth century when the Mogul imperial structure was disintegrating. The Portuguese missionary Father Sebastian Manrique, who was in India in 1629 and again in 1640–1641, noticed that the land tax in Bengal was not only increased repeatedly but also collected four to six months in advance. The cause of this, he said, was the constant change of officials, who were invariably dismissed or transferred after a short term in office. "On this account they always used to collect the revenue in advance, often by force, and when the wretched people have no means of paying, they seize their wives and children, making them into slaves and selling them by auction, if they are heathens" [1] (that is, Hindus rather than Moslems as were the ruling Moguls).

Yet even in such trying periods the Indian village was not transformed in any basic respect. Individual regions were ravaged, but eventually the cultivators returned to resume their traditional institutions and their traditional ways of life. This timeless and indestructible quality of the Indian village was noted and emphasized as late as 1830 by Charles Metcalfe, a British governor.

> The village communities are little republics, having nearly every thing they want within themselves, and almost independent of any foreign relations. They seem to last where nothing else lasts. Dynasty after dynasty tumbles down; revolution succeeds to revolution; Hindu, Pathan, Mahratta, Sikh, English, are masters in turn; but the village communities remain the same. In times of trouble they arm and fortify themselves; a hostile army passes through the country; the Village Community collect their cattle within their walls, and let the army pass unprovoked; if plunder and devastation be directed against themselves and the force employed be irresistible, they flee to friendly villages at a distance, but when the storm has passed over they return and resume their occupation. If a country remains for a series of years the scene of continual pillage and massacre, so that the villages cannot be inhabited, the villagers nevertheless return whenever the power of peaceable possession revives. A generation may pass away, but the succeeding generations will return. The sons will take the place of their fathers, the same site for the village, the same position for the houses, the same lands will be re-occupied by the descendants of those who were driven out when the village was depopulated; and it is not a trifling matter that will drive them out, for they will often maintain their posts through times of disturbance and convulsion, and acquire strength sufficient to resist pillage and oppression with success. [2]

II. BRITISH CONQUEST

The Indian village was relatively unchanging and self-sufficient until the coming of the British. But before examining the impact of these Western intruders we shall consider the reasons why they were able with comparatively little difficulty to conquer the whole of India during the late eighteenth and nineteenth centuries. This is a real question, because for 250 years after Albuquerque had captured Goa early in the sixteenth century (see Chapter 3) the position of the European nations in India had remained substantially the same. For 250 years they had been able only to cling to a few stations along the coasts. Then within a few decades the balance of power shifted decisively and the whole of the Indian subcontinent fell under British rule.

This denouement may be explained in part by the growing economic and military strength of the Western nations. But this is not the only factor, for it does not explain why India succumbed to the West so much earlier than did China. It is necessary, therefore, to take into account the conditions prevailing within India itself. First and foremost there was the decline of Mogul power and authority (see Chapter 3, section IV). This enabled Moslem warlords and provincial governors to declare their independence and establish personal dynasties in various regions. In this fashion the Nizam of Hyderabad came to power in 1724, and Hyder Ali and his son Tipu Sultan ensconced themselves in Mysore (the father in 1761, the son later). At the same time the Hindus asserted themselves by organizing the powerful [Maratha] confederacy with its center in the city of Poona. The Marathas won control of the entire Deccan and then, about 1740, began to invade northern India with the intention of displacing the declining Moguls. Thus India was in an anarchical state in the eighteenth century, with various officials seeking to convert their posts into hereditary princedoms and intriguing with any power, whether Indian or foreign, in order to realize their ambitions. The British consequently were able to play off one Indian prince against another until they became the masters of the entire peninsula. This was altogether different from China, where the Manchu imperial structure remained intact and compelled all foreigners to deal directly with the Emperor in Peking. In other words, India experienced in the eighteenth century a degree of fragmentation that China was spared until the overthrow of the Manchus and the rise of the provincial warlords in the twentieth century.

Another important factor that contributed substantially to the vulnerability of India was the rise of a powerful merchant class whose economic interests were bound up with those of the Western companies. These companies were allowed to trade relatively freely in India (they were almost entirely excluded in China). During the sixteenth century India's economy was little affected by the trade because it was confined largely to spices and textiles. But in the seventeenth century various commercial crops such as indigo, mustard seed, and hemp, as well as saltpeter, were exported in large quantities. Bengal was the center of this trade, and in that province there now arose wealthy native merchants who dominated the local economy and who were becoming increasingly restless under the corrupt and inefficient rule of the Mogul officials. It was one of these merchants, Jagat Seth, who bought the allegiance of the generals who supposedly were under the orders of the nawab, or governor, of Bengal. At the Battle of Plassey (1757) these generals refrained from fighting against the British, who lost only sixty-five men in that fateful encounter. As one Indian historian has put it, Plassey was "a transaction, not a battle."

The British now were the actual rulers of Bengal, though they continued to recognize puppet nawabs as a matter of form. In 1764, after defeating the Mogul's forces, the English East India Company was granted the *Diwani,* or the right of tax collection, in the rich provinces of Bengal, Bihar, and Orissa. This opened up manifold opportunities for profit making and outright extortion, which the English agents exploited to the full. By raising the taxes, controlling the trade, and accepting numerous "gifts" from native officials, they amassed fortunes for themselves and their superiors in London. Company officials and their Indian agents, too, were not subject to the high duties levied on Indian merchants. "To engineer a revolution," state two English historians, "had been revealed as the most paying game in the world. A gold-lust unequalled since the hysteria that took hold of the Spaniards of Cortes' and Pizzaro's age filled the English mind. Bengal in particular was not to know peace again until it had been bled white." [3] Richard Beecher, a servant of the company, wrote to his masters in London on May 24, 1769, as follows: "It must give pain to an Englishman to have reason to think that since the accession of the Company to the *Diwani* the condition of the people of this country has been worse than it was before. . . . This fine country, which flourished under the most despotic and arbitrary government, is verging towards ruin." [4]

The foothold in Bengal gave the British the base and the resources necessary for further expansion in India. At that time there were four other contenders for the Mogul domains—the French, the rulers of Mysore and of Hyderabad, and the Maratha Confederacy. The French were eliminated during the course of the Seven Years' War, being forced to surrender virtually all their posts in India by the Treaty of Paris of 1763 (see Chapter 7, section VI). Then during the American Revolution the British were challenged in India also by a coalition of the three principal native powers. The governor-general, Warren Hastings, managed to hold out and later took the offensive. By 1800 only the British and the Marathas were left, and during the following years the British gradually prevailed because of dissension within the Maratha Confederacy. By 1818 the back of the Marathas had been broken, though some fighting continued with them as well as with the Sikhs in the Punjab.

After having established themselves in the heart of the subcontinent, the British began pushing northward in a search for natural frontiers. To the northeast, in Himalayan Nepal, they defeated the Gurkhas who henceforth fought on the side of the British. Likewise to the northwest they finally defeated the proud Sikhs of the Punjab. Thus by the middle of the nineteenth century the British were the masters of all India, from the Indus to the Brahmaputra, and from the Himalayas to Cape Comorin. A few major kingdoms still survived, including Kashmir, Hyderabad, Baroda, and Travancore, but these were now dependent territories, isolated from each other, and powerless against the might of Britain.

With their authority firmly established in India, the British now overran neighboring states. Previous rulers of India had, with one exception, not attempted expansion across the ocean because they lacked seapower. The British, by contrast, had no rivals in Eastern waters, and they also had the great resources of a united India behind them. As early as 1819 Sir Stamford Raffles had occupied Singapore on the Malay Peninsula. The significance of this acquisition was fully realized at the time. "You have only to glance at the map . . . our station completely outflanks the Straits of Malacca and secures a passage for our China ships at all times and in all circumstances. What Malta is in the West, Singapore may become in the East." [5] The British next turned to Burma, on India's eastern border. They fought three wars with this state, the first in 1824, the second in 1852, and the last, which ended in annexation, in 1886.

In addition to these outright annexations, the British surrounded India with a defensive network of alliances and spheres of influence. With an eye on expansionist Russia in Central Asia, the British, though pursuing different policies under successive Conservative and Liberal governments, generally sought to build a protective buffer zone around their Indian Empire. This explains their two invasions of Afghanistan in 1839 and 1879. Eventually the British recognized the independence of this state and granted it a subsidy in return for the right to control its foreign relations. Likewise, rumors of Russian penetration in Tibet caused the British to send an expedition to that country in 1904. An agreement followed whereby Tibet undertook not to admit any foreign agents. Further to the west the British clashed repeatedly with the Russians for paramount influence in Persia. The struggle veered back and forth until the two rivals agreed, in the Anglo-Russian Entente of 1907, to divide Persia into a British sphere of influence in the south, a Russian sphere in the north, and a buffer zone in the center.

The rationale behind these military moves and diplomatic arrangements was stated clearly and frankly by Lord Curzon, viceroy of India between 1899 and 1905.

> India is like a fortress, with the vast moat of the sea on two of her faces, and with mountains for her walls on the remainder; but beyond these walls, which are sometimes of by no means insuperable height and admit of being easily penetrated, extends a glacis of varying breadth and dimension. We do not want to occupy it, but we also cannot afford to see it occupied by our foes. We are quite content to let it remain in the hands of our allies and friends, but if rivals and unfriendly influences creep up to it and lodge themselves right under our walls, we are compelled to intervene, because a danger would thereby grow up that one day might menace our security. That is the secret of the whole position in Arabia, Persia, Afghanistan, Tibet, and as far eastwards as Siam. He would be a short-sighted commander who merely manned his ramparts in India and did not look beyond. [6]

It might be added that at the same time that the British were establishing themselves in India and the surrounding territories. The French were conquering Indochina. They compelled the Chinese government to relinquish its claims to suzerainty in Indochina in 1883. Siam escaped foreign domination because of the desire of the British to preserve a buffer state between British Burma and French Indochina. The East Indies remained under the rule of the Dutch, who had conquered them from the Portuguese in the seventeenth century (see Chapter 7, section III).

III. British Rule

We have seen that the East India Company was at first outrageously exploitive in its administration of the Indian territories it controlled. The excesses aroused public opinion in Britain, and this, together with political considerations, prompted Parliament to pass acts in 1773 and 1784 that placed the company under the supervision of the London government. The company continued to trade, and its servants and soldiers continued to govern and fight in India, but it functioned under the watchful eye of Parliament and the British government. The next change came in 1833, when the company lost its commercial monopoly and served henceforth as a largely administrative body under the Crown. The main privilege and justification for the existence of the company now was the appointment of civil servants, which constituted very substantial and influential patronage. But an act of 1853 took away this patronage by instituting an open competitive examination for the recruitment of civil servants. The continued existence of the company now could scarcely be justified, and, in fact, its early demise was forecast by many. Undoubtedly it would eventually have been formally abolished even if the Indian Mutiny of 1857 had not suddenly forced the issue.

The Mutiny was not the national movement or war of independence that some Indian writers have called it. Rather it was primarily a military outbreak that was exploited by certain discontented princes and landlords whose interests had been harmed by the British. Lord Dalhousie, the governor-general between 1848 and 1856, had dispossessed many princes and aroused uneasiness and suspicion amongst those who remained. Other groups, too, were dissatisfied: Conservative elements of the Indian population were deeply disturbed by the introduction of the railway and telegraph, the opening of Western-type schools, the aggressive activities of certain Christian missionaries, the legalization of widow remarriage, and the abolition of practices such as infanticide and suttee, or the self-cremation of widows on their husbands' funeral pyres. The Sepoys, as the Indian soldiers serving in the British forces were called, were disaffected because of prolonged campaigning in distant lands and the refusal of extra allowances for such service. The spark that set off the uprising was the introduction of cartridges that were greased with cow and pig fat, obnoxious to both the Hindus and the Moslems. All these factors combined to make the Mutiny assume the proportions of a popular uprising in certain scattered regions.

When the Mutiny began on May 10, 1857, the British were caught by surprise and forced to the defensive. But the revolt did not spread throughout the country, being confined largely to the north. Even there most of the important native states remained loyal to the British and gave invaluable assistance. Thus after about four months the British were able to counterattack, and by July, 1858, the Mutiny had been crushed. Both sides were guilty of brutality, the Indians murdering many captives, and the English burning down villages and indiscriminately killing the inhabitants.

A month after the suppression of the Mutiny, Parliament passed the India Act ending the rule of the East India Company and substituting that of the Crown. Henceforth India was ruled by a vast hierarchy with its base in India

The storming of Delhi during the Indian Mutiny.

and its apex in London in the person of the Secretary of State for India. This official was a member of the cabinet and generally was allowed a free hand by his colleagues. The top official in India was the governor-general, or viceroy, acting as the direct representative of the Crown, and usually appointed for a five-year term. The viceroy was assisted by an executive council of five members, none of them Indian until 1909. Beneath these top officials was the famous Indian Civil Service which collected the revenues, maintained law and order, and supervised the judicial system. Prior to 1919 almost all the members of this small but elite group consisted of British graduates of Oxford and Cambridge. The Civil Service in turn supervised a subordinate provincial service that was exclusively Indian in personnel. It was through these Indian officials in the lower ranks of the bureaucracy that the authority of the government penetrated to the masses.

The efficiency of British rule in India is reflected in the fact that in 1900 there were a total of 4,000 British civilian administrators in the country compared to 500,000 Indian. And in 1910 the Indian army comprised 69,000 Britishers and 130,000 Indians. It should be noted that Britain's position in India was based not only on the army and the bureaucracy but also on the surviving Indian princes. Prior to the Mutiny the British often had no compunction about taking over principalities when it suited them to do so. But this policy was reversed following the Mutiny, so that India remained thenceforth a crazy-quilt pattern of some 550 native states intermingled with British Indian provinces. The reason for this change of policy was made clear in 1860 by Lord Canning, the first viceroy following the Mutiny: "if we could keep up a number of Native States without political power, but as royal instruments, we should exist in India as long as our naval supremacy was maintained." [7] Another viceroy, Lord Lytton, declared two decades later that "the Crown of England should henceforth be identified with the hopes, the aspirations, the sympathies and the interests of a powerful native aristocracy." [8]

It goes without saying that the British officials in India, no matter how sincere they may have been, had little direct contact with Indian opinion. Most of them conscientiously sought to understand and to correct the abuses inherent in a large and unrepresentative system of bureaucratic government. But their preconceptions were naturally British, and this prevented them from perceiving the full implications and repercussions of their decisions. As Britishers, for example, they generally viewed the introduction of English law as a great boon, when in fact it frequently served as a medium for social disruption. We shall now consider the impact of Britain, intentional or otherwise, upon her Indian Empire.

IV. BRITISH IMPACT

Economic

The British impact upon India was felt first in the economic field, and naturally so since the British arrived in India in search of markets and commodities. Particularly after they became masters of the country, the British affected its economy decisively, though often unwittingly. This was the case when Lord Cornwallis introduced, with his fateful Permanent Settlement of 1793, a form of private property in land in the lower Ganges basin. Hitherto the tax collectors had been state officials charged with securing the state's share of the crop from a number of villages assigned to them. But now these revenue collectors were transformed into English-type landlords, or zamindars, while most of the villagers, who formerly had enjoyed hereditary use of the land, now were reduced to the status of tenants-at-will.

The new landlords were expected to collect a little more than £3,000,-000 annually as rent from the peasantry, but they were required to pass on ten-elevenths to the British authorities, leaving one-eleventh for themselves. The "permanent" feature of this arrangement was that the annual sum expected of the zamindars was to remain the same for all time to come. This proved a windfall for the new landlords, who were collecting between £12,000,000 and £20,000,000 annually by World War II, while continuing to pay the original £3,000,000 to the state. The motive behind this strange contract was explained by a later governor-general, Lord William Bentinck, as follows:

> If . . . security was wanting against popular tumult or revolution, I should say that the Permanent Settlement, which, though a failure in many other respects and in its most important essentials, has this great advantage at least, of having created a vast body of rich landed proprietors deeply interested in the continuance of British Dominion and having complete command over the mass of the people.[9]

The British did secure the allegiance of the zamindars, but they also effected a revolution in the villages that they did not entirely foresee. The old communal land arrangements now gave way before individual ownership, contract law, mortgage, distraint, and forced sale. Formerly, the land tax had been collected with considerable flexibility, but now the tax was a fixed sum and had to be paid on a set day or the property was put up for tax sale. Furthermore, these strange new laws were enforced by alien officials speaking an alien language and usually ill acquainted with local problems and practices. Under these circumstances many of the Indian peasants lost their lands or sank hopelessly into debt. Gradually but inexorably the traditional non-commercial and self-sufficient life of the Indian village came to an end.

In order to meet their new financial obligations the peasants had to abandon their ancient subsistence economy and turn to the production of commodities that could be sold on the world markets. These commodities were transported to the seaports by a newly built railroad network totaling 4,000 miles by 1870, 7,000 miles by 1880, and 41,000 miles by 1939. The opening of the Suez Canal also facilitated the export of Indian raw materials by reducing the distance traversed by freighters between London and Karachi from 10,800 miles to 6,100 miles. Thus India became one of the world's important sources of raw materials. Wheat poured out of the Punjab, cotton out of Bombay, and jute out of Bengal.

Furthermore, the same railroads that carried away the commercial crops brought back cheap, machine-made, industrial products to the villages. These undermined the position of the village artisans who had plied their trades since time immemorial. Fewer and fewer of them were able to subsist on what they received for their services to their fellow-villagers. Precisely the same thing had happened earlier in England and other European countries with the advent of industrialization. But in these cases the artisans had been able to find employment in the new factories appearing in the cities. In India, however, no such industrialization occurred to absorb the displaced multitudes. Britain made no attempt to encourage manufacturing in India, and on crucial occasions actively discouraged it. Even in the early nineteenth century British cotton and silk goods entering India paid a duty of 3½ per cent and woolen goods 2 per cent, while Indian cotton goods imported into Britain paid 10 per cent, silk goods 20 per cent, and woolen goods 30 per cent. In the three decades between 1814 and 1844 the number of pieces of Indian cotton goods imported into Britain fell from 1,250,000 to 63,000, while British cottons exported to India rose from less than 1,000,000 yards to over 51,000,000 yards. Not only the Indian spinners and weavers, but also the tanners and smelters and smiths and shipwrights and many others succumbed to the tidal wave from British factories. And where could these displaced millions go? They could only fall back on agriculture, thereby producing the terrible overpressure on land that remains to the present day one of the most pressing problems of the Indian economy. And at the same time this population pressure was intensified by steady population growth. Thanks to Western medical science, health measures, and famine relief arrangements, India's population rose from 255 million in 1872 to 305 million in 1921.

Social

These economic developments naturally had a profound effect upon the Indian people, but whether beneficial or detrimental is a matter of debate.

The facts do not all support either one viewpoint or the other. There is no doubt that British rule enhanced India's economic development: this is reflected in the great extension of irrigation works, the building of the railroad network, the opening up of the Bengal coal fields and the Burma oilfields, the establishment of modern ironworks at Raniganj, the development of tea and coffee plantations, and the growth of banking facilities and of joint stock organization. All this meant greater productivity, which enabled India to support a much larger population in 1914 than could possibly have been kept alive in the eighteenth century.

But the question still remains whether this larger population was better off than the smaller one of the pre-British period. The evidence is so incomplete that a definitive answer cannot be given. Certainly there was widespread distress from the changes in the land tenure system and the decline of village handicrafts. This produced not only population pressure and underemployment in the countryside but also social dislocation and psychological insecurity. The peasant no longer had hereditary claims to a share of the village land. Instead, he became a defenseless tenant working for a grasping landlord, or a peasant proprietor subject to a fluctuating world market that he could neither understand nor control. With the passage of time a larger and larger percentage of the agricultural land fell into the hands of moneylenders and great magnates.

Furthermore, the transformation of the village economy undermined the village social institutions. The joint family weakened as members found employment opportunities outside the village and as the traditional communal spirit gave way to individualism. The caste system remained a religious and ritual institution, but its significance and effectiveness decreased as the outside world impinged on daily village life. Likewise the Panchayat withered away as various government bureaus took over more and more of its functions. All this change undoubtedly was most unsettling and uncomfortable for the average Indian villager.

The economic and social dislocation in the countryside should be balanced by the opportunities afforded in the new urban centers. The growth of commerce and industry led to the development of large metropolitan cities like Bombay, Madras, and Calcutta, and industrial towns like Ahmedabad and Jamshedpur. In these centers appeared a middle class comprising the owners of landed estates and urban property, government officeholders, merchants, and members of various professions such as lawyers, doctors, and journalists. By 1914 the urban population amounted to about 10 per cent of the total population of the country. That this was inadequate to absorb the displaced multitudes from the countryside is the basic reason why the Indian people were no better off as a result of the Western impact, and quite possibly were worse off. It should be noted, however, that the rising middle class in the cities represented a political innovation of major significance. It replaced the old ruling circles that had been ousted by the British conquerors, and it provided the dynamism behind the burgeoning nationalist movement and the new intellectual currents that were revivifying India.*

* See "British Impact: Economic and Social," *EMM*, No. 83.

Intellectual

For about half a century after their conquest of India the British made no attempt to impose their culture upon the country. They were too busy working out administrative, financial, and judicial arrangements. Accordingly, they left the existing system of education undisturbed, but also unsupported. Elementary education continued to be given in village schools, both Hindu and Moslem. But higher learning declined because it no longer received the customary patronage from the native princes and nobles. By 1811, Governor-General Lord Minto was warning that Indian science and literature were deteriorating so rapidly that, unless the government intervened, the revival of letters might become hopeless from lack of books and of teachers. The government did respond two years later by providing an annual grant of £10,000 for "the revival and improvement of literature and the encouragement of the learned natives."

Nothing was done to implement this legislation until 1823, when a Committee on Public Instruction was appointed to expend the grants that had accumulated. This body decided that it should encourage not an English but an Oriental type of education based on Sanskrit, Arabic, and Persian. This is not surprising, for English scholars had discovered India's cultural heritage and were tremendously impressed, especially by the common origin of the Aryans of India and Europe. Sir William Jones, for example, was extolling Sanskrit for its "wonderful structure; more perfect than the *Greek,* more copious than the *Latin,* and more exquisitely refined than either." [10] On the other hand, some Indians objected to this decision because they wished to learn English in order to get jobs with the new government. The more far-seeing of these objectors favored an English-type of education in order to make available to their countrymen the whole corpus of Western learning. Most outstanding was the distinguished Bengali scholar Ram Mohan Roy, whose career we shall consider shortly. Roy sent a letter to the governor-general in 1823 protesting that the traditional type of education would merely "load the minds of youth with grammatical niceties and metaphysical distinctions of little or no practical use to the possessors or to society." He appealed instead for "a more liberal and enlightened system of instruction, embracing mathematics, natural philosophy, chemistry, anatomy, with other useful sciences." [11]

The controversy split the Committee on Public Instruction into two factions, the "Anglicists" and the "Orientalists." The issue was not altogether clearcut, since the Orientalists were willing to introduce courses in the English language and even on Western thinkers, but only within the framework of the traditional curriculum. The deadlock persisted until Thomas Babington Macauley was appointed president of the Committee in 1834. The following year he prepared his famous Minute on Education in which he adopted wholeheartedly Roy's viewpoint and concluded "that English is better worth knowing than Sanscrit or Arabic. . . ." Macauley added that "it is impossible for us, with our limited means, to attempt to educate the body of the people. We must at present do our best to form a class who may be interpreters between us and the millions whom we govern; a class of persons, Indian in blood and color, but English in taste, in opinions, in morals, and in intellect." [12]

Macauley worked hard to implement his recommendation as soon as it was officially adopted. During the following decades a national system of education was worked out, consisting of universities, training colleges for teachers, high schools, and vernacular elementary schools designed for the masses. Between 1885 and 1900 the number of students in colleges and universities rose from 11,000 to 23,000, and those in secondary schools from 429,000 to 633,000. At the same time the introduction of the printing press greatly stimulated intellectual life in India. Sanskrit works became public property rather than the jealously guarded monopoly of Brahmins. And newspapers appeared published in the various modern Indian languages as well as in English.

These developments affected the intellectual climate of India profoundly. They did not touch the masses, which remained completely illiterate. Nor, at first, did they reach the Moslems, who remained generally hostile to the new schools and books. For half a century the Moslems clung to their traditional culture, and studied only the law, literature, and theology of Islam. Thus, English education become almost the exclusive possession of a small Hindu upper class. But this was enough to start off a chain reaction that has continued to the present day. In the first place, English education created a new class of Indians familiar with foreign languages and cultures, and committed to liberal and rational ideologies. These men had broken out of the traditional mold of religion and caste and custom. They had become, as Macauley had predicted, "Indian in blood and color, but English in taste, in opinions, in morals, and in intellect."

This development, in turn, had two far-reaching repercussions. One was that it provided for the first time a common language and a common cultural background for men in all parts of India. Hitherto they had been separated by the barriers of linguistic, regional, and cultural differences, but now these barriers were shattered by the new language and literature and thought from England. English education also had political repercussions. Western thought, together with the new conditions of all-Indian unity, inevitably gave birth to political self-consciousness and to the demand for Indian self-government. The English had introduced their language and culture in India in order to modernize the country and to create a Western-educated class that would help them in the work of administration. They did attain these objectives, but at the same time they undermined fatally their rule in India. For it was precisely this Western-educated class that used European ideology to attack British domination and to organize a nationalist movement that eventually culminated in an independent India.*

V. INDIAN RENAISSANCE

Britain's intellectual impact stimulated an upsurge and a creativity in Indian thought and culture that is commonly known as the Indian Renaissance. To appreciate the significance of this movement, it should be noted that when

* See "British Impact: Intellectual," *EMM*, No. 84.

the British arrived upon the scene, Hinduism was for the most part in a depressed and demoralized state. During the preceding 700 years of Moslem domination, Hinduism had been looked down upon as the idolatrous religion of a subject race. It lacked prestige, organization, and active leadership. But when the British overthrew Mogul rule, Hinduism for the first time in seven centuries stood on a plane of equality with Islam. And when the British opened their schools, the Hindus, in contrast to the Moslems, flocked to them eagerly. By so doing, they benefited in two ways: they filled the posts in the new bureaucracy, and they experienced an intellectual revival by virtue of their Western contacts.

The stimulus of the West provoked three type of reaction or three schools of thought amongst the Hindus, although the lines were by no means clearcut, and there was much overlapping. The first was wholeheartedly and uncritically pro-Western and antitraditional: everything Western was accepted as *ipso-facto* superior and preferable.

The second reaction was one of complete rejection. The West was admittedly stronger, but its ideas were subversive and its customs repugnant. No true Indian, Hindu or Moslem, should compromise with the evil thing. Rather he should withdraw so far as possible from contact with the foreigner and live his own life in the traditional way. Proponents of this view regarded caste rule as immutable, accepted textual authority without reservations, and opposed such reforms as the abolition of suttee or of infanticide.

The third and most common reaction to the West represented a compromise between blind worship and outright rejection. It accepted the essence of Western secularism and learning, but it also sought to reform Hinduism from within and to preserve its basic truths while ridding it of corruptions and gross encrustations. The outstanding leader of this school of thought was Ram Mohan Roy, widely venerated as "The Father of Modern India." Born in 1772 in a devout Brahman family of Bengal, he broke with his parents over the spectacle of his sister's torture on the funeral pyre of her husband. An insatiable student, he mastered Persian, Arabic, and Sanskrit, and then learned English and entered the service of the government. He was fascinated by Western thought and religions, and studied Greek and Hebrew in order to read the Scriptures in the original. Roy rejected formal doctrinal Christianity while accepting its humanitarian message. His book, *The Precepts of Jesus: The Guide to Peace and Happiness,* is a personal interpretation of Christianity —a reply to the missionaries rather than a call to his fellow-countrymen. Roy also reinterpreted Hinduism in his *Brahmo Samaj,* or Society of God, a new reformed sect of Hinduism which he founded. The Samaj was not a Christian dilution of Hinduism, as is often stated, but rather a synthesis of the doctrines of the European Enlightenment with the philosophical views of the Upanishads. Roy was above all a rationalist who believed that Hinduism rested squarely upon reason. This principle established, he proceeded both to prune current Hindu practices and to borrow freely from the West. Thus he left his followers a creed that enabled them to face the West without losing their identity or their self-respect.

The Brahmo Samaj remained for two generations after Roy's death in 1833 the focus of efforts to purify Hinduism. Then the initiative passed to Swami Dayananda (1824–1883), who rejected the "Brahmos" of his day as being too much under Western influence and ignorant of their own Hindu culture and traditions. Dayananda founded the *Arya Samaj,* or Aryan Society. The name emphasized that the new organization stood for Indian as against "foreign" principles. The Arya Samaj program stressed Sanskrit education and the authority of the Vedas. Dayananda was by no means a reactionary, for he used the Vedas as his authority in attacking untouchability, child marriage, sex inequality, and idol worship.

Two other outstanding leaders of India's renaissance were Sri Ramakrishna (1836–1886) and Swami Vivekananda (1863–1902). Ramakrishna was a saintly mystic whose natural purity and selfless devotion to God attracted disciples throughout India and even abroad. His most famous disciple was Vivekananda, who attracted international attention when he addressed the First World Parliament of Religions at Chicago in 1893. After four years of lecturing in the United States and Europe, he returned to India a national hero. He then devoted himself to the regeneration of his fellow-countrymen, dedicating the Ramakrishna Mission to both social work and religious education. He died at the age of thirty-nine from overwork, but his success in preaching to the world the principles of Hinduism had given his countrymen a sense of dignity and of pride. The Hindu response to the Western challenge had thus made a full circle from rejection and imitation to critical re-evaluation and confident assertiveness.

VI. INDIAN NATIONALISM

Ram Mohan Roy was the pioneer leader not only of India's religious renaissance but also of her political awakening, or nationalist movement. This was a new phenomenon in India, where hitherto there had been cultural unity and regional loyalties but no all-Indian feeling of patriotism. Nationalism developed under British rule for several reasons. One was the "superiority complex" of the English—their conviction that they were a racial elite and divinely ordained to rule India permanently. As the British statesman John Strachey relates,

> Especially after the Mutiny, the fatal doctrine of racial superiority came more and more to dominate the imaginations of the British in India. Perhaps the deterioration in this respect can be made concrete from the records of my own family. During the eighteenth and early nineteenth centuries two of my collatoral ancestors, Colonel Kirkpatrick and Edward Strachey, had married what the late-nineteenth-century British would, so offensively, have called native women. Kirkpatrick had married a Bengali lady of a distinguished family and Strachey a Persian princess, in each case, so far as the family records go, without exciting the least adverse comment or injuring their careers in any way. How unthinkable such alliances would have been to my great-uncles, Sir John and Sir Richard Strachey, who were members of the Governor-General's Council in the eighteen-seventies. This terrible withdrawal of genuine human community went far to undo—in some respects it more than undid—the good which the immense improvement in British conduct might have done for the relations of the two great peoples.[13]

This racism, which was particularly strong following the Mutiny, manifested itself in all fields—in the army and the bureaucracy, where Indians could not rise above certain ranks regardless of their qualifications, and in social life, where Indians were excluded from certain hotels, clubs, and parks. In these circumstances it was perhaps inevitable that an opposing sense of cultural and national consciousness should have gradually developed.

The British also stimulated nationalism by virtue of the unprecedented unity that they imposed on the Indian Peninsula. For the first time the whole of India was under one rule, and throughout the land Pax Britannica prevailed. The British also forged a physical unity with their railways and telegraph and postal services. Equally important was the unprecedented linguistic unity that followed the adoption of English as the common speech of the educated.

The British system of education, which introduced into the country the whole body of Western literature and political thought, also furthered Indian nationalism. The principles of liberalism and nationalism, of personal freedom and self-determination, inevitably were turned against the foreign British rule. The Indian leaders used not only Western political principles but also Western political techniques. Newspapers, platform oratory, pamphleteering, mass meetings, and monster petitions—all were used as grist for the nationalist mill. "On the political side," writes one of the nationalist leaders, "Indian nationalism has been inspired and strengthened by the forces of European nationalism. . . . The nationalist calendar of great men followed by Young India contains such names as those of Washington, Cavour, Mazzini, Bismarck, Kossuth, Emmett, Parnell, by the side of Partap, Ramdas, Guru Govind Singh, Sivaji, Tipu Sultan, and the Rani of Jhansi." [14] A striking example of the close relationship between the Western and Indian independence movements is to be found in the following excerpts from the American Declaration of Independence and the pledge taken by members of the Indian National Congress on "Independence Day" (January 26, 1950). [15]

American Declaration of Independence

We hold these truths to be self evident: that all men are created equal; that they are endowed by their Creator with certain inalienable rights; that among these are life, liberty, and the pursuit of happiness; that to secure these rights governments are instituted among men, deriving their just powers from the consent of the governed; that whenever any form of government becomes destructive of these ends, it is the right of the people to alter it or abolish it.

National Congress Pledge

We believe that it is an inalienable right of the Indian people, as of any other people, to have freedom and enjoy the fruits of their toil and have the necessities of life, so that they may have full opportunities of growth. We believe also that if any government deprives a people of these rights and oppresses them, the people have a further right to alter it or to abolish it.

Ram Mohan Roy laid the foundations of Indian nationalism with his agitation for political and social reform. An indication of his strong interest in these matters is the dinner that he gave to celebrate the 1830 Revolution in Paris. It was largely his campaign against suttee that induced the British government to prohibit the practice. Roy also worked for administrative and judicial reforms, and helped to establish English-language schools and newspapers. Many of the outstanding future leaders of Indian nationalism first came into contact with the new teachings at the famous Hindu College in Calcutta with which Roy was associated.

Among the early Indian nationalist leaders, three are especially noteworthy. The first is Dadabhai Naoroji (1825–1917), an Indian businessman who resided many years in London and who, in fact, was elected in 1892 to the House of Commons on the Liberal ticket. Naoroji emphasized the drain of India's wealth to Britain, and secured the appointment of a parliamentary commission to investigate the financial administration of British India. M. G. Ranade (1842–1901), another distinguished leader, was disqualified from entering active politics because he was a judge, so he concentrated on social and economic reform. After careful study of India's problems, he concluded that the greatest need was for rapid industrialization under British auspices, and he bent his efforts towards the realization of this goal. Ranade's disciple was G. K. Gokhale (1866–1915), who also was interested primarily in economic problems. As a member of the Legislative Council he raised the cry "No taxation without representation," and his annual speeches on the imperial budget forced many tax reductions and financial reforms.

All these men were "moderates," in the sense that they accepted British rule and sought merely to secure certain concessions. Accordingly, they cooperated in supporting the Indian National Congress founded in 1885. The expressed aim of this body was to provide "an unanswerable reply to the assertion that India is still wholly unfit for any form of representative institutions." But this aspiration for parliamentary government was in no way incompatible with a sincere loyalty to Britain. Naoroji, who served as president of the Congress on three separate occasions, declared in one of his presidential addresses:

> Well, then, what is it for which we are now met on this occasion? . . . I put the *question* plainly: Is this Congress a nursery for sedition and rebellion against the British Government (cries of "no, no"); or is it another stone in the foundation of the stability of that Government (cries of "yes, yes")? There could be but one answer, and that you have already given. . . . Let us speak out like men and proclaim that we are loyal to the backbone (cheers); that we understand the benefits English rule has conferred upon us; that we thoroughly appreciate the education that has been given to us, the new light which has been poured upon us, turning us from darkness into light and teaching us the new lesson that kings are made for the people, not people for their kings; and this new lesson we have learned amidst the darkness of Asiatic despotism only by the light of free English civilization (loud cheers).[16]

This first generation of Indian nationalists, then, were admirers of Great Britain and apostles of cooperation. But after 1890 these "moderates" were challenged by the extremists led by Bal Gangadhar Tilak (1856–1920), the "father of Indian unrest." Tilak was a militant crusader who sought to transform the nationalist cause from an upper-class to a popular mass movement.

This may explain his dogmatic support of many Hindu social customs, going so far as to organize a cow-protection society and to support child marriage. Yet at the same time he fought for a minimum wage for labor, freedom for trade union organization, creation of a citizen army, universal franchise, and free and compulsory education without distinction as to sex. Tilak was a brilliant orator and journalist, and made his newspaper, the *Kesari* ("Lion") a powerful organ of propaganda and education. He won followers throughout the country with slogans such as "Educate, Agitate, and Organize," "Militancy, not mendicancy," and "Freedom is my birthright and I will have it."

Tilak was aided in his crusade by a series of famines and plagues in the 1890's that gave impetus to the growing sense of grievance. Indian militancy was also aroused by the revolution in Russia in 1905 and by Japan's defeat of Russia in the same year. The latter event was particularly exciting, being taken as a practical and signal refutation of the claim of Western superiority. At this point the Indian government passed in 1905 an act for the partition of Bengal into two provinces: the new East Bengal with 18 million Moslems and 12 million Hindus, and the remaining Bengal with 42 million Hindus and 12 million Moslems. The government's professed aim was to improve administration, for the original province had been too large and the area east of the Ganges had been neglected. But to the Indian nationalists it appeared that by dividing Bengal into predominantly Moslem and predominantly Hindu sections, the British were following a policy of divide and rule. This issue united the nationalists throughout the country to an unprecedented degree. They fought the government very effectively with the slogans *"Swaraj,"* or self-government within the British Empire, and *"Swadeshi,"* or boycott of British goods. Students in large numbers participated in the picketing of stores, and for the first time women became active in politics and appeared in the picket lines. The strong feelings aroused by the Bengal issue enabled the Extremists to control the 1906 meeting of the Indian Congress, and to secure a majority vote in favor of Swaraj and Swadeshi. Some of the nationalists went further, and, following the example and methods of the underground in Ireland and Russia, resorted to acts of terrorism. In Bengal alone, between 1906 and 1917, there were 168 outrages that took the lives of 61 persons.*

Widespread though it was, this nationalist movement was predominantly Hindu. Under the leadership of Sir Sayyid Ahmad Khan, the Moslems had for the most part stayed out of the Indian Congress. They foresaw that if the Congess' demand for representative government were satisfied, the Moslems would suffer as a permanent minority. The Moslems also were alarmed by the increasing strength and militancy of Hindu nationalism, particularly since some of the most ardent Hindu patriots referred to the Moslems as "foreigners." In self-protection the Moslems organized the Moslem League, which, like the Indian Congress, held annual meetings. The British naturally welcomed and supported the League as a makeweight against the Congress. But the existence of the League was due basically not to British machinations but rather to the error of many nationalist leaders, such as Tilak, in basing their campaign on a revival of Hinduism. The formation of cow-protection societies, for example, undoubtedly aided the nationalist movement, but it

* See "Rise of Indian Nationalism," *EMM,* No. 85.

also alienated Moslem Indians who naturally felt apprehensive about their future in a Hindu-controlled India.

Meanwhile, the spread of terrorism and the growing dissatisfaction of even the "moderates" convinced the British government that some concession was necessary. Accordingly, in 1909 the Secretary of State for India, Lord Morley, and the Viceroy, Lord Minto, presented the so-called Morley–Minto Reforms. These provided that a very small group of Indian voters, selected on the basis of high property, income, or education qualifications, should elect a majority of the members in the Legislative Councils of the provincial Governors, and a minority of members in the Viceroy's Legislative Council. A specified proportion of the legislative seats were reserved for Hindus and Moslems, and Moslem representation was weighted very considerably. For example, to become an elector, the Moslem had to pay income tax on an income of 3,000 rupees a year, the non-Moslem on an income of 300,000 rupees. Furthermore, even where an elective majority existed, as in the provincial councils, the British government could, and was prepared to, override any opposition. Thus the Reforms were in no way designed to introduce responsible government. Rather they were intended to permit an element of representative government while leaving full power and final decisions in British hands. Lord Morley himself made this quite clear during the debates in the House of Lords:

> If it could be said that this chapter of reforms led directly or in-directly to the establishment of a parliamentary system in India, I, for one, would have nothing at all to do with it.
>
> There are three classes of people whom we have to consider in dealing with a scheme of this kind. There are the Extremists who nurse fantastic dreams that some day they will drive us out of India. . . . The second group nourish no hope of this sort, but hope for autonomy or self-government of the colonial species and pattern. And then the third section of this classification ask for no more than to be admitted to co-operation in our administration.
>
> I believe the effect of the Reforms has been, is being and will be to draw the second class, who hope for colonial autonomy, into the third class, who will be content with being admitted to a fair and full co-operation.[17]

This strategy succeeded in large part. The moderate nationalists, who had regained control of the Congress, passed a resolution expressing "deep and general satisfaction at the Reform proposals." They were further placated when the British made several more concessions in 1911, including the annulment of the unpopular partition of Bengal, the release of certain political prisoners, and the granting of substantial sums for educational purposes. Thus although individual acts of terrorism continued sporadically, India was relatively tranquil between 1910 and 1914.

Throughout this period, the nationalist movement was confined largely to the intellectuals. It is true that the National Congress had grown remarkably during the quarter-century following its establishment in 1885. Its membership was drawn from all parts of British India rather than from Bengal and a few cities on the west coast, as was originally the case. Yet the fact remains that it was almost exclusively a middle-class movement of lawyers, journalists, teachers, and merchants. These people were more familiar with John Stuart Mill, Herbert Spencer, and Charles Darwin than with the misery and grievances and aspirations of the masses of their own countrymen in the villages. Not unnaturally, there was little rapport between the nationalist leaders and the illiterate peasants. The gulf persisted until bridged by Mohandas Gandhi in the postwar period. And Gandhi succeeded because he sensed the essentially religious outlook of his people, and preached, not political abstractions, but religious concepts to which he gave a political meaning (see Chapter 21, section V).

VII. CONCLUSION

The impact of the West on India was quite different from its impact on Russia or the Middle East. In the case of Russia, the West exerted decisive cultural and economic influence, but Russia remained politically and militarily strong and independent. The Near East, on the other hand, was dominated economically and militarily by the West, yet, because of strategic considerations, the Ottoman Empire managed to retain its independence until World War I. India, by contrast, was conquered outright by Britain during the late eighteenth and nineteenth centuries. British rule lasted for nearly two centuries in Bengal and for more than one century in the Punjab. Consequently, the Western impact on India was more direct and all-embracing than in other regions. The Indians did not have the privilege of picking and choosing those features of European civilization that most appealed to them. Certain features that they disliked were imposed upon them, and others that they admired and wished to adopt were denied them.

An example is to be found in Western military technique, which the Indians, like the Russians, the Turks, and the Chinese, and Japanese, desired to learn and utilize. In fact, Indian princes engaged European adventurers to train their troops, and the former disorderly feudal arrays gave way to disciplined battalions. The Sikhs in the Punjab, for example, developed an army that was as well-trained as the British, and that was superior in its use of artillery. In the end, the British prevailed not because of purely military factors, but because of their greater economic resources and because of their cohesiveness, in contrast to the division amongst the Indian rulers. Once the British won out, the Indians no longer could keep up with Western military technique. The British did not allow them to rise above a certain rank in their armed forces, and excluded them altogether from their artillery and air units. Thus the Indians, who started out in this military field in precisely the same manner as other non-European peoples, were forced to follow a different pattern because of the British conquest. This was the case also, as we have seen, in other areas—economic, political, and cultural—with the result that India felt the Western impact more indiscriminately and probably more profoundly, than any other major region of Asia.

SUGGESTED READING

An excellent survey of the historical literature on India is provided in the pamphlet by R. I. Crane, *The History of India: Its Study and Interpretation* (Washington: Service Center for Teachers of History, 1958).

The most recent general history of India is the fine study by P. Spear, *India: A Modern History* (Ann Arbor: Univ. of Michigan, 1961). Other standard histories are by E. Thompson and G. T. Garratt, *Rise and Fulfilment of British Rule in India* (London: Macmillan, 1934); R. C. Majumdar, H. C. Raychaudhuri, and K. Datta, *An Advanced History of India* (London: Macmillan, 1960); W. H. Moreland and A. C. Chatterjee, *A Short History of India* (London: Longmans, 1957); and K. M. Panikkar, *A Survey of Indian History,* 3rd ed. (Bombay: Asia Publishing House, 1956).

For general studies of British rule in India, there is the excellent brief analysis by R. P. Masani, *Britain in India* (New York: Oxford Univ., 1961); as well as P. Woodruff, *The Men Who Ruled India* (London: J. Cape, 1954–1955), 2 vols.; R. Coupland, *Britain and India, 1600–1941* (London: Longmans, 1943); and the excellent collection of readings reflecting various viewpoints, in M. D. Lewis, ed., *The British in India: Imperialism or Trusteeship* (Boston: Heath, 1962). Another very useful collection of readings presenting various interpretations of the Indian Mutiny is available in A. T. Embree, ed., *1857 in India: Mutiny or War of Independence?* (Boston: Heath, 1963).

The most thorough study of Europe's impact on India is by L. S. S. O'Malley, *Modern India and the West* (New York: Oxford Univ., 1941). See also P. Spear, *India, Pakistan and the West* (New York: Oxford Univ., 1958); and P. Griffiths, *The British Impact on India* (London: Macdonald, 1952).

For the intellectual and nationalist trends in India, see B. T. McCully, *English Education and the Origins of Indian Nationalism* (New York: Columbia Univ., 1940); W. R. Smith, *Nationalism and Reform in India* (New Haven: Yale Univ., 1938); and the authoritative study of the outstanding pre-1914 nationalist leaders by S. A. Wolpert, *Tilak and Gokhale: Revolution and Reform in the Making of Modern India* (Berkeley: Univ. of California, 1962).

The historian who grasps the true secret of
Japan's success in rapid Westernization has a
key to modern Far Eastern history.

JOHN K. FAIRBANK

Chapter

16

China and Japan

T he Far East was the last major region of Eurasia to feel
the impact of expanding Europe. Various factors explain why China
and Japan, in this respect, followed behind Russia, the Near East, and
India. First, and most obvious, is the fact that the Far East, by
definition, is that portion of the Eurasian continent that is farthest
removed from Europe. China and Japan are not contiguous to Europe,
as were the Russian and Ottoman Empires; and they are much further
to the east and north than India. Probably more significant than geographic isolation was the political unity of the two Far Eastern
countries. The European intruders were not able to employ in China
and Japan the divide-and-rule policy that had proven so effective in
India. There were no independent local potentates who could be enlisted against the central governments in Peking and Tokyo. And,
thanks to the rigid seclusion policies of both these governments, there
were no potential fifth column elements that could be exploited by
the Europeans. The large body of Christian converts in Japan had
been ruthlessly wiped out during the seventeenth century, and the
rigid curtailment of trade with the outside world prevented the growth
in China and Japan of a considerable merchant class, like that of
India, whose ties were more with foreign companies than with their
own governments.

Consequently, the Far Eastern countries were able to limit their contact with Europe to a mere trickle of closely supervised trade. But in the mid-nineteenth century this situation changed suddenly and drastically. First China, and then Japan, were forced open and compelled to accept Western merchants and missionaries and consuls and gunboats. The impact was not quite so overwhelming as in India, where a conquered people had little opportunity to pick and choose what they wanted of the foreign culture. But both the Far Eastern countries were fundamentally affected, though in very different ways. Japan was able to adopt and to utilize the principles of Western power and to exploit them for self-defense and, later, for aggrandizement. China, by contrast, proved incapable of reorganizing herself along modified Western lines. On the other hand, she was too large and cohesive to be conquered outright, like India and the countries of Southeast Asia. Thus China remained in uncomfortable and unstable limbo until World War I, and even for some decades thereafter.

I. OPENING OF CHINA

Over a period of 4,000 years the Chinese people developed a unique and self-contained society at the extreme eastern end of the Eurasian landmass. This society, like others in Asia, was based on agriculture rather than trade, and governed by landlords and bureaucrats rather than by merchants and politicians. It was a distinctly self-centered and self-assured society that regarded the rest of the world as inferior and subordinate.

The Chinese first came into direct contact with the West when the Portuguese appeared off the southeast coast in 1514. After the Portuguese came the Dutch and the British, who also arrived by sea, and in the north appeared the Russians, who came overland to the Amur valley. The Chinese resolutely kept all these intruders at arm's length (see Chapter 4, section IV). They restricted commercial relations to a few ports, and refused to establish diplomatic relations on a full and equal basis. The fact is that the Chinese were profoundly uninterested in the outside world. This is reflected in their invincible ignorance of Europe and the Europeans. They had little notion of the location of Europe and cared less. They were completely confused concerning the various European nationals, and preferred to lump them together as the "long-nosed barbarians." They felt no need whatsoever for the products of Europe, as Emperor Ch'ien lung made painfully clear in his famous letter to George III in 1793 (quoted in Chapter 9, section III).

The Chinese were forcefully jarred out of their seclusion and complacency by three disastrous wars: the first with Britain in 1839–1842, the second with Britain and France in 1856–1858, and the third with Japan in 1895. The humiliating defeats suffered in these wars compelled the Chinese to throw open the gates, to end their condescending attitude toward the West, and to reappraise their own traditional civilization. The outcome was a chain reaction of intrusion and response that produced a new China and induced repercussions that are still convulsing the Far East and the entire globe.

Britain was able to take the lead in opening up China because she had a powerful base in India as well as control of the seas. Britain's main objective in forcing the issue was to remove the innumerable obstacles that the Chinese placed in the way of trading operations. It should be borne in mind that by the mid-nineteenth century the British had come to believe in almost a divine right to trade anywhere in the world, and considered it unnatural and reprehensible for governments to close their countries to free commerce.

The immediate issue that provoked hostilities between Britain and China was the trade in opium. European sailors had introduced opium smoking in China in the seventeenth century, and the habit spread rapidly from the ports. The demand for opium solved the British problem of paying for Chinese products. Hitherto the British had been forced to pay mostly in gold and silver, because the Chinese were little interested in Western goods. But now the market for opium reversed the balance of trade in favor of the British. The Peking government issued decrees in 1729 and 1799 prohibiting the importation of opium, but the trade was so profitable that Chinese officials could be bribed to permit smuggling. By 1833 this nefarious trade had reached an annual value of $15 million.

The first Anglo-Chinese War, or Opium War, as it is frequently called, broke out when the Chinese attempted to enforce their prohibition of the opium traffic. The Emperor appointed as special Imperial Commissioner a man of proven integrity and firmness, Liu Tse-hsu. Liu seized 20,000 chests of opium worth $6 million, and destroyed them at a public ceremony. Complications following this action led to a clash between Chinese war junks and British frigates, and war began in November, 1839. The course of the following hostilities made clear the hopeless military inferiority of the Chinese. With a squadron of ships and a few thousand men, the British were able to seize port after port at will. The Chinese fought valiantly, their garrisons often resisting to the last man. But the odds were much more uneven than they had been between the Conquistadors and the Aztecs. European warships and artillery had been developed immeasurably between the sixteenth and nineteenth

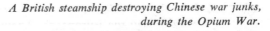

A British steamship destroying Chinese war junks, during the Opium War.

A scene from the Sino-Japanese war. (From a Toshihide print. Victoria & Albert Museum. Crown copyright.)

centuries, while Chinese military technology had stagnated at a level little above that of the Aztecs. In 1842, the Peking government capitulated and accepted the Treaty of Nanking, the first of a long series of unequal treaties that were to nibble away much of China's sovereignty.

By the Nanking Treaty China ceded the island of Hong Kong and opened five ports to foreign trade—Canton, Foochow, Ningpo, Amoy, and Shanghai. At these ports British consuls could be stationed and British merchants could lease land for residential and business uses. China also agreed to a uniform tariff fixed at 5 per cent ad valorem, to be changed only by mutual agreement. This provision deprived China of tariff autonomy and hence of control over her national revenue. Furthermore, a supplementary treaty concluded the following year granted Britain extraterritoriality in criminal cases, and also included a most-favored nation clause assuring Britain any additional privileges that China might grant other powers in the future. Probably neither side quite realized at the time that these provisions were to lead eventually to an elaborate system of foreign settlements and concessions located in all parts of the country each constituting a foreign city under foreign government.

The Nanking Treaty did not end the friction between the Chinese and the Europeans. The latter were disappointed because the opening of the treaty

ports did not lead to so great an expansion of trade as they had anticipated. The remedy, they believed, was to secure even more concessions. "Our trade with China," declared the Manchester Chamber of Commerce, "will never be fully developed until the right to sell and purchase is extended beyond the ports to which we are now restricted." [1] The Chinese, on the other hand, felt that the treaties had granted too many privileges and constantly evaded fulfillment of the treaty obligations. Furthermore, the European merchants and the numerous adventurers of unsavory character who now flocked to the treaty ports aroused strong antiforeign feelings amongst the Chinese populace. A placard distributed in the Canton region in 1841 expressed these feelings in vigorous terms. Addressed to the "rebellious barbarian dogs and sheep," it asked rhetorically, "Although you have penetrated our inland rivers . . . what goods have you? . . . Except for your ships being solid, your gunfire fierce and your rockets powerful, what other abilities have you?" The poster then threatened the foreigners with the most dire consequences if they persisted in remaining in China. "If we do not completely exterminate you pigs and dogs, we will not be manly Chinese able to support the sky on our heads. . . . We are definitely going to kill you, cut your heads off and burn you to death!" [2]

With such sentiments prevailing on both sides it is not surprising that hostilities began again in 1856. The occasion this time was the imprisonment by Chinese officials of the Chinese crew on board a Chinese ship flying the British flag. When the Peking government refused to release the crew, the British bombarded Canton. The French also entered the war, using the murder of a French priest as a pretext. The British operations were delayed for some time because of the outbreak of the Mutiny in India. But once reinforcements arrived, the Anglo-French forces proved as irresistible as in the first war. In June, 1858, the Chinese were compelled to sign the Tientsin Treaties, but they refused to carry out the provisions and delayed formal ratification. The Anglo-French forces renewed the attack, capturing the capital and forcing China to sign the Peking Conventions in 1860. The Tientsin and Peking agreements opened several more ports on the coast and in the interior, redefined and extended extraterritoriality, and permitted the establishment of foreign legations in Peking and of Christian missions throughout the country. It should be recalled that it was at this time that the Russians took advantage of China's difficulties to secure by diplomatic means large areas in the Amur Valley and along the Pacific coast (see Chapter 13, section III).

The third defeat suffered by China was the most humiliating, for it was at the hands of the small neighboring kingdom of Japan. We shall see later in this chapter that the Japanese, in contrast to the Chinese, had been able to adapt Western technology to their needs and to build an efficient military establishment. Having accomplished what no other Oriental state had been able to achieve thus far, Japan now pressed certain shadowy claims in Korea. Traditionally, the Koreans had recognized the suzerainty of China, but they also had periodically submitted tribute to Japan. Thus when China sent a small force to Korea in 1894 in response to an appeal for aid in suppressing a revolt, the Japanese also landed a detachment of marines. The two forces clashed, and war was formally declared by China and Japan in August, 1894. The Chinese armies again were easily routed, and in April, 1895, Peking was forced to accept the Treaty of Shimonoseki. Its terms required China to pay an indemnity, recognize the independence of Korea, cede to Japan the island of Formosa, the Pescadores Islands, and the Liaotung Peninsula, and open four more ports to foreign commerce. Some of the European powers were not at all pleased with the appearance of a new rival for concessions in China. Accordingly, Russia, France, and Germany joined in a demand that the strategic Liaotung Peninsula be returned to China, a demand to which Japan yielded reluctantly.

The Japanese war was a shattering blow to the pride and complacency of China. The great empire had been shown up to be completely helpless before a despised neighbor equipped with modern instruments of war. Furthermore, the European powers during the preceding years had been taking advantage of China's weakness and annexing outlying territories that traditionally had recognized Peking's suzerainty. Russia took the Amur Valley, the Maritime Provinces, and for a while occupied the Ili region in Central Asia. France seized Indochina, Britain took Burma, and Japan, having established her predominance in Korea by defeating China, proceeded to annex the country outright in 1910. In addition to these territorial acquisitions, the Western states divided China proper into spheres of influence in which were recognized the political and economic primacy of the respective powers concerned. Thus Yunnan and the area bordering on Indochina became a French sphere, Canton and the Yangtze Valley and the large area in between was a British sphere, Manchuria was Russian, Shantung was German, and Fukien Japanese.

The state of China at the end of the nineteenth century was roughly comparable to that of the Ottoman Empire. Just as the European powers had annexed former Turkish tributary regions such as the trans-Danubian territories, southern Russia, Egypt, and North Africa, so the Great Powers annexed former Chinese tributary regions such as Indochina, Burma, Korea, and the Amur Valley. In the remaining provinces of the Chinese Empire, Western control was more direct and extensive than in the remaining provinces of the Ottoman Empire. Whereas European gunboats patrolled China's inland waterways, the Turks were left in control of their Straits. And while the Europeans did enjoy extraterritorial privileges in the Ottoman Empire, they never infringed upon Turkish suzerainty to the extent that they did upon Chinese in the various concessions, and especially in the Shanghai International Settlement. Generally speaking, Europe dominated China in the same manner that she dominated Turkey, though the control was more direct and extensive in the case of China. On the other hand, China did escape the outright conquest and direct foreign rule that India suffered. The main reason for this difference is that by the time China's defenselessness had become fully apparent, more than one power was interested in the country, and so none had the freedom of action that Britain had enjoyed and exploited in the early nineteenth century in India.

The humiliations and disasters that China experienced in the latter half of the nineteenth century forced the traditionally self-centered Middle Kingdom to undertake a painful self-searching, reappraisal, and reorganization. We will now trace the course of this process, noting how the Chinese slowly and grudgingly tried to follow the Western model, first in the military field, then in the economic, later in the social and intellectual, and finally in the political.

II. MILITARY IMPACT

During the Opium War between China and Britain, a certain general who was a cousin of the Chinese Emperor conceived a plan for the defeat of the Western barbarians. He proposed tying firecrackers to the backs of monkeys, which should then be flung on board the English warships anchored off the coast. The plan was approved, and nineteen monkeys were brought in litters to the Chinese headquarters. But no one could be found who dared go within throwing range of the warships.

This incident reflects the grotesque disparity between Chinese and Western military technology in the mid-nineteenth century. Liu Tse-hsu, the Chinese commissioner who had tried to stem the flow of opium and who had borne the brunt of the first British attack, realized the superiority of foreign arms. In a letter to a friend he described the impossibility of coping with British warships, and concluded that "ships, guns, and a water force are absolutely indispensable." But Liu was by no means willing to broadcast these views. "I only beg you to keep them confidential," he requested his friend. "By all means, please do not tell other persons." [3]

352

His aversion to publicity indicated that he feared a hostile reaction among his colleagues and superiors. This fear was by no means unjustified. The scholar-officials who ruled China remained, with a few exceptions, profoundly antipathetic and scornful of everything Western. The shock of defeat compelled them to take certain measures toward imitating Western arms and techniques. But in actual practice they did little more than go through the motions. The mandarins were hopelessly incompetent in mechanical matters even if they were sincerely desirous of imitating the West, which fundamentally they were not. Thus China did little during the interwar years of 1842 to 1858 to face the challenge of European expansionism.*

III. Economic Impact

The second defeat at the hands of the Western powers forced a few forward-looking Chinese intellectuals again to reconsider their traditional values and policies. Their response was what they called the "self-strengthening" movement. The phrase itself is from the Confucian classics, and was used in the 1860's to mean the preservation of Chinese civilization by grafting on Western mechanisms. In this regard the leaders of China now were ready to go beyond purely military matters to include railroads, steamship lines, machine factories, and applied science generally. In the words of one of the reformers of this period, "China should acquire the West's superiority in arms and machinery, but retain China's superiority in Confucian virtue." [4] This "self-strengthening" movement was doomed to failure because the basic assumption on which it rested was fallacious. Westernization could not be a half-way process; it was all or nothing. Westernization in tools led inevitably to westernization in ideas and institutions. So Western science could not be used to preserve a Confucian civilization; rather it was bound to undermine that civilization.

The fallacy of half-way modernization was apparent to the conservative Chinese scholar-bureaucrats, who consequently rejected westernization outright. Since they comprised a large majority of China's ruling class, they effectively blocked the attempt to modernize China in economic matters, as they had checked the earlier attempt at military modernization. An example of their influence is to be found in the fate of the mission of 120 long-gowned Chinese students who were sent to school at Hartford, Connecticut, in 1872. Old-style Chinese teachers accompanied them in order to prepare these prospective modernizers of China for the traditional classics examinations that still were a prerequisite to an administrative career. Every measure was taken to ensure that this unprecedented contact with the West did not contaminate the young students' Confucian morals. Despite elaborate precautions, there was much misgiving concerning the wisdom and desirability of the undertaking. Finally a conservative reaction led to the recall of the entire group in 1881 before the program of studies had been completed.

Similar attitudes handicapped the few attempts at industrialization. For

* See "China's Response to the West: Technological Phase," *EMM*, No. 86.

example, the China Merchants Steam Navigation Company was established in 1872 to build steamships for transporting rice from the Yangtze Delta to the capital in the north. The steamer fleet needed coal, so the Kaiping coal 353 mines were opened north of Tientsin in 1878. To transport this coal, China's first permanent railroad began operations in 1881. This integrated complex of enterprises had a sound economic basis and should have prospered. But its directors were motivated, in the traditional Chinese fashion, more by family than by corporate considerations. They appointed needy relatives and greedy henchmen to the various posts, with the result that the entire under-taking fell heavily into debt and eventually passed under foreign control.

China's failure to build up her economy and her armed forces led inevita-bly to increasing Western penetration and control. Numerous loans were made to the Peking government, frequently under pressure and on conditions that gave the creditors control over segments of China's economy. Another means of economic influence was the concessions held by the European powers in various Chinese ports. Most important was the "international settlement" of Shanghai which developed into a sovereign city-state in which Chinese laws did not apply and Chinese courts and police had no jurisdiction. These con-cessions profoundly affected China's economy, which traditionally had been self-sufficient and land-based. But now it was becoming increasingly dependent upon the foreign-controlled coastal cities, and particularly upon Shanghai. The Western powers also dominated the great inland waterways as well as the coastal ports. They maintained fleets of gunboats that patrolled the Yangtze River between Shanghai and Chunking, a distance of 1,500 miles across the heart of China. In fact, Britain maintained an officer with the revealing title of Rear-Admiral Yangtze! *

IV. Social and Intellectual Impact

In the late nineteenth and early twentieth centuries, the Chinese response to the West's challenge broadened from the military and economic spheres to the social and intellectual. This broadening is reflected in the changing nature of the Western books that the Chinese were selecting for translation. In the period 1850 to 1899 the translated works in natural and particularly in applied science outnumbered those in the social sciences and humanities four to one; in the years 1902 to 1904, the latter outnumbered the former two to one, and in the period 1912 to 1940 they outnumbered the natural and applied sciences three to one.

One reason for this shift in interest was the defeat by Japan in 1894–1895, a crushing blow to the pride and complacency of the ruling scholar-official class. The other reason was the massive and seemingly irresistible intrusion of the West. In the years following the war with Japan, this intrusion reached such proportions in every field that the very existence of the Chinese state seemed endangered. As a result, a growing number of Chinese leaders were being forced to the conclusion that drastic change was essential for survival, and that this change could not be limited to military and economic matters.

* See "China's Response to the West: Institutional Phase," *EMM*, No. 87.

Furthermore, the very process of Western penetration created forces and conditions that were propitious to change.

The extension of foreign business into the interior of the country stimulated the growth of a Chinese merchant class, which soon took over the distribution of Western goods. As early as 1869 a British official reported that "owing to superior knowledge of language and markets and lower overhead charges, the Chinese were almost monopolising the business of administration." [5] Later, Chinese manufacturers began to establish match factories, flour mills, cotton mills, and silk-spinning factories. These new economic leaders tended to be an independent political force. They disliked European domination because of the privileges it conferred upon foreign business competitors. But they also had little use for the reactionary imperial court in Peking, which neither offered effective resistance to the foreigners nor showed any understanding of the nature and needs of a modern economy. Thus, these Chinese merchants felt no more loyalty toward the Manchu regime in Peking than the Indian merchants had felt earlier for the Mogul regime in Delhi. Consequently it was they who provided the dynamism behind the revolutionary nationalist movement that developed at the turn of the century. It was not accidental that the first antiforeign boycotts were organized in the coastal cities, and that the 1911 revolution that overthrew the Manchu dynasty also broke out in those cities.

The perilous situation of China also affected the ruling scholar-bureaucrats, though they were impelled in the direction of reform rather than revolution. Because of their official positions and vested interests, they wanted only "change within tradition." They still held that China's Confucian civilization could be renovated to meet modern needs. An outstanding exponent of this view was the fiery Cantonese scholar K'ang Yu-wei (1858–1927), who startled his colleagues with his study *Confucius as a Reformer*. This iconoclastic work depicted Confucius as a champion of the rights of the people, rather than imperial authority. One of K'ang's disciples spelled out this radical notion as follows:

> In general, when the power of the empire comes from one person, it is weak. When it comes from millions of people, it is strong. . . . If the scholars, merchants, and common people can all feel concern about the dangers and difficulties of the nation, then the people will be intelligent; otherwise ignorant. Therefore, unless we rely on the people's authority, it is impossible to change our disunited spirit to one of concentration, and our ignorance to wisdom.[6]

This advocacy of people's rights and of their participation in government was something new for China. Hitherto the Western concepts of democracy and nationalism had been conspicuously absent. Instead, the emphasis had been on the family, and, so far as a broader allegiance was concerned, it took the form of "culturalism" rather than nationalism. By culturalism is meant identification with the native cultural tradition, which was viewed simply as the alternative to foreign barbarism. China's ruling scholar-bureacracy was steeped in this tradition, and many of its members still avowed that it was "better to see the nation die than its way of life change." [7] But against the standpatism of this traditional culturalism the reform leaders now affirmed revolutionary Western concepts. "What does nationalism mean?" asked one of these reformers. "It is that in all places people of the same race, the same language, the same religion, and the same customs, regard each other as brothers and work for independence and self-government, and organize a more perfect government to work for the public welfare and to oppose the infringement of other races. . . . If we wish to promote nationalism in China, there is no other means of doing it except through the renovation of the people." [8]

V. POLITICAL IMPACT

The new reform spokesmen in China were able to win a hearing following the defeat at the hands of the Japanese in 1895. They gained the ear of the young emperor, Kuang-hsü, who momentarily broke away from the influence of the empress dowager, Tz'u-hsi. The latter had determined China's policy since 1860, but now the reformers won the emperor over to their side. So impressed was he by their oral and written presentations that he issued in the summer of 1898 a series of sweeping reform decrees that are collectively called the Hundred Days Reform. These decrees were to provide a basic reorganization of most phases of Chinese society. Numerous sinecures were to be eliminated, the provincial governments were to be more centralized under Peking, new schools were to disseminate European learning, Western-style production methods were to be encouraged, and a national conscript army was to be organized along Western lines.

These measures never got beyond the paper stage. The reformers were inexperienced, and their decrees had to be carried out by a conservative bureaucracy that was predominantly unsympathetic. Convinced that their program would fail unless the opposition leadership was removed, the reformers plotted to remove the empress dowager and the diehard elements gathered about her. But the empress dowager moved first, and with the support of the military she effected a coup and deposed the unfortunate emperor. Then she declared herself regent, rescinded all the reform decrees, and executed six of the reform leaders.

The collapse of the Hundred Days Reform gave the reactionaries full power. In their zeal they actively channeled social and political discontent against the foreigners. Antiforeign secret societies, incited by court reactionaries and provincial governors, organized local militias to combat foreign aggression. Chief among these societies was the I Ho T'uan, or Righteous Harmony Fists, popularly termed Boxers. With official connivance the Boxers began to attack foreigners, and by 1900 numerous Chinese Christians and foreigners had been killed in North China. When European naval detachments began to land at Tientsin, the Boxers declared war on all foreigners and besieged the foreign legations in Peking. Within a few months, international armies relieved the legations, and the Imperial Court fled from the capital. Once more China was forced to accept a peace with humiliating terms, including further commercial concessions and payment of an indemnity of $333 million.

The fiascos of the Hundred Days Reform and of the Boxer Rebellion dramatically demonstrated the futility of trying to modernize China by reform from above. The alternative was revolution from below, and this did take place in 1911, when the Manchu dynasty finally was overthrown and its place taken by a republic.

The leader and ideologist of the revolutionists was Dr. Sun Yat-sen (1866–1925). Compared to the reform leaders who had hitherto been prominent, Sun was a strange and anomalous figure. He was not one of the upper-class literati; in fact, his training was as much Western as Chinese, and his knowledge of the traditional classics was far from secure. He was born in the Canton Delta, which had been subject to foreign influence longer than any other area in China. At the age of thirteen he joined his brother in Honolulu where he remained five years and completed a high-school course in a Church of England boarding school. Then he went to Queen's College in Hong Kong, and after graduation he enrolled in the Hong Kong Medical College and received his medical degree in 1892. Thus Sun acquired an excellent scientific education that he could have used to acquire wealth and status; instead he identified with the poor and always felt a passionate concern for their welfare. "I am a coolie and the son of a coolie," he declared on one occasion. "I was born with the poor and I am still poor. My sympathies have always been with the struggling mass." [9]

With such sentiments, he did not remain long in professional practice. The defeat by Japan in 1895 convinced him that the government of his country was rotten to the core and that nothing short of a revolution would provide the remedy. So he embarked on the career of a revolutionary and went first to Japan, then to America, and later to London. In the latter capital he was kidnapped in the streets and carried off to the Chinese legation where he was kept hidden for twelve days. But he was able to get word to Sir James Cantlie, his former teacher at the Hong Kong Medical College, who now lived in London near the legation. Cantlie promptly informed the British authorities and secured Sun's release. This undoubtedly saved Sun's life, for the legation officials had planned to smuggle him back to China where he certainly would have been executed.

After this escapade Sun proceeded to the continent of Europe and spent the next few years studying social and political institutions. It was at this time that Sun became definitely republican in his thinking. He had for long been a revolutionary in the sense that he wished to overthrow the Manchu dynasty. But hitherto his constructive proposals had been limited to training competent personnel and carrying out technological improvements. Now he decided that the aim of revolution should be the establishment of a democratic republic. At a conference held in Tokyo in 1905 Sun founded the T'ung-meng-hui, or League of Common Alliance. Its program called for a republican government elected by "the people of the country" and also for the division of the land amongst the peasantry.* It is significant that no one had earlier raised the issue of land distribution as a possible element in self-strengthening or reform. The explanation is that no one had seriously considered the idea of a fundamental revolution in the Chinese way of life. No one, before Sun, had proposed the notion that the peasant masses might be transformed into literate, property-owning, and politically active citizens.

* See "China's Response to the West: Revolutionary Phase," *EMM*, No. 88.

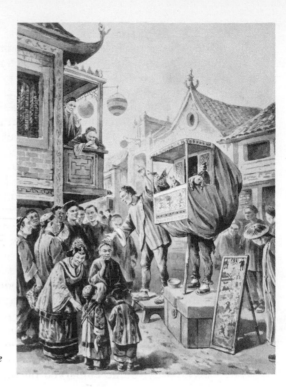

A Chinese Punch and Judy show used by the
Boxers as antiforeign propaganda.

Sun Yat-sen derived his main support from Chinese merchants and laundry-men overseas. Within the country only a few students and merchants were influenced by his ideas, while the mass of the population remained illiterate and apathetic. When the revolution came in 1911, it was partly the work of landlord gentry and commercial interests in the provinces which were opposed to the belated efforts of the Manchu regime to nationalize railway construction. The provincial leaders fomented strikes and riots, ostensibly on the ground that nationalization would lead to foreign control, but actually because they feared it would exclude them from profit possibilities. In any case, the revolutionists exploited the discontent and worked effectively amongst students and soldiers. A small-scale republican uprising in Canton was suppressed, but on October 10, 1911, an accidental explosion in a revolutionist bomb factory at Hankow led to mutiny among nearby imperial troops. Despite lack of coordination, the revolutionary movement spread rapidly throughout the country. Sun Yat-sen, who was in the United States at the time, hurried back and on December 30, 1911, was elected President of the United Provinces of China by a provisional revolutionary assembly.

The movement that overthrew the Manchus obviously represented a good deal more than the revolutionary leadership supplied by Sun Yat-sen. Consequently, Sun was unable to control the country even though he was the nominal leader. Actual power was in the hands of an able and ambitious imperial official, Yuan Shih-k'ai (1859–1916), who commanded the most

357

effective army in China. Rather than risk a civil war that would invite foreign intervention, Sun, in February, 1912, yielded the presidency to Yuan, and the latter agreed to work with a parliament and a responsible cabinet. This arrangement, however, did not really settle the basic question of what form of government would replace the fallen Manchu regime. Yuan was all for Western military technology and administrative methods, but Western political institutions, including control of the executive by representatives of the people, he regarded as antithetical to China's traditions and certainly antithetical to his personal ambitions.

The issue was joined with little delay. Sun Yat-sen founded a new political party, the Kuomintang, or National Peoples' party. To organize his own followers, Yuan formed the Chinputang, or Progressive party. When the National Assembly was elected in April, 1913, the majority of seats was held by the Kuomintang. But this setback did not unduly restrict Yuan, for he had the backing of the army, the bureaucracy, and the foreign powers. In fact, the showdown came over a loan of £25 million, which Yuan borrowed from a group of five powers. Realizing that Yuan would use some of this money to strengthen his hold on the government, the Kuomintang leaders warned the governments that the constitution required parliamentary approval of loans, and since the Assembly would never approve this particular loan, it would not be legally binding. But the Powers preferred to back the strongman Yuan, as they had backed the Manchu dynasty in earlier years. So Yuan received the money, and, as the Kuomintang had feared, he used it to consolidate his position. The measures that he now took, including the assassination of a top Kuomintang leader, led Sun Yat-sen to resort to an armed uprising in the summer of 1913. The move was premature and Yuan suppressed the revolt with ease.

Sun fled to Japan with his principal followers, and Yuan made preparations to fulfill his ill-concealed ambition to establish himself as emperor. In October, 1913, he had himself elected permanent president. Then he ordered the dissolution of both the Kuomintang and the Parliament. With the oppostion out of the way, he engineered "spontaneous" requests that he fulfill his duty to his country and become emperor. In December, 1915, Yuan announced that he would assume the title of emperor on January 1, 1916. The unexpectedly strong negative response was foreseen by a Chinese philosopher who wrote at this time,

> We carve wood or mold clay in the image of a person and call it a god. Place it in a beautiful temple, and seat it in a glorious shrine and the people will worship it and find it mysteriously potent. But suppose some insane person should pull it down, tread it under foot and throw it into a dirty pond and suppose someone should discover it and carry it back to its original sacred abode, you will find the charm has gone from it.[10]

It turned out as he intimated. A revolt broke out in Yunnan in December, 1915, and quickly spread. Yuan found it necessary first to postpone and finally, in March, 1916, to abandon the restoration of the monarchy. Humiliated and embittered, Yuan died in June of the same year. After his death the army commanders who had served under him divided the country amongst themselves. Until 1926, these warlords paid little attention to the republican government that nominally ruled from Peking. Rather, they pillaged the countryside mercilessly and dragged China down to a brutalizing anarchy. The early years of the republic marked one of the worst periods in the history of China.

Several factors account for this wretched outcome of several decades of response to the West. First there is the sheer size of China, which for many years left the interior of the country unaffected by Western contact. This interior functioned as a vast reservoir, out of which tradition-minded civil service candidates continued to appear for several decades. The bureaucracy that they formed consisted of intellectuals who were steeped in the Confucian classics and who consequently placed much greater emphasis upon ethical principles than upon the manual arts or the technology of warfare. This ruling class was further inhibited by the fact that, apart from Buddhism, China had little or no tradition of borrowing from abroad. Thus it is not surprising that although China did change in the second half of the nineteenth century, the tempo of her change was far below that of other countries responding to the West.

However, the bureaucracy cannot be shouldered with the entire responsibility for China's failure. The young Western-trained Chinese also were partly to blame. Some of them played leading roles in the early days of the republic, but they tried to set up in China carbon copies of the institutions they had observed and studied abroad, and especially in the United States. What they established naturally had no meaning for the Chinese people and quickly crumbled before the realities of Chinese politics.* An American authority has vividly described this failure of amateur statesmen:

> It was absurd to set up in China in 1911 an imitation of the American republic. . . . That kind of a republic was a fiasco because it had no roots in Chinese history, traditions, political experience, institutions, instincts, beliefs, attitudes, or habits. It was alien and empty. It was superimposed on China. It washed off with time, a very short time. It did not represent political thought but a caricature of political thought, a crude, callow, schoolboy caricature. . . . The republic sank wretchedly to its end, a squalid failure. Yet it was not a republic that failed . . . it was a generation.[11]

VI. Japan in Seclusion

Historians have proffered several factors in explanation of the difference between the Chinese and the Japanese response to the challenge of the West. The physical compactness of the Japanese islands facilitated both the forging of national unity and the spread of new values and new learning throughout the country. It also made the country vulnerable to, and aware of, foreign pressures. Perry's ships sailed within sight of the capital, Edo, and within a few weeks all of Japan knew of this fateful event. By contrast, the vast, densely populated, interior provinces of China were for long inaccessible and

* See "Chinese Intellectuals and the West," *EMM*, No. 89.

impervious to Western influences, and served instead as reservoirs of traditional attitudes and forces. Furthermore, Japan's long tradition of borrowing from the great Chinese cultural world made similar borrowing from the Western world in the nineteenth century less jarring and painful. Japan had adapted selected aspects of Chinese culture with the slogan "Japanese spirit and Chinese knowledge." Now she borrowed what she wished from the West with the slogan "Eastern morale and Western arts." And Japanese government and society were pluralistic in structure in comparison with the monolithic features of the Chinese Empire. The clan tradition and regional particularism of Japan were reinforced by geographic compartmentalization—by the broken mountainous terrain. The merchant class in Japan had more autonomy and economic strength, and, as we shall see, was rapidly extending its power at the critical moment of the West's intrusion. The military elements in Japan were at the top of the social ladder, rather than at the bottom, as was the case in China. This meant that Japan had a ruling class that was much more sensitive and responsive to Western military technology than were the Chinese literati. In sum, geography, cultural traditions, and pluralistic organization combined to make Japan more vulnerable to Western intrusion than China, and more quick to respond to that intrusion.

Despite these basic differences, Japan, like China, remained in seclusion until the mid-nineteenth century. It is true that the Japanese welcomed the Portuguese in the sixteenth century and embraced Christianity in large numbers (see Chapter 4, section VIII). But the Tokugawa shoguns perceived that Western religion and trade represented an unsettling force that threatened their authority. For this reason they severed one by one the ties between Japan and the Western world. By the mid-seventeenth century the sole remaining contact was the handful of Dutch traders who were confined to the islet of Deshima, and even they were subjected to the most restricting and humiliating regulations.

The aim of the Tokugawa leaders was to keep Japan isolated and unchanging in order to perpetuate their regime. But despite their efforts, certain developments did occur that gradually altered the balance of forces in the country and undermined the *status quo*. The long peace enforced by Tokugawa rule stimulated population growth, economic expansion, and the strengthening of the merchant class. The population jumped from 18 million in 1600 to 26 million in 1725. Cities grew disproportionately, Edo approaching the million mark by 1700, and Osaka and Kyoto each reaching 300,000. The population spurt increased the demand for commodities and encouraged merchants and rich peasants to invest surplus capital in new forms of production, including the domestic, or putting-out, system. They provided materials and equipment for peasants and craftsmen, and marketed the finished products. It appears that in certain areas this industrial development had reached the level of factory organization by the end of the Tokugawa period. Regional specialization based on available raw materials and local skills became widespread, so that particular areas were noted for their lacquerware, pottery, textiles, or rice wine.

The rising production led to wide-scale exchange of goods, which in turn led to the development of money economy. At first money was imported from China and Korea, but in the seventeenth century a gold mint was established.

The aristocrats became dependent on brokers to convert their rice into money, and upon merchants to satisfy their consumption needs. In these transactions the aristocrats lost out because of merchant manipulation of prices through monopolies, and because the price of rice failed to keep up with the soaring costs of other commodities. The aristocrats, besides, had acquired a taste for luxuries and tended to compete with each other in ostentatious living. The net result was that they generally became indebted to the merchants, even though the latter ranked far below in the social scale. In time the merchant families bought their way into the aristocracy by intermarriage or adoption. These families dominated not only the economy but also the art and literature of the eighteenth and early nineteenth centuries.

These changes, it should be noted, affected not only the top levels of the aristocracy, but also the samurai, whose services were not so much in demand during this long period of peace. The mass of the peasants also suffered severely with the lag of the price of rice. Many of them migrated to the cities, but not all were able to find employment, for the growth of the national economy was not keeping pace with the growth of population.

Thus, Japanese society was in a state of transition. It was experiencing profound economic and social change, and this engendered political tensions that were reaching the breaking point when Admiral Perry forced Japan's doors open to trade. One reason the Japanese proved so ready to reorganize their society under the impact of the West was precisely that many of them were all too aware that this society needed reorganizing.

Foreign pressure upon Japan had been mounting since the early nineteenth century because of the increasing commercial activity in northern Pacific waters. Ships engaged in whaling and fur trading needed Japanese ports to obtain provisions and to make repairs, but they were denied all access. Instead, the Japanese normally killed or maltreated foreign seamen shipwrecked on their shores. Toward the middle of the century the introduction of the steamship aggravated the situation by creating a need for coaling stations. Finally the United States government decided to take the initiative and to force the issue. On July 8, 1853, Commodore Matthew Perry cast anchor in Edo Bay and delivered a letter from President Fillmore asking for trading privileges, coaling stations, and protection for shipwrecked Americans. Within a week he sailed away after warning that he would be back for an answer the following spring. When he returned in February, 1854, he made it clear that the alternative was a treaty or war. The Japanese yielded and on March 31 signed the Treaty of Kanagawa. Its terms opened the ports of Shimoda and Hakodate for the repair and provisioning of American ships, provided for proper treatment and repatriation of shipwrecked Americans, permitted the appointment of consular representatives if either nation considered it necessary, and promised most-favored-nation treatment for the United States.

In accordance with the provisions of this treaty, the United States sent Townsend Harris, an unusually able man, as the first consul to Japan. With his extraordinary tact and patience, Harris gradually won the confidence of the Japanese and secured the Commercial Treaty of 1858. This opened four more ports to trade, provided for mutual diplomatic representative, gave to Americans both civil and criminal extraterritoriality, prohibited the opium trade, and gave freedom of religion to foreigners. Soon after signing these two treaties with the United States, Japan concluded similar pacts with Holland, Russia, Britain, and France.

362   This series of treaties did not attract much attention in the Western world. But for Japan they represented the great divide of her history. Almost three centuries of seclusion had come to an end. For better or for worse, Japan, like China before her, now had to suffer the intrusion of the West. But her response to that intrusion was altogether different from that of the Middle Kingdom.

VII. MODERNIZATION OF JAPAN

The first effect of the Western encroachment was to produce a crisis that precipitated the downfall of the Tokugawa Shogunate. With the signing of the treaties the shogun was subject to conflicting pressures: on the one hand from the foreign powers, which demanded implementation of all the provisions, and on the other from the Japanese population, which was strongly anti-foreign. This popular sentiment was exploited by the anti-Tokugawa clans, especially the Satsuma, Choshu, Hizen, and Tosa, often referred to as the Satcho Hito group. Between 1858 and 1865, attacks were made upon Europeans and their employers with the slogan "Honor the Emperor! Expel the barbarians!" The foreign powers retaliated by bombarding the Satsuma port of Kagoshima in 1863 and the Choshu coastal defenses in 1864. This action impressed the clan leaders, who now dropped their antiforeignism and sought to obtain Western armaments. With the death two years later of both the emperor and the Tokugawa Shogun, the way was clear for the so-called Meiji Restoration. The Tokugawa clansmen were shorn of their power and fiefs, and their place was taken by the Satcho Hito clans, which henceforth controlled the government in the name of the new Meiji Emperor. It was young samurai in the service of these clans who now provided Japan with extraordinary leadership that made possible successful modernization.

It should be noted that Japan at this point had fallen fully as much under Western control as China. Foreign settlements were being established in the ports, and these settlements were utilizing their extraterritoriality privileges to set up municipal organizations along the lines of those in the Chinese treaty ports. The foreign communities fully expected that, with dissension rampant in the country, Japan would speedily fall under Western domination as had the other Asian countries. But in contrast to China's literati, Japan's young new leaders realized that they were retarded in certain fields, and, more important, they were willing and able to do something about it, and they knew what needed to be done.

This is not altogether surprising if it is noted that even during their centuries of seclusion the Japanese leaders had gone out of their way to keep informed of developments in Europe. In fact, the Dutch were allowed to continue trading primarily so that they could be questioned concerning the outside world. Both the Shogunate and the clans promoted military industry and maintained schools for the study of foreign languages and foreign texts. The general level of knowledge rose to the point where, in the natural sciences, physics was separated from chemistry, and, in medicine, students were trained in special fields such as surgery, pediatrics, obstetrics, and internal medicine. In the Nagasaki naval school, instruction was given in navigation and gunnery only after a solid base had been laid in mathematics, astronomy, and physics. In other words, the Japanese all along had been much more appreciative of, and responsive to, Western culture. This is strikingly illustrated in the following eulogy of England written by a Japanese scholar about the same time that the Emperor of China was scornfully informing King George III that China had no use for anything from the barbarian West.

When it comes to grand edifices, no country in the world can compare with England. There is no country comparable to England in the manufacture of very fine things. Among the articles which have been imported into Japan by the Dutch, there have been none more precious than the watches. Some of them are so exquisite that hairs are split to make them. London is considered to produce the finest such workmanship in the world. Next comes Paris, in France, and then Amsterdam in Holland. In these three capitals live people virtually without a peer in the world, who are the handsomest of men. . . . Why is it that the people of these three cities, who are human beings like everyone else, have attained such excellence? [12]

In the light of this background, it is understandable why the Japanese acted quite differently from the Chinese once the Westerners forced their way in. The difference was evident from the beginning, and was described at the time in the following remarkable passage by a British official, Lord Elgin:

One result of the difference between the habits and the mode of feeling of the Chinese and the Japanese is undoubtedly this, that as the Chinese are steadily retrograding and will in all probability continue to do so until the Empire falls to pieces, the Japanese, if not actually in a state of progressive advancement, are in a condition to profit by the flood of light that is about to be poured into them and to take advantage of these improvements and inventions which the Chinese regard with contemptuous scorn, but which the Japanese will in all probability, when they come to know us better, be both able and anxious to adopt.[13]

The correctness of Lord Elgin's prophecy was speedily demonstrated. In 1868 the emperor promulgated an imperial oath (known as the Charter Oath) that was designed to quiet the general unrest and to clarify the objectives of the new regime. This document emphasized two general points: that "all matters shall be decided by public discussion," and that "the evil customs of the past shall be broken off. . . . Knowledge shall be sought throughout the world." [14] In fact, Western ideas and Western material objects became the craze of the 1870's. It became fashionable to eat beef, to wear trousers, to carry an umbrella, and to sport a watch and diamond rings. The best illustration of this attitude is a children's song composed in 1878. According to G. B. Sansom, "It was called the 'Civilization Ball Song' and was designed to impress on young minds the advantages of western culture. They were to count the bounces of the ball by reciting the names of ten objects deemed to be the most worthy of adoption—namely, gas lamps, steam engines, horse-carriages, cameras, telegrams, lightning-conductors, newspapers, schools, letter post, and steamboats." [15]

364

Japan's new leaders disapproved of this indiscriminate adulation of all things Western. They were interested not in Western civilization per se, but only in those features that enhanced national power. During the period of seclusion (when Ram Mohan Roy in India was corresponding with Condorcet on the ideology of the Enlightenment), the Japanese had followed European achievements in mathematics, science, and economics, but had paid no attention to literature, philosophy, and the social sciences. Likewise now they launched a remarkable reform program that was carefully designed to build up a strong Japan rather than to create a replica of a Western state.*

In the field of religion, for example, the Meiji statesmen supported Shinto as the state cult because it identified the national character with the emperor, and held that the emperor was descended from the Sun Goddess. In other words, Shinto stimulated national unity and patriotism, and these attributes were properly deemed necessary if Japan were to hold her own in the modern world. In education, it was explicitly stated that the objective was the furtherance of state interests rather than the development of the individual. Compulsory elementary education was decreed because the state needed a literate citizenry. Large numbers of foreign educators were brought to Japan to found schools and universities, and thousands of Japanese studied abroad and returned to teach in the new institutions. But the entire educational system was kept under close state supervision to ensure uniformity of thought as well as of administration. The Educational Rescript issued in 1890 exhorted all students to "offer yourselves courageously to the State; and thus guard and maintain the prosperity of Our Imperial Throne, coeval with heaven and earth." [16]

In military affairs the Japanese abolished the old feudal levies and organized modern armed forces based on the latest European models. They built a conscript army with the aid of a German military mission, and a small navy under the guidance of the British. The Meiji leaders foresaw that the new military forces required a modern economy to supply their needs. Accordingly, they secured the establishment of the needed industries by granting subsidies, purchasing stock, or forming government corporations. In order to facilitate industrial growth they concentrated at first on financial institutions, commodity exchanges, shipping companies, railways, and telegraph lines. The government leaders were careful to support not only light industries such as textiles, but also heavy industries such as mining, steel, and shipbuilding, which were necessary to fill military needs. Once these enterprises were founded, the government generally sold them to various favored private interests at extremely low prices. It was in this manner that a few wealthy families, collectively known as the Zaibatsu, gained a stranglehold on the national economy that has persisted to the present. It might be added that the capital for this industrial expansion was obtained largely from agriculture. A substantial increase in agricultural yield was attained at relatively low cost by introducing better seed strains, improving land use, and expanding irrigation and drainage. Between 1878 and 1892 the area under cultivation increased

* See "Pioneer Japanese Advocate of Westernization," EMM, No. 90.

by 7 per cent, the yield by 21 per cent, and the population by 15 per cent. The resulting agricultural surplus was siphoned off by taxes which furnished the capital for industrialization.

The Japanese also overhauled their legal system. This was in such a state when the Westerners appeared that their demand for extraterritoriality was at least understandable. The laws were chaotic and harsh, individual rights were disregarded, the police were arbitrary and all-powerful, and prison conditions were revolting. In 1871 a judicial department was organized, and in the following years new codes were adopted and a distinction made between judicial and administrative powers.

At the same time various political innovations were made in order to provide Japan with at least the trappings of parliamentary government. A cabinet and a privy council were first established, and then a constitution was promulgated with due ceremony in 1889. This document promised the citizens freedom from arbitrary arrest, protection of property rights, and freedom of religion, speech, and association. But in each instance the government was given authority to curb these rights when it so desired. In general, the constitution borrowed much more from the German model than from the French or English. The reason is that Japan, like Germany, was then in the process of consolidation, and consequently was more interested in building up national strength than in safeguarding civil liberties. Hence the constitution provided Japan with a parliamentary façade while preserving oligarchic rule and emperor worship. Indeed, the first article of the constitution provided that "The Empire of Japan shall be reigned over and governed by a line of Emperors unbroken for ages eternal," and the third article likewise stipulated that "The Emperor is sacred and inviolable."

With the adoption of the constitution and of the legal reforms, the Japanese were in a position to press for the abolition of the unequal treaties. They could fairly argue that Japan now had taken her place in the comity of civilized nations and that there was no longer any need for extraterritoriality and for the other infringements on their sovereignty. After prolonged diplomatic efforts they were able in 1894 to persuade Britain and the United States to terminate extraterritoriality and consular jurisdiction in five years. In the same year the Japanese won their unexpected and spectacular victory over the Chinese Empire. Henceforth there could be no more question of treating Japan as an inferior country, and the other powers soon followed Britain and the United States in yielding their special privileges. By 1899 Japan had gained legal jurisdiction over all foreigners on her soil, and in doing so, she became the first Asian nation to break the chains of Western control.*

VIII. EXPANSION OF JAPAN

Having modernized herself, Japan embarked on a career of expansion on the mainland. This is not surprising in view of Japan's warlike tradition and the immense prestige that her military leaders enjoyed from earliest times. Furthermore, the Far East was then most patently an area of international

* See "Social Changes in New Japan," *EMM,* No. 91.

366

rivalry and of jostling for position. The practical-minded leaders of Japan drew the obvious conclusion that each people must grab for themselves and that nothing would be left to the weak and the timid. A civilian bureaucrat expressed this viewpoint as follows: "This is like riding in a third-class train; at first there is adequate space but as more passengers enter there is no place for them to sit. If while rubbing shoulders and supporting yourself with your arms you lose your place you can't recover the same position. . . . The logic of necessity requires the people to plant both feet firmly and expand their elbows into any opening that may occur for, unless this is done, others will close the opening." [17]

Japan's first expansionist move was in Korea. The Japanese government initially was interested in ensuring Korea's independence, particularly as against China. As noted earlier in this chapter, this policy led to an armed clash in 1894 that precipitated the Sino-Japanese War. The course of the hostilities revealed to a startled world how far Japan had progressed in two decades. The Chinese troops fought bravely but hopelessly against a modern military machine. By the Treaty of Shimoneseki of 1895, Japan acquired Formosa, the Pescadores, and the Liaotung Peninsula, though the latter had to be restored on the insistence of France, Russia, and Germany. It is instructive to note that during the peace negotiations the following exchange took place between the Chinese representative, Li Hung-chang, and the Japanese envoy, Ito Hirobumi.

> *Ito:* Ten years ago when I was at Tientsin, I talked about reform with the grand secretary [Li Hung-chang]. Why is it that up to now not a single thing has been changed or reformed? This I deeply regret.
>
> *Li:* At that time when I heard you, sir, talking about that, I was overcome with admiration, and furthermore I deeply admired, sir, your having vigorously changed your customs in Japan so as to reach the present stage. Affairs in my country have been so confined by tradition that I could not accomplish what I desired.
>
> *Ito:* "The providence of heaven has no affection, except for the virtuous." If your honorable country wishes to exert itself to action, Heaven above would certainly help your honorable country to fulfill its desires. It is because Heaven treats the people below without discrimination. The essential thing is that each country should do its own best.[18]

After defeating China, the Japanese were faced by a much more serious adversary, Russia. Not only had Russia acted with France and Germany to force Japan to restore the Liaotung Peninsula, but in addition Russia now encroached upon both Korea and Manchuria. During the Sino-Japanese War, Korea signed a treaty agreeing to accept Japanese guidance and capital. Immediately after the war, the Japanese minister to Korea began a comprehensive reform program and placed Japanese officials in strategic positions. But the Korean queen, who led the conservative faction, opposed the Japanese minister. The latter organized a conspiracy resulting in the murder of the queen, but the coup was short-lived. The king now turned to Russia, replacing Japanese advisers with Russians, and granting a timber-cutting concession to a Russian company.

At the same time that the Russians were supplanting the Japanese in Korea, they were also winning concessions in Manchuria. We noted earlier the secret Chinese-Russian treaty of 1896 that allowed Russia to construct a railroad across Manchuria to Vladivostok (see Chapter 13, section III). We also noted that in 1898 Russia obtained a twenty-five year lease of the Liaotung Peninsula, and two years later occupied the entire province of Manchuria during the Boxer Rebellion. These Russian advances engendered warm debates among the ruling group in Tokyo. Some favored trying to reach an accord with Russia that would be based on a division of the spoils. Others preferred an alliance with Great Britain as the country with which Japan most nearly had common cause. With such an alliance to back her up, Japan would then be able to stand up to Russian expansionism.

Feelers were sent out to both the British and the Russian capitals, and it was soon evident that London was as receptive as St. Petersburg was intractable. The old policy of splendid isolation had by this time lost its splendor for the British. Confronted by a rising Germany and an aggressive Russia, they welcomed an ally in the Far East that could serve as a check on Russia. On January 30, 1902, the Anglo-Japanese alliance was signed, providing for the independence of China and Korea, and recognizing Britain's special interests in Central China and Japan's special interests in Korea. If either Japan or Britain became involved in war with a third power, the other party would remain neutral, but if another power intervened, then the other party was bound to aid its ally. Since Russia and France had been allied for the past eight years, the Anglo-Japanese alliance obviously was designed to keep France from aiding Russia in the event of war.

Japan was now in a position to force the issue with Russia. In mid-1903 Japan offered to recognize Russia's primacy in Manchuria if Russia would reciprocate concerning Japan's position in Korea. The negotiations dragged on, with the overconfident Russians temporizing and evading. The Japanese concluded, with good reason, that the Russians were not negotiating in good faith, and severed diplomatic relations on February 6, 1904. Two days later, without an ultimatum or declaration of war, the Japanese attacked the Russian base at Port Arthur on the Liaotung Peninsula.

As noted above, the Japanese won an even more unexpected victory over the Russians than they had won a decade earlier over the Chinese. By the Treaty of Portsmouth (September 5, 1905) Japan acquired the southern half of Sakhalin Island and Russia's Liaotung leasehold, and secured recognition of her special interests in Korea. In retrospect this war stands out as a major turning point in the history of the Far East, and even of the world. Certainly it established Japan as a major power and altered the balance of forces in the Far East. But much more significant is the fact that for the first time an Asian state defeated a European state, and a great empire at that. This had an electrifying effect on all Asia. It demonstrated to millions of colonial peoples that European domination was not divinely ordained. For the first time since the days of the conquistadors the white man had been beaten, and a thrill of hope ran through the nonwhite races of the globe. In this sense the Russo-Japanese War stands out as a landmark in modern history; it represents the prelude to the great awakening of the non-European peoples that today is convulsing the entire world.

SUGGESTED READING

For background references, see the bibliography for Chapter 4. The best over-all survey of the impact of the West on East Asia is by E. O. Reischauer, J. K. Fairbank, and A. M. Craig, *A History of East Asian Civilization,* Vol. II, *East Asia: The Modern Transformation* (Boston: Houghton, 1965). See also the excellent study by G. M. Beckmann, *The Modernization of China and Japan* (New York: Harper, 1962). The most important work on the West's impact on China is the following collection of documents with explanatory essays: Ssu-yu Teng and J. K. Fairbank, *China's Response to the West: A Documentary Survey, 1839–1923* (Cambridge: Harvard Univ., 1954). Also noteworthy is J. K. Fairbank, *The United States and China,* rev. ed. (Cambridge: Harvard Univ., 1958), which provides an excellent bibliography. For China's domestic politics, see Li Chien-nung, *The Political History of China, 1840–1928* (Princeton: Van Nostrand, 1956).

The outstanding works on the West's impact on Japan are the documentary collection by R. Tsunoda, *Sources of the Japanese Tradition* (New York: Columbia Univ., 1958) and the masterly analysis by G. B. Sansom, *The Western World and Japan* (New York: Knopf, 1950). Also noteworthy are E. O. Reischauer, *Japan Past and Present,* rev. ed. (New York: Knopf, 1953); C. Yanaza, *Japan Since Perry* (New York: McGraw, 1950); H. Borton, *Japan's Modern Century* (New York: Ronald, 1955); and W. W. Lockwood, *The Economic Development of Japan: Growth and Structural Change, 1868–1938* (Princeton: Princeton Univ., 1954).

For Western diplomacy in the Far East, see W. L. Langer, *The Diplomacy of Imperialism, 1890–1902,* rev. ed. (New York: Knopf, 1956). The problem of the contrasting response of China and Japan to the Western intrusion is considered in the following studies: N. Jacobs, *The Origin of Modern Capitalism and Eastern Asia* (Hong Kong: Hong Kong Univ., 1958); E. Swisher, "Chinese Intellectuals and the Western Impact, 1838–1900," *Comparative Studies in Society and History,* I (October, 1958), 26–37; W. W. Lockwood, "Japan's Response to the West," *World Politics,* IX (October, 1956), 37–54; J. K. Fairbank, "China's Response to the West: Problems and Suggestions," *Journal of World History,* III, No. 2 (1956), 381–406; J. K. Fairbank, "The Influence of Modern Western Science and Technology on Japan and China," *Explorations in Entrepreneurial History,* VII, No. 4 (1955), 189–204; and J. Numata, "Acceptance and Rejection of Elements of European Culture in Japan," *Journal of World History,* III, No. 1 (1956), 231–53.

*For better or for worse the old Africa is gone
and the white races must face the new situation
which they have themselves created.*

JAN CHRISTIANN SMUTS

Chapter
17

Africa

Europe's impact on sub-Saharan Africa was felt considerably later than that upon Eurasia. The European powers fastened their rule upon India, the East Indies, and much of North Africa, before they expanded south of the Sahara. France acquired Algeria in 1830 and Tunisia in 1881, while England occupied Egypt in 1882 (see Chapter 14, section III). European penetration southward came generally later because of various reasons, including adverse climate, prevalence of disease, geographic inaccessibility, and the superior organization and resistance of the Africans compared to the American Indians or the Australian aborigines (see Chapter 5, section I). Also there was a lack of exploitable riches to entice Europeans into the interior, as was the case with the bullion of Mexico and Peru. Thus sub-Saharan Africa, apart from certain coastal regions, remained largely unaffected by Europe until the late nineteenth century. In the last two decades of that century, however, the European powers made up for lost time, partitioning virtually the entire continent and exploiting its material and human resources. By 1914 the African peoples had, in many respects, come under European influence even more than had the Asians, though many villagers in the interior regions continued to live largely unaffected by the European intruder.

I. SLAVE TRADE

For centuries the most valuable of African resources for Europeans were the slaves, but these were obtainable at coastal ports, without any need for penetration inland. Although the slave stations were restricted to the coast, the slave trade nevertheless had profound repercussions upon considerable areas of sub-Saharan Africa. The trade began in 1442 when two captains of Prince Henry the Navigator took twelve African slaves to Lisbon. It is true that slavery already was an established and widespread institution in Africa. Prisoners of war were enslaved, as were also debtors or individuals guilty of serious crimes. But these slaves usually were treated as part of the family; they had clearly defined rights, and their status was not necessarily hereditary. In Europe, by contrast, slavery was a very different institution and had a very different history. From the beginning it was primarily economic, so that slaves were being worked to death in mines during classical times. This impersonalism was reinforced by racism when the Europeans became involved in the African slave trade on a large scale. Perhaps as a subconscious rationalization they gradually came to look down upon Negroes as inherently inferior savages, and therefore preordained to serve their white masters. Rationalization also may have been involved in the Europeans' resort to religion to justify the traffic in human beings. Enslavement, it was argued, assured the conversion of the African heathen to the true faith as well as to civilization. Typical is the following statement of a contemporary observer on the advantages of slavery in Portugal over freedom in Africa.

> And so their lot was quite contrary of what it had been; since before they had lived in perdition of soul and body; of their souls in that they were yet pagans, without the clearness and the light of holy faith; and of their bodies, in that they lived like beasts, without any custom of reasonable beings—for they had no knowledge of bread or wine, and they were without the covering of clothes, or the lodgement of houses; and worse than all, through the great ignorance that was in them, in that they had no understanding of good, but only knew how to live in bestial sloth.[1]

In this self-satisfying spirit the Portuguese shipped thousands of African slaves to their homeland. The numbers were so large, and the intermarriage was so free, that the racial composition of certain parts of Portugal was significantly affected. But this was a petty prelude to the new and fateful phase of the slave trade that began in 1510 when the first shipload of African slaves was shipped to the New World. The venture proved highly successful, for there was urgent need for labor in the Americas, especially on the sugar plantations. The market for slaves was almost limitless, and several other countries entered the slave trade to share in the rich profits. Portugal dominated the trade in the sixteenth century, Holland during most of the seventeenth, and Britain in the eighteenth. The west African coast was dotted with about forty European forts which were used for defense against the rival trading nations and for storing the slaves while awaiting shipment across the Atlantic.

The typical voyage of the slave traders was triangular. The first leg was from the home port to Africa, with a cargo including salt, cloth, firearms, hardware, beads, and rum. These goods were bartered for slaves brought by fellow-Africans from the interior to the coast. The unfortunate victims were packed under atrocious conditions in the vessels and shipped across the Atlantic on the so-called "middle passage." At their New World destinations the slaves were either sold at once or held in stockades to be retailed on demand. The final lap was the voyage home with plantation produce such as sugar, molasses, tobacco, or rice.

Thanks to the prevailing trade winds the "middle passage" was normally swift and brief. Nevertheless, the average death rate during the trip was over 10 per cent. The casualties were brought about by the inhuman crowding, the stifling heat, and the poor food. Maize and water once every twenty-four hours was the standard diet. If the slaves refused to eat they were lashed and, if that failed, hot irons were used to force them to eat. When epidemics broke out, as they often did under the foul conditions, the sick slaves were drowned in order to prevent infection from spreading. Not infrequently the slaves jumped overboard rather than endure the misery. Indeed, this became so common that nets were fixed all around the decks in order to prevent suicides. It is revealing that slave ships carried insurance against the death of slaves and also against insurrections aboard ship.

Even greater casualties were suffered earlier, during the overland march to the coast. Raiding parties plundered villages and broke up families in their search for strong young men and women. The captives were then driven from dawn to dusk in the blazing heat and pouring rain, through thick jungles or over dry plains, and tormented by stinging insects that gave them no peace. If they faltered through sheer exhaustion they were mercilessly beaten, and if they failed to stumble on, they were finished off by a sword or a club. The survivors who reached the coast were driven naked into the market like cattle. Then they were branded with the name of the company or buyer, and herded into the forts to await shipment across the ocean. It is not surprising that for every 1,000 Africans kidnapped from their villages, an estimated 300 survived to work in the Americas. Five hundred normally perished during the march to the coast, 125 in the packed holes of the slave ships, and another 75 died soon after landing in the New World.*

Despite these horrors, Europeans continued to buy and sell Africans for over four centuries. The profits were so great that powerful vested interests resolutely opposed any proposals for control or abolition. There were first of all the African chiefs who received as much as £20 or 30 for a single able-bodied slave. One of the chiefs, when told to stop his trade said, "What! Can a cat stop catching mice? Will not a cat die with a mouse in its mouth? I will die with a slave in my mouth." [2] The African middlemen who had reaped handsome profits from the trade were violently opposed to all abolition proposals. Indeed, riots against Europeans were organized on African soil in defiance of the abolition movement.

* See "The Slave Trade: Eyewitness Reports," *EMM*, No. 92.

The plantation owners in the Americas likewise supported the slave trade, especially the Barbados planters who held an important bloc of seats in the British Parliament in the eighteenth century. There were European vested interests also that championed the slave trade, both amongst the traders and the various merchants at home who provided the rum and the manufactured goods. According to one estimate, Britain shipped to Africa manufactures valued at one million pounds a year, and the other European countries sent an equal amount for the same purpose. The return on this outlay was so extraordinarily high that in the eighteenth century the prosperity of cities such as Liverpool and Bristol depended heavily on this traffic. A considerable number of distilleries were built to provide the slave ships with rum. English woolens, and later, cottons, also were shipped in large quantities to Africa. The metallurgical industry provided chains, locks, bars, and guns of all kinds. The shipyards, too, were kept busy by the slave trade, since over 200 English ships alone were engaged at the end of the eighteenth century. The famous abolitionist leader William Wilberforce properly observed that "Interest can draw a film over the eyes so thick that blindness itself could do no more." [3]

The champions of the slave trade used military as well as economic arguments to support their case. The large number of vessels involved not only supported shipyards but also provided jobs for thousands of seamen. So it was maintained that any country that took the lead in abolition would weaken itself as a naval power. Various intellectual rationalizations in defense of slavery were made by such men as James Boswell, the famous Scottish biographer of Samuel Johnson, who wrote that "To abolish a status which in all ages God has sanctioned and many have continued, would not only be robbery to an innumerable class of our fellow subjects, but it would be extreme cruelty to the African savages, a portion of whom it saves from massacre and introduces to a happier life." [4]

Despite these formidable obstacles, a small group of reformers campaigned vigorously for abolition. In 1787 they established in England the Society for the Abolition of the Slave Trade. In 1823 they founded the Anti-Slavery Society to end the institution of slavery as well as the slave trade. These abolitionists were aided by the progress of the Industrial Revolution, which was rendering slavery obsolete. Advancing technology called for overseas markets rather than for a cheap supply of human power. In fact, the abolitionists argued that the slave trade was inefficient, and insisted that a more profitable "legitimate" trade could be developed in Africa.

The first success of the abolitionists was a law in 1807 providing that no British ships could participate in the slave trade, and prohibiting the landing of slaves in British colonies. Finally, in 1833 Parliament passed a decree completely abolishing slavery on British territory, and providing 20 million pounds as compensation for the slaveholders. The British government went further and persuaded other European countries to follow its example in allowing British warships to seize slave ships flying other flags. At one period, a fourth of the whole British navy was patrolling the coasts of Africa, Cuba, and Brazil with a force of 56 vessels manned by 9,000 sailors. In twenty years these patrol ships captured over 1,000 slaves and set free their human cargoes. Needless to say, many traders continued to slip through the blockade, lured on by the fortunes awaiting them in the Americas. Complete success was not possible until the various countries in the New World gradually abolished slavery as an institution—as did Haiti in 1803, the United States in 1863, Brazil in 1888, Cuba at about the same time, and so forth.

While the slave trade was being stamped out on the west coast of Africa, it continued to be carried on by the Arabs in Central and East Africa. The Arabs had been engaged in this trade long before the appearance of the Europeans, and they continued through the nineteenth century and even into the twentieth. The captives were marched across the Sahara to North African fairs, or they were taken to east coast ports and then shipped to Zanzibar, Madagascar, Arabia, Turkey, Persia, and even India. This traffic was much more difficult to suppress than that on the west coast. Despite British naval patrols in the Red Sea and the Indian Ocean, it persisted until World War I and later. Even today slavery may exist in remote parts of Ethiopia, and the selling of slaves is by no means unknown, especially in the states of the Arabian Peninsula.

Over four centuries of slave trading in West Africa, and double that span in Central and East Africa, inevitably affected profoundly the development of the continent. As noted earlier, the effects were positive as well as negative (see Chapter 9, section III). There was loss of manpower and also the disruptive effect of slave raids on the political and social structure of Africa. But the Africans did receive certain economically productive commodities in return for the slaves, and they did benefit tremendously from newly introduced food plants from the Americas, which increased very substantially the food supply, and hence the population, of the continent.

II. EXPLORATION OF AFRICA

The agitation for the abolition of slavery contributed directly to the exploration and opening up of the "Dark Continent." The abolitionists hoped to curtail the slave trade by pushing into the interior where the slaves were captured and they sought to develop "legitimate" or regular commerce that would replace the traffic in slaves. At the same time, a growing scientific fad for geography made Europeans intensely curious about unexplored lands. These factors all combined to bring to Africa in the nineteenth century a number of remarkable and colorful explorers.

The systematic exploration of the continent began with the founding of the African Association in 1788. It was headed by the noted British scientist, Joseph Banks, and its purpose was "to promote the cause of science and humanity, to explore the mysterious geography, to ascertain the resources, and to improve the conditions of that ill-fated continent." [5] The Association's attention was directed first to the problem of the Niger. As yet the river was only a name. Even before the beginning of the European slave trade rumors had circulated about fabulous cities on the banks of a great river called the Niger. No one knew where it rose or where it ended. To solve the mystery, the Association in 1795 sent out a Scottish physician, Mungo Park. After enduring blistering heat, sickness, captivity, and hunger, he succeeded in reaching the Niger, but illness compelled him to return to the coast instead of following the river to its mouth. In 1805 Park returned at the head of a sizeable

Stanley's expedition in search of Livingstone.

expedition, but most of his companions died during the overland trek before even reaching the river. The spirit of the explorers of this period is reflected in a letter that Park wrote home:

> I am sorry to say that of forty-five Europeans who left the Gambia in perfect health, five only at present are alive, viz., three soldiers (one deranged in his mind), Lieutenant Martyn and myself. . . . My dear friend Mr. Anderson and likewise Mr. Scott are both dead, but though all the Europeans who are with me should die, and if I could not succeed in the object of my journey, I would at least die on the Niger.[6]

Park did die on the Niger, as did his eighteen-year-old son who set out to find his father. Many others tried to unlock the mystery of the Niger until finally Richard Lander followed it to its mouth in 1830. In doing so, Lander proved that the so-called Oil Rivers, long known to Europeans as a source of palm oil and slaves, comprised the delta of the Niger. The exploration of West Africa was furthered the most during the 1850's by Dr. Heinrich Barth. This remarkable German visited the most important cities of the western Sudan and then crossed the Sahara and returned to England in 1855. His journey is one of the greatest feats in the history of African travel. Barth's account of his travels is equally outstanding because of his thorough exposition of the geography, history, and ethnology of the lands he visited.

Interest shifted to East Africa after a disastrous trading expedition up the Niger proved that commercial opportunities were scanty there. The big question in East Africa was the source of the Nile. Hostile natives, vast marshes, and innumerable rapids had defeated all attempts to follow the river upstream to its headwaters. In 1856 two Englishmen John Speke and

Richard Burton started inland from the African east coast. They discovered Lake Tanganyika, and with Burton ill, Speke pushed on another two hundred miles to discover Lake Victoria. On a second trip (1860–1863) Speke saw the White Nile pouring from Lake Victoria at Ripon Falls, and then followed the great river to Khartoum and on through Egypt to the Mediterranean.

Head and shoulders above all the other explorers stands the figure of the great David Livingstone. He had trained himself originally to become a medical missionary in China, but the outbreak of the Opium War diverted him to Africa where he landed at Capetown and worked his way northward.* In 1849 Livingstone crossed the Kalahari River to see what fields for missionary enterprise lay beyond. He discovered Lake Ngami where he heard that the country ahead was populous and well-watered, in contrast to the desert he had just crossed. In 1852 he set forth on the great journey that was to take him first to the Atlantic and then back across the continent to the Indian Ocean, which he reached in 1856. Livingstone then returned to England and delivered at Cambridge University his historic address that stimulated interest in Africa throughout the Western world.

Between 1857 and 1863 Livingstone headed an expedition that explored the Zambezi region, and in 1866 he set forth again to settle various questions concerning the source of the Nile. Disappearing into the African bush, he was unable to send word to the outside world for five years. Finally the New York *Herald* sent Henry M. Stanley, a famous foreign correspondent, to find Livingstone. Stanley did find him in 1871 on Lake Tanganyika in one of the memorable episodes of African exploration. Although Livingstone

* See "Livingstone and the Rain Doctor," *EMM*, No. 93.

Timbuktu in 1828.

was weak and emaciated, "a mere ruckle of bones" in his own words, he refused to return home with Stanley. Instead he continued his explorations until May 1, 1873, when his followers found him dead in a praying position beside his cot.

Stanley was so inspired by Livingstone's character and career that he returned to Africa to solve some of the problems left by "the Good Doctor." He discovered that the Lualaba River, thought by Livingstone to flow into the Nile, instead became the Congo, which flowed westward to the Atlantic. Stanley arrived in Boma on the west coast on November 26, 1877, exactly 999 days after leaving Zanzibar. The last of the four great African rivers had at last been traced from source to mouth.

Two years later, in 1879, Stanley was again on the Congo River, but this time he was functioning as the agent for King Leopold of Belgium rather than as an explorer. The age of African exploration had given way to the age of African partition.

III. Partition of Africa

Prior to 1870 the European powers had insignificant holdings in Africa. They consisted mostly of seaports and fortified trading stations, together with bits of adjacent territory acquired as adjuncts to trade rather than as bases for territorial expansion. With the termination of the European slave trade, most of these coastal footholds were virtually abandoned since the legitimate trade was insufficient to support them. The only significant exceptions to this general picture were at the opposite ends of the continent, in French Algeria and British South Africa, where actual colonization was taking place. But even there the activities were haphazard, with no definite plans for expansion and annexation. European statesmen during this early period repeatedly made clear their opposition to the acquisition of colonies. Bismarck, for example, declared himself "not a colonialist," and likened German colonies to the silken sables on the back of a Polish noble who had no shirt beneath. Likewise, in Britain a House of Commons Committee appointed to consider West African affairs agreed unanimously in 1865 "that all further extension of territory or assumption of government, or new treaty offering any protection to native tribes, would be inexpedient."

After 1870 a combination of factors (see Chapter 10, section VII) produced a reversal of this anticolonial attitude. Colonies now were regarded as assets for the mother country, and the continent of Africa, being unoccupied and defenseless, became the vortex of imperialist aspirations. A typical expression of the new colonialism was that of the French economist Paul Leroy-Beaulieu, who wrote in 1874, "Colonization is for France a question of life and death: either France will become a great African power, or in a century or two she will be no more than a secondary European power; she will count for about as much in the world as Greece and Roumania in Europe." [7]

The leader of the imperialist drive in Africa was King Leopold of Belgium. A shrewd monarch, he sensed the opportunities offered by the great interior plateaus that were being opened up by the explorers. In 1876 he convened a conference in Brussels, ostensibly to help introduce civilization into Africa. In his opening address he declared, "The object which unites us here today is one of those which deserve in the highest degree to occupy the friends of humanity. To open to civilization the only part of our globe where it has not penetrated, to pierce the darkness which envelops entire populations, is, I venture to say, a crusade worthy of this century of progress."[8] The Brussels Conference resulted in the founding of the International Association for the Exploration and Civilization of Central Africa. Although ostensibly an association of several national groups, the executive committee was controlled by Leopold.

At the outset Leopold was interested primarily in East Africa. But with Stanley's exploration of the Congo Basin in 1876–1877, he at once perceived the potentialities of this great central region. In fact Stanley himself saw the opportunity but he was unable to enlist support in England. So in 1878 Stanley entered Leopold's service, and the following year he returned to the Congo. Between 1879 and 1880 Stanley signed numerous treaties with chiefs, handing over no less than 900,000 square miles to the International Association of the Congo, a new organization set up under Leopold's direction. The chiefs had no way of knowing that signing the pieces of paper and accepting token payments meant permanent loss of their tribal lands. An African chief traditionally was entrusted with his people's land. His selling was like a mayor's selling "his" city hall. Yet this was the standard procedure all over the continent, and repercussions are being felt to the present day.*

The immediate effect of Leopold's machinations was to jolt the other European leaders to action. The French already had sent their famous explorer, Count de Brazza, to the lower Congo, and he was able to acquire for his country the lands to the north of the river. The Germans also entered the race, obtaining in 1884 South-West Africa, Togoland, and the Cameroons. Now the Portuguese joined in, especially since they had been claiming for some time the west coast as far north as 5° 12′ S., that is, both sides of the Congo mouth and inland indefinitely. Britain never had been willing to recognize these Portuguese claims but she now changed her mind in hopes of checking the aggressive Belgians and French. So an Anglo-Portuguese Convention was signed on February 26, 1884 recognizing Portuguese sovereignty over the mouth of the Congo and providing for Anglo-Portuguese control of navigation on the river.

The treaty was furiously denounced by the other powers, so an international conference was held in Berlin in 1884–1885 to prepare rules for the further acquisition of African territories. It was agreed that no power should annex land or establish a protectorate without first giving notice of intent; that recognition of territorial claims must depend on effective occupation; and that disputes were to be settled by arbitration. The conference also recognized the rights of Leopold's International Association of the Congo to much of the Congo Basin, to be known as the Congo Free State. Finally, high-sounding declarations were made about uplifting the natives, spreading the Gospel, and stamping out slavery. All these were to be conspicuous by their absence in the so-called Free State.

* See "Partition of Africa: African View," *EMM,* No. 95.

Now that an international code for territorial aggrandizement was agreed upon, the entire continent was partitioned in less than two decades. In the Congo, Leopold bought out in 1887 all non-Belgian interests in order to eliminate possible criticism of his enterprise. Then he reimbursed himself by reserving a crown district of the richest rubber lands, ten times the size of Belgium. Here, as elsewhere in the Congo, special monopolies for the exploitation of natural products, including rights of native labor, were awarded to commercial concerns in most of which Leopold was a heavy stockholder. His profits, therefore, were derived both from the stipends paid to the state by the concessionaires and from the dividends earned in the course of their immensely successful operations. In the final analysis, the fortunes that were made in the Congo were extracted by ruthless exploitation of the native peoples. So unbelievably brutal were the various methods of forced labor that the population of the Congo declined by one-half (from 20 to 10 million) between 1885 and 1908 when it was ruled by Leopold.

If the Africans did not bring in the required amount of rubber and ivory, they were mutilated or shot. Mutilation meant chopping off a hand or a foot or both. To prove that they were doing their job properly, the bosses of the labor gangs brought to their superiors baskets full of human hands. And because the climate was hot and humid, the hands were sometimes smoked in order to preserve them. A traveler in the Congo Free State recorded his observations as follows: "The inhabitants have disappeared. Their homes have been burned; huge heaps of ashes amid neglected palm-hedges and devastated abandoned fields. Inhuman floggings, murders, plunderings, and carryings-off. . . . The people flee into the wild or seek protection in French or Portuguese territory." [9]

News of these atrocities leaked out and Leopold was forced to hand over his Congo possessions to the Belgian government in 1908. What had been private property now became a Belgian colony. The government took measures to end the atrocities, though a modified form of forced labor did continue. Leopold, the mercenary promoter to the end, induced the Belgian parliament to compensate him handsomely for his "sacrifice" of the Congo.

In the rest of West Africa the French were the most active. Starting from their old trading posts on the Ivory Coast, in Dahomey, and on the north bank of the Congo, they conceived a grand plan for pushing inward and founding a French West African Empire that would stretch from Algeria to the Congo and from the Senegal to the Nile or even the Red Sea. Since the Germans and the British also had footholds along the west coast, the French had to out-flank their rivals in a race for the hinterland. By and large they were successful. Only the British in Nigeria and the Germans in the Cameroons were able to expand significantly into the interior. All the rest of West Africa, together with the vast Sahara, became a great French domain ruled from Paris.

In order to extend their holdings eastward across the whole of Africa, the French sent Colonel Marchand on a perilous expedition. It took him from the French Congo to Fashoda on the Nile, which he reached in July 1898. A few weeks later, General Kitchener arrived at the head of an expedition that had ascended the Nile from Egypt. In the name of Britain, Kitchener demanded that Marchand withdraw from Fashoda. The two men then sensibly decided to refer the dispute to their respective governments. For some months

Britain and France were on the brink of war, but in the spring of 1899 France gave way, leaving Britain in possesion of the Upper Nile.

In East Africa the Portuguese had held Mozambique since the sixteenth century and France had claims to Madagascar. The chief rivals for the remaining territory were the Germans and the British. At the end of 1884, while the Berlin Conference was in session, a young German colonial enthusiast, Dr. Carl Peters, landed secretly in East Africa. Within ten days he had persuaded the local chiefs to sign away more than 60,000 square miles, an area almost one-third the size of his own homeland.* The following year the German government proclaimed a protectorate over the region obtained by Carl Peters.

The German activities aroused the British who proceeded to sign treaties giving them the territory in the Kenya area. This land grabbing drew repeated protests from the Sultan of Zanzibar who for long had held sovereignty over the East African coast opposite his island. Both the British and the Germans ignored his protests and signed two agreements in 1886 and 1890 settling their respective territorial disputes. The Germans retained the huge area known as the German East Africa Protectorate, to be named Tanganyika after 1919; the British were allotted their East Africa Protectorate, later to be known as Kenya Colony, together with a protectorate over Uganda. The Sultan of Zanzibar retained possession of his island, but had to recognize Britain as his suzerain.

Meanwhile, the Italians had belatedly joined the scramble for African territory. They managed to obtain two barren colonies on the Red Sea coast, Eritrea and Somaliland, and later, in 1896, they gambled for higher stakes by sending an army to conquer the kingdom of Ethiopia. The Christian Ethiopians were not a primitive tribal people like those in most other parts of Africa. Their Emperor Menelik had an army of 80,000 men trained by French officers and armed with French weapons. He was able to defeat the small Italian army of 10,000, and his kingdom remained free from European rule. Except for the small republic of Liberia on the west coast, by 1914 Ethiopia was the only independent state on the whole continent. And even Liberia, set up in 1822 as a settlement for freed American Negroes (named from the Latin *liber,* meaning "free"), became a virtual United States protectorate in 1911 because of bankruptcy and internal disorders.

Meanwhile, on the southern tip of the continent the British were roused to action by the establishment of a German protectorate in South-West Africa and by Portuguese plans for the linking of Angola on the west coast to Mozambique on the east. The British took control of three areas—Basutoland, Bechuanaland, and Swaziland—all of which were made into native reservations and placed under British commissioners. North of the Limpopo River the British were attracted by rich goldfields and healthy plateau lands that were suitable for white colonization. In 1889 the British government granted a charter to the British South Africa Company whose field of operations was defined as "to the north and west of the South African Republic, and to the west of the Portuguese dominions." Settlers began to move in and in 1890 the town of Salisbury was laid out on the beautiful and salubrious

---

* See "Partition of Africa: European View," *EMM,* No. 94.

plateau between the Limpopo and the Zambesi. These British settlements did not take root without challenge from two sources—the native King Lobengula who tried belatedly to oust the white intruders, and the neighboring Portuguese who had ambitions of their own. Lobengula was forced to yield to superior force, while the Portuguese in 1891 signed a treaty that left most of the disputed territory to the British. After World War I the British company gave up its charter and its lands were organized as the two colonies of Northern and Southern Rhodesia.

The British also had difficulties in South Africa proper, where a long smoldering feud with the Boer settlers flared up into full-scale war in 1899. After the war the British granted self-government to the Boers in the Orange Free State and the Transvaal, and in 1907 these two colonies joined with Natal and Cape Colony to form the Dominion of the Union of South Africa.

The net result of this unprecedented territorial aggrandizement was the partitioning of the entire continent of Africa among the European powers. The only exceptions, as note above, were the precarious states of Liberia and Ethiopia. Table 1 gives a specific analysis of the African continent in 1914.

TABLE 1. Political Divisions in Africa in 1914

	Square miles
French (Tunisia, Algeria, Morocco, French West Africa, French Congo, French Somaliland, Madagascar)	4,086,950
British (Union of South Africa, Basutoland, Bechuanaland, Nyasaland, Rhodesia, British East Africa, Uganda, Zanzibar, Somaliland, Nigeria, Gold Coast, Sierra Leone, Gambia, Egypt, Anglo-Egyptian Sudan)	3,701,411
German (East Africa, South-West Africa, Cameroon, Togoland)	910,150
Belgian (Congo State)	900,000
Portuguese (Guinea, West Africa, East Africa)	787,500
Italian (Eritrea, Italian Somaliland, Libya)	600,000
Spanish (Rio de Oro, Muni River Settlements)	79,800
Independent States (Liberia, Ethiopia)	393,000
TOTAL	11,458,811

IV. EUROPE'S IMPACT

Economic

Since economic motives were prominent in the partitioning of Africa, it is not surprising that drastic economic changes followed the partitioning. Europe no longer was content with boatloads of slaves at the coastal ports. The industrialized West no longer needed human slaves; technology had provided an abundance of the mechanical variety. Instead the West had need for the raw materials found in the interior of Africa, and it now had the technological means to extract these materials.

The first important step in the exploitation of Africa's resources came with the discovery of diamonds in Kimberley (1867) and gold in the Witwatersrand (1884). Equally great mineral wealth was discovered in the Rhodesias (gold and copper) and in the Congo (gold, copper, and diamonds). Many portions of the west coast yielded rich supplies of such tropical forest products as palm oil, rubber, and ivory. European and American companies bought vast plantations in such regions as the Congo, the Cameroons, and French Equatorial Africa, one example being the Firestone Corporation, which in 1926 was given a 90-year lease on 100,000 acres of land in Liberia.

Not only did foreign companies lease large tracts of land, but foreign settlers took over much of the good agricultural land. Explorers had reported that some of the interior plateaus had fertile soil as well as a pleasant climate. Consequently, European settlers flocked in, particularly to Southern Rhodesia and East Africa. Before long they had gained possession of the most desirable agricultural properties in these regions.

In order to transport the minerals and the agricultural commodities now being produced, the Europeans proceeded to build a network of railways in Africa as they already had done in Asia. These railways were designed to facilitate the export of produce rather than to stimulate general economic development. Thus the railway system in West Africa ran only north to south, with no direct connection between east and west.

The expansion of production and the construction of transportation facilities stimulated trade to the point where the traditional barter gave way to a monetary system. No longer did the Africans exchange slaves, golddust, feathers, and ivory for the Europeans' salt, glassware, cloth, rum, and gin. By the end of the nineteenth century there was fairly widespread use of English silver coins and of Austrian and American dollars.

All of these economic developments naturally had profound effects upon the native peoples. The inhabitants of the temperate plateau areas were affected most by the loss of the lands taken by white settlers. In some cases whole districts were reserved for exclusive white use, and the land could not be tilled by the Africans, even though it sometimes lay fallow. Consequently, the Africans were forced to work for wages on the white man's plantations, while some even "squatted" on the land of the white farmers for whom they worked to gain the privilege of tilling a small plot for themselves. In other regions the Africans found it necessary to leave their families and go to work in the mines. If the Africans refused to provide the labor needed for the plantations and mines, various types of forced labor were used. The most common was the levying of a head tax compelling the African to work in order to earn the money to pay the tax. These various developments reduced the traditional economic self-sufficiency of the African. No longer did he work simply to feed himself and his family, increasingly he was involved in a money economy and was affected by world economic conditions. For example, a depression in the industrialized countries immediately affected the operation of copper mines, while a slump in the world price for palm oil immediately lowered the income of a large number of individual producers in West Africa. We can see, then, that the effect of Europe's economic impact was twofold: to entangle the Africans in a world-wide money economy, and to subordinate them, directly or indirectly, to the white man who was everywhere the "boss." *

Cultural

Together with the trader, the investor, and the settler from Europe came the European missionary. He had a profound effect upon African culture because he was the first European who consciously sought to change it. The others affected it indirectly and incidentally, as when they forced Africans to leave their ancestral villages to work in cities or mines. But the missionary came with the avowed purpose of changing the African way of life, and he used three instruments to carry this out: education, medicine, and religion.

Schools offering a Western education and Western ideals were an integral part of every mission station. These schools were particularly influential since most colonial governments left education to the missionaries. In many respects the mission schools were constructive in their influence: Often they taught the pupils how to build better houses, improve their agricultural methods, and observe the rudiments of hygiene and sanitation. They also taught reading and writing in African as well as European languages. The missionaries reduced the African languages to writing and so laid the foundations for indigenous African literature. The great majority of those Africans who chose literary careers were educated in missionary schools.

On the other hand, these schools inevitably had a subversive influence on the African people; they often taught that the traditional way of life was primitive and wrong. In time the students listened less to their parents and elders and more to their European teachers whom they learned to respect. In addition, the mission schools used European books that taught more about Europe than about Africa. Early history text books used in the French colonies began with lessons dealing with "our ancestors the Gauls." Missionary education encouraged individualism, which was contrary to the communal African way of life. It is not surprising that Africans subjected to several years of this type of education were usually loathe to return to their villages. Instead they looked for jobs with the colonial governments, missions, or private businesses, thus moving further away from their traditional culture.

The missions also brought medical knowledge and facilities that saved the lives of many Africans. But besides saving lives, medicine also forced Africans to question their traditional ideas of what caused illness and death. The White Man had the power to make people well even after the proper petitioning of spirits had not worked. So traditional religion no longer could be counted upon to meet all emergencies and to provide all the answers. Even though the majority of Africans clung to their old faiths, traditional religion no longer was as effective a cement in holding together the African's whole way of life as it previously had been.†

* See "Europe's Impact: Economic," *EMM,* No. 96.
† See "Europe's Impact: Cultural," *EMM,* No. 97.

Europe's imprint was as marked in the political field as it was in the economic and cultural fields. To start, the boundaries of the various colonies had to be fixed (here the outcome depended purely upon the European balance of power). No attention was paid to the indigenous people concerned, so that they often found themselves under the rule of two or even three European powers. Some of the Somali, for example, were ruled by the French, others by the British, still others by the Italians, and a number even found themselves within the boundaries of Ethiopia.

Once the boundaries had been settled, the problem of organizing some administrative system arose. The European governments did not have enough manpower to rule directly all the peoples of the vast African continent, so they resorted to various forms of indirect rule; administration was conducted through tribal chiefs who were allowed to retain some of their authority. Usually the British allowed the chiefs more leeway than did the French, but even the French could not control everything because their African possessions were so vast and their supply of officials was so limited.

On the surface, then, the Africans retained their traditional political institutions. They still had their councils of elders, their laws, their courts, and their chiefs. But in practice this political structure was undermined. The chiefs could be appointed or removed by the local European administrators, and their decisions no longer had the force of law since tribesmen could go over their heads to the European officials whose word was final. The extent to which the authority of the chiefs was curtailed is evident in the following account by a colonial official who tells how he administered his territory:

> In mid-1917, I arrived at a remote, unadministered part of [Tanganyika] . . . with orders to set up at least a rudimentary civil authority. I had my servants, an African sergeant, porters for my goods, and some twenty police uniforms and rifles and a little ammunition for them. Arrived at the chosen place—a mission station—I summoned the local chiefs, explained that I was the government and would they please provide me with twenty men to be policemen? Would they also please note that from now on people must not kill their wives or children whose teeth appeared in the ill-omened order; nor must chiefs make war on their neighbors without consulting me. In fact, a whole lot of customary and often agreeable things must be given up." [10]

Perhaps the most important factors undermining the traditional political systems were the economic and cultural changes brought about by European rule. Chiefs often were believed to have been given their authority by the tribal gods, so that their religious leadership buttressed their political power. Obviously both their religious leadership and political power were weakened where the people were converted to a new religion or where their faith was shaken in the old. Likewise, people who gained money wealth by working in cities or mines acquired a status and independence that would have been in-

384

conceivable had they remained in their villages. In some cases these newly rich people actually had more prestige and power than the old chiefs.

The most serious and direct challenge to the traditional tribal authorities came from the class of Western educated Africans that gradually developed in almost all the colonies. They tended to challenge not only the native chiefs but also the European officials. They usually were the first to demand that educated Africans should be allowed to participate in the administration of their countries. These people were the first nationalists; they laid the foundations for the powerful nationalist movement of today. They did so because they had imbibed in Western schools certain political ideas such as individual liberty and political freedom, and they saw no reason why the principles of liberalism and nationalism should be applicable in Europe and not in Africa. They were also moved to political agitation by the discrimination frequently encountered in government and private employment. Usually they were not allowed to be more than poorly paid clerks in European firms or very minor officials in the colonial administration. Again they could not see why, when they had the required education and experience, they should be kept in subordinate positions simply because their skins were dark. The Christian religion, and especially Protestantism, stimulated nationalism because it emphasized individual judgment and initiative. This point was made by a writer in an Angolan journal: "To tell a person he is able to interpret the Bible freely is to insinuate in him an undue autonomy and turn him into a rebel. . . . A Protestant native is already disposed towards—not to say an active agent in—the revolt against civilized peoples." [11]

This was the combination of forces that moved the Western-educated Africans to take over the political leadership of their peoples. They were not demanding full independence before 1914, but they were insisting on more participation in government, and thereby preparing the ground for the triumphant nationalist movements of today.*

V. Conclusion

The above survey indicates that in many basic respects Europe had a much deeper imprint on Africa than on Eurasia. There was no parallel in the latter area to the draining of African manpower through the slave trade, even though the continent's general demography had not thereby been drastically affected. With the exception of Southeast Asia, there was also no parallel to the alienation of agricultural lands, even though this was limited to East Africa and South Africa. Likewise, there was no parallel in Eurasia to the virtually total European domination of transport, finance, foreign trade, mining, and manufacturing. Finally, there was no parallel, with the exception of the Philippines, to the widespread diffusion of European Christianity and European languages, and to the proliferating cultural influence of the European missionaries with their schools and their medical facilities.

The basic reason for this contrast in degree of European influence is to be found in the corresponding contrast in the level of general development that

* See "Europe's Impact: Political," *EMM,* No. 98.

had been attained in Africa and in Eurasia. This contrast prevailed in all fields—in the sophistication of cultures, in the development of economies and technologies, and, consequently, in the density of populations. It was this contrast that made sub-Saharan Africa infinitely more vulnerable to European missionaries, entrepreneurs, and settlers.

And yet this very underdevelopedness of sub-Saharan Africa provided a natural resistance at the village level (as distinct from the European-influenced urban centers). In most parts of the continent prior to 1914, the interior villages retained their economic self-sufficiency and their integrated traditional cultures, which made them largely impervious to the West. While acknowledging the decisive impact of Europe in certain basic respects, one must still realize that even to the present day, probably over half the villages of sub-Saharan African remain relatively unchanged in their traditional patterns of life.

Suggested Reading

For general histories of Africa, see the bibliography for Chapter 5 and also the comprehensive survey of historical literature on this area by P. D. Curtin, *African History* (Washington: Service Center for Teachers of History, 1964), No. 56. Two excellent recent studies of the slave trade are by B. Davidson, *Black Mother: The Years of the African Slave Trade* (Boston: Little, 1963) and D. P. Mannix, *Black Cargoes: A History of the Atlantic Slave Trade, 1518–1865* (New York: Viking, 1962). For the story of the abolition movement, see W. E. B. Dubois, *The Suppression of the African Slave Trade* (New York: Longmans, 1896) and R. Coupland, *The British Anti-Slavery Movement* (London: Butterworth, 1933). E. Williams, *Capitalism and Slavery* (Chapel Hill: Univ. of North Carolina, 1944), emphasizes the economic factors assisting the abolition movement.

The accounts of the explorers provide colorful material on the opening up of the continent, outstanding being M. Park, *Travels in the Interior Districts of Africa* (London: J. Murray, 1816–17), 2 vols.; *Barth's Travels in Nigeria: Extracts from the Journal of Heinrich Barth's Travels in Nigeria, 1850–1855*, selected and edited, with an introduction by A. H. M. Kirk-Greene (New York: Oxford Univ., 1962); *Livingstone's African Journal, 1853–1856*, ed. by I. Schapera (Berkeley: Univ. California, 1963), 2 vols.; *The Exploration Diaries of H. M. Stanley*, ed. by R. Stanley and A. Neame (New York: Vanguard, 1962); and Sir Richard Burton, *The Lake Regions of Central Africa* (London: Sidgwick, 1961), 2 vols. A convenient collection of explorers' accounts is available in M. Perham and J. Simmons, *African Discovery: An Anthology of Exploration* (London: Faber, 1942). A readable survey of the history of African exploration is given in H. Schiffers, *The Quest for Africa: Two Thousand Years of Exploration* (London: Odhams, 1957).

A brief survey of the partitioning of Africa is available in H. L. Haskins, *European Imperialism in Africa* (New York: Holt, 1930). A broader and more detailed analysis is presented in M. E. Townsend and C. H. Peake, *European Colonial Expansion Since 1871* (Philadelphia: Lippincott, 1941). For specialized aspects of the partitioning of Africa, see H. I. Priestley, *France Overseas:*

A Study of Modern Imperialism (New York: Appleton, 1939); H. Rudin, *The Germans in the Cameroons, 1884–1914* (New Haven: Yale, 1938); R. Coupland, *The Exploitation of East Africa, 1856–1890* (London: Faber, 1939); and M. E. Townsend, *The Rise and Fall of Germany's Colonial Empire* (New York: Macmillan, 1930).

Finally for the impact of the West on Africa there is H. A. Wieschhoff, *Colonial Policies in Africa* (Philadelphia: Univ. of Pennsylvania, 1944); R. L. Buell, *The Native Problem in Africa* (New York: Macmillan, 1928), 2 vols.; K. Little, "African Culture and the Western Intrusion," *Journal of World History,* III (1957), 941–63; K. O. Dike, *Trade and Politics in the Niger Delta, 1830–1885* (New York: Oxford, 1956); T. Hodgkin, *Nationalism in Colonial Africa* (New York: New York Univ., 1957), and the documentary collections in F. Wolfson, *Pageant of Ghana* (London: Oxford Univ. 1958); and T. Hodgkin, *Nigerian Perspectives* (New York: Oxford Univ., 1960).

*Afterwards the Spaniards resolved to go and
hunt the Indians who were in the mountains
[of Cuba], where they perpetrated marvellous
massacres. Thus they ruined and depopulated
all this island which we beheld not long ago;
and it excites pity, and great anguish to see it
deserted, and reduced to a solitude.*

BARTOLOMÉ DE LAS CASAS, *1552*

*The disappearance of these people [Australian
aborigines] before the white invaders is just as
certain as the disappearance of wolves in a
country becoming civilized and populous.*

JAMES STEPHEN, *1841*

Chapter 18

The Americas and
the British Dominions

Even more far-reaching than Europe's impact upon Asia
and Africa during the nineteenth century were its effects upon the
Americas and the British Dominions. The title of this chapter, then,
refers not to "impact," but to outright Europeanization.

Europeanization involves more than just political domination or
cultural penetration. It involves actual biological replacement, the
physical substitution of one people by another—as happened in the
relatively empty territories of the Western Hemisphere and the South
Pacific. The scanty indigenous populations were either wiped out or
pushed aside, and tens of millions of European emigrants swarmed in
and occupied their lands, bringing with them their political institutions, their ways of earning a living, and their cultural traditions. Thus
the ethnic Europeanization of overseas territories was followed inevitably by political, economic, and cultural Europeanization.

I. ETHNIC EUROPEANIZATION

Early Migrations

An earlier chapter explained why Europe was able to supply so
many emigrants, and why these millions of people were willing to leave

their ancestral homes and brave unknown dangers in far-off continents. The thin ribbons of European settlement that existed in 1763 had stretched by 1914 to cover entire continents, including Australia and New Zealand, which had still been untouched at the earlier date.*

Tables 1–3 show that the majority of European emigrants went to the Americas. This is understandable, because the earliest European colonies were established in the Americas, and also because those continents offered much greater natural resources and economic opportunities. However, since the first European settlements were in Central and South America, it is surprising that so many more of these emigrants settled in North America.

The basically different character of the Spanish and Portuguese colonies, compared to the English explains it.† The Spaniards and the Portuguese settled in territories with relatively dense Indian populations. Although estimates of the number of Indians in the Americas before the coming of the Europeans vary tremendously, it is agreed that the Indian populations were concentrated in what came to be Latin America. These native peoples supplied all the labor that was needed, so European settlers were not required for that purpose. Accordingly, emigrants to the Spanish and Portuguese colonies in the Americas were mostly soldiers, members of the clergy, government officials, and a few necessary craftsmen.

North of the Rio Grande. by contrast, the Indian population was relatively sparse and provided no reservoir of labor power. The English along the Atlantic Seaboard and the French on the banks of the St. Lawrence had to

TABLE 1.   Racial Distribution in the Americas (in millions)

	White		Negro		Indian
	1835	1935	1835	1935	1935
North America	13.8	124.3	2.6	12.4	1.8
Central America	1.9	6.9	2.7	8.4	21.4
South America	2.9	40.9	4.5	18.7	29.2
TOTAL	18.6	172.1	9.8	39.5	52.4

Source: See Table 3.

TABLE 2.   Racial Distribution in Africa

	Whites		Africans
	1835	1935	1935
Mediterranean countries *	20,000	1,660,000 †	30,000,000
Union of South Africa	66,000	1,950,000	6,600,000
Rest of South Africa ‡	3,000	190,000	12,200,000
Rest of continent	1,000	100,000	87,700,000
Islands	45,000	100,000	4,500,000
TOTAL	135,000	4,000,000	141,000,000

Source: See Table 3.
* Egypt, Libya, Tunis, Algeria, Moroccos, Spanish North Africa, Tangier.
† Includes only the settlers of European origin.
‡ Angola, S.W. Africa, Rhodesias, Nyasaland, Bechuanaland, Basutoland, Swaziland, Mozambique.

* See "Europe's Great Migrations," *EMM*, No. 99.
† See "Immigrants in Argentina," *EMM*, No. 101.

do their own work, whether it was cutting the forests, plowing the cleared land, or fishing the coastal waters. Under these circumstances North America wanted all the settlers it could get, and so the British North American colonies 389

TABLE 3. Racial Distribution in Oceania

	Date	Whites	Natives
Australia	June, 1935	6,674,000	81,000
New Zealand	Dec., 1935	1,486,000	76,000
Papua (Australia)	June, 1933	1,000	275,000
Fiji Islands (Br.)	Dec., 1934	5,000	107,000
New Guinea (Austr.)	June, 1935	4,000	679,000
Other islands (15)	1930's	109,756	464,525
TOTAL (of 19 areas)		8,279,756	1,682,525

Source: R. R. Kuczynski, *Population Movements* (Oxford: Clarendon, 1936), pp. 91, 95, 102–3, 109–10, 118.

were opened to immigrants of all races, languages, and faiths. By 1835 there were 4.8 million European settlers in all of Central and South America as against 13.8 million in North America.*

Nineteenth Century Migrations

In the second half of the nineteenth century European emigration steadily

* See "Peopling of North America," *EMM,* No. 100.

A French settlement in the St. Lawrence Valley. (From a watercolor by James Duncan. The Public Archives of Canada.)

increased, reaching its height between 1900 and 1910 when almost one million people left each year. This unprecedented flood poured into every continent, so that Australia, South Africa, and South America now were peopled by substantial numbers of Europeans, although North America continued to be the main beneficiary.

So far as the specific sources of immigration were concerned (see tables in Chapter 11, section VII), the Latin American countries were peopled, as might be expected, mostly by emigrants from the Iberian Peninsula, though considerable numbers also came in the late nineteenth century from Italy and Germany. The great majority of the emigrants to North America were, until 1890, from northwestern Europe. After that date, approximately one-third came from northwestern Europe, and the remaining two-thirds came from eastern and southern Europe. In the case of the British Dominions, immigration restrictions limited the supply largely to the British Isles. After World War I, however, the Dominions liberalized their immigration policies in order to get more people into their wide open spaces. The Australians are particularly sensitive about their comparative lack of population because of the teeming Asian lands nearby, and the white South Africans, likewise, are concerned because of the large Negro majority.

Ethnic Results

The net result of these migrations has been the ethnic Europeanization of the Americas and the British Dominions. These areas have become largely European in population, although there are certain important exceptions such as the native Indian strain remaining predominant (58% of the total population) in Central America, and comprising one-third of the total population of South America. The substantial Negro element introduced into the Americas as a result of the slave trade is another exception to ethnic Europeanization. It is estimated that approximately 15 million slaves were shipped from Africa to the New World. Their descendents today comprise about 10 per cent of the total population in North America, 30 per cent in Central America, and 21 per cent in South America. South Africa represents the third exception to ethnic Europeanization; there the native Africans outnumber the whites (whether of Boer or British origin) by more than three to one.

The Indian and Negro elements in the New World are not of decisive political significance, even when they comprise the majority—as do the Indians in Central America—because in no major country in the New World are the Indians or the Negroes in a ruling position. Everywhere they have accepted the political domination and the culture of the whites of European origin. The significance of the Negro majority in South Africa is very different. Although this majority has been denied equal political and social rights from the beginning, its attitude still differs greatly from that of the Indians or Negroes in the New World. The South African Negroes feel that they have behind them over 175 million fellow Negroes now living on the rest of the continent, most of whom have won their independence. They have, in other words, the confidence of Negroes on an overwhelming Negro continent, whereas the Negroes and Indians of the Americas feel much less secure in a new world where Whites are far superior to them in numbers and power.

II. POLITICAL EUROPEANIZATION

Colonial Period

From the beginning, Europe's colonies had a wide variety of political institutions. Such a variety arose from the different political backgrounds of the mother countries. For example, Spain was ruled autocratically by the Madrid court, so naturally the Spanish colonies were ruled in the same manner. The officials that were sent to the colonies had virtually absolute authority, so that the colonists had little choice but to take orders. Very rarely was a colonist given a government post. Of the 672 viceroys, captains-general, and governors who held office in colonial Hispanic America, only 18 were permanent residents of the colonies; the remaining 97.4 per cent were permanent residents of Spain. The French colonies were also ruled autocratically, with power concentrated in the hands of the governors, who were responsible for the defense of each colony, and the intendants who handled economic affairs.

By contrast, the English colonies had popularly elected representative institutions that reflected the flourishing parliamentary government of the mother country. The precise nature of these institutions varied somewhat from colony to colony. In Virginia the settlers were granted permission to elect a local legislature as early as 1619. This body gradually grew in power until by the time of the American Revolution it had more influence than the royal governor. In New England, instead of individual settlers braving the wilderness, groups of people migrated to the frontier to set up new towns. There they developed a type of town government with regular "town meetings" at which decisions were made and various officials were elected. Despite these differences in the precise forms of government, the Thirteen Colonies had one thing in common: popular participation in public affairs, which led to constant friction between the elected representatives and the royal officials. In 1774 one of these officials William Knox plaintively contrasted the noisy intractability of the English colonies with the quiet discipline of the French:

> The government of the French colonies particularly deserves our attention, and is worthy of our imitation; they take every precaution of a wise and prudent nation, to secure good order and government; a governor is appointed with a proper power, and a council established to give him assistance, as well as to guard the rights of the crown. . . . Without any of those pompous ideas of popular governments, which our countrymen are elated with, the people are happy. . . . Happy would it be for this kingdom, were such plans adopted for the government of our colonies.[1]

Revolutionary Period

Knox's concern over the "pompous ideas" of the British colonials proved to be fully justified. These ideas prompted the call to arms in 1776 that would lead to the establishment of the independent United States of America.

Furthermore, the revolution of the Thirteen Colonies triggered a chain reaction of similar uprisings that swept all the colonies in the New World during the six decades between 1776 and 1837.

Various factors contributed to the revolts in Latin America, one of which was the example of the Thirteen Colonies whose successful revolution was followed closely and sympathetically. Latin Americans were as well-acquainted with what they called the philosophy of Philadelphia, as they were with the teachings of the French *philosophes*. The writings of the latter were smuggled in large quantities across the Atlantic in what were called "the ships of the Enlightenment." According to one historian, so many copies of Rousseau's *Social Contract* were received in Venezuela that torn-out pages were used in 1807 to wrap food in the shops. Spain's colonial policy, especially the economic exploitation and the lack of self-government, was another obvious factor promoting revolution. The concentration of power in the hands of officials from Spain alienated the creoles (Spaniards born in America) and the mestizos (people of Spanish and Indian blood). The long years of the French Revolution and the Napoleonic Wars, when Spain was preoccupied in Europe and her colonies were left to shift for themselves, also stimulated revolutionary ideas. The Spanish colonies were unwilling to give up the new freedom they had tasted and enjoyed, and they were backed up by foreign powers interested in liquidating Spain's colonial empire.

Napoleon Bonaparte's domination of Spain and the establishment of his brother, Joseph, on the Madrid throne was the immediate cause of revolution in Latin America. The Spanish colonials refused to recognize Joseph and proclaimed allegiance to the deposed Ferdinand VII. Their professions of loyalty did not convince the Spanish authorities, and widespread fighting broke out in 1809 between the patriots and the loyalists. The wars of independence dragged on until 1825, with the British giving help as decisive to Latin American victory as French aid had been to that of the Thirteen Colonies.

The great revolutionary hero in northern South America was General Simon Bolivar, the "Liberator." For fifteen years this brilliant leader fought unceasingly, virtually creating the independent states of Colombia, Venezuela, Panama, Ecuador, and Bolivia, the last being named after him. The outstanding leader in the southern part of the continent was General José de San Martin. After freeing Argentina in 1816, San Martin made an historic crossing of the Andes and participated in the liberation of Chile and Peru.

The revolution in Mexico began in 1810 under the creole priest Manuel Hidalgo and was continued after his death by another liberal curate, José Maria Morelos. These men attempted to combine the creole ideal of independence with a program of social reform that would aid the mestizos and the Indians. The plan was considered too radical by the creole conservatives, and they combined with the royalists to suppress the revolt in 1815. Later, these conservatives feared that the 1820 liberal revolution in Spain might endanger their privileges, so they worked for separation from the mother country. A creole officer Agustín de Iturbide devised a compromise program that united most factions. Royalist forces were easily overcome, and in September 1822 a national congress proclaimed the independence of Mexico.

It proved possible to win independence in Brazil without bloodshed. Following the occupation of Portugal by French troops in 1807–1808, the Emperor John VI left Lisbon to establish the Portuguese government-in-exile in Rio de Janeiro. John returned to Lisbon in 1821 but left his son, Dom Pedro, temporarily in charge of public affairs in Brazil. Dom Pedro eventually decided against following his father to Lisbon and declared the independence of Brazil. Rather than sending an army against his own son, John accepted the declaration and Brazil became an independent state.

In this way, almost all Latin America won its independence from European rule. The only exceptions were British, Dutch, and French Guiana to the north of Brazil, certain Caribbean islands such as Jamaica, which remained British until the winning of independence in 1962, the Virgin Islands, which were under Denmark until 1917, and Cuba, which was under Spanish rule until 1898.

The Latin American wars of independence were over by 1825, but revolution in the Americas was not. In 1837, a little over a decade later, insurrection broke out in two British colonies, Upper and Lower Canada. The roots of this uprising go back to 1763 when Britain acquired the colony of New France on the banks of the St. Lawrence, and to 1774 when the Quebec Act of that year extended the boundaries of Quebec to the Ohio and Mississippi rivers, and forbade frontiersmen to cross over the Alleghenies into the Ohio Valley. We have already seen that this restriction contributed to the outbreak of the American Revolution in 1776. But the Revolution, paradoxically enough, was responsible for making French Canada British territory. Thousands of Tories—or United Empire Loyalists, as they are known in the Empire —emigrated during and after the Revolution. Some returned to Britain, others fled to various British islands in the Caribbean, but many headed northward to the Maritime Provinces (Nova Scotia, New Brunswick, and Prince Edward Island) and to the wilderness that is now Ontario. These loyalists proved to be Canada's Pilgrim Fathers. Their settlements, together with those of the earlier French, created the basis of the great Dominion of Canada.

These loyalists who settled in what is now Ontario were dissatisfied because according to the terms of the Quebec Act, they did not have the representative type of government they had enjoyed in the Thirteen Colonies. Accordingly, the British Parliament passed the Constitutional Act of 1791, dividing Quebec into Upper and Lower Canada, and setting up elective assemblies in both parts. But now the same conflict recurred between imperial authority and colonial self-government that had convulsed the Thirteen Colonies. In both Canadas a constitutional struggle developed between the governors and the appointed councils on the one hand and the popular elective assemblies on the other. The specific points of conflict were such issues as patronage abuses, control of revenue and of the judiciary, and the allocation of public lands exclusively for the established Anglican Church, even though the Methodists and Presbyterians claimed to have more members.

By 1837 affairs had reached a bitter deadlock and the popular leaders (William Lyon Mackenzie in Upper Canada and Louis Joseph Papineau in Lower Canada) decided to use force. Although some fighting took place around Montreal and Toronto, the mass of the people remained passive. The rebels were easily defeated and the leaders fled to the United States. The British government responded by sending out Lord Durham as governor-general of all the Canadian provinces, with sweeping powers for administration and investigation.

Durham remained in Canada only five months, but he made full use of his time by hearing all shades of opinion in all the provinces. On his return he submitted the historic report that constitutes a landmark in the evolution of the British Empire. Apart from his recommendation that the two Canadas be reunited once more, his great contribution was the radical proposal for granting "responsible government" to the colonies:

> The wisdom of adopting the true principle of representative government and facilitating the management of public affairs by entrusting it to persons who have the confidence of the representative body has never been recognized in the government of the North American colonies. . . . I know not how it is possible to secure . . . harmony in any other way than by administering the government on those principles which have been found perfectly efficacious in Great Britain. . . . But the Crown must submit to the necessary consequences of representative institutions; and if it has to carry on the government in unison with a representative body, it must consent to carry it on by means of those in whom that representative body has confidence.[2]

Lord Durham meant by responsible or representative government that the traditional conflict between imperial authority and colonial self-government be resolved in favor of the latter. He was ready to grant colonial assemblies as much authority as was enjoyed by the British parliament, though with certain reservations: The imperial government would retain control of foreign relations, regulation of trade, disposal of public lands, and determination of colonial constitutions.

If this daring and unprecedented recommendation had been proposed and adopted earlier, the American colonies probably would never have revolted. Even in 1839, when the report was submitted, it was widely attacked as a utopian document that would surely undermine the Empire. But the pressure of further events soon forced British statesmen to try out Lord Durham's novel principle. The test was made cautiously and tentatively, but it proved an immediate success. Responsible government was then extended to other colonies, with equal benefit. And so Lord Durham's concept provided the basis on which the British Commonwealth was to be organized during the decades following the ill-fated Canadian rebellions. This is the historic significance of the rebellions and of the memorable report they inspired.

National Period

Once the former European colonies had won independence or autonomy, they proceeded to develop individual political institutions and practices that varied widely, depending on such factors as geographic background and past experiences during the colonial period.

UNITED STATES. The Articles of Confederation of 1777 constituted the first document prepared for the governing of the new United States. It was the work of liberals who were convinced that tyranny and centralization were indissolubly linked, and that popular liberties could best be preserved by dispersing power. Accordingly, the creators of the Confederation allowed the central government jurisdiction over purely national affairs, and left all other matters to state control. Article 2 provided that "Each state retains its sovereignty, freedom and independence, and every Power, Jurisdiction and right, which is not by this confederation expressly delegated to the United States, in Congress assembled."

Such an arrangement did not give the national government enough authority over the states or individuals to keep them under control. This became clear during the depression of 1785–1787, when the federal government found there was little it could do to help. In some regions the unemployed organized marches on the state capitals to secure relief by force (Shays' Rebellion of 1787 in Massachusetts). In other states, where the lower classes gained control of the legislatures, laws were passed to ease debtors' burdens. These developments convinced the conservative men of property that a strong central government was needed to keep "mobocracy" in check. All this provided the background for the Constitutional Convention that met in Independence Hall, Philadelphia, on May 25, 1787.

The document that emerged from Constitution Hall was carefully designed to curb popular democracy. Its chief characteristic was an elaborate system of checks and balances. There were to be four separate units of government —a House of Representatives, a Senate, a President, and a Supreme Court— chosen by distinct methods serving different terms of office. The elective House of Representatives was controlled by several devices: suffrage restrictions, a bicameral system that provided a Senate to check an over-impetuous House, a presidential veto that Congress could override with only a two-thirds veto of each house, and a Supreme Court with judicial review power over Congress. When the framers ended their sixteen weeks of debate on September 17, 1787 and adjourned to the City Tavern for a last dinner together, they had every reason to view with pride the product of their labors. The Constitution welded together thirteen states to form the first durable federal government in the world's history.

The framers provided that the new Constitution would go into operation as soon as conventions in nine of the states acted favorably upon it. The choice of delegates to these conventions occasioned the first national political campaign in American history. On one side were the so-called Federalists: the wealthy merchants, lawyers, and landowners who stood to gain the most from the new frame of government. On the other side were the opponents of the Constitution—small farmers, workers, and artisans who wanted nothing to do with a document that left them little political power. The latter constituted the majority of the population but were defeated because they were scattered, disorganized, and unprepared. The Constitution was ratified after a bitter contest, and the first President and Congress were elected in the fall of 1788.

Not until April 30, 1789 did enough congressmen straggle into New York to inaugurate George Washington, the unanimous choice of the electoral college for first President of the United States. Staggering problems faced these pioneering officeholders: no bureaucracy, no funds or revenue system, and no precedents on which to base the new government were available. Yet stabili-

396

zation took a surprisingly short time, and the federal government was soon functioning. The able leadership of President Washington, the lifting of the depression that had plagued the country during the postwar years, and the Constitution itself all aided in making the system work. Although the Constitution provided for strong national leadership, it was, at the same time, elastic enough to adjust to changing times and conditions. An early example of this was the adoption in 1791 of a Bill of Rights, despite the opposition of most of the well-to-do. A number of privileges for citizens were spelled out by the Bill, including free speech, freedom of religion and assembly, freedom of the press, and right to counsel.

One of the unique contributions of the Founding Fathers was their solution for the difficult problem of federalism. They carefully distributed governmental power between national and state governments in such a way as to minimize competition for authority. If issues arose anyway, provision was made for adjudication by an independent court system. In fact, one of the first acts of Congress under the new Constitution was to pass a Judiciary Act spelling out clearly the functions and the authority of federal courts. The Northwest Ordinance of 1787 provided that new states, identical in all legal respects with the old, except for the exclusion of slavery, should be formed in the territories north of the Ohio River. This ensured that the western lands, as they qualified for statehood, would join the federal union under the same principle and conditions. Under these circumstances the United States steadily extended its frontiers westward from the Alleghenies to the Pacific. Vast territories were acquired by various means: the Mississippi Valley by the Louisiana Purchase, from France; the Southwest by conquest and purchase, from Mexico; the Northwest by negotiation with Britain; and Alaska by purchase, from Russia. Out of these new lands were carved a succession of states, mounting finally to the fifty that comprise the present-day United States of America.

LATIN AMERICA. Political developments in Latin America during the national period were very different from those in the United States. The trend in Latin America was toward political fragmentation rather than unification. Mountain and jungle barriers separated one region from another, and lack of communication facilities meant that the regions often had closer contact with Europe than they did with each other. Fragmentation was also promoted by the centuries of isolation under Spain, which fostered separatist tendencies. And the personal ambitions of individual leaders who preferred prominence in a small state to obscurity in a large union must also be taken into account. The original eight Spanish colonies have now become no fewer than eighteen separate countries: The old Viceroyalty of the United Provinces of the Rio de la Plata has become the separate republics of Argentina, Paraguay, Bolivia, and Uraguay; the former Viceroyalty of New Granada has become the countries of Columbia, Ecuador, Venezuela, and Panama; the Captaincy-General of Guatemala has been divided into the separate states of Guatemala, Costa Rica, El Salvador, Honduras, and Nicaragua.

The chronic instability reflected in the frequent overthrow of governments by military coup is another characteristic of Latin American politics in the national period. By contrast, the United States has retained the Constitution of 1787 to the present day, albeit with numerous amendments. In addition, the United States has enjoyed relative political stability during most of its history; usually two parties have succeeded each other in office on the basis of the returns of regular elections. In Latin America, on the other hand, 20 republics have adopted since independence a total of 186 constitutions, or an average of 9.3 each. The rise and fall of governments has been much more frequent. Indeed the Brazilian Emperor Dom Pedro II (1831–1889) is said to have remarked when he visited the Philadelphia Exposition in 1876 that Latin America had more revolutions per minute than many of the new machines he saw on display.

However, almost all these Latin American "revolutions" are revolutions in name only. A true revolution is one that produces a fundamental change in a system, a basic reorganization of the social and political order. Most of the so-called "revolutions" in Latin America simply involve the replacement of one military dictator by another without fundamental changes in the existing order. This intervention of the military in political affairs arises partly from the sharp class distinctions and the political apathy or exclusion of the masses in many of the Latin American states, and has enabled a handful of wealthy landowners and high military officers to conduct politics like a game. A procession of military and civilian leaders have succeeded each other, with little attention being paid to the wishes of the people or to the needs of the countries involved. It is not surprising that over 80 per cent of the presidents of Peru have been military men, and that the students in the military schools in Ecuador are taught that "the last step in a military career is the Presidency of the Republic." [3]

CANADA.   In contrast to Latin America and the United States, the British possessions during the nineteenth century gradually won self-government while preserving the imperial tie. The basis of this unique evolution, as noted earlier, was the principle of responsible government propounded by Lord Durham in 1839. Too novel and radical a concept to accept at once, the British government did act promptly on his recommendation that the two Canadas be reunited. The Canada Act, which came into force in 1841, provided for a united Canadian legislature consisting of a legislative council appointed for life by the governor-general, and an assembly elected on a fairly wide franchise. The executive ministers were to be selected by the governor-general, which left it open to him to appoint those belonging to the majority party in the assembly, and thus to establish responsible government.

For a few years the British government hesitated to take the plunge. In 1839 the Colonial Secretary, Lord John Russell, pointed out why he considered responsible government impractical: "It may happen that the Governor receives at one and the same time instructions from the Queen, and advice from his executive council, totally at variance with each other. If he is to obey his instructions from England, the parallel of constitutional responsibility entirely fails; if, on the other hand, he is to follow the advice of his council, he is no longer a subordinate officer, but an independent sovereign. . . . I thus see insuperable objections to the adoption of the principle [of responsible government]." The way out of this impasse, stated Lord Russell, was for each side "to exercise a wise moderation. The Governor must only oppose the wishes of the Assembly where the honour of the Crown, or the interests of the empire are deeply concerned; and the Assembly must be ready to modify some of its measures for the sake of harmony, and from a reverent attachment to the authority of Great Britain." [4]

Such a compromise course proved impractical in practice and one governor after another failed to stifle the demand for full responsibility. In 1846 a new Colonial Secretary, Lord Grey, perceived that it was impossible to stop short of what Durham had advocated. In his instructions to the governor of Nova Scotia he declared boldly that ". . . it is impossible to allow the Legislative Council to obstruct permanently the passing of measures called for by public opinion, and sent up by the popular branch of the Legislature. . . . It cannot be too distinctly acknowledged that it is neither possible nor desirable to carry on the government of any of the British provinces in North America in opposition to the opinion of the inhabitants." [5]

And so responsible government was applied first in Nova Scotia and immediately thereafter in Canada, resulting in a triumphant vindication of Lord Durham's foresight. After a few years of administration by responsible government, the governor of Canada concluded: "I have been possessed with the idea that it is possible to maintain on this soil of North America, and in the face of Republican America, British connection and British institutions, if you give the latter freely and trustingly. Faith, when it is sincere, is always catching. . . ." [6] The most striking tribute was paid by William Lyon Mackenzie, leader of the 1837 rebellion. Returning on pardon after ten years of exile, he observed: "Had I seen things in 1837 as I do in 1848, I would have shuddered at the very idea of revolt, no matter what our wrongs might have been." [7]

In this manner a complete revolution was inaugurated in the relations between England and her North American colonies. And because the principle of responsible government was extended to other colonies, the British Empire was transformed into the durable Commonwealth that is still flourishing today.

Further major political development in Canada—the achievement of Confederation in 1867—was necessary because the Maritime Provinces, and even the reunited province of Canada, were too sparsely populated to effectively stand alone. Furthermore, the vast Canadian West, with its unexplored resources, was waiting to be developed, and this was Canada's responsibility. The conclusion of the Civil War in the United States was followed by spread-eagle oratory on the part of American super-patriots who covetously eyed the British colonies to the north, so unity promised military security as well as economic advantages. After surprisingly short discussion the Canadian statesmen agreed on the terms of union, and the Dominion of Canada was created by the passage of the British North America Act on July 1, 1867. During the following decades the Dominion extended its domain westward to the Pacific after the manner of the United States. Manitoba became a province in 1870, British Columbia in 1871, and Alberta and Saskatchewan in 1905.

AUSTRALIA AND NEW ZEALAND. Meanwhile, similar developments were taking place in other parts of the Empire settled by Europeans. The colonization of Australia began in 1787 when an expedition arrived from England with 750 convicts and 250 guards. With the loss of the Thirteen Colonies, Australia had been selected as the new dumping ground for convicts. By 1793 free settlers began to arrive, and colonies were established in what are now Queensland, Victoria, South Australia, Tasmania, and even distant Western Australia.

At the same time bands of whalers, sealers, and traders made their way even further afield to the islands of New Zealand, and by 1792 they were arriving frequently, despite the native Maoris, a Polynesian people who were much more advanced and militant than the primitive Australian aborigines. By 1839 there were 2,000 settlers, and London formally proclaimed New Zealand as British territory. A steady stream of colonists arrived from Britain during the following decades, primarily because of the activities of Edward Gibbon Wakefield, an energetic promoter who founded land settlement companies and sent out a considerable number of settlers to both Australia and New Zealand.

By the middle of the nineteenth century a string of settlements had taken root along much of the coast line of Australia and New Zealand, and as they grew more populous and stable, they began to demand control of their own affairs. Agitation for self-government became increasingly frequent, as it had earlier in Canada, but the Canadian precedent now served as a model that eased the way for the Pacific colonies. In 1850 the British parliament passed the Australian Colonies Government Act granting the colonies the right to constitute their own legislatures, fix the franchise, alter their constitutions, and determine their own tariffs, all subject to royal confirmation. But confirmation was forthcoming, in accordance with the procedure tested and proven in Canada. Likewise, in New Zealand a constitution was granted in 1852 that set up six provinces with larger powers of local government, and a general assembly for local purposes. Four years later responsible government was formally sanctioned in New Zealand.

The final task of unifying the six widely separated Australian settlements into a federation was carried out more leisurely in Australia than it had been in Canada because the pressure of an expansionist neighbor was missing. But by the end of the century even isolated Australia was feeling the pull of outside influences. Foreign nations were annexing Pacific islands that Australians regarded as being within their security zone. In addition, the problem of Asiatic immigration was considered a threat to white supremacy in Australia; consequently, a referendum in 1899 returned a majority in every colony in favor of federation. A bill was passed by the British Parliament in 1900, and on January 1, 1901 the Commonwealth of Australia formally took its place in the family of nations.

SOUTH AFRICA. The colony of South Africa, as noted earlier, was established by the Dutch but came under British rule in 1814. The Dutch farmers, or Boers as they called themselves, were a hard-bitten, intractible lot who wanted only to be left alone to pasture their herds on vast interior tracts, and to rule over their families and native slaves like patriarchs of old. When the British interfered with their treatment of the natives the Boers started on their Great Trek of 1836. Some settled in the country beyond the Orange River while others pushed on beyond the Vaal. But the British continued to claim dominion over them, and planted a colony of English settlers at Natal on the east coast.

Cape Colony obtained representative institutions in 1853, although responsible government was withheld until 1872; Natal did not reach the same stage until 1893. In both cases the delay was largely due to the preponderance of natives, whose treatment was a matter of concern to the imperial government. In addition, continual friction existed between the two white peoples, the Boers and the English. At one point it seemed that the problem had been solved by the Convention of Bloemfontein (1854) by which the British accepted the Orange River as their northern frontier, and recognized the independence of the Boer republics of the Orange Free State and the Transvaal. But in 1871 diamonds were found at Kimberley to the north of the Orange River, and by 1890 some six tons of diamonds were mined, valued at £39 million. Equally important was the discovery of gold in southern Transvaal in 1886. Within four years 450 companies had been organized with capital totaling £11 million.

Such great wealth naturally attracted hordes of miners from all over the world, and this in turn caused complications that rendered obsolete the Bloemfontein Convention. On the one hand the Boers resented the intruders and sought to restrict their privileges, while on the other hand the British government was being strongly pressured to annex the rich mineral territories despite the Bloemfontein commitment. The most vigorous advocate of expansionism was the legendary Cecil Rhodes who began his career as a sickly immigrant and ended it as a multimillionaire exponent of imperialism. Like the earlier conquistadors, he amassed great wealth with single-minded ruthlessness, first in the diamond fields and then in the gold mines. But wealth for Rhodes was not an end in itself; it was the means to a greater goal—the aggrandizement of the British Empire. "That's my dream—all English," he would say when he was a mere youth at Kimberley, waving his hand comprehensively northward toward the vast interior of Africa.

Having made his fortune, he entered politics, became premier of Cape Colony, and then proceeded to scheme and work for the realization of his dream. Because the London governments vacillated, some accepting Rhodes's plans and others strongly opposing them, Rhodes decided to force the issue by violent methods. In 1895 he financed a revolution against Paul Kruger, President of the Transvaal, and organized a raid into the Transvaal under his friend Dr. L. S. Jameson. Both the revolution and the raid failed, and Rhodes was forced to resign as premier. But these incidents further embittered British-Boer relations until finally, in 1899, full-scale war broke out.

The Boers resorted to guerrilla tactics, which prolonged the war for three years and compelled the British to mobilize 300,000 troops against the 60,000 to 75,000 Boers. Eventually the Boers had to sign the Treaty of Vereeniging (1902) accepting British sovereignty, but in return they were promised representative institutions as soon as circumstances should permit. At first the British hesitated to confer full responsibility on a people who had so recently been fighting for full independence, but the new Liberal government that took office in 1905 decided on a policy of conciliation and equality. Accordingly, in 1907 both the Transvaal and the Orange River Colony were granted constitutions providing for full responsible government. The following year these two colonies, together with Cape Colony and Natal, began negotiations for a union. A draft constitution was agreed upon, and the British parliament incorporated it into the South Africa Act of 1909. The following year the Act came into effect and the Union of South Africa became a member of the self-governing British communities.

CONCLUSION. It is apparent that a great variety of political institutions and practices were developed by Europeans in their overseas settlements. The differences are so marked that a Canadian or Australian or New Zealand political leader would have been quite lost if he had found himself at the head of an American political party with its precarious balance of sectional interests, nationality blocs, and big city machines. He would have been even more bewildered by Latin American politics and their unceasing succession of constitutions and caudillos. Yet beneath these obvious differences certain underlying similarities stem from the common European origin of all these political systems. This common origin explains the similarity in law codes: Anglo-Saxon law in the United States and the British Dominions, Roman law in Latin America and Quebec—and it also explains the commitment to constitutionalism, despite the diversity in the methods of observing or evading the commitment.

III. ECONOMIC EUROPEANIZATION

Colonial Period

Europeanization prevailed as much in the economic as in the political field. So far as the European powers were concerned, their economic objectives and methods were basically the same at the outset. All believed in the mercan tilist doctrine of subordinating colonial economies to those of the mother countries. The following instructions sent from London to Governor Murray in Quebec in 1763 were in no way different from the countless other instructions on this subject despatched from Paris or Madrid or Lisbon:

> . . . it is Our Express Will and Pleasure, that you do not, upon any Pretence whatever, upon pain of Our highest Displeasure, give your Assent to any Law or Laws for setting up any Manufactures and carrying on any Trades, which are hurtful and prejudicial to this Kingdom; and that You do use your utmost Endeavours to discourage, discountenance and restrain any Attempts which may be made to set up such Manufactures, or establish any such Trades.[8]

Despite this common mercantilist background, the various European settlements soon developed distinctive economies that differed in many respects from each other as well as from those in Europe. We shall see that this diversity was produced by several factors, including differences in the economic development of the mother countries and in the natural and human resources in the colonies.

LATIN AMERICA. One of the most important single factors affecting the economic development of Latin America was the existence of relatively dense and settled native populations. It is true that in large areas such as northern

Mexico and Argentina the Indians were neither numerous nor settled; in those regions the process of economic development was the same as in the United States—protracted Indian wars followed by extermination or relocation of the natives, and their replacement by mass immigration from Europe. But this did not take place in Latin America until the nineteenth century. In the earlier colonial period, the Spaniards were attracted to the Aztec and Inca lands where a sedentary native population was available for exploitation. These lands were divided by the Spanish conquerors into large estates or *encomiendas*. The Indians on these estates lived and worked as serfs, providing a vast reservoir of free labor that affected profoundly and permanently the economic evolution of Latin America.

Immigration from Europe was limited largely to officials, churchmen, soldiers, and artisans because of the supply of native labor. The free labor supply was also responsible for the early development of a one-crop economy—the single crop being precious metals. In 1747, for example, when the colonial economy had been fully organized, the American colonies sent to Spain 34.6 million pesos in gold, silver, and precious stones, compared with less than 4 million pesos worth of all other products. Of course not all the Indians worked in mines, but almost all those who did not were employed in producing foodstuffs for their masters, though not for world trade. Thus Latin America's economy was extraordinarily static. It consisted largely of self-sufficient haciendas and mines whose product was shipped to Spain, buried in treasure vaults, or worked into church ornaments. Needless to say, technological progress was quite superfluous; the abundance of manpower obviated any need for the gadgets being introduced in the English colonies to the north.

THIRTEEN COLONIES AND NEW FRANCE. The economic history of the Thirteen Colonies and of New France was basically different from that of Latin America because a native labor supply and precious metals were lacking. This situation compelled the English and French settlers to do their own work and to develop from the available natural resources some type of viable economy. Both the Paris and London governments attempted from the beginning to mold the economic growth of their colonies along traditional lines. On the banks of the St. Lawrence a seignorial system was established that was patterned after the feudalism of France. The habitant was required to pay to his seignior dues in money and labor. Likewise, in the Thirteen Colonies attempts were made to impose various rigid economic systems. Companies similar to modern corporations settled Virginia and Massachusetts, with money being raised from stockholders on the promise of profits from their investments. The Virginia Company started out to establish an economic system under which no one who came to Virginia owned land privately and everyone worked for the company. All goods produced were put into a common storehouse and people could draw only what they needed from this company store.

These regulations and restrictions proved unenforceable in both the French and English colonies, and the reason in both cases was the abundance of land to which a dissatisfied settler could turn. These colonies could not depend upon the mother country for the award of feudal *encomienda* with an abundant supply of native labor, as did Latin America. The habitant did pay dues to the seignior, but they were much lighter than those customary in France.

The church tried to collect as tithe one-thirteenth of the habitant's produce, but had to settle for only half of that proportion. And every effort of the authorities to prevent young men from running off and becoming coureurs de bois failed before the lure of the wilderness and the lucrative fur trade. So New France developed along its own lines, with most of the population engaged in self-sufficient agriculture, and a minority carrying on the fur trade, which produced the only important export commodity.

Similarly, in the Thirteen Colonies the companies were not able for long to keep control over their settlers. A governor in Virginia reported that when he arrived he found the people "engaged in their usual activities, bowling in the streets." Strengthened by the fact that land was more plentiful than labor, the English colonists worked out their own economic institutions and practices. The majority necessarily turned to agriculture, with geography determining the type and the success of the farming.

In the warm, rich, southern colonies, settlers found their best crops were tobacco, rice, and indigo. In the middle colonies—Pennsylvania, New Jersey, Delaware—grain grew well and this area quickly became the breadbasket of the colonies. Most of New England also turned to agriculture, but the long winters and rocky soil were a severe handicap. So they resorted to other occupations, mainly fishing, shipping, and manufacturing.

We see, then, that the economy of the Thirteen Colonies was much more diversified than that of Latin America, and it was more dynamic because native laborers, held down to a level of bare subsistence, did not form its basis. In place of Indian serfs who toiled century after century, using the same tools and techniques, there were in the Thirteen Colonies clipper ships sailing the seven seas, a string of factories along the river fall line, and individual frontiersmen who, with rifle and ax, won homesteads in the wilderness and steadily pushed westward the line of settlement.

Revolutionary Period

THIRTEEN COLONIES. Precisely because the economy of the Thirteen Colonies was so dynamic, it created difficulties with the mother country, making it hard to control and to subordinate to England's own economic interests. New England's manufacturing and shipping ran afoul of mercantilist legislation such as the Navigation Laws, and after the liquidation of the French colonies in 1763, the British government began to crack down on infractions of their decrees. In order to avoid trouble with the Indians, they forbade settlers to cross the Appalachians into the Ohio Valley. The colonists protested loudly and repeatedly against these restrictions, and eventually they resorted to arms. The American Revolution was a struggle for economic as well as political independence.

The war itself caused colonial manufacturing to grow tremendously in order to meet the needs of the American armies as well as of the civilians who formerly had been supplied by the British. American shipping, expanded and converted into a make-shift navy during the Revolution, continued in its expanded form after the winning of independence. Yankee sea captains opened a highly profitable trade with California and with China only a few years after the peace treaty. The Revolution profoundly affected agriculture, in which the great majority were still engaged. State legislation now abolished

404

obsolete systems of land tenure embodied in the laws of primogeniture and entail that were designed to perpetuate a landed aristocracy. Large estates, especially in the South, were divided amongst the farmers, and the lands west of the Appalachians were opened to the frontiersmen for settlement. The dynamic American economy was freed in these various ways for rapid expansion overland and overseas.

LATIN AMERICA. Economic grievances contributed to the revolutions in the Spanish as well as the English colonies. Conflict existed between the Spaniards born in the colonies (the creoles) and those born in Spain (the peninsulares); the latter were favored in appointments to government positions and in the right to enter certain professions. Consequently, the revolutionary movements in many colonies were organized and led by creoles who wished to end this discrimination. Equally important in stimulating revolution was Spain's mercantilist legislation limiting colonial trade with the mother country. This was especially burdensome because Spain could neither absorb the new materials produced in the colonies, nor provide in return the needed manufactured goods as cheaply and as well made as could England and other European countries. And so an immense contraband trade developed, particularly during the years when Spain was locked in desperate struggle with Napoleonic France and could not maintain normal economic relations with her colonies. When the war ended and Spain attempted to reimpose her trade restrictions, the colonists finally took up arms in protest. They were encouraged and assisted by the British, who had built up a lucrative trade with Spanish America. The following impassioned appeal made in 1809 by a spokesman for Argentine cattlemen reflects the economic motives behind revolution in Latin America:

> Is it just that the fruits of our agricultural labours should be lost, because the unfortunate provinces of Spain can no longer consume them? Is it just that the abundant productions of the country should rot in our magazines, because the navy of Spain is too weak to export them? . . . Is it just, that, when the subjects of a friendly and generous nation present themselves to our ports, and offer us, at a cheap rate, the merchandize of which we are in want, and with which Spain cannot supply us, we should reject the proposal, and convert, by so doing, their good intentions to the exclusive advantage of a few European merchants, who, by means of a contraband trade, render themselves masters of the whole imports of the country? [9]

The winning of independence did not stimulate economic growth in Latin America as it did in the United States, basically because the Latin American economy continued to be dominated by mines and haciendas manned by Indians laboring at subsistence level. Free trade did bring greater economic activity along the coasts, but this had little impact on the static interior. Lacking capital, technological skills, and a healthy socioeconomic structure, independent Latin America held a stagnant position in the world economy.

BRITISH COLONIES. Economic grievances contributed to the outbreak of the Canadian Rebellions in 1837, an outstanding factor of which was the

The driving of the golden spike to signalize the completion of the Main Line of the Canadian Pacific, November 7, 1885. (The Public Archives of Canada)

popular resentment against the Crown and Clergy Reserves, each amounting to one-seventh of the total lands of the province. These huge tracts were set aside to defray the expenses of the government and of the established Anglican Church. They were bitterly resented because they blocked the progress of settlement and because only a minority of the population adhered to the endowed church. In addition, a small privileged group known as the Family Compact enjoyed the same official favors in Canada as the peninsulares did in Latin America. Furthermore, the Canadian provinces were not as prosperous as the American states across the border, and many held British rule responsible for the economic discrepancy. The following charge levelled by the rebel leader William Lyon Mackenzie makes this apparent:

> Suppose, for instance, that the Mississippi River had been the western boundary of Upper Canada. What would Michigan, Indiana, Illinois or the Wisconsin Territories have been at present? Would they, in the short space of a few years, have been swarming with hundreds of thousands of inhabitants actuated by the industry, public spirit and enter-

406

prise characteristic of the people of the Western States? Or would they have been held back, and their energies crippled by the same accursed drag chains which have hitherto withered the prospects, and retarded the progress of our own misgoverned Province? [10]

Such was the sentiment that culminated in the Rebellions of 1837. Since these proved futile, no radical reform took place in Canada during the following years. Instead, the country developed modestly and quietly: Population grew steadily and new districts were opened for settlement; roads and canals were built; a few industries were started to meet local needs—sawmills to supply lumber for building, gristmills to provide flour, carding and woolen mills to prepare the wool for spinning and to weave it into cloth, and cheese factories to process the farmers' surplus milk. Yet Canada did not have the rich and varied resources of the republic to the south, so that the disparity in the rate of economic development continued after 1837 as it had before.

National Period

The process of economic Europeanization was most thorough and most spectacular during this national period when most of the overseas colonies

An undated lithograph from the collection of the Chicago Historical Society.

settled by Europeans had won their independence. The unprecedented economic growth and expansionism of Europe during those years basically explains this paradox. As noted earlier, this was the period of mass migration from Europe, and this migration meant not only ethnic Europeanization but also stronger economic ties between Europe and overseas settlements. Scientific and technological advances made it possible for Europe to provide the railways, steamships, machine guns, and agricultural machinery that were essential for the conquest and effective exploitation of vast continents. In addition to exporting the capital necessary to finance these costly operations, Europe afforded a market for the flood of foodstuffs and industrial raw materials from overseas. These developments all added up to an unparalleled economic impact by Europe upon the rest of the globe, and especially upon those areas settled by European emigrants.

UNITED STATES. The American economy expanded at a fast rate between the Revolution and the Civil War. This was especially true of industry following the adoption of a protective tariff in 1816. In the cotton industry the number of spindles rose from 87,000 in 1810 to 250,000 in 1820, and to over 2,000,000 by 1860. The iron industry spread westward from the eastern seaboard, reaching Lake Superior by 1860. At the same time, roads were improved and canals and railroads were constructed. Railroad mileage rose from nothing in 1830 to over 30,000 by 1860.

It was during the decades following the Civil War, however, that the United States experienced its most spectacular economic growth. The Civil War itself stimulated a vast industrial expansion, and this continued after the War with the opening of the West and the building of transcontinental railroads. Great quantities of foodstuffs and various raw materials were hauled by railroads and steamships to the burgeoning urban centers of eastern United States and western Europe. At the same time, the millions of immigrants provided an abundant supply of cheap labor and further expanded the domestic market for American industrialists and farmers. The net result was that the United States economy spurted ahead in the second half of the nineteenth century at a rate unequaled to that time: In 1860 the United States was ranked fourth in the industrial nations of the world; by 1894 it was the first. Between 1860 and 1900 the number of industrial establishments increased three times, the number of industrial wage earners four times, the value of manufactured products seven times, and the amount of capital invested in industry nine times. By 1890 the value of manufactured goods equaled that of agricultural products, and by 1900 it was worth twice as much. In 1860 manufacturing was still largely concentrated on the eastern seaboard, but by 1900 it had spread to the Great Lakes and also to many portions of the South and West.

LATIN AMERICA. For several decades after the winning of its independence, Latin America, as noted above, remained economically stagnant; however, after the mid-nineteenth century, rapid strides began to be made. Europe's mounting demand for foodstuffs such as meat, coffee, sugar, and cocoa, and for industrial commodities such as minerals, lumber, wool, and hides was as important as its role in building railroads, steamships, and refrigerated ships, and in providing the capital necessary for such equipment. The statistics in Table 4 concerning British trade with, and investments in, Argentina illustrate this.

TABLE 4.   Anglo-Argentine Trade and Investment
(in thousands of pounds)

Year	British imports from Argentina	British exports to Argentina	British capital in Argentina
1857	1,574	1,287	2,605
1865	1,014	1,951	5,375
1874	1,271	3,128	23,060
1885	1,879	4,660	45,602
1900	13,080	7,143	189,040
1910	28,933	19,120	291,110

Source: F. S. Ferns, *Britain and Argentina in the Nineteenth Century* (Oxford: Clarendon, 1960), pp. 492–93.

Similar statistics may be presented for other Latin American countries such as Chile with its nitrate and copper, Mexico with its gold and silver, Brazil with its coffee and rubber, and Bolivia with its tin. And so Latin America entered the world economy as it had never done before. On the other hand, this economic growth was in many respects one-sided and unhealthy. Most Latin American countries experienced booms in one or two commodities, while the rest of their economies remained static. The semifeudal hacienda system of land tenure and labor relations remained virtually unchanged, so the mass of people continued to exist as peons at subsistence level. And foreign economies penetrated and controlled most of the profitable enterprises, whether railways, public utilities, or mining properties. The benefits of this economic expansion, instead of being widely diffused as they were in the United States, accrued to a small number of foreign and native landlords, merchants, and concessionaires, producing a social friction and political instability that has persisted to the present.

BRITISH DOMINIONS.   Like Latin America, the British Dominions also lagged behind the United States in rate of economic growth. The cause in this case, however, was not a semifeudal social system but rather inferior natural resources compared to those of the United States. Canada, for example, does possess abundant resources, but it was not profitable to exploit them until the mid-twentieth century when air transportation made them accessible, and when more readily available resources in the United States had been depleted. In the nineteenth century, however, Canada was in no position to compete with her prosperous neighbor. The barren Laurentian Plateau was an insuperable obstacle to the progress of settlement. Canada had no counterpart to the fertile Midwest, the cotton South, and the industrialized East, each supplementing and stimulating the other. Instead, the Canadian settler faced 1,500 miles of muskeg to the west and arctic wasteland to the north, leaving him no choice but to cross over to the American states, which he did in droves. The pull of the American magnet was such that in the decade 1881–1891, when the total population of Canada was less than five million, over one million crossed over to the United States. It is estimated that two young people who married in Canada fifty years ago would today have half their descendants living in the United States.

409

The other British dominions were even less favorably endowed than Canada. Australia, New Zealand, and South Africa are all located in the Southern Hemisphere; all are far removed from the great population and industrial centers of Western Europe. It makes a good deal of difference that Perth is 9,500 miles from London and Capetown is 6,500, compared to the 3,000 miles between New York and Liverpool. In addition, these three dominions do not approach the United States in the richness and diversity of their resources. This is true even of Australia, which is as large as continental United States without Alaska. Yet Australia is largely arid, its rivers are of little use for irrigation, and it lacks forests, oil deposits, and base metals.

These drawbacks are all relative to the uniquely endowed United States. The British Dominions still had plentiful resources for substantial economic development. In Canada the first transcontinental railroad was completed in 1885, and was followed by two more in 1915. The railroads, together with heavy immigration, speeded the settlement of the three prairie provinces of Alberta, Saskatchewan, and Manitoba. Between 1906 and 1911 their populations doubled. Industry also grew considerably, especially after the adoption of the protectionist "National Policy" in 1878.

In Australia sheep raising was the mainstay of the economy for a long time. The number of sheep rose precipitously from 200,000 in 1820 to 20 million in 1860 and 100 million by 1890. The country was as dependent on this industry as the American South was on cotton. A gradual diversification of industry included sugar cane cultivation in Queensland and, more important, gold mining (with the great gold rush of the 1850's). In the decade 1851–1860 Australia produced 39 per cent of the world's output of gold (compared to the 41 per cent produced in the United States), and the population of the country jumped from 431,000 in 1841 to 1,140,000 in 1860 (compared to 31,400,000 in the United States in the latter year).

New Zealand, like Australia, developed an economy dependent on the European market. It concentrated largely on sheep raising and dairy farming, and exported mostly wool, beef, cheese, and butter.

The economy of South Africa was based upon the diamond mines opened at Kimberley in 1870 and the gold fields discovered at the Witwatersrand in 1886. In addition, some tobacco, sugar, tea, and other tropical produce were exported in modest quantities by 1914.

CONCLUSION. The national period to 1914 was a time of rapid economic growth in the Americas and the British Dominions, but one should bear in mind that this was the product of economic Europeanization. It was Europe that provided in large part the manpower, the capital, the technology, and the markets.* Europe's contributions were as vital for the independent countries as for the dominions that retained their ties with the mother country. It is perhaps understandable that British capital should have financed the building

---

* See "British Capital in the Americas and the Dominions," EMM, No, 102.

410

of Canada's transcontinental railroads and the development of South Africa's mines. But British capital, and commerce as well, were fully as active in lands where the Union Jack did not fly. After the Thirteen Colonies won their independence, for example, trade with Britain rose steeply instead of declining. In 1765, the last year of normal trade before the Revolution, Britain exported £1,944,114 of goods to the Thirteen Colonies; the corresponding figure for 1784, the first normal postwar year, was £3,679,467. Between 1820 and 1830, 36 per cent of all American exports went to Britain, and 43 per cent of all American imports came from Britain. European capital —mostly British, Dutch, and German—poured into the United States during the nineteenth century, especially in the building of railways. By 1914 total foreign investments amounted to no less than 7.2 billion dollars. And in the comparatively underdeveloped Latin American countries, European investments usually dominated the national economies. As late as 1932 Will Rogers wrote from Buenos Aires: "Englishmen have got this country sewed up tighter than Borah has Idaho."

IV. CULTURAL EUROPEANIZATION

Latin America

Cultural Europeanization inevitably accompanied the ethnic, political, and economic Europeanization, and this was true almost as much of the regions that won independence as of those that remained within the British Commonwealth. In Latin America the predominant cultural pattern is Spanish, with the exception of Portuguese Brazil; this pattern is evident in the Spanish language spoken by the majority of the people, and in the Roman Catholicism they profess. One sees it also in architectural forms such as the patio or courtyard, the barred window, and the house front that is flush with the sidewalk. Town planning, based on the central plaza rather than on the main street, is equally revealing. Much of the clothing is Spanish, including the men's broadrimmed hats of felt or straw, and the women's cloth head coverings—mantilla, head shawl, or decorative towel. In family organization the typical Spanish pattern of male dominance and close supervision of girls, including chaperoned dates, is followed, as is the tendency to regard physical labor as undignified and unsuitable for gentlemen.

Although Latin American culture is basically Spanish or Portuguese, a strong Indian influence prevails, especially in Mexico, Central America, and the northwestern part of South America where the Indians comprise a large percentage of the total population. This influence (see Chapter 9, section V), is evident in cooking, clothing, building materials, and religious practices.

Latin American culture also has a considerable African element, brought over by the millions of slaves imported to work on plantations. This African influence is strongest in the Caribbean area where most of the slaves settled, although examples of their influence, especially music, can be found in most parts of Latin America; here the Negroes contributed their traditional drums.

United States

The culture that developed in the United States was less influenced by the native Indian population than was Latin American culture, the main reason being that the Indians were fewer in number and less advanced. Nevertheless, Indian influence was not altogether negligible: 25 states bear Indian names; at least 300 Indian words are now part of the English language; and many Indian inventions are commonly used, including moccasins, canoes, toboggans, and snowshoes.

Likewise, the United States has been less influenced by African culture than have certain Latin American states in the Caribbean area. Still, the influence here has been considerable; Negroes comprise 10 per cent of the total population of the country compared to the one-half of one per cent comprised of Indians. The chief impact of the Negroes has been in the field of folk culture. One example is their folk stories, such as those popularized by Joel Chandler Harris in the Uncle Remus cycle; Another is their folk music, including so-called spirituals or religious songs, and secular songs such as work songs, prison songs, railroad and steamboat songs, narrative ballads like "Frankie and Johnny" and "John Henry," and the world famous jazz.

Despite these Indian and African elements, American culture is overwhelmingly European in origin, although its European characteristics were drastically modified during the process of transplantation and adaptation. This has been noted by European travelers since colonial days. The question posed in 1782 by the Frenchman Jean Crèvecoeur was a typical one: "What then is the American, this new man?" It is a basic question involving the national character of the American people, and many have sought to answer it, from Crèvecoeur's day to the present.* From the mass of contradictory responses a definite image of "this new man" does emerge.

In a country where unceasing labor had been necessary first to establish the colonies and then to conquer the continent, it was natural for this man to believe that toil was virtuous and idleness sinful. President Theodore Roosevelt expressed this national sentiment when he said, "I pity the creature who doesn't work—at whichever end of the social scale he may be." [11] The fact that the English Who's Who lists hobbies while the American does not is also revealing.

Closely related to the American's belief in social equality was his belief in social mobility. He considered himself as good as the next man, and insisted that all men should be free to rise on the basis of ability and effort rather than of class origin.

Reflecting his farm and frontier background, the American was an inveterate tinkerer, constantly engaged in devising gadgets to speed up the work that had to be done. "Would any but an American," remarked a mid-nineteenth century observer, "have ever invented a milking machine? or a machine to beat eggs? or a machine to black boots, scour knives, pare apples, and do a hundred things that all other peoples have done with their ten fingers from time immemorial?" [12]

* See "What Then is the American, this New Man?" EMM, No. 103.

Where his future was concerned, the "new man" was an optimist: he had a sturdy faith in the inevitability of progress. The same observer who noted the mechanical ingenuity of the Americans also wrote: "Americans are sanguine enough to believe that no evil is without a remedy, if they could only find it, and they see no good reason why they should not try to find remedies for all the evils of life." [13] Often this optimism was expressed in the national love of bragging. Living in a country of great resources and equally great opportunities, Americans found it natural to glorify the future and to talk as though it had already materialized. Frontier humor was based on "tall tales," and the folk heroes were supermen like Paul Bunyon and Pecos Bill.

In the more sophisticated realm of formal arts and letters, the nineteenth century American felt distinctly inferior to his European contemporary—and for very good reasons. He had been too busy taming the wilderness to find time for gentility and aesthetics. Besides, the Puritan tradition placed greater value on hard work and saving of souls than it did on cultivation of the arts. The French traveler Alexis de Tocqueville wrote in 1835, "People who spend every day in the week in making money, and Sunday in going to church, have nothing to invite the Muse of Comedy."

As late as 1820, fully 80 per cent of all books in the United States were imported from Britain, and by 1830 the figure was still as high as 70 per cent. So far as European intellectuals were concerned, American culture was non-existent.* A typical attitude was that of the English critic Sydney Smith who asked rhetorically in 1820: "In the four corners of the globe, who reads an American book? or goes to an American play? or looks at an American picture or statue?" This condescension was generally accepted by the Americans themselves. "All through life," wrote Henry Adams, "one had seen the American on his literary knees to the Europeans." [14]

Accordingly, the nineteenth century Americans earnestly strove to imitate European culture. They went to school in London, Paris, Vienna, and Rome, built Greek temples for public buildings and churches, and imported European musicians and singers to help establish opera houses and orchestras. Some millionaire tycoons sent agents to Europe to buy up "old Masters." Some even purchased castles, which they took down stone by stone and then re-erected in America. As might be expected, such efforts did not impress most European intellectuals; they continued to look down upon Americans as a "whittling, spitting, guessing, reckoning, gambling, slave-beating, dram-drinking people."

Toward the end of the nineteenth century some change in this attitude began to be noticeable. Walt Whitman and Mark Twain were fully and truly American, the latter in particular, with "everything European fallen away, the last shred of feudal culture gone, local and western yet continental." [15] Significant also was the publication in 1888 of James Bryce's appreciative masterpiece, *The American Commonwealth*. As the century closed, European intellectuals were becoming increasingly aware of a growing galaxy of American stars: John Dewey, William James, Oliver Wendell Holmes, Thorstein Veblen, and William Dean Howells. Yet Europe's tutelage remained hard to shake. At the end of the century, Henry Cabot Lodge still could write, "The

---

* See "Europe's Scorn for Nineteenth Century American Culture," *EMM*, No. 104.

first step of an American entering upon a literary career was to pretend to be an Englishman in order that he might win the approval, not of Englishmen, but of his own countrymen." [16]

British Dominions

Europe's cultural influence was stronger in the Dominions than in the United States or Latin America. One reason was the preservation of the imperial bonds, which occasioned more interaction with the mother country. Also, with the exception of South Africa, a much larger percentage of the peoples of the Dominions were of European origin than was the case in the United States and Latin America with their substantial Negro and Indian elements. This does not mean, however, that the Dominions all developed a uniform culture; distinctive local environments created distinctive local cultures.

Canada's cultural development, for example, has been molded by two over-ruling factors: a French Canadian bloc comprising one-third of the total population, and geographic proximity to the United States. The large French Canadian minority has made Canada officially bilingual, as can be seen in the coinage, the paper money, government proclamations, and inscriptions on nationally distributed commodities. More important is the outlook and national role of the French Canadians. In a very real sense they are a people without a mother country. Abandoned by France in 1763, they have been taught by their all-powerful Catholic Church to turn their backs on republican and secular France, and to scorn what they consider to be the commercialism and materialism of the English-speaking Canadians and the Americans. Consequently, their main desire is to be left alone and to preserve their identity in a predominantly Protestant, Anglo-Saxon continent.

Perhaps even more important for Canada is the overwhelming impact of the colossus to the south, whose influence has led not only to the wholesale draining of Canadian manpower, as noted above, but also to a decisive molding of Canadian ways of living and thinking. The average Canadian will be awakened in the morning by an alarm clock of American manufacture, will then brush his teeth with American-made toothpaste and toothbrush, and will shave with shaving cream and razor of American make. One quarter of the news items that he will read in his morning newspaper will deal with the United States. He will drive to work in an American car, enter an American-made elevator in his office building, and work during the day with office equipment that is mostly from the United States. When he returns home he is likely to end the day with an American radio or television program, or an American novel or magazine, or he may decide to drive to his neighborhood theatre to see an American movie.

All this does not mean that Canadian culture is an exact carbon copy of the culture to the south. There are, for example, few resemblances between the Canadian and American versions of political conventions and campaigns, advertising and salesmanship, or law enforcement and court procedures. Nevertheless, a well-known Canadian journalist has concluded that "Canada is a confederation but not a nation." [17] In 1949 the Canadian government appointed a "Royal Commission on National Development in the Arts, Letters and Sciences." The report of this Commission included the following passage:

> American influences on Canadian life to say the least are impressive. There should be no thought of interfering with the liberty of all Canadians to enjoy them. Cultural exchanges are excellent in themselves. They widen the choice of the consumer and provide stimulating competition for the producer. It cannot be denied, however, that a vast and disproportionate amount of material coming from a single alien source may stifle rather than stimulate our own creative effort; and, passively accepted without any standard of comparison, this may weaken critical faculties. We are now spending millions to maintain a national independence which would be nothing but an empty shell without a vigorous and distinctive cultural life.[18]

The cultural development of Australia and New Zealand has been greatly affected by their ethnic homogeneity. These dominions have neither a one-tenth Negro minority, as does the United States, nor a one-third French Catholic minority, as does Canada. Despite considerable non-British immigration since World War II, the population of Australia remains 90 per cent British in origin, and that of New Zealand, 98 per cent. As a result, both dominions maintained exceptionally close cultural ties with the mother country. New Zealanders commonly regarded England as "home" and New Zealand as a place in which to make a living. Australians did not have quite so strong an emotional attachment, partly because of a considerable proportion of Irish immigrants. Yet during World War I Australian troops fought as stoutly as the New Zealanders at Gallipoli and elsewhere. By contrast, in Canada the French Canadians rioted fiercely because they felt no commitment to fight for any cause other than the defense of their own lands.

It is perhaps worth noting that since World War II, Australians and New Zealanders have expressed the same concern about American cultural penetration as Canadians did. The impact of the United States has extended as far as the South Pacific, partly because of heavy American investments made in recent years, and also as an aftermath of the stationing of American troops there during World War II. A young Australian writer Robin Boyd has expressed the alarm of many of his countrymen: "Australia is sinking [culturally] into the Pacific, and a new state is rising which we might call Austerica. . . . Austerica's chief industry is the imitation of the froth on the top of the American soda-fountain drink. Its religion is 'glamor' and the devotees are psychologically displaced persons who picture Heaven as a pool terrace of a Las Vegas hotel." [19]

Conclusion

We have seen that in culture, as in politics and economics, wholesale transplanting of European civilization took place, though with a good deal of modification. This cultural diffusion and adaptation is most strikingly evident in the field of language.* An Englishman who visits Australia, the United States, or Canada can easily understand the variations of his language spoken in those countries, although it is true that in Australia he would be mystified by such words as "aboes" (aborigines), "sheilas" (girls), "galahs" (chatterboxes), and "dills" (fools), and in both Canada and the United States he would soon learn that his petrol, silencer, boot, and demister, have become gas, muffler, trunk, and windshield wiper. He would also find instances where the Canadians have maintained their individuality against both English and American influences. If he asked for a "chesterfield," he would receive a man's coat in England, a pack of cigarettes in the United States, and an over-stuffed sofa in Canada.

Such miscellaneous differences, however, are too often exaggerated at the expense of the underlying, basic similarities. Actually, very few words would cause trouble to the Englishman traveling throughout the widely scattered English speaking world. The same would be true of a Frenchman in Quebec, a Portuguese in Brazil, or a Spaniard in the rest of Latin America. Most of the peculiar usages that are found overseas can be traced back to provincial dialects in the mother country. A Spaniard could find in his own country most of the variations he would encounter abroad, and the same would hold true for an Englishman or a Frenchman.

We may conclude, then, that the cultural Europeanization of the Americas and the British Dominions has been both pervasive and enduring. A European need only visit New York, Mexico City, Montreal, or Melbourne, and then visit Cairo, Delhi, Tokyo, or Peking to sense the reality and the extent of the overseas diffusion of his culture.

SUGGESTED READING

The over-all picture of migrations in modern times is given in W. F. Willcox, *et al., International Migrations* (New York: National Bureau of Economic Research, 1929, 1931), 2 vols.; A. M. Carr-Saunders, *World Population* (London: Oxford Univ., 1936); W. S. and E. S. Woytinsky, *World Population and Production* (New York: Twentieth Century Fund, 1953), Chap. 3; and R. R. Kuczynski, *Population Movements* (Oxford: Clarendon, 1936). For the migration to individual regions, see M. L. Hansen, *The Atlantic Migration, 1607–1860: A History of the Continuing Settlement of the United States* (Cambridge: Harvard Univ., 1940); O. Handlin, ed., *Immigration as a Factor in American History* (Englewood Cliffs, N. J.; Prentice-Hall, 1959); W. D. Forsyth, *The Myth of Open Spaces: Australian, British and World Trends of Population and Migration* (Melbourne: Melbourne Univ., 1942); E. M. O'Brien, *The Foundation of Australia, 1786–1800: A Study in English Criminal Practice and Penal Colonization in the Eighteenth Century* (Sydney: Angus, 1937); and L. G. Reynolds, *The British Immigrant: His Economic and Social Adjustment in Canada* (London: Oxford Univ., 1935). For penetrating interpretations of the above studies, see F. Thistlethwaite, "Migration from Europe Overseas in the Nineteenth and Twentieth Centuries," *Rapports, International Committee of Historical Sciences*

* See "The English Language Overseas," *EMM,* No. 105.

(Stockholm, 1960), V, 32–60; and F. D. Scott, *Emigration and Immigration* (Washington, D. C., Service Center for Teachers of History, 1963), No. 51.

416

The best general survey of the process of Europeanization is by E. Fischer, *The Passing of the European Age* (Cambridge: Harvard Univ., 1948). Much valuable material has been published on this subject in numerous studies of the applicability of Frederick Jackson Turner's frontier hypothesis. Outstanding are F. J. Turner, *The Frontier in American History* (New York: Holt, 1920); R. A. Billington, *Westward Expansion* (New York: Macmillan, 1959), rev. ed.; E. A. Walker, *The Frontier Tradition in South Africa* (London: Oxford Univ., 1930); F. Alexander, *Moving Frontier: An American Theme and its Application to Australian History* (Melbourne: Melbourne Univ., 1947); F. Landon, *Western Ontario and the American Frontier* (Toronto: Ryerson, 1941); G. F. G. Stanley, "Western Canada and the Frontier Thesis," *Canadian Historical Association Report* (1940), 105–17; P. J. Coleman, "The New Zealand Frontier and the Turner Thesis," *Pacific Historical Review,* XXVII (August, 1958), 221–38; P. Sharp, "Three Frontiers: Some Comparative Studies of Canadian, American and Australian Settlements," *Pacific Historical Review,* XXIV (1955), 369–77; and the series of articles in W. D. Wyman and C. B. Kroeber, *The Frontier in Perspective* (Madison: Univ. of Wisconsin, 1957). Finally, see the excellent bibliographical survey in R. A. Billington, *The American Frontier* (Washington: Service Center for Teachers of History, 1958) and the application of the frontier hypothesis to modern world history in W. P. Webb, *The Great Frontier* (Boston: Houghton, 1952).

Other important sources for the Europeanization process are the studies of the comparative history of the Americas: H. E. Bolton, "The Epic of Greater America," *American Historical Review,* XXXVIII (April, 1933), 448–74; "Have the Americas a Common History?" *Canadian Historical Review,* XXIII (June, 1942), 125–56; A. P. Whitaker, *The Western Hemisphere Idea* (Ithaca: Cornell Univ., 1954); and S. Zavala, "A General View of the Colonial History of the New World," *American Historical Review,* LXVI (July, 1961), 913–29.

More specialized works on individual regions are as follows:

LATIN AMERICA. A bibliographical essay by C. Gibson, *The Colonial Period in Latin American History* (Washington: Service Center for Teachers of History, 1958); an imaginative general history by W. L. Schurz, *This New World: The Civilization of Latin America* (New York: Dutton, 1954); an admirable collection of readings in B. Keen, *Readings in Latin American Civilization* (Boston: Houghton, 1955); and important study in economic history in H. S. Ferns, *Britain and Argentina in the Nineteenth Century* (New York: Oxford, 1960); and studies in aspects of cultural history in P. H. Urena, *Literary Currents in Hispanic America* (Cambridge: Harvard Univ., 1945) and J. T. Lanning, *Academic Culture in the Spanish Colonies* (London: Oxford Univ., 1940).

UNITED STATES. The early interpretative analyses of American civilization by Crevecoeur, de Tocqueville, and Bryce have recent counterparts in M. Lerner, *America as a Civilization* (New York: Simon and Schuster, 1957) and the essay by A. M. Schlesinger, "What Then Is the American, This New Man?" *American Historical Review,* XLVIII (January, 1943), 225–44. Recent evaluations by foreign students are D. W. Brogan, *The American Character* (New York: Knopf, 1944) and F. Thistlethwaite, *The Great Experiment* (Cambridge: Cambridge Univ., 1955). On specific topics, see V. L. Parrington, *Main Cur-*

rents in American Thought (New York: Harcourt, 1927–1930), 3 vols.; A. H. Kelly and W. A. Harbison, *The American Constitution* (New York: Norton, 1948); E. C. Kirkland, *A History of American Economic Life,* rev. ed. (New York: Appleton, 1951); H. C. Allen, *Great Britain and the United States: A History of Anglo-American Relations, 1783–1952* (London: Odhams, 1954); R. H. Heindel, *The American Impact on Great Britain* (Philadelphia: Univ. of Pennsylvania, 1940); C. Strout, *The American Image of The Old World* (New York: Harper, 1964); and S. Skard, *The American Myth and the European Mind: American Studies in Europe, 1776–1960* (Philadelphia: Univ. of Pennsylvania, 1961).

BRITISH DOMINIONS. See first the interpretative essay and bibliography by C. F. Mullett, *The British Empire-Commonwealth: Its Themes and Character* (Washington: Service Center for Teachers of History, 1961) and the study of Commonwealth literature by A. L. McLeod, ed. *The Commonwealth Pen* (Ithaca: Cornell Univ., 1961). On Canada there is the survey by R. W. Winks, *Recent Trends and New Literature in Canadian History* (Washington: Service Center for Teachers of History, 1959); the sprightly analysis by J. MacCormac, *Canada: America's Problem* (New York: Viking, 1940); the study of French-Canadianism by M. Wade, ed., *Canadian Dualism* (Toronto: Univ. of Toronto, 1961); H. G. J. Aitken, *The American Economic Impact on Canada* (Durham, N. C.: Duke Univ., 1961); W. L. Morton, *The Canadian Identity* (Madison: Univ. of Wisconsin, 1961); and the invaluable two volumes of *Report,* and *Royal Commission Studies,* of the Royal Commission on National Development in the Arts, Letters, and Sciences (Ottawa: E. Cloutier, 1951). On South Africa, see F. A. Van Jaarsveld, *The Awakening of Africaner Nationalism 1868–1881* (Cape Town: Human and Rousseau, 1961); G. W. de Kiewiet, *The Imperial Factor in South Africa* (London: Cambridge Univ., 1937); and L. M. Thomson, *The Unification of South Africa, 1902–1910* (New York: Oxford Univ., 1960). Finally, on Australia and New Zealand there is C. H. Grattan, *The United States and the Southwest Pacific* (Cambridge: Harvard Univ., 1961); the same author's *The Southwest Pacific to 1900* (Ann Arbor: Univ. of Michigan, 1963); C. S. Belshaw, "The Changing Cultures of Oceanic Peoples During the Nineteenth Century," *Journal of World History,* II (1957), 647–64; G. Greenwood, ed., *Australia: A Social and Political History* (New York: Praeger, 1955); R. Ward, *The Australian Legend* (New York: Oxford Univ., 1958); R. Boyd, *The Australian Ugliness* (Melbourne: Cheshire, 1961); A. A. Philips, *The Australian Tradition* (Melbourne: Cheshire, 1961); and J. C. Beaglehole, "The Development of New Zealand Nationality," *Journal of World History,* II (1954), 106–23.

Chapter 19

*Above all I wish to urge upon you once again the
immense vista of difficulty and possibility of
danger opened up by the newly awakened
ambitions and aspirations of the Eastern races.
What may be the final outcome of the collision
. . . it is impossible to foretell. This, however, is
certain—that contact with Western thought and
Western ideals has exercised a revivifying influence
upon all the races of the East. Those that have
come into sharpest contact with it have exhibited
most markedly its effects.*

LORD RONALDSHAY, *1909*

Significance of the Period
for World History

The period between 1763 and 1914 stands out in world
history as the period when Europe became master of the entire globe,
whether directly or indirectly. Europe's hegemony was evident not
only in the political sphere—in the form of great colonial empires—
but also in the economic and cultural spheres. On the other hand,
the decade before 1914 also witnessed the first serious challenges
to Europe's predominance, the most significant one being Japan's
defeat of Russia. The contemporary revolutions in Turkey and Persia,
and the underground rumblings in various colonial or semicolonial
regions were also noteworthy. Let us now consider Europe's political,
economic, and cultural predominance, and then the early challenges
to this predominance.

I. EUROPE'S POLITICAL DOMINANCE

Between 1500 and 1763 Europe had emerged from obscurity
by gaining control of the oceans and the relatively empty spaces of
Siberia and the Americas. But so far as Asia and Africa were concerned, Europe's impact still remained negligible at the end of the
eighteenth century. In Africa there were only a string of slave-
trading stations along the coasts and an insignificant settlement of

Boers on the southern tip of the continent. Likewise, in India the Europeans were confined to their few coastal trading posts and had not yet begun to affect substantially the vast hinterland. In East Asia the Westerners were rigidly restricted to Canton and Deshima despite their pleas for further contacts. If by some miracle the relations between Europe on the one hand and Africa and Asia on the other had been suddenly severed in the late eighteenth century, there would have been little left to show for the three centuries of interaction. A few ruined forts and churches would have been almost the only reminders of the intruders who had come across the sea. Everyday life would have continued along traditional lines as in the past millennia.

By 1914 this situation had changed fundamentally. Europe's impact had grown immeasurably, both in extent and in depth; the vast portions of the globe—the United States, Latin America, Siberia, and the British Dominions —had been Europeanized. Europeans had migrated to those territories en masse, displacing to a greater or lesser degree the indigenous peoples. It is true that by 1914 the United States and Latin America had won political independence, while the British Dominions were self-governing. Nevertheless, as we have seen, these had become Europeanized lands; they were intimately related to Europe as regards ethnic composition, economic ties, and cultural institutions.

Vast territories, including the entire continent of Africa, with the exception of Liberia and Ethiopia, and the greater part of Asia, had become outright colonial possessions of the European powers. Of the 16,819,000 square miles comprising Asia, no less than 9,443,000 square miles were under European rule. These included 6,496,000 square miles under Russia, 1,998,000 under Britain, 587,000 under Holland, 248,000 under France, 114,000 under the United States, and a paltry 193 for Germany. In contrast to these tremendous colonial territories, Japan, the only truly independent Asian nation in 1914, accounted for a mere 161,000 square miles.

The remaining portion of the globe, apart from these colonial possessions and the Europeanized territories, consisted of countries that were nominally independent but actually semicolonial. These included the great Chinese and Ottoman empires as well as such smaller states as Iran, Afghanistan, and Nepal. All these countries were dominated by European economic and military power; they were allowed to retain a nominal political independence simply because the European powers could not agree on the details of their dismemberment.

In this manner the entire globe had come under Europe's hegemony by 1914. It was the extraordinary climax of the long process started half a millennium earlier when Portuguese captains began to feel their way down the coast of Africa. One peninsula of the Eurasian landmass now was the center of the world, with a concentration of power altogether unprecedented in past history.*

II. EUROPE'S ECONOMIC DOMINANCE

That Europe's hegemony in 1914 was unprecedented not only in extent but also in depth was evident in the economic control that Europe exercised.

* See "Europe Dominates the World," *EMM,* No. 106.

Europe had become the banker of the world, providing the capital needed for building transcontinental railroads, digging interoceanic canals, opening mines, and establishing plantations. By 1914 Britain had invested abroad 4 billion pounds, comprising one-fourth of her total national wealth; France had invested 45 billion francs, equal to one-sixth of her national wealth; and Germany, 22–25 billion marks, or one-fifteenth of her total wealth.

Europe had become not only the banker but also the industrial workshop of the world. By 1870 Europe was responsible for 64.7 per cent of the world's total industrial output, the only rival being the United States with 23.3 per cent. Even though the United States had forged ahead by 1913 to 35.8 per cent, Europe's factories in that year still turned out 47.7 per cent of the world's total production.

The effect of Europe's great outpouring of capital and technology was an unprecedented global economic unity: By 1914 over 516,000 kilometers of cables had been laid on ocean beds, as well as a vast network of telegraph and telephone lines on the land surface of the globe. By 1914 over 30,000 ships with a total tonnage of 50 millions carried goods from one part of the world to another. Several canals were built to facilitate world commerce, the most important being the Suez (1869), which shortened the route between Western Europe and India by 4,000 miles, and the Panama (1914), which reduced the distance between New York and San Francisco by almost 8,000 miles. Continents were opened for economic exploitation by the construction of several transcontinental railroads, the first in the United States being completed in 1869, the first in Canada in 1885, the trans-Siberian in 1905; the Berlin to Bagdad and the Cape to Cairo railroads were almost completed by 1914.

This economic integration of the continents led to a spectacular increase in over-all global productivity. World industrial production multiplied no less than six times between 1860 and 1913, while the value of world trade increased twelve times between 1851 and 1913. Europe, as might be expected, benefited the most from this economic leap forward. Statistics are not available for conditions all over the globe, but one economist has estimated that living standards in colonial or semicolonial regions were between one-fifth and one-tenth of those in the European metropolitan countries. More specifically, we know that Britain experienced in the last quarter of the nineteenth century a drop of one-third in the cost of living, while wages rose slightly by about 5 per cent during the same period, adding up to a rise of over 35 per cent in living standards. Other Western European countries made comparable advances during these years.*

III. Europe's Cultural Dominance

The everyday life of the peasant masses in colonial territories had been drastically affected by the shift from a traditional natural economy to a money economy. Money had been used in the earlier period but only in a peripheral manner, and production had been carried on by the peasant households

* See "Europe's Impact: Economic and Social," *EMM,* No. 107.

primarily to satisfy family needs. A few commodities might have been sold in the local market, but not for the purpose of making a profit. Rather the aim was to secure a little money to meet any tax obligations and to buy a few essentials such as salt and a little iron. Frequently the transactions and obligations were met by simple barter, and no money at all changed hands. But a new market economy was introduced when the Europeans appeared with their railroads, their machine-made goods, and their insatible demands for foodstuffs and industrial raw materials. Before long the peasants found themselves producing for an international market rather than for themselves and their neighbors, which in turn meant that they became subject to the vagaries of economic fluctuations as well as to the mercies of merchants and moneylenders who now flourished in this new economy. The transition from a closed and static natural economy to a dynamic money and market economy was beneficial so far as productive capacity was concerned, but certainly its initial effects were disruptive and uncomfortable. The following wry reflections of a Croatian peasant in the mid-nineteenth century must have echoed again and again amongst the millions of peasants in overseas lands:

421

> We live in a time of wonders
> Wise people tell me that carts roll without horses to pull them,
> That proud ships sail fast as an arrow without sail or wind,
> That wondor-doctors can cut off legs or hands and one feels no pain or
>   utters any cry,
> That, on a wire stretched across the earth, news can travel around the
>   world faster than one counts to three,
> That, of itself, the scythe mows, the spinning wheel runs, and the plow
>   cuts a furrow,
> And still the hunger for bread is amongst us as it has ever been.[1]

The way of thinking as well as the way of life was affected by Europe's intrusion.* However, this intellectual change involved primarily the small upper class in the colonial world rather than the peasant masses; it was the few members of the thin upper crust who knew some Western language, who read Western newspapers and books, and who were familiar with European history and current politics. The initial response to this exposure to the alien culture was often an enthusiastic, uncritical admiration of everything Western, but was usually followed by a reaction against the West and an attempt to preserve and foster at least some elements of the traditional culture. This ambivalent response to Western culture is clearly expressed in the following reminiscence written in 1925 by a prominent Indian:

> Our fore fathers, the firstfruits of English education, were violently pro-British. They could see no flaw in the civilization or the culture of the West. They were charmed by its novelty and its strangeness. The enfranchisement of the individual, the substitution of the right of private judgement in the place of traditional authority, the exaltation of duty over custom, all came with a force and suddenness of a revelation to an

* See "Europe's Impact: Cultural," EMM, No. 108.

THE BLACK BABY.

Mr. Bull. "WHAT, ANOTHER!!—WELL, I SUPPOSE I MUST TAKE IT IN!!!"

A cartoon from Punch, *April 21, 1894. (From the Collections of the Library of Congress)*

Oriental people who knew no more binding obligation than the mandate of immemorial usage and of venerable tradition. . . . Everything English was good—even the drinking of brandy was a virtue; everything not English was to be viewed with suspicion. . . . In due time came the reaction, and with a sudden rush. And from the adoration of all things Western, we are now in a whirlpool that would recall us back to our ancient civilization and our time-honored ways and customs untempered by the impact of the ages that have rolled by and the forces of modern life.[2]

IV. WHITE MAN'S BURDEN

The political, economic, and cultural dominance of Europe at the turn of the century naturally led Europeans to assume that their primacy arose from the superiority of their civilization, and that this in turn reflected the superiority of themselves as a race. It was confidently believed that God had created man unequal. He had made the Whites more intelligent so that they could direct the labor and guide the development of the inferior races who had broad backs and weak minds. Hence the concept of the White Man's Burden *—a preaching that cloaked the imperialism of the times with a mantle of idealistic devotion to duty. In the well-known lines of Rudyard Kipling, written appropriately at the end of the century (1899):

* See "White Man's Burden," *EMM,* No. 109.

Take up the White Man's Burden—
Send forth the best ye breed—
Go bind your sons to exile
To serve your captives' need. . . .[3]

423

On all continents the European masters accepted the homage of the "lesser breeds" as part of the divine nature of things—as the inevitable outcome of the "survival of the fittest." In India they were addressed respectfully as "sahib," in the Middle East as "effendi," in Africa as "bwana," and in Latin American as "patron." Under these circumstances it is scarcely surprising that Europeans came to view the world with a myopia and a self-centeredness that today seems incredible. Arnold Toynbee has described the *Weltanschaung* of his fellow countrymen at the turn of the century: "As they saw it, history for them was over. It had come to an end in foreign affairs in 1815, with the Battle of Waterloo; in home affairs in 1832, with the Great Reform Bill; and in imperial affairs in 1859, with the suppression of the Indian Mutiny. And they had every reason to congratulate themselves on the permanent state of felicity which this ending of history had conferred on them. . . . This *fin de siècle* middle-class English hallucination seems sheer lunacy, yet it was shared by Western middle-class people of other nationalities." [4]

The hallucination was indeed not confined to the British Isles. Across the Atlantic, President Theodore Roosevelt in a message to Congress in 1904 warned Latin America that ". . . chronic wrong doing, or an impotency which results in a general loosening of the ties of civilized society, may in America, as elsewhere, ultimately require intervention by some civilized nation." [5] Most spectacular was the supreme self-confidence and aggressiveness of Cecil Rhodes, who was ahead of his time in dreaming of other planets to conquer: "The world is nearly parcelled out, and what there is left of it is being divided up, conquered, and colonized. To think of these stars that you

Reception of Siamese ambassadors by Queen Victoria, 1857.

see overhead at night, these vast worlds which we can never reach. I would annex the planets if I could; I often think of that. It makes me sad to see them so clear and yet so far." [6]

424

V. First Challenges to Europe's Dominance

Europe's global hegemony seemed in 1914 to be unassailable and eternal, but in the clearer light of retrospect one can easily perceive the lurking nemesis of a colonial world slowly awakening and striking the first blows against the Western imperium.

Throughout history, whenever a weaker society has been threatened by one more vigorous and aggressive, there have been two contradictory types of reactions: One severs all contact with the intruding forces, withdraws into isolation, and seeks refuge in traditional beliefs and practices. The other tries instead to adopt as many features of the alien society as are necessary to meet it on equal terms and thus to resist it effectively. The first reaction represents retreat and escapism; the other, adjustment and adaptation. The slogan of the first is "Back to the good old days"; that of the second is, "Learn from the West in order to fight the West."

There were many cases during the nineteenth century of both types of reaction to the Western intrusion, classic examples of the escapist variety being the Indian Mutiny in 1857–1858 and the Boxer Rebellion in 1900. We have seen that the Mutiny was the work of discontented Sepoys incited by princes and landlords whose interests had been harmed by the British and who wished to return to the ways of the past. Likewise, the Boxer Rebillion was an uprising of antiforeign secret societies encouraged behind the scenes by reactionary court officials and provincial governors steeped in traditional Confucianism (see Chapter 15, section III, and Chapter 16, section V for details). Both the Mutiny and the Rebellion were bitter, bloody affairs, yet neither of them seriously challenged Europe's supremacy because they were essentially negative revolts, seeking to oust the hated Europeans by force in order to restore the good old days. Obviously utopian and doomed to failure, this approach could neither force out nor keep out the Western powers. The power of Western arms and the dynamism of Western economic enterprise were irresistable. But it was an entirely different matter when native peoples began to adopt Western ideas and technology in order to use them against the West.

The Japanese were the first Asian people to successfully carry out this policy of resistance by adaptation. As noted earlier, a fortuitous combination of circumstances enabled them to take over Western economic and military technology, and then to free themselves from the unequal treaty system that had been imposed upon them as upon the Chinese. The Japanese further imitated their European mentors by undertaking a program of overseas expansion: They defeated the weak Chinese Empire in 1894–1895, and then the mighty Russian Empire in 1904–1905 (see Chapter 16, sections VII and VIII for details).

The triumph of a small Asian kingdom over a giant European power marks a turning point in recent world history. It was an event that sent a tremor of hope and excitement throughout the colonial world. As influential as the outcome of the Russo-Japanese War was the great Russian Revolution, stimulated in part by the war (see Chapter 13, section IV). The news that the Tsarist autocracy was on the verge of downfall was as exciting to oppressed peoples everywhere as the reports from the battlefields of Manchuria. A Britisher who was in Persia at this time sensed an undercurrent of aroused emotions and expectations in all the colonial lands. In a letter of August 1906 he reported:

> It seems to me that a change must be coming over the East. The victory of Japan has, it would appear, had a remarkable influence all over the East. Even here in Persia it has not been without effect. . . . Moreover, the Russian Revolution has had a most astounding effect here. Events in Russia have been watched with great attention, and a new spirit would seem to have come over the people. They are tired of their rulers, and, taking example of Russia, have come to think that it is possible to have another and better form of government . . . it almost seems that the East is stirring in its sleep. In China there is a marked movement against the foreigners, and a tendency towards the ideal of "China for the Chinese." In Persia, owing to its proximity to Russia, the awakening would appear to take the form of a movement towards democratic reform. In Egypt and North Africa it is signalized by a remarkable increase in fanaticism, coupled with the spread of the Pan-Islamic movement. The simultaneousness of these symptoms of unrest is too remarkable to be attributed solely to coincidence. Who knows? Perhaps the East is really awakening from its secular slumber, and we are about to witness the rising of these patient millions against the exploitation of an unscrupulous West.[7]

This analysis proved prophetic. In the next few years a series of explosions broke out in all parts of Asia, from the Ottoman Empire in the West to the Chinese Empire in the East. These eruptions were inspired to a greater or lesser degree by the Russo-Japanese War and the Russian Revolution, though naturally the local conditions and historical traditions were more basic and decisive factors. The effect of these revolutions was to challenge both the European powers and the decrepit local dynasties that usually served to camouflage foreign control.

The revolution that took place in Persia in December 1905 is a good example of the uprisings in the colonial and semicolonial lands at this time. We have seen that this was primarily a movement against Western economic domination and against ineffective and irresponsible leadership by the native Kajar dynasty. We have also seen that Russia contributed substantially to the Persian Revolution because of the 1905 Revolution which not only offered a provocative example but also prevented the Tsar for a time from crushing the reformers in Persia.

Noteworthy, too, is the 1908 Young Turk Revolution that ended Abdul Hamid's autocratic rule in Constantinople. This revolution was appreciably influenced by the earlier upheavals in Russia and Persia. A British diplomat in Constantinople reported to his government at the time:

426

Colonial reactions to the Europeans. (center, and top right) Carved figures of a French colonial official in Madagascar, and the wife of such an official. It is symbolic of nineteenth century colonialism that these Europeans, depicted with such insight, seem unaware that they are being observed. (left) A door jamb for the house of a chief in Bana, Cameroons, shows an arrogant German on horseback, and African troops armed with rifles. (bottom right) Many Indians of Latin America worked for Spanish-Americans as laborers. This don is depicted in unflattering terms by one of his employees. (Chicago Natural History Museum)

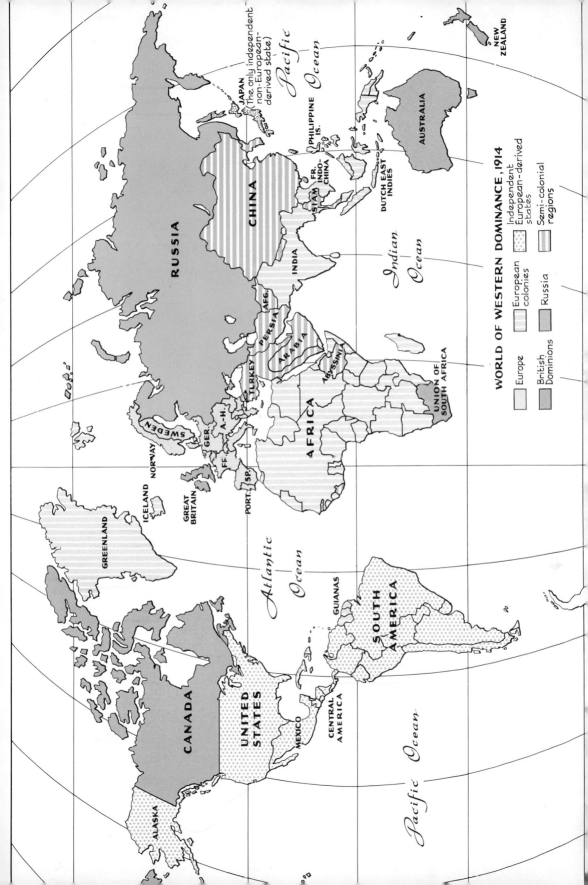

WORLD OF WESTERN DOMINANCE, 1914

Europe

British Dominions

Independent European-derived states

European colonies

Russia

Semi-colonial regions

JAPAN
The only independent non-European-derived state

RUSSIA

CHINA

AFG.

PERSIA

INDIA

PHILIPPINE IS.

SIAM

FR. INDO-CHINA

DUTCH EAST INDIES

AUSTRALIA

NEW ZEALAND

Pacific Ocean

Indian Ocean

TURKEY

ARABIA

ABYSSINIA

AFRICA

UNION OF SOUTH AFRICA

SWEDEN

NORWAY

A.-H.

GER.

FR.

ITALY

SP.

PORT.

ICELAND

GREAT BRITAIN

GREENLAND

Atlantic Ocean

CANADA

UNITED STATES

MEXICO

CENTRAL AMERICA

GUIANAS

SOUTH AMERICA

ALASKA

Pacific Ocean

The success of Japan over Russia the traditional enemy of the Turk made every fibre of the latter's body tingle. His national pride—that of a race with a great past, was wounded at seeing the "contemptible" Persians making a bid for a new national life, at a time when Turkey, owing to the despotism of the Sultan was more than ever threatened by the degrading and increasing tutelage of Western Powers in the European provinces.[8]

The impact of the Russian and Persian Revolutions was felt even in the African provinces of the Ottoman Empire. A Cairo newspaper, for example, made frequent references to the developments in Russia and Persia, and urged its readers to implement "the sublime ideas of the Russian Revolution" or "to blush for shame" before what had been accomplished in Persia.[9]

Russian influence in the Ottoman Empire was reinforced by the influx of large numbers of Moslem Tatar refugees fleeing from the Russification measures of the Tsarist regime. Many had arrived before the 1905 Revolution, and still more with the reaction following the failure of the Revolution. The refugees brought with them revolutionary literature, newspapers, and pamphlets, which were circulated widely in Turkey.

We have seen that when the Young Turk leaders unfurled the flag of revolt in July 1908, they did so for reasons very similar to those that had motivated the reformers in Persia. They wished to curb the authority of the aging autocrat, Abdul Hamid, whose rigid opposition to change was imperiling the existence of the empire. Equally important was the fear that Britain and Russia were about to divide the Ottoman Empire into spheres of influence, as they already had divided Persia.

The Turkish revolutionaries were successful, in contrast to their counterparts in Persia, mainly because the European Powers were not able to act as freely and high handedly in Constantinople as they were in Teheran. The cause of revolution was doomed in Persia once Britain and Russia joined forces. But many other powers were interested in the Ottoman Empire and were in a position to assert themselves. Consequently, the Young Turks were able to overthrow the Sultan and to become the masters of the empire. However, their efforts to Westernize and revitalize the empire were frustrated by the irreconcilable nationalism of the subject nationalities and by the series of wars with Italy, the Balkan states, and the Allied Powers. Effective Westernization had to wait until the emergence of the Turkish Republic out of the shambles of World War I.

China, at the other end of Asia, also experienced revolution directed against Western intervention and weak native leadership. In this case, the spectacle of Russia's defeat at the hands of Japan was particularly exciting, since the war was fought mostly on Chinese soil. Furthermore, large numbers of Chinese students were studying in Japan: 8,000 in 1905 and 17,860 by 1907. It is not surprising that Sun Yat-sen later asserted, "We regarded the Russian defeat by Japan as the defeat of the West by the East. We regarded the Japanese victory as our own victory." [10] When the War was followed by revolution in Russia, again there was significant response in China. A Chinese reformer wrote an article in which he interpreted events in Russia as a warning of what could happen to the Manchu dynasty. He pointed out that Tsarist

428

Russia—"the one and only despotic state on the globe"—had not been able to escape revolution. Since the Romanoff dynasty was more strongly entrenched than the Manchu, he concluded that the latter could save itself only by immediate reforms.[11]

The Manchus failed to heed the warning, and the outcome, as prophesied, was a revolution that overthrew the dynasty and established a republic (see Chapter 16, section V). No one could have foreseen the decades of anarchy and misery that were to follow this uprising in 1911. But the point to be noted here is that the aim of the Chinese Revolution, like that of the earlier ones in Persia and Turkey, was to adopt Western technology and institutions in order to resist the West.

India was less affected by the disturbances of these years, partly because of remoteness from the centers of trouble, but also because of the dampening effect of direct British rule. Yet even the moderate leader Dadabhai Naoroji raised the following pointed questions before the Indian National Congress in 1906:

> At the very time that China in East Asia, and Persia in West Asia, are awakening, when Japan has already awakened, and Russia is struggling for liberation from despotism, is it possible for the free citizens of the British Empire in India—the people who were among the first to create world civilization—to continue to remain under the yoke of despotism? [12]

We may conclude that although Europe's global hegemony in 1914 seemed irresistible and everlasting, it actually was being challenged at many points and in many ways. In some cases the challenge was direct, as in India and in Central Asia where a few pioneer nationalists were beginning to demand independence from Britain and Russia. In other cases the challenge was indirect, being aimed against the weak Ottoman, Kajar, and Manchu dynasties because of their failure to resist Western aggression. In this pre-1914 period the European Powers were able to suppress the opposition, either by direct force or by supporting the Shah against the *majlis* or the conservative Yuan Shih-kai against the radical Sun Yat-sen. Yet this early opposition did represent a beginning—the genesis of the nationalist movements that, after World War I, and especially after World War II, were to sweep everything before them.*

SUGGESTED READING

Europe's role in world affairs at the turn of the century is surveyed in C. J. H. Hayes, *A Generation of Materialism, 1871–1900* (New York: Harper, 1941). The pre-1914 challenges to Europe's supremacy are analyzed by E. Fischer, "Rebellion Against the European Man in the Nineteenth Century," *Journal of World Affairs,* II (1954), 363–80, and by I. Spector, *The First Russian Revolution: Its Impact on Asia* (Englewood Cliffs, N. J.: Prentice-Hall, 1962; a Spectrum book). For the revolutions in Persia, the Ottoman Empire, and China, see the bibliographies for Chapters 14 and 15.

* See "First Challenges to Europe's Domination," *EMM,* No. 110.

WORLD OF
WESTERN DECLINE
AND TRIUMPH, 1914-

The Great War of 1914–1918 was from the
Asian point of view a civil war within the
European community of nations.

K. M. PANIKKAR,
Indian diplomat and historian

World War I:
Global Repercussions

In the autumn of 1914, as one European country after another was being dragged into the holocaust of World War I, the British Foreign Secretary, Earl Grey, remarked, "The lamps are going out all over Europe." His comment was indeed fully justified, and to a much greater degree than he could have foreseen at the time. World War I was destined to bring down in ruins the Europe with which Earl Grey was familiar. It wiped out the centuries-old Hapsburg, Hohenzollern, Romanoff, and Ottoman dynasties. In their places appeared new leaders, new institutions, and new ideologies that aristocrats such as Earl Grey only dimly comprehended. The Europe of 1918 was as different from that of 1914 as the Europe of 1815 had been different from that of 1789.

World War I also marked the end of the Europe that had dominated the globe so completely and abnormally during the nineteenth century. By the end of the war Europe's control had manifestly weakened and was everywhere being challenged. In one way or another the challenges were successfully resisted in most parts of the world. But the respite lasted only two decades, for the Second World War completed the undermining process begun by the First, and left the European empires everywhere in shambles.

From the viewpoint of world history as well as European, World War I stands out as a historic turning point. The purpose of this chapter is to analyze the roots, the course, and the global repercussions of this fateful episode.

432

I. ROOTS OF WAR

The Versailles Treaty terminating World War I included an article specifically stating that the War was provoked "by the aggression of Germany and her allies." This "war guilt" clause was of more than academic interest, for it was used by the Allies to justify their claim for reparation payments from the defeated Central Powers. Consequently, it stimulated a passionate and prolonged controversy that led to the publication of great collections of documents totaling over 60,000 in all, as well as more thousands of articles and books. By the mid-1930's the polemics had quieted down and relatively scholarly studies appeared that paid less attention to "war guilt" and more to historical conditions and forces that produced war. Most historians now distinguish between background causes that had been operative for some decades, and the immediate causes that came into play during the hectic weeks following the assassination of the Archduke Francis Ferdinand on June 28, 1914. The most important of the background factors are four in number: economic rivalries, colonial disputes, conflicting alliance systems and irreconcilable nationalist aspirations.

Economic Rivalries

Most of the major European powers became involved in tariff wars and in competition for foreign markets. For example, Italy and France waged a tariff war between 1888 and 1899, Russia and Germany between 1879 and 1894, and Austria and Serbia between 1906 and 1910. The most serious economic rivalry developed between Britain and Germany because of the latter's extraordinarily rapid rate of industrialization in the late nineteenth century. In 1870 Britain produced 31.8 per cent of the world's total industrial output, compared to Germany's 13.2 per cent. By 1914 Britain's share had dropped to 14 per cent, due largely to the spectacular upsurge of the United States from 23.3 to 35.8 per cent. Germany's production, however, had risen sufficiently so that her share rose slightly to 14.3 per cent, or a shade greater than that of Britain.

Germany's spurt in industrial production meant stiff competition for Britain in overseas markets. Britain was able to retain her economic predominance in her own colonies, but in Latin America, the Middle East, and the Far East, she lost heavily to the aggressive German businessmen. It is impossible to define precisely the political repercussions of this economic rivalry, but it manifestly strained the relations between the two countries. It further contributed to international tension by stimulating competition in naval armaments. In both countries it was argued vociferously that it was essential to build up naval strength in order to safeguard trade routes and merchant shipping.

Colonial Disputes

Economic rivalries also fomented colonial disputes, for additional colonies were eagerly sought after in order to be assured of protected overseas markets for surplus capital and manufactures. Since the Germans did not enter the colonial race until after their national unification in 1871, they were particularly aggressive in their demands for an empire commensurate with their growing economic strength. The Pan-German League pointed to the substantial colonial possessions of small countries like Portugal, Holland, and Belgium, and insisted that Germany also must have her "place in the sun." But in almost every part of the globe the Germans found themselves blocked by the farflung possessions of the British, whom they bitterly accused of "dog in the manger" selfishness.

The competition for colonies, however, was by no means restricted to Britain and Germany. Almost all the major powers were involved in the scramble for empire in the late nineteenth century, so they repeatedly clashed in one region or another: Britain and Germany clashed in East Africa and Southwest Africa; Britain and France, in Siam and the Nile Valley; Britain and Russia, in Persia and Afghanistan; and Germany and France, in Morocco and West Africa.

Alliance Systems

These colonial rivalries in turn contributed to the forging of conflicting alliance systems that were in large part responsible for the coming of war. When war broke out in August, 1914, a German official remarked despairingly: "It all came from this damned system of alliances, which were the curse of modern times."

This judgment was by no means without foundation. The alliance system began in 1879 when the German chancellor, Otto von Bismarck, concluded the Dual Alliance with Austria-Hungary. This was a defensive pact, designed to protect Germany against the French, who aspired to recover the Alsace-Lorraine provinces lost in 1871, and also to protect Austria-Hungary against the Russians, with whom they continually clashed in the Balkans. In 1882 the Dual Alliance became the Triple Alliance with the adhesion of Italy. Again the objective was defensive: to protect Italy against France because of sharp conflict over Tunis. The Triple Alliance, then, was definitely not aggressive in intention or in its provisions. Germany and Austria-Hungary were both satiated powers interested primarily in preserving the *status quo* on the Continent.

But from the other side of the fence the Triple Alliance appeared quite differently. For France and Russia it meant an overwhelming bloc that dominated Europe and left them isolated and vulnerable. Furthermore, France and Russia both had serious difficulties with Britain over colonial issues in several regions. Bismarck was quite aware of the danger of a Franco-Russian *rapprochement* when he concluded the Dual Alliance, but he was able by astute diplomacy to prevent its materialization. In 1890, however, he resigned as chancellor, and his successors proved incapable of continuing his delicate diplomatic jug-

434

gling. The result was the Franco-Russian Alliance, concluded in 1894 with the double purpose of countering the Triple Alliance and resisting Britain in colonial disputes. The Franco-Russian Alliance became the Triple Entente with the signing of the Anglo-French Entente in 1904 and the Anglo-Russian Entente in 1907. Both of these arrangements were essentially colonial in nature. Britain and France, for example, agreed to recognize their respective interests in the Nile Valley and Morocco, while Britain and Russia likewise agreed to divide Persia into spheres of influence.

Thus all the major powers now were aligned in rival alliance systems, with disastrous results for international relations. Whenever any dispute of consequence arose, the members of both blocs felt compelled to support their respective allies who were directly involved, even if they entertained doubts regarding the issues. Otherwise they feared that their alliances would disintegrate, leaving them alone and exposed. Each dispute consequently tended to be magnified into a major crisis involving, willy-nilly, all the members of both alliances. In the middle of the 1914 crisis, for example, the Austro-Hungarian foreign minister, Count Berchtold, declared, ". . . we are playing a great game, in which there are serious difficulties to overcome, and in which we might fail, unless the Powers of the Triple Alliance hold firmly together." This attitude explains why crises became increasingly frequent during the decade prior to 1914, and why they became increasingly difficult to resolve as the bloc members fearfully and compulsively supported each other.

Nationalist Aspirations

The final background cause was the rising nationalist aspirations of Europe's subject minorities. This was difficult enough in Alsace-Lorraine, where the French remained unreconciled to German rule. But it was a nightmare in Central and Eastern Europe, where the multinational empires were in danger of being literally torn to pieces by the growing demand for self-determination. In the Hapsburg Empire, for example, the ruling Austrians and Hungarians were confronted by the resurgent Italians and Rumanians as well as the great Slavic multitude: Czechs, Slovaks, Ruthenians, Poles, Slovenes, Croats, and Serbs. Very understandably the Hapsburg officials decided that firm measures were necessary if the empire was to survive. This was especially true regarding the militant Serbs who were clamoring for unification with the independent Serbia across the Danube. Hence the stiff terms sent to Belgrade when the Archduke was murdered by a Serb patriot at Sarajevo. But behind Serbia was Russia, and behind Russia were France and Britain. Austria-Hungary, likewise, was backed by Germany and, theoretically, by Italy. Thus this combination of national self-determination and conflicting alliance systems brought Europe to Armageddon.*

II. Sarajevo

On June 28, 1914, Archduke Francis Ferdinand and his wife were assassinated in Sarajevo, the capital of the recently annexed province of Bosnia. The murder was committed by a young Bosnian Serb student named Gavrilo

* See "Background to Sarajevo," *EMM,* No. 111.

Princip. In the trial that followed, Princip boldly stated his beliefs and motives. "I have no regret because I am convinced that I have destroyed a scourge and done a good deed. . . . I have seen our people going steadily downhill. I am a peasant's son and know what is happening in the villages. . . . All this had its influence on me and also the fact of knowing that he [the archduke] was a German, an enemy of the Slavs. . . . As future Sovereign he would have prevented our union and carried out certain reforms which would have been clearly against our interests." [1]

435

Princip was not alone in carrying out the murder. Behind him was the secret Serbian organization *Ujedinjenje ili Smrt,* or "Union or Death," popularly known as the Black Hand. Founded in Belgrade in 1911, the Black Hand had as its avowed aim the realization of "the national ideal: the union of all Serbs." Its bylaws stated, "This organization prefers terrorist action to intellectual propaganda, and for this reason must be kept absolutely secret from non-members." [2] In keeping with this conspiratorial injunction, the initiation of new members took place in a darkened room, lighted only by a wax candle, before a small table covered with a black cloth, on which lay a crucifix, a dagger, and a revolver. The Society's seal bore a skull and crossbones, dagger, bomb, and a bottle of poison, with the inscription *Ujedinjenje ili Smrt.*

These extravagances reflected the fanatical earnestness and singlemindedness of the members, who were particularly active in Bosnia. The Serbian government was not behind this society, which indeed it regarded as dangerously radical and militant. But this did not prevent the Black Hand from organizing an underground revolutionary organization that conducted an effective campaign of agitation and terrorism. A Serbian diplomat stationed in Vienna at this time testified: "The year 1913 in Bosnia was the year of revolutionary organization. . . . 'Action, action, enough of words' was the cry on all lips. The young dreamed of nothing but bombs, assassinations, explosives to blow up and destroy everything." [3]

The unfortunate Francis Ferdinand played into the hands of these Serb revolutionaries by agreeing to pay an official visit to the Bosnian capital. The day selected, June 28, was Vidovdan, or St. Vitus' Day, commemorating the battle of Kosovo in which the Turks in 1389 conquered the medieval Serbian Empire. The decision was unpardonably shortsighted, for this was a day when Serbian nationalist sentiment was bound to be inflamed, particularly in view of the current Black Hand agitation. When the archduke and his duchess paid their visit on a radiant Sunday morning, no less than six assassins, armed with bombs and revolvers, were waiting along the designated route. As fate would have it, the procession stopped at the very corner where Princip was stationed. He drew his revolver and fired two shots, one at Francis Ferdinand and the other at General Potiorek, the Governor of Bosnia. The second shot went wild and hit the duchess instead. Before medical aid arrived, both the archduke and his wife were dead.

Now the "damned system of alliances" began to operate relentlessly and fatally. First Germany assured Austria-Hungary of full support regardless of what course she decided upon. This famous "blank check" from Berlin did not signify that the Germans wanted war. Rather they assumed that Russia would not dare support Serbia against both Germany and Austria, and that it was therefore in the interest of peace to make this common front perfectly clear at the outset. The assumption was understandable in view of the fact that

436

this is precisely what had happened in 1908 when Austria annexed the province of Bosnia from the Turks. The Serbs, who for long had eyed this Slavic province, reacted violently against the annexation and were backed by Russia. But when Germany supported Austria, the Russians decided they were in no condition to risk war and backed down.

This sequence was not to be repeated in 1914, however, because Russia was now in a stronger position than she had been in 1908. She had recovered from the defeat of 1904–1905 in the Far East. She now had firm support from France, as she had not had in 1908, when France had been lukewarm to make an issue of Bosnia. Thus, the German assumption that the Sarajevo crisis could be localized proved a miscalculation, and the stage was set for the great catastrophe.

On July 23, Austria presented Serbia a stiff ultimatum, which included demands for explanations and apologies, suppression of anti-Austrian publications and organizations, participation of Austrian officials in the inquiry regarding responsibility for the crime, and judicial proceedings against those accessory to the plot. The Serbian reply on July 25 appeared conciliatory at first glance, but actually was so hedged with qualifications as to be evasive and unsatisfactory. Austria promptly broke off diplomatic relations, and on July 28 declared war on Serbia.

Russia now retaliated by ordering full mobilization on July 30. The next day Germany sent a twelve-hour ultimatum to Russia demanding that mobilization be stopped. When no reply was received, Germany declared war against Russia on August 1 and against Russia's ally, France, on August 3. On the same day Germany began actual hostilities by invading Belgium. This aggression provided a welcome pretext for Britain's declaration of war on Germany on August 4. Thus the great powers of Europe were at each others' throats five weeks after the murder at Sarajevo.*

III. EUROPEAN PHASE OF THE WAR, 1914–1917

1914: War of Attrition in the West

World War I began with cheering crowds and marching soldiers singing the "Marseillaise," or "In der Heimat," or "Tipperary." Troop trains on both sides bore the chalked inscription "Home by Christmas." All peoples confidently expected a brief and victorious war. Instead, they soon found themselves embroiled in a prolonged and brutalizing ordeal that was unprecedented in its toll of material wealth and human lives. The war was equally destructive of social institutions and political structures. When the Tsar signed the order for general mobilization on July 30, he protested to his ministers, "Think of the responsibility you are advising me to take; think of the thousands and thousands of men who will be sent to their death." Little did he realize that he was signing the death warrant of millions rather than thousands, including that of his own family and dynasty.

The explanation for the bloody stalemate that gutted European civilization

* See "Coming of War," *EMM,* No. 112.

is to be found in the failure of traditional war strategy. The General Staffs of all the European armies had for years been carefully preparing for war against any neighbor or combination of neighbors. The Germans had a plan devised in 1905 by their Chief of Staff, Count Alfred von Schlieffen. This Schlieffen Plan called for a speedy and overwhelming attack upon France before turning against the slow-moving Russians in the East. The bulk of the German forces were to be concentrated in the north and were to attack through Belgium and Luxembourg in a vast wheeling movement that would roll up the French army to the east of Paris and thus end the war in thirty days.

On August 4 this plan went into operation, when German forces crossed the frontier of Belgium, of whose neutrality Germany was herself a guarantor. At the same time the French launched an attack on Alsace-Lorraine, as determined to reach Berlin as the Germans were to take Paris. But the French were stopped in their tracks with heavy losses, primarily because they were inadequately equipped with machine guns, which quickly proved their effectiveness in this war. Meanwhile the Germans were rushing through Belgium and northern France according to plan. They reached the Marne River, and by September 2 were at Chantilly, only 25 miles from Paris.

Now the tide unexpectedly began to turn. German military headquarters had failed to coordinate the movements of their rapidly advancing forces, so that a gap 30 miles wide developed between the first and second armies. French airplanes spotted the break, and General Joffre promptly exploited the opportunity. He brought up troops from the Alsace-Lorraine sector and from the Italian border, Italy still remaining neutral, and hurled them at the German weak point. Outnumbered 4 to 3, and exhausted by their long advance, the Germans retreated to the natural defense line of the Aisne River. The opposing armies now began a series of flanking and counterflanking movements that ended only when the battle front extended from the coast of Flanders to the frontier of Switzerland.

This line did not shift by more than ten miles in either direction during the next three years despite repeated offensives that took a ghastly tool in lives. The reason for the bloody deadlock was that from the beginning of the war defensive weapons proved superior over offensive. The traditional mode of attack was the massed infantry charge supported by a preliminary artillery barrage. But this was of no avail against the combination of deep trenches, barbed wire entanglements, ingenious land mines, and machine-gun nests. Thus the casualties on the western front during the first four months were 700,000 Germans, 850,000 French, and 90,000 British. Contrary to the plans of all General Staffs, the struggle in the west now became a war of position and attrition.*

This was not the case on the Russian and Balkan fronts, where vast distances and scanty transportation facilities necessitated a fluid war of movement. The Russians led off with a surprisingly fast and powerful offensive into East Prussia, designed to relieve the pressure on the French in the west. The strategy worked, for the Germans transferred four divisions from Belgium to the east. Before they reached their destination, the issue had been decided by smashing victories over two Russian armies advancing into East Prussia. The German commanders, Hindenburg and Ludendorff, used their superior

* See "Trench Fighting," EMM, No. 113.

railway network to concentrate their forces against first one Russian army and then the other. By the middle of September, East Prussia was cleared of her invaders.

On the Balkan front the Austrians meanwhile were suffering humiliating setbacks. General Potiorek, who had barely escaped Princip's bullet in Sarajevo, was impatient to destroy "the viper's nest." On August 12 he crossed the Drina River into Serbia with 250,000 men. But he was met by a Serbian army of 350,000, of whom 90 per cent were seasoned veterans of the Balkan Wars of 1912–13. In less than two weeks these Serbs had forced the Austrians back across the river with a loss of one-third of their numbers. Potiorek returned to the attack in September and succeeded in taking Belgrade on December 2. But again the Serbians counterattacked, and by the end of the same month the Serb commander triumphantly announced, "On the territory of Serbia there remains not one free enemy soldier." [4]

1915: Russian Retreat in the East

The 1915 campaigns were dominated by the decision of the new German Commander-in-Chief, Erich von Falkenhayn, to reverse the Schlieffen Plan. In view of the stalemate on the western front he concentrated his forces on the east in an effort to knock out the Russians. Combined German and Austrian armies attacked with stunning effect on May 1, blasting a thirty-mile hole in the enemy lines. The Russian soldiers, handicapped by inferior leadership and inadequate arms, retreated precipitously. By the end of the summer the Central Power armies had advanced an average of 200 miles. In addition to military casualties totalling 2,500,000 men, Russia had lost 15 per cent of her territories, 10 per cent of her railways, 30 per cent of her industries, and 20 per cent of her civilian population. The Tsarist regime had suffered a blow from which it never was able to recover.

Meanwhile, on the western front the war of attrition continued. General Joffre clung to his belief that intensive artillery bombardment plus massed frontal attack would bring victory. But repeated offensives left the lines unchanged and resulted only in appalling loss of life.

At the same time the Western Powers were attempting to force the Straits in order to knock out Turkey and open a supply route to Russia. When Turkey joined the Central Powers on November 2, 1914, the Straits automatically were closed to the Allies, thus making it difficult to ship much-needed supplies to Russia. Accordingly, on March 18, 1915, a squadron of fourteen British and four French battleships steamed into the Straits with guns blazing. On the first day three ships were sunk and two others badly battered. The damage was done more by mines than by the coastal artillery. The British admiral in command decided that the losses were prohibitive and gave orders to withdraw. In doing so he allowed one of the greatest opportunities of the war to pass. It is known now that the Turks had used up most of their ammunition and had given up hope of holding out the following day. The chief German officer at the Straits reported, "We expect the British will come back early tomorrow morning, and if they do, we may be able to hold out for a few hours." [5] It is fascinating to speculate how different the course of world history might have been if the squadron had returned. Constantinople would have been taken, Turkey would have been forced out of the war, Russia would have received the supplies she needed, her armies would have fared better than they did, and quite possibly the Tsarist regime might have been saved or at least the Bolshevik Revolution averted.

439

As it was, the Allied ships withdrew, and an attempt was made to take the Straits by land. Landings were made on the Gallipoli beaches on April 25, but only shallow footholds were secured in the face of withering machine-gun fire. The Turks held on to the heights above the beaches until the Allies finally faced facts and withdrew permanently in January, 1916.

The failure at the Straits together with the disaster on the Russian front persuaded Bulgaria to join the Central Powers on October 14, 1915. This intervention spelled the end for the gallant Serbs. An overwhelming number of German, Austrian, and Bulgarian divisions attacked Serbia on October 6 from three sides. By the end of the year the entire country was occupied. In one of the great epics of the war, remnants of the Serbian army fled across the Albanian mountains in the dead of winter. The few who survived the cold, disease, and starvation, not to mention hostile Albanian bands, were picked up on the Adriatic coast by Allied ships.

To counterbalance these setbacks in the Balkans, the Allies were strengthened by the decision of Italy to join their cause. Although the Italians technically had been allies of the Central Powers, they decided at the outset of the war to remain neutral. The bulk of the Italian people favored this course, especially since it was Austria that held the "unredeemed" lands across the Adriatic. The Allies now freely offered these lands to Italy, together with additional territories at the expense of Turkey. The bait proved effective, and on April 29 Italy signed the Treaty of London agreeing to enter the war in one month in return for these territorial promises. Actually Italy's intervention scarcely affected the course of the war, apart from compelling the Austrians to divert a few divisions from the eastern front.

1916: Verdun and the Somme

By 1916 the Central Powers had reached the height of their military fortunes. Their armies had overrun Belgium, northern France, Poland, and Serbia. The Allied expedition to the Straits had failed, and repeated Italian attacks against Austria had produced insignificant results. But for all their victories the Central Powers still had not won *the* victory. Although they controlled the continent of Europe from Hamburg to the Persian Gulf, they still were not able to force a peace settlement on the Allies.

At Christmas of 1915 General Falkenhayn submitted a memorandum to His Majesty the Kaiser in which he analyzed this dilemma and proposed a way out. After a survey of the situation on the various fronts, he pointed out that, with Russia on the ropes, France now was the most vulnerable Allied Power. England remained secure behind the Channel, but France was near the breaking point after the bloodletting of 1915. Accordingly, he proposed an all-out attack on Verdun, a key French fortress that was easy to attack but hard to defend. The French High Command, he reasoned, would be forced to throw in every reserve to hold Verdun, and thus France would be bled white and her will to resist would be broken.

440

The battle for Verdun began on February 21, 1916. The Germans concentrated 1,400 guns on a short front of eight miles. After a devastating bombardment they took Fort Douaumont. As expected, the French rushed in reinforcements and raised the battle cry "They shall not pass." The Germans continued their attacks until July, when they went over to the defensive. The net result was French casualties totaling 350,000 men, and German casualties almost as great. The Verdun bloodbath did not bring the decision that Falkenhayn had hoped for. Indeed, the French counterattacked toward the end of the year and regained the positions lost in the spring.

While the Battle of Verdun raged, the British were launching a great offensive to the northwest at the Somme. After a week's cannonade, the attack began on July 1. On the first day the British lost 60,000 men, including more than half the officers engaged—the highest rate of casualties in either World War I or II. The slaughter continued until November, when operations bogged down in rain and mud. The maximum advance was about seven miles, and the total cost was 400,000 British lives, 200,000 French, and 500,000 German.

To everyone's surprise, the Russians mounted a successful offensive on the eastern front in 1916. The Austrians had thinned their lines in Galicia in order to reinforce an attack against Italy. Consequently, when General Brusilov started what was intended at first to be merely a feint to relieve the pressure on Verdun, the Austrian front "broke like a pie crust" for a distance of 200 miles. The surprised Russians poured all reserves into the gap and overran the province of Galicia.

The failure of the Germans at Verdun and the unexpected success of the Brusilov offensive encouraged Rumania to intervene in the war on the side of the Allies on August 27, 1916. The Central Powers now decided to make an object lesson of Rumania as a warning to other neutrals contemplating following her course. German, Austrian, Bulgarian, and Turkish forces descended in full speed and overwhelming force. By the end of the year the Rumanians had lost two-thirds of their country, including their capital.

The involvement of Rumania in the war left Greece as the only neutral in the Balkans. That country was fairly evenly divided on the issue of neutrality or intervention. The most prominent statesman, Eleutherios Venizelos, was all for joining the Allies, but King Constantine, who was the Kaiser's brother-in-law, insisted on neutrality. The deadlock was broken in 1917 when the Allies decided that Greek assistance was essential to succeed in Macedonia, where they had been fighting inconclusively against the Bulgars. Accordingly, the Allies resorted to various extralegal measures, such as seizing the Greek fleet, blockading Greek ports, and even landing troops at Piraeus. Finally, on June 27, 1917, Greece entered the war on the Allied side, thereby paving the way for the 1918 offensives in Macedonia that knocked Bulgaria out of the war.

1917: Bloodletting and Defeatism

Meanwhile, the terrible bloodletting was continuing unabated on the western front. Whereas in 1916 the Germans had assumed the offensive at Verdun, now in 1917 the Allies took the lead. The cautious General Joffre was replaced by the audacious General Nivelle who had distinguished himself in the Verdun fighting. Nivelle preached with persuasive fervor a new type of lightning offensive that would bring victory with few casualties. Despite the opposition of many military leaders, both French and British, Nivelle's aggressive strategy was accepted.

441

The Germans at the same time had replaced Falkenhayn with their eastern front team of Hindenburg and Ludendorff. After the shattering experience of the previous year at Verdun and the Somme, they decided to go on the defensive on the western front while opening unrestricted submarine warfare at sea. They hoped thereby to starve England into submission, leaving France isolated on the Continent. They were well aware that submarine warfare involved the risk of American intervention, but they gambled that England would be broken before American aid became effective.

We shall see shortly that this gamble came within an ace of being won, though in the end it brought disaster. But the defensive strategy on land paid off handsomely. In order to consolidate and strengthen his front lines, Hindenburg withdrew his forces to a new fortified position, the Siegfried Line, or as it was more commonly called, the Hindenburg Line. This was straighter, shorter, and more heavily fortified. The withdrawal badly upset Nivelle's offensive plans, but he persisted in going through with them. French, British, and Canadian troops went over the top as scheduled, but they suffered one of the bloodiest repulses of the war. Nivelle nevertheless pressed the attack with reckless obstinacy until finally French army units revolted in protest against the senseless massacre. The *buveur de sang,* or "blood-drinker," as Nivelle was now called, was replaced by General Pétain, who fell back on the defensive and did what he could to meet the grievances of the men. Further north, an all-British campaign under General Haig proved equally costly and equally futile. Hindenburg's defensive strategy had served the Germans well. They inflicted 400,000 casualties on the Allies, while incurring only 250,000 themselves.

By this time the peoples of Europe were enduring the fourth year of the most devastating and murderous war in history. Despite all the sacrifices and grief, no end was yet in sight. War weariness and defeatism appeared not only in the trenches but also amongst the civilians in both camps.* One of the most spectacular manifestations was the passage of a Peace Resolution by the German Reichstag on July 19, 1917, by a vote of 212 to 126. In Austria-Hungary the death of the respected old Emperor Francis Joseph on November 21, 1917, removed a venerable symbol of loyalty and discipline. The subject nationalities, always restive under Hapsburg rule, now began to take concrete measures for independent statehood. The young new Emperor Charles doubted that the ramshackle imperial structure would hold together through another winter, and sent his brother-in-law, Prince Sixtus, to France to make peace overtures. Likewise in England, a former Foreign Secretary, Lord Lansdowne, wrote an open letter prophesying the collapse of Western civilization unless some way was found to end the conflict. English soldiers in the trenches expressed the same antiwar sentiment in a song that included the lines

> I want to go home! I want to go home!
> The bullets they whistle, the cannon they roar;
> I don't want to stay here any more. . . .

* See "War Weariness," *EMM,* No. 114.

IV. GLOBAL PHASE OF THE WAR: 1917 RUSSIAN REVOLUTIONS

From European to Global Phase

The war weariness and defeatism that appeared all over Europe during 1917 were most intense and widespread in Russia, where in March and November there occurred two great revolutions that profoundly affected not only the course of the war but also the pattern of world history in the postwar years. In fact, 1917 proved to be the year of decision because of two fateful developments—the Russian Revolutions and the intervention of the United States. These events changed the character of the war—from an essentially European affair fought over primarily European issues, to a war of global proportions. It is true that Japan had entered the war on August 23, 1914, but she had done little more than help herself to scattered German colonial possessions in the Pacific. But now the entry of the United States involved a great non-European power that quickly decided the outcome of the war.

The American intervention and the Russian Revolutions also introduced a new ideological element that immediately had worldwide repercussions. Wilson's Fourteen Points and Lenin's revolutionary slogans were universal and disruptive in their impact, in contrast to parochial European issues such as the fate of Alsace-Lorraine or of the Hapsburg subject nationalities. It was in 1917, then, that the transition occurred from the European to the global phase of World War I.

Roots of Revolution

Russians of all classes rallied behind their government when war with Germany began on August 1, 1914. In contrast to the Japanese War of 1904–1905, this conflict was popular with the masses of the people, who were convinced it was a war of defense against the aggression of their traditional Teutonic enemies. When the Duma met on August 8, the Cadet Party leader, Professor Miliukov, who hitherto had been extremely critical of the government, now declared, "We must concentrate all our forces upon defending the country from a foreign foe who is bent on pushing us aside, on his way towards world domination. . . . We fight for the freedom of our native land from foreign invasion, for the freedom of Europe and Slavdom from German domination. . . ." [6] A Jewish deputy expressed similar sentiments, despite the fact that his coreligionists had long suffered discrimination and persecution. "We, the Jews, have lived, and continue to live, under exceptionally harsh legal conditions. Nevertheless, we . . . will, as one man, take our stand under the banners of Russia. . . . The Jewish people will do their duty to the last." [7]

The only exception to this closing of ranks came from the extreme left-wing Bolsheviks. Their leader, Lenin, branded the war as an imperialist struggle over markets and colonies. There was no reason, therefore, why the workers of the world should sacrifice themselves in such a conflict. Instead, Lenin called upon them to turn against the imperialist instigators of war.

Tirelessly he repeated the slogan "Turn the imperialist war into a class war!" This, however, was the only discordant note in 1914, and at that time it was unnoticed and insignificant. The Bolsheviks were a tiny faction within Russia, and their outstanding leaders were in exile abroad, including Lenin who was in Switzerland and Trotsky in New York. Consequently, Bolshevik agitation did not mar the impressive national unity behind the Tsarist regime.

The Russians not only were united against the Germans but they also were confident that they would win the war in short order. In fact, a public collection was made of a large sum of money that was to be granted to the first Russian soldier who entered Berlin. But instead of quick victory, Russia suffered disastrous defeats. It is true that the Russian war effort contributed significantly to the final Allied victory. The unexpectedly rapid Russian advance into East Prussia in 1914 compelled the Germans to transfer troops from the western front and thus contributed significantly to the halting of the Germans at the Marne. Yet the fact remains that the two Russian armies that penetrated into East Prussia in 1914 suffered crushing defeats. In the following year came the great rout, when Russian armies reeled back before a great German-Austrian attack. The most densely populated and highly industrialized provinces of the empire were lost to the Central Powers. The disasters of 1915 proved to be the beginning of the end of the Tsarist regime.

One reason why Russia never recovered from the military setbacks is that she simply lacked the economic strength to wage modern warfare against first-class industrial powers (see Chapter 13, section V). What this meant concretely for the Russian soldiers at the front is vividly described in the following comments made in the summer of 1915 to the French ambassador by a Russian general:

> Imagine in several infantry regiments which took part in the last engagements, one third of the men had no rifles! The poor devils waited patiently, in a storm of shrapnel, until they could pick up the rifles of their fallen comrades. It was a miracle that under such conditions there was no panic. . . . How long will our soldiers bear the trial? The carnage is frightful! [8]

This economic weakness became much worse with the loss of the industrialized portions of the empire in 1915. In addition, Russia's war effort was handicapped by incompetent military leadership. When hostilities began, Tsar Nicholas selected his uncle, Grand Duke Nicholas, to serve as Commander in Chief. The Grand Duke was eminently unqualified for the position, as indicated in this estimate by a competent Russian general: "He appeared to be a man entirely unequipped for the task, and, in accordance with his own statement, on the receipt of the Imperial order, he spent much of his time crying because he did not know how to approach his new duties." [9]

The Russians were handicapped also by political dissension on the home front. The Duma and the imperial bureaucracy were constantly feuding over their respective jurisdictions and prerogatives. Both of them, in turn, clashed with the military in assigning responsibility for the shortage of war supplies and, ultimately, for the defeats at the front. This discord might have been minimized and controlled if there had been strong leadership at the top. Unfor-

444

tunately, Tsar Nicholas was a well-meaning but weak and vacillating ruler with limited intelligence and imagination. His strong-willed but highstrung and unstable wife constantly urged him to assert his authority and crack the whip. "You have never lost an opportunity to show your love and kindness; now let them feel your fist." But Nicholas remained an irresolute and pathetic figure, usually following the advice of whoever spoke to him last. His crowning error was his decision in August, 1915, in the midst of disaster at the front, to dismiss Grand Duke Nicholas and to assume personal command of military operations. He was even less qualified to do so than his uncle, and proved to be a nuisance at General Headquarters. Yet he had a mystical belief that his self-sacrifice might save the situation. "Perhaps a sin offering is needed to save Russia. I shall be the victim. God's will be done." Ultimately he was indeed the victim, for henceforth he was held personally responsible for military defeats. Thus, the final outcome was the destruction of his family, the ending of the Tsarist regime, and the advent of the Bolsheviks.*

March Revolution

Two revolutions occurred in Russia in 1917: the first, in March, ended Tsarism and created a Provisional Government, while the second, in November, toppled the Provisional Government and substituted Soviet rule. The first revolution was an unplanned affair that took everyone by surprise. Strikes and riots broke out in Petrograd on March 8 because of the desperate shortage of food and fuel arising from inadequate transportation facilities. The authorities ordered the army to restore order, but, instead, the soldiers mutinied and fraternized with the demonstrators. The Tsar, always distrustful of the Duma, suspected it of complicity and ordered its dissolution on March 11. The Duma leaders refused to comply with the order, and the Tsar discovered that he no longer could enforce obedience. This realization of powerlessness was to all intents and purposes the revolution itself. Suddenly it became apparent that the Tsarist government was a government in name only, that it did not possess the means for asserting its authority. Russia, in other words, no longer had a functioning government. This was the situation legally as well as factually when Tsar Nicholas abdicated on March 15 in favor of his brother Michael, and when Michael in turn gave up the throne the following day.

Nobody had expected, let alone plotted, this first Russian Revolution. Rather, it was a case of the decrepit and corrupt Tsarist regime being undermined by the stresses and disasters of war until the whole rickety structure came tumbling down. Some new structure had to be erected quickly lest the radical elements in the streets take over. On March 12 a Provisional Government was organized to administer the country until a Constituent Assembly could be elected. The new government was headed by the liberal Prince Georgi Lvov and included the Cadet leader, Professor Paul Miliukov, as minister for foreign affairs, and Alexander Kerensky, the only socialist, as minister of justice.

This was a bourgeois, liberal, middle-of-the-road cabinet, which favored reform up to a certain point. In fact, it did proclaim freedom of speech, press, and assembly; it declared an amnesty for political and religious offenses; rec-

* See "Roots of Russian Revolution," *EMM,* No. 115.

ognized the legal equality of all citizens without social, religious, or racial discrimination; and passed labor legislation, including the eight-hour day.* Despite this reform record the Provisional Government never sank roots in the country. For eight months it strove desperately but in vain to provide an adequate administration. At the end of that time the new government was not overthrown; rather, it collapsed as helplessly and ignominiously as the Tsarist regime had in March. The Provisional Government was then succeeded by an entirely new political system—that of the soviets.

445

Between Revolutions

The period between March and November, 1917, was one of struggle for power between the Provisional Government and the soviets. In this struggle the Provisional Government was fatally handicapped because from the beginning it refused to consider the two things that most Russians wanted—peace and land. Prince Lvov and his ministers insisted that such a fundamental reform as redistribution of land must wait for a Constituent Assembly that would be truly representative of the people and would have the authority to decide on such a basic issue. Likewise, the government refused to end the war, because Russia had certain commitments to her allies that could not be violated. These arguments were sensible and understandable, but politically suicidal. While the government was temporizing and pleading for patience, the soviets were winning over the masses by demanding immediate peace and immediate distribution of land.

The origin of the soviets goes back to the 1905 Revolution when the workers elected councils, or soviets, to coordinate their struggle against Tsarism. Although suppressed at that time, the soviets had proven their value as organs for agitation and direct action. They had precisely that quality which the Provisional Government conspicuously lacked—intimate rapport with the masses. An observer of the 1905 Revolution described this characteristic in the case of the Petrograd soviet as follows:

> It was, in the beginning, a confused and mixed assembly towards which the people turned nevertheless as to something that really represented them. It became the meeting place of soldiers who had escaped from their barracks, of workmen on strike, of domestic servants, of cab drivers. . . . It was the refuge, the port, the pound. One went there to palaver, to drink, to smoke, even to sleep. It truly was the house of the people.[10]

Very naturally, soviets reappeared with the crisis precipitated by the World War. Because of their origin and composition, they had none of the Provisional Government's squeamishness about waiting for elections before proceeding with peace negotiations and land distribution. Without hesitation or reservations they gave voice to popular yearnings, and in doing so attracted more and more mass support. Soviets soon were appearing in the villages and in military units as well as in the cities. Thus the Soviet movement mushroomed throughout the country, developing virtually into a grass-roots government that con-

* See "First Russian Revolution: March 1917," EMM, No. 116.

tinually challenged that in Petrograd. Village soviets were organizing seizures of nobles' estates; city soviets were behind the unceasing demonstrations and riots in the streets; while the soldiers' soviets were gradually usurping the authority of the officers to the point where they had control of all weapons and countersigned all orders before they could be executed.*

At the beginning, the delegates elected to the soviets were predominantly Socialist Revolutionaries and Mensheviks. The Bolsheviks remained relatively insignificant until the return of their leaders from Switzerland. On April 16, Lenin and several of his lieutenants arrived in Petrograd, having been transported through Germany in a sealed carriage. The German High Command calculated that these revolutionaries would undermine the pro-Allied Provisional Government, and their calculation proved correct. Lenin promptly issued his famous "April Theses" demanding immediate peace, land to the peasants, and all power to the soviets.

In the light of what was to come, Lenin's demands may seem natural and logical. Actually they aroused much opposition within the soviets amongst the Socialist Revolutionaries and Mensheviks, and even some of the Bolsheviks. Especially controversial was the demand for "all power to the soviets." This seemed at the time preposterous and irresponsible. As Marxists, most delegates to the soviets regarded the March Revolution as a bourgeois uprising, and believed that a second, or socialist, revolution was out of the question until Russia had undergone long-term economic development. Consequently, their strategy was to allow the Provisional Government to remain in office, while constantly prodding it for desired reforms and social change.

Lenin was almost alone in challenging this policy and calling for a second revolution at once. Time, however, was on his side, for the longer the war continued, the more the public discontent mounted, and the more popular his demands became. Slogans that seemed bizarre in April were to sound perfectly reasonable half a year later. By late 1917 many were ready to fight for "all power to the soviets" in order to be rid of the Provisional Government that stood in the way of the much-desired peace and land and bread.

An early indication of shifting public opinion was the forced resignation of Foreign Minister Miliukov on May 17. His insistence that Russia remain in the war made him so unpopular that he was dropped, and a new Provisional Government formed under Lvov and Kerensky. It remained in office until July 20, when Kerensky, who had been steadily emerging as the strongman, organized a new government with himself as premier. By this time the temper of the country had swung so far to the left that the new ministers were mostly Socialist Revolutionaries and Mensheviks. Gone were the days when the Cadets were regarded as the radicals of Russian politics. Now Kerensky was cooperating with the Mensheviks and the Socialist Revolutionaries in order to withstand Lenin and his Bolsheviks.

Bolshevik Revolution

Kerensky declared that his main objective was "to save the revolution from the extremists." In an effort to halt the growing seizure of estates he warned that the future Constituent Assembly would not recognize land transfers made after July 25. He also tried to restore some semblance of discipline

* See "Provisional Government versus Soviets," *EMM,* No. 117.

in the armed forces by reintroducing the death penalty for certain offenses. These measures naturally made Kerensky very unpopular with the Bolsheviks and other radicals. Unfortunately for him, he did not thereby attract the support of the military men and other conservatives. They regarded him as a weak, loud-mouthed politician, and demanded that he take immediate steps to crush the soviets. When he refused to do so, a certain General Lavr Kornilov staged an army revolt against Kerensky with the avowed aim of freeing the government from soviet domination.

The effect of Kornilov's revolt was precisely the opposite from that which was intended. It was the soviets that took the lead in organizing resistance against Kornilov and in conducting propaganda amongst his troops until many deserted. Thus Kornilov was defeated primarily by the soviets, and Kerensky consequently found himself under their domination. Furthermore, the Bolsheviks by this time were becoming increasingly influential within the soviets as public opinion veered more and more to the left. By October they had a majority in both the Petrograd and Moscow soviets. Lenin now decided that the time had come to overthrow Kerensky and effect the socialist revolution. But his own party still was not ready for the final plunge, fearing that they would not be able to retain power even if they were able to topple the Provisional Government. Lenin replied that 240,000 Bolshevik party members could govern Russia in the interest of the poor against the rich as easily as 130,000 landlords previously had governed in the interest of the rich against the poor. Finally, after threatening to resign, Lenin persuaded the Central Committee of his party to vote for revolution, and the date was set for November 7.

The actual revolution was anticlimactic. With almost no resistance the Bolshevik forces seized key positions in Petrograd—railway stations, bridges, banks, and government buildings. Blood was shed only at the Winter Palace, and casualties there totaled one Red soldier and five Red sailors. Kerensky managed to escape, and after a futile attempt to organize resistance, fled to exile abroad. Thus fell the Provisional Government with a humiliating casualness reminiscent of the end of Tsarism. There was no fighting, because Kerensky had as few dedicated supporters in November as Nicholas had had in March.*

The easy victory of the Bolsheviks did not mean that they commanded the support of all the Russian people, or even the majority. This was demonstrated by the composition of the Constituent Assembly that was finally elected on November 25: Socialist Revolutionaries, 370; Bolsheviks, 175; Left Socialist Revolutionaries, 40; Cadets, 17; Mensheviks, 16; national groups, 86. The Assembly met in Petrograd on January 18, 1918, and, after holding one session, was dispersed by the Bolsheviks, who now had military power. Nevertheless, the make-up of the Assembly is revealing of the relative following enjoyed by the various parties at that time.

Brest-Litovsk Treaty

Meanwhile, Lenin was earnestly striving for peace, if for no other reason than that Russia was in no condition to resume fighting. On November 25, Trotsky broadcast to all belligerents a radio message inviting them to conclude

* See "Second Russian Revolution: November 1917," *EMM*, No. 118.

448

an immediate armistice. The Allies, unwilling to accept peace on the basis of the Bolshevik slogan of "No annexations and no indemnities," evaded an answer. But the Central Powers were willing to negotiate, and on December 5 they signed an armistice with the Bolsheviks. In the negotiations that followed, the Germans demanded the cession of Poland and the Baltic provinces, supposedly on the basis of self-determination. When the Bolsheviks demurred, the Germans broke the armistice and advanced on Petrograd. Lenin now decided to capitulate, partly because he lacked the means to resist, but also because he calculated that the Germans would lose the war and so would not be able to retain their conquests.

On March 3, 1918, he accepted the Brest-Litovsk Treaty, whose Draconian terms were much harsher than those originally demanded. He surrendered not only Poland and the Baltic provinces, but also Finland, the Ukraine, and parts of the Caucasus. These cessions involved 62 million people and 1¼ million square miles of territory producing three-fourths of Russia's iron and coal, and including half of her industrial plants and a third of her crop area.

In this manner Russia dropped out of World War I, and the new Bolshevik rulers proceeded to organize the Union of Soviet Socialist Republics with repercussions still being felt in all parts of the globe.*

V. Global Phase of the War: American Intervention

When World War I began, President Wilson immediately called upon his fellow countrymen to observe strict neutrality. In his message to the American people on August 19, 1914, he declared, "I venture to speak a solemn word of warning to you against that deepest, most subtle, most essential breach of neutrality which may spring out of partisanship, out of passionately taking sides. The United States must be neutral in fact as well as in name during these days that are to try men's souls."

This appeal met with general approval, for the great majority of Americans wished to avoid involvement in the war. And yet, by 1917, Wilson himself was leading the country into war. Why the intervention in the face of this strong proneutrality sentiment?

One factor was the campaign for military preparedness. The National Security League, founded on December 1, 1914, was vigorously supported by military men, munitions makers, and politicians seeking an issue. They publicized the possibility of war with Germany and demanded compulsory military training and very substantial increases in the standing army and the navy. Wilson at first opposed this agitation, but for political reasons he could not ignore it altogether. In the end, he himself led preparedness parades in New York and Washington, and he sponsored the National Defense Act of June 3, 1916, which doubled the standing army, reorganized the National Guard, and provided for the training of officers in colleges and summer camps. Two months later another bill authorized a three-year program for major expansion of the navy. The intensive agitation and publicity connected with this

* See "Lenin Proclaims the New Order," *EMM*, No. 119.

military preparedness helped to prepare the nation psychologically for intervention in the war.

Very similar was the effect of the armed American incursion into Mexico between March, 1916, and February, 1917. This was precipitated when Francisco (Pancho) Villa, a half revolutionary and half bandit, raided the border town of Columbus in New Mexico, leaving behind nineteen dead. Villa's aim was to provoke American intervention and thereby to discredit and overthrow President Carranza. Wilson did respond by promptly ordering a punitive expedition under General John Pershing. Although over 100,000 men were sent across the border, it proved impossible to pin down Villa and his followers. Instead, Villa struck again at Glen Springs in Texas, killing four more persons. This aroused a great clamor in the United States for a declaration of war and occupation of northern Mexico. Both Carranza and Wilson, however, wished to avoid hostilities, and arrangements finally were worked out making possible the withdrawal of American troops. Nevertheless, this strange interlude contributed to the building up of a war spirit in the United States by providing the thrills of military action without the grief and sacrifice.

Another factor operating in favor of intervention was the American financial and industrial commitment to the Allied cause. Bryan foresaw this pressure and urged from the beginning a "moral embargo" on loans to belligerents. This was rejected by Wilson, so that by the end of 1914 the House of Morgan was already "coordinating" Allied purchases of war material in the United States. To pay for these purchases the Allied powers first gave cash, then sold the bonds and stocks they held in the United States, and finally had to resort to large-scale borrowing. This situation inevitably generated pressures for American involvement in the war. Booming industries in the United States were dependent upon continued Allied orders, while American bankers had safes full of British and French paper that would become worthless if Germany emerged victorious.

Also noteworthy are the propaganda campaigns conducted by both sets of belligerents to influence American thinking. The Allies on the whole were more successful, partly because of superior skill and communication facilities, but also because their case was easier to justify and defend. British highhandedness on the seas paled before the German invasion and occupation of Belgium. The alleged starvation in Germany resulting from England's blockade was soon forgotten when the U-boats began taking their toll of American lives.

This leads to what proved to be the most important single factor responsible for American intervention—Germany's submarine campaign against merchant ships. Germany refrained from waging unrestricted submarine warfare until 1917 for a simple military reason—there were not enough submarines available to guarantee Britain's defeat before the military strength of the United States could be brought to bear. But the number of U-boats rose rapidly—from 27 in February, 1915, to 74 in August, 1916, and to 103 in February, 1917. Thus by the beginning of 1917 the German military believed that if they were given a free hand, England could be brought to her knees within six months. This was the basic reason why the German government ordered unrestricted submarine warfare beginning on February 1, 1917. The order was issued with full realization that it would lead almost inevitably to American intervention. But it was logically calculated that the United States as a belligerent could not give more economic support to the Entente than it was already providing as a neutral, and that its armies would arrive too late in Europe to save Britain from being forced to surrender.

Wilson now cut diplomatic relations with Germany, but he still drew back from actual war. In a message to Congress he declared that he could not believe the Germans would carry out their threat to destroy American lives and ships. If he were proven wrong, he would return to Congress for legislative authority to protect the rights of Americans on the high seas.

Wilson's restraint failed to halt what was now an inexorable drift to war. On March 1, 1917, the American press made public the notorious Zimmermann telegram sent by the then German foreign secretary to his minister in Mexico City. In case of war with the United States, the minister was to propose to the Carranza government an alliance whereby Mexico would intervene on Germany's side and would receive in return "generous financial aid" and also the restitution of the "lost territory in Texas, New Mexico, and Arizona." Carranza also should be asked to mediate between Germany and Japan, who were then at war, and invite Japan to join the coalition. This telegram had been intercepted and decoded by the British, who transmitted it to Ambassador Page. When it was released to the American press, public opinion in the United States naturally was deeply shocked. The references to Japan and to territorial cessions to Mexico aroused war sentiment in the Middle and Far West, where there had been relative apathy. At the same time the Germans were torpedoing American ships and American lives were being lost. To cap it all, the Tsarist regime was now overthrown, and the United States recognized the new Russian Provisional Government on March 20. Without reservations the United States now could join a league of democratic powers battling the autocracies of Central Europe.

On April 2 Congress convened for an extraordinary session. President Wilson read his War Message to the assembled legislators: * "We are glad to fight for the ultimate peace of the world and for the liberation of its peoples. . . . The world must be made safe for democracy. . . . We desire no conquest, no dominion. . . . We are but one of the champions of the rights of mankind. . . ." On April 4 and 6, the Senate and the House passed a joint resolution declaring a state of war between the United States and Germany. The presidential proclamation followed, and the United States went to war.

Wilson's enunciation of objectives in his War Message was necessarily couched in abstract and general terms. But in his address to the joint session of Congress on January 8, 1918, he set forth specific and detailed war aims in the form of his famous Fourteen Points. Outstanding among these were "open covenants of peace" as against secret diplomacy, freedom of the seas, removal of barriers to international trade, reduction of armaments, impartial adjustment of all colonial claims on the principle that the interests of the colonial peoples must have equal weight with the claims of colonial powers, and the application of the principle of self-determination in dealing with the various subject minorities in Central and Eastern Europe.

* See "United States Enters World War I," *EMM*, No. 120.

VI. ALLIED VICTORY   451

Eminent British and American naval experts are agreed that only a few more submarines would have enabled Germany to win the war. How close the decision was is evident in the figures on ship losses and ship construction presented in Table 1. These figures show that the Allies won out not only by

TABLE 1. Allied and Neutral Ships Lost and Constructed
During World War I (gross tons)

Period	Lost	Constructed
1915	1,744,657	1,202,000
1916	2,799,772	1,688,000
1917	6,623,623	2,937,786
1918		
1st quarter	1,146,920	870,317
2nd quarter	963,370	1,243,274
3rd quarter	892,546	1,384,130

Source: David Lloyd George, *War Memoirs* (Boston: Little, 1934), III, 132–33. By permission of the Beaverbrook Foundations.

stepping up ship construction but also by cutting down on ship sinkings. This was achieved by a variety of methods, including the development of an efficient convoy system, the camouflaging of merchantmen, the use of depth bombs containing large charges of high explosives, and the invention of hydrophones, which made possible the detection of nearby submarines. Thanks to this variety of devices the Allies passed the danger point early in 1918, when the construction of new ships for the first time surpassed the tonnage destroyed.

Once the U-boat threat was overcome, the United States was able to make effective use of her enormous economic potential. How decisive this was is made clear in the statistics concerning the productivity of the belligerents shown in Table 2.

TABLE 2. Production of the Belligerent Powers
(in millions of tons)

	August 1, 1914		September 15, 1914		1917	
	Allies	Central Powers	Allies	Central Powers	Allies	Central Powers
Pig Iron	22	22	16	25	50	15
Steel	19	21	16	25	58	16
Coal	394	331	346	355	851	340

Source: F. Sternberg, *Capitalism and Socialism on Trial* (New York: Day, 1951), pp. 166–67.

The intervention of the United States gave the Allies decisive superiority in manpower as well as in war supplies. In the month of March, 1918, a total of 84,889 American soldiers reached the western front, and in July the number rose to 306,350. Thus a fresh new army was made available to the Allied commanders each month. The German High Command made a final desperate effort to avoid defeat by launching an all-out drive on Paris in the spring of 1918. Their effort was aided by the Brest-Litovsk Treaty which enabled them to transfer divisions from the eastern to the western front. In the greatest offensive of the war to that date, the Germans managed to reach within forty miles of the capital, but then were stopped. The turning point came when the Allies on July 18 launched a counterattack supported by fleets of tanks. The attack not only proved the value of the tank as an instrument for trench warfare, but also disclosed for the first time widespread defeatism in the German ranks. Whole battalions of Germans surrendered, sometimes to single infantrymen, while retiring German troops greeted fresh units going up to the line with shouts of *"Streikbrecher," "Kriegsverlängerer"* ("Strike breakers" and "War prolongers").

Meanwhile, Germany's allies were in even worse straits. The Bulgarian front crumbled when General Franchet d'Esperey, commander of the Allied forces in Saloniki, attacked in mid-September. On September 29, 1918, Bulgarian representatives signed an armistice, and on October 3 King Ferdinand abdicated in favor of his son Boris. Likewise in Turkey, British imperial forces were advancing victoriously in a two-pronged drive—one from Egypt up the Levant coast, and the other from the Persian Gulf up the Mesopotamian valley. At the same time an Allied force from Saloniki was marching upon Constantinople. Staggered by these setbacks and isolated by Bulgaria's surrender, the Turks accepted an armistice on October 30, 1918.

Most desperate was the position of Austria-Hungary. The numerous minorities were organizing national assemblies and proclaiming their independence. Even German-Austrians and Hungarians, who hitherto had ruled the empire, now were talking in terms of independent states of their own. At the same time the Italians were breaking through on the Piave, while Franchet d'Esperey was advancing up the Danube. On November 3 an Austro-Hungarian Armistice Commission accepted the terms of the Italian High Command, and on November 6 Count Michael Karolyi, a liberal Hungarian leader, signed a separate armistice at Belgrade in behalf of Hungary. The ancient Hapsburg Empire finally reached its end on November 11, when Emperor Charles renounced his sovereign rights.

Meanwhile, the German position on the western front had steadily deteriorated. With American soldiers pouring in, Marshal Foch, the Allied commander in chief, was able to strike where and as he pleased. German casualties were outstripping replacements, and deserters were crowding into depots and railroad stations. These setbacks, together with the news of Bulgaria's surrender, shook the nerve of General Ludendorff. In something of a panic he demanded on September 29 that the government initiate armistice negotiations "without delay" while the army was still reasonably intact. In preparation for the negotiations the Kaiser appointed his cousin, Prince Max of Baden, as the new chancellor. Prince Max, who had the reputation of a liberal and pacifist, requested President Wilson for negotiations on the basis of the Fourteen Points. There followed an exchange of notes between Berlin and Washington that extended over several weeks. A principal stumbling block was the Kaiser's adamant refusal to abdicate. His hand was forced, however, by mutiny in the German fleet at Kiel on November 3. The mutiny spread rapidly from port to port and then into the interior. Prince Max forced the issue by announcing the abdication of the emperor November 9. Two days later the armistice was signed and fighting ceased on the western front.

Thus ended the First World War—a war that lasted four years and three months, involved thirty sovereign states, overthrew four empires, gave birth to seven new nations, took approximately 8,500,000 combatant lives and 10,000,000 noncombatant, and cost $180.5 billion directly and $151.6 billion indirectly.

VII. Peace Settlement

Separate peace treaties were signed with each of the Central Powers: the Versailles Treaty with Germany, June 28, 1919; the St. German Treaty with Austria, September 10, 1919; the Trianon Treaty with Hungary, March 22, 1919; the Neuilly Treaty with Bulgaria, November 27, 1919; and the Sèvres Treaty with Turkey, August 20, 1920. Three features of this over-all peace settlement are of significance for world history: the establishment of the League of Nations, the application of the principle of self-determination in Europe, and the failure to apply this principle outside Europe.

The League of Nations stands out in world history as the first worldwide association of nations pledged to mutual protection against aggression and to resolution of disputes by nonviolent methods. The idea of a league of this sort had been frequently proposed during the course of the war. In 1915 a League of Nations Society had been founded in Britain, and a League to Enforce Peace, in the United States. Various world leaders, including Pope Benedict XV, Lord Robert Cecil, then British Under Secretary for Foreign Affairs, and General Smuts, then South African Minister of Defense, presented suggestions for the future organization of peace. In the last of his Fourteen Points, President Wilson declared that "a general association of nations must be formed under specific covenants for the purpose of affording mutual guarantees of political independence with territorial integrity to great and small states alike." Thus the League was the only problem of the peace to which serious thought had been given when the war ended.

The League Covenant, which was an integral part of the Versailles Treaty, came into effect in January, 1920. In a world made safe for democracy—as was then hoped—it was natural that the Covenant should provide the standard democratic pattern of parliament, cabinet, and civil service. The Assembly was the League's parliament, and each of the forty-two original member states had one vote in the Assembly. The Council was the League's cabinet, and consisted of the representatives of the five "Principal Allied and Associated Powers," each with a permanent seat, and in addition the representatives of four other powers "selected by the Assembly from time to time in its discretion." The original permanent members were England, the United States, France, Japan, and Italy, but the United States did not join the League. Subsequently, Germany and Russia were given permanent seats, and the number of nonpermanent members was increased to ten. Finally, there was the Secretariat, which functioned as the League's civil service, and consisted of a Secretary General and a staff.

The primary purpose of the League was to preserve the peace. Its members were to afford each other mutual protection against aggression, to submit disputes to arbitration or inquiry, and to abstain from war until three months after an award. The secondary purpose of the League was to concern itself with health, social, economic, and humanitarian problems of international scope. For this purpose there were established specialized League bodies such as the Health Organization, the Committee on Intellectual Cooperation, and the International Labor Organization, as well as numerous temporary advisory commissions. By and large, the League succeeded brilliantly in its secondary functions. It proved invaluable in improving international labor conditions, promoting world health, combatting the narcotic and slave traffics, and coping with economic crises. But we shall see that the League was not able to keep the peace, and since this was its *raison d'être,* the failure spelled the end of the entire organization.

The post–World War I settlement was characterized also by the redrawing of European frontiers on the basis of the principle of self-determination. This had been propounded fairly explicitly in the Fourteen Points, and was then officially implemented in the various peace treaties. The net result was a drastic revision of the map of Europe. Alsace-Lorraine was returned to France without question. Russia was deprived of most of her Baltic coastline by the establishment of the independent states of Finland, Latvia, Estonia, and Lithuania. An independent Poland was created, carved out of former Russian, German, and Hapsburg provinces. The new state of Yugoslavia also appeared, comprising prewar Serbia and Montenegro together with various former Hapsburg territories inhabited by South Slavs. Rumania more than doubled in size as a result of her acquisitions from Austria-Hungary, Russia, and Bulgaria. Finally, from the remains of the old Hapsburg Empire, there emerged the two rump states of Austria and Hungary.

It does not follow that the principle of self-determination was invariably respected in the drawing of the new frontiers. Indeed, there were bitter protests concerning the sizable German minorities in Poland and Czechoslovakia, the Hungarian minorities in Yugoslavia, Rumania, and Czechoslovakia, and the Russian minorities in Poland, Czechoslovakia, and Rumania. The explanation is to be found partly in the fact that the numerous ethnic groups in Central and Eastern Europe were so inextricably mixed that no frontiers could be drawn without creating considerable minorities on one side or the other. The inevitable minorities, however, were substantially increased because frontiers sometimes were drawn to comply with strategic considerations as well as to satisfy nationalist aspirations. This was why the Sudeten Germans were left in Czechoslovakia, why the Tyrol Germans were left in Italy, and why the union of Austria and Germany was specifically forbidden by the St. Germain Treaty even though it would have been in accord with popular will, at least in the immediate postwar years. Yet despite these deviations, the new frontiers were infinitely more in accord with nationalist aspirations than the old. The number of the minority peoples was much smaller after World War I than before.

It is sometimes charged that the peacemakers erred in following the self-determination principle to the point of dissolving the Hapsburg Empire altogether. Winston Churchill, for example, has written that "The cardinal tragedy was the complete break-up of the Austro-Hungarian Empire by the Treaties of St. Germain and Trianon. . . . There is not one of the peoples or provinces that constituted the Empire of the Hapsburgs to whom gaining their independence has not brought the tortures which ancient poets and theologians had reserved for the damned." [11] While it is true that self-determination did not usher in the millennium that some idealists naïvely expected, it is equally true that the St. Germain and Trianon Treaties were not responsible for the dissolution of the Hapsburg Empire. The breakup began in the later stages of the war as a result of the military defeats and the subversive impact of Wilson's Fourteen Points on the subject peoples. In a desperate effort to halt the crumbling of the imperial structure, Emperor Charles issued a manifesto on October 16, 1918, transforming Austria into a federative state. In Hungary, Count Michael Karolyi likewise granted the minority peoples full autonomy. But both offers were unhesitatingly rejected. The Czechs proclaimed their independence in Prague, the Germans did likewise in Vienna, the South Slavs declared for union with Belgrade, and the Rumanians of Transylvania for union with Bucharest.

Thus the subject nationalities turned their backs upon both the autocratic old Hapsburg Empire and the proposed new federated version. However desirable it might have been for the Hapsburg Empire to have been preserved in one form or another, the fact remains that it lacked any substantial popular support upon which it could have been based. The Hapsburg Empire, like the Romanoff, Hohenzollern, and Ottoman, was the victim not of shortsighted diplomats but rather of triumphant nationalism, which now was coming into its own throughout Central and Eastern Europe where it had for so long been repressed.

Although the peacemakers generally applied self-determination in Europe, they definitely did not do so outside Europe. This discrimination was clearly evident in Wilson's Fourteen Points, which specifically spelled out how the aspirations of the various European minorities were to be satisfied. By contrast, Point 5 declared that in the colonies "the interests of the populations concerned must have equal weight with the equitable claims of the government whose title is to be determined." The significant point here is the reference to the "interests" rather than to the "wishes" of the colonial peoples. Needless to say, it was the Europeans themselves who decided what these "interests" were, and the outcome was a modified form of imperial rule known as the mandate system.

Article 22 of the League Covenant referred to the inhabitants of the colonies taken from the Central Powers as "peoples not yet able to stand by themselves under the strenuous conditions of the modern world." The article accordingly provided that the "tutelage of such peoples should be entrusted to advanced nations who, by reason of their resources, their experience, or their geographical position, can best undertake this responsibility . . . and that this tutelage should be exercised by them as Mandatories on behalf of the League." It is significant that this provision for "tutelage" under "Mandatories" was not extended to the colonies of the victorious Allies, whose inhabitants in many cases were at a similar level of development or lack of development.

456   The Mandates article divided the foreign and overseas territories of Germany and the Ottoman Empire into Class A, B, and C mandates. The category varied according to the level of development of the territory concerned. On this basis the former Ottoman possessions were put in Class A, and the German colonies in B and C. Of the Ottoman territories, Mesopotamia and Palestine were alloted to Britain as the Mandatory Power, and Syria and Lebanon to France. Of the German colonies, the greater part of Tanganyika went to Britain and the remainder to Belgium; Togoland and the Cameroons were divided between Britain and France; South-West Africa was allotted to the Union of South Africa; and Germany's Pacific islands north of the equator went to Japan, and those south of the equator to Australia and New Zealand.

The Mandatory Powers assumed specific obligations toward the inhabitants of the mandated territories. For fulfillment of these obligations they were accountable to the Permanent Mandates Commission, and were required to report annually to the Council of the League of Nations. Though neither the Commission nor the League itself had authority to coerce a recalcitrant Mandatory Power, yet it is significant that European states for the first time accepted certain specified procedures. The procedures varied according to the type of mandate. In the case of Class A, the Mandates article looked forward specifically to the granting of independence as soon as feasible. The duty of the Mandatory Power was merely "the rendering of administrative advice and assistance . . . until such time as they [the people of the mandated territory] are able to stand alone. The wishes of these communities must be a principal consideration in the selection of the Mandatory." But for B and C Class mandates, there was no reference to eventual independence. The obligation rather was to provide administration in accord with the interests of the inhabitants.

Although the mandate system represented a certain improvement over the traditional division of colonial booty by the victors in a war, nevertheless it is strongly reminiscent of the 1815 settlement in its ignoring of national aspirations. We shall see that the inhabitants of the Ottoman territories did not want mandated status, and were violently opposed to France as Mandatory Power. Their wishes were directly flouted when Syria and Lebanon were allotted to France. Even in the case of some of the Class B mandates in Africa, there was acute dissatisfaction with the arrangements made. It is not surprising, then, that just as the ignoring of nationalist wishes in 1815 led to a long series of revolutions in Europe during the nineteenth century, so this mandate system was to lead to uprisings in the colonial world during the postwar years.

It is paradoxical that Europe's subject minorities required a full century to win independence, while most of the overseas colonial peoples, in many cases less advanced than the Europeans, were to attain freedom within half a century. The explanation presumably is to be found partly in the effect of modern mass-communication media. Thanks to the radio blaring forth in village squares everywhere, the contemporary Indonesian or Egyptian of Pakistani is aware of, and responsive to, world events and trends to a degree never imagined by a nineteenth century Galician or Bosnian or Albanian. The contemporary colonial awakening is to be explained also by the two World Wars that weakened the European powers much more than the series of relatively minor conflicts between 1815 and 1914.

457

VIII. WORLD WAR I IN WORLD HISTORY

A glance at the globe before and after World War I reveals comparatively few changes. Europe's frontiers were different because of the disappearance of four empires, but so far as the world as a whole was concerned, European dominance appeared undiminished. Britain, France, and the other imperial powers still ruled as many overseas colonies as before 1914. Indeed, their possessions were even greater, for they now controlled territories in the Middle East that formerly had been under the sultan. Thus, Europe's global hegemony appeared to be more complete after World War I than before.

Beneath the surface, however, the situation was entirely different. In fact, the overriding significance of World War I from a global viewpoint is precisely that it began the undermining of Europe's supremacy—a process that was completed following World War II. The undermining was evident in at least three regards: the economic decline, the political crisis, and the weakening hold over the colonies.

Before 1914, Europe's economy was dependent to a considerable degree upon massive overseas investments, yielding massive annual returns. During World War I, however, Britain lost a quarter of her foreign investments, France a third, and Germany lost all. The reverse of this trend may be seen in the new financial strength of the United States. Prior to the war, America depended on Europe for her capital requirements. By 1914 the United States owed about $4 billion to European investors, a trifling sum by contemporary standards, but three times the national debt of the period. The war, however, reversed this relationship, for the Allied governments were forced to sell their American holdings to pay for war materials, and then to borrow in the United States from both the government and from private sources. Thus, by 1919 the United States had become a creditor nation to the tune of $3.7 billion; by 1930 this had risen to $8.8 billion.

The same pattern is evident in industry, for many European industrial areas were devastated, while American factories mushroomed spectacularly under the impetus of unlimited wartime demand. By 1929 the United States was responsible for no less than 42.2 per cent of world industrial output, an amount greater than that of all the countries of Europe, including Russia. Thus, the economic relationships between Europe and the United States were reversed as a result of World War I. Europe no longer was the banker and the workshop of the world, as she had been during the nineteenth century. Leadership in both areas had crossed the Atlantic.

The war gutted Europe politically as well as economically. Prior to 1914 Europe had been the source of the basic political ideas and institutions of modern times. Their impact, as we have seen, had been felt in all corners of the globe. The holocaust of war, however, left Europeans demoralized and unbelieving. In all parts of the Continent the old order was being questioned and challenged. In a confidential memorandum of March, 1919, the British premier, David Lloyd George, wrote, "There is a deep sense not only of discontent, but of anger and revolt, amongst the workmen against pre-war conditions. The whole existing order in its political, social and economic aspects is questioned by the masses of the people from one end of Europe to the other." [12]

In this revolutionary crisis, many Europeans looked for guidance to two non-Europeans, the American Wilson and the Russian Lenin. Wilson's Fourteen Points had stirred up a ferment of democratic hope and expectancy. When he stepped on the bloodsoaked soil of Europe in December, 1918, huge crowds greeted Wilson with delirious enthusiasm as "King of Humanity," "Savior," "Prince of Peace." They listened avidly to his plans for a future of peace and security.

At the same time another gospel of salvation was coming from the East. The millions of dead and wounded, the smoking ruins of cities and villages, made large masses receptive to the call for revolution and for a new social order. In imitation of the Bolshevik Revolution, soviets were set up in Berlin, Hamburg, and Budapest. Demonstrations were staged in the streets of London, Paris, and Rome. Wilson's confidante, Colonel House, wrote in his diary on March 22, 1919: "Rumblings of discontent every day. The people want peace. Bolshevism is gaining ground everywhere. Hungary has just succumbed. We are sitting upon an open powder magazine and some day a spark may ignite it." [13]

In the eighteenth and nineteenth centuries, European ideas had awakened and inspired the Americans and Russians. Now the opposite was the case. The Europeans were looking elsewhere for leaders and for ideas. In the following chapter we shall see that Europe remained "an open powder magazine" until the 1920's, and then settled down to a few years of quiet and prosperity before the economic hurricane of 1929.

Finally, Europe's hegemony was undermined by World War I because of the repercussions in the overseas colonies.* The spectacle of one bloc of European powers fighting another to the bitter end damaged the prestige of the white master irreparably. No longer was he regarded as almost divinely ordained to rule over colored multitudes. Equally disruptive was the participation in the war of millions of colonials as soldiers or as laborers. Indian divisions fought on the western front and in Mesopotamia; many Africans in French uniform fought in northern France; and large numbers of Chinese and Indochinese served in labor battalions behind the lines. Needless to say, the colonials who returned home after such experiences were not likely to be as deferential to European overlords as before. For example, a French administrator observed that "the 175,000 soldiers enrolled during the years 1914–1918, dug the grave of the old Africa in the trenches of France and Flanders." [14] And a French Governor-General of Indochina wrote in 1926: "The war which covered Europe with blood has . . . awakened in lands far distant from us a feeling of independence. . . . All has changed in the past few years. Both men and ideas and Asia herself are being transformed." [15]

Revolutionary ideas in the colonies were also spread by propaganda associated with the conduct of the war. It is true that Wilson's Fourteen Points had referred only to the "interest" rather than to the desires of the colonial peoples. But this was an overfine distinction in a time of war, and the revolutionary

* See "World War I in World History," *EMM*, No. 121.

phrase "self-determination of peoples" left its imprint on the colonial world as well as upon Europe. Equally influential were the ideologies of socialism and communism. Before World War I, Asian intellectuals had been inspired by Western liberalism and nationalism. They had quoted Voltaire, Mazzini, and John Stuart Mill. But their sons now were likely to quote Marx, Lenin, or Harold Laski. Dr. Sun Yat-sen, on July 25, 1919, gave evidence of this shift when he declared, "If the people of China wish to be free . . . its only ally and brother in the struggle for national freedom are the Russian workers and peasants of the Red Army." [16]

All these repercussions of World War I on the colonial world inevitably had profound political consequences. The peace treaties had left the colonial territories under European tutelage, but Europe now had to fight to assert her authority. In a great sweep from Morocco through the Middle East and across South Asia to China, subject peoples stirred and struck out for freedom. We shall see in the following chapter that, after very considerable effort, the European powers were able to re-establish their rule. But this was to last for only a few more years. World War I had sapped the foundations of European colonial empires, and World War II was to sweep away the tottering structure.

SUGGESTED READING

The standard works on the origins of World War I are by L. Albertini, *The Origins of the War of 1914,* trans. and ed. by I. M. Massey (New York: Oxford Univ., 1953), 2 vols.; S. B. Fay, *The Origins of the World War,* rev. ed. (New York: Macmillan, 1934), 2 vols.; and B. E. Schmitt, *The Coming of the War, 1914* (New York: Scribners, 1930), 2 vols. A convenient collection of readings and a good bibliography on this subject is available in D. E. Lee, ed., *The Outbreak of the First World War* [Problems in European Civilization] (Boston: Heath, 1958).

An excellent summary of World War I is provided by H. W. Baldwin, *World War I: An Outline History* (New York: Harper, 1962); B. H. Liddell Hart, *The Real War, 1914–1918* (Boston: Little, 1964); and C. R. M. F. Cruttwell, *A History of the Great War, 1914–1918* (New York: Oxford Univ., 1936). Outstanding works on specific aspects are by B. W. Tuchman, *The Guns of August* (New York: Macmillan, 1962) for the first month's operations leading to the deadlock; Winston S. Churchill, *The Unknown War: The Eastern Front* (New York: Scribner, 1931); A. Moorehead, *Gallipoli* (London: Hamilton, 1956); and J. C. Adams, *Flight in Winter* (Princeton: Princeton Univ., 1942), for the Serb 1914 campaigns and the 1915 flight through Albania.

The most thorough study of the Russian Revolutions is the fascinating account by E. H. Carr, *The Bolshevik Revolution, 1917–1923* (New York: Macmillan, 1951–1953), 3 vols. Convenient brief bibliographies and collections of readings are provided by R. H. McNeal, *The Russian Revolution* [Source Problems in World Civilization] (New York: Holt, 1959) and A. E. Adams, *The Russian Revolution and Bolshevik Victory* [Problems in European Civilization] (Boston: Heath, 1960). Fascinating documentary materials are provided in F. A. Golder, *Documents of Russian History, 1914–1917* (New York: Appleton, 1927); J. Bunyan and H. H. Fisher, *The Bolshevik Revolution, 1917–1918* (Stanford;

Stanford Univ., 1934); and R. P. Browder and A. F. Kerensky, *The Russian Provisional Government, 1917* (Stanford: Stanford University, 1962), 3 vols.

The literature on American intervention is expertly summarized and analyzed in R. W. Leopold, "The Problem of American Intervention, 1917: An Historical Retrospect," *World Politics,* II (1950), 405–25, and in E. R. May, *American Intervention: 1917 and 1941* (Washington: Service Center for Teachers of History, 1960), No. 30.

Finally, for the Versailles settlement see the convenient collections of readings, and also the bibliographies, in I. J. Lederer, ed., *The Versailles Settlement: Was It Foredoomed to Failure?* [Problems in European Civilization] (Boston: Heath, 1960) and T. P. Greene, ed., *Wilson at Versailles* [Problems in American Civilization] (Boston: Heath, 1957).

Since the day of Japan's victory over Russia, the peoples of Asia have cherished the hope of shaking off the yoke of European oppression, a hope which has given rise to a series of independence movements—in Egypt, Persia, Turkey, Afghanistan, and finally in India. . . . If we want to regain our rights, we must resort to force.

SUN YAT-SEN, *1924*

Chapter

21

Nationalist Uprisings in the Colonial World

World War I was followed by a wave of revolutions in the colonial territories. The roots of these revolutions go back to the pre-1914 years, but it was the war itself that provided the immediate stimulus. The final outcomes varied, with the Turks at one extreme winning most of their objectives, the Rif tribesmen at the other going down to bloody defeat, and, in between, the Egyptians, Iraqis, Indians, and others winning modest constitutional concessions. In the light of retrospect, these uprisings represent the prelude to the elemental upheavals that finally ended the European empires during the two decades following World War II.

I. TURKEY

The most spectacular and successful of all the post–World War I colonial revolts against European domination was that of the Turks. They had suffered disastrous defeat during the war, and had then been compelled to accept humiliating armistice and peace terms. Yet they bounced back, defeating their enemies in armed conflict, and winning a new treaty with more favorable terms. Thus, of all the Central Powers, only primitive and despised Turkey proved capable of turning upon the victorious Allies and forcing them to accept a revision of the peace settlement. To understand this extraordinary outcome it is necessary to review the tangled wartime diplomacy concerning the Ottoman Empire.

Wartime Diplomacy

Britain was the prime mover behind most of the diplomacy involving the Middle East during the war years. She was responsible for three sets of often-conflicting agreements—with her own allies, with Arab representatives, and with the Zionists.

The agreements among the Allies consisted of four secret treaties providing for the partitioning of the Ottoman Empire. The first of these was the Constantinople agreement comprising diplomatic exchanges between Russia, Britain, and France during a five week period in March–April, 1915. The Western powers reluctantly agreed that in the event of victory, Russia should annex Constantinople, the Straits, and considerable hinterland on each side. In exchange, Britain and France stipulated that they would later define their own claims in Persia and the Arabian Peninsula as well as the Ottoman Empire. A few weeks later, on April 26, 1915, the three Entente powers signed the secret Treaty of London with Italy in order to secure that country as an ally. In addition to territory in the Alps and along the Dalmatian coast, Italy was to receive the province of Adalia in southwest Asia Minor, and also was given full sovereignty over the Dodecanese Islands, which she had occupied during the Italo-Turkish War of 1911–1912.

The most far-reaching of the secret treaties—the Sykes-Picot Agreement of April 26, 1916—defined the over-all claims of Britain, France, and Russia. Russia was alloted the already promised Constantinople and Straits, together with Armenia and parts of Kurdistan and northern Anatolia. Britain obtained Mesopotamia and an enclave about Haifa and Acre on the Mediterranean. The French sphere was to include Syria north of Tyre, the Adana vilayet, and the Cilicia region in southwest Anatolia. Finally, Palestine west of the Jordan River and from Gaza to Tyre was to be under an international administration because of its Holy Places.

The Italians, upon hearing of the Sykes-Picot arrangements, extended their claims and insisted on diplomatic ratification. This was granted with the British-French-Italian Saint-Jean-de-Maurienne Treaty of April, 1917, by which Italy was to receive most of the west coast of Asia Minor in addition to Adalia province already assigned.

These secret treaties marked the death warrant of the Ottoman Empire. They provided for the amputation of not only the Arab provinces but also of most of Asia Minor itself. The French, Italian, and Russian spheres left to the Turks only 20,000 square miles in the northern section of their homeland. More important, these secret treaties were in direct conflict with certain agreements that Britain was concluding at this time with Arab representatives.

Even before the outbreak of World War I, Britain had shown interest in the Arabs as a counterweight to the Turks, who were then drifting toward Germany. Some Arab circles were definitely interested, particularly because of the Turkification policies of the Young Turks, noted in Chapter 14, section III. The leading dignitary among the Arabs was Emir Hussein of the Hashimite family, Keeper of the Holy Places and Prince of Mecca. Early in 1914 Hussein's second son, Abdullah, in passing through Cairo, sounded out the British about possible aid for an Arab uprising against the Turks. As soon as Turkey joined the Central Powers in November, 1914, the British eagerly renewed these contacts. Protracted negotiations between Hussein and Sir Henry McMahon, British High Commissioner in Egypt, culminated in a military alliance and in an ambiguous political understanding that was to cause endless troubles in later years. In return for an Arab revolt against the Turks, the British agreed to recognize the independence of the Arab countries south of the 37th latitude, including the Arabian Peninsula. In the course of the correspondence, which dragged on between July, 1915, and March, 1916, McMahon stipulated that the agreement could not infringe upon unspecified French interests in Syria. Hussein replied that he would not consent to any Arab land becoming the possession of any power, meaning France. In order to avoid delay of the Arab revolt, this disputed point remained unclarified, with unfortunate results a few years later.*

While the British Foreign Office was dealing with Hussein, the India Office was negotiating with Ibn-Saud, Sultan of the Nejd, whose territories were nearer the Persian Gulf. On December 26, 1915, an agreement was reached by which the India Office recognized Ibn-Saud's independence in return for his benevolent neutrality during the war. That a different British government agency was involved did not alter the fact that contradictory commitments had been made to Ibn-Saud and to Hussein.

More ominous for the future was another conflicting commitment, this one to Lord Rothschild of the World Zionist Organization. Zionism was a nationalist movement that had developed among European Jews in the last quarter of the nineteenth century as a reaction against mounting anti-Semitism. The World Zionist Organization, established in Basle in 1897, had repeatedly sought permission from the Ottoman government to set up a Jewish settlement company in Palestine. The Turks, already plagued by the demands of various subject nationalists, rejected the Zionist petitions. The Zionists, in turn, rejected a British offer for a settlement in Uganda; Zionism without Zion was inconceivable.

With Turkey's involvement in World War I, Zionist leaders in England and the United States seized the opportunity to press for an Allied commitment to create a Jewish commonwealth in Palestine upon the demise of the Ottoman Empire. Political pressure to this end was exerted, and slowly the leading government leaders in Britain were won over to the Zionist position. They were influenced partly by the desire to earn for the Allied cause the support of numerous and influential Zionist organizations in Russia and the United States. Also it was feared, with some justification, that Germany and Turkey were ready to make concessions to attract international Zionist support. Consequently, on November 2, 1917, Lord Balfour wrote to Lord Rothschild that the British Government favored the establishment in Palestine of a "national home for the Jewish people . . . it being clearly understood that nothing shall be done which may prejudice the civil and religious rights of existing non-Jewish communities in Palestine. . . ." It is evident

* See "Hussein-McMahon Correspondence, 1915–1916," EMM, No. 125.

that this Balfour Declaration conflicted with both the Sykes-Picot and the Hussein-McMahon agreements.

464   Given this bundle of contradictions, it is scarcely surprising that no permanent decisions regarding the Middle East were reached by the peacemakers in Paris.* In the end it was Britain and France who determined the settlement, for the United States was withdrawing into isolation, Russia was convulsed by civil war and intervention, while Italy was immobilized by internal dissension. The Treaty of Sèvres (August 10, 1920), then, was essentially of Anglo-French origin, and its provisions reflected its origin. France secured Syria as a mandate, while Britain obtained Mesopotamia and Palestine, in addition to a protectorate over Egypt. The Dodecanese Islands were ceded to Italy, while Greece, thanks to the artful diplomacy of her Premier Venizelos, obtained several Aegean islands, Eastern Thrace, and the right to administer the Smyrna region for five years, after which its final disposition was to be determined by a plebiscite. Armenia and the Kingdom of Hejaz were recognized as independent. Finally, Soviet Russia, in armed conflict with Allied interventionist forces and having published and repudiated the secret treaties that the Tsarist ministers had signed, did not obtain Constantinople and the Straits. Instead, this strategic territory was left under Turkish sovereignty, though the Straits were to be demilitarized and placed under international control.

These provisions, so contrary to the promises made to the Arabs and to the professed Allied principle of self-determination, aroused a wave of armed resistance throughout the Middle East. A combination of factors enabled the Turks to scrap the Sèvres Treaty altogether, while the Arabs won piecemeal concessions after years of stubborn struggle.

Republican Victory

The George Washington of modern Turkey is Mustafa Kemal, later known as Atatürk, or Foremost Turk. He won fame for his successful defense of the Dardanelles during the war, but he did not rise to the top because he was at odds with the Young Turk clique that had embroiled Turkey in the war. Kemal's opportunity came after the fighting ceased, when he led the opposition to the Sèvres Treaty. He was perfectly willing to surrender the Arab provinces of the old empire, but he refused to accept the cession of Eastern Thrace and the provisions concerning Constantinople and the Straits. Furthermore, the victorious Allies had gone further and divided Asia Minor into spheres of influence, so that the rump Turkey that was left seemed destined to a fate comparable to that of China.

Having made himself obnoxious in Constantinople with his defiant nationalism, Kemal was sent to eastern Asia Minor to supervise demobilization. There he was safely away from the guns of the Allied fleet anchored off Constantinople. He traveled about in the Turkish hinterland, organizing resistance to the Allies and their puppet sultan in the capital. By September, 1919, Kemal had summoned a nationalist congress which adopted a National Pact consisting of six principles. These included self-determination, abolition

* See "T. E. Lawrence on the Arab Revolt," *EMM*, No. 126.

of capitulations, security for Constantinople, and a new Straits settlement. In the elections of October, 1919, Kemal's followers won a majority, and when Parliament met in January, 1920, it adopted the National Pact.* The Allies retaliated by occupying Constantinople on March 16 to check the spread of the nationalist agitation. Kemal now made the final break by summoning his nationalist deputies to Angora in central Asia Minor. There, on April 23, 1920, they denounced the Sultan's regime and established a provisional government with Kemal as president.

The nationalists triumphed over seemingly overwhelming odds. One reason was the courageous and inspired leadership of Kemal. Another was the loyal support of the mass of the Turkish people, who were united to an unprecedented degree by the highhandedness of the Allies in Constantinople, and even more by the landing of Greek troops in Smyrna in the spring of 1919. Finally, Kemal exploited serious differences amongst the Allies to conclude separate treaties with them, thereby isolating the Greeks in Smyrna and paving the way for their defeat. The Allied dissension arose from the fact that both the French and the Italians felt, with justification, that the British and their Greek protégés had gotten the lion's share of the spoils in the Middle East. Accordingly, the Italians were willing to sign a pact on March 13, 1921, in which, in return for certain economic concessions in southeastern Asia Minor, they agreed to withdraw their forces from that area and to give diplomatic support to the Turks in their efforts to regain Smyrna and Eastern Thrace. The French soon followed the Italian example. On October 20, 1921, they signed an agreement with the Turks defining the frontier between Syria and Turkey and settling various railroad and other economic issues.

Meanwhile, the Turks had also been negotiating with the Russians. These traditional enemies now were attracted to each other because they both were at war with Britain. On March 16, 1921, they signed a treaty defining their common frontier in the Caucasus, and the Russians followed this with arms and money for the Turkish nationalists.

This series of treaties fundamentally transformed the balance of power in the Middle East. Turkey and Russia now presented a united front, while the Allies were so divided that only Britain and Greece were left to enforce the terms of the Sèvres Treaty. And Britain, because of her worldwide commitments and the state of public opinion at home, could do no more than maintain her ships in Constantinople and the Straits. In other words, the Greeks now were left alone in Smyrna to face the Turkish nationalist upsurge in Asia Minor.

Fighting between the Greeks and the Turks began at the end of March, 1921. At first the Greeks met with weak resistance, because the opposition consisted of little more than guerrilla bands. But the further they advanced, the stiffer became the opposition, and the population was so hostile that fully two-thirds of Greek manpower had to be used to guard transportation lines. The turning point came when the invaders reached the Sakarya River in the heart of Asia Minor. Kemal struck back, and the overextended Greeks were stopped dead and then pushed back. Retreat brought demoralization and

* See "Turkish National Pact, January 28, 1920," *EMM*, No. 122.

eventually a stampede. By September 9, 1922, Kemal was riding triumphantly into Smyrna. Not only the Greek army, but also Greek civilians who had lived for centuries in the Smyrna region, were evacuated.

Kemal now was in a position to demand revision of the Sèvres Treaty. After protracted negotiations the Lausanne Treaty was signed on July 24, 1923. This returned to Turkey Eastern Thrace and some of the Aegean Islands. Also Turkey was to pay no reparations, and the capitulations were abolished in return for a promise of judicial reform. The Straits remained demilitarized, and open to ships of all nations in time of peace or war if Turkey remained neutral. If Turkey was at war, enemy ships, but not neutrals, might be excluded. Finally, a separate agreement provided for the compulsory exchange of the Greek minority in Constantinople for the Turkish minority in Western Thrace and Macedonia.

New Turkey

The Lausanne Treaty represented a great personal triumph for Kemal. The decrepit Ottoman Empire at long last was dead after half a millennium of checkered history. On October 29, 1923, the Turkish Republic was formally proclaimed with Kemal as president. Having created the new Turkey, Kemal now turned to the equally difficult task of creating new Turks. He had set forth his guiding principle in 1921 in the midst of the struggle for survival.

> As regards the philosophical outlook of our movement, our eyes are turned westwards. We shall transplant Western institutions to Asiatic soil. We shall transform our schools on the Western model. No more Pan-Islamism, but nationalism, Asia's new watchword. . . . We wish to be a modern nation with our minds open to admit current ideas, and yet to remain ourselves. We do not wish to be regarded as an Asiatic people, anxious to remain isolated behind moral barriers.[1]

In accordance with these views, Kemal ruthlessly swept away the outdated institutions of the past. Reform followed reform in a great torrent of change.

> October 14, 1923—Capital of the Turkish state moved from Constantinople to Angora in the heart of Turkish Anatolia.
>
> March 3, 1924—Caliphate abolished, and all members of the Ottoman dynasty banished from Turkey.*
>
> April 20, 1924—Adoption of a constitution providing for a president, premier, cabinet, and a grand national assembly elected quadrenially by indirect vote.†
>
> September 2, 1925—All religious orders and houses suppressed, and individuals prohibited from living as members of orders and from wearing the costumes or bearing the titles associated therewith.

* See "Abolition of the Caliphate and Banishment of the Imperial Ottoman Family, March 3, 1924," *EMM,* No. 123.
† See "Constitution of the Turkish Republic, April 20, 1924," *EMM,* No. 124.

November, 1925—Officials and private citizens required to wear hat in place of the traditional fez. The use of the veil by women was made optional but discouraged.

January–February, 1926—Introduction of new civil, criminal, and commercial law codes, based respectively on Swiss, Italian, and German systems.

August 17, 1926—Polygamy abolished.

September 1, 1926—Civil marriage made compulsory.

November 3, 1928—Latin alphabet introduced in place of intricate Arabic script, the change being applied first to newspapers and then to books.

March 28, 1930—Place names changed: Constantinople to Istanbul; Angora to Ankara; Smyrna to Izmir; Adrianople to Edirne, and so forth.

December 14, 1934—Women given the right to vote and to sit in the assembly.

By the time of Kemal's death on November 10, 1938, the New Turkey was definitely established. It is true that the newness was more horizontal than vertical. A large proportion of the peasantry, which constituted the great majority of the population, still clung to their age-old Moslem ideas and customs. On the other hand, the new elite that governed the country had been Europeanized in its way of life and way of thought. Many of the peasants also had changed sufficiently to have established rapport with the government unprecedented in past centuries. To a much greater degree than any other Moslem country, Turkey had become, as Kemal had planned, a "modern nation."

II. Arab Middle East

Pattern of Revolt

While the Turks were successfully scrapping the Sèvres Treaty, the Arabs were stubbornly resisting the Mandatory Powers to which they had been assigned. Contrary to the Hussein-McMahon Agreement, Syria-Lebanon had been given as a mandate to France, Mesopotamia and Palestine had been made British mandates, and full British control had been established in Egypt. This high-handed parceling out of Arab lands was bound to lead to trouble, because the war itself had stimulated tremendous national sentiment among the Arabs. Allied propaganda concerning national self-determination inevitably had its effect on Arab opinion. The successful operations of Arab military units also aroused national consciousness and pride. Arab soldiers had fought side by side with British in a campaign that liberated Damascus, Aleppo, and other historic Arab centers. Equally significant was the widespread suffering and outright starvation caused by the disruption of trade during the war. It is estimated that at least 300,000 people died of hunger or of diseases due to malnutrition.

Finally there was the all-important religious consideration, especially for the fellahin in the villages. In the 1950's an Egyptian sociologist concluded, after first-hand research, that "for the villagers, the world is classified into believers and nonbelievers on the basis of the Moslem faith," and that "they are hardly aware of concepts like race or class." [2] This religion-bound outlook undoubtedly was even more pronounced in the immediate post–World War I years. This is borne out by the fact that Arab nationalist leaders in the cities often were surprised by the degree of support they received from the peasantry with whom they had little contact. The inference is that the village uprisings were spontaneous movements motivated by religious feelings against the infidel foreign rulers.

This combination of factors explains the postwar Arab struggle for independence.* A common pattern is discernible in the evolution of the struggle. First, an explosion of defiance and armed revolt occurred during the years immediately following the peace treaties. Then Britain and France gradually restored order and reasserted their authority. Finally they granted varying degrees of autonomy, which did not entirely satisfy the nationalists, but which did preserve an uneasy peace until World War II.

Course of Revolt

In Egypt, the mandatory relationship, strictly speaking, did not exist. But the situation was essentially similar because Britain at the beginning of the war had repudiated the nominal Ottoman suzerainty and had declared the country a British protectorate. Immediately, the nationalist Wafd party organized violent opposition. In 1922 Britain proclaimed Egypt "an independent sovereign state" but reserved for herself control of foreign affairs and of external security, as well as protection of minorities and of foreign interests. The nationalists rejected this illusory independence and continued the struggle. One of their weapons was terrorism, and they succeeded in 1924 in assassinating the British head of the Egyptian army, Sir Lee Stack. The nationalists also could count on popular support, which was manifested in the repeated electoral victories they won. Finally in 1936 a compromise settlement was reached with the signing of a twenty-year alliance treaty. Britain undertook to end her military occupation of the country and to arrange for Egypt's admission to the League of Nations. In return, Egypt agreed to stand by Britain in time of war; to accept the British garrison stationed for the defense of the Suez Canal; and also to continue the joint British-Egyptian administration of the Sudan. Nationalist leaders were far from satisfied with this settlement. But they accepted it as the best available under the circumstances and they waited for the first opportunity to abolish the obnoxious vestiges of foreign control.

Nationalist opposition in Iraq followed much the same course as in Egypt. A widespread armed revolt broke out in 1920. The British first restored order and then attempted to conciliate nationalist feeling by enthroning as king the third son of Hussein, Prince Faisal. The following year, in 1922, the British negotiated a treaty of alliance in which they retained such controls as they deemed necessary to protect their interests. The nationalists remained dissatisfied and continued their agitation. Finally an alliance treaty was concluded in 1930, by which Britain agreed to terminate the mandate

* See "Syrian Opposition to Mandates," *EMM,* No. 127.

and to support Iraq's application for admission to the League of Nations. In return, Iraq agreed that Britain should maintain three air bases in the country and also should have full use of railways, rivers, and ports in time of war. In 1932 Iraq became a member of the League of Nations, the first Arab country to gain that distinction. As in the case of Egypt, however, nationalist circles remained dissatisfied. They claimed that only outward forms had changed, and that Britain had retained all the desired privileges through the expedient of an alliance.

In Syria and Lebanon, the French proved less flexible than the British and therefore less successful. Nationalist outbreaks occurred periodically, the most serious being in 1925, when the French were forced to shell Damascus in order to retain control. Finally in 1936 the French government negotiated treaties with Syria and Lebanon modeled after the Anglo-Iraqi treaty of 1930. Neither of these treaties, however, was ratified by the French Chamber of Deputies, so that the conflict remained unresolved when World War II began.

Palestine Triangle

In Palestine the situation was unique because it quickly deteriorated into a bitter three-way struggle involving Britain, Arabs, and Jews. The Arabs maintained that the Balfour Declaration concerning a Jewish "national home" was in flagrant contravention of prior commitments made to the Arabs in the McMahon correspondence. Britain attempted to appease the Arabs by setting apart in 1921 the interior portion of the country as the independent state of Transjordan. This was exempt from all the clauses of the mandate concerning the establishment of a Jewish home. Furthermore, the British installed Faisal's elder brother, Abdullah, as ruler of Transjordan. This tactic proved eminently satisfactory so far as Transjordan itself was concerned. Abdullah always cooperated loyally with the British, particularly since the poverty of his country made him dependent on subsidies from London. Probably the most effective military unit in the Arab world was Transjordan's Arab legion, supported by British funds and lead by the British General John Glubb.

In Palestine proper, however, the triangle conflict became increasingly fierce as Jewish immigrants poured in and the apprehensive Arabs struck back against both the Jews and the British. Article 6 of the mandate required Britain to "facilitate" Jewish immigration and to "encourage close settlement by Jews on the land." But the same article also provided that "the rights and position of other sections of the population" were to be safeguarded. The British apparently felt at the time that the two orders were not necessarily contradictory. They expected that Jewish immigration would never reach such proportions as to impinge upon "the rights and position" of the Arabs. They could not have foreseen the repercussions of Hitler's rise to power in 1933. Jewish immigration jumped from 9,553 in 1932 to 30,327 in 1933, 42,359 in 1934 and 61,854 in 1935. The total Jewish population in Palestine rose from 65,000 in 1919 to 450,000 in 1939.

So long as the Jewish influx had been modest, the Arabs had not raised serious objections. In fact they had welcomed the Jews with their money and energy and skills. They themselves had benefited substantially from the miracles the Jews had performed in restoring exhausted land, founding industries, and checking diseases. But when the stream of immigration became a torrent, the Arabs reacted violently, and understandably so. As one Arab remarked in alarm and bewilderment, "I don't understand their languages; I don't understand their ways; they make me feel like a foreigner in my own country." [3] Other Arabs pointed out that there was no reason why they should lose their country because of western anti-Semitism. "Anti-Semitism is a deplorable Western disease. . . . We aren't anti-Semites; we are also Semites. Yet this Western problem is being smoothed over at our expense. Is that your idea of right?" [4]

Arab attacks against the Jews became increasingly frequent and serious. Highlights were the Wailing Wall disorders in 1929, the Arab "National Political Strike" in 1936, and the Arab Rebellion of 1938. The British response was to send out Royal Commissions following the major outbreaks. By the time of World War II several commissions had investigated the situation and had vacillated in their recommendations as they sought to satisfy three distinct and conflicting interests—Jewish Zionist aspirations, Arab nationalist demands, and British imperial interests. The White Paper of May, 1939, for example, proposed that Palestine become an independent state in ten years, and that definite limits be placed on Jewish immigration and land purchases. The concluding paragraph included the philosophical observation that "His Majesty's Government cannot hope to satisfy the partisans of one party or the other in such controversy as the Mandate has aroused." This proved thoroughly justified. Both Arabs and Jews rejected the British proposals, and the Palestine controversy remained as far from settlement as ever when World War II began.

III. NORTH AFRICA

The territory west of Egypt, known as the Maghreb, had gradually fallen under European rule during the nineteenth century (see Chapter 14, section III). France began the aggression in Algeria in 1830, and Italy completed it in Libya in 1911. The latter invasion provoked a stubborn resistance that lasted into the postwar period and that represented the beginning of the Maghreb's general struggle for liberation.

The Italians had little difficulty in defeating the small Turkish garrisons in Libya in 1911. But the native Arab and Berber population continued the struggle with arms left by the departing Turks. The Senussi religious order organized and led the resistance so effectively that by the summer of 1915 the Italians were confined to half a dozen points along the coast. After World War I the Italians again tried to impose their authority over the entire country, but with little success. They held the coast, but much of the interior remained under Arab control.

The Italian failure in Libya was a serious blow to European prestige, but it was soon overshadowed by the spectacular defeats inflicted on the Spaniards by the Rif mountaineers of Morocco. For centuries the Spanish possessions in Morocco had been limited to four tiny enclaves along the

Mediterranean coast. Meanwhile, France had been pushing out from Algeria, establishing a protectorate over Tunisia in 1881, and beginning the occupation of Morocco after the Algeciras Conference of 1906. This stimulated the Spaniards to similar action, so they reached an agreement with the French for the division of Morocco between them, and began in 1909 to advance into the interior. Their pace was slow, so that for several years there was little resistance. Then suddenly, in the summer of 1921, they suffered a disastrous defeat—the worst inflicted on a Western army since the Ethiopians defeated the Italians at Adowa in 1896.

Abd-el-Krim, leader of the Rif tribesmen, was responsible for the unexpected blow. Having been well educated in Spain, he knew the value of Western technology and how to use it. The startled Spaniards poured in 150,000 men, but failed to recover much ground. In the summer of 1923 they offered Krim autonomy, but, flushed with victory, he demanded full independence. By 1924 the Spaniards again were confined to the coast, except for a few interior garrisons, which were usually encircled by the Rif. For all practical purposes Krim now was the master of virtually all of Spanish Morocco.*

The following year Krim challenged the French as well as the Spaniards—a move that led directly to his downfall. The blunder was due partly to his need for some grain-producing lands behind the French lines, and partly to his miscalculation of the French political scene. He overestimated the extent of war weariness among the French, and also was too impressed by pledges of support from the French Communist party. On September 20, 1924, the Communist leader Jacques Doriot sent a telegram to Krim congratulating him on his victories over the Spaniards and expressing the hope that, "in liaison with the proletariat of France and of Europe he would carry on the struggle against all imperialism, French imperialism included, until the complete liberation of the soil of Morocco." [5] Doriot undoubtedly was sincere in his good wishes, but he was not in a position to back them up with effective aid.

Krim began his offensive on April 13, 1925, before reinforcements could arrive from France. The Rif warriors penetrated the French lines and aroused some of the tribes in the interior. The French fortified posts, cut off from their bases, had to be evacuated one after the other. Complete disaster was averted only because of the loyalty of the non-French elements that comprised a large majority of the Foreign Legion and the regular French army. So serious was the situation that Spain and France concluded a pact for joint action against the Rif, including a land and sea blockade of Rif territory in order to stop gunrunning. Nevertheless, Krim's failure to win victory in his initial offensive meant the beginning of the end. The combined Franco-Spanish resources were so overwhelmingly superior that eventual defeat of the Rif was inevitable.

By the fall of 1925, the 60,000 Rif troops were facing Franco-Spanish forces totaling 280,000 men. The odds were too great, especially since Krim did not succeed in raising a general revolt in the French rear. During the winter and spring he suffered a succession of defeats, until he surrendered on May 27, 1926. He was exiled to Réunion Island in the Indian Ocean.

* See "Guerrilla Tactics of the Rif in Morocco," EMM, No. 128.

Krim's exploits, although they had failed to drive out the French, had aroused the entire Maghreb and inspired the various nationalist parties that were organized in the 1930's and that successfully fought for freedom after World War II.

IV. PERSIA

Shortly before World War I, Persia had been divided into British and Russian spheres of influence (see Chapter 14, section IV). When the war began, the shah announced an official policy of neutrality; because he lacked the power to enforce this policy, the northern sections of the country were soon overrun by Turkish and Russian troops, and the southern by British. The authority of the Persian government scarcely extended beyond the environs of the capital. The general chaos was so intense and widespread that it contributed to the famine of 1918 in which an estimated two million people died of starvation.* The appallingly low level of public life is indicated by the report of a foreign observer that "There is not the slightest doubt that the distress of the 1918 famine was gravely accentuated by manipulation on the part of those in high authority." 6

The end of the war found the British in control of most of the country, thanks to the revolution and civil war that occupied the Russians. The British were determined to maintain this control both because of the importance of Persia for India's defense and because of the oil properties of the Anglo-Persian Oil Company, whose crucial significance for the imperial navy had been amply demonstrated during the war. Accordingly, the British, with the aid of heavy bribery, persuaded the Persian prime minister and two of his cabinet members to sign an agreement on August 9, 1919, providing for a loan, the revision of the customs tariff, the provision of British advisers in the principal ministries, and of British officers to organize the gendarmerie, rebuild the army, and construct a railroad. These terms were so manifestly in Britain's favor that many feared the two-power control of the prewar years would now be replaced by that of a single power. After much agitation, the Persian majlis (legislature) refused to ratify the treaty and it lapsed.

Meanwhile, the Russians had not been idle. On January 14, 1918, they denounced the 1907 Anglo-Russian convention and "the preceding as well as the subsequent [Tsarist] treaties which, in whatever form, limit and restrict the right of the Persian people to a free and independent existence." More specifically, on June 26, 1918, they announced the nullification of all Russian concessions and special privileges in Persia and all Persian debts to Tsarist Russia. Being faced with civil war and intervention, the Bolsheviks presumably made these sweeping concessions in the hope of placating their Persian neighbors and stimulating anti-Western popular uprisings in the colonial world. These calculations probably explain similar concessions the Bolsheviks made to the Turks and the Chinese at this time.

Pursuing their policy further, the Russians signed a formal Persian-Soviet Treaty of Friendship on February 26, 1921. Of benefit to the Persians were

* See "Old Regime in Persia," *EMM,* No. 129.

the official cancellation of all outstanding debts, surrender of all physical commercial installations in Persia, and the nullification of all concessions, extraterritorial rights, and other special privileges. On the other hand, certain provisions favored the Russians, including the denial to Persia of the right to grant the surrendered concessions in the five northern provinces to any other power, and the right of the Russians to send troops into Persia if any foreign power were using Persian territory as a base of operations against Russia.

While this treaty was under negotiation, Persian political life was becoming ever more anarchical. One prime minister, for example, resigned on January 19, 1921, resumed office four days later, formed on February 3 a cabinet which resigned on the 6th, and formed another cabinet on the 16th, which was overthrown by a coup d'état on the 21st. The coup was engineered by Reza Khan, a colonel in the Persian Cossack Brigade that had been organized by the Russians before World War I. For the new two decades the story of Persia is the story of this dominating personality who rose to become the great reforming shah of his country.

Reza was an austere, single-minded military man of exceptional courage and determination. Through sheer ability and concentration on military duties he rose from the ranks and won the respect and loyalty of his men. His chance came when the British compelled the Russian officers of the Cossack Division to resign their commissions in the fall of 1920. Reza moved into the power vacuum, and by February, 1921, he was strong enough to lead the coup that overthrew the government. From now on his rise was rapid. Immediately after the coup he became commander in chief of the Persian army. A few weeks later he was appointed Minister of War. After making and unmaking several ministries, he became Prime Minister himself on October 28, 1923. The ruler, Ahmad Shah of the Kajar dynasty, now left Persia for the Riviera, and two years later, on December 15, 1925, Reza assumed the throne, founding the Pahlevi dynasty which has survived to the present.

Despite his eccentricities and excesses, Reza Shah's reign was like a breath of fresh air in the prevailing atmosphere of corruption, incompetence, and obscurantism. Indeed, the Shah is reminiscent of Kemal, whom he admired and imitated. His first move was to modernize and strengthen the army in order to forestall the threatened partition of the country. Before he came to power the Russian-officered Cossack division controlled the northern provinces, the British-officered South Persian Rifles the southern, while a Swedish-officered *gendarmerie* theoretically upheld Persian national interest. Having already been relieved of the Russian officers through the action of Great Britain, Reza Shah now got rid of their British and Swedish colleagues. He then combined the disbanded units into a unified and modern national army of 40,000, upon which he lavished much attention and money. With this military force at his command, the Shah was able to resist undue foreign pressures and also to assert the central government's authority over tribal chieftains who had been *de facto* independent since the mid-nineteenth century.

Reza Shah also sought to modernize his country's economy. The most spectacular manifestation was the building of the trans-Iranian railroad. This

474

had long been a dream of both the British and the Russians, the former seeking to connect India with the European network through Iran, the latter wishing to extend their line, which already reached Tabriz, to the Persian Gulf. The Shah, heeding neither the British nor the Russians, laid out his own route. It was spectacular, if not economically practical, requiring over 4,000 bridges and 200 tunnels in its course of 870 miles. Completed in 1939, it was destined to play a key role in transporting military supplies to the Soviet Union during World War II.

The railroad was typical of the Shah's economic ventures. There was no coordinated plan, and individual projects were not conceived in the light of the over-all economic needs of the nation. By the time of the Shah's abdication in 1941, a considerable number of factories had been built, including textile mills, cement plants, sugar refineries, and cigarette factories; yet despite high protective tariffs, almost all operated at a loss.

Like Kemal, Reza Shah attacked various symbols of the past. He forbade the use of honorary titles, abolished the veil for women, and ordered men to wear European hats or caps. Above all else, nationalism was emphasized, and foreign influences were rooted out wherever possible. Arabic words were purged from the Persian language, and modern buildings were modeled after the Achaemenid style of architecture found in the ruins of the magnificent palaces of old. Typical of this nationalism was the adoption in 1934, in place of "Persia," of the name "Iran," harking back to Indo-European ancestors three millennia removed.

Reza Shah's reign ended abruptly with his abdication on September 16, 1941. During the preceding years he had been leaning increasingly toward Nazi Germany. Trade with Germany rose to number one place, while German technicians, teachers, merchants, and tourists increased steadily in numbers. With Hitler's attack on the U.S.S.R. in June, 1941, the Shah received several joint Soviet-British notes requesting him to expel the Germans from Iran. His replies were considered unsatisfactory, and on August 25, 1941, Soviet and British forces occupied the country. On September 16 Reza Shah abdicated in favor of his son, Mohammed Reza Pahlevi, the present ruler.

In retrospect, Reza Shah did not have so profound an impact on his country as Kemal did on Turkey. Kemal profited from a preceding military disaster of such magnitude that it made it easier to abolish outmoded institutions and practices. And the Turks, having been subject to Western influences longer, were more receptive to them. Nevertheless, Reza Shah stands head and shoulders above his predecessors, and his reign represents a major turning point in modern Iranian history.*

V. INDIA

At the turn of the century British rule in India seemed perfectly secure for the foreseeable future. In 1912, a great imperial durbar was held in Delhi to celebrate the coronation of King George V. The ceremony was held in the great audience hall of Shah Jehan (1592–1666) builder of the Taj Mahal. Amidst pageantry and splendor, King George received the hom-

* See "Reza Shah: Persia's Strong Man," *EMM,* No. 130.

age of India's princes and potentates without a voice being raised in dissent. In 1914, India rallied solidly behind Britain at war. The princes contributed generous financial aid, while no less than 900,000 Indians served in the British army as combatants and another 300,000 as laborers. Gandhi was particularly earnest in his support of the British cause. "I would make India," he wrote to Viceroy Lord Hardinge, "offer all her able-bodied sons as a sacrifice to the Empire at its critical moment . . . we can but accelerate our journey to the goal [of Home Rule] by silently and simply devoting ourselves heart and soul to the work of delivering the Empire from the threatening danger." [7]

Only three decades after World War I British rule in India came to an end. One reason for this extraordinary outcome was the impact of the war itself—the influence of slogans about self-determination, and the unsettling effect of overseas service upon hundreds of thousands of soldiers who returned with new ideas and attitudes. Unrest was stimulated also by a series of disasters in the immediate postwar years. The failure of the monsoon in 1918 brought famine to many parts of India. A year earlier the bubonic plague left a trail of death, but it was trifling compared to the influenza epidemic of 1918–1919, which killed no less than 13 million people! Another factor contributing to unrest was the repressive policy followed by Britain after the war, contrary to Gandhi's expectations. The Rowlatt Acts of March, 1919, authorized the government to intern agitators without trial and entitled judges to try cases without juries. Gandhi struck back by organizing a campaign of passive resistance and noncooperation. During the riots that followed, the British General Dyer perpetrated the infamous Amritsar Massacre of April 13, 1919. Seeking to impress the populace with the strength of the government, he ordered his troops to fire without warning on a crowded political meeting of unarmed civilians. Nearly 400 were killed and 1,000 wounded. A committee of the House of Commons censured the general, who was relieved of his command. But the House of Lords supported Dyer, and a solatium of £26,000 was raised for him by public subscription. A wave of bitter protest swept the nation, and Gandhi denounced the government as "satanic."

Gandhi was by all odds the outstanding figure in this postwar anti-British movement. The Indian Congress, organized in 1885, did not seriously threaten the British prior to 1914 (see Chapter 15, section VI). It had remained essentially a middle-class movement with negligible support from village masses. Gandhi's great contribution was that he managed to break through to the villagers, establish rapport with them, and involve them in the struggle for independence. Although a London-trained lawyer, Gandhi remained profoundly Indian and non-Western—indeed anti-Western—so that he was able to communicate with his people in meaningful terms.*

Gandhi's message was simple and appealing. He pointed out that in 1914 the British were ruling 300 million Indians with a mere 4,000 administrators and 69,000 soldiers. This was possible only because all classes of the population were cooperating with the British in one way or another. If this cooperation were withdrawn, British rule inevitably would collapse. The task, then, was to educate and prepare the people for *satyagraha*, or nonviolent

---

* See "Gandhi and Nehru," *EMM*, No. 131.

passive resistance. Gandhi also called on the people to practise *hartal,* or boycott of British goods. In place of imported machine-made goods, Gandhi preached the wearing of homespun cloth. This would undermine the economic basis of British rule and also revive village industries. He himself wore a loin cloth of homespun material, and publicly worked at his spinning wheel. The combination of *satyagraha* and *hartal,* Gandhi taught, would make possible the realization of *swaraj,* or home rule. Once India's villagers comprehended these teachings and acted upon them, the days of the British *raj* were numbered.

In an effort to forestall the gathering storm, the London government introduced on December 23, 1919, the Montagu-Chelmsford reforms establishing an administrative system known as "dyarchy." This left the central government in Delhi much the same as before, with an appointed viceroy and executive council, and a legislative assembly of 140 members, of whom 100 were elected by a very restricted suffrage. The dyarchy principle operated in the provincial governments, each of which consisted of an appointed governor and executive council, and a legislative council which was 70 per cent elective by a rigidly limited suffrage. Important matters were "reserved" for the governor and his executive council; the less important, such as sanitation, agriculture, medical relief, and education, were to be "transferred" to the Indian ministers. The theory was that more matters would be transferred from the "reserved" to the "transferred" list if this "dyarchy," or division of responsibility, proved workable.

The National Congress, led by Gandhi, rejected the British reform proposal, partly as a reaction to the Dyer affair, partly because of a practical political consideration—the readiness of the Moslems for the first time to join forces with the Hindus. Indian Moslems were shocked by what they considered to be the overly harsh Sèvres Treaty imposed by Britain and her allies on the Ottoman Empire. The so-called Khalifat movement was organized to lend support to the beleagured Turks. Gandhi grasped the opportunity to form an entente with the Moslems, so that all Indians now were united in demanding *swaraj* for India as well as revision of the Sèvres Treaty. In September, 1920, an all-out noncooperation campaign was launched.* The response was impressive, but it gradually got out of hand. Gandhi insisted on strict nonviolence, yet strikes and riots broke out in the cities, while in the countryside the peasants rose against landlords and money-lenders. The climax came on February 4, 1922, when insurgent peasants attacked the police station at Chauri Chaura and killed 22 policemen.

The shocked Gandhi promptly ordered suspension of the noncooperation campaign, but he was nevertheless arrested and sentenced to six years' imprisonment. He was released after two years because of his precarious health, but the nationalist campaign had largely petered out by then, owing to confusion among the Hindus and the cooling ardor of the Moslems who were dismayed by Kemal's abolition of the Caliphate and his strongly secularist program.

For several years after his release from prison, Gandhi stayed out of politics. During this period new and more radical nationalist leaders were emerging, including Jawaharlal Nehru. Up to this time the leadership of

* See "Non-cooperation Campaign," *EMM,* No. 132.

the National Congress had been largely upper and middle class in its origins and views. By the mid-1920's workers groups began to appear, with a socialist or communist political orientation. This trend resulted in the growth of a left-wing element within the National Congress, and in the organization of an All-India Independence League with Nehru as president. The distinguishing feature of the League is that it demanded not only complete independence from Britain but also basic social change within India along socialist lines. As Nehru wrote, "The younger men and women of the Congress who used to read Bryce on democracies, and Morley and Keith and Mazzini, were now reading, when they could get them, books on socialism and communism and Russia." [8]

Nehru himself provides a good illustration of the new trend. The son of a wealthy lawyer, he was educated at Harrow and Cambridge, and was admitted to the bar in 1912. On his return, he plunged into the nationalist struggle for freedom, becoming a follower and admirer of Gandhi. Nehru, however, was very different from his mystical and ascetic leader. He was a nationalist, a socialist, and a firm believer in science and technology as the means for liberating mankind from its age-old misery and ignorance. He parted company with Gandhi when the latter rejected the modern world in this denunciation: "India's salvation consists in unlearning what she has learned during the last fifty years. The railways, telegraphs, hospitals, lawyers, doctors, and suchlike have all to go, and the so-called upper classes have to learn consciously, religiously, and deliberately the simple peasant life, knowing it to be a life giving true happiness. . . . Everytime I get into a railway car or use a motor bus I know that I am doing violence to my sense of what is right." [9]

Nehru nevertheless recognized Gandhi's extraordinary service in arousing India's peasantry. Even the National Congress, rent with personal rivalries and doctrinal disputes, was dependent on Gandhi. He returned to political life in December, 1928, and persuaded Congress to accept a compromise resolution acceptable to both the radical and conservative elements. A few months later the British Labour Party defeated the Conservatives and formed a new government. The outlook seemed promising, for the Labourites consistently had criticized the Conservatives for tardiness in extending self-government to India. The promise, however, was not realized; the decade 1930–1939 proved a disappointment.

One reason was the vacillation of the government between cycles of repression and concession. Nationalist violence was followed by large-scale arrests and deportations, and then, in turn, by attempts at conciliation through slow granting of responsibility to elective institutions. Much of the responsibility, however, lies with the Indians, for they increasingly divided into warring Hindu and Moslem blocs. As early as 1919 the All-India Moslem League had been founded, but for many years it had little following. Not only were the Moslems less than a quarter of the total population of the subcontinent, but the National Congress claimed it represented all Indians, regardless of religion. Indeed, the Congress did have a Moslem wing headed by the distinguished Abul Kalam Azad. Thus the Moslem League was of little significance until after 1935, when it came under the leadership of a Bombay lawyer, Mohammed Ali Jinnah. He offered to cooperate with the Congress on a coalition basis, but Congress rejected this and would deal only with Moslems who joined the party as individuals. Jinnah retaliated by appealing to the Moslem masses with the cry "Islam is in danger." The response was enthusiastic, for many Indian Moslems felt they had more in common with the rest of the Moslem world than with their Hindu neighbors. Jinnah's electoral successes made possible the future establishment of the independent Moslem Pakistan.

Meanwhile the viceroy, Lord Irwin, had announced in October, 1929, that Britain definitely planned dominion status for India and that a conference would be held to make arrangements. The National Congress, however, passed a resolution on December 31, 1929, demanding complete independence. On March 12, Gandhi began another civil disobedience campaign to force the British to get out of India. His tactic was the great salt march to the sea, 170 miles away. There he dipped up sea water and placed it on a fire, a symbolic act of defiance against the government's salt tax, which he denounced as iniquitous. It was a shrewd, as well as a highly dramatic and well publicized move, for the peasant mass bitterly resented this tax and actively supported Gandhi. Widespread disorders broke out, including attacks on government salt works, terrorist assaults on officials, and rioting by unemployed factory workers who were hard hit by the worldwide depression. On May 5, Gandhi was again arrested and imprisoned, along with some 60,000 of his followers.

Lord Irwin was aware that force alone offered no solution. After order had been somewhat restored, he released Gandhi on January 26, 1931, and persuaded him to sign the Delhi Pact on March 4. The government agreed to release political prisoners who had not been guilty of violence, and in return the Congress was to end the disobedience campaign and also to participate in the roundtable conferences that had started a few months earlier. Gandhi personally attended the conferences in London, but no agreement was reached, partly because the Labour Government meanwhile had been replaced by the predominantly Conservative "National Government" which was less flexible. When Gandhi returned to India, he was once more arrested in January, 1932. Disobedience again flared up, but by this time the country was weary, and the compaign petered out in a few months.

Finally on August 2, 1935, the British Parliament passed the Government of India Act as the constructive half of the dual policy of repression of violence and advance toward self-government. It provided that Burma and Aden were to be separated from India and to become crown colonies. India itself was to become a federal union of the provinces and the princely states, subject to the latter's concurrence. As in the 1919 constitution, the viceroy retained authority in foreign affairs and defense, but all other federal matters were entrusted to a legislature of two branches, the majority of whose members to be chosen by a restricted electorate of about 6 million. In the provinces, in place of the dyarchy scheme that had proved unworkable, there were to be provincial legislatures and ministries answerable to them. Approximately 38 million Indians were given the right to elect the legislatures, which were to have complete autonomy in provincial affairs. In the event that a provincial government failed to function for any reason, the local British governor had authority to carry on public business.

The federal union provided in this 1935 act proved stillborn. The Indian princes, distrustful of the Nationalists, refused to cooperate. Consequently, the central administration that had been set up in 1919 continued to function. The new provincial arrangements, however, were put into operation with the election of the provincial legislatures in 1937. The Nationalists gained control in seven of the eleven provinces, and promptly proceeded to liberate political prisoners, restore civil liberties, and prepare agrarian reform. In 1939 all this abruptly ended when the viceroy proclaimed that India was a party to the new World War. Since the Indians were in no way consulted, the Nationalist ministries in the seven provinces resigned. British governors then took over and governed by decree. Once again the Nationalists raised the cry for complete independence, while the Moslems under Jinnah demanded that the subcontinent be partitioned into two states, one Hindu, and the other Moslem and to be called Pakistan.

VI. CHINA

Although nominally independent, China experienced an anti-Western movement after World War I comparable to that of India. China entered the war in 1917 in hope of recovering Shantung province, which Japan had occupied in 1914. When the lost province was not restored by the peacemakers at Versailles, wild demonstrations broke out among the students and intellectuals in Peking. The protests soon spread to other cities, and the merchants joined by closing their shops. This developed into a boycott of Japanese goods attended by clashes with Japanese residents. Newly organized labor unions also participated in the protest movement by staging strikes. All in all, this proved to be the most intense and widespread demonstration of national feeling that China had ever seen.

The Western powers also were the targets of this violent outburst, because of their willingness to allow Japan to retain her booty on the mainland. Soviet Russia, by contrast, was regarded with sympathy and admiration. One reason was the understandable appeal of Lenin's antiimperialistic teachings. Another was that the Soviet government had renounced Tsarist special privileges in China, as it also did at this time in Turkey and Persia. It is understandable that Chinese nationalists now looked increasingly to the Soviet Union as against the Japanese and the Westerners.

These changes gave Dr. Sun Yat-sen the opportunity to make a fresh start with new policies and methods. He had come on hard times following the 1911 revolution that established the republic (see Chapter 16, section V). Yüan Shih-k'ai had shunted him aside, while the provincial warlords ignored the central government and ruled as independent potentates. Sun now decided that his Kuomintang Party had to be strengthened to defeat the warlords and to create a unified and modernized state. He appealed for international aid but was turned down by the Western governments. The Soviets, however, responded positively, and thus began the Kuomintang-Communist Entente that lasted to 1927.*

In January, 1923, Dr. Sun and the Soviet representative, Adolf Joffe,

* See "Sun Yat-sen Seeks Foreign Aid," *EMM,* No. 133.

agreed that the purpose of the entente was not to establish communism in China but rather "to achieve national unification and attain full national independence." The Russians followed up by sending their able Mikhail Borodin to Canton, where he became Sun's right-hand man. Together they were able to bring about three basic changes: they remodeled the Kuomintang Party along communist lines, organized an efficient modern army, and developed a more effective and appealing political ideology.

In the reorganization of the Kuomintang, Sun came to exercise control through a Central Executive Committee elected by a Party Congress.* For the first time the party was now able to function as a disciplined unit from headquarters to the smallest subdivision. At the same time a new army was being organized with the help of Russian arms and officers led by General Vasili Blücher. In May, 1924, the Whampoa Military Academy was established in Canton to train officers. Officially, its director was Chiang Kai-shek, Sun's chief of staff, who had just returned from a period of study at the Red Army Academy in Moscow, but its real head was Blücher. It might be noted that its secretary was Chou En-lai, later to become foreign minister and premier of Communist China. Finally, Sun recast the ideology of his party into the form of his famous Three Principles of the People: Nationalism, Democracy, and Livelihood. The Principle of Democracy looked toward the achievement of democratic government, though a period of tutelage under one-party rule was deemed necessary. The Principle of Livelihood sought economic betterment for the people through equitable distribution of the land, and state management or control of industry.

Sun Yat-sen died in 1925, at the very time when the instruments had been forged to fulfill his ambitions.† Although he did not live to see the warlords humbled and the country united, he is today recognized, both by the mainland Communists and the Taiwan Nationalists, as one of the great creators of modern China. Dr. Sun's death made it possible for Chiang Kai-shek to become the leading figure in the Kuomintang. In May, 1926, he assumed command of the "Northern Expedition," a campaign to unify China by crushing the warlords in the north. The Kuomintang forces, preceded by propaganda corps, swept everything before them, reaching the Yangtze by October. The capital was now moved to Hankow, which was dominated by left-wing and communist elements.

This pointed up a growing split within the Kuomintang between the left wing ensconced in Hankow and the right wing under General Chiang. The latter favored nationalism but not social revolution. He had become alarmed by the activities of the leftist propaganda corps that had been operating ahead of his divisions. Working among the peasantry and the city workers, these propagandists whipped up a revolutionary movement against the landed gentry, the urban bourgeoisie, and the Western business interests. Although Chiang had worked closely with his Russian advisers, he was definitely anti-communist and determined to prevent the leftists from getting control of the Kuomintang.

The showdown came when Nanking fell on March 24, 1927. As had happened in other cities, worker and student battalions were organized as

* See "The Three People's Principles," *EMM*, No. 134.
† See "Sun Yat-sen's Message to the Soviet Union," *EMM*, No. 135.

the Kuomintang army approached. They waged a general strike and were able to take over control of the city during the interval between the departure of the warlord forces and the arrival of Chiang. The latter was not at all happy to be greeted by a revolutionary committee that included Chou En-lai. With the backing of conservative elements in the Kuomintang and of financial interests in Shanghai, Chiang now carried out a bloody purge of communists and their leftist allies. Borodin returned to Russia, and Chiang reorganized the Kuomintang so that he was the undisputed head. In June, 1928, his armies took Peking, destroying the power of the northern warlords and completing the official unification of the country. The capital of the new China was moved to Nanking.

Chiang now visited the Buddhist temple outside Peking where Sun Yat-sen's body had lain in state. He reported to the spirit of the dead leader that victory had been achieved. Compared to the immediate post–World War I years, China was indeed infinitely better off. And during the following decade the country made appreciable progress under Chiang's guidance. Railway mileage almost doubled, and that of modern roads quadrupled. Internal tariff barriers, of which there had been about 500, were abolished in 1932. Likewise, a unified currency was created for the first time. Significant progress was also made in governmental procedures, in public health, in education, and in industrialization. Equally striking were the government's successes in the diplomatic field. Control of the tariff was regained, some of the territories ceded to foreign nations were recovered, and many of the special privileges wrested by the Western powers were returned. By 1943 extraterritorial rights had been surrendered by all foreign nations.

But there were serious gaps in Chiang's reform program, and these ultimately proved fatal. Badly needed land reform was neglected because the Kuomintang Party in the rural areas was dominated by landlords who opposed any change. And Chiang's authoritarian, one-party government prevented the growth of democracy, so that opposition groups could not assert themselves by constitutional means; revolution was the sole alternative. Finally, the Kuomintang failed to develop ideas that could attract the support of the people. Nationalist appeals had little attraction for land-hungry peasants and poverty-stricken city workers. Chiang realized that something was missing, so he fell back on old-fashioned Confucian preachings about propriety and righteousness. These were as quaint as they were ineffective in the China of the twentieth century.

These weaknesses of the Kuomintang regime might have been gradually overcome if it had been given a long period of peace. But it did not have this opportunity because of two mortal enemies, the Communists at home and the Japanese abroad. The Chinese Communist party was organized in Shanghai in May, 1921, and in the following years branches appeared in all parts of the country. Many students and intellectuals joined the ranks, attracted by the call for action and the assurances of a classless and equitable society for the future. As we have seen, the Communists first cooperated with Sun Yat-sen and then broke with Chiang Kai-shek in 1927. Most of the Communist leaders were killed off by Chiang, but a number managed to escape to the mountainous interior of South China. One of their leaders was Mao Tse-tung, who now worked out a new revolutionary strategy in defiance of the Communist

International in Moscow. He rejected the traditional Marxist doctrine that only the city proletariat could be depended upon to carry through a revolution. From firsthand observation in the countryside he concluded that the poor peasants, who comprised 70 per cent of the population, were "the vanguard of the revolution. . . . Without the poor peasant there can be no revolution." This was pure heresy in Moscow, but Mao went his way, organizing the peasants and building up a separate army and government in the south.

Chiang responded by launching five "bandit extermination campaigns," as they were called. The Communists managed to survive, thanks to the support of the peasants who were won over by the Communist policy of dividing large estates without compensation to the owners. The fifth campaign did succeed in dislodging the Communists, who were completely surrounded by the Kuomintang armies. Finally 90,000 managed to break through, and of these, less than 7,000 survived a 6,000 mile trek of incredible hardship. During this historic "Long March" of 368 days (October 16, 1934 to October 25, 1935) they fought an average of almost a skirmish a day with Kuomintang forces totaling more than 300,000. Finally the Communist survivors reached the northwest provinces, where they dug in and established a base. Their land reform policies again won them peasant support, so that they were able to build up their strength to the point where they became serious rivals of the Kuomintang regime in Nanking.

While Chiang was involved in this domestic struggle with the Communists, he was being attacked from the outside by the Japanese. We shall see later (Chapter 24, section I) that this aggression began with the occupation of Manchuria in 1931, and continued until the Japanese were in control of the entire eastern seaboard by the beginning of World War II. This combination of Communist subversion and Japanese aggression culminated in 1949 in Chiang's flight to Taiwan (Formosa), leaving Mao to rule the mainland from his new capital in Peking.*

SUGGESTED READING

General surveys of the post-World War I colonial uprising are available in the relevant sections of H. Kohn, *The Age of Nationalism: The First Era of Global History* (New York: Harper, 1962); M. Edwardes, *Asia in the European Age, 1498–1955* (London: Thames, 1961); and J. Romein, *The Asian Century* (London: Allen, 1962).

World War I diplomacy involving the Middle East is analyzed in H. N. Howard, *The Partition of Turkey: A Diplomatic History, 1913–1923* (Norman, Okla.: Univ. of Oklahoma, 1931); E. Kedourie, *England and the Middle East: The Destruction of the Ottoman Empire, 1914–1921* (London: Bowes, 1956); and L. Stein, *The Balfour Declaration* (New York: Simon and Schuster, 1961). For the relevant documents, see the convenient collection by J. C. Hurewitz, *Diplomacy in the Near and Middle East: A Documentary Record, 1914–1956* (Princeton: Van Nostrand, 1956), Vol. II.

For Turkey's revival under Kemal, see E. D. Smith, *Turkey: Origins of the Kemalist Movement and the Government of the Grand National Assembly,*

* See "Sun Yat-sen on the Colonial Revolution," *EMM*, No. 136.

1919–1923 (Washington: Judd & Detweiler, 1959); the personal account of the Turkish nationalist movement in Halidé Edib, *The Turkish Ordeal* (New York: Appleton, 1928); the sympathetic biography by H. C. Armstrong, *Grey Wolf, Mustafa Kemal* (London: Barker, 1932); and the detailed analysis by D. E. Webster, *The Turkey of Ataturk: Social Process in the Turkish Reformation* (Philadelphia: Am. Acad. Pol. and Soc. Sci., 1939).

The basic study of the Arab nationalist uprising is by G. Antonius, *The Arab Awakening: The Story of the Arab National Movement* (London: Hamilton, 1938). See also H. Kohn, *Nationalism and Imperialism in the Hither East* (London: Routledge, 1932); N. Safran, *Egypt in Search of Political Community* (Cambridge: Harvard Univ., 1961); Z. N. Zeine, *The Struggle for Arab Independence: Western Diplomacy & the Rise and Fall of Feisal's Kingdom in Syria* (Beirut: Khayat, 1960); and A. J. Toynbee, *Survey of International Affairs, 1925,* Vol. I, *The Islamic World Since the Peace Settlement* (London: 1927; Oxford, Royal Institute of International Affairs).

An important first-hand account of post-war Persia is given by Sir Percy Sykes, commander of the South Persia Rifles, in the first volume of his *History of Persia* (London: Macmillan, 1930). Another British first-hand account is by J. M. Balfour, *Recent Happenings in Persia* (London: Blackwood, 1922). For the Persian view of these years, see N. S. Fatemi, *Diplomatic History of Persia, 1917–1923* (New York: R. Moore, 1952). Dependable brief histories are by J. M. Upton, *The History of Modern Iran: An Interpretation* (Cambridge: Harvard Univ., 1960) and R. N. Frye, *Iran* (New York: Holt, 1953).

On the outstanding figures in India, there are M. K. Gandhi, *An Autobiography: The Story of My Experiments with Truth,* first published in Ahmedabad in 1927 and then as a Beacon Press Paperback in Boston, 1957; *All Men Are Brothers: Life and Thoughts of Mahatma Gandhi as Told in His Own Words* (New York: UNESCO, 1958); Louis Fischer, *Gandhi: His Life and Message for the World* (New York: New Am. Lib., 1954, Signet Key Book); *Toward Freedom: The Autobiography of Jawaharlal Nehru* (New York: Day, 1941); the valuable biography by M. Brecher, *Nehru: A Political Biography* (New York: Oxford Univ., 1959); and for the Moslem side, the biography *Jinnah* by H. Bolitho (London: J. Murray, 1954). An acute analysis of the British position is given by G. Wint, *The British in India,* 2nd ed. (London: Faber, 1955). Finally, see the relevant chapters in the following standard surveys: W. N. Brown, *The United States and India and Pakistan* (Cambridge: Harvard Univ., 1955); T. Walter Wallbank, *A Short History of India and Pakistan* (New York: New Am. Lib., 1958; A Mentor Book); and P. Spear, *India* (Ann Arbor: Univ. of Michigan, 1961). For further references, see R. I. Crane, *The History of India: Its Study and Interpretation* (Washington: Service Center for Teachers of History, 1958).

On the outstanding figures in China, there is L. Sharman, *Sun Yat-sen* (New Day, 1934); E. Hahn, *Chiang Kai-shek: An Unauthorized Biography* (New York: Doubleday, 1955); R. S. Elegant, *China's Red Master* (New York: Twayne, 1951); and A. Fremantle, ed., *Mao Tse-tung: An Anthology of His Writings* (New York: New Am. Lib., 1962, A Mentor Book). Various aspects of the interwar period in China are analyzed in F. G. Liu, *A Military History of Modern China, 1924–1949* (Princeton: Princeton Univ., 1956); Hu Shih, *The Chinese Renaissance* (Chicago: Univ. Chicago, 1934); J. de Francis, *Nationalism and*

484

Language Reform in China (Princeton: Princeton Univ., 1950); M. J. Levy, Jr., *The Family Revolution in Modern China* (Cambridge: Harvard Univ., 1949); and E. Snow, *Red Star Over China* (New York: Random, 1938), the latter being a classic first-hand account of Communist leaders and strategy in 1936. For further references see C. O. Hucker, *Chinese History: A Bibliographic Review* (Washington: Service Center for Teachers of History, 1958).

*The failure to strangle Bolshevism at its birth
and to bring Russia, then prostrate, by one
means or another, into the general democratic system, lies heavy upon us today.*

WINSTON CHURCHILL, *April 1, 1949*

Chapter

22

Revolution and Settlement
in Europe to 1929

At the same time that the colonial world was in the throes
of national revolution, Europe itself was seething with social revolution. All over the Continent the old order was being questioned, partly
because of the trauma of the World War, and partly because of the
impact of the great Russian Revolution. Thus, European history during the decade to 1929 was largely a history of struggle between revolutionary and counterrevolutionary forces. In Russia, communism
emerged triumphant after years of civil war and intervention. In
Central Europe the extremist revolutionary forces were crushed and
a variety of non-Communist regimes appeared, ranging from the liberal Weimar Republic in Germany to the rightist Horthy government
in Hungary and to the fascist Mussolini state in Italy. Western Europe
was spared such violent upheavals, but even here, the authority of
traditional parliamentary institutions was being strained by economic
difficulties, mass unemployment, and cabinet instability. By the late
1920's, some measure of order seemed to be returning to Europe.
Prosperity was growing, unemployment was on the decline, and various international issues appeared to be resolved by the Dawes Plan,
the Locarno Pacts, the Kellogg–Briand Pact, and the commitment of
the Soviet Union to Five Year Plans rather than to world revolution.
Europe was returning to a normal state, or so it seemed, until the

Great Depression precipitated the series of domestic and international crises that were to culminate in World War II.

I. Communism Triumphs in Russia

Origins of Counterrevolution and Intervention

By signing the harsh Brest-Litovsk Treaty on March 3, 1918 (see Chapter 20, section IV), the Bolsheviks hoped that at last they would be able to turn from war to the more congenial task of building a new social order. Instead, they were destined to fight on for three more years against counterrevolution and foreign intervention. The counterrevolution was in part the work of members of the propertied classes—army officers, government officials, landowners, and businessmen—who for obvious reasons wished to be rid of the Bolsheviks. Equally ardent in their counterrevolutionary activities, however, were the various elements of the non-Bolshevik Left, of whom the Socialist Revolutionaries were by far the most numerous. They agreed with the Bolsheviks on the need for social revolution, but they bitterly resented the Bolshevik monopolization of the revolution. They regarded the Bolshevik coup of November 7, 1917, as a gross betrayal, particularly because the Constituent Assembly elected on November 25, 1917, included only 175 Bolsheviks as against 370 Socialist Revolutionaries and 159 other assorted representatives (see Chapter 20, section IV). Accordingly, the non-Bolshevik Left took the lead in organizing underground opposition, while the rightist elements led armed forces in open revolt, beginning in the Cossack territories.

These anti-Bolshevik groups were encouraged and assisted by the Western powers, the latter being motivated by various considerations such as the strident Bolshevik campaign for world revolution. Both in Europe and in the colonial regions the Bolsheviks called on the "toiling masses" to "convert the imperialist war into a class war." Many Western leaders naturally responded by seeking to crush these Marxist incendiaries before they could ignite the smoldering tinder of revolution scattered throughout the world. Also, certain British and French statesmen erroneously regarded the Bolsheviks as tools of the German general staff, and wished to be rid of them in order to bring Russia back into the war. Closely related was the problem of the disposition of Allied war materials that had been accumulated in Russia in huge quantities—over 160,000 tons in Murmansk and 800,000 tons in Vladivostok, the Western powers were worried lest the Bolsheviks, willingly or unwillingly, allow these supplies to fall into German hands. And there were economic motives behind the Allied intervention: Bolshevik nationalization of foreign properties and repudiation of foreign debts naturally alienated powerful vested interests, which used their influence in behalf of intervention.

Course of Civil War

Under these circumstances several counterrevolutionary governments were set up soon after the Brest-Litovsk Treaty all along the borders of Russia—in the northern Archangel-Murmansk region, the Baltic provinces, the

Ukraine, the Don territories, Transcaucasia, and Siberia. These governments were generously provided with funds and war materials, as well as with military advisers and small detachments of troops on certain fronts. Soon after operations had gotten under way, the war ended in the West, raising the question of whether the Allied intervention should be pressed further. The original arguments about bringing Russia back into the war and preventing the Germans from seizing military supplies were now irrelevant.

The issue of whether to continue the intervention was debated by the Allied leaders in conference at Paris. Both President Wilson and Prime Minister Lloyd George favored immediate cessation of hostilities. Georges Clemenceau, however, maintained that the whole of Europe was menaced by the threat of revolution and that Bolshevism must be crushed in its place of origin. Having to leave the conference in order to attend to political duties at home, Wilson and Lloyd George were unable to back up their views. The deputies they left behind, Secretary of State Robert Lansing and Secretary of War Winston Churchill, held positions closer to Clemenceau's. Hence a decision was reached for continued intervention, a fateful choice that was to mean three more years of war and a bitter legacy of international mistrust for the postwar years.*

At first the Bolsheviks suffered one reverse after another, simply because the old Russian army had disintegrated and there was nothing else to take its place. The Commissar for Defense, Leon Trotsky, gradually built up a new Red Army, which numbered about 500,000 men by the end of 1918. At times this force had to fight on two dozen different fronts, as revolts broke out in all parts of the country and Allied forces landed in coastal areas.

The chief opponents of the Bolsheviks in 1919 were Admiral Kolchak in Siberia, General Denikin in the Crimea and the Ukraine, and General Yudenich in Estonia. A common pattern is evident in their campaigns. Beginning with sudden attacks from their bases, they gained easy initial victories, came within reach of full victory, then were stopped, gradually pushed back, and finally routed and "liquidated," to use a favorite Bolshevik expression. In March, 1919, Kolchak captured the city of Ufa to the west of the Urals; in August, Denikin had advanced north to Kiev, and by October, Yudenich had penetrated to the very suburbs of Petrograd. Lenin's regime now was limited to the Petrograd-Moscow regions, an area about equal to the fifteenth century Muscovite principality. However, by the end of 1919 the tides had turned: Denikin had been driven back to the Crimea, Yudenich to the Baltic, and Kolchak was not only forced back over the Urals, but was captured and shot.

It appeared early in 1920 that the ordeal was finally over. But another full year of fighting lay ahead, owing to the appearance of the Poles and renewed large-scale intervention by the French. The Poles, determined to extend their frontiers as far eastward as possible, took advantage of the confusion and exhaustion to invade the Ukraine in April, 1920. The pattern of the previous year's operations was now repeated. The Poles advanced rapidly and took Kiev on May 7, but five weeks later they were driven out of the city, and by mid-July were back in their own territory. The triumphant Bolsheviks pressed on, reaching the outskirts of Warsaw on August 14. But the Poles, strongly supported by the French, stopped the advancing Russians and managed to

* See "Allied Intervention in Russia," *EMM*, No. 137.

488

push them back. The campaign ended in mid-October, and on March 18, 1921, the Treaty of Riga defined the Polish-Russian frontier that prevailed until World War II.

Meanwhile, General Wrangel, who had replaced Denikin, had overrun much of southern Russia with the generous assistance of the French. But after the Bolsheviks were through with the Poles, they turned their forces against Wrangel, driving him south to the Crimea. This peninsula, once the playground of tsars and grand dukes, was now crowded with a motley host of refugees—high ecclesiastics, tsarist officials, aristocratic landowners, and the remnants of White armies. As many as possible were evacuated in French warships and scattered in ports from Constantinople to Marseilles; the remainder were left to the mercy of the victorious Red Army.

The only foreign troops now left on Russian soil were the Japanese operating from Vladivostok. Originally there had been American and British as well as Japanese contingents in eastern Siberia, but the first two were withdrawn in 1920. The Japanese stayed on, hoping to retain control of these vast but sparsely populated regions through the medium of a puppet regime. The United States repeatedly brought diplomatic pressure on the Japanese to leave, and finally persuaded them to do so at the Washington Naval Disarmament Conference in 1922.

Roots of Bolshevik Victory

With the departure of the Japanese, the tragic period of civil war and intervention mercifully came to a close. Lenin's Communist party was now in control of the entire country. Few would have predicted this outcome in 1919 when the beleaguered Communists appeared to be doomed by forces of counterrevolution that were backed by the might of the Allied powers. But the fact is that, contrary to the claims of Soviet historians, the Allied powers never concentrated their attention and their resources on the struggle going on in Russia. Aside from certain passionately dedicated anti-Bolsheviks who occupied subordinate posts, the Allied leaders regarded the intervention as little more than a sideshow, and they supported it fitfully with varied and conflicting motives. They did provide the Whites with abundant funds and military supplies, but they sent very few troops. Only in northern Russia did these Allied contingents participate significantly in actual combat. In fact, in eastern Siberia the Japanese, American, and British forces were more often engaged in intrigues against each other than in action against the Reds. The American diplomat-historian George Kennan has concluded that intervention "served everywhere to compromise the enemies of the Bolsheviki and to strengthen the Communists themselves. So important was this factor that I think it may well be questioned whether Bolshevism would ever have prevailed throughout Russia had the Western governments not aided its progress to power by this ill-conceived interference."[1]

Allied disunity and vacillation was one reason for the triumph of the Bolsheviks. Even more disunity prevailed amongst the Whites, partly because of the conflicting ambitions of individual leaders, but also because of the basic incompatibility of the leftist Socialist Revolutionaries and the assorted right-wing elements. The Communists, by contrast, enjoyed certain advantages that proved decisive in the end. Their monolithic party organization imposed a cohesion and discipline that was unmatched on the other side.* The Communist party was effectively supported by an efficient secret police organization, the Cheka, that ruthlessly ferreted out opposition groups. The Commissar of War, Leon Trotsky, skillfully combined the enthusiasm of proletarian volunteers with the indispensable technical knowledge of former Tsarist officers to forge a formidable new Red Army. Furthermore, this army enjoyed the substantial advantage of having internal lines of communication, in contrast to the tremendous distances separating the White forces from each other and from their sources of supplies in Western Europe and the United States. Finally, the Bolsheviks were generally more successful in winning the support of the peasant masses. This does not mean that the Russian peasants were won over to Marxist ideology; indeed, most of them were fed up with both the Reds and the Whites, and would rather have been left alone. But when forced to make a choice, they more frequently decided in favor of the Reds who, they thought, were on their side and would allow them to keep the plots they had seized from the landlords.†

In retrospect, the protracted civil war and intervention was a disaster for all parties concerned. It left the Russian countryside devastated from the Baltic to the Pacific, and the Russian people decimated by casualties, starvation, and disease. Equally serious was the poisoning of relations between the new Soviet state and the Western world. The Soviet leaders were confirmed in their Marxist fears of "capitalist encirclement," while Western statesmen took all too seriously the futile manifestos of the Communist International established in 1919. So deep and lasting was this mutual distrust that it envenomed international relations during the following decade and contributed significantly to the coming of World War II.

II. COMMUNISM FAILS IN CENTRAL EUROPE

Balance of Power in Germany

While civil war was raging in Russia, the crucial question for Europe was whether communism would spread westward. Lenin and his fellow Bolsheviks assumed that if this did not occur, their cause would be doomed. In line with Marxist ideology, they could not conceive that their revolution might survive and take root in a single country, least of all in predominantly agrarian Russia. Accordingly, they followed closely and hopefully the course of events in Central Europe—especially Germany, which was clearly the key country. If it went communist, the combination of German industrial strength and Russian natural resources would be unbeatable, and the future of the revolution would be assured.

At first it appeared that these Bolshevik hopes might be realized. The Kaiser was forced to abdicate on November 9, 1918, following a mutiny in the navy and the spread of revolution from the Baltic ports into the interior (see Chapter 20, section VI). Workers' and Soldiers' Councils, similar to the

* See "H. G. Wells on the Bolshevik Victory," *EMM*, No. 138.
† See "The Peasants and the Revolution," *EMM*, No. 139.

Russian Soviets, appeared in all the major cities, including Berlin. So strong was the revolutionary movement that it seemed probable that communism would engulf the Continent, at least to the Rhine. The final outcome, however, was not a Soviet Germany but the bourgeois German Republic.

Several factors that escaped attention at the time explain this fateful outcome, one being the prosperity of prewar Germany, which left the working class relatively contented and in no mood for revolution. It is true that the German Social Democratic party in 1914 was the strongest party in Europe, but it was conservative, committed to social reform rather than to revolution. Equally important was the prosperity of the German peasants, who were infinitely better off than those of Russia. They had not fared too badly during the war years, so that the Bolshevik slogan "Land to the Peasants," which had been so effective in Russia, made very little impact on Germany. Also, the war had already ended at the time of the German revolution, again in contrast to the situation in Russia. The demand for peace, which probably helped the Bolsheviks more than anything else, was irrelevant in Germany. Furthermore, although the German army was defeated, it was far from being as demoralized and mutinous as the Russian army of 1917.* The opponents of revolution in Germany were able to call upon reliable military forces when the showdown came.

A final factor of major significance was the split in the ranks of the German socialists. This, of course, was not unique. All the European socialist parties had splintered to a greater or lesser extent in 1914 over the question of whether to support or oppose the war. In Germany, the Majority Social Democrats, led by Friedrich Ebert and Philipp Scheidemann, had supported the German war effort from the beginning. Being relatively conservative, they now strenuously opposed the revolutionary Workers' and Soldiers' Councils. "I hate the social revolution," Ebert declared candidly, "I hate it like sin." At the other end of the spectrum was the Spartacist League, the counterpart of Lenin's Bolsheviks, led by two able and outstanding revolutionaries, Karl Liebknecht, of a well-known German socialist family, and Rosa Luxemburg, of Polish-Jewish origin. The Spartacists, as might be expected, supported the Workers' and Soldiers' Councils and wished to establish a Soviet-type regime in Germany. Between the Majority Socialists and the Spartacists was the Independent Socialist party; it also favored a Soviet Germany but in addition wished to cooperate with the Majority Socialists.

Establishment of Weimar Republic

When Prince Max announced the abdication of the Kaiser, he himself resigned the chancellorship and handed the government over to Friedrich Ebert. The latter formed a cabinet, or council, of "Six Commissars," composed of three Majority Social Democrats and three Independent Socialists. The Spartacists chose to remain outside for the simple reason that they were interested only in forcing the revolution further to the Left. Philipp Scheidemann had proclaimed the establishment of the German Republic from the balcony of the parliament building, but Liebknecht at the same time had

* See "Discipline of the German Army," *EMM,* No. 140.

proclaimed a Soviet Germany from the balcony of the Imperial Palace a mile away. The great question now was which side would prevail.

The situation was comparable to that in Russia when the Provisional Government was established in March, 1917. Ebert was very much aware of the outcome in that country, and had no desire to be another Kerensky. Accordingly, on November 10, the day after the Kaiser's abdication, he formed a secret alliance with General Wilhelm Groener, Chief of the General Staff, for the suppression of the Spartacists and the Workers' and Soldiers' Councils.* Every night between 11:00 P.M. and 1:00 A.M., the two men talked on a special telephone linking the chancellory at Berlin and headquarters at Spa. With this powerful support, Ebert moved aggressively against the extreme Left. The Independent Social Democrats refused to go along and resigned from the cabinet, but this made little difference. On December 30, the Spartacists renamed themselves the Communist Labor Party of Germany and made plans for revolt, but before these were completed, Karl Liebknecht and Rosa Luxemburg were arrested and shot "while trying to escape." Over a thousand of their followers were killed during the ruthless street fighting that followed. By mid-January, 1919, the danger from the Left was over.

The critical turning point had been passed, and on January 19, 1919, elections were held throughout Germany for a National Assembly rather than for a Congress of Soviets. The delegates elected were overwhelmingly of the moderate Left. The Assembly met in Weimar, partly to escape the disorders of Berlin and partly to associate the new Germany in world public opinion with peaceful cultural symbols such as Goethe and Schiller. Ebert was elected the first president of the Republic, and Scheidemann the first chancellor.

The constitution adopted in July, 1919, was unimpeachably democratic, at least in principle. It embodied all the devices then favored by the democracies, including universal suffrage, proportional representation, a bill of rights, and separation of church and state, and church and school. The president, who was elected for a term of seven years, appointed the chancellor, who in turn chose a cabinet that had to have the support of the majority in the *Reichstag,* or lower house. The *Reichsrat,* or upper house, composed of delegates from the eighteen states, could delay but not prevent legislation.

Behind this new constitutional façade, much of the old Germany remained unchanged. The bureaucracy, the judiciary, and the police survived intact. In the universities, the most undemocratic and anti-Semitic faculties and fraternities continued untouched on the grounds of academic freedom. The new *Reichswehr* was the old imperial army in miniature. Except for the legal eight-hour day, virtually no social reforms were introduced. The industrial cartels and monopolies continued as before; the Junkers of East Prussia retained their landed estates, as did the Kaiser and the various local rulers. In short, the German revolution had preserved more than it had changed. Power was left largely in the hands of the old ruling elements, which never accepted the new order. At first the Weimar Republic did succeed in stabilizing itself with foreign financial aid. But when the Great Depression undermined the foundations of the state, most of these unreconciled bureaucrats, army officers, and landed gentry turned upon the Republic and helped in its destruction.

* See "The 'Ebert–Groener Deal,' " *EMM,* No. 141.

This built-in Achilles' heel of the Weimar Republic was described by an American observer:

> Imagine a republic that allows its laws to be interpreted by monarchist judges, its Government to be administered by old-time functionaries brought up in fidelity to the old regime; that watches passively while reactionary school teachers and professors teach its children to despise the present freedom in favor of a glorified feudal past. . . . This remarkable Republic paid generous pensions to thousands of ex-officers and civil servants who made no bones of their desire to overthrow it.[2]

Revolution and Reaction in Central Europe

The suppression of the Spartacists and the establishment of the Weimar Republic ensured that the rest of Central Europe would not go communist. Nevertheless, for a number of years this part of Europe seethed with unrest and revolt. The peasant masses between the Baltic and the Aegean were politically awake and active to an unprecedented degree, one reason being that millions of peasant army recruits had widened their horizons immeasurably as a result of their war experiences. They had observed not only the differences between city and village life, but also the differences in living standards and social institutions among various countries. The peasants were also profoundly affected by the overthrow of the Hapsburg, Hohenzollern, and Romanoff dynasties. In the light of centuries-old traditions, this was a seismic shock that aroused nationalist aspirations and class consciousness. Finally, the unprecedented destructiveness and suffering that took place during the long years of war aggravated the revolutionary situation, especially in the countries that had suffered defeat.

The precise manifestation of this revolutionary ferment varied from country to country according to local circumstances. The Communist parties did not play an outstanding role except in the case of Hungary, where on November 16, 1918, Count Michael Karolyi, an aristocrat of socialist and pacifist learnings, had proclaimed the Hungarian People's Republic. Karolyi cut the ties with Austria and then attempted to liberalize the Hungarian state by such reforms as universal suffrage, freedom of speech and assembly, separation of church and state, and expropriation of large estates. This failed to win over the Czech, Yugloslav, and Rumanian minorities, who wanted independence rather than reform, and looked to Prague, Belgrade, and Bucharest rather than to Budapest. In addition, the allies were demanding armistice terms so stringent that Karolyi could not accept them. In March, 1919, he resigned his office and left the country.

The vacuum was filled by the International Revolutionary Hungarian Socialist party, which included both communists and socialists. With the support of the Workers' and Soldiers' Councils, this party established a Soviet Republic. Its leading figure was Bela Kun, a middle-class Jew who had been an officer in the Hungarian army and who had lived as a war prisoner in Russia. There he met Lenin and other Bolsheviks, and returned home a professional revolutionary. Catapulted to power by the course of events, he was unable to hold on to his authority. The peasants in the countryside remained generally hostile and refused to sell their provisions for the Communist paper money. Meanwhile, Rumanian troops were invading the country, and on August 4, 1919, they occupied Budapest, forcing Bela Kun to flee to Vienna. When the Rumanians departed in February, 1920, a right-wing government headed by Admiral Miklós Horthy was established with Allied support. Horthy remained in power for the whole interwar period, during which time Hungary was unique in Central Europe for the almost complete absence of agrarian or other reforms.

In most of the other Central European countries, agrarian or peasant parties were giving voice to popular discontent. The following peasant leaders assumed office in the postwar years: Aleksandr Stamboliski in Bulgaria in 1919, Stefan Radich in Yugoslavia in 1925, Wincenty Witos in Poland in 1926, and Iuliu Maniu in Rumania in 1928. Owing to their pacifism and distaste for violence, however, none of them was able to retain power for long. They were left vulnerable to the entrenched military and bureaucratic elements that did not hesitate to forcefully seize power when their interests were threatened. Another reason for their failure was the increasing control that lawyers and urban intellectuals, who were attracted by the political opportunities, gained over the peasant parties. Under this leadership, the parties usually represented the interests of the wealthy peasants and had little contact with the great mass of poor peasants.

One after another the peasant leaders were ousted from office. Stamboliski was assassinated in 1923, and a dictatorship was established by King Boris. Radich was assassinated in 1928, and the following year King Alexander set up his dictatorship. In Poland, Witos lasted only a few days before he was removed by General Joseph Pilsudski, who dominated the country until his death in 1935. Maniu was eased out of office in 1930 by King Carol II, who made and unmade governments until forced to flee Rumania a decade later.

The same pattern prevailed in Austria and Greece where, for various reasons, agrarian parties never took hold. Yet Austria ended up with an authoritarian government under Chancellor Dollfuss in 1934, and Greece with an avowedly fascist regime under General Metaxas in 1936. Thus, by World War II the whole of Central Europe was under dictatorial rule, with one exception—Czechoslovakia. This country possessed certain advantages that explain its uniqueness: a high level of literacy; a trained bureaucracy inherited from the Hapsburgs; the capable leadership of Jan Masaryk and Eduard Beneš; and a balanced economy that provided higher living standards and greater security than was possible in the predominantly agrarian countries to the east.

III. Italy Goes Fascist

While bolshevism, agrarianism, and traditional parliamentarianism battled for primacy in Eastern and Central Europe, an entirely new ism was coming to the force in Italy—fascism, the outstanding political innovation in Europe in the postwar years. Bolshevism had a history going back at least to the Communist Manifesto of 1848, while agrarianism was taking political form with the appearance of peasant parties at the turn of the century. Fascism, by contrast, appeared unexpectedly and dramatically with Mussolini's march on Rome in October, 1922.

494   Postwar conditions in Italy provided fertile soil for a violent, melodramatic, and anti-intellectual movement such as fascism. The Italy of 1919 had behind it only two generations of national independence and unity. Parliamentary government was, in practice, a morass of corruption in which party "bosses" manipulated short-lived coalition blocs. This unstable political structure was further weakened in the postwar years by serious economic dislocation. Many of the demobilized millions were unable to find jobs. Foreign trade and tourist traffic were declining in the aftermath of war. Emigration, which for decades had served as a safety valve and a source of overseas remittances, now petered out because of restrictive legislation in the United States and other countries. The popular unrest engendered by this economic stress was aggravated by the slighting of Italian claims at the Paris peace conference. The expenditure of blood and treasure appeared to have been in vain, and the resulting frustration and injured pride produced an inflammable situation.

This became evident with the November, 1919, elections, which returned 160 for the Socialist party and 103 for the Catholic Popular party as against 93 and 58 respectively for the traditional Liberal and Radical parties. When parliament opened, the Socialists refused to greet the King and shouted "Long Live Socialism!" The climax came in September, 1920, when workers throughout north Italy began taking over factories. Giovanni Giolitti, the old prewar political manipulator who had formed a cabinet in June, 1920, decided to leave the "campers" in possession on the assumption that they would bungle the operation of the factories and be forced to evacuate them on their own accord. In the end, the workers did agree to leave in return for wage increases and a share of control in industry.

The "sit-ins" had shed a sudden light on the contemporary scene, demonstrating the inert and powerless positions of both government and factory owners. More important, they emphasized the futile "maximalism" of the Italian socialists. Although these vociferous revolutionaries sounded like Lenin in their demands for immediate socialization, they had no intention of or plans for seizing power. They certainly had every opportunity to take over, for Giolitti had not taken action against the "sit-ins," partly because he did not know whether the soldiers would obey orders or join the workers. All the classical conditions for a revolution were present—except for the will to start one. The Socialist watchword at this time was "the revolution is not made. The revolution comes." Within two years this slogan was proven wrong by one who was ready to make revolution.

Benito Mussolini was of working-class origin, being the son of a socialist blacksmith in a poverty-stricken Romagnese village. Somehow he managed to earn a teacher's diploma, but he made little use of it. By temperament he was more suited for revolutionary agitation than for classroom instruction. During the Tripolitan War of 1911 he attracted attention by his inflammatory speeches in which he referred to the Italian flag as "a rag fit only to be planted on a dung heap." The following year he became editor of the official Socialist paper *Avanti*! When World War I began in August, 1914, he was still a revolutionary and a pacifist, but the following month his great transformation took place, facilitated by funds from the French government, which was desperately anxious at this point to secure Italy as an ally. Mussolini was enabled to start his own newspaper, *Il Popolo d'Italia,* in which he conducted a passionate interventionist campaign.

495

Called to battle in September, 1915, Mussolini fought in the trenches for a few weeks until he was wounded and invalided out of the army. He languished in obscurity until 1919, when he formed his first "combat troops," or *fasci di combattimento.* The *fasces*, a bundle of rods tied around the haft of an ax, was the emblem carried by the Roman lictors who attended the magistrates. Thus it was a symbol for unity and authority, which became Mussolini's watchwords against the political anarchy and social strife of the period. At the outset he attracted the support of only a handful of frustrated students and demobilized soldiers. In the November, 1919 elections he ran two candidates, one being himself; neither he nor the other candidate was elected. He polled a mere 4,795 votes as against 180,000 for his Socialist opponent. But in the elections of May 15, 1921, the Fascist party won 22 seats, while the Socialist representation declined from 160 to 122. The big gainer was the Liberal party with 275, while the Catholic Popular party remained about the same with 107, and the new Communist party won 16 seats.

Mussolini was still far from a position of authority, but at least his party had a nationwide organization with about 250,000 members at election time. From then on it forged rapidly ahead, partly because the passivity of the Socialists had created a vacuum that Mussolini promptly filled. Equally important was the substantial support that Mussolini was now receiving from industrialists, landowners, and other members of the propertied classes. Terrified by the widespread seizure of factories and estates, they now looked hopefully to the Fascist *squadristi,* or armed bands, as a bulwark against the dreaded social revolution. Actually, the danger of revolution had passed with the evacuation of the factories in late September, 1920. Now it was the Fascist bands, aided by the benevolent neutrality of the police, that were disturbing the peace. With impunity they attacked trade union offices and Socialist party headquarters, raided working-class districts, drove out mayors and other officials who were Socialists, and wrecked opposition newspaper offices. The government and the wealthy elements of society tolerated, and even secretly aided, this campaign of violence and terrorism.*

In the fall of 1922, Mussolini prepared for a coup by winning over both the monarchy and the Church with specific assurance that their interests would be respected. Since the regular army and the police already had manifested their benevolent neutrality, Mussolini proceeded with assurance to mobilize his Blackshirts for a widely publicized march on Rome. Prime Minister Luigi Facta asked King Victor Emmanuel to proclaim martial law, but the King refused and instead called on Mussolini to form a government. Thus only a token march on Rome by the Blackshirts was necessary, while Mussolini arrived anticlimactically in Rome on October 27 in a sleeping-car.

Mussolini had become premier by technically constitutional methods, but it soon became apparent that he had no intention of respecting constitutional procedures. His party had won 35 seats in the 1921 elections, but these comprised only 6 per cent of the total number. Mussolini warned Parliament, "I

* See "Mussolini's 'Authorized Lawlessness,' " *EMM,* No. 142.

could have made of this sordid, gray assembly hall a bivouac for Squadristi . . . but I did not want to, at least not for the present." Parliament and the King gave Mussolini dictatorial powers until December 31, 1923, to restore order and introduce reforms. During this period he allowed a degree of liberty to the press, to the trade unions, and to the parliamentary parties. But at the same time he was gaining control of the state machinery by appointing prefects and judges of Fascist sympathies and organizing a voluntary Fascist militia.

The showdown came with the elections of April 6, 1924. Through liberal use of the *squadristi,* the Fascist party polled 65 per cent of the votes and won 375 seats, compared to the 35 they had previously held. Two months later a prominent Socialist deputy, Giacomo Matteotti, was found murdered. He had written a book, *The Fascisti Exposed,* presenting detailed case histories of hundreds of illegal acts of Fascist violence. It was widely suspected, and later proven, that Matteotti had been killed on orders from Mussolini himself. Most of the non-Fascist deputies walked out of the chamber, vowing not to return until the Matteotti affair had been cleared up. Mussolini faced a major crisis but managed to survive, thanks to the indecisiveness of the opposition and the unwavering support of the king.

By the fall of 1926, Mussolini felt strong enough to take the offensive. He declared the seats of the absent deputies vacant, disbanded the old political parties, tightened censorship of the press, and established an organization of secret police. Italy had become a one-party state, with the Chamber functioning as a rubber-stamp body for passing Facist bills.

The new Fascist regime gradually evolved certain distinctive features.* One was the corporative state in which deputies were elected as representatives not of geographical constituencies but rather of trades and professions. Theoretically it eliminated class conflict by bringing capital and labor together under the benevolent auspices of the state. Actually, only capital enjoyed true self-government, while labor was denied the right to strike or to select its own leaders. Neither the position of the workers nor that of the peasants was basically improved under the corporative state.

Another feature of Mussolini's Italy was the elaborate public works program designed to provide employment and to erect impressive structures for the glorification of fascism. Monuments of the past were restored, and many cities were adorned with large new buildings, workers' tenements, and stadiums. Certain marshlands were drained and made available for cultivation. Tourists were particularly impressed by the trains that "ran on time" and by the extensive new highways or *autostrade.*

The Fascist regime pursued an aggressive foreign policy based on what was then a novel doctrine—the intrinsic merits and desirability of war and of imperial expansion. "Only war" wrote Mussolini in the official *Enciclopedia Italiana,* "carries human energies to the highest level and puts the seal of nobility upon peoples who have the courage to undertake it. . . . Fascism regards the tendency to empire . . . as a manifestation of vitality." In 1923 Mussolini attempted to put these theories into practice by using the murder of certain Italian officials in Greece as a pretext to occupy the Greek island of Corfu. The international climate was then unfavorable for such adventures,

---

* See "The Doctrine of Fascism," *EMM,* No. 143.

and Mussolini found it necessary to withdraw after receiving certain compensations. But in the 1930's the diplomatic balance of power changed, giving him greater freedom of action. He quickly took advantage of it to invade Ethiopia and to forge the Rome-Berlin Axis (see Chapter 24, sections III, IV).

497

IV. Problems of Democracy in Western Europe

In Western Europe there were no upheavals comparable to the civil war in Russia or to the bitter clash between Right and Left in Central Europe. Democratic institutions had stronger and deeper roots in the West, and the prevailing social structures were healthier and enjoyed more popular support. In addition, the Western powers had been the victors rather than the losers in the war, a fact that further contributed to political and social stability. It does not follow, however, that Western Europe experienced no difficulties in the postwar years. There were many problems, the most serious being economic in nature, though with far-reaching social and political repercussions. The experiences of the two leading Western countries, Great Britain and France, illustrate this.

Great Britain

The chief problem in Britain was, by all odds, the severe and chronic unemployment. There was a short-lived boom immediately after the war when factories operated overtime to meet long pent-up consumer demands. But the bust came in 1920, and by March of 1921, over 2,000,000 people were out of work. Unemployment persisted through the 1920's, and the situation grew worse in the 1930's. Thus the depression actually began in Britain in 1920 rather than in 1929, and continued without significant respite to World War II.

To understand this prolonged ordeal it should be noted that Britain's prewar economy had been based on the importation of food and raw materials and the exportation of manufactured goods. On the eve of the First World War Britain was building two-thirds of the world's new ships and exporting seven-ninths of the cotton cloth she produced, one-third of the coal, and one-quarter of the iron and steel. In addition, Britain received a substantial invisible income from overseas investments, financial services, and merchant shipping.

The World War upset this economic balance by stimulating the industrialization of such countries as the United States, Japan, and the British Dominions, which meant reduced overseas markets, especially in the case of textiles where Britain faced stiff Japanese competition. The destruction of much of Britain's merchant marine also caused the invisible revenues to be reduced, as did the fact that Britain was no longer the world's financial center. The Bolshevik revolution further hurt the British economy, wiping out an important market for manufactured goods as well as subtantial investments.*

At least as important as the war in explaining Britain's economic difficulties was the failure of the British themselves to keep up with the rest of the world

* See "Britain's Postwar Problems," *EMM,* No. 144.

in industrial efficiency. Initially, they had led the world in the Industrial Revolution, but now they lagged behind in modernizing their equipment. Because they tended to keep machines until they were worn out rather than until they had become obsolete, productivity per man-hour lagged in comparison with other countries. For example, taking the year 1913 as 100, the output per man-shift in British mines rose by 1938 to a mere 113, compared to 164 in the German mines, and 201 in the Dutch.

Faced with the competition of more efficient foreign industries, British manufacturers often resorted to cutting wages and making agreements amongst themselves to fix prices, allocate production, and share the shrinking foreign markets. These measures did not face up to the basic problem of the growing obsolescence of British industry. The failure to do so arose in part from the traditional values of British society. The ablest graduates of the British universities were more likely to enter the civil service than business, so that the management of industries was often left to individuals of inferior ability and inadequate technical training. Too often they regarded their function as being more to combat unions and keep wages low, than to raise plant efficiency and productivity. At the same time, labor fought not only to keep up wages but also, very often, to prevent any technological advances that might reduce jobs.

This combination of circumstances was responsible for the almost unrelieved depression that gripped Britain during the interwar period. Millions of families subsisted on state relief, or the "dole" as it was popularly called. A whole generation grew up without an opportunity to work. Such a situation was as unhealthy psychologically as it was economically. Eventually the unemployed became demoralized, depending on the dole without hope for the future.

These conditions inevitably resulted in political repercussions. Most important was the decline of the Liberal party as the workers turned increasingly to the Labor party in the hope of finding relief. Thus the economic crisis tended to polarize British politics, with the propertied classes generally voting Conservative, the workers supporting Labor and the middle class fluctuating between the two. Each party had its panacea for the country's ills: the Conservatives called for protection; the declining Liberals, for free trade; and Labour, for a capital levy and for the nationalization of heavy industry. The net result was a succession of alternating Conservative and Labour ministries, none of which was able to improve significantly the national fortunes.

With the ending of the war, Prime Minister Lloyd George held the so-called Khaki Election on December 14, 1918. His coalition government won a large majority—484 seats—on an ultranationalistic platform, including full repatriations for war damages and punishment of the German "war criminals." Despite his majority, Lloyd George's position was precarious, because 70 per cent of his supporters were Conservatives, while the Liberals were divided between those who supported him and a mere 26 who still followed Asquith in opposition. This left Labour as the chief opposition party, but with its 63 seats it could not hope to challenge the overwhelming predominance of the Conservatives.

Lloyd George was embarrassed from the outset by the perennial Irish problem. The outbreak of war in 1914 ended the Liberal party's efforts to give Ireland home rule. The new Sinn Fein party had won 73 seats in the 1918 elections, and it was now demanding full independence. Refusing to take their seats in Westminster, these delegates met in Dublin in January, 1919, and declared Ireland an independent state, thus precipitating cruel guerrilla warfare that dragged on until Lloyd George agreed in 1922 to an Irish Free State with status similar to that of the Dominions.

These Irish troubles, together with the mounting unemployment, undermined Lloyd George's position. In October, 1922, he was ousted in favor of Andrew Bonar Law, who organized an all-Conservative government. The elections held the following month returned a Conservative majority, but the Labourites won the surprising number of 142 seats, while the Liberals remained divided and impotent. In May, 1923, Bonar Law resigned because of ill health and was succeeded by Stanley Baldwin. The new prime minister proposed higher protective tariffs as the solution for unemployment, and he called an election for December, 1923, to pass on this radical departure from Britain's tradition of free trade. The Conservatives lost their majority but retained a plurality, followed by the Labourites with 192 seats, and the newly united Liberals with 158.

Baldwin declined to form a new government, so Ramsey MacDonald headed the first labour ministry with Liberal support. He remained in office only ten months—January to November, 1924—and accomplished little, apart from adopting a more conciliatory policy toward Germany and recognizing the Soviet Union. The latter move gave the Conservatives the issue they needed to overthrow the government. They raised a "Red" scare and used it to defeat the Labourites in the ensuing elections, in which they won a majority of 200 seats. Baldwin now formed a government that lasted for five years. Its policies reflected the cautious mediocrity of its leader. Unemployment continued unchecked, culminating in the general strike of 1926. Despite the support of two and one-half million workers the strike failed, and the government triumphantly passed a Trades Disputes Act that declared illegal all "sympathetic" strikes.

The term of parliament came to a statutory end, and general elections were held in May, 1929. Baldwin's characteristic slogan was "Safety First," but this did not catch on in the face of increasing unemployment. The Labourites captured 289 seats, the Conservatives, 259, and the Liberals, 58. MacDonald formed his second government with the backing of the Liberals. He could not have known that within half a year the country would be hit by the Great Depression that was to cripple Britain's economy still more, ultimately sweeping away MacDonald's new administration.

France

France, too, was plagued by economic difficulties in the postwar years, although in certain respects she was better off than most of her neighbors. France had a well-balanced economy, so that she was not as vulnerable as the predominantly agrarian or industrial countries. The peace settlement strengthened her economy by adding the Saar Basin with its coal mines, and the Alsace-Lorraine region with its textile industry and rich potash and iron ore deposits. Conversely, France had been weakened by the loss of 1.4 million men who had been in the prime of life, and by unprecedented destruction of property. The war on the western front had been waged mostly on French soil, causing 23 billion dollars worth of damage to villages, towns, factories, mines, and railways. Also France had financed the war by loans rather than taxes, and this now meant that further loans would be needed for reconstruction purposes. The government resorted to printing more money, which led to the depreciation of the franc, which, in turn, resulted in political repercussions.

In contrast to Britain's two or three parties, France had several, so that a government's life depended on its ability to muster a large enough coalition or bloc of these parties to secure majority support. This explains the relatively rapid turnover of governments in France compared to that in Britain. The leading parties, from Left to Right, were the Communists and Socialists, who represented mostly urban and rural workers; the Radical Socialists, who were in the center and were supported by the lower middle class; and various parties on the Right, such as the Republican Democratic Union and the Democratic Alliance, which were usually strongly Catholic and represented big business and high finance.

As had happened in Britain, elections in 1919 returned a predominantly conservative and nationalistic parliament in France. For the next five years France was ruled by National Bloc ministries based mostly on the parties of the Right. The dominant personality during this period was Raymond Poincaré, who was determined to make the Germans pay the costs of reconstruction. His policy culminated in the French occupation of the Ruhr in 1923, an expensive operation that yielded little revenue. By early 1924 the franc had fallen from its prewar value of 19.3 cents to little more than 3 cents. The French public was alienated by this financial instability and by the Ruhr adventure, which aroused fears of renewed warfare. Accordingly, the May, 1924, elections returned a majority for the Cartel des Gauches, or Left Bloc. Edouard Herriot, leader of the Radical Socialists, became premier with the support of the Socialists. In foreign affairs he ended the Ruhr occupation, agreed to a settlement of the reparations issue, and recognized the Soviet Union. But the financial dilemma remained unsolved, and on this matter the laissez-faire Radicals and the quasi-Marxist Socialists were unable to reach agreement. The Socialists demanded a capital levy, Herriot was opposed, and his government fell in April, 1925. The franc immediately decreased in value; by the following year it was worth only two cents—one-tenth of its prewar value.

France now turned once more to the Right. In July, 1926 Poincaré formed a National Union ministry of all parties except the Socialist and Communist. To indicate the seriousness of the situation, the new government included six former premiers, among them Herriot. Poincaré adopted orthodox, but stringent measures to reduce expenditures and increase revenues. By the end of 1926, the franc stood at 4 cents, and was stablized at that level. Since this was only one-fifth of its prewar value, the government had relieved itself of four-fifths of its debts, though this was achieved at the expense of French bondholders. The devaluation attracted many tourists, especially the Americans, and also facilitated the exportation of French goods. Poincaré's success enabled him to remain premier for three years, an interwar record. He retired in the summer of 1929, just in time to escape the economic cyclone that was to destroy the precarious stability he had achieved.

V. STABILIZATION AND SETTLEMENT IN EUROPE 501

Reparations Settlement: Dawes Plan

The period from 1924 to 1929 was one of peace and settlement in Europe. The negotiation in 1924 of the Dawes Plan, an agreement concerning reparations payments, was the first phase of this process of stabilization. Germany had been required by the Versailles Treaty to accept responsibility for the war and to promise to make payments for the losses sustained. No agreement was reached at Versailles concerning the amount and the schedule of payments, and during the following years this issue was a perennial source of discord amongst the Allies as well as between them and Germany.

The Reparations Commission, a body that had been appointed to work out the details, decided in 1920 that the payments from Germany should be divided as follows: 52 per cent to France, 22 per cent to Britain, 10 per cent to Italy, 8 per cent to Belgium, and the remaining 8 per cent to the other allied powers. The following year the Commission set the total German indemnity at $32 billion, to be paid both in cash and in kind (coal, locomotives, textile machinery, and other products of German factories and mines). Allied business interests soon protested because these commodities were providing a source of competition for their own goods. Accordingly, Germany was required to pay mostly in cash, but this was feasible only if her exports were substantially greater than her imports, which, of course, was out of the question, because tariffs were being raised all over the world and Germany was stepping up her imports to meet the needs of reconstruction.

Some payments were made in 1921 and 1922, but at the same time Germany was undergoing a disastrous inflation. The mark, worth 25 cents in 1914, had fallen to 2 cents by July, 1922, and a year later it was worthless—two and one-half trillion to the dollar. Under these circumstances the Germans requested a two-year moratorium on payments. The British, suffering from unemployment and being anxious to hasten the revival of international trade, responded favorably to the request. The French, however, having suffered the heaviest damages, were convinced that the Germans could pay if they wished to, and proceeded to use force. In the face of British criticism, a French army, with Italian and Belgian contingents, occupied the Ruhr industrial region in January, 1923.

The Germans responded with a general strike, so that the French were forced to spend more on the occupation than they got out of it. With the German economy prostrate and the French stymied, the reparations issue was deadlocked, and so a commission of economic experts, headed by an American banker, Charles Dawes, was called in. On September 1, 1924, the so-called Dawes Plan was approved by both sides and went into effect. Based on the slogan, "Business, not politics," the plan called for annual payments beginning at $238 million and reaching a maximum of $595 million. These amounts were adjustable depending on the index of prosperity for a given year. Also, Germany was to cancel her inflated currency and reorganize her *Reichsbank* under

Allied supervision. In return, she was to receive a foreign loan of $200 million, and France was required to evacuate the Ruhr.

However, this arrangement, like so many others, was to be swept away by the onslaught of the Great Depression. Even during the four years that it operated, up to September, 1928, the Germans paid in cash and in kind only about half of what they borrowed from foreign markets, mostly American. Nevertheless, the Dawes Plan did ease tensions in Europe and prepare the way for the settlement of political issues.

Quest for Peace: Locarno Pacts

European diplomacy in the years immediately following the war was dominated by France and her allies in Central and Eastern Europe. Owing to the disappearance of Austria-Hungary and the prostration of Germany and Russia, France was now the first power on the Continent. Because sooner or later both Germany and Russia would obviously seek to reassert themselves, the aim of French diplomacy was to organize some dependable and lasting basis for national security.

Theoretically, the League of Nations provided general security with Article 10 of the Covenant, which required member states "to respect and preserve against external aggression the territorial integrity and existing political independence of all members of the League." The difficulty rested in the League's lacking the power necessary to enforce this article. The Council could invite members to bring to bear an economic boycott, or even armed reprisal, against an aggressor, but any such measures of economic or military restraint could be applied only by the governments of individual states. The League itself possessed no weapons and no armed force; a French proposal to place an international police corps at its disposal was voted down. Consequently, in the final analysis the weight of a League decision was dependent upon international public opinion, which was usually confused and divided over major issues.

Having experienced two German invasions in less than 50 years, France refused to entrust her security to a League without authority. First she proposed a British-French-American triple alliance that would guarantee Anglo-American aid to France in case of German aggression. When this plan failed because the United States Senate refused to ratify the Treaty, France turned to the smaller European states that shared her interest in supporting the peace settlement and opposing treaty revision. She negotiated a formal military alliance with Belgium in September, 1920, with Poland in 1921, and with Czechoslovakia in 1924. Czechoslovakia had already organized the so-called "Little Entente" with Rumania and Yugoslavia in 1920–1921 for the purpose of providing mutual aid in case of either an attack by Hungary or the restoration of the Hapsburg dynasty. Poland was attached to the Little Entente in 1921 through an alliance with Rumania in which the two guaranteed reciprocal help in the event of attack by Russia. France's relationship with the Little Entente enabled her, then, to extend her own alliance system to include Rumania in 1926 and Yugoslavia in 1927.

This alliance system was basically anti-German, its primary purpose being to protect France and her allies by isolating Germany. About 1925, however,

Franco-German relations improved, thanks to the temporarily successful operation of the Dawes Plan, and also to the mutually conciliatory attitudes of the foreign ministers of the two countries, Aristide Briand of France and Gustav Stresemann of Germany, who decided that the security of their respective countries could be enhanced by direct negotiations and agreements. They were encouraged by the British foreign minister, Sir Austen Chamberlain, who also brought the Italians around to this view. The outcome was a series of agreements known as the Locarno Pacts, signed in October, 1925.

503

These provided that Germany should enter the League of Nations and become a permanent Council member. In return, Germany agreed not to seek treaty revision by force and to settle peacefully every dispute with France, Belgium, Czechoslovakia, and Poland. Germany did reserve the right to seek modification of her eastern frontiers by peaceful means, but she recognized the permanence of her western frontiers. Germany, France, and Belgium undertook to respect for all time their mutual borders, and Britain and Italy guaranteed observance of this provision.

The Locarno Spirit

The Locarno Pacts made a deep impression at the time. Chamberlain expressed the prevailing view when he declared that they marked "the real dividing line between the years of peace and the years of war." Likewise, Briand made eloquent speeches about "the Locarno spirit," which banned war and substituted "conciliation, arbitration, and peace." In the afterglow of this optimism, the American Secretary of State, Frank Kellogg, acting on a suggestion of Briand, proposed that nations pledge themselves to renounce war as "an instrument of national policy." The proposal was implemented, and on August 27, 1928, the Kellogg–Briand Pact was signed. Since the pact only involved renunciation of war and made no provision for sanctions, it was quickly signed by over 60 countries. Although it depended exclusively on the moral pressure of world public opinion, the mere fact that so many countries signed contributed to a further lessening of international tension.

Equally promising were the improved relations with Germany. That country was admitted into the League of Nations in 1926, and was made a permanent member of the Council. Also, a further settlement was reached with Germany concerning the payment of reparations. The Dawes Plan had not stipulated the sum total of reparations that Germany should pay, so in 1929, a second commission of economic experts, under the chairmanship of another American financier Owen Young, met in Paris and prepared a new payment schedule that was adopted early in 1930. The total amount to be paid by Germany was set at $8 billion, and the installments were to be extended over 58 years. In return for Germany's acceptance of the Young Plan, France evacuated the Rhineland in 1930, four years earlier than was required by the Versailles Treaty.

At the same time, a series of disarmament conferences was being held, partly because of the pressure of international public opinion, but also because the Allies had forced Germany to disarm with the expressed intention of initiating "a general limitation in the armaments of all nations." Furthermore, the Covenant of the League stated that "the maintenance of peace requires the reduction of national armaments" and provided that the League Council "shall formulate plans." However, despite these pledges, no general limitation of armaments was achieved in the interwar period. The countries with conscript armies did not wish to include trained reserves as effectives, while those with volunteer armies insisted that they should be included. Some countries wanted armaments to be limited on the basis of financial expenditures, but Britain and the United States were strongly opposed, because their expenditures were much higher per soldier. In addition, France and her allies insisted on international control and supervision of armaments, while Britain and the United States preferred reliance on good faith. The basic difficulty was that, given the absence of an international security system, each country sought security in its own armed forces. Some progress was made in limiting navies, partly because the number of naval powers was smaller than the number of military powers. But even here agreement was restricted to the ratio of tonnages in certain categories, instead of limiting the total tonnage.

Despite the failure in disarmament, there was a general feeling in the late Twenties that Europe had at last returned to normalcy: Germany and her former enemies appeared to be reconciled; French troops were out of the Rhineland and the Germans were in the League; the problem of reparations appeared to be finally resolved; over 60 nations had renounced war "as an instrument of national policy"; prosperity was on the rise, and unemployment was correspondingly declining. Even the news from the Soviet Union was encouraging, for that country had launched in 1928 a novel and gradiose Five Year Plan (see Chapter 23, section I). Most authorities in the West regarded the Plan as impractical and doomed to failure, but at least it diverted the Russians from international adventures to internal economic development. Thus the "Locarno spirit" appeared to have meaning and substance, and it was assumed that Europe now could settle back to enjoy decades of peace and prosperity as it had in the nineteenth century.*

SUGGESTED READING

The standard account of the civil war and intervention in Russia is the three-volume work by E. H. Carr, *The Bolshevik Revolution, 1917–1923* (New York: Macmillan, 1951–1953). Briefer comprehensive studies are available in G. F. Kennan, *Russia and the West Under Lenin and Stalin* (Boston: Little, 1961); and D. Footman, *Civil War in Russia* (New York: Praeger, 1962). The numerous accounts of regional developments include J. A. White, *The Siberian Intervention* (Princeton: Princeton Univ., 1950) and L. I. Strakhovsky, *Intervention at Archangel* (Princeton: Princeton Univ., 1944).

For interpretations of why Bolshevism failed outside Russia, see J. A. Schumpeter, *Capitalism, Socialism and Democracy* (New York: Harper, 1942) and F. Sternberg, *Capitalism and Socialism on Trial* (New York: Day, 1951). Several works deal with the critical developments in Germany in 1918 and after, including E. G. L. White, *Vanguard of Nazism: The Free Corps Movement in Post War Germany, 1918–1923* (Cambridge: Harvard Univ., 1952); R. Coper, *Failure*

* See "Years of Contentment," *EMM*, No. 145.

of a Revolution: Germany in 1918–1919 (New York: Cambridge University Press, 1955); E. Waldman, *The Spartacist Uprising of 1910* (Milwaukee: Marquette Univ., 1958); A. Rosenberg, *The Birth of the German Republic, 1871–1918* (New York: Oxford Univ., 1931); and W. T. Angress, *Stillborn Revolution: The Communist Bid for Power in Germany, 1921—1923* (Princeton: Princeton Univ., 1964).

The best survey of the forces molding Central and Eastern Europe in these years is by H. Seton-Watson, *Eastern Europe Between the Wars, 1918–1941* (London: Cambridge Univ., 1946). See also L. S. Stavrianos, *The Balkans Since 1453* (New York: Holt, 1959) and W. E. Moore, *Economic Demography of Eastern and Southern Europe* (Geneva: League of Nations, 1945).

For Mussolini's coming to power, see G. Megaro, *Mussolini in the Making* (Boston: Houghton, 1938); A. Rossi, *The Rise of Italian Fascism, 1918–1922* (London: Methuen, 1938); and G. Salvemini, *Under the Axe of Fascism* (New York: Viking, 1936). For the later period, see H. Finer *Mussolini's Italy* (London: Gollancz, 1935); D. A. Binchy, *Church and State in Fascist Italy* (New York: Oxford Univ., 1941); C. F. Delzell, *Mussolini's Enemies: The Italian Anti-Fascist Resistance* (Princeton: Princeton Univ., 1961); and F. Chabod, *A History of Italian Fascism* (London: Weidenfeld, 1963). The best analysis of Mussolini as a man as well as a political leader is by I. Kirkpatrick, *Mussolini: A Study in Power* (New York: Hawthorn, 1964). See also C. F. Delzell, "Benito Mussolini: A Guide to the Biographical Literature," *Journal of Modern History* (December 1963), 339–53.

Various aspects of Britain's development are analyzed in the general but meticulous survey by C. L. Mowat, *Britain Between the Wars, 1918–1940* (Chicago: Univ. of Chicago, 1955) and in the specialized studies by R. Graves and A. Hodge, *The Long Week End: A Social History of Great Britain, 1918–1939* (New York: Macmillan, 1941); K. Hutchison, *Decline and Fall of British Capitalism* (New York: Scribner, 1950); and S. Pollard, *The Development of the British Economy, 1914–1950* (London: Arnold, 1962). See also the excellent bibliographical guide by H. R. Winkler, *Great Britain in the Twentieth Century* (Washington: Service Center for Teachers of History, 1960), No. 28. On France, see the detailed presentation by D. W. Brogan, *France Under the Republic, 1870–1939* (New York: Harper, 1940); the more lucid account by D. Thomson, *Democracy in France* (New York: Oxford Univ., 1952); and the various works by the well-informed journalist A. Werth, especially *France in Ferment* (London: Jarrolds, 1935).

The most stimulating analysis of diplomatic developments is by E. H. Carr, *International Relations between the Two World Wars* (London: Macmillan, 1947). A number of interpretative essays are available in G. A. Craig and F. Gilbert, eds., *The Diplomats: 1919–1939* (Princeton: Princeton Univ., 1953). On specific topics, there are P. S. Wandycz, *France and her Eastern Allies, 1919–1925* (Minneapolis: Univ. of Minnesota, 1962); J. T. Shotwell, *War as in Instrument of National Policy and its Renunciation in the Pact of Paris* (New York: Harcourt, 1929); F. P. Walters, *A History of the League of Nations* (New York: Oxford Univ., 1952), 2 vols.; and W. E. Rappard, *The Quest for Peace Since the World War* (Cambridge: Harvard Univ., 1940).

*The year 1931 was distinguished from previous
years in the "post-war" and in the "pre-war"
age alike—by one outstanding feature.
In 1931, men and women all over the world
were seriously contemplating and frankly dis-
cussing the possibility that the Western system of
Society might break down and cease to work.*

ARNOLD J. TOYNBEE

The Five Year Plans
and the Great Depression

As the 1920's drew to a close, Europe seemed to be settling
down to an era of peace, security, and relative prosperity. This comfortable prospect was, however, destroyed completely by the onset of
the Great Depression, and the resulting economic dislocation and
mass unemployment undermined the foundations of the settlement
that had been reached in the preceding years. Everywhere governments rose and fell under the pressure of mounting distress and discontent. Such political instability affected directly—and disastrously—
the international situation; some governments resorted to foreign adventures as a means for diverting domestic tension, while others ignored the acts of aggression because of their own pressing problems
at home. Thus the Depression represents the Great Divide of the
interwar period. The years before 1929 were years of hope, as Europe
gradually resolved the various issues created by the First World War.
By contrast, the years after 1929 were filled with anxiety and disillu-
sionment, as crisis followed crisis, culminating finally in World War II.

The impact and significance of the Great Depression was heightened by Russia's Five Year Plans. At a time when the West's economy
had slowed down almost to a standstill, the Soviet Union was proceeding with its unique experiment in economic development. Although accompanied by rigid repression and mass privation, the Five
Year Plans were substantially successful. The Soviet Union rose rap-

idly from a predominantly agrarian state to the second greatest industrial power in the world. This unprecedented achievement had international repercussions, particularly because of the economic difficulties besetting the West at the time.

And so the Five Year plans and the Great Depression stand out in the interwar period, the one accentuating the other, and each having repercussions that are being felt to the present day.

I. FIVE YEAR PLANS

War Communism

When the Bolsheviks, to their surprise, found themselves the masters of Russia, they faced the challenge of creating the millennium about which they had preached so long. They soon discovered it a challenge they were quite unprepared to meet. There was no model in past history to follow, and Marxist literature was of little use since it was concerned almost exclusively with how to seize power rather than with what to do once this had been accomplished. The traditional definition of a socialist society—one in which the state owns the means of production—was no guide for the actual materialization of the society. Lenin himself admitted, "We knew when we took power into our hands, that there were no ready forms of concrete reorganization of the capitalist system into a socialist one. . . . I do not know of any socialist who has dealt with these problems. . . . We must go by experiments." [1]

At first there was little opportunity for experimenting because the struggle for survival took precedence over everything else. The so-called "War Communism" that prevailed between 1917 and 1921 evolved out of the desperate measures taken to supply the battle front with needed materials and manpower. One feature of War Communism was the nationalization of land, banks, foreign trade, and heavy industry. Another was the forcible requisitioning of surplus agricultural produce needed to feed the soldiers and the city dwellers. The original plan was to compensate the peasants with manufactured goods, but this proved impossible because almost all factories were producing for the front.

The ending of the civil war meant that this stopgap system of War Communism was no longer needed, so it was promptly dropped. The peasants were up in arms against confiscation without compensation. As one of them put it: "The land belongs to us: the bread to you; the water to us: the fish to you; the forest to us: the timber to you." [2] At the same time, the economy of the country was paralyzed, owing largely to the uninterrupted fighting between 1914 and 1921. Industry had fallen to 10 per cent of prewar levels, while the grain crop declined from 74 million tons in 1916 to 30 million tons in 1919. The crowning disaster was the widespread drought of 1920 and 1921, which contributed to the worst famine in Russia's history. Millions of people died of starvation, and millions more were kept alive only by the shipments of the American Relief Administration. Even the Kronstadt sailors, hitherto the staunchest supporters of the Bolsheviks, now revolted with the slogan "The Soviets without the Bolsheviks.'

New Economic Policy

508

The practical-minded Lenin realized that concessions were unavoidable—hence the adoption in 1921 of the New Economic Policy, or NEP as it was commonly known, which allowed a partial restoration of capitalism, especially in agriculture and trade. Peasants were permitted to sell their produce on the open market after paying to the state a tax in kind that consisted of about 12 per cent of their output. Private individuals were allowed to operate small stores and factories. Both the peasants and the new businessmen, or Nepmen as they were called, could employ labor and retain what profits they made from their operations. Lenin, however, saw to it that the state kept control of title to the land and of what he termed "the commanding heights" (banking, foreign trade, heavy industry, and transportation). So far as Lenin was concerned, the NEP did not mean the end of socialism in Russia; rather it was a temporary retreat, "one step backward in order to take two steps forward."

The great question in the following years was how these "two steps forward" should be made. The NEP did give the people a breathing spell, and it did allow the economy to recover from the utter prostration of 1921. By 1926, industrial and agricultural production had reached pre-1914 levels; but this was not enough so far as the Soviet leaders were concerned. The population had increased by eight million since 1914, so the prewar per capita standards had not been reached. Furthermore, these standards had been inadequate for nineteenth century Tsarist Russia, not to speak of the twentieth century Soviet state. Even more disturbing was the growing strength of the well-to-do peasants, or kulaks (*kulak* means "the fist"), and their supporters. They were openly hostile to the Soviet regime because agricultural prices had fallen to just over half what they had been in 1913, while the prices for manufactured goods had nearly doubled. The kulaks, who produced most of the surplus foodstuffs, retaliated by reducing their output or keeping it from the market in order to force prices upward. Thus the Soviets found it increasingly difficult to feed the urban population; the hostile kulaks were in a position to starve the cities at will. Such was the unpleasant state of affairs more than a decade after the great revolution that was to have heralded the new socialist society.

Gosplan

Lenin died in 1924, and the economic issue concerning the replacement of the NEP was tied up with the political issue of Lenin's successor. One faction within the Bolshevik party wanted essentially to continue the NEP, but also thought that price concessions should be made to the kulaks in order to encourage them to increase their output. Some of the surplus produce could then be sold abroad and the proceeds used for developing industry. This program was opposed by another faction on the grounds that it would not yield the amount of capital necessary for industrialization. Accordingly, this group wished to speed up industrial growth by over-all planning, counting on the increased industrial output to encourage the peasants to raise their levels of productivity. When Joseph Stalin emerged triumphant as the Party leader, he adopted the second group's proposal for planned industrialization, but he made as significant contribution of his own: the collectivization of agriculture, a plan designed to force the peasants to produce surplus food without economic concessions, and thus to make available the capital necessary for industrialization. In 1928, Stalin launched the first of a series of Five Year Plans designed to put this program into effect. For reasons of national security, all resources and all means of persuasion and compulsion were used to hasten the materialization of the Plans.*

These Plans were without precedent in that they provided a blueprint and a mechanism for the reorganization and operation of a nation's entire economy. At the center was the State Planning Commission (Gosplan), appointed by the Council of Peoples Commissars, the Soviet counterpart of a Western cabinet. The function of the Gosplan to the present day is to prepare the plans on the basis of the general directives received from the government and the statistical data received from all parts of the country.

The government (actually the Communist party leadership) makes the basic decisions, such as whether a particular Plan should concentrate on producing armaments or building up heavy industry or turning out more consumer goods or reducing grain crops in favor of industrial crops. With these directives as a guide, the Gosplan sets to work on the huge mass of statistical information that is constantly pouring into headquarters. All Soviet organizations— whether agricultural, industrial, military, or cultural—are required by law to provide the Gosplan with specified data concerning resources and operations. This mass of information is processed by a highly trained staff of statisticians, economists, and technical experts, who proceed to work out a provisional Five Year Plan. After consultation and countersuggestions from the organizations concerned, a final Plan is drafted. The first of these Five Year plans, though primitive when compared with the current computer-prepared ones, comprised a three-volume text of 1,600 pages, including tables and statistics that ranged over heavy industries, light industries, finance, cooperatives, agriculture, transportation, communications, labor, wages, schools, literature, public health, and social insurance.

Collectivization of Agriculture

Stalin once stated that the kulak resistance to collectivization was the most dangerous challenge he ever encountered. Yet, he had no choice but to force his plan on them, for collectivization was the foundation of the new economy he had blueprinted. The kulaks naturally opposed the collective farms that they had to enter on the same terms as the poor peasants who brought little with them. In some cases, the kulaks burned the buildings of the collectives, poisoned the cattle, and spread rumors to frighten away other peasants. The Soviet government crushed such resistance without mercy and incited class warfare in the villages by goading the poor peasants to oppose the kulaks.† The police uprooted hundreds of thousands of kulak families from their villages, putting them in prisons and in Siberian labor camps. In the end, the government had its way, so that by 1938 almost all peasant holdings had been amalgamated into 242,400 collective farms, or *kolkhozy,* and 4,000 state farms, or *sovkhozy.*

* See "The Motive," *EMM,* No. 146.
† See "The Carrot and the Stick," *EMM,* No. 147.

510

Most of the land on the kolkhozy is worked cooperatively by the farmers, who divide the profits at the end of the year on the basis of the amount and the skill of the work contributed. Each family is allowed to own its house, furniture, a little livestock, tools, unlimited poultry, and a surrounding garden of one-quarter to two and one-half acres. In this garden each family can grow what it wishes, and may either consume the produce or sell it in the open market of a nearby town. By contrast, the output of the collectively worked fields is sold at lower prices to the government or to industrial enterprises or municipalities. The government also determines, in fact if not in theory, what each collective farm must produce and who its manager should be.

The sovkhozy differ from the kolkhozy in two respects: their workers are paid set wages as though they were factory hands, and they are much larger in acreage—about five times larger in 1938—than the kolkhozy. The sovkhozy are designed to serve primarily as experimental, or model, farms for the surrounding kolkhozy, and their produce belongs to the government which is the owner-operator.

Although the Soviet government was successful in eliminating almost all private farms, the output of its collectivized agriculture has been very disappointing. Even today about half of the population of the Soviet Union is needed to provide food for the other half, whereas in the United States, only 10 per cent of the population is engaged in farming. After World War II, Nikita Khrushchev devoted much time and energy to the agricultural problem. He consolidated the collective farms into larger units, imported high-yielding hybrid corn from the United States, and sent thousands of settlers to farm vast new lands in Siberia and the Kazakh Republic. Yet agriculture is still the Archilles' heel of the Soviet economy, and is widely considered to have been one of the principal reasons for the downfall of Khrushchev in October, 1964.

Although collectivization has not been successful from the viewpoint of production, it has nevertheless provided the essential basis for the Five Year Plans. It has eliminated the kulaks who at one time threatened the very existence of the Soviet regime. The peasants are no longer an independent political force, and Soviet authority is firmly established in the countryside. This, in turn, has enabled the Soviet government to foist much of the cost of industrialization upon the peasantry. Surplus produce has been siphoned off by the state in the form of tax levies, and then exported in order to finance the cost of industrialization. Even though the peasants have been dragging their heels, the collectivist system of agriculture has enabled the government to squeeze enough out of them to feed the city dwellers and to help pay for the new industrial centers. The decision of Khrushchev's successors to invest very large amounts of capital in agriculture may represent a basic shift from the traditional policy of taxing the peasants for the benefit of industry.

Growth of Industry

While Soviet agriculture lagged, industry was forging ahead; indeed, the two trends were directly related. Agriculture lagged partly because the peasants preferred private farms to the government-imposed collectives, but also because the government directly sacrificed agriculture in siphoning off capital for the benefit of industry. In order to make Russia militarily and economically independent of the rest of the world, it was essential that the Soviet leaders give top priority to heavy industry.

Whereas most of the farms are run as cooperatives, the factories are mostly
owned and operated by the government. Besides providing industry with the necessary capital, the government also employs a combination of the "carrot" and the "stick" to stimulate maximum production. Both workers and managers are required to meet certain quotas on pain of fine or dismissal. On the other hand, if they surpass their quotas, they are rewarded with bonuses. Trade unions are allowed and recognized, but are denied the basic right to strike—for strikes would be incompatible with the goals and functioning of the Soviet-planned economy. The purpose of a strike is to secure for the workers, in the form of higher wages, a larger proportion of what is produced; but the Gosplan has already decided how much will go to workers and how much to the government for reinvestment in industry.

In actuality, Soviet industry has grown as rapidly as it has because the government withdraws about 40 per cent of the national income for reinvestment; in comparison, the United States withdraws about 20 per cent of its national income. Furthermore, in a planned economy the government is able to allocate investment capital as it wishes. Thus about 70 per cent of the total Soviet industrial output consists of capital goods, and 30 per cent, of consumer goods, whereas in the United States, the ratio is roughly the reverse. By the end of the first Five Year Plan, in 1932, the Soviet Union had risen in industrial output from fifth to second place in the world. This extraordinary spurt was due not only to the increase of productivity in the Soviet Union, but also to the decline of productivity in the West that was brought about by the Depression. Nevertheless, Soviet gross national product, which included the lagging agricultural as well as the industrial output, increased three and a half times during the quarter century between 1928 and 1952—a rate of growth surpassing that of any other country during this period. Today the Soviet Union remains the second greatest industrial power in the world, though its output is only about half that of the United States.

It should be emphasized that Soviet economic growth has been achieved at the expense of the Soviet citizens, who have been forced to work hard for the future and to endure privation in the present, regardless of what their wishes might be. Consumer goods are, according to plan, scarce, expensive, and of poor quality. The United States, with a population approximately 17 per cent less than that of the Soviet Union, produced in 1961 roughly 37 times as many passenger cars, 3 times as many television sets, 4 times as many radios, and 3 times as much meat as the Soviet Union. And, according to U.S. Department of Labor statistics for 1964, the average Soviet citizen had to work 6 times as long as his U.S. counterpart to buy a loaf of bread, 10 times as long to buy a pound of butter, and 18 times as long for a pound of sugar.*

Significance for World History

From the point of view of global impact, it is likely that the Gosplan will prove to be of greater significance than the Communist International. The

* See "The Results," EMM, No. 148.

512

Five Year Plans attracted worldwide attention, particularly because of the concurrent breakdown of the West's economy. Socialism was no longer a dream of visionaries; it was a going concern. The American journalist Lincoln Steffens returned from the Soviet Union with the pronouncement, "I have seen the future and it works." Thus, the original skepticism gave way to genuine interest and, in some cases, to imitation. Economic policies were influenced, consciously or unconsciously, by the Soviet success in setting priorities for the investment of national resources, which is the essence of planning. Some countries went so far as to launch Plans of their own, of varying duration, in the hope of alleviating their economic difficulties.

The Five Year Plans do not seem to have impressed the Western countries as much as the underdeveloped nations, one reason being that by Western standards, Soviet citizens were grossly exploited. Western visitors to Russia were struck by the shabby clothing, the monotonous diet, the wretched housing, and the scarcity of consumer goods. They were also appalled by the lack of individual freedom as reflected in the one-party political structure, the hobbling of trade unions, the regimentation of education, and the rigid control of all communication media. Soviet society, despite the achievements of the Five Year Plans, did not seem to most Westerners a Socialist paradise worthy of emulation.

Former colonial peoples in the underdeveloped world reacted very differently. To them, the Soviet Union was the country that succeeded in transforming itself within a generation from a backward agrarian state into the second greatest industrial and military power in the world. The institutions and the techniques that made this dramatic change possible were of vital concern to these peoples. Although most of them had recently won political independence, they were still far from economic independence. And so they regarded Soviet living standards with envy rather than commiseration. Less attention was paid to the absence of individual liberties in the Soviet Union because these people had not customarily enjoyed such liberties in their own countries.

That the Soviet Union is a great Asian as well as European state is an important fact. Its frontiers stretch from Korea, past Mongolia, Sinkiang, Afghanistan, and Iran, to Turkey. In almost all these regions, kindred people exist on both sides of the frontier, thus facilitating interaction and comparison of conditions. In most cases, the Soviet Union has fared well by comparison, thanks to the revivifying effect of the Five Year Plans on its eastern regions. The other side of the long frontier has had few counterparts to the substantial material advances made in the Soviet Central Asian republics: the 185-mile Ferghana irrigation canal, the 900-mile Turksib Railway, the new textile mills, the Karaganda coalfields, the Lake Balcha copper-smelting works, the fertilizer and farm-machinery plants, as well as the rise in literacy from about 2 per cent in 1914 to 75 per cent in 1940, and to nearly 100 per cent today.

Soviet policies in Central Asia have not met with unanimous approval. Between 100,000 and 200,000 Kazaks fled into Chinese Sinkiang to escape the repression of the early days of the Plans. Many of the older generation have been bitterly opposed to the growing Russification of their republics—a result of deliberate government policy and mass Slavic immigration. But this internal dissatisfaction has not affected substantially the attraction that the

Soviet planned economy has held for many who live in former colonial
territories.* The reason for this is made clear in the following report by an
American correspondent who traveled extensively in Central Asia in 1953. The
global implications of his observations are self-evident.

513

> From Mandalay to Cairo, from the Khyber Pass to Malabar and from
> China to the Suez, the Tashkent transmitters carry the Soviet Union's
> message every day to the farthest ends of the vast and restless continent.
>
> If the message is heard by an increasingly receptive audience through-
> out Asia, not the least of the many reasons for it is that the metropolis
> of Tashkent itself provides a kind of show window. . . .
>
> There are not many Americans who can locate Tashkent on their maps,
> but there are few literate Asians who cannot tell you where it is and what
> it signifies. . . .
>
> What is it that gives Asian visitors to Tashkent such [favorable]
> impressions? It is the sight of a . . . huge Asian city with excellent
> health standards, education, sanitation, clean streets, rapidly improving
> housing, electric facilities, substantial if not fancy consumers' goods, an
> abundance of food, an abundance of work, a rapidly widening indus-
> trialization program and constantly improving agricultural productivity.
>
> Along with this they see equality of races under the law and the
> participation of large numbers of Uzbeks and other Central Asian peoples
> in government, industry and education.
>
> Against this background the Asian visitor is not likely to be too much
> influenced by Western arguments about democracy nor does the in-
> dividual human factor impress the Asian visitor so strongly since he is
> more likely to know the mortality tables of his own country.
>
> While the European visitor to Tashkent might reach one set of con-
> clusions based on comparisons with Europe and on a lack of facilities to
> which he has been accustomed, an Asian might arrive at directly the
> opposite conclusions. It is the Asian's conclusions that are important,
> since Tashkent has prime importance as a symbol for Asia rather than for
> Europe.[3]

II. THE GREAT DEPRESSION

Origins of the Crash

With the opening of the year 1929, the United States appeared to be
flourishing. The index of industrial production in that country averaged only
67 in 1921 (1923–1925 = 100) but rose to 110 by July, 1928 and to 126 by
June, 1929. Even more impressive was the performance of the American stock
market. During the three summer months of 1929, Westinghouse stock rose
from 151 to 286, General Electric, from 268 to 391, and United States
Steel, from 165 to 258. Businessmen, academic economists, and government
leaders were all expressing confidence in the future. The financier Bernard
Baruch wrote in June, 1929, "the economic condition of the world seems on

* See "Global Repercussions: The Central Asian Showcase," *EMM*, No. 149.

514

the verge of a great forward movement." Professor Irving Fisher of Yale University declared in the fall of 1929, "Stock prices have reached what looks like a permanently high plateau." The Secretary of the Treasury, Andrew W. Mellon, assured the public in September, 1929, "There is no cause for worry. The high tide of prosperity will continue." [4]

This confidence proved unjustified; in the fall of 1929, the bottom fell out of the stock market, and a worldwide depression, unprecedented in its intensity and longevity, followed. The serious international economic imbalance that developed when the United States became a creditor nation on a large scale (following World War I) seems to have been one reason for this unexpected denouement. Britain had been a creditor nation before the war, but she had used the proceeds from her overseas investments and loans to pay for her chronic excess of imports over exports. The United States, by contrast, normally had a favorable trade balance, accentuated by tariffs that were kept at high levels for reasons of domestic politics. In addition, money poured into the country in the 1920's in payment of war debts, and the American gold hoard rose between 1913 and 1924 from $1.924 to $4.499 billion, or half the world's total gold supply.

This imbalance was neutralized for several years by large-scale American loans and investments abroad: between 1925 and 1928, the average annual total for American foreign investments amounted to $1.1 billion. In the long run, this, of course, intensified the imbalance and could not be continued indefinitely. As payments came due, debtor countries were forced to curtail imports from the United States, and certain branches of the American economy, especially agriculture, were hurt. In addition, some countries found it necessary to default on their debts, which shook certain financial firms in the United States.

As serious as the imbalance of the international economy was that of the American economy, the basic reason being that wages lagged behind the rising productivity. Between 1920 and 1929, hourly industrial wages rose only 2 per cent, while the productivity of workers in factories jumped 55 per cent. At the same time, the real income of the farmers was shrinking because agricultural prices were falling while taxes and living costs were rising. Whereas in 1910 the income per farm worker had been slightly less than 40 per cent that of the nonfarm worker, by 1930, it was just under 30 per cent. Such poverty in the countryside was a serious matter, because the rural population then comprised one-fifth of the total population.

The combination of stationary factory wages and falling farm income resulted in severe maldistribution of national income. In 1929, 5 per cent of the American people received one-third of all personal incomes (compared to one-sixth by the end of World War II). This meant inadequate purchasing power for the masses, combined with a high level of capital investment by those who were receiving the high salaries and dividends. Production of capital goods during the 1920's rose at an average annual rate of 6.4 per cent, compared to 2.8 per cent for consumer goods. Eventually this led to the clogging of the economy; the low purchasing power was unable to support such a high rate of capital investment. As a result, the index of industrial production dropped from 126 to 117 between June and October, 1929, creating a slump that contributed to the stock market crash that autumn.

The weakness of the American banking system was a final factor contributing to the crash of 1929. A great number of independent banking firms were operating, and some of these lacked sufficient resources to weather financial storms. When one closed its doors, panic spread, and depositors rushed to withdraw their savings from other banks, thus setting in motion a chain reaction that undermined the entire banking structure. This weakness was accentuated by a speculative fever that permeated the economy in 1929 and led some business and banking firms to abandon normal precautions and to pursue get-rich-quick ventures.

Worldwide Depression

The stock market crash in the United States began in September, 1929. Within one month, stock values dropped 40 per cent, and apart from a few brief recoveries, the decline continued for three years. During that period, United States Steel stock fell from 262 to 22, General Motors, from 73 to 8. Every branch of the national economy suffered correspondingly. During those three years, 5,000 banks closed their doors. General Motors had produced 5.5 million automobiles in 1929, but in 1931, they produced only 2.5 million. The steel industry in July, 1932 was operating at 12 per cent of capacity. By 1933, both general industrial production and national income had slumped by nearly one-half, wholesale prices, by almost one-third, and merchandise trade, by more than two-thirds.

The Great Depression was unique not only in its intensity but also in its worldwide impact. American financial houses were forced to call in their short-term loans abroad; naturally, there were repercussions. In May, 1931, the Credit-Anstalt, the largest and most reputable bank in Vienna, declared itself insolvent, setting off a wave of panic throughout the Continent. On July 13, the German Danatbank followed suit, and for the next two days all German banks were decreed on holiday; the Berlin Stock Exchange, the Börse, closed for two months. In September, 1931, Britain went off the gold standard, to be followed two years later by the United States and nearly all the major countries.

The breakdown of the financial world had its counterpart in industry and commerce: the index of world industrial production, excluding the Soviet Union, fell from 100 in 1929 to 86.5 in 1930, 74.8 in 1931, and 63.8 in 1932, a drop of 36.2 per cent. The maximum decline in previous crises had been 7 per cent. Even more drastic was the shrinking of world international trade, from $68.6 billion in 1929 to 55.6 in 1930, 39.7 in 1931, 26.9 in 1932, and 24.2 in 1933.[5] Again it might be noted that the maximum drop in international trade in the past had been 7 per cent, during the 1907–1908 crisis.

Social Repercussions

These economic cataclysms gave rise to social problems of corresponding magnitude. Most serious and intractible was the problem of mass unemployment, which reached tragic proportions. In March, 1933, the number of people out of work in the United States was estimated conservatively at over 14 million, or a fourth of the total labor force. In Britain, the jobless were

516

numbered at nearly 3 million, representing about the same proportion of the workers as in the United States. Germany was the worst off with no less than 6 million out of work: trade-union executives estimated that more than two-fifths of their members were wholly unemployed, and another fifth had only part-time work. France was the least affected, owing to the better balance of agriculture and industry; the number of unemployed in that country never exceeded 850,000, though this figure did not include substantial under-employment in the rural areas. (This was even more true of the predominantly agrarian countries of Eastern Europe, where many workers left the cities and returned to the already overpopulated villages to share the misery of their relatives.)

Unemployment on this scale drastically lowered living standards in all countries. Even in the wealthy United States there was wholesale misery and privation, especially in the beginning, when relief was left to private and to local agencies with inadequate funds. These were years of bread lines, of soup kitchens, and of veterans selling apples on street corners. Thousands of men, and even some women, "rode the rods" back and forth, from coast to coast, hoping to find jobs, or simply because there was nothing else to do. Thousands more left the Texas and Oklahoma dustbowls for California, as described in John Steinbeck's *Grapes of Wrath*.

In England, where unemployment had been chronic throughout the 1920's, the situation now became even worse. A substantial proportion of a whole generation was growing up with little opportunity or prospect of finding employment. Some bitterly referred to their purposeless existence as a "living

A breadline in Oklahoma. (Wide World Photos)

death." Others gave up hope and became resigned to their fate: "You've got as much chance of picking up a job nowadays as of winning the Irish Sweep." In Germany, with its higher percentage of jobless people, the frustrations and tensions were more acute; they eventually made possible the triumph of Hitler. Perhaps most tragic of all was the plight of the peasant masses of Eastern Europe. They had always lived at subsistence level, but a survey made in 1939 of the Drina region of Yugoslavia, an area reasonably representative of southeastern Europe, revealed that out of 219,279 households, 46.4 per cent had no beds, 54.3 per cent had no latrines of any sort, and 51.6 per cent had floors of packed earth. In human terms, this meant an infant mortality rate (deaths under one year per 1,000 live births) of 183 in Rumania, 144 in Yugoslavia and Bulgaria, and 99 in Greece, compared to 60 in Germany, 55 in Britain, and 37 in the Netherlands.*

Political Repercussions

Social dislocation on such a large scale inevitably had profound political repercussions. Even in the United States, with its superior resources and its tradition of political stability, these were years of strange ideas and agitations: a Bonus Army composed of uprooted war veterans; technocracy, an anti-capitalist movement for rule by engineers; a Farm Holiday amounting to a sit-down strike in agriculture; and various proposals for income redistribution, including the Townshend Plan for munificent old-age pensions, and the Share-Our-Wealth movement of Senator Huey Long of Louisiana. Another manifestation of the political turbulence was Franklin Roosevelt's sweeping electoral victory in 1932. The New Deal that followed served as an escape valve for the political discontent, and effectively neutralized the extremist movements.

Political developments in Britain and France during these years were generally the same as in the United States. Both countries were hit by political storms but managed to ride them out within the framework of their traditional institutions. The British Labour party, which had come into office in June, 1929, was faced almost at once with the problem of paying "dole" to ever greater numbers of unemployed. At the same time, American firms were re-calling their short-term loans and refusing to consider new loans unless the British government carried out certain economies. In August, 1931, Prime Minister Ramsay MacDonald capitulated to these pressures, agreeing to disband his Labour government and to head a new National government. Like Lloyd George's coalition of 1916 to 1922, this proved to be a mere façade for Tory rule, with the Conservatives comprising the majority of the cabinet. Although the new government had been formed to save the pound, it promptly abandoned the gold standard, and the pound fell from $4.86 to $3.49. The adoption in 1932 of a protective tariff and of a limited amount of preferential trade treatment for the member states of the Empire represented another break with the past. Three years later, the aging and ailing MacDonald resigned in favor of Stanley Baldwin, and so Britain passed under virtual Conservative rule, though the coalition still existed nominally.

In France, too, the Left was forced out of office by the pressures of the

* See "Social Repercussions," *EMM,* No. 150.

518

Depression. It won the 1932 elections, and the Radical Édouard Herriot formed a government with Socialist support as had been done in 1924. On this occasion also, the Left ministry was undermined by mounting financial difficulties. The Radicals and the Socialists were hopelessly divided on the question of how to cope with the economic crisis. Herriot held office for only six months, and four other premiers followed in rapid succession. The showdown came in December, 1933, with the Stavisky scandal, involving a Russian-born promoter and a provincial pawnshop in a fraudulent bond issue; according to rumors, various important officials and politicians were implicated. Extreme rightist groups took advantage of the opportunity to stage street riots in an effort to overthrow the republic itself. Although they failed to do so, they did force the government to resign in February, 1934. A number of conservative ministries followed, none of which proved capable of coping with the country's basic ills.

Much more dramatic and fateful was the rise of Hitler to power in Germany. The Depression affected the course of political events directly and decisively in that country, also. A Western-type republic had been established with the adoption of the Weimar Constitution in 1919 (see Chapter 22, section II). During its first year, the new republic had to face Communist uprisings in Bavaria and the Ruhr, as well as the monarchist Kapp *Putsch* in Berlin. The instability persisted through 1923 when French and Italian forces occupied the Ruhr because of the reparations imbroglio. At the same time, inflation swept the country, wiping out the savings of all classes. Only with the negotiation of the Dawes Plan and the evacuation of the Ruhr in 1924 did Germany finally begin to settle down. During the following years, Germany accepted the Locarno Pacts and entered the League of Nations, and her economy steadily improved, thanks to generous American loans.

The Depression hit Germany with particular severity, leaving two-fifths of the labor force unemployed and another fifth partially employed. The government at the time was a Left-Center coalition led by the Socialist Chancellor Herman Müller, while the conservative old war hero Paul von Hindenburg was functioning as president. Like Socialist ministries elsewhere, the Müller ministry in Germany was undermined by dissension over how to cope with unemployment and other problems created by the Depression. The Left favored increased unemployment relief, while the Right insisted on retrenchment and a balanced budget. The latter course was supported by most economists, for the rationale of deficit financing had not yet been worked out in theory or in practice. The Müller cabinet was forced to resign in March, 1930, and from then on, Germany was ruled by parties of the Center and Right.

At first a coalition government was organized by Heinrich Brüning, an intelligent and upright, though cold and rigid, Centrist, who commanded more respect than friendship. It was the tragedy of this well-meaning patriot that he dug the grave of German democracy. Lacking a parliamentary majority, he fell back upon Article 48 of the constitution, which empowered the president, in case of emergency, to issue decrees that would have the force of law unless specifically rejected by majority vote of the Reichstag. The Reichstag did, in fact, vote against the first emergency decrees, but Brüning countered by persuading Hindenburg to dissolve the Reichstag and order new elections for September, 1930. Brüning expected that a majority for the various Center and Right parties would be returned, enabling him to govern the country in regular parliamentary fashion. Instead, the elections marked the emergence of Hitler's National Socialist party as a national force.

The son of a minor Austrian customs official, Adolf Hitler went to Vienna early in life, aspiring to be a painter. Lacking talent, he spent, according to his own account—which seems to be greatly exaggerated—five miserable years working at the most menial jobs to keep body and soul together. His misery, real or fancied, together with his undoubted professional failure, help to explain the passionate convictions he now acquired: a hatred of Marxists and Jews, a detestation of parliamentary government, and a contempt for the affluent bourgeoisie and its "decadent" culture. From Vienna, Hitler drifted to Munich, where in 1914 he enlisted in a Bavarian regiment. Although he fought bravely through the war, was thrice wounded, and was awarded the coveted Iron Cross, he apparently displayed no particular aptitude, because he rose no higher than a corporal despite his devoted service. Yet his army years were among the happiest of his life, the military discipline providing a sense of direction he had hitherto lacked.

TABLE 1.   Reichstag Elections, 1919–1933
(Number of deputies and percentage of total votes *)

Party	1/19/19	6/6/20	5/4/24	12/7/24	5/20/28	9/14/30	7/31/32	11/6/32	3/5/33
Communist									
No. dep.	0	4	62	45	54	77	89	100	81
% vote		2.1%	12.6%	9.0%	10.6%	13.1%	14.6%	16.9%	12.3%
Social Democratic									
No. dep.			100	131	153	143	133	121	120
% vote			20.5%	26.0%	29.8%	24.5%	21.6%	20.4%	18.3%
Ind.									
No. dep.	22	84							
% vote	7.6%	17.9%							
Maj.									
No. dep.	165	102							
% vote	37.9%	21.6%							
Democratic									
No. dep.	75	39	28	32	25	20	4	2	5
% vote	18.6%	8.3%	5.7%	6.3%	4.9%	3.8%	1.0%	1.0%	0.8%
Centrum									
No. dep.	91	64	65	69	62	68	75	70	74
% vote	19.7%	13.6%	13.4%	13.6%	12.1%	11.8%	12.5%	11.9%	11.7%
Bavarian People's									
No. dep.	0	21	16	19	16	19	22	20	18
% vote		4.4%	3.2%	3.7%	3.0%	3.0%	3.2%	3.1%	2.7%
Economic									
No. dep.	4	4	10	17	23	23	2	1	0
% vote	0.9%	0.8%	2.4%	3.3%	4.5%	3.9%	0.4%	0.3%	0
German People's									
No. dep.	19	65	45	51	45	30	7	11	2
% vote	4.4%	13.9%	9.2%	10.1%	8.7%	4.5%	1.2%	1.9%	1.1%
National People's									
No. dep.	44	71	95	103	73	41	37	52	52
% vote	10.3%	14.9%	19.5%	20.5%	14.2%	7.0%	5.9%	8.8%	8.0%
National Socialist									
No. dep.	0	0	32	14	12	107	230	196	288
% vote			6.5%	3.0%	2.6%	18.3%	37.4%	33.1%	43.9%

* Under the electoral system provided for in the Weimar Constitution, each party received approximately one representative for every 60,000 popular votes cast for its candidates. Various small parties, not listed here, were underrepresented in the Reichstag.

520

At the end of the war, Hitler turned violently against the new Weimar Republic. "I regard the present German Reich as neither a democracy nor a republic, but a Marxistic-Jewish-international pigsty." In 1919, he joined a struggling group called the National Socialist German Workers' party, of which he soon became the leader, or Führer. After making rabble-rousing speeches on nationalist and anti-Semitic themes, he joined Field Marshal Ludendorff in an *opéra-bouffe* uprising in Munich in 1923. It was easily put down by the police, and Hitler was imprisoned for nine months. There, at the age of thirty-five, he wrote *Mein Kampf*—"My Battle"—a long and turgid autobiographical reflection into which he poured his hatred of democracy, Marxism, and Jews, and which specified how a defeated Germany could become "the lord of the earth." "Racial purity" was the key to this mastery: "A State, which in the age of racial poisoning devotes itself to the fostering of its best racial elements, must one day become the lord of the earth."

Upon release from prison, Hitler resumed his agitation but with disappointing results. In the December, 1924, elections, his Nazi party won only 14 seats and a mere 908,000 votes, and in May, 1928, won even fewer—12 seats and 810,000 votes, or 2.6 per cent of the total number. The turning point came with the September, 1930, elections when the Nazis won 107 seats and 6,407,000 votes, or 18.3 per cent of the total. This avalanche of ballots did not come from the workers; the Socialist and Communist parties between them gained 13 more seats in 1930 than in 1928. Hitler was getting his new-found support from the middle-class elements that were looking desperately for safety in the fierce economic storm (This is evident in Table 1, which shows the marked drop in the votes received from 1930 onward by all the Center and Right parties except the Catholic Centrum).

To the minor functionaries and bankrupt tradesmen, the Nazi platform offered comfort and hope. It called for abolition of unearned income and "interest slavery," nationalization of all trusts, profit sharing in large concerns, and the death penalty for usurers and profiteers. At the same time, all patriotic Germans were promised the smashing of the Versailles chains and the persecution of the Jews, who were branded as being both exploiting financiers and materialistic Communists. It should be emphasized that Hitler had been campaigning on this platform for years, with little response. The Depression was directly and primarily responsible for the change in his political fortunes. Before its full effects were felt, he had been regarded by most Germans as a loud-mouthed but quite harmless fanatic; when almost half the labor force was unemployed, he became for increasing numbers the beloved Führer who supplied scapegoats for their misery, and a program of action for individual and national fulfillment.

With the September, 1930, elections, the Nazis increased their Reichstag representation from 12 to 107, thus becoming the second largest party in the country. This unexpected outcome undermined parliamentary government in Germany because it denied a majority to both a Center-Right coalition desired by Brüning and a Center-Left coalition that had functioned under Müller. Consequently, Brüning had to rely for over two years on presidential decrees for all necessary legislation. The extent of his dependence on Hindenburg was demonstrated when he proposed legislation for the breakup of East Prussian estates; President Hindenburg, himself a Junker landowner, was strongly opposed, and forced Bruning to resign in May, 1932.

The new chancellor was Franz von Papen, nominally a member of the Center. Actually he was a reactionary aristocrat, well described as "an elegant, gracious, suave nonentity, clever to the point of stupidity." Papen headed a weak coalition government with negligible Reichstag support, so he held new elections in July, 1932, in the hope of strengthening his position. Instead, the Nazis were the big winners: their votes jumped to 13,799,000, or 37.4 per cent of the total number, and their seats to 230. Again, these gains were made at the expense of the Right and Center parties, because, compared to 1930, the combined Socialist and Communist seats actually increased by two.

Hitler was now the head of the number one party in the country. In negotiations with President Hindenburg, he demanded complete executive power. "And what do you imply by that request?" asked Hindenburg. Hitler replied, "I want precisely the same power as Mussolini exercised after the march on Rome." Hindenburg refused, being unimpressed by the "Bohemian corporal," as he called him. But parliamentary government was now impossible. Since neither the Nazis nor the Communists would enter a coalition, no majority support could be organized.

In November, 1932, Papen held still another election in an attempt to break the deadlock. This time the Nazis lost 2 million votes and 34 seats in the Reichstag, reducing them to 196 deputies. They were still the strongest party in the country, but they could no longer pose as the irresistable wave of the future. Indeed, panic seized the party leaders. Hitler's lieutenant, Joseph Goebbels, wrote in his diary on December 8, 1932: "Deep depression throughout the organization. Lack of money is making it impossible to do things thoroughly well. For hours the Leader paces up and down the room in the hotel. It is obvious that he is thinking very hard. . . . Suddenly he stops and says: 'If the party once falls to pieces, I shall shoot myself without further ado.' A dreadful threat, and most depressing." [6]

Less than two months later, the would-be suicide was the Chancellor of Germany. One reason for this startling reversal was the large-scale financial support now given to the Nazi party by German business leaders, who were worried that millions of votes might shift to the Left if the party disintegrated. Hitler met with the Cologne banker Kurt von Schroeder on January 4, and from then on, the "lack of money" that Goebbels had complained about was no longer a problem. The other reason was the morass of intrigues and cabals that passed for government in Berlin at the time. The aged Hindenburg was now senile and could function lucidly only a few hours each day. Persuaded to get rid of Papen, he appointed in his place General Kurt von Schleicher, who was even more devious than his predecessor.

Schleicher decided to try demagogy. He cancelled the cuts in wages and relief that Papen had made, revived plans for partitioning East Prussian estates, and began an investigation of illegal profits made by landowners through government agrarian legislation. Both the landowners and the businessmen denounced him bitterly, and won over Hindenburg. Schleicher was vulnerable for the same reason that Brüning and Papen had been: inability to organize a majority in the Reichstag. On January 28, 1933, Schleicher was forced to resign, and two days later, Hitler became chancellor with a coalition cabinet of Nationalists and Nazis.

522   Within six months Hitler had regimented Germany, on the basis of his ideas concerning race and leadership.* A new Reichstag was elected on March 5 following a campaign of unprecedented propaganda and terrorism. The Nazis received 288 seats and five and a half million votes, but they still comprised only 44 per cent of the total cast. When the representatives met, Hitler declared the Communist seats null and void, and then made a deal with the Catholic Center that gave him enough votes to pass the Enabling Act on March 23, 1933. This gave him authority to rule by decree for four years. But by the summer of 1933, he had eliminated or leashed virtually all independent elements in German life—trade unions, schools, churches, political parties, communications media, the judiciary, and the states of the federation.† As early as April 22, 1933, Goebbels was noting in his diary, "The Leader's authority is now completely in the ascendant in the Cabinet. There will be no more voting. The Leader's personality decides. All this has been achieved much more quickly than we had dared hope." [7]

Thus Hitler became master of Germany, and by technically legal methods, as he never ceased to boast. The Depression had made his triumph possible, though by no means inevitable; the possibility was translated into actuality by a combination of other factors, including Hitler's own talents, the support afforded by assorted vested interests, and the myopia of his opponents who underestimated him and failed to unite in opposition.‡ On August 2, 1934, Hindenburg conveniently died, enabling Hitler to combine the offices of president and chancellor in his own person. The following month the Nazi Party Congress assembled in Nuremberg, and Hitler proclaimed, "The German form of life is definitely determined for the next thousand years."

International Repercussions

The British Foreign Minister, Sir Austen Chamberlain, comparing the international situation in 1932 with that of the Locarno era, observed:

> I look at the world to-day and I contrast the conditions now with the conditions at that time, and I am forced to acknowledge that for some reason or other, owing to something upon which it is difficult to put one's finger, in these last two years the world is moving backward. Instead of approaching nearer to one another, instead of increasing the measure of goodwill, instead of progressing to a stable peace, it has fallen back into an attitude of suspicion, of fear, of danger, which imperils the peace of the world. [8]

That "something" that Chamberlain could not identify was the Depression and its manifold repercussions, international as well as national. Various international agreements of the Locarno era were rendered unworkable, particularly those concerning reparations and war debts. It soon became obvious that

* See "Hitler and Race," *EMM*, No. 154.
† See "The Leadership Principle," *EMM*, No. 153.
‡ See "Political Repercussions," *EMM*, No. 151.

governments, pushed to the brink of bankruptcy by their slumping economies and mounting unemployment, would not be able to meet commitments undertaken a few years earlier. In July, 1931, on the initiative of President Hoover, the powers agreed to a moratorium on all intergovernmental debts. The moratorium showed that there was, in fact, a close connection between inter-Allied debts and reparations, though Hoover reiterated that there was no such connection. The following summer, at the Lausanne Conference, the powers in fact, if not in theory, cancelled German reparations entirely. Simultaneously, the payment of war debts to the United States came to an end, though a few token payments were made in the following years. And so the sticky old issue of reparations and war debts was finally swept away by the economic storms let loose by the Depression.

Another effect of the storms was to accentuate the endemic economic nationalism to the point where it disturbed international relations. In the general spirit of *sauve qui peut,* self-protective measures by individual nations took such forms as higher tariffs, more rigid import quotas, clearing agreements, currency control regulations, and bilateral trade pacts. These measures inevitably fomented economic friction and political tensions among states. Various attempts were made to reverse the trend but without success. The World Economic Conference that met in London in 1933 was a dismal fiasco, and "autarchy," or economic self-sufficiency, gradually became a commonly accepted national goal.

Closely related was the petering out of disarmament efforts, which gave way to massive rearmament programs. The Disarmament Conference that met intermittently for twenty months, beginning in February, 1932, was as futile as the Economic Conference. As the 1930's progressed, countries devoted more and more of their energies to rearming. The trend proved impossible to stop because armament manufacturing provided jobs as well as imagined security. Unemployment in the United States, for example, was not substantially reduced until the country began to rearm on the eve of World War II. Likewise, Hitler quickly disposed of the unprecedented unemployment he faced by launching a gigantic rearmament program. It is sobering to realize that he was the most successful in pulling his country out of the slump because he was the most thorough in preparing his country for war. Furthermore, the social ravages of the Depression and the attendent unemployment had cut so deeply that the masses everywhere welcomed new jobs, even in armament factories. Probably no single measure endeared Hitler so much to his people as did the wholesale rearming that gave work to the desperate unemployed.

The armaments now being accumulated were bound sooner or later to be used, and their use required some justification; the most obvious was that of *Lebensraum,* or living space. This was the term coined by Hitler, but similar expressions and arguments were employed by Mussolini in Italy and by the military leaders in Japan. The unemployment and general misery, according to this doctrine, arose from the lack of *Lebensraum.* A few fortunate countries had seized all the colonies and underpopulated lands overseas, leaving the other nations without the natural resources needed to support their people. The obvious way out was to expand, by force if necessary, to remedy the injustices inflicted in the past. Such were the arguments used by the so-called "have-not" countries against the "haves."

524

The reasoning was manifestly specious in view of the fact that the Depression had devastated equally and impartially the United States, Canada, and Britain, along with Germany, Italy, and Japan. Nevertheless, the *Lebensraum* ideology served to unite the people of the "have-not" countries in support of the expansionist policies of their respective governments. It also gave a superficial moral justification to aggression committed for the avowed purpose of providing food for the needy and work for the jobless. Indeed, certain elements even within the "have" countries accepted these rationalizations and defended the aggressions that followed. Even Western statesmen who refused to swallow these sophistries were sometimes obliged to close their eyes to aggressive acts because of pressing problems at home. The blatant and repeated violations of the League Covenant during the 1930's were successful in part because of the overwhelming domestic problems that had first claim to the attentions of Western leaders.*

Such, then, was the combination of forces behind the "suspicion," the "fear," and the "moving backward" that Chamberlain had observed in 1932. During the following years, these forces undermined completely the settlement that had been reached in the Twenties and precipitated one crisis after another, culminating finally in World War II.†

SUGGESTED READING

The most recent, and most readable, survey of the Five Year Plans is the paperback by R. W. Campbell, *Soviet Economic Power: Its Organization, Growth and Challenge* (Boston: Houghton, 1960). The organization and role of trade unions is analyzed in I. Deutscher, *Soviet Trade Unions* (New York: Oxford Univ., 1950). For current developments, see the *Current Digest of the Soviet Press,* a weekly publication providing translations of the most important materials appearing in the Soviet press. Finally, the global impact of the Five Year Plans is described by E. H. Carr, *The Soviet Impact on the Western World* (New York: Macmillan, 1954), and by O. Lattimore in his following studies: *Solution in Asia* (Boston: Little, 1945), *The Situation in Asia* (Boston: Little, 1949), and *Nomads and Commissars: Mongolia Revisited* (New York: Oxford Univ., 1962).

A brief and readable analysis of the Depression is available in J. K. Galbraith, *The Great Crash, 1929* (Boston: Houghton, 1955). For the effect on the United States, see D. A. Shannon, *The Great Depression* (Englewood Cliffs, N. J.: Prentice-Hall, 1960; A Spectrum Book); on Britain, see W. H. Beveridge, *Full Employment in a Free Society* (New York: Norton, 1945); and on the world, see F. Sternberg, *Capitalism and Socialism on Trial* (New York: Day, 1951). On Hitler's rise to power there is a convenient collection of materials reflecting different viewpoints in J. L. Snell, *The Nazi Revolution: Germany's Guilt or Germany's Fate?* [Problems in European Civilization] (Boston: Heath, 1959). This also provides an excellent brief bibliography. See also the spirited account by W. L. Shirer, *The Rise and Fall of the Third Reich* (New York: Simon and

---

* See "International Repercussions," *EMM,* No. 152.
† See "Two Appraisals: Toynbee and Nehru," *EMM,* No. 155.

Schuster, 1960); the competent biography by A. Bullock, *Hitler: A Study in Tyranny* (New York: Harper, 1952); the important analysis by A. Schweitzer, *Big Business in the Third Reich* (Bloomington: Indiana Univ., 1964); and the bibliographical survey by H. C. Meyer, *Five Images of Germany: Half a Century of American Views on German History* (Washington: Service Center for Teachers of History, 1960).

*This is not Peace.
It is an Armistice for twenty years.*

MARSHAL FOCH, *1919*

Drift to War, 1929-1939

Τhe late 1920's were years of prosperity, stabilization, and settlement; the 1930's were years of depression, crises, and war. In Europe, the settlement of the Twenties was based on the French system of alliances, and in the Far East, on the Washington Conference agreements, the objective in each case being to preserve the *status quo* in the two regions. This objective was realized in the 1920's, but during the next decade, everything was suddenly and decisively upset. New leaders appeared in Germany and Japan who were determined to revise the territorial settlement of World War I and who possessed the means and the will to do so. Their massive rearming programs and their breath-taking aggressions drastically altered the balance of power. No longer was the relatively weak Italy the only revisionist state attempting ineffectually to challenge the *status quo;* the Third Reich and Imperial Japan also gave strength to the revisionist drive, resulting in an entirely new power configuration. A triangle situation developed, with Britain, France, and their Continental allies supporting the *status quo,* Germany, Italy, and Japan driving for revision, and the Soviet Union, strengthened by the Five Year Plans, playing an increasingly important role. The interplay of these three forces explains the recurring crises of the 1930's and the final outbreak of World War II.

I. JAPAN INVADES MANCHURIA

The first major act of aggression was made by Japan, in pursuance of long-cherished territorial ambitions on the mainland. The Japanese had entered World War I promptly in order to exploit what appeared to be a golden opportunity. They took over with little difficulty the German islands in the Pacific and the German holdings on the Shantung Peninsula. The full extent of their ambitions, however, was manifested by the Twenty-one Demands made upon China in January, 1915. If implemented, these would have transformed China into a Japanese protectorate. The maintenance of the Japanese expeditionary force in Siberia after the British and American troops had been withdraw in 1920 was another indication of their continental ambitions.

These Japanese aspirations were, for the most part, unsatisfied. The Twenty-one Demands were successfully resisted, owing in part to a warning by Secretary of State, William Jennings Bryan, that the United States would recognize no treaty infringing the integrity of China or the principle of the Open Door. At the Paris Peace Conference Japan did retain control of the former German islands, but as Class C mandates rather than as outright possessions. President Wilson strenuously opposed Japanese claims to the undisputably Chinese territory of Shantung. As a compromise, Japan was confirmed in "temporary" possession of the peninsula, but she conceded that it was her "policy" to restore the territory to China at an unspecified date, "retaining only the economic priviliges [hitherto] granted to Germany."

At the Washington Naval Conference Japan formally renounced any territorial ambitions she may still have cherished. The nine powers at the conference signed a Nine-Power Treaty (February 6, 1922) guaranteeing the territorial integrity of China and reiterating the principle of the Open Door. At the same conference the United States, Britain, France, and Japan signed the Four-Power Treaty (December 13, 1921) by which they agreed to respect one another's rights in "insular possessions" in the Pacific and to settle any future differences by consultation. In addition, Japan, after energetic American mediation, agreed to restore Shantung to China and to evacuate her troops from Siberia; both commitments were fulfilled in 1922.

Having finished with foreign adventures, at least for the time being, Japan now turned to domestic problems: the aftermath of the disastrous 1923 earthquake, which destroyed three quarters of Tokyo and inflicted 160,000 casualties and $2 billion worth of property loss; and the troublous suffrage issue, which provoked riots and political upheavals until the acceptance of universal male suffrage in 1925 increasing the number of voters from 3 to 14 million.

Most acute was the economic problem, particularly that of the impoverished peasantry. Japan, like the United States, had prospered greatly during World War I, supplying munitions and merchant shipping. Between 1914 and 1920, the value of foreign trade increased almost four times, from $1.2 billion to $4.3 billion. The prosperity, however, was poorly distributed, because of the unprecedented concentration of economic power in the so-called Zaibatsu (*Zai* means wealth, *batsu*, clique). This was the general name given to four giant family corporations (Mitsui, Mitsubishi, Sumitomo, and Yasuda) that by World War II controlled three-fourths of the combined capitalization of all Japanese firms, and held one-third of all deposits in Japan's private banks, three-fourths of all trust deposits, and one-fifth of all life insurance policies. The peasants, comprising one-half the total population, were impoverished by high rents and heavy debts. Only 7 per cent of these families owned five acres or more of land; the average holding was less than three acres. City workers suffered from high food prices, low wages, and lack of trade-union freedom. Speculators drove prices so high that rice riots broke out in 1918, necessitating the use of troops to restore order.

The depressed living standards of the workers and peasants meant a severely restricted domestic market. Consequently, Japanese industry was particularly dependent upon foreign markets for the disposal of its products; this dependence spelled disaster with the coming of the Depression. Between 1929 and 1931, foreign trade decreased by almost 50 per cent. The peasants, who had supplemented their meager incomes by silk cultivation, were badly hurt by the sharp slump in silk exports to depression-ridden America. City workers suffered correspondingly from unemployment.

Army leaders and other champions of territorial aggrandizement were now able to argue persuasively that the source of Japan's trouble was her dependence upon foreign markets. Japan should conquer an empire that would make her self-sufficient and economically independent of the rest of the world. Military spokesmen had been preaching this doctrine for years, but the ravages of the Depression now provided them with a responsive audience, as had happened in the case of Hitler in Germany. In 1927, Prime Minister General Tanaka wrote in a memorial to the Emperor that England had available the raw materials of India and Australia, while the United States had the resources of Canada and South America. "But in Japan her food supply and raw materials decrease in proportion to her population. If we merely hope to develop trade, we shall eventually be defeated. . . . In the end we shall get nothing. . . . Our best policy lies in the direction of taking positive steps to secure rights and privilieges in Manchuria and Mongolia. . . ." [1]

The Japanese expansionists were not only motivated by economic considerations. They were also concerned about the growing strength of the Soviet Union and the increasing success of Chiang Kai-shek in unifying China. In addition, they were fully aware of the unemployment situation and other problems that were then engrossing the attention of Western statesmen. These calculations are reflected in a memorandum submitted by General Honjo to the Minister of War in the summer of 1931, only six months before the Japanese army struck in Manchuria:

> In order to strengthen the position of our country and its powers, it is necessary immediately to take advantage of the difficult world economic position, as well as the circumstance that the Five Year Plan in the Soviet Union has not yet been completed and that China is not a united country. All these factors must be utilized for the purpose of the more intense occupation of Manchuria and Mongolia and for realizing the active aims of the former Siberian expedition. The unity of China, the existence of the Soviet Union, and the penetration of America in the Far East, all does not accord with our interests. [2]

It was not accidental that both Tanaka and Honjo specified Manchuria as the first objective in their program of expansionism. This province in the northeast corner of China had the double advantage of being loosely connected with the central Nanking government and possessing abundant natural resources, including iron, coal, and extensive fertile plains. Furthermore, Japan had obtained through past treaty arrangements certain special privileges in Manchuria; these could be used to find pretexts for justifying aggressive measures. This was precisely what was done when the Japanese military decided in the fall of 1931 that the time had come to strike.

On the evening of September 18, 1931, an explosion wrecked a small section of track on the Japanese-controlled South Manchuria railway to the north of Mukden. Since a southbound train passed over that track several minutes later without difficulty, and since the Japanese refused for five days to allow newsmen to visit the scene of the "incident," as the Japanese delicately called it at the time, most contemporaries regarded the whole affair as a fabrication. It is now definitely known to have occurred, because of the testimony of Baron Shidehara before the International War Crimes Tribunal in Tokyo in June, 1946. The Baron, who was Foreign Minister in 1931, admitted that army officers had staged the incident that he had vainly tried to stop. His testimony is supported by the speed and precision with which the Japanese army quartered in the Kwantung Peninsula—the Kwantung army, as it was called—swung immediately into action. Without declaring war, it captured Mukden and Changchun in the space of twenty-four hours, and then fanned out in all directions. The taking of Harbin in late January, 1932, signified the end of all organized resistance in Manchuria. In March, 1932, the victors renamed their conquest Manchukuo, the "State of Manchu." Needing a puppet emperor, they dragged out of retirement Henry P'u Yi, the surviving head of the old Manchu dynasty that had fallen in 1911, and solemnly installed him as Regent.

Meanwhile, the Chinese government had appealed to the League of Nations under Article 11, and to the United States under the Paris Pact (Kellogg–Briand Pact). The result was much deliberation but no practical aid. Secretary of State Henry L. Stimson expressed "whole hearted sympathy" yet declined to invoke the Paris Pact. The League Council convened on September 19, October 13, and again on November 16, to discuss the Manchurian situation; the sessions were marked by delay and confusion as well as by courtesies and compliments. Many in Geneva and in Washington clung to the belief that the Japanese cabinet would be able to curb the army and end the crisis. On November 21, the Japanese delegation accepted the orginal Chinese proposal for an impartial commission of inquiry, but the members were not chosen until January 14, 1932, and they did not actually reach Mukden until April 21; by that time, Manchuria had become Manchukuo.

On January 7, 1932, the United States government proclaimed its so-called Stimson Doctrine, which stipulated that no treaty would be recognized that impaired the independence or territorial integrity of China, infringed the Open Door policy, or was brought about by means contrary to the Paris Pact. This had little practical effect, for the Japanese military were responsive only to superior force, and no power at this time was strong enough to stand up to Japan in the Far East. Besides, all Western governments were distracted by pressing domestic problems. President Hoover, for example, faced both a

national election and the Depression, which was then at its nadir. It is understandable that he should have expressed a desire "to get out" of international
530 complications and concentrate on internal matters.

In the meantime, the League Commission, known as the Lytton Commission after its chairman, Lord Lytton, had collected evidence in Japan, China, and Manchuria. Its report, submitted in October, 1932, was carefully worded to avoid offending the Japanese. It denied that the Japanese aggression could be justified as a defensive measure and branded the new Manchukuo state a Japanese puppet regime. On the other hand, it refrained from ordering Japan to get out. Instead, the report proposed a settlement recognizing Japan's special interest in Manchuria and making that province an autonomous state under Chinese sovereignty but under Japanese control. On February 25, 1933, the League adopted the report, and the following month, Japan withdrew from that body.

In retrospect, the Manchurian affair stands out as the first serious blow leveled at the League of Nations and at the entire diplomatic structure designed to maintain the *status quo*—the Versailles settlement, the Washington Conference agreements, and the Paris Pact. The ease with which Japan had acquired its vast and rich new possession was not lost upon the revisionist leaders of Italy and Germany; Manchuria set off a chain reaction of aggressions that ultimately led to World War II.

II. Diplomatic Reactions to Hitler

The Japanese conquest of Manchuria was a rude challenge to the *status quo* in the Far East, but even more upsetting was Hitler's threat to the *status quo* in Europe. Hitherto the French system of alliances had dominated the continent with little difficulty. Mussolini had tried to organize a counter bloc, but his agreements with third-rate revisionist states such as Austria, Hungary, Bulgaria, and Albania were of little value. Likewise, the Soviet Union was cut off by the "cordon sanitaire" and, in any case, was engrossed in "building socialism in one country." Only Germany was left, and under Stresemann, this country had made peace with its wartime enemies when it accepted the Locarno Pacts and entered the League of Nations.

This comfortable situation was drastically altered when Hitler became chancellor in 1933. The Nazi leader had for sometime been demanding more *lebensraum* for the German people. The following selections from *Mein Kampf* (1924) reflect his basic ideas and objectives, which he repeated incessantly and without significant change in the years that followed.

. . . oppressed territories are led back to the bosom of a common Reich, not by flaming protests, but by a mighty sword.

To forge this sword is the task of a country's internal political leadership; to safeguard the work of forging and seek comrades in arms is the function of diplomatic leadership. . . .

The demand for restoration of the frontiers of 1914 is a political absurdity of such proportions and consequences as to make it seem a crime . . . the Reich's frontiers in 1914 were anything but logical. For in reality they were neither complete in the sense of embracing the people of German nationality, nor sensible with regard to geo-military expediency. . . .

And so we National Socialists consciously . . . take up where we broke off six hundred years ago. We stop the endless German movement to the south and west, and turn our gaze toward the land to the east. If we speak of soil in Europe today, we can primarily have in mind only Russia *and her vassal border states . . . the new Reich must again set itself on the march along the road of the Teutonic Knights of old, to obtain by the German sword sod for the German plow and daily bread for the nation.*[3]

It is scarcely surprising that there were immediate diplomatic repercussions when the author of these statements became the master of Germany, the first being the revitalization of the Little Entente, which had been dormant for several years. In February, 1933, Czechoslovakia, Yugoslavia, and Rumania established a permanent council of their foreign ministers to facilitate the coordination and implementation of their diplomatic policies. Likewise, in that spring, the French foreign minister, Louis Barthou, toured the Little Entente capitals and also Warsaw, strengthening the bonds between France and her eastern allies.

Even Mussolini, who later was to form the Rome-Berlin Axis with Hitler, at first reacted strongly against his fellow dictator. In view of the substantial German minority in the South Tyrol, Mussolini was apprehensive of an expansionist Nazi regime with its slogan of *"Ein Volk, ein Reich, ein Führer."* Accordingly, he took the initiative in concluding the Four-Power Pact on July 15, 1933 with Britain, France, and Germany. The agreement reiterated the adherence of the signatories to the League Covenant, the Locarno Treaties, and the Kellogg–Briand Pact, and also prohibited any changes in the Versailles Treaty without the consent of all four powers. This proved to be a futile exercise, for Hitler repeatedly violated these commitments—without even a reference to his fellow signatories. In October, 1933, he announced Germany's withdrawal from the Disarmament Conference and from the League of Nations. Although he did not immediately reveal his rearming program, its existence, if not its pace and magnitude, became generally known.

These developments stimulated the formation of another regional bloc comprised of Turkey, Greece, Rumania, and Yugoslavia, the last two having considerable German minorities. On February 9, 1934, the four countries signed the Balkan Pact which provided for cooperation to preserve the *status quo* in southeastern Europe.

More significant than the formation of the Balkan Entente was the basic shift now occurring in Soviet foreign policy. Traditionally, the Soviet leaders regarded the League as a concert of predatory imperialist powers. But when asked in December, 1933 by the American correspondent, Walter Duranty, whether the Soviet attitude to the League would always be negative, Stalin replied:

No, not always and not under all circumstances. You perhaps do not quite understand our point of view. Notwithstanding the withdrawal of

Germany and Japan from the League of Nations—or perhaps just because of this—the League may become something of a check to retard the outbreak of military actions or to hinder them. If this is so . . . then it is not impossible that we should support the League of Nations in spite of its colossal defects.[4]

This statement reflected the Soviet government's deep concern over the advent of Hitler. Because of their apprehension, the Soviets now viewed the League as a possible instrument for organizing collective resistance to ward off the anticipated aggression of the Nazis. This new attitude was encouraged by the French foreign minister, Louis Barthou. A conservative in domestic matters, Barthou's simple and consistent objective in foreign affairs was to build up a coalition that would be strong enough to dissuade Hitler from expansionist ventures. In addition to cementing the ties between France, the Little Entente, and Poland, Barthou now sought to add the Soviet Union to the *status quo* bloc. It was due largely to his efforts that the League of Nations invited the Soviet Union to join its ranks, and that the invitation was accepted on September 19, 1934.

The following month, an assassin's bullets killed Barthou, along with King Alexander of Yugoslavia, in Marseilles. It was a turning point in Europeon diplomacy, for Barthou's successors followed a relatively devious and ambivalent policy vis-à-vis Germany. This was particularly true of Pierre Laval, whose machinations on one occasion goaded the Rumanian foreign minister, Nicolae Titulescu, to explode, "Ce cochon de Laval." [5] Typical was the settlement that Laval concluded with Mussolini on January 7, 1935, in which the two agreed to cooperate in case of action by Hitler; they also settled various differences concerning their African possessions. France ceded to Italy certain desert territories adjoining the Italian colonies of Libya and Eritrea, and Mussolini, in turn, gave up claims in Tunis, where there was a considerable Italian population. However, a verbal understanding regarding Ethiopia was to lead to much controversy: Mussolini claimed that he had been promised a completely free hand in that country, while Laval insisted that the understanding had been limited to economic matters. Anthony Eden concluded, "The truth of what was said will never be known. . . . These two masters of chicanery were to go on arguing . . . after Laval's fall from power. . . . My own opinion, having heard and read their explanations, is that Laval was sufficiently equivocal to give Mussolini the chance to exploit his attitude. Certainly the Duce got the worst of the bargain on paper and the best in licence.[6]

Two months later, on March 16, 1935, Germany formally renounced the clauses of the Versailles Treaty concerning her disarmament, reintroduced conscription, and announced that her army would be increased to 36 divisions. Britain, France, and Italy responded on April 11 at the Stresa Conference where they agreed on common action against the German menace. The "Stresa front" proved as futile as the Four-Power Pact two years earlier. Each of the signatories promptly proceeded to go its own way: Italy busied herself preparing to invade Ethiopia; Britain made a separate naval agreement with Germany on June 18 permitting the latter to build up to 35 per cent of British strength; France concluded on May 2 a five-year alliance with Russia, each promising to aid the other in case of unprovoked attack. On May 16, Czechoslovakia signed a similar pact with Russia, though Russian aid to Czechoslovakia was made contingent upon France also providing aid as required by the 1924 alliance.

In conclusion, Hitler's accession to power had stimulated within two years several new diplomatic groupings—the Balkan Entente, the revived Little Entente, the French-Russian alliance and the Czech-Russian alliance—all designed to block any aggressive moves on the Führer's part. On the other hand, there were serious fissures in this diplomatic lineup, such as the British-German Naval Pact, which was resented in Paris, the German-Polish Non-aggression Pact of January, 1934, which also was not appreciated in Paris, and the unpredictability of Laval who basically distrusted his Soviet ally and preferred to make his own private deals on the side. With the outbreak of the Ethiopian crisis, these fissures became gaping chasms that completely undermined the League of Nations and the entire postwar diplomatic structure.

III. Italy Conquers Ethiopia

On October 3, 1935, Mussolini's legions invaded the independent African kingdom of Ethiopia. Behind this naked aggression were several motivations, one being the fascist glorification of empire-building for its own sake. "The growth of Empire," proclaimed Mussolini, "is an essential manifestation of vitality, and its opposite a sign of decadence." This yen for imperial glory was sharpened by memories of the defeat at Adowa in 1896 when an Italian army of 25,000 suffered crushing defeat at the hands of the tribesmen. The impact of the Depression also left its mark, for the number of unemployed Italians rose from 110,000 in 1926, to 730,000 in 1931, and to over 1,000,000 in 1933, thus giving rise to the usual rationalizations that concluded colonial expansion was needed to relieve the economic pressures at home. The Italians were particularly ardent on this point because Britain and France had obtained all the choice territories in Africa, leaving them only the sandy wastes of Libya, Eritrea, and Somaliland.

This determination to expand was expressed at the time by an Italian engineer who complained that he could find no gold in Eritrea. "But in Abyssinia," he added, "there is platinum as well, and it costs next to nothing to recover. But it is all locked up in the earth. Nobody does anything except loaf in the sunshine. When you look at it properly it is immoral to think that a people, from sheer laziness, can put an embargo on incalculable treasure, while others have to fight against all the forces of nature in sterile ground." [7] Mussolini decided to move when he did because he considered the diplomatic situation favorable. He believed that Laval had given him the green light, and he assumed that the opposition from other quarters would not be sufficiently resolute to stop him—an assumption that proved quite justified.

The pretext for the Italian aggression was reminiscent of the incident staged by the Japanese in Manchuria. On December 5, 1934, Ethiopian and Italian troops clashed at Walwal near the border between Italian Somaliland and Ethiopia. Emperor Haile Selassie offered to leave to an arbitration commission the question of whether Walwal was on Italian or Ethiopian territory. Musso-

534

lini refused to accept this and instead made various demands while preparing openly for invasion. On September 11, 1935, the British Foreign Secretary, Sir Samuel Hoare, delivered a famous speech before the League Assembly, in which he pledged Britain's support against aggression: "In conformity with its precise and explicit obligations, the League stands, and my country stands with it, for the collective maintenance of the Covenant in its entirety, and particularly for steady and collective resistance to all acts of unprovoked aggression. . . ." [8] This speech, as one delegate observed, was "one of the most electrifying moments in the history of the League." But Hoare seems to have been addressing himself to the British electorate that was about to vote, for his subsequent actions paralyzed rather than supported "collective resistance to unprovoked aggression."

A little more than a week after the Italians began their invasion, the League Council declared Italy the aggressor, and the Assembly voted for economic sanctions under Article 16 of the Covenant. These sanctions, which went into effect on November 18, 1935, included embargoes on arms, credits, and certain raw materials, but did not include the key ones—oil, coal, iron, and steel. Despite such limitations, the sanctions did represent a significant beginning toward stopping the Italian advance. Also, world public opinion expressed itself overwhelmingly against Mussolini's aggression. The Ethiopians were resisting stoutly, though the initial difficulty of the Italians in making headway was due more to the almost complete absence of roads than to the military effectiveness of their opponents.

At this point, the wily Laval squandered what little chance there was of stopping the Italians. Early in December, 1935, he persuaded Hoare to accept a plan by which Italy would be given outright about half of Ethiopia, and would control the remaining half of the country as a "zone of economic expansion and settlement." The two negotiators agreed to maintain secrecy until the plan had been submitted to the interested parties: Italy, Ethiopia, and the League. Laval, however, anticipated difficulties in Britain, so he permitted the plan to come to the attention of the French press. To his astonishment, the news of the deal aroused a storm of indignation in both London and Paris. Hoare was forced to resign, and was succeeded by Anthony Eden. The following month, Laval also had to go, after a drubbing at the hands of the Chamber.

For a while it seemed like a clean sweep for the supporters of the League against aggression, but the basic issue still was whether the sanctions would be made effective by adding the key materials, particularly oil. Eden was in favor of doing so, but the new French foreign minister, Pierre Flandin, persisted in dragging his feet. "Flandin's attitude," reported Eden, "was indistinguishable from Laval's, but was more skilfully and consistently presented." [9] Flandin's chief argument was that Mussolini would quit the League if oil sanctions were voted; he insisted that another attempt be made to reach a settlement. Since the British cabinet was not united behind Eden, Flandin had his way and effective sanctions were never enforced. The significance of this decision is apparent in the following revelation by Hitler's interpreter, Dr. Paul Schmidt:

> In 1938, on the eve of the Munich Conference, Mussolini admitted that the League of Nations had very nearly succeeded in countering

aggression by means of collective security. "If the League of Nations had followed Eden's advice in the Abyssinian dispute," he said to Hitler, "and had extended economic sanctions to oil, I would have had to withdraw from Abyssinia within a week. That would have been an incalculable disaster for me." [10]

The death blow to any remaining hope of effective sanctions came with Hitler's occupation of the Rhineland on March 7, 1936. A fateful move that had far-reaching repercussions (see the following section), it made the British and French governments even more sensitive to the German threat and more determined to placate Mussolini in order to keep him on their side and within the League of Nations. Consequently, the League Council voted on April 20, 1936 to continue the sanctions without oil, thus spelling the doom of the Ethiopian armies that in the meantime had been fighting the Italians with gallantry but with little else.

Mussolini, determined to eliminate any possibility of another Adowa disaster, had prepared an army of 250,000 men, which with African auxiliaries and labor battalions reached a total of 400,000. This force was armed with a formidable array of tanks, motorized units, and planes. The Ethiopians, by contrast, numbered less than 300,000, and almost all of them were more poorly armed than the Italian noncombatants. As serious as the need for tanks, planes, and heavy artillery, was the incredibly poor leadership of the Ethiopians. The victories of the Rif in Morocco had demonstrated the effectiveness of guerrilla tactics against superior European armies, but the Ethiopian tribal leaders, in their suicidal pride and ignorance, scorned guerrilla warfare as unworthy and demeaning. Instead, they attempted to wage a war of position, and were mercilessly bombarded, strafed, and even sprayed with mustard gas.

After a campaign of seven months, Marshal Badoglio triumphantly entered Addis Ababa on May 5, 1936. The same day, Mussolini proclaimed "a Roman peace, which is expressed in this simple, irrevocable, definite phrase— 'Ethiopia is Italian.' " Four days later, the King of Italy assumed the title "Emperor of Ethiopia." And so, at a cost of 3,000 men and $1 billion, Mussolini had won an empire of 350,000 square miles, ten million inhabitants, and rich natural resources.

So far as Europe and the rest of the world were concerned, the significance of the Ethiopian affair was that it undermined the League of Nations. Many small countries such as Greece, Rumania, and Yugoslavia had loyally supported the League during the crisis and enforced the sanctions against Italy, but their only rewards were heavy economic losses and exposing themselves to the wrath of the triumphant Duce. The obvious moral was that, given the pusillanimity of the leading Western powers, collective security was a snare and a delusion. Accordingly, the small countries henceforth followed a policy of *sauve qui peut* and turned their backs on the League of Nations. Ironically, the sacrifice of the League did not keep Italy on the side of the Western powers against Germany, which had been the great objective of those who insisted on placating Mussolini. Instead, the appeasement had precisely the opposite effect; both Mussolini and Hitler were impressed by their striking victories in Ethiopia and the Rhineland, and perceived the vast possibilities to which coordinated, aggressive activities could give rise. The final outcome was not the isolation of Nazi Germany but the formation of the Rome-Berlin Axis.

IV. ROME-BERLIN AXIS

At the beginning of the Ethiopian crisis Hitler played a wait-and-see game. If Mussolini failed, a rival in Central Europe would be eliminated; if he won, then the collective security system would be undermined, and Hitler's *Lebensraum* plans would be correspondingly enhanced. On March 7, 1936, Hitler dramatically ended this passive policy by sending a force of 35,000 marching into the Rhineland. The Versailles Treaty had stipulated that Germany should have no fortifications or armed forces on the left bank of the Rhine, nor in a zone of 50 kilometers from the right bank. Hitler's violation of this provision was a move of first-rate strategic significance: The French system of alliances was based on the accessibility of Central Europe to the French army; with the reoccupation of the Rhineland and the building of the Siegfried Line fortifications, which was immediately started, the French no longer had this accessibility. France was cut off from her allies while Germany's strength was immeasurably increased because her vitals were no longer left vulnerable by a demilitarized Rhineland. In short, Hitler's Rhineland coup represented a tremendous upset in Europe's military and diplomatic balance of power.

France was unable to respond appropriately to this momentous challenge because the country was preparing for elections and a stopgap ministry was in office. Premier Sarraut and Foreign Minister Flandin wanted to stop Hitler by mobilizing the army and dispatching an ultimatum. This plan would have worked, for it is now known that Hitler had decided on the Rhineland move against the advice of nearly all his generals. The German armed forces were not yet ready to wage serious war, so with only two exceptions, the German military leaders opposed the reoccupation, which they naturally assumed would lead to conflict with France. Accordingly, Hitler ordered that his divisions should retire without firing a shot if France mobilized and sent her army across the frontier. Hitler, like Mussolini, was bluffing, and the tactics worked for both men.

Sarraut and Flandin were dissuaded from action partly because their military advisers opposed any moves that involved the risk of war, but also because the British government held back as much as the French government had done during the Ethiopian crisis. When Flandin consulted Prime Minister Baldwin, the latter refused to have anything to do with the proposal to mobilize the French army and send it into the Rhineland. "You may be right," declared Baldwin, "but if there is *even one chance in a hundred* that war would follow from your police operation, I have not the right to commit England. . . . England is not in a state to go to war." [11]

The French government, being itself divided, was incapable of decisive action without Britain's support, and since this was not forthcoming, Hitler won a major victory with no opposition. One result of this triumph was the beginning of the end of the French system of alliances. Not only did the Siegfried Line cut off France from Central and Eastern Europe, but at the same time, Germany conducted an economic offensive in southeastern Europe that made that region virtually an economic dependency. By 1936, Germany was taking 51 per cent of Turkey's total exports, 48 per cent of Bulgaria's,

36 per cent of Greece's, 24 per cent of Yugoslavia's, and 23 per cent of Hungary's. Such close economic ties inevitably resulted in political repercussions, especially since the dictatorial regimes now appearing in southeastern Europe felt a certain ideological predilection for the German and Italian fascist regimes as against the Western democracies. Certainly the foreign policies of General Metaxas, King Carol, and Prince Paul were quite different from those of Venizelos, Titulescu, and King Alexander.

The Rhineland coup also served to bring together the hitherto antagonistic Führer and Duce. Mussolini deeply appreciated Hitler's role in distracting the attention of the League at a time when oil sanctions were still a possibility. Within a short time, the two dictators had formed a working partnership that quickly made a shambles of the existing diplomatic structure.

With the Austro-German accord of July 11, 1936, Hitler undertook to respect the integrity of Austria, thus removing the main source of discord between Rome and Berlin. A week later, civil war broke out in Spain, a tragic episode (see the following section) that was to drag on for three years, during which time Hitler and Mussolini worked together to encompass the downfall of the Spanish Republic. On October 24, 1936, the Rome-Berlin Axis was formerly constituted; Italy and Germany agreed on general cooperation as well as on such specific issues as German recognition of Italian Ethiopia in return for economic concessions. The following month Japan associated herself with the Axis by concluding anti-Communist pacts with Germany and then with Italy.

And so by the end of 1936, the diplomatic balance was entirely different from what it had been when Hitler came into office. Italy and Germany now had a working partnership. France had lost her former hegemony and declined into relative isolation. Her old allies in Central Europe were drifting away, while the new alliance with the Soviet Union remained largely a paper creation. The French governments distrusted the Soviet regime to the point of refusing to conclude the military convention needed to make their alliance fully effective. Likewise, the relations of the French and the British were far from being close or trustful. Such disarray of the *status quo* bloc, together with the crippling of the League of Nations, as a result of Manchuria and Ethiopia, enabled the Rome-Berlin Axis to seize the initiative during the next three years and to score triumph after triumph with virtually no opposition.

V. SPANISH CIVIL WAR

The Spanish Civil War was of more than ordinary significance because it was essentially two wars in one—a deep-rooted social conflict generated by the decay and tensions of Spanish society, and a dress rehearsal for World War II arising from the clash of ideologies and of Great Power interests.

Spain in the twentieth century was very different from what it had been in the sixteenth, when that country was the most powerful and feared nation in Europe. Symbolic of the decline during the intervening centuries was the Spanish-American War of 1898; with humiliating ease, the United States stripped Spain of most of her remaining colonial possessions. The war exposed not only the military weakness of Spain, but also the corruption and

538

inefficiency of the entrenched oligarchy that ruled the country. Three principal elements made up this oligarchy: the large landowners, the army, and the church.

The large landowners consisted of the old aristocracy and the wealthy upper middle class that had bought many estates. About 35,000 of these landowners possessed approximately 50 per cent of the total arable land. Conditions varied substantially from province to province, the most glaring inequalities in land ownership being in the south and west. The north, by contrast, had few large estates, though the peasants there could barely eke out a living because of the small size of their plots. Agricultural productivity in the country as a whole was very low, and the peasants, comprising 70 per cent of the entire population, were as depressed as any in other parts of Europe. The landowners contributed nothing, being of the absentee type who squandered their incomes in Madrid or in foreign capitals.

The Spanish army was noteworthy for two reasons: the extraordinarily large number of officers in proportion to the number of rank and file, and the constant intervention of the military in the politics of the country. Indeed, the officers felt they had a right to supervise political affairs and they acted accordingly; specifically, this meant the safeguarding of the *status quo* against all challengers, whether of the Republican Center or the parties of the Left.

The established Roman Catholic Church, an enormously wealthy and influential institution, had lost its landed property in the early and mid-nineteenth century, but in compensation, it had acquired industrial stocks and had received a substantial subsidy from the government, amounting to 2 per cent of the annual budget in the 1920's. The relations of the church in Spain with the state were similar to those of the Russian Orthodox Church with the Tsarist regime. The bishops were nominees of the king, and some of them were members of the Senate; but most important of all, the church controlled most of the education of the country. Spain had no comprehensive state educational system as had the rest of Western Europe, so that most of the existing schools were under church jurisdiction. In addition, the church exerted much influence through certain important newspapers, labor groups, and a variety of lay organizations. As had occurred in other countries where Catholicism played a similar role, this formidable power engendered a strong anticlerical movement in Spain. The widespread attacks on priests and nuns, and the wholesale destruction of church property during the Civil War were by no means unique in Spanish history.

Such was the Spain that Alfonso XIII was called upon to rule when he ascended the throne in 1902. Between that date and the establishment of the Rivera dictatorship in 1923, there were 33 different cabinets as well as a liberal number of strikes, mutinies, and assassinations. Spain's neutrality during World War I brought relative prosperity, but this lasted only for the duration of the war; with the peace, the chronic aliments and disorders returned. These were accentuated during the 1920's by the disasters suffered by the Spanish armies in Morocco at the hands of the Rif. The resulting discontent paved the way for the military coup d'état of General Primo de Rivera in September, 1923.

The new "strong man" admired Mussolini and imitated him in destroying the remnants of constitutional government, censoring the press, and restricting the universities. He also followed the Duce's example in building highways and staging international exhibitions. But these were merely surface gestures, for underneath, traditional Spanish society creaked on with its inequities and anachronisms. Finally, Primo de Rivera lost the support of the army and the King, and was forced to resign in January, 1930.

539

With the dictator gone, popular discontent was turned against the King himself. The Depression made the situation still more precarious, until at last Alfonso decided to restore the constitution and to hold municipal elections in April, 1931. The vote went heavily against the regime, the Republicans carrying 46 of the 50 provincial capitals. The state of public opinion was evident, and Alfonso prudently left the country, as four of his predecessors had done since 1789.

A republic was proclaimed on April 14, 1931, and elections were held for a constituent assembly, or cortes. When this body assembled in July, its members fell into three broad groupings: Right, Center, and Left. The Right represented the interests of the aristocracy, the army and the church. It wanted to preserve the *status quo;* if change proved unavoidable, then it should at least be directed to authoritarian channels. The Center reflected primarily the views of the lower middle class, the intellectuals and professional people. Republican for the most part, it espoused the liberal principles emanating from the French Revolution, including anticlericalism, personal freedoms, and a modest degree of social reform. The Left was comprised of various groups of Socialists, Stalinist and Trotskyite Communists and Anarcho-Syndicalists, the latter being particularly numerous and usually unwilling to work with any other groups. Although bitterly divided amongst themselves, these left-wing parties were all agreed on the need for fundamental institutional change, social and economic as well as political.

The Center and the Left, which together comprised a large majority, combined to adopt a markedly liberal constitution. Spain was declared to be a "democratic republic of workers of all kinds," with universal suffrage for both sexes, and a ministry responsible to a single-chamber cortes. In addition, the constitution proclaimed complete religious freedom, separated church and state, secularized education, and nationalized church property.

The first prime minister under the new constitution, the able Republican, Manuel Azaña, was supported also by the moderate socialists, and laws were promptly passed to implement the provisions of the constitution: Government subsidies to the church were abolished, certain monastic orders were banned, the pay of farm laborers was raised above the usual $.20 per day, a few large estates were divided among the peasants with partial compensation for the owners, hundreds of army officers were retired, and home rule was granted to the province of Catalonia. These were typical middle-of-the-road reforms that antagonized both the Right and the Left. In fact, the government had to use armed force to put down a military uprising in Seville led by General José Sanjurjo, and a revolt of Syndicalists and Anarchists in Barcelona and other cities.

With the dissolution of the Constituent Assembly at the end of 1933, the first elections for a regular cortes returned a conservative majority. The *bienio negro,* the "black" two years of clerical reaction, followed. Autonomy for Catalonia was revoked and much of the legislation concerning the church and

540

land distribution was either repealed or not enforced. Again, armed resistance flared up, especially among the miners of the Asturias, who were finally suppressed only by the use of Moroccan troops.

In preparation for the elections of February, 1936, the parties of the Left and the Left-Center now banded together to form a Popular Front similar to that which had just appeared in France. The coalition won a narrow victory and Azaña formed a new Republican cabinet which the Left parties supported but did not enter. Catalan autonomy was restored and anticlerical measures along with mild social reform were resumed. In retrospect, the Republicans appear to have blundered in emphasizing anticlericalism rather than Agrarian reform, which most Spaniards accepted. This policy alienated the fervent Catholics and much of the middle class. At the same time, the Great Depression, with its widespread unemployment, strengthened the extremist and weakened the moderate parties. To hold the desperate workers, the Socialists had to move steadily to the extreme Left; reacting to this, much of the middle class allied itself with the extreme Right—hence the mounting ideological passions and the polarization of political life to the point where parliamentary government became increasingly tenuous.

At this juncture, the Spanish rightists, with the connivance of Germany and Italy, and under the leadership of General Francisco Franco, raised the standard of counterrevolution. On July 17, 1936, the army in Morocco revolted, and the next day a number of mainland generals took up arms. The rebels, or self-styled Nationalists, quickly overran the southern and the western regions, and these sections of the country remained their main bases throughout the protracted struggle. Franco had hoped that with the advantage of surprise, he would be able to capture quickly the main cities and fortresses and so gain control of the entire country. Instead, the struggle dragged on for almost three years with a savagery reminiscent of the sixteenth century Wars of Religion.

After losing about one-half the country in the first few weeks of the revolt, the Loyalists rallied and managed to retain control of Madrid in the center, the Basque provinces in the north, and the highly developed east coast with the large cities of Barcelona and Valencia. The Loyalists were now in a strong position, for they had behind them the industrial centers, the most densely populated regions, and the capital, with its exceptionally large gold reserve. Despite these advantages, the Loyalists were eventually beaten, the main reason being that they were unable to obtain arms from abroad in quantities approaching those received by the Nationalists.

That such a turn of events should take place was paradoxical, because the Loyalists had both the money to import arms and the right to do so under international law, since they constituted the legal government of the country. The British and French governments, however, refused to allow the sale of arms to the Republican regime. They were inhibited by the sharp division of public opinion in their respective countries concerning the civil war, and they feared that an unrestricted flow of arms to the contending parties might escalade into a European war. Accordingly, Britian and France took the lead in sponsoring a nonintervention agreement, which was accepted by Germany, Italy, and the Soviet Union, as well as by several smaller countries.

The agreement provided that the signatories should refrain from shipping arms to Spain, but Germany and Italy violated their pledge from the beginning, and the Soviet Union soon was doing likewise. Italy sent not only arms but also regular army units, which rapidly increased in numbers as the war continued. According to official Italian sources, during the four months between December, 1936 and April, 1937, Mussolini despatched 100,000 men along with 40,000 tons of munitions and 750 cannon. Russia, like Germany, sent no ground troops but did provide war materials of all types in addition to technical advisers and pilots. The Loyalists were also aided by the International Brigades, which first went into action in November, 1936 in the defense of Madrid. The Brigades consisted of volunteers—mostly young idealists from Britain, France, and the United States—as well as antifascist émigrés from Italy and Germany. The majority were not Communists when they enlisted, but most of those few who survived did become members of the organization, partly because of their experiences and also because of indoctrination by their political commissars. Sustaining the strong sympathy for the Spanish Republic that was so widespread among Western European intellectuals in the late 1930's, was perhaps the chief significance of the Brigades.

541

Foreign intervention affected the Civil War in two important respects: it favored by all odds the Nationalists and was the decisive factor behind their victory; it also served to bring the Nationalists closer to fascism and the Republicans closer to communism, the latter trend being the more pronounced. At the outset, the Anarchists and the Socialists were predominant on the Republican side, with moderate Socialists filling the leading posts in the Loyalist administration throughout the Civil War. But the Communists became increasingly dominant with the Loyalist dependence on Soviet war materials, and by late 1937, the Russian-controlled International Brigades, Russian aircraft, and Spanish Communist generals were leading the Loyalist armies and dictating policy. Increased effectiveness usually resulted, but it also meant the destruction or overshadowing of non-Communist groups, particularly the Anarchists, who had a large following.

If the Loyalists had won, a new civil war might well have followed, with the Communists ranged against the Socialists, Anarchists, and Trotskyites. As it turned out, the Axis supplies of both ground troops and war materials proved irresistible, especially when Stalin decided to abandon the Spanish Republic. For two years there had been a stalemate, with the Nationalists controlling the Agrarian western and southern regions, and the Loyalists, the more developed northern and eastern sections, together with the Madrid salient. But in mid-1938, the Soviet government decided to cut its losses and stop the aid to Spain, in view of the continued refusal of the Western democracies to end the nonintervention farce, thus enabling Franco's armies to break the stalemate. In late December, 1938, the Nationalists began their great offensive against Catalonia; within a month they had taken Barcelona. Madrid and Valencia were now helpless, but they held out for two more months. With their fall in late March, the Civil War ended.

For Spain, the long ordeal involved three-fourths of one million casualties out of a population of 25 million, and one of every seven of the uninjured was left without shelter. For the Western powers, the Civil War represented another stunning defeat. As in the case of Ethiopia, they had again shown themselves weak and vacillating in the face of Axis aggression, a pattern that had also manifested itself during the German annexation of Austria, which had occurred in the course of the Spanish Civil War.

542

VI. Annexation of Austria

1938 was the year of the great bloodless victories of the Axis powers. At the center of these fateful developments was Neville Chamberlain, who succeeded Stanley Baldwin as Prime Minister in May, 1937, and who was taking over little by little the direction of British foreign policy even though Anthony Eden was his Foreign Secretary. Winston Churchill has left a characteristically pungent and penetrating estimate of the man who was to influence so decisively the course of European diplomacy at this critical juncture:

> Neville Chamberlain . . . was alert, business-like, opinionated, and self-confident in a very high degree. Unlike Baldwin, he conceived himself able to comprehend the whole field of Europe, and indeed the world. Instead of a vague but none the less deep-seated intuition, we had now a narrow, sharp-edged efficiency within the limits of the policy in which he believed. . . . He had formed decided judgments about all the political figures of the day, both at home and abroad, and felt himself capable of dealing with them. His all-pervading hope was to go down to history as the Great Peacemaker; and for this he was prepared to strive continually in the teeth of facts, and face great risks for himself and his country. Unhappily, he ran into tides the force of which he could not measure, and met hurricanes from which he did not flinch, but with which he could not cope.[12]

Hitler's interpreter, describing the fateful Munich Conference of 1938 which marked the end of Czechoslovakia and a radical shift in the Central European balance of power, has left a similar estimate of Chamberlain:

> Chamberlain kept on asking who would compensate the Czecho-Slovak Government for the buildings and installations which would pass to Germany with the Sudeten territory? It was obvious here that not the Prime Minister and politician, but the former Chancellor of the Exchequer and business man was speaking. Hitler became more and more restive. "These installations and buildings are the result of taxes paid by the Sudeten Germans," he kept saying with growing impatience, "and there can be no question of indemnification." But this failed to satisfy Chamberlain's sense of tidiness in matters affecting property. Hitler finally exploded. "Our time is too valuable to be wasted on such trivialities," he shouted at Chamberlain. This was when Chamberlain, for full measure, also raised the question of whether cattle were to remain in Sudeten territory or whether some of the livestock might not be driven into what remained of Czecho-Slovakia.[13]

The first clash between Chamberlain and his Foreign Secretary was over the policy to be followed in dealing with Mussolini. Chamberlain was determined to conciliate the Duce and to tempt him out of the newly formed Axis and back into the Western fold. He hoped to accomplish this by recognizing Italian sovereignty over Ethiopia, but his idea was opposed by Eden, who still upheld the ideals of collective security and the League of Nations. The issue came to a head in January, 1938, when President Roosevelt sent a personal letter to Chamberlain suggesting a conference in Washington between interested powers to discuss the deteriorating international situation. "Here," wrote Churchill, "was a formidable and measureless step." [14] But without consulting his Foreign Secretary, Chamberlain sent a chilling reply suggesting postponement of the proposed conference because it might imperil his negotiations with Italy regarding Ethiopia.

This incident, which led to Eden's resignation in February, 1938, revealed the motivations of those who now determined British foreign policy. "The truth," wrote Eden, "was that some of my seniors in the Cabinet . . . could not believe that Mussolini and Hitler were as untrustworthy as I painted them. After all, had not Mussolini defeated the reds and made the trains in Italy run on time? Moreover, as old-fashioned Conservatives they felt little sympathy with Roosevelt whom they instinctively regarded as something of a demagogue." [15] This outlook explains in large measure the stunning Axis victories of these years. The Conservatives felt that they could do business with the dictators, and that this was preferable to cooperation with President Roosevelt in "wooly" and "idealistic" projects based on the principle of collective security. Their counterparts in France likewise preferred to deal with Mussolini and Hitler rather than to turn to the Russians with whom they were nominally allied. The direct outcome of this way of thinking was the sacrifice of the independent states of Austria, Albania, and Czechoslovakia—a sacrifice that led not to "peace in our time" as was fondly imagined, but to World War II.

On the first page of *Mein Kampf* Hitler had written, "German-Austria must return to the great German mother country. . . . One blood demands one Reich." In line with this philosophy, a band of Austrian Nazis attempted in July, 1934, to seize control of the state. They killed Chancellor Dollfuss and occupied the Vienna radio station, but there was no popular uprising and the *putsch* failed. Two years later, in order to dispel Mussolini's suspicions, Hitler signed an agreement with Austria promising to respect the independence of that country. For some time thereafter, Hitler was effusive in his protestations of peace and goodwill, but at the same time, Germany was rearming at breakneck speed. In 1937, he spent $4.5 billion on armaments compared to a combined expenditure of less than $2 billion spent by Britain and France. The disparity the following year was as great, though both sides spent larger sums. This massive rearming, together with the successful remilitarization of the Rhineland in 1936, strengthened Germany's military position to the point where Hitler could strike out for his objectives with confidence.

On February 12, 1938, Hitler invited Austria's Chancellor, Kurt von Schuschnigg, to his Bavarian mountain retreat at Berchtesgaden. There the scholarly, modest, and pious Schuschnigg was subjected to long hours of table-pounding and invective.

> I have only to give an order, and in one single night all your ridiculous defense mechanisms are blown to bits. You don't seriously believe that you can stop me or even delay me for half an hour, do you? . . . Don't think for one moment that anybody on earth is going to thwart my decisions. Italy? I see eye to eye with Mussolini. . . . And England? England will not move one finger for Austria. . . . And France? Well, three years ago we marched on the Rhineland with a handful of battalions, that was the time I risked everything. If France had stopped us then we would have had to retreat. . . . But now it is too late for France.[16]

When Hitler had finished, the softening-up process was resumed by German generals and Nazi leaders, Austrian as well as German. Thus Schuschnigg was bullied into accepting various demands, such as an amnesty for imprisoned Austrian Nazis, and the appointment of Nazis to various posts, including the key Ministry of Interior. On his return to Vienna, Schuschnigg delivered a radio speech in which he made clear his determination to preserve Austria's independence. "We know exactly that we were able to go, and did go, to that boundary line beyond which, clearly and unequivocally appear the words: "So far and no further.' " Then he forbade the display of swastikas, the wearing of brown shirts, or the holding of Nazi demonstrations. These firm measures aroused sufficient popular support so that Schuschnigg was emboldened to schedule a plebiscite on March 13 on the following question: "Are you for a free and independent, German and Christian Austria?" [17]

This defiance infuriated Hitler, who began to concentrate troops on the frontier. In the ensuing crisis, he was proven justified in his warning to Schuschnigg that no Great Power would lift a finger to help Austria. France had no government at all, being caught between two ministries. Mussolini was unhappy and resentful, especially since he had not been forewarned by his fellow dictator, but his hands were tied by the Rome-Berlin Axis, so he had to inform Schuschnigg that he could offer "no advice under the circumstances." Chamberlain had already proclaimed his hands-off policy in a speech to the Commons on February 22: "Does anybody here believe that the League, as it is constituted to-day, can afford collective security? . . . If I am right, as I am confident I am, in saying that the League . . . is unable to provide collective security for anybody, then I say we must not try to delude ourselves and, still more, we must not try to delude small weak nations into thinking that they will be protected by the League against aggression and acting accordingly when we know that nothing of the kind can be expected." [18]

On March 11, Schuschnigg, in the face of two ultimatums, was compelled first to cancel the plebiscite and then to hand over the chancellorship to the Nazi Ministry of Interior, Dr. Artur von Seyss-Inquart. The latter, who had been in continual telephonic communication with Berlin, now issued a statement that had been dictated from Berlin and that requested the German government "to send in German troops as soon as possible . . . to restore peace and order . . . and to prevent bloodshed." Because of a misunderstanding, the troops actually crossed the border two hours before the request was made. On March 13, decrees from Berlin and Vienna declared Austria a part of Germany, and the next day Hitler made his triumphant entry into the land of his birth. Thus Austria was taken over by telephone; the event was not mentioned in the League of Nations.

VII. END OF CZECHOSLOVAKIA

With Austria safely annexed, Hitler turned against the neighboring state of Czechoslovakia, a larger and much stronger country, with an efficient modern army and a considerable industrial establishment, as well as the only surviving democratic institutions in East-Central Europe (see Chapter 22, section II). But the presence of a three-million German minority in the Sudeten borderlands made Czechoslovakia vulnerable to Nazi propaganda and subversion. The fact is that the Sudeten Germans had been treated far more liberally than other minorities in Europe, so that they had remained relatively contented and quiet. After Hitler came to power, Nazi agents set to work, and their agitation, combined with the discontent arising from heavy unemployment due to the Depression, turned most of the German minority against Prague.

With the *Anschluss,* the Sudeten problem suddenly became a serious menace for Czechoslovakia. The country was now surrounded on three sides by the enlarged Reich. Even more serious were certain indications that the British and French governments were ready to abandon Czechoslovakia as they had Austria. On March 24, Chamberlain had declared in the Commons that he could not pledge assistance to Czechoslovakia, or to France if she went to the aid of Czechoslovakia, because British interests "are not concerned in the same degree as they are in the case of France and Belgium." France, in contrast to Britain, was bound by treaty obligations to help Czechoslovakia in case of unprovoked aggression. But the French generals were warning that their army could not fight beyond the national frontiers since the entire military establishment was geared to the defensive Maginot Line fortifications. Thus the French government was theoretically bound to honor its treaty commitments, but it was actually far from willing to do so, and when the showdown came, it flatly refused.

The Czechoslovak crisis began on September 12, when Hitler delivered an inflammatory speech in which he violently attacked President Beneš for his "persecution" of the Sudeten Germans, and warned that, "if these tortured creatures can find no rights and no help themselves, they will get both from us." Hitler was supported in his demands by Lord Runciman, a wealthy British businessman having no experience in Central European affairs, who had been sent by Chamberlain to Czechoslovakia as his personal "investigator and mediator." Runciman now reported that "a very large majority of the inhabitants desire amalgamation with Germany" [an unproven assumption since the Sudeten Nazis had hitherto demanded autonomy rather than secession, and had won the support of the Sudeten Germans with this program] and he accordingly recommended secession for the areas with "important German majorities," and local autonomy for those where the German minority was "not so important."

Such was the background of the famous Berchtesgaden meeting of Chamberlain and Hitler where Czechoslovakia's fate was decided. The meeting was precipitated by widespread rioting on the part of the Sudeten Germans

546

following Hitler's speech. The Prague government proclaimed martial law, Nazi leaders fled to German, and Hitler concentrated troops along Czechoslovakia's frontier. Chamberlain feared that if Hitler actually invaded, a chain reaction might be unleashed that would embroil France and ultimately Britain. To avert this danger, Chamberlain, in agreement with Premier Daladier, proposed to Hitler a personal conference. The latter accepted, and Chamberlain arrived at Berchtesgaden on September 15.

Hitler baldly set forth his demand for annexation of the Sudeten areas on the basis of self-determination, and indicated his readiness "to risk a world war" to attain his end. Chamberlain returned home and persuaded first his own cabinet, and then the French, to accept Hitler's terms. The two governments in turn urged acceptance upon the Czechoslovak government; when the latter resisted, they brought every pressure to bear, including the threat of desertion. Prague finally capitulated on September 21, in return for an Anglo-French guarantee for the new frontier.

The next day Chamberlain flew to Godesberg in the belief that he only needed to work out with Hitler the technical details for the transfer of the territories. Instead, the Führer made new demands: immediate surrender of the predominantly German areas without waiting for plebiscites and without any removal or destruction of military or economic establishments. In addition, Hitler now supported territorial claims on Czechoslovakia made by Poland and Hungary.

These new demands precipitated an acute international crisis. Czechoslovakia ordered full mobilization, France called up 600,000 reservists, while the Soviet foreign minister, Maxim Litvinov, declared on September 21 before the League Assembly: "We intend to fulfill our obligations under the Pact, and together with France to afford assistance to Czechoslovakia by the ways open to us."

"This public and unqualified declaration," as Churchill pointed out, was treated by the Western powers with "indifference—not to say disdain." Instead, they acted on Mussolini's suggestion for a four-power conference of Britain, France, Germany, and Italy. The meetings were held in Munich on September 29, and without either Czech or Soviet participation, it was decided that Hitler should be granted all his demands, the only modifications being the face-saving provisions that the Sudeten lands should be occupied in stages and that the final delimitation of the frontier should be determined by an international commission.

As Churchill pointed out in the Commons: "All that the Prime Minister has gained for Czechoslovakia has been that the German dictator, instead of snatching the victuals from the table, has been content to have them served to him course by course." Yet the fact remains that the Munich surrender was popular with the masses in both Britain and France. Chamberlain and Daladier were hailed as peacemakers by enthusiastic crowds. Loud cheers greeted Chamberlain when he declared "I believe it is peace in our time." Hitler was gratefully believed when he avowed, "This is the last territorial claim I have to make in Europe." The events of the next year were to prove with cataclysmic finality the worth of such statements.

The first sign that further demands were in the offing was the gradual taking of substantial border regions of the Czechoslovak state. In accordance with the provisions reached at Munich, an international commission was appointed to determine the new frontiers. It soon became apparent that, despite their commitments, Britain and France had no interest in the proceedings of the commission. Accordingly, no plebiscites were held, and the decisions were made by two German generals who were members of the commission. In the end, Germany acquired 10,000 square miles of Czechoslovak territory with a population of 3,500,000, of whom about one-fifth were Czechs. At the same time, Poland seized the Teschen area with its rich coal fields, while Hungary occupied generous portions of Slovakia and Ruthenia. The truncated Czechoslovak state now disintegrated, with Germany's help, into three fragments: an autonomous Slovakia, an autonomous Ruthenia, and the Czech provinces of Bohemia and Moravia.

The finale came in March, 1939, when the puppet heads of the Czech and Slovak lands were summoned to Berlin to hear from Hitler the dissolution of their respective states; on March 15, German troops entered Prague. Bohemia and Moravia were declared a protectorate of the Reich, and Slovakia was also placed under German protection. Simultaneously, the Hungarians were allowed by Hitler to invade and annex Ruthenia in the east. So ended the state of Czechoslovakia, as well as the illusion that Hitler's objective was simply the redemption of German-populated lands. The partitioning of Czechoslovakia with its predominantly Slavic population was a rude awakening for those who had taken the Führer at his word. Chamberlain was particularly shocked, for as an orthodox British businessman, he had assumed that Hitler would keep his pledge that he had no further territorial ambitions in Europe. The breaking of this promise forced Chamberlain, as well as Daladier, to painfully reappraise their policy and to take a firmer stand when Hitler now turned upon Poland.

VIII. Coming of War

With Austria and Czechoslovakia taken, and with Spain and Hungary in the Axis camp, it was becoming apparent that the Western powers and the Soviet Union needed to work together in order to stem further aggression. "The key to a Grand Alliance," wrote Churchill, "was an understanding with Russia." The Russian government, on its part, was more than ready for such an "understanding." On March 18, it informed Berlin that it refused to recognize the partitioning of Czechoslovakia. Three days later, the Soviet government proposed a six-power conference (Britain, France, Russia, Poland, Rumania, and Turkey) to consider measures against future aggression. London replied that the proposal was "premature," and so it was not pursued further. In a private letter of March 26, Chamberlain gave the reasons for his negative response:

> I must confess to the most profound distrust of Russia. I have no belief whatever in her ability to maintain an effective offensive, even if she wanted to. And I distrust her motives, which seem to me to have little connection with our ideas of liberty, and to be concerned only with getting everyone else by the ears. Moreover, she is both hated and sus-

pected by many of the smaller states, notably by Poland, Rumania and Finland.[19]

In the same month, however, Hitler forced Lithuania to hand over the city of Memel, and he sent stiff demands to Warsaw concerning Danzig and the Polish Corridor. Faced by the prospect of limitless German expansion, Chamberlain, on March 31, pledged Anglo-French aid to the Poles in the case of "any action which clearly threatened Polish independence." A week later this was expanded into a pact of mutual assistance. The next move of the Axis was Italy's invasion and conquest of Albania, which began on April 7. Again Britain and France countered by pledging on April 13 full support to Rumania and Greece in the event that their independence was clearly threatened. The following month, Anglo-Turkish and Franco-Turkish mutual assistance pacts were signed.

These commitments to various East European countries represented a revolutionary departure in British foreign policy. Half a year earlier, Chamberlain had refused to lift a finger in behalf of Czechoslovakia because it was a "faraway country" and no vital British interests were involved. Now he was promising to go to the aid of countries that were even more remote and inaccessible, and where no greater British interests were at stake. In fact, their very inaccessibility made his promises worthless unless Britain acted in concert with the Soviet Union. As Churchill declared in the Commons on May 19, "Without an effective eastern front, there can be no satisfactory defence of our interests in the West, and without Russia there can be no effective eastern front." [20] Chamberlain finally opened negotiations with the Russians on April 15.

By this time, there was so much distrust on both sides that little headway was made. The Western leaders were still beset by the doubts and fears voiced earlier by Chamberlain concerning the effectiveness of the Red army, the motives of the Soviet leaders, and the reactions of Russia's neighbors. Likewise, Stalin's doubts had been steadily mounting with the successive Axis triumphs in Spain, Austria, and Czechoslovakia. More and more, he suspected that the basic aim of Western diplomacy was to divert German expansion eastward against the Soviet Union, a suspicion that manifested itself in his abandonment of the Spanish Republic in mid-1938 and in his replacement on May 3, 1939 of Litvinov, the indefatigable supporter of the League of Nations, with Vyacheslav M. Molotov, the grimly impassive Party veteran.

This mutual distrust aborted the negotiations between the Soviet Union and the two Western powers during the summer of 1939, with the question as to which side was responsible for this failure remaining a matter of dispute to the present day. Two American historians have concluded, "All in all, the Soviet policy in this latter phase was one of shameless deception." [21] By contrast, a British historian maintains, "However one spins the crystal and tries to look into the future from the point of view of 23 August 1939 [the German-Soviet Nonaggression Pact], it is difficult to see what other course Soviet Russia could have followed." [22] Perhaps there is substantial truth in each of these estimates, since there was so much mutual suspicion that both sides not only contemplated the possibility of a deal with Hitler but also took steps in that direction.

On the surface, both Russia and the Western powers favored the organization of a "Peace Front." However, given the current atmosphere, this was easier said than done. For example, on May 31, Molotov declared that no Peace Front was possible unless Britain and France accepted the elementary principle of reciprocity and equal obligations. Specifically, he demanded that the border states of the Soviet Union—Finland and the three Baltic countries—must be given the same guarantees as had been extended to Poland, Greece, Rumania, and Turkey. But the Baltic states had concluded nonaggression pacts with Germany and refused any Soviet-Western guarantees. London took the position that this ended the possibility of guarantees, whereas the Russians interpreted it as legalistic quibbling and evading of the issue. Likewise, the Poles refused to agree to allow the Red army to operate on Polish territory in case of war. Soviet aid, they insisted, should be limited to the providing of war materials. From the Polish viewpoint this was understandable, but the Soviet Marshal Voroshilov retorted, "Just as the British and American troops in the past World War would have been unable to participate in military collaboration with the French armed forces if they had no possibility of operating in French territory, the Soviet armed forces could not participate in military collaboration with armed forces of France and Great Britain if they are not allowed access to Polish territory." [23]

Behind this sparring was the gnawing suspicion in London that the real objective of the Soviets was to obtain legal justification for marching into Poland and the Baltic states at their pleasure; it was reinforced when the Russians insisted that the guarantee to the Baltic states should provide for cases of indirect as well as direct aggression. This meant that the Soviet Union would take immediate action if a change of government in a Baltic state seemed to favor an aggressor. To London, such an arrangement represented an intolerable invitation to Soviet expansionism.

The Russians, on their part, feared that if they agreed to go to war in the event of an attack on Poland, and could not send their army into Polish territory to meet the advancing Germans, the latter would quickly overrun Poland and reach the Soviet frontier. Would Britain and France then wage serious war against Germany, or would they sit back and leave the Soviet Union to face the onslaught alone? Their apprehension was strengthened when, in July, two representatives of Chamberlain, acting on his instructions, broached to a German official in London the possibility of a British-German non-aggression pact that would enable Britain to rid herself of her commitments to Poland. Thus Chamberlain, who was not very happy about the guarantee to Poland, and was even less happy about the negotiations with the Soviet Union, was feeling out the Germans with a view to reviving his appeasement policy. The German government showed no interest in these British advances, but they undoubtedly served to confirm the Kremlin's suspicion that Chamberlain was interested basically in isolating the Soviet Union and pushing Hitler eastward.

All of this was behind Stalin's fateful decision to turn to his hitherto mortal Axis enemies. In mid-August, he informed the Führer that he was ready for negotiations. Molotov talked with the German foreign minister, Joachim von Ribbentrop, as one realist to another. On August 23, they announced the diplomatic revolution that shook the world. The sworn enemies had signed a nonaggression pact and agreed to remain neutral if either were attacked by a third power. Significantly enough, the pact did not contain the so-called "escape clause," characteristic of Soviet nonaggression pacts with other countries, that would render the agreement inoperative if either party committed aggression against a third state. Perhaps this omission was related to a secret protocol in the pact stipulating that in the event of "a territorial or political rearrangement," Lithuania and western Poland were to come under the German sphere of influence, and the remainder of Poland, together with Finland, Estonia, Latvia, and Bessarabia, were to fall to the Russian sphere.

Now that he was protected on his eastern flank, Hitler felt free to strike. On August 25, he ordered his army to begin the invasion of Poland at 5:45 the next morning. In doing so, Hitler hoped that the Western powers, deprived of Russian support, would refrain from attempting to go to the help of Poland. But on the contrary, on the very same day that Hitler issued his orders, British government representatives officially signed the alliance pact with Poland. At the same time, Hitler heard that Mussolini had decided he would not fight, at least for the time being. These two setbacks persuaded Hitler that a temporary retreat was necessary, and during the evening of August 25, he countermanded his invasion order.

The Nazi leader now waited hopefully for another diplomatic Munich. During the following days, proposals for a variety of compromises, mediations, and plebiscites emanated from the Foreign Offices of Europe; none of these last minute efforts produced concrete results. Meanwhile, the German generals were reminding Hitler that only one month remained before the autumn rains would make tank maneuvers impossible on the Polish plains. Accordingly, on August 31, the Führer issued the final orders to march. At the same time, he published a rather moderate sixteen-point proposal for the Polish government to consider; this was merely for the record. Before the proposal had been transmitted to Warsaw, Hitler announced that it had been rejected, and with this hocus-pocus, he sought to justify the onslaught upon Poland that now took place. Early in the morning of September 1, 1939, without a declaration of war, German troops, tanks, and planes crossed Poland's frontier all along the line. On September 3, both Britain and France declared war on Germany. Mussolini, despite his oratory about the Axis "pact of steel," remained neutral. World War II had begun.*

SUGGESTED READING

General surveys of the diplomacy of this decade from various viewpoints are provided by D. E. Lee, *Ten Years: The World on the Road to War, 1930–1940* (Boston: Houghton, 1942); G. M. Gathorne-Hardy, *A Short History of International Affairs, 1920–1939,* 4th ed. (New York: Oxford Univ., 1950); D. F. Fleming, *The Cold War and Its Origins, 1917–1960* (New York: Doubleday, 1961), 2 vols.; and A. J. P. Taylor, *The Origins of the Second World War* (London: Hamilton, 1961).

For the background to Japanese expansionism, see D. M. Brown, *Nationalism in Japan* (Berkeley, Univ. of California, 1955); Y. C. Maxon, *Control of Japa-*

* See "The Origins of the Second World War," *EMM,* No. 156.

nese Foreign Policy: A Study of Civil-Military Rivalry, 1930–1945 (Berkeley, Univ. of California, 1957). Details concerning the actual expansion are available in J. M. Maki, *Conflict and Tension in the Far East: Key Documents, 1894–1960* (Seattle: Univ. of Washington, 1961); D. Borg, *The United States and the Far Eastern Crisis of 1933–38* (Cambridge: Harvard Univ., 1964); and F. C. Jones, *Japan's New Order in East Asia: Its Rise and Fall, 1937–1945* (New York: Oxford Univ., 1954). The Italian invasion of Ethiopia is considered in the survey by M. H. H. Macartney and P. Cremona, *Italy's Foreign and Colonial Policy, 1914–1937* (London: Oxford Univ., 1938) and in the sprightly account by G. Salvemini, *Prelude to World War II* (London: Gollancz, 1953). For the Spanish Civil War, see G. Brenan, *The Spanish Labrynth: An Account of the Social and Political Background of the Civil War* (New York: Macmillan, 1943); J. M. Sanchez, *Reform and Reaction: The Politico-Religious Background of the Spanish Civil War* (Chapel Hill: Univ. of North Carolina, 1964); D. A. Puzzo, *Spain and the Great Powers, 1936–1941* (New York: Columbia Univ., 1963); and the well-written account of the war itself by T. Hugh, *The Spanish Civil War* (New York: Harper, 1961).

551

The rapid drift to war after the Ethiopian invasion and the outbreak of the Spanish Civil War is described from various viewpoints by F. W. Deakin, *The Brutal Friendship: Mussolini, Hitler and the Fall of Italian Fascism* (London: Weidenfeld, 1962); I. Kirkpatrick, *Mussolini: A Study in Power* (New York: Hawthorn, 1964); M. Beloff, *The Foreign Policy of Soviet Russia, 1929–1941* (London: Oxford Univ., 1948), 2 vols.; G. F. Kennan, *Russia and the West* (Boston: Little, 1960); A. Wolfers, *Britain and France Between Two Wars* (New York: Harcourt, 1940); E. H. Carr, *German-Soviet Relations Between the Two World Wars* (Baltimore: Hopkins, 1951); L. B. Namier, *Diplomatic Prelude, 1938–1939* (London: Macmillan, 1948); W. Evans, *Alliance Against Hitler: The Origins of the Franco-Soviet Pact* (Durham: Duke Univ., 1963); J. Gehl, *Austria, Germany and the Anschluss, 1931–1938* (New York: Oxford Univ., 1963); G. Shepherd, *The Rape of Austria* (New York: Macmillan, 1963); and K. Eubank, *Munich* (Norman: Univ. of Oklahoma, 1963). See also the collection of readings and extensive bibliography in J. L. Snell, *The Outbreak of the Second World War: Design or Blunder?* (Boston: Heath, 1962).

Finally, there are the memoirs or published collections of the papers of numerous personalities of the period, some of the more significant being those of Winston S. Churchill, Anthony Eden, Neville Chamberlain (K. Feiling), Kurt von Schuschnigg, Paul Joseph Goebbels, Joachim von Ribbentrop, Galeazzo Ciano, Georges Bonnet, and Pierre-Etienne Flandin. For the Soviet side, see J. Degras, ed., *Soviet Documents on Foreign Policy* (New York: Oxford Univ., 1951–1953), 3 vols.; the interpretation by the Soviet diplomat, I. Maisky, *Who Helped Hitler?* (London: Hutchinson, 1964); and the polemical pamphlet *Falsificators of History* (Moscow: Soviet Information Bureau, 1948) the latter being a reply to the American government publication, *Nazi-Soviet Relations, 1939–1941: Documents from the Archives of the German Foreign Office* (Washington: Department of State, 1948).

*The next World War
will be fought with stones.*

ALBERT EINSTEIN

World War II:
Global Repercussions

In signing the pact with Stalin, Hitler's aim was to secure Russia's neutrality while he disposed of Poland. Then he could, and did, marshal his armed forces against Britain and France. He declared privately at the time, "Let us think of the pact as securing our rear." As for Russia, that country also was on his list of future victims. "At present she is not dangerous," he stated. "We can oppose Russia only when we are free in the West. For the next year or two, the present situation will remain." [1] Thus, Hitler from the beginning had charted his schedule of conquest: first Poland, then the West, and finally Russia. He adhered to this schedule, and in doing so determined the course of World War II until Russia and the West became strong enough to seize the initiative.

The Second World War, like the First, began as a European conflict precipitated by the issue of minorities in Eastern Europe. During the first two years the campaigns were waged on European battlefields. Then Japan's attack on Pearl Harbor in 1941 transformed World War II into a global struggle, just as America's intervention in 1917 had transformed World War I. At this point, however, the similarity between the two wars ends. With Japan's lightning conquest of the entire East and Southeast Asia, World War II came to involve much more of the globe than the preceding war had involved. The two wars differed fundamentally in the strategy and weapons employed. During the first war, the defense, based on trenches and machine-gun nests, proved superior to the offense; during the second war the offense, based on tanks and planes, proved stronger than the defense. This explains the extraordinary fluidity of battle lines that characterized the later struggle. Whole countries, and even continents, changed hands back and forth in striking contrast to the bloody stalemate on the western front between 1914 and 1918.*

I. European Phase of the War

Partitioning of Poland

In Poland the Germans demonstrated for the first time the deadly effectiveness of their new type of *Blitzkrieg,* or "lightning war." First came waves of dive bombers, or *Stukas,* blasting communication lines and spreading terror and confusion. Then followed the armored tank divisions, or *Panzers,* smashing holes in the enemy lines, penetrating deeply into the rear, destroying transportation and communication facilities, and cutting the opposing forces into ribbons. Finally the lighter motorized divisions and the infantry moved in for the "mopping up" of the splintered and battered enemy forces, supported where necessary by air and artillery cover.

Unfortunate Poland was a "set-up" for this type of warfare. The country was almost entirely a great plains area, with few natural obstacles to hinder the tanks. The Polish army was hopelessly obsolete, possessing twelve cavalry brigades fully horsed, booted, and spurred, but only a single armored brigade. Furthermore, the Polish High Command had spread out its forces thinly along the entire frontier in the vain hope of defending all the national territory. With little difficulty the *Panzers* broke through at selected points, cutting supply lines and encircling the Polish infantry divisions, while the *Luftwaffe* bombed its targets with feeble opposition from the small Polish air force. The resulting confusion allowed only two-thirds of Poland's army of 1,700,000 men to be mobilized, and less than half of these were able to reach their concentration areas.

Within ten days the campaign had been virtually decided. The German tank-plane teams raced through the Polish countryside against declining resistance. The speed of the German advance forced Stalin to move in order to take over the territories he had staked out in his pact with Hitler. On September 17, the Red Army crossed over into Eastern Poland, and two days later established contact with the triumphant Germans. On September 27, Warsaw fell, the Polish government leaders fleeing to Rumania and thence to France. Their country was partitioned two days later, the Germans taking 37,000 square miles with 22 million people, and the Russians 77,000 square miles with a population of 13 million. Within less than a month one of the largest countries of Europe had disappeared completely from the map.

The Soviet government now took advantage of the secret protocol of the Moscow Pact to strengthen its strategic position in the Baltic area. In

* See *"Blitzkrieg," EMM,* No. 157.

September and October, 1939, it compelled Estonia, Latvia, and Lithuania to accept Russian military bases on their territories. Lithuania, by way of compensation, received the long-desired district and city of Vilna, hitherto a part of Poland. The Soviets next demanded from Finland certain territorial cessions in the Karelian Isthmus and around Petsamo on the Arctic Ocean. Although the Russians offered substantial territorial compensation elsewhere, the Finns refused, for it would have meant the loss of their Mannerheim Line, a formidable fortification system in the Karelian region. Since these fortifications were within artillery range of Leningrad, the Russians pressed their demands, and finally on November 30, the Red Army attacked.

Finland appealed to the League of Nations, and that body expelled the Soviet Union from membership, the only state, it may be noted, to have been so treated. The Finns resisted the Russian onslaught with unexpected success, repulsing repeated attacks on the Mannerheim Line. Public opinion in the West was overwhelmingly behind Finland. Volunteers, especially from Sweden, joined the embattled Finns, and by February, 1940, the British and French governments were seriously considering the dispatch of an expeditionary force to help Finland. By this time, however, the Russians, who had grossly underestimated Finnish strength, were launching a major offensive with regular forces rather than local units. They cracked the Mannerheim Line with heavy artillery bombardment and by mid-March had forced the Finns to sue for peace. The ensuing treaty yielded the Russians somewhat more territory than they originally demanded, including the Petsamo region, the port of Viipuri, several islands in the Gulf of Finland, and a naval base at Hanko.

Perhaps the chief significance of these Russian moves against Finland and the other Baltic states was that they reflected the rivalry and distrust that existed behind the façade of Russo-German cooperation. This was underscored by the evacuation to Germany, on Russia's insistence, of the Baltic Germans who for centuries had dominated urban centers such as Memel and Riga.

Conquest of Denmark and Norway

Meanwhile, the western front had been disconcertingly quiet. The British and the French had stood helplessly by while Poland was being partitioned. They could not enter the Baltic Sea which the Germans had sealed tight; their air forces were unable to operate across the breadth of the Reich; while their ground troops were confronted by the elaborate fortifications built by Hitler following his 1936 occupation of the Rhineland. Thus the French were forced to sit tight behind their Maginot Line, while the Germans made no move from behind their Siegfried Line or West Wall. Hitler took advantage of the stalemate to make peace overtures to the Western powers. He was promptly rebuffed, but the inactivity persisted, and the conflict was popularly dubbed the "phony" war, the *drôle de guerre,* the *Sitzkrieg.*

This surface calm proved deceptive. On April 9, 1940, the *Wehrmacht* suddenly erupted into action, sweeping through Denmark and making landings on the coast of Norway. The main objective was to gain control of the Norwegian fiords which could provide invaluable bases for German submarines and also safeguard the shipment of Swedish iron ore down the coast to

Germany. The Danes could offer no resistance, but the Norwegians, with
British support, fought back stubbornly. In the end, German control of the
skies proved decisive. By the end of April the Allies were forced to evacuate   555
the south and center of Norway. In the north, around the port of Narvik,
resistance continued for another month. But by early June France herself
was in mortal peril, so the Allied expeditionary forces sailed away, accompanied by the Norwegian government, which took refuge in London. The
Germans set up their own administration in Norway under the collaborationist
Quisling, whose name became a synonym for the self-seeking traitor.

Fall of France and the Low Countries

The Allied setback in Norway was soon dwarfed by the stunning *Blitzkrieg*
that overran France and the Low Countries in seven weeks. On May 10 the
Germans attacked Holland and Belgium, and two days later France. The
Dutch defense collapsed in five days. The Belgians held out longer, but by
May 28 King Leopold surrendered in person, and the Belgian army capitu-
lated. Meanwhile the Germans had skirted the northern end of the Maginot
Line, which had never been extended to the sea, and drove through the
Ardennes Forest, smashing a fifty-mile breach in the French lines at Sedan.
The *Panzer* divisions now raced westward through Amiens to Abbéville on
the English Channel, reaching it on May 21.

The German breakthrough left the British, French, and Belgian forces in
the north cut off from the main French armies. The French High Command
attempted counterthrusts to sever the ribbonlike salient that the German
tanks had cut across northern France. But the general confusion and stupe-
faction prevented effective action, and the German mechanized forces continued to fan out along the Channel coast. The Allied armies in Flanders,
mostly British, retreated to Dunkirk, the only port still free of the enemy. The
prospects for evacuation appeared hopeless, with the harbor half destroyed
and only a few miles of open beach. It was hoped that perhaps 45,000 men
could be saved; in fact, 366,000 were ferried back to Britain. This "Miracle
of Dunkirk" was made possible partly by Hitler's decision to regroup his
forces to the south for the crucial struggle for France rather than to strive for
complete victory in what had become a peripheral operation. Equally significant was the mettle of the British Admiralty, which assembled a motley
rescue fleet of 850 vessels of every vintage and description, including river
tugs, motor launches, fishing boats, and seaside paddle steamers. The Royal
Air Force covered the evacuation, scoring its first victory over the *Luftwaffe*.
Yet the British were forced to leave behind all their precious equipment, as
well as 13,000 dead and 40,000 prisoners.

With the completion of the Dunkirk evacuation on June 4, the agony of
France began. On the following day the German forces resumed their advance
southward. By June 13 Paris was occupied, undefended and abandoned by
the government. Two days later the Germans were in Verdun, where they had
suffered bloody defeat in 1916. By this time the French Premier, Paul Rey-
naud (who had succeeded Daladier in late March) was thoroughly demoralized and under the influence of appeasers within his cabinet. Originally he
had planned to move his government to North Africa, but on June 16 he
wearily resigned the premiership to Marshal Pétain. It was this "hero of

Verdun" who, ironically, now sued for peace. On June 22, at Compiègne, the site of the signing of the 1918 German armistice, the French accepted the severe armistice terms, including release of all German prisoners of war, disbandment of French military forces, surrender of French warships, and occupation by Germany of slightly over half of France, including the principal industrial and food-producing areas and the entire French coastline down to the Spanish border.

The staggering impact of the German *Blitzkrieg* is reflected in the incredibly low casualty figures. During the entire campaign the French lost about 100,000 men, the other Allies 20,000, and the Germans 45,000. These losses were less than half those sustained in single offensives during World War I. This speedy collapse by what was considered to be the strongest Western power came naturally as a most painful shock. Charges of treason and cowardice were leveled in explanation for the great disaster. Though these charges were not altogether unwarranted, other factors appear to have been more decisive. One was the effect of the Russo-German pact, which enabled Hitler to concentrate his forces on a single front. France in 1914 had been substantially aided by the Tsarist armies operating on the eastern front; now France had to face Germany alone, with relatively slight support from Britain. Perhaps most important was the German superiority in several fields, especially in the number of planes and tanks, and in the development of the new *Blitzkrieg* technique. The French High Command was handicapped not only by inadequate equipment, but even more by its inability to utilize effectively the men and materials it did possess.*

Battle of Britain

After Dunkirk and after the fall of France, Hitler not unnaturally assumed that Britain would see reason and would come to terms. But he failed to reckon with the British people and with Winston Churchill. A born fighter and maverick, Churchill was the descendant of Marlborough and the son of Lord Randolph Churchill and of Jennie Jerome, daughter of a former proprietor of *The New York Times*. Before he was twenty-six years old Churchill had already seen action in Cuba, on the northwest Indian frontier, in the Sudan, and in South Africa, where, during the Boer War, he was captured and then made his escape. In the First World War his reputation was almost ruined by the failure of the Gallipoli Expedition, of which he had been the prime supporter. In the late 1930's he conducted almost singlehanded a campaign for rearmament, even though this was an unpopular cause at the time. It was typical of him to refuse to count popularity by avoiding thorny issues or by compromising. Thus he took the lead in demanding a firm stand against Axis aggression during the years of appeasement under Chamberlain.

This record of courage and forthrightness made him the natural successor to Chamberlain when the latter was forced to resign on May 10, 1940, because of the bungling of aid to Norway and the general failure to mobilize the country for a war of survival. Churchill formed an all-party cabinet, including the Labour party leaders, Clement Attlee and Ernest Bevin, as well as the Conservative Anthony Eden, who had resigned as Foreign Minister in 1938 in pro-

*See "Fall of France," *EMM,* No. 158.

test against the current appeasement policies. From the beginning, Churchill proved himself an incomparable war leader. With characteristic resoluteness and audacity he told his people—and the world: "We shall fight on the beaches. We shall fight on the landing grounds. We shall fight on the fields and in the streets. We shall fight in the hills; we shall never surrender." His countrymen responded in kind, and buckled down with fortitude and self-confidence to the grim task that lay ahead.

Meanwhile Hitler was marking time, unsure what the next step should be. The unexpectedly rapid fall of France had caught him by surprise. First he tried to make a deal with the British, for whom he always had genuine respect. When his overtures were ignored, he issued on July 16, 1940, his directive "Sea Lion" for the invasion of the island. But time was needed to organize an amphibious operation for which the German High Command had neither the proper equipment nor—excepting Norway—the necessary experience. And much time was wasted in acrimonious debate amongst the German service chiefs over the formidable technical problems of the Channel crossing. They were all agreed, however, that "Sea Lion" would be impossible without command of the air. Accordingly, Reichmarshal Hermann Göring unleashed his *Luftwaffe,* confident that it could subdue Britain by air attack alone, without resort to a hazardous sea crossing.

The ensuing air assault developed into the critical Battle of Britain, one of the major turning points of World War II. In this epic struggle in the skies, the *Luftwaffe* had the advantage of numbers—2,670 planes against the Royal Air Force's 1,475. But the RAF Spitfires and Hurricanes were more advanced planes, because Britain had gone into mass production a couple years later than Germany. The British also had the use of radar, a new invention that enabled enemy aircraft to be "sighted" fifty to a hundred miles before reaching their targets. Even so, the almost 2 to 1 numerical superiority of the *Luftwaffe* might have proven decisive if it had concentrated on the RAF fields and fighter forces. Instead, Göring kept shifting his targets: first the southeast ports and Channel shipping, then the RAF fields and radar stations, and finally, in September, 1940, London, Coventry, and other industrial centers. For a month these cities were bombed daily, but loss of life was surprisingly light, and industrial production was not seriously affected. Public morale, far from being broken, was, according to doctors, raised and strengthened by the ordeal. Furthermore, Göring's switch to the cities was tacit admission that he was unable to destroy the RAF fighter strength. On September 17, Hitler gave orders that "Sea Lion" was to be postponed until the following spring. In actual fact, the plan for the invasion of Britain had been shelved forever. A few thousand British and Dominion fighter pilots, with a scattering of Poles, Czechs, French, and Belgians, had successfully repulsed the *Luftwaffe*. "Never in the field of human conflict," said Churchill at the height of the battle, "was so much owed by so many to so few." *

Conquest of the Balkans

On July 31, 1940, two weeks before the Battle of Britain, Hitler held a conference with his top army and navy commanders. He was advised that a

* See "Battle of Britain," *EMM,* No. 159.

558

successful invasion of Britain that fall was highly improbable. Hitler thereupon made his momentous decision to invade Russia the following spring. He reached his decision through the following reasoning:

> In the event that invasion [of England] does not take place, our action must be directed to eliminate all factors that let England hope for a change in the situation. . . . *Britain's hope lies in Russia and the United States.* If Russia drops out of the picture America, too, is lost for Britain, because elimination of Russia would tremendously increase *Japan's power* in the Far East. . . . *Russia is the factor on which Britain is relying the most.* . . . *With Russia smashed, Britain's last hope will be shattered.* Germany then will be master of Europe and the Balkans.
>
> *Decision: Russia's destruction must therefore be made a part of this struggle. Spring 1941.*
>
> *The sooner Russia is crushed, the better.* Attack achieves its purpose only if Russian state can be shattered to its roots with one blow. . . . If we start in May 41, we would have five months to finish the job in.[2]

Preparing for the projected invasion of Russia, Hitler sent troops into Rumania in October, 1940. He informed Moscow that these were "training troops" dispatched to "instruct" the Rumanian army. But at the same time a secret German order stated that the "real task" of the troops was to prepare the Rumanian army to participate in the forthcoming invasion of the Soviet Union.

At this point, when Hitler was occupying Rumania, Mussolini launched his blundering invasion of Greece. *Il Duce,* who for long had fancied himself the dean of the dictators, had become jealous of the spectacularly successful *Führer.* Although formally allied by the Axis Pact, Hitler had gone on from triumph to triumph without consulting or notifying his Italian partner. "Hitler always faces me with a *fait accompli*," complained Mussolini to his son-in-law and foreign minister, Count Ciano. "This time I am going to pay him back in his own coin. He will find out from the papers that I have occupied Greece." [3]

What Mussolini assumed would be an effortless occupation proved in fact to be a humiliating fiasco. On October 28, 1940, Italian troops crossed over from Albania into Greece, expecting a triumphal procession to Athens. But after pushing some distance across the Greek-Albanian frontier, they suffered a decisive defeat at the battle of Metsovo on November 11. The crack Italian Alpine "Iulia" division, counting on its tanks and supporting air force, had advanced along the valleys toward Metsovo without bothering to occupy some higher positions to their rear. Greek mountain regiments made a forced night march and occupied the heights overlooking the Italians in the valleys. At dawn they swooped down, and, after some hard fighting, the Italians broke and fled.

The Metsovo battle served as the model for future Greek victories. Taking advantage of the difficulties of the ponderous Italian armored divisions in the mountains of Epirus, the Greeks invariably made for the high ground and from there cut off and surrounded the enemy below. By mid-November they had driven the Italians back across the frontier into Albania. In the following weeks they captured the large Albanian towns of Koritsa, Argyrokastron, and Porto Edda. For a while it appeared that Mussolini might even have to endure a Dunkirk in the Adriatic.

At this point Mussolini was rescued from his mortifying predicament by the intervention of his Axis ally. Hitler was not motivated by sentiments of loyalty to his partner; in fact, he was furious that the war had been extended to the Balkans. But he could not sit back and watch the Italians flounder, particularly because the British were landing air units in Greece. Furthermore, Molotov had demanded on November 25, 1940, that Germany recognize Soviet primacy in Bulgaria and in the Bosporus and Dardanelles. Hitler gave no reply; instead, he issued in December his directives for Operation Marita and Operation Barbarossa—directives that were to prove so fateful for the entire world. Marita called for "the occupation of the Aegean North coast by way of Bulgaria, and if necessary . . . the entire Greek mainland." Barbarossa stipulated that "The German Armed Forces must be prepared *to crush Soviet Russia in a quick campaign* even before the conclusion of the war against England. . . . Preparations are to be completed by May 15, 1941." [4]

In preparation for Marita, Hitler forced Bulgaria to accept the entry of German troops that had been massed across the Danube on Rumanian soil. When these troops appeared in Bulgaria in January, 1941, Churchill countered by dispatching troops to Greece, though at the cost of weakening General Wavell's current offensive in North Africa. Finally, the Yugoslav government was forced by a virtual ultimatum to accept a pact (March 25) aligning the country with the Axis Powers. But so unpopular was this capitulation that the government was overthrown the following night by a military coup. Enthusiastic crowds paraded in the streets of Belgrade shouting "Better War than the Pact."

Less than a fortnight later, on April 6, war did come. As in Poland and France, the *Panzer* divisions and the *Luftwaffe* swept everything before them. The mountainous terrain of the Balkan Peninsula did not prove an effective obstacle, as had been hoped, while the British ground and air units were too weak to halt the tide. By April 13, the Germans had entered Belgrade, and ten days later the British were evacuating their forces from southern Greece to Crete. The Germans then launched an airborne invasion of Crete, catching by surprise the British who did not expect an air attack from the Greek mainland 180 miles to the north. Though they suffered heavy losses, the Germans finally gained complete control of the island by the beginning of June.

Hitler now had a golden opportunity in the Mediterranean which he might have exploited with every chance of success and with the prospect of overrunning the entire Middle East. In addition to the triumph in the Balkans, his armies had won an equally impressive victory in North Africa under the able and energetic General Erwin Rommel. Wavell had gained the initial success in North Africa when, between December, 1940, and February, 1941, he pushed the Italians back from the Egyptian frontier to Tripolitania. Immediately thereafter the British forces were weakened by the withdrawals for the Greek campaign. At the same time the Germans rushed reinforcements to North Africa to bolster their Italian allies. British intelligence underestimated

560

the strength of these reinforcements, so that when Rommel attacked on March 31, 1941, he was able to sweep all before him. In less than a month he captured Benghazi, Bardia, and all of Cyrenaica.

The victories in the Balkans and in North Africa presented Hitler with the opportunity to execute a gigantic pincer operation upon the Suez through Libya and Egypt on the one side and Turkey and Syria on the other. But the *Führer* allowed this opportunity to pass because, as a German diplomat observed, Hitler was moving "along a mental one-way street against Russia." [5] Instead of exploiting the promising situation in the Middle East, he moved his divisions from the Balkans to the eastern front. When the mighty *Wehrmacht* finally crashed across the Soviet frontier on June 22, 1941, it was a precious five weeks behind schedule because of the Balkan campaign.

II. Global Phase of the War

Invasion of Russia

Stalin signed the pact with Hitler in August, 1939, for a variety of reasons, including deep distrust of the Western leaders and desire to gain time to strengthen his military and industrial establishments. He also calculated that sooner or later Germany and the Western powers would clash in a war of attrition, while Russia, thanks to the pact, would be free to remain aloof until it was profitable for her to intervene. "If war begins," he told his comrades, "we cannot simply sit back. *We will have to get into the fighting, but we must be the last to join in.* And we shall join so as to cast the decisive weight on to the scales, the weight that will tip the balance." [6] This strategy was shrewd, yet it boomeranged and came very close to destroying the Soviet state. It was based on the assumption that the German and Western forces were evenly matched and would decimate each other, leaving the Red Army the dominant force on the Continent. Instead, the *Wehrmacht* crushed all opposition with incredible ease, leaving Germany the master of the Continent and the Soviet Union isolated and imperiled.

Stalin was by no means the only one surprised by the swiftness and decisiveness of Hitler's victories. What is not understandable is why Stalin was caught unprepared by the German onslaught on June 22. According to Khrushchev's later testimony, Stalin simply refused to believe the growing evidence of German preparations. He ignored the repeated warnings of Winston Chuchill and of his own intelligence services. Instead, he continued to the last minute to feed Hitler's war machine with ever increasing quantities of provisions and of war materials. Why Stalin, the cynical realist, should have been so tragically blind in his relations with Hitler remains one of the bizarre mysteries of World War II.*

At first it seemed that Russia would collapse as ignominiously as had Poland and France. The *Panzer* divisions, in their now familiar fashion, smashed through the frontier defenses and drove deeply into the rear, encircling entire Soviet armies and taking hundred of thousands of prisoners. By the end of the year the *Wehrmacht* had penetrated 600 miles eastward, overrunning the most industralized and populous regions of the Soviet Union.

* See "Hitler Attacks Russia," *EMM,* No. 160.

One reason for the German triumph, apart from the important factor of surprise, was numerical preponderance at the outset. Hitler struck with an army of about three million as against approximately two million on the other side. The Russians, of course, had huge reserves to draw upon, but the *Luftwaffe* bombing made it difficult to utilize them promptly and efficiently. The German forces also had the telling advantage of battle experience under varied conditions in Poland, France, and the Balkans. In addition, recent Russian publications have revealed hitherto unsuspected weaknesses in the Soviet armed forces. A large part of the Red air fleet had been concentrated on small fields near the frontier, where most of it was destroyed on the very first day. The Red Army lacked sufficient antitank guns to cope with the massive *Panzer* onslaught that sometimes reached 100 tanks per kilometer. And whereas in 1941 most German infantrymen had Tommy guns, the Russians had only rifles. Finally it should be recalled that this was not a struggle between the Soviet Union and Germany, but rather between the Soviet Union and the European continent. This meant that the Red Army had to cope with substantial Finnish, Rumanian, and Hungarian forces as well as German, and that Soviet armament plants were in competition with those of France and Czechoslovakia as well as Germany. Thus whereas Soviet steel output in 1941 was almost equal to Germany's, it was considerably less than half that of Germany and the rest of the Continent.

Hitler's strategy was to advance all along the thousand-mile front from Finland to Rumania, and to push eastward to a line running from Leningrad to Moscow to Kharkov to Rostov. The Red Army was to be encircled and destroyed to the west of this line, so that the *Wehrmacht* would not need to overextend its lines to the Urals and beyond. Thanks to the factors indicated above, the Germans attained almost all their territorial objectives. They captured both Kharkov and Rostov, and almost completely encircled Moscow and Leningrad. In the latter city the daily ration was reduced to four ounces of more or less ersatz bread. One-third of the civilian population of nearly three million perished from starvation before the terrible winter was over.

Despite these impressive gains, the 1941 German campaign failed in its basic strategic objectives. Neither Moscow nor Leningrad was taken, while the Red Army, though badly mauled, remained intact. In fact, it was able on December 10 to launch a counteroffensive that broke the German pincers around Moscow and Leningrad, and also recaptured Rostov—the first city of any size that the *Wehrmacht* had taken and then been forced to surrender. Thus, despite its severe losses, the Red Army had done much better than expected. Nor was "General Winter" responsible for its survival, as is commonly assumed. During the first and greatest German attack on Moscow in October, the weather was unseasonably mild. Not until the second assault, after November 16, did the winter weather hamper the Germans; and it was equally destructive of the Russians' counteroffensive, which otherwise might have been more successful than it was.

Pearl Harbor

The Second World War was transformed from a European to a global conflict with the Japanese attack on Pearl Harbor on December 7, 1941. At the beginning of the war, almost all Americans were determined to remain neutral. President Roosevelt, like Woodrow Wilson, publicly expressed this determination; "there will be no blackout of peace," he declared to the nation on September 3, 1939. But Hitler's unexpected victories, and particularly the fall of France, compelled American policy makers to question whether neutrality automatically afforded protection against involvement. If Hitler were to conquer England and then gain control of the Atlantic—eventualities that seemed by no means improbable at the time—might not the New World be next on the schedule of conquest?

These considerations led Washington to conclude that the best way to avoid involvement in the war was to give all aid short of war to those still fighting Germany. This explains the steady drift of the United States from neutrality to nonbelligerency with the Destroyers-Bases Agreement (September 2, 1940), and from nonbelligerency to undeclared war with the Lend-Lease Act (March 11, 1941), the signing of the Atlantic Charter (August 12, 1941), and the orders (August–September, 1941) to provide naval escorts for all belligerent and neutral merchantmen between Newfoundland and Iceland, and to shoot on sight any Axis warships in those waters.

While striving to limit Axis expansion in the West, President Roosevelt also had attempted to restrain Japan from aggression in the Pacific. Successive Tokyo governments, however, became increasingly bellicose in response to what appeared to be golden opportunities provided by the course of events in Europe. Hitler's victories had left almost undefended the rich French, British, and Dutch possessions in East and Southeast Asia. Accordingly, on September 27, 1940, Japan signed the Tripartite Pact with Germany and Italy. This recognized the hegemony of Germany and Italy in Europe and of Japan in Asia, and called for full mutual aid if any of the signatories were attacked by the United States.

The Japanese, however, had no direct interest in the war in Europe. In pursuit of their own advantage, they concluded a treaty with Russia on April 13, 1941, in which each power pledged neutrality should the other "become the object of hostilities on the part of one or several third powers." When Hitler invaded Russia in June, 1941, he pressed Japan to join him and to attack from the east. The Japanese refused to oblige, distrusting German intentions in Asia. Furthermore, they perceived greener fields in Southeast Asia, which was seething with unrest and which offered obvious opportunity for them. By the summer of 1941 they had occupied bases in French Indochina, signed an alliance treaty with Thailand, and were demanding the oil and rubber output of the Dutch East Indies. The British were so hard-pressed in Europe that they had withdrawn from Shanghai, and maintained only feeble forces in Hong Kong and Singapore. Thus the entire East and Southeast Asia appeared ripe for plucking if only the United States would not intervene.

Japan's leaders were divided on the question of relations with the United States. The army was ready to challenge Britain, France, and the United States directly, but the navy, the diplomats, and the industrialists mostly held back. The turning point came with the resignation in October, 1941, of the Premier, Prince Fumimaro Konoye, who favored a settlement with the United States. He was succeeded by General Hideki Tojo, "Razor Brain," at the head of a cabinet of army and navy officers—a cabinet, it was said, that "smelled of gunpowder." Tojo decided to settle accounts with the United States, by diplomacy or by force, before the end of the year. The Japanese ambassador in Washington, Admiral Kichisaburo Nomura, joined by a special envoy, Saburo Kurusu, held an eleventh hour series of conversations with Secretary of State Cordell Hull. The positions taken by the two sides were so far apart that a compromise was out of the question.

Hull at this time knew of the day-to-day decisions of the Tokyo government because the Japanese radio code had been cracked. Accordingly, repeated "alert" warnings were sent to Pearl Harbor and to General Douglas MacArthur, commander of the United States armed forces in the Far East, stationed in the Philippines. The last warning was sent on December 7 from Washington to Pearl Harbor by General George C. Marshall, Chief of Staff. Static difficulties barred the use of the Army radio, so the message was sent instead through commercial channels. In Honolulu the telegram was given to a messenger boy who pedaled off on his bicycle. While he was on his way, a little after 7 A.M., Japanese bombs began to fall on the island. Within a few hours five of the eight battleships in Pearl Harbor had been destroyed, as well as three cruisers and three destroyers. At the same time another Japanese task force destroyed most of the United States Army's planes in the Philippines.

In conformity with the terms of the Tripartite Pact, Germany and Italy declared war on the United States. Thus America was fully involved in the war, both in Europe and in Asia. The acrimonious debate that had been carried on in Washington over war or peace was suddenly ended.* Speaking to a nation now united, the President proclaimed, "We are now in this war. We are in it all the way. Every single man, woman, and child is a partner in the most tremendous undertaking of our American history." America's role as partner was to become "the arsenal of the democracies." At the peak of output in 1943–44 this "arsenal" was producing one ship a day and one plane every five minutes; and during the six years of war it produced 87,000 tanks, 296,000 planes, and 53,000,000 tons of shipping.

1942: Year of Axis Triumphs

During the year 1942, Germany, Italy, and Japan were almost everywhere victorious. Great offensives overran large parts of Russia, North Africa, and the Pacific, like a huge three-taloned claw grasping the Eurasian hemisphere. At the same time, German submarines and surface craft were threatening Allied communication lines, their toll averaging about 400,000 tons a month in 1942.

The most spectacular triumphs were won by the Japanese, who quickly conquered a vast Pacific empire, stretching from the Aleutians to Australia, and from Guam to India.† The Japanese were successful partly because they struck at a time when opposition was virtually impossible. France and Holland were occupied, Britain was struggling desperately for sheer survival, and the United States was only starting to convert from a peace to a war economy. Thus, the Japanese moved into a vacuum and filled it rapidly and easily. The Western powers' traditional treatment of their colonial subjects

* See "Responsibility for Pearl Harbor," *EMM*, No. 161.
† See "Vacuum in Southeast Asia," *EMM*, No. 162.

564

as providers of raw materials and consumers of manufactured goods also contributed to Japan's success. Profitable though this arrangement may have been for the mother countries, it left the colonial territories economically stunted. Even India, with its vast resources and manpower, could not produce a single jeep or plane or landing craft. This meant that all basic war materials had to be transported several thousand miles from Europe or the United States. The traditional political policies of the colonial powers also boomeranged at this time of showdown: the average Indian or Burmese or Indonesian saw no reason why he should fight in defense of regimes that he regarded as alien and oppressive. Instead, he took a plague-on-both-your-houses attitude, when he did not actively welcome and assist the Japanese invaders. The latter shrewdly exploited this sentiment with slogans such as "Asia for the Asians." Significantly enough, the only serious resistance encountered by the Japanese was in the Philippines, which were to become an autonomous republic in 1946, and which possessed their own national army of 100,000 men.

Three days after Pearl Harbor the Japanese scored another victory when their land-based aircraft sank the British battleship *Prince of Wales* and the battle cruiser *Repulse* in the Gulf of Siam. Because these were new warships manned by select crews, their loss was as much of a shock to the British as Pearl Harbor had been to the Americans. "In all the war," Churchill later wrote, "I never received a more direct shock . . . how many efforts, hopes and plans foundered with these two ships. . . . There were no British or American capital ships in the Indian Ocean or the Pacific except the American survivors of Pearl Harbour, who were hastening back to California. Over all this vast expanse of waters Japan was supreme, and we everywhere weak and naked." [7]

By Christmas, little more than two weeks after Pearl Harbor, the Japanese already had captured Guam, Wake, and Hong Kong. They invaded the jungles of the Malay Peninsula, hitherto considered to be impregnable. Thanks to years of experience against guerrilla forces in China, the Japanese had trained their men to infiltrate around enemy positions and to attack on the flanks and the rear. They moved quickly with light mortars, light tanks, bicycles, and local transport and supplies in areas with poor ground communications. These tactics proved so successful that by February 15, 1942, the great Singapore fortress fell, with a demoralized army of 80,000 British, Australian, and Indian troops surrendering to 50,000 Japanese. Churchill described the loss as "the worst disaster and largest capitulation of British history." [8] It was more than that. Singapore for long had stood as a glittering symbol of Western imperialism in Asia. Its fall was as significant for the second half of the twentieth century as the Russian defeat at Tsushima Straits had been for the first.

Essentially the same pattern was repeated in Burma and Indonesia. Japanese troops crossed the Burmese frontier on December 10, 1941. By April they had taken Rangoon and Mandalay, and mixed British, Indian, and Chinese forces were fleeing to India along obscure jungle trails. In Indonesia the Dutch commander in chief capitulated with his army at Bandung on March 8. Nor had the Japanese more trouble landing in the Philippines and capturing Manila on January 2. But a mixed American-Filipino army under MacArthur, and later under General Wainwright, held out in the mountainous Bataan

Peninsula until May 6. Further afield, the Japanese took the Andaman Islands in the Indian Ocean and the Attu and Kiska islets in the Aleutian chain. Thus, in five months, at a cost of only 15,000 killed and wounded, the Japanese had won an empire that had a population of over 100 million and that had supplied 95 per cent of the world's raw rubber, 90 per cent of the hemp, and two-thirds of the tin. As Churchill secretly confided to the Commons: ". . . the violence, fury, skill and might of Japan had far exceeded anything that we had been led to expect."

Meanwhile, on the Russian front, Hitler had launched another massive offensive in June, 1942. Since Moscow and Leningrad had proven impregnable the previous year, he now directed his armies southward. His objective was to reach the Volga and the Caspian, thereby cutting the Soviet Union in two and depriving the Red Army of its oil supplies from the Caucasus. As in 1941, the *Panzer* divisions at first rolled swiftly across the flat steppe country. In early July they took the great Sevastopol fortress in the Crimea, and at the end of the month they recaptured Rostov. Then they crossed the Don River and fanned out southeast toward the Caucasus oil fields and northeast toward Stalingrad on the Volga. By August 22, Nazi tanks had taken the Maikop oil center, though they fell short of the major oil fields at Grozny. Hitler had assigned much of his armored force to this Caucasus drive, though General Ewald von Kleist later testified, "I did not need its aid, and it merely congested the roads I was using." According to Kleist, Stalingrad could have been taken "without a fight" at the end of July. But it was not until a month later that the *Panzers,* coming up belatedly from the Caucasus, were able to drive through to the Volga slightly to the north of Stalingrad. By this time the Russians had poured reinforcements into the city, and it was no longer available for plucking. Nevertheless, the amount of territory overrun by the Germans in 1942 was most impressive. In Berlin, Hitler proclaimed that his troops had reached the banks of the Volga in the heart of Russia and would never be dislodged.

In North Africa also, 1942 was a year of victory for the Germans. This was partly because the British had weakened their forces on that front by their ill-fated attempt to stop the German drive down into Greece. At the same time the British Mediterranean fleet was decimated by mines and submarines, while the *Luftwaffe* bombed Malta so severely that the island was temporarily useless as an aerial and naval base. Hitler, besides, had decided early in 1941 to bolster the wavering Italians by sending to North Africa one of his most capable commanders, General Erwin Rommel. Although not a member of the Prussian military caste, Rommel had risen rapidly because of his outstanding performance during the French campaign. A keen strategist and a dashing leader of men, he quickly whipped into shape his famous Afrika Korps. In March, 1941, he launched an offensive that drove the British back across Libya to the Egyptian border. In May, 1942, he resumed the attack, crossed into Egypt and reached El Alamein, a scant fifty miles from Alexandria. So confident was Rommel of complete victory that he selected a white stallion for his triumphal entry into Cairo, while the grateful *Führer* promoted him to the rank of field marshal.

Even on sea, the Germans in 1942 were alarmingly successful. Both the British and the Americans were operating at the end of supply lines thousands of miles long, while the Russians also were dependent to a considerable degree on war materials shipped via North Cape or the Persian Gulf. This was a made-to-order situation for the Japanese and German naval forces, respectively the third and fourth strongest in the world (after the American and the British). The Germans inflicted much greater losses on Allied shipping than did the Japanese, primarily because the German submarine fleet was larger, more efficient, and closer to the main Allied shipping lanes. In the course of the entire war the Allies and the neutrals lost a total of 23,506,000 gross tons of shipping, half again as much as during World War I. Three-fourths of this tonnage was lost in the Atlantic, 70 per cent of this sunk by submarines as against 30 per cent by mines, surface ships, and aircraft. The rate of sinkings rose from 3,992,000 tons in 1940 to 4,329,000 in 1941 and to a high of 8,330,000 in 1942. Then the losses declined in the next two years to 4,065,000 and 1,495,000 tons. The shipping crisis came in 1942, and it was not until the autumn of that year that the output of Allied shipyards surpassed the losses.

On every front the Axis powers were at the height of their fortunes in 1942. In North Africa Rommel was preparing to strike for Cairo, in Russia the *Wehrmacht* had reached the Volga, in the Pacific the Japanese appeared to be ready to spring on Australia and India, while the shipping battle on the high seas remained close until the end of the year.

1943: Turning of the Tide

During the first three years of the war the Axis powers had everything their own way. The turning point began at the end of 1942 with the epic Russian victory at Stalingrad, the British breakthrough in Egypt, the Allied landings in French North Africa, the fall of Mussolini, the mounting serial bombardment of Germany, and the defeat of Japanese fleets in the Pacific.

Stalingrad was a difficult city to defend, sprawling as it did for thirty miles along the banks of the mile-wide Volga, over which Soviet troops and supplies had to be ferried. Nevertheless, Stalin's orders were to hold the city at all costs. It was a major industrial center, producing tractors in peacetime and tanks during war. It was strategically important, also, being located at the westernmost bend of the Volga. If it fell to the Germans, the country would be effectively cut in two, and Caucasus oil no longer could be shipped up the Volga to the northern battlefields. The fall of Stalingrad would have been equivalent to the loss of Detroit or Chicago, and the cutting off of traffic along the Great Lakes and the Mississippi.

The battle for the city began on August 22. By mid-September the Germans had fought their way into the center, and there they bogged down. Their planes had reduced the city to a great sea of rubble. This, paradoxically, prevented the Germans from exploiting their tank superiority that had proven so effective in the open steppe. Instead of mobile warfare, the battle of Stalingrad became the *Rattenkrieg* (War of the Rats), as men fought hand to hand in cellars, on rooftops, in alleys and courtyards and sewers. For days on end the sun was almost blotted out by the dust rising from the pulverized rubble. "Stalingrad," wrote one observer, "was a monstrous graveyard of shattered buildings, shaking walls, and rotting flesh."

Meanwhile, Stalin had been preparing a vast winter counteroffensive. On November 19, 1942, it was launched under the direction of General Georgi Zhukov. Two new armies crossed the Volga from the east, one attacking to the north of the city and the other to the south. The besiegers were in danger of becoming the besieged. The German commander, General Friedrich Paulus, wished to fight his way out of the threatening trap, but Hitler ordered him to hold on, and Göring promised to supply him by air. Meanwhile, the Russian armies had driven forward and closed around the Germans in a gigantic pincers movement. A German relief army from the southeast was thrown back with heavy losses, while the Russians progressively occupied more and more airfields, thereby immobilizing Göring's air transports. The Germans now were hopelessly stranded. Thanks to Hitler's obstinacy, they were to endure a martyrdom of starvation, disease, and freezing. The end came on February 2, 1943, when Paulus surrendered with 120,000 men, the miserable survivors of the original army of 334,000. Hitler had expected Paulus, whom he had recently promoted to field marshal, to commit suicide and ascend to "eternity and national immortality"; instead, the *Führer* observed acidly, "he prefers to go to Moscow." *

567

At the same time that the Russians were destroying the German army at Stalingrad, they launched a series of offensives at other points along the front. By the end of March, they had regained all the territory they had lost in 1942. In a desperate effort to check the relentless advance of the Red Army, the Germans made an out-out attack on a Soviet salient at Kursk. Though they concentrated 160 tanks per mile, they gained only 20 miles, and this at a cost of 40,000 men, 1,400 planes and 3,000 tanks. On July 12 the Russians counterattacked, quickly rewon their positions, and then rolled on until logistic difficulties forced them to halt.

The Kursk battle marks the turning point in the Russo-German War. It was the last major Nazi offensive on the eastern front. Henceforth the Russians had the initiative, and the Germans fought defensive actions to prevent their retreat from becoming a rout. This shift in the balance of power was effected partly by the large-scale aid from the West that reached the Red Army, beginning about the time of the Stalingrad battle. But the 400,000 jeeps and trucks, 22,000 planes (mostly fighters), and 12,000 tanks that reached Russia from the West amounted only to about 10 per cent of the total war material used by the Red Army. The Russian victories would have been impossible if the Soviet economy had not been able to produce the other 90 per cent, and if the Soviet High Command had not been able to raise and train new armies despite the appalling military and economic losses of the first two years.

Hitler himself contributed to the Russian victories with his racist policy of extermination or degradation of the "inferior" Slavic peoples of the East in order to make room for German settlers. Hitler stated explicitly that he was prepared to wage a "conventional, gentlemanly" war against Britain and France. But in the East the Russian state was to be destroyed, its ancient capitals were to be obliterated, its officials and intellectuals liquidated, and its peasant masses decimated and reduced to hewers of wood and drawers of water for the master race. This policy left the millions of Russians in the occupied territories no alternative but to resist for sheer survival. It could have

* See "Stalingrad," *EMM,* No. 163.

568

been very different, for the large-scale desertions and surrenders in the early stages of the war indicate that a considerate proporation of the Russian people were at least lukewarm toward the Bolshevik regime. If Hitler had offered these people something more than Stalin had given them, they might have responded in sufficient numbers to have influenced decisively the course of the war. Instead, Hitler's policy of *Lebensraum* for the master race drove the Slavs throughout Eastern Europe into the underground and the guerrilla bands.

While the Germans were being forced back in Russia, they and their Italian allies were being driven out completely from North Africa. In late August, 1942, Rommel attempted to resume his offensive into Egypt but was heavily repulsed. The British now had a new commander on this front, Sir Bernard Montgomery, a flamboyant personality but a strict disciplinarian and a cautious strategist. With the aid of new and heavier tanks from the United States, Montgomery unleashed his own offensive on October 23. A preliminary barrage from 1,000 guns prepared the way for the advancing tanks. After twelve days' hard fighting, the Germans and Italians were routed. As they fell back along the coastal road, they were harried by air and naval bombardment. By January 24, 1943, Montgomery had captured Tripoli, and the road to Tunisia lay open.

Meanwhile Anglo-American troops had landed on November 7–8, 1942, at the other end of North Africa, in Morocco and Algeria. The strategy was to squeeze the Axis forces in a great pincers operation from east and west, and thus remove them once and for all from this theater. On the night of November 7, 1942, some 850 ships in three great convoys, one from the United States and two from England, arrived at Casablanca, Oran, and Algiers. In three weeks 185,000 men landed against token resistance by Vichy French forces. The Anglo-American forces drove toward Tunisia, which was to be subdued by Christmas. This plan was upset, however, as Hitler rushed reinforcements across the Mediterranean. The fighting in Tunisia was hard, with the Anglo-American forces from the west supported by Montgomery advancing from the east and by a Fighting French unit from the south. Eventually, by the middle of May, 1943, Tunisia was subdued by the Allied forces.

These military developments had been accompanied by a bitter political struggle behind the scenes. The Allies had recognized as the head of occupied French Africa a certain Admiral Jean-François Darlan. He was a prominent supporter of the Vichy regime that was headed by Marshal Pétain and that ruled the southern part of France left unoccupied by Hitler. The selection of Darlan, frankly made on grounds of military expediency, infuriated the Free French leader, General de Gaulle, as well as liberal circles throughout the West. Darlan was killed by an assassin's bullet on Christmas Eve of 1942, but de Gaulle was again bypassed, largely because of Roosevelt's personal antipathy to him. The new leader selected was General Henri Giraud, a gallant but politically ineffectual figure. When it soon became apparent that he lacked the popular following of de Gaulle, Roosevelt was finally persuaded to allow the Free French leader to go to Algiers to share power. Giraud from the beginning was overshadowed by his dynamic rival, and by the autumn of 1943 Giraud was out, and de Gaulle was the head of what was in fact, if not in name, a provisional government of the French Empire. Since Hitler had occupied Vichy France as soon as the Allies invaded Morocco and Algiers, de Gaulle now stood out as the undisputed leader of all Frenchmen who had not sold out to the Germans.

Following their conquest of North Africa, the Anglo-Americans pressed on to Sicily, which they invaded on July 10. The German troops fought hard, but the Italians, discouraged by constant defeats and alienated by their domineering partners, offered only token resistance. The Sicilian capital, Palermo, fell on July 22, and by mid-August, allied troops were following the retreating enemy across the Messina Straits to the mainland.

Mussolini paid for these disasters with his office and eventually with his life. King Victor Emmanuel III was persuaded by monarchists and Fascist dissidents to dismiss Mussolini and to place him in prison. This was done on July 25, three days after the fall of Palermo. Supreme authority was now vested in the king and in Marshal Pietro Badoglio, the conquerer of Ethiopia. The latter sought to take Italy out of the war with as little further bloodshed and destruction as possible. In this objective he doubtless had the support of the great majority of Italians, who were heartily sick of the war and of the alliance with the detested Germans. But peace was not so easily attained; the Italians had yet to face a second phase of the war that was to prove much crueler than the first.

Badoglio, with the approval of the king, concluded an armistice agreement with the Allies on September 3. At the same time, British troops landed at Calabria on the toe of the Italian Peninsula, while Americans attacked at Salerno, south of Naples. The Germans responded promptly by seizing Rome and occupying the central and northern parts of the country. In a bold raid, Nazi parachutists rescued Mussolini from prison. The shopworn *Duce* established a "Fascist Republic" in northern Italy and proclaimed his intention of fighting to the bitter end. His new regime was, of course, completely dependent on the Germans. General Albert Kesselring was in charge of military operations, and he was able to confine the Allies to their coastal footholds in the south. Although Churchill repeatedly had referred to southern Europe as the "soft underbelly" of the Continent, the fact is that the mountainous terrain made it anything but soft as a military objective. For the next year and a half Italy was to be a divided and war-wracked country; the Germans with their puppet Mussolini in the north, and the Allies with Badoglio's provisional government in the south.

Meanwhile, the soil of the Third Reich itself was being subjected to steadily increasing aerial bombardment. It first got under way after June, 1941, when the diversion of most of the *Luftwaffe* to the Russian front gave the RAF superiority in the west. In 1942, British raids were extended to the Ruhr Valley and to all the large cities in north Germany. By 1943, the Americans joined in, so that round-the-clock bombing became possible, the British raiding by night and the Americans by day. German cities were subjected to what were termed "concentrated" attacks of 800 bombers per hour, and "superconcentrated," or "saturation," attacks of 1,800 bombers per hour. More explosives were now dropped on German cities in one hour than had been loosed during the entire Battle of Britain. Civilian deaths from air raids in Germany throughout the war have been estimated at 305,000. This unprecedented aerial assault was used by the Western powers as a partial answer to

570

the growing Soviet demand for a second front in France. Yet the effectiveness of all this bombing remains a matter of dispute. Factories and railroads usually were in full operation within days after a major raid. The German munitions output, according to German figures, reached its highest point in 1944, the year when the bombing also was at its heaviest.

Meanwhile, the Japanese were suffering reverses comparable to those of their Axis partners in Europe. After their spectacular victories in the first six months, the Japanese finally were stopped and then were pushed back at an accelerating pace. The basic reason for this shift in the course of the war was the overwhelming superiority of American resources and productivity. When the war began, the Japanese economy was roughly comparable to the French in productivity. But compared to the American it was paltry, as Table 1 indicates:

TABLE 1.   Percentage of World Production

	U.S.A.		Japan	
	1942	1944	1942	1944
Coal	35	55	6	5
Oil	60	72	6	2
Iron ore	30	50	6	5
Steel	40	55	5.5	4

Source: J. Romein, *The Asian Century: A History of Modern Nationalism in Asia* (Berkeley: Univ. of Calif., 1962), p. 338.

It is apparent why the American economy, once it was converted to a war footing, simply swamped Japan's despite the fanatic courage of the Japanese. For example, the disasters during the early part of the war left the United States with only 3 first-line aircraft carriers, but within two years of Pearl Harbor the number had jumped to 50. Likewise, the number of navy planes rose from 3,638 in 1941 to 30,070 in 1944, and the construction of submarines increased from 11 in 1941 to 77 in 1944. Most impressive was the production of landing craft, ranging from tiny rafts to 300-foot transports that landed tanks and infantry. The total number of such vessels skyrocketed from 123 in 1941 to 54,206 in 1945.*

The Japanese could not even begin to match this flood from American factories. The empire they had conquered had an abundant supply of raw materials, but they could not convert these into war goods. One reason was the decimation of their merchant marine by American planes and submarines. At the beginning of the war, Japan had about seven million tons of merchant shipping; by the summer of 1945 scarcely one million tons remained. Thus, the Japanese found it increasingly difficult to keep supplies flowing to their factories at home as well as to their armed forces abroad. Equally serious was the weakness of Japanese heavy industry. Even if raw materials had been available in adequate quantities, Japan lacked the industrial resources to utilize them. Manpower also was in short supply, despite the 73 million people who were then crowded on the home islands. No less than 40 per cent of this population was engaged in intensive rice cultivation, leaving no surplus for

* See "American War Production," *EMM*, No. 164.

substantial expansion of industry. If Japan could have had a decade or two of peace to exploit her newly won territories, she might well have become a great world empire. But instead of peace, she was to suffer catastrophic defeat.

The first step on the long road to Tokyo was taken at Guadalcanal, where United States Marines landed on August 7, 1942. Slowly, and at heavy cost, American and Australian forces captured vital bases in New Britain and New Guinea. Very few Japanese were taken prisoners, for capture was considered a disgrace and was rarely accepted. Suicidal *banzai* charges by officers and soldiers refusing to surrender became almost a routine climax to the taking of Japanese positions. In the face of such resistance, the American counter-offensive overwhelmed Munda in New Georgia, Rabaul in New Britain, Sala-maua and Lae in New Guinea, Tarawa in the Gilbert Islands, Kwajalein in the Marshalls, and Attu and Kiska in the Aleutians. By mid-1944 Saipan and Guam in the Marianas were taken, bringing the Japanese home islands within range of the new B-29 superfortresses. It was the beginning of the end of Japan's brief hour of glory.

Liberation of Europe

Europe was liberated in 1944–1945 primarily by the Red Army advancing from the east and by Anglo-American forces invading from the Normandy landing beaches in the west. Fighting also continued in Italy during this period, but it was peripheral compared to the campaigns in the north. In an attempt to end the Italian war quickly, the Allies in January, 1944, made a landing at Anzio, only 30 miles from Rome, and also attacked the German stronghold at the Monte Cassino monastery. Both operations failed, and the Italian campaign bogged down to a dreary stalemate. Not until mid-May was Cassino captured, thanks largely to Free French mountain troops from North Africa. The way to Rome now lay open, and American and French troops pushed up the western flank of the peninsula while Britishers and Poles advanced on the eastern. On June 5, the Fifth American Army of General Mark Clark entered Rome, tempestuously welcomed by its inhabitants. Rome was the first of the Continental capitals to be freed from Nazi rule, but this triumph was overshadowed by the Allied landings in Normandy on the following day.

As early as February, 1944, the Allies had begun to prepare the way for Operation "Overlord" by bombing enemy industrial plants, railway and sea transportation facilities, and coastal defenses. In the last few days before D-Day the Allies had absolute aerial supremacy over the Channel and were sending over waves of 1,000 bombers, each carrying 5,000 tons of explosives. In England, the invasion planners were able to profit from the earlier amphibious operations in the Mediterranean and the Pacific, though Overlord was on an entirely different scale. A million and a half men together with all their equipment, including heavy guns, trucks, and tanks, had to be transported across the Channel and kept supplied as operations unfolded. Two huge prefabricated harbors, each as large as Dover Harbor, were built for emplacement on the invasion beaches. Meanwhile, on the other side of the Channel, the Germans were busy strengthening their Atlantic Wall made up of pill-boxes, machine-gun nests and artillery, as well as mines and underwater obstructions.

Stormy weather threatened to postpone the expedition indefinitely as the time was running out when moon and tide would permit a crossing to the Continent. The Supreme Allied Commander, General Dwight Eisenhower, postponed the expedition for one day, and then decided to take a chance and proceed with the invasion on June 6. Fortunately, the storm abated somewhat, though the seas were choppy and many of the soldiers arrived miserably seasick. The vast armada comprised 4,000 merchant vessels and 700 warships. At 6:30 A.M. landings began, and by the end of the first day 326,000 men and 20,000 vehicles reached the shore. Bitter fighting occurred at Omaha and Utah beaches, and for some hours the fate of the entire expedition hung in balance. Fortunately for the Allies, the German High Command suspected that the Normandy landings were only a feint and that the main attack would come at Calais, where the Channel was narrowest. Accordingly, the German armored forces were kept in reserve until it was too late to dislodge the invaders. By D-Day plus five, the beachheads had been merged along a front of sixty miles.* From the beginning, it should be noted, the Allied forces received invaluable aid from the French underground bands (*maquis*), which wrecked bridges, cut communication lines, and derailed German troop trains.

The Allied plan of campaign, generally credited to Montgomery, was for the British and Canadian forces on the left to repel the main enemy attacks, while the American forces on the right, trained and equipped for mobility, broke out of the bridgehead and took the Germans in the rear. On July 25, the Americans, aided by 1,500 heavy bombers that blasted a gap in the enemy lines, fought their way into open country at Saint-Lô. As they advanced, they trapped 100,000 of the enemy in the Cherbourg Peninsula. By early August the dashing tank commander General George Patton was rushing headlong across northern France toward Paris. On August 15, a new American army under General Alexander M. Patch, with strong French reinforcements, landed on the Riviera beaches and advanced rapidly up the Rhone valley. Meanwhile, central France was being liberated by the *maquis* who descended from the hills and attacked enemy garrisons and communication lines. Belabored from all sides, the Germans now made a general withdrawal toward their own frontiers. On August 19, resistance forces began open insurrection in Paris, and six days later a French armored division and an American infantry division completed the liberation of the capital. General de Gaulle, now universally recognized as the leader of the French people, drove in triumph to Notre Dame for the *Te Deum* of thanksgiving.

These sweeping victories raised hopes for an end to the war by Christmas. The German armies had pulled back behind the Siegfried Line and in front of the Rhine River for a desperate last stand. Eisenhower now dropped about 3,000 American and British paratroopers near Arnhem in the eastern Netherlands. It was a bold gamble taken in the hope of capturing the Rhine bridges and clearing the way for an attack across the river into the heart of Germany. The operation succeded at first, but the relief forces were unable to fight their way through, and the Germans closed in and wiped out the bridgehead. Only a quarter of the paratroopers were evacuated back to the Allied lines. Meanwhile, Patton's tank army was running short of fuel, while the French and

* See "D-Day," *EMM*, No. 165.

Americans advancing from the south were meeting stiff resistance in Alsace. By October it was apparent that victory was out of reach for that year.

While the Western powers were liberating France, the Red Army was advancing rapidly from the East. Having driven the *Wehrmacht* from the Crimea and the Ukraine by the spring of 1944, it then began a general offensive against approximately two million Germans (compared to the one million facing the Allies in France and Italy). In the north the Russians knocked Finland out of the war by September; in the center they crossed both the old and new frontiers of Poland and drove to the gates of Warsaw; in the south they reached the mouth of the Danube in the heart of Rumania. Young King Michael of Rumania seized the opportunity to pull his country out of the war in September, thus opening the Balkan Peninsula to the Red Army. Bulgaria followed this example by suing for peace and re-entering the war on the side of the Soviet Union. The German armies in the Balkans were now in danger of being trapped and began to pull out as fast as possible. As they did so, the Communist-led resistance forces in Yugoslavia and Greece descended from the mountains and took over control of their respective countries—a development that was to contribute to the forthcoming Cold War between Russia and the Western powers. Aided by the local Communist-led guerrillas, the Red Army drove up the Danube Valley until it was stopped in Hungary by stiffening German resistance.

At this point the Allies were caught off guard by a sudden offensive launched by the Germans on December 16, 1944, in the Ardennes in Belgium. Using much heavy armor and helped by foggy weather that hampered Allied aerial counterattacks, the Germans carved out a salient or "bulge" fifty miles in depth and as broad at the base. They came uncomfortably close to capturing the key supply base of Antwerp, which would have upset the entire Allied plan of operations. Finally the weather cleared on December 24, and 5,000 Allied planes pounded German supply lines, while Patton counterattacked from the south and Montgomery from the north. By the end of January, 1945, the Germans had been forced back to their original positions, and thereafter they were forced steadily backward under relentless Allied pressure.

While the "Battle of the Bulge" was raging in the west, the Russians were advancing steadily in Poland and Hungary. Both Warsaw and Hungary were taken by February, 1945, though only after bitter fighting that left the two capitals in ruins. Thanks to an exceptionally mild winter, the Red Army soldiers were able to press on into Austria and Germany. On April 13, they took Vienna, while to the north they overran East Prussia and Silesia. By late March, they were fighting their way across the Oder, only forty miles from Berlin.

Meanwhile, the American, British, Canadian, and French armies were making corresponding progress on the western front. After recovering from the shock at Ardennes they cracked the West Wall and fought their way through to the Rhine. There they discovered to their astonishment that the retreating Germans had neglected to blow up the Ludendorff railway bridge at Remagen, south of Bonn. The Allies swarmed over, and within a month they had conquered the Rhineland and taken a quarter-million prisoners. Seven Allied armies now raced eastward through the collapsing Reich. On

April 25, an American patrol linked up with the Soviet vanguard at the village of Torgau on the Elbe, cutting Germany in two.

574

At the same time General Mark Clark was clearing the Germans out of Italy with his agglomeration of Britons, Anzacs, South Africans, Indians, Palestinians, Poles, French, Brazilians, and Free Italians, as well as Americans of white, colored, and nisei varieties. With the noteworthy assistance of Italian guerrillas, who harassed the enemy as the *maquis* did in France, a final offensive was launched on April 10. Within a fortnight the German lines had crumpled and the Allies streamed down into the Po valley and beyond to the Alps. In Milan and other industrial cities, the resistance fighters organized successful risings and won control before the Allies arrived. On May 2, the German commanders in Italy signed terms of unconditional surrender. Five days earlier Mussolini had been apprehended by guerrillas while attempting to escape to Switzerland and was summarily shot. His body, and that of his mistress, were hung up on display in Milan.

Hitler meanwhile was still holding out, even though both his eastern and western fronts had caved in. He clung to the hope that total disaster could be averted by playing off Russia against the Western powers. Propaganda minister Goebbels referred continuously to "new weapons" that would confound the enemy, and assured his countrymen, "I know for certain that the *Führer* will find a way out." This whistling in the dark was futile. On April 16, Marshal Zhukov opened his final offensive upon the German capital. Nine days later he had the city surrounded, and shells were thudding around Hitler's concrete bunker in the chancellery garden. On the last day of the month Hitler and his companion, Eva Braun, whom he had married a few days earlier, committed suicide. Their bodies were burned with gasoline in the chancellery courtyard, and no traces were ever found. On May 2, Berlin surrendered to the Russians, and during the next week Nazi emissaries surrendered unconditionally to the Western powers at Rheims and to the Soviet Union in Berlin.

Surrender of Japan

The surrender of Germany made even bleaker the prospects for the Japanese in the Pacific. Already by mid-1944 their home islands were being bombed by superfortresses based on the Marianas. At the end of the year American forces landed in the Philippines, and by late February, 1945, they had forced the Japanese garrisons to surrender. More serious for the enemy was the taking of Iwo Jima in March by three divisions of American marines. The ferocity of the fighting is reflected in the casualty figures: 20,000 of the 30,000 marines were killed or wounded, and 20,000 Japanese were killed and 200 taken prisoners. Iwo Jima was only 750 miles away from the Japanese homeland, and Okinawa, which was taken in June after another savage struggle, was only 350 miles distant.* Using these two islands as bases, American airmen now subjected Japan's crowded cities to the same storm of explosives that had wracked Germany. The Japanese were even more vulnerable, for their flimsy wood and paper structures went up in flames like so much kindling In the nine months from November, 1944, to the surrender in September, 1945, B-29 superfortresses made 32,000 sorties against Japan, or more than

* See "Okinawa," *EMM,* No. 166.

a hundred a day. The toll of dead or homeless Japanese soared beyond eight million.

To make matters worse, the Japanese had to prepare also for an attack from the East, for the Soviet government had terminated the Russo-Japanese Nonaggression Pact in April, 1945. Yet the militarists who had been responsible for Japan's intervention in the war were loathe to acknowledge their error and to begin serious peace negotiations. While they were hesitating and seeking to preserve their dignity, a series of unprecedented cataclysms abruptly ended their indecision.

On August 6, 1945, an American superfortress dropped an atomic bomb on Hiroshima, demolishing three-fifths of the city and killing 78,150 inhabitants.* The following day President Truman announced in a radio address, "Sixteen hours ago, an American plane dropped one bomb at Hiroshima, an important Japanese army base. That bomb had more power than 20,000 tons of TNT. It had more than 2,000 times the blast power of the British 'Grand Slam,' which is the largest bomb ever used in the history of warfare." On the following day, August 8, Russia declared war on Japan, and the Red Army promptly drove across the frontier into Manchuria. Russia's invasion came exactly three months after Germany's surrender, fulfilling an obligation assumed by Stalin during his meeting with Roosevelt and Churchill at Yalta in February, 1945. In addition to Russia's land invasion, Britain's Pacific Fleet, after sailing 25,000 miles in sixty days, joined in the mounting naval attack upon Japan. The final blow was the dropping of a second atomic bomb on August 9 upon the city of Nagasaki, with results as devastating as at Hiroshima. The extreme Japanese militarists still opposed a general surrender, and it seemed at one point that the war would deteriorate into a struggle of individual guerrilla groups led by diehard officers. But the Emperor, on the advice of the Cabinet and the Elder Statesmen, decided to capitulate, and on August 14 the Allied ultimatum was accepted. The formal ceremony of surrender took place on board the U.S.S. Missouri in Tokyo Bay on September 2 in the presence of General MacArthur, Admiral Nimitz, and ranking Allied officers.

III. WORLD WAR II IN WORLD HISTORY

World War II completed the undermining of Europe's global hegemony that had been started by World War I. Thus, in a general sense the two wars had a similar significance for world history. There were variations in detail, however, that are of prime significance for the contemporary scene. The Nazis and the Japanese militarists were infinitely more destructive of the old orders in Europe and Asia than the Hohenzollerns and the Hapsburgs had ever been. The Germans had overrun the entire continent of Europe; and the Japanese, the whole of East and Southeast Asia. But these vast empires proved short-lived. They disappeared in 1945, leaving behind two great power vacuums embracing territories of primary economic and strategic significance. It was the existence of these vacuums, as much as any ideological considerations, that was responsible for the outbreak of the Cold War and the inability to conclude a general peace settlement immediately after 1945.

* See "Hiroshima," *EMM,* No. 167.

Another difference between the two postwar periods was the successful upsurge of colonial subjects after 1945, in contrast to the enforcement of imperial authority after 1918. Within a period of two decades the farflung European empires had all but disappeared. In this sense, these were decades of European decline, political and military. Yet at the same time, thanks to the accelerating unification of the globe, Western ideas and institutions and technology were spreading throughout the globe at an unprecedented pace. Thus the post–World War II years constitute, paradoxically, a period of European triumph as well as decline.

SUGGESTED READING

One of the most important and sprightly sources for World War II is Winston S. Churchill, *The Second World War* (Boston: Houghton, 1948–1953) 6 vols. Two excellent anthologies of war reporting are by D. Flower and J. Reeves, eds., *The Taste of Courage: The War, 1939–1945* (New York: Harper, 1960), and L. L. Snyder, ed., *Masterpieces of War Reporting: The Great Moments of World War II* (New York: Messner, 1962). A French historian has provided the standard account of the collapse of his country: J. Benoist-Méchin, *Sixty Days That Shook the West: The Fall of France: 1940* (New York: Oxford Univ., 1963). The German-Russian war is authoritatively and interestingly analyzed by A. Werth, *Russia at War, 1941–1945* (New York: Dutton, 1964), who also provides an excellent bibliography. Hitler's extermination policies and actions in Eastern Europe are set forth in I. Kamenetsky, *Secret Nazi Plans for Eastern Europe: A Study of Lebensraum Policies* (New York: Bookman, 1961) and R. Hilberg, *The Destruction of the European Jews* (Chicago, Quadrangle, 1961).

The diplomacy leading to Japan's intervention is analyzed by H. Feis, *The Road to Pearl Harbor* (Princeton: Princeton Univ., 1950). The circumstances of the attack are authoritatively analyzed by R. Wohlsetter, *Pearl Harbor: Warning and Decision* (Stanford: Stanford Univ., 1964). For the human aspects of Pearl Harbor, see W. Lord, *Day of Infamy* (New York: Holt, 1957). The Japanese officer in charge of planning the Malaya campaign describes Britain's defeat at Singapore in M. Tsuji, *Singapore: The Japanese Version* (New York: St. Martins, 1962). An excellent anthology of the Pacific War, edited by D. Congdon and published as a Dell paperback is *Combat: The Pacific Theater: World War II* (1959). The fateful atomic bombing of Hiroshima is the subject of F. Knebel and C. W. Bailey, II, *No High Ground* (New York: Harper, 1960) and J. Hersey, *Hiroshima* (New York: Knopf, 1946). Two of the most outstanding novels on the Pacific War are by J. Jones, *From Here to Eternity* and N. Mailer, *The Naked and the Dead,* both available as New American Library–Signet paperbacks.

*It is not so difficult to keep unity in time of war
since there is a joint aim to defeat the
common enemy, which is clear to everyone. The
difficult task will come after the war when
diverse interests tend to divide the Allies.*

STALIN, *at Yalta*

Chapter

26

Grand Alliance to Cold War

W orld War I was followed by revolution in Central and Eastern Europe and by the threat of revolution in Western Europe. World War II stimulated no comparable disturbances. Revolutions did not convulse the Continent, despite the fact that the Second War inflicted greater material damage and political dislocation than the First. One reason was the sheer fatigue of the civilian populations. For six years they had been subjected to constant bombardment from the air, to wide-ranging ground operations, and to mass uprooting through flight, forced labor, or imprisonment. More than 15 million soldiers were killed, as well as 10 million civilians, including 6 million Jews. This was approximately twice the casualties and thirteen times the material damage of World War I.

Those who survived had experienced unprecedented privation and dislocation. In the first three and a half years of the war alone, 30 million Europeans had fled or were driven from their original homes. At the end of the hostilities, Allied armies and international relief agencies returned home more than 12 million "displaced persons," yet there still remained a hard core of more than a million— mostly anti-Communists from Eastern Europe—who refused to go home. This wholesale reshuffling of peoples, together with the accompanying cold, hunger, and disease, left most Europeans too exhausted and dispirited to think of revolution.

578

Equally decisive was the occupation of all Europe by the forces of the victorious Allies. The Red Army, no less than the British and the American, stamped out opposition and disorder. A revolution in the social structure did occur in Eastern Europe, but it was an imposed revolution directed from Moscow. The Communist parties throughout Europe were obedient instruments of Soviet foreign policy rather than fomenters of indigenous revolutions. Thus, Russia and Britain and the United States effectively controlled developments in Europe after the downfall of Hitler. It was these powers that were responsible for the policies and events that gradually disrupted the wartime Grand Alliance and brought on the Cold War.

I. WARTIME UNITY

During the war years, the Western powers and the Soviet Union were forced to present a common front against the menace of a mortal enemy.* On the very day of Hitler's invasion of Russia, Churchill proclaimed: "The Russian danger is . . . our danger, and the danger of the United States, just as the cause of any Russian fighting for his hearth and home is the cause of free men and free peoples in every quarter of the globe." [1]

Two months later, on August 14, 1941, Churchill and Roosevelt issued their Atlantic Charter, in which they set forth in idealistic terms their common aims and principles. More specific expressions of Allied cooperation were the twenty-year mutual-aid pact signed by Great Britain and the Soviet Union in May, 1942, and the American-Russian Lend-Lease Agreement of the following month. Another manifestation of cooperation was the decision of the Russians in May, 1943, to abolish the Communist International which they had established in 1919 to overthrow world capitalism. In view of their friendly relations with the Western powers, the Russians now decided that the Comintern had outlived its usefulness, though it should be noted that this decision meant little in practice because the top Comintern officials had been transferred by 1939 to the Party Secretariat, where they continued to function. Still another result of Allied wartime cooperation was the establishment in November, 1943, of the United Nations Relief and Rehabilitation Administration (UNRRA). This international agency followed in the wake of the armed forces and provided relief of all kinds to the liberated countries until the new national administrations could assume responsibility. It began work in the spring of 1944, and by the time of its dissolution in September, 1948, it had distributed 22 million tons of supplies including food, clothing, and medicines, mostly of American origin. Its main operations were in Greece, Yugoslavia, Poland, Czechoslovakia, Austria, and Italy. Without its contributions the deprivation and distress in postwar Europe would have been substantially worse than it was.

As the war neared its end, this cooperation forced by mutual danger began to falter. The partners were more ready to sacrifice unity for what they considered to be their postwar national interests. Thus with peace, the Grand Alliance was rent by discord, and within two or three years was replaced by a Cold War that constantly threatened to become hot.

* See "Roots of the Grand Alliance," EMM, No. 168.

The breakup of the Grand Alliance was hastened by the failure of the Allied statesmen to plan seriously during the war years regarding the postwar settlement. Early in the war they did prepare the Atlantic Charter, signed by Churchill and Roosevelt on the deck of the United States cruiser *Augusta* on August 14, 1941. It provided for a postwar world free from want and fear, in which there should be no territorial changes without the consent of the people concerned, self-determination regarding form of government, equal economic opportunity for all nations, and disarming of aggressive powers. Unfortunately, little effort was made to apply these idealistic principles specifically and realistically to the manifold issues that awaited the conclusion of peace. The conferences held in 1943 in Casablanca, Quebec, and Teheran were all devoted primarily to military strategy, postwar matters being referred to only incidentally and in general terms.

By the fall of 1944, political issues no longer could be evaded. The advance of the Red Army up the Danube Valley was forcing the Germans to evacuate the Balkan Peninsula, and the Communist-led resistance fighters were filling in the vacuum. The prospect of a Communist-dominated Balkans prompted Churchill to meet with Stalin in Moscow in October, 1944. These two leaders quickly agreed upon spheres of influence in the disputed peninsula. Bulgaria and Rumania were to be in the Russian sphere, Greece in the British, and Yugoslavia to be a buffer zone under joint British-Russian influence. Thus Churchill was forced, by the exigencies of an unfavorable strategic situation, to accept Soviet predominance in the northern Balkans in order to preserve Britain's traditional primacy in Greece.*

At the same time that Churchill was bargaining with Stalin in Moscow, British troops were beginning to land in Greece. They advanced northward on the heels of the retreating Germans, but found the Greek resistance forces preceding them in all the towns and cities. No opposition was offered by these forces, led by disciplined Communists who obediently followed the current Kremlin line. It is interesting to speculate whether these Communists would have been so accommodating had they known of Stalin's cavalier disposition of their country. In any case, they welcomed the small British units, though, had they wished, they could then have easily barred them as the nationalist-minded Tito was doing at the time in Yugoslavia.

Despite the compliance of the Greek resistance forces, the fact remained that they were the preponderant military power in the country as the Germans withdrew. This was an intolerable situation for Churchill. On November 7 he informed his foreign minister, Anthony Eden: "In my opinion, having paid the price we have to Russia for freedom of action in Greece, we should not hesitate to use British troops to support the Royal Hellenic Government under M. Papandreou." [2] Churchill's problem, specifically, was how to secure the disarming of the resistance forces so as to transfer state power to the legal royal government. Various disarmament formulas were proposed, but none satisfied both sides. This dispute precipitated an armed clash that developed into the bitter and bloody Battle of Athens. British and Indian troops were rushed in from Italy, and after a month of fighting the resistance forces withdrew from the Athens area.

On February 12, a peace agreement (the Varkiza Pact) was signed by

* See "Churchill and Stalin Divide the Balkans," *EMM*, No. 169.

which the resistance troops surrendered their arms in return for a promise of elections and a plebiscite on the question of the return of the king. Thus Churchill secured the sphere allotted to him in Moscow: Greece was to be on the side of the West during the postwar years. Equally significant was Stalin's eloquent silence while Churchill was dispersing the leftist resistance fighters. The British-Russian deal on the Balkans was in operation and was working.

II. YALTA CONFERENCE

The fighting in Athens had barely ceased when, in February, 1945, Roosevelt, Churchill, and Stalin met at Yalta for the last of their wartime conferences. With the Allied armies converging upon Germany from all sides, the problems of a postwar settlement now had to be considered specifically and realistically. Little difficulty was encountered in reaching an agreement on the Far East. Stalin agreed to declare war against Japan within sixty days after the end of hostilities in Europe. In return, Russia was to regain the Kuril Islands and also the concessions and territories lost to Japan in 1905, including the southern part of Sakhalin Island, the lease of the Port Arthur naval base, and joint Russo-Chinese operation of the Chinese Eastern and South Manchuria railroads.

On Germany, the conference postponed decision on most issues, including reparations and frontiers. It was agreed, however, that the country should be divided into four occupation zones (including one for France) under an Allied Control Council. Berlin, located within the Soviet zone, was to be occupied and administered jointly. A cause for serious postwar conflict was the failure to conclude a specific agreement guaranteeing Western access to the capital.

Most of the negotiating at Yalta had to do with the newly liberated countries in Eastern Europe. Stalin was in a strong position in this area, for his armies had done the liberating and were in actual occupation. Furthermore, it had been agreed earlier that until the end of the war each great power would supervise political developments in those regions through which its armies passed in the course of military operations. As one of the American delegates, James F. Byrnes, later put it: "It was not a question of what we would *let* the Russians do, but what we could *get* the Russians to do."

Given this context, the agreements that were made on Eastern Europe were, *on paper,* eminently satisfactory from the Western viewpoint. As regards frontiers, Russia was to receive the Polish territory east of a modified Curzon Line, which had been drawn after World War I but subsequently ignored. Poland was to be compensated with territory in East Germany; this was agreed upon in principle, though a final and specific decision was postponed. As regards the Polish and Yugoslav governments, Stalin agreed that the Communist regimes already established under Soviet auspices should be broadened by the admission of representatives from the West-oriented governments-in-exile. The latter were understandably apprehensive about this arrangement, which left the Red Army and the Communist governments in physical and legal control. Their doubts were met, in theory, by a broad statement of policy known as the Yalta Declaration on Liberated Europe. This committed the three powers to assist the liberated peoples of Europe "to form interim governmental authorities broadly representative of all democratic elements in the population and pledged to the earliest possible establishment through free elections of governments responsive to the will of the people. . . ."

Taken at face value, this Declaration represented a substantial concession on the part of Stalin. Despite his domination of Eastern Europe he had consented to free elections that might well bring to office anti-Soviet governments. The substance of this concession, however, was negligible. The Declaration proved to be meaningless, and a constant source of friction, because it was interpreted very differently by the various signatories. The United States interpreted it literally—that is, free elections and no spheres of influence in Eastern Europe. The United States was free to take this position because it was not bound by the agreement reached by Churchill and Stalin in Moscow the previous October. Britain, on the other hand, was ambivalent about the Declaration because the Moscow agreement had enabled her to secure her position in Greece. Yet the Declaration was alluring, because, if literally enforced, it would give Britain a chance to regain positions in Rumania and Bulgaria that she had abandoned.

Stalin, by contrast, clung to the Moscow agreement and regarded the Declaration as mere window dressing. He had scrupulously kept quiet while the British crushed the Greek resistance forces. He expressly assured Churchill during the Yalta negotiations that he had "complete confidence" in his Greek policy. In return, Stalin expected the Western powers to respect his primacy in the northern Balkans. He was surprised and outraged when the British gradually joined the Americans in demanding strict enforcement of the Declaration. Stalin refused to budge on this point, regarding "friendly" governments in Eastern Europe as prerequisite for Russian security.

This crucial issue became clear at the next three-power conference held at Potsdam in July–August, 1945. James Byrnes, then American Secretary of State, told his Russian counterpart, Molotov: "The United States sincerely desires Russia to have friendly countries on her borders, but we believe they should seek the friendship of people rather than of any particular government. We, therefore, want the governments to be representative of the people." [3] If Byrnes was unaware that his proposal was inherently contradictory, Stalin was ready to enlighten him with brutal frankness: "A freely elected government in any of these countries would be anti-Soviet and that we cannot allow." [4] The contradiction between "friendly" and "freely elected" governments was one of the main causes for the disruption of the Grand Alliance in the months to come.

This, however, still remained for the future. Although there had been plain speaking and hard bargaining at Yalta, the proceedings had been generally amicable, and the decisions reached were greeted at the time as eminently reasonable and promising. It was not believed then, as some were to claim later, that there had been a "giveaway" to Stalin. Rather, the Yalta Conference was generally interpreted and welcomed as the culmination of the Grand Alliance.[*]

[*] See "Yalta in Retrospect," EMM, No. 170.

582

III. UNITED NATIONS

The cooperation of the wartime allies was again manifested with the organization of the United Nations. The initial drafts of the charter of this body had been worked out by the four "sponsoring powers"—the United States, the Soviet Union, Britain, and China—at Dumbarton Oaks, in Washington, in the autumn of 1944. The final charter was signed by the representatives of 50 nations at the conclusion of a conference held in San Francisco from April to June, 1945, and by Poland some four months later. By the end of 1964, UN membership had risen to 115 (it dropped to 114 in March, 1965, when Indonesia withdrew from membership). Some of the newcomers were wartime enemies or neutrals, but the majority were newly independent states in Asia and Africa, which totaled 59 in 1964, as against 13 of the original 51 in 1945.

The UN, like its predecessor the League, was set up to accomplish two basic tasks: to preserve peace and security, and to cope with international economic, social, and cultural problems. Also like the League, the UN was established as an association of sovereign states, the charter specifying that the organization might not "intervene in matters which are essentially within the domestic jurisdiction of any state."

The task of maintaining peace was entrusted primarily to a Security Council consisting of five permanent members—the United States, the Soviet Union, Britain, France, and China—and six other members elected for two-year terms by the General Assembly on the recommendation of the Council. In all substantive matters the unanimous vote of the permanent members was required (together with the vote of two of the nonpermanent members), for it was recognized that peace could be maintained only if the Great Powers were in agreement. The Security Council was given a wide range of powers for the settlement of international disputes. It could employ peaceful methods, such as mediation or arbitration, or it could impose economic or political sanctions. If these measures proved inadequate, the Council was empowered to take "such action by air, sea, or land forces as may be necessary to maintain or restore international peace." For this purpose the charter provided for an "international police force" to be supplied by member nations. When the disruptive effect of the Cold War prevented such a force from materializing, the UN resorted to military units organized on a temporary basis for its intervention during the Korean, the Suez, and the Congo crises.

The Cold War seriously reduced the effectiveness of the Security Council because the Soviet Union used its veto on all the critical issues on which it clashed with the Western powers. This immobilization of the Council enabled the General Assembly to assume a more important role than was originally planned for it, because in 1950 the Assembly was empowered to consider Security Council business when the latter group, owing to lack of unanimity of the permanent members, failed to maintain international peace and security. It should be noted further that the influx of Afro-Asian nations shifted the balance of power within the Assembly. All UN member states are represented in this body, with each having only one vote. Decisions on important matters require a two-thirds majority; otherwise a simple majority is adequate. Since the Afro-Asia nations have come to constitute an absolute majority of the total membership, it is obviously necessary to pay serious attention to their views (see Chapter 27, section X).

The second task of the UN—the fight against hunger and disease and ignorance—was entrusted to the Economic and Social Council, which established programs designed to provide more food for the half of the world's people who were hungry, cure the one-eighth of the world's population that had malaria, save the 40 per cent of the children who died before the end of their first year, and teach the 50 per cent of the world's adults who were illiterate to read and write. To attain these objectives, the Economic and Social Council set up numerous specialized agencies, including, among others, the International Labor Organization; Food and Agriculture Organization; UN Educational, Scientific, and Cultural Organization; World Health Organization; and International Monetary Fund.

Like the League of Nations, the UN has been quite successful in these various nonpolitical activities. But again like the League, the UN has had a spotty record in its main job of keeping the peace. It has helped to prevent all-out war between the Great Powers by providing a medium for maintaining rapport. It has stopped fighting in areas such as Indonesia, Israel, and Kashmir, where vital interests of the major powers were not involved. But it was not able to forestall a series of local, or "brush-fire," wars in Korea, Algeria, Egypt, and Vietnam. Nor was there any consultation of the UN during the highly dangerous Cuban crisis of 1962. Particularly on the continent of Europe, the UN proved almost powerless. There the Cold War widened the gap between the Communist and non-Communist blocs until it was too wide to be bridged. Consequently, the major powers went their separate ways, organizing their rival security systems and reacting independently to each crisis. The basic difficulty of the UN, as of the League, was that in a world of sovereign states it could provide machinery for settling disputes but could not enjoin use of the machinery.

IV. PEACE TREATIES

Two months after the establishment of the UN, Japan surrendered, and the war in the Far East was over. The victorious Allies now could devote full attention to the making of peace. Their foreign ministers conducted the protracted negotiations in London, Paris, and New York, finally signing peace treaties in Paris on February 10, 1947, with Italy, Rumania, Hungary, Bulgaria, and Finland. All the treaties imposed reparations on the defeated countries, limited their armed forces, and redrew their frontiers. Italy lost the Dodecanese Islands to Greece, Saseno Island to Albania, small enclaves to France, Venezia Giulia to Yugoslavia, and the Trieste region, which was set up as a Free Territory. When the last-named arrangement had proved unworkable by 1954, Italy annexed the city itself with its predominantly Italian population, while Yugoslavia took the surrounding rural part of the Free Territory. Italy's African colonies were placed under the temporary trusteeship of Great Britain, their ultimate status to be determined later.

In the Balkans, Bulgaria restored the Greek and Yugoslav territories that she had occupied, but she acquired southern Dobruja, which she had lost to Rumania in 1919. Rumania lost Bessarabia (which had been Russian from 1812 to 1918) and the northern Bucovina (inhabited largely by Ukrainians) to the Soviet Union, but she regained northern Transylvania, which Hungary had seized during the war. Other territorial changes in Eastern Europe not covered by the satellite treaties included the acquisition by Russia of the predominantly Ukranian Carpathian-Ruthenia from Czechoslovakia, and of the three Baltic states—Latvia, Lithuania, and Estonia. Though Russia claimed the Baltic states on the ground that they had been a part of the Tsarist empire, the Western powers withheld official recognition of their annexation.

As significant as the provisions of the satellite treaties was the protracted diplomatic wrangling involved in their negotiation, which underscored the breakup of the Grand Alliance and the imminence of the Cold War. The atmosphere during this bargaining was very different from that at Yalta. Russia strove hard to gain favorable terms for those Axis satellites that were now within her sphere, while the Western powers for similar reasons championed the interests of Italy. By the time the treaties were signed, Italy had been accepted as a military ally of the West, while Bulgaria, Hungary, and Rumania had become obedient Soviet satellites. Perhaps these treaties will be remembered in the future for the fact that they sanctioned the new Communist regimes in Eastern Europe. Churchill had frequently declared during the war that he would not allow the Soviet zone to extend westward to a line from Stettin in the north to Trieste in the south. Yet this is precisely what the Western powers accepted when they signed the peace treaties at Paris. In doing so they recognized a new balance in Europe—a balance in which Bucharest, Sofia, and Budapest, along with Prague and Warsaw, now looked toward Moscow rather than toward Paris or Berlin.

V. Roots of East-West Conflict

The satellite treaties were not followed by corresponding pacts with the other enemy countries. Several years elapsed before peace agreements were concluded with Japan and Austria, and none has yet been arranged with Germany. The breakdown in peacemaking reflected the growing dissension between East and West. This, in turn, may be explained to a large degree by the immense power vacuums in Europe and Asia following the collapse of the German and Japanese empires. Vacuums are as unnatural and transitory in the political world as in the physical. They obviously were destined to be filled as soon as the fighting ceased. The question was how and by whom.

This vital question involved fundamental readjustments of power relationships. Under the best of circumstances such readjustments are difficult to arrange and fraught with danger, as evidence by the crises following the Napoleonic Wars and World War I. Now, after World War II, the process of readjustment was made even more complicated and perilous by the addition of ideological issues to the traditional power struggle.

In the Far East, the situation was simplified by the fact that the United States had the lead role in the war against Japan, and did not hesitate to assume a corresponding role in the peace settlement and in postwar affairs.

In Europe, the issues were considerably more complicated. The United States was ambivalent about its position in that area because of the traditional American aversion to peacetime involvement in the Old World. This aversion was expressed in the popular clamor to "get the boys back home" without delay—a task that in fact was accomplished so promptly that within two years after the end of the war the American armed forces had fallen from 12 to 1½ million men.

American policy makers assumed that their precipitous withdrawal from Europe would be balanced by the UN's handling of the larger problems of political, social, and economic rehabilitation. They assumed, too, that the provisional regimes established at the end of the war in the liberated European countries would shortly be succeeded by freely elected governments. And they expected that a balance would be struck in the Old World, with the Soviet Union predominant in Eastern Europe, Britain in the Mederiterranean and Middle East, France in Western Europe, and all the wartime allies cooperating to keep Germany firmly in check.

One by one these assumptions were proven unjustified. The UN Security Council was paralyzed by Soviet vetoes. In place of democratically elected governments in Eastern Europe appeared the "People's Democracies," thinly disguised instruments of Soviet control. The expected balance in Europe was upset by the fact that Britain and France, though still given the courtesy title of Great Powers, were really no match for the Soviet Union.

While the United States was withdrawing from Europe, the Soviet Union by contrast was entrenching itself within its East European preserve. Its objectives were territorial expansion toward the pre–World War I Tsarist frontiers, large-scale reparations to help pay for the crushing war devastation, and "friendly" governments in Eastern Europe that would prevent more invasions from the West. In striving for these objectives the Soviet Union came into direct and progressively sharper conflict with the Western powers. The latter opposed strenuously the Peoples Democracies as being representative more of the Soviet proconsuls than of the peoples concerned. In reply, the Soviets repeatedly drew attention to the reports of rightist terrorism in Greece, where the governments, since the Battle of Athens, were supported by Britain. As James Byrnes observed: "Whenever the Soviets were faced with an issue that annoyed them or placed them on the defensive it was standard operating procedure for them to gather up a sheaf of British and American press reports from Greece and launch a counterattack." [5]

More serious was the East-West clash in Germany, where the stakes were higher. The end of the war had left Germany with no central government. Only local officials were left, and in the East even these were lacking as they fled before the advancing Red Army. For purposes of occupation the Allies divided Germany into four zones—the Russians in the east, the British in the northwest, the Americans in the south, and the French in a smaller southwest zone bordering on their own country. A similar four-way division of Berlin was arranged, with an Allied Control Council located in the city to ensure uniformity of policy.

When the occupying powers faced the concrete problems of administering Germany, they discovered basic differences in aims and policies. The Russians wanted substantial reparations and also a social revolution that would transform their zone, and the whole nation if possible, into another Peoples

586

Democracy. For this reason they favored a centralized German state that would facilitate its eventual communization. The French, like the Russians, were determined to exact heavy reparations, but they preferred a loose federative union, which they regarded as less dangerous to their national security. The British and the Americans were with the French in favoring a federative state, but they opposed both the French and the Russians in economic matters.

In September, 1944, Roosevelt and Churchill had accepted the harsh Morgenthau Plan—proposed by the American Secretary of the Treasury, Henry Morgenthau, Jr.—for transforming Germany into a pastoral country with a greatly reduced industrial structure. Alluring though this goal was at the time, is was eventually discarded as impractical, unless a large percentage of the German people were to be allowed to starve. Economic realities became even clearer when both the United States and Britain found it necessary to import large quantities of food into their densely populated zones. Large numbers of German refugees had streamed into these zones from East Germany and from various regions in Central-Eastern Europe where German minorities had lived for centuries. In order to support this swollen population, London and Washington realized that more, rather than less, industrial production was needed. The Russians not unnaturally reacted with suspicion and resentment.

The issue came to a head over reparations. It had been agreed at the Potsdam Conference in July, 1945, that Russia was to receive $10 billion indemnity from Germany, to be collected from German foreign assets and through the removal of industrial equipment—from the Russian zone, and from the Western zones insofar as the equipment was not needed by the local economies. The Russians promptly proceeded to dismantle and ship East German factories to their own country, and also to tap current German factory output. The latter practice was a violation of the Potsdam agreement, as was also the refusal by the Russians to allow any inspection of the East German economy. In retaliation, the Americans and the British stopped the delivery of reparations from their zones in May, 1946, and repeatedly raised the permitted level of German industry. The next step occurred in December, 1946, when the British and the Americans combined their zones into an economic "Bizonia."

By early 1947 the four-power administration of Germany had broken up. In an effort to resolve the conflict, a Big Four conference was held in Moscow in March, 1947. The Americans and the British insisted on the economic unification of Germany; the French and the Russians were opposed. After six weeks of futile wrangling, the conference adjourned. Its failure, together with the proclamation of the Truman Doctrine at the same time, are considered by some to mark the beginning of the Cold War.*

VI. TRUMAN DOCTRINE AND MARSHALL PLAN

The most dramatic manifestation of the oncoming Cold War was President Truman's intervention in the Greek Civil War in March, 1947. Communist-led guerrillas had appeared the preceding fall in the mountains of northern

* See "Approach of the Cold War," *EMM*, No. 171.

Greece. One reason for the renewed civil strife was the wretched economic condition that drove many impoverished peasants to the rebel ranks. Another was the deteriorating international situation, which led the Soviet bloc to incite and aid the guerrillas against the British-supported Athens government. Finally there was the rightist persecution of political opponents despite the provision for amnesty and normal political procedures in the Varkiza Pact terminating the Battle of Athens. The rightest repression was sufficiently serious to cause Prime Minister Clement Attlee to telegraph to Athens on August 5, 1945, that he was concerned over reports "of right-wing excesses in contravention of the Varkiza Agreement."

These circumstances engendered considerable popular support for the insurrection, which spread from the northern mountains to the Peloponnesus and the larger islands. The likelihood for suppressing the revolt appeared bleak, so that Greece faced the prospect of prolonged civil war with the possibility of an eventual Communist victory. The situation became critical when on February 24, 1947, the British government announced that it could not afford the large-scale aid necessary to ensure victory over the rebel bands. Without further aid from London, the Athens regime probably would not have survived the year. President Truman met the emergency by proclaiming the doctrine named after him. Enunciating the principle that "it must be the policy of the United States to support free peoples who are resisting attempted subjugation by armed minorities or by outside pressures," he stated that "the very existence of the Greek state is today threatened," and requested Congress to appropriate $400 million for aid to Greece and Turkey. Thus Britain surrendered her century-old primacy in Greece, and the United States assumed the responsibility for preventing the extension of Communist influence in the eastern Mediterranean.*

The task proved more onerous than anticipated. The United States dispatched economic and military missions to Athens, and between March, 1947, and June, 1949, spent approximately $400 million for military purposes and $300 million for economic aid. Even with this lavish support the Greek government armies were unable to crush the enemy. When hard-pressed, the guerrillas simply dispersed and dug in again in new positions. Both the 1947 and 1948 campaigns proved inconclusive. In 1949 the balance shifted decisively in favor of the government. The Tito-Stalin split led Marshal Tito to to close the Yugoslav border and stop all aid to the guerrillas who had sided with Stalin. At the same time the Athens armies were being retrained by American officers to fight a mobile offensive war instead of garrisoning key towns and communication routes. Thus, in the fall of 1949 the national armies were able to drive the guerrillas from their mountain strongholds and to reach and seal the northern frontiers.

The counterpart to the Truman Doctrine in the economic sphere was the Marshall Plan. Speaking at Harvard University on June 5, 1947, Secretary of State George Marshall pointed out that for the next few years at least the requirements of Europe far exceeded her ability to pay for them. "It is logical," he added, "that the United States should do whatever it is able to do to assist in the return of normal economic health in the world, without which there can be no political stability and no assured peace." This offer of aid was followed up by the establishment in the following spring of the European

* See "Truman Doctrine," EMM, No. 172.

588 Recovery Program, commonly known as the Marshall Plan. By the time of its termination on December 31, 1951, a total of $12.5 billion was spent in support of Marshall Plan operations. This extraordinary investment, together with the human and material resources of Europe, made possible a rapid recovery that raised production and living standards to above prewar levels. But from the viewpoint of East-West relations, the Marshall Plan marked the final step toward the Cold War. The offer of aid had been directed to all countries, irrespective of ideology. Moscow, however, interpreted the offer as an anti-Communist maneuver and ordered back the Czechs and Poles who had been inclined to respond. Instead, Moscow established in January, 1949, the Council for Mutual Economic Assistance (Molotov Plan), as the Eastern counterpart to the Marshall Plan.*

Thus the line was drawn between the Communist and Western worlds. The Cold War now was in full sway, and for the next half decade one crisis followed closely on another in tragic sequence.

VII. Cold War in Europe

In order to wage the Cold War effectively, the Communist parties of Eastern Europe combined with those of France and Italy to establish in September, 1947, the Communist Information Bureau, or Cominform. The title suggested that the new body was designed merely for information purposes, but in practice it resumed the work of the Communist International disbanded in May, 1943. It coordinated the activities of the member parties in the struggle against "Anglo-American imperialism," supporting, for example, such activities as an insurrectionary general strike waged at the end of 1947 by the Communist-dominated trade unions in France.†

In February, 1948, the Communists eliminated the last bridgehead of Western influence in the Soviet sphere when they seized full control in Czechoslovakia. That small republic had tried to steer a middle course between East and West. In foreign affairs the Czechs had followed the lead of the Soviet Union, but in domestic affairs they tried to preserve some of the personal freedoms that had made their country the democratic exception in Central-Eastern Europe in the interwar years. This attempt to maintain democracy was ended when the Communists used their control of the police and of their militant "action committees" to take over the government. In March, 1948, Foreign Minister Jan Masaryk, known for his Western learnings, was reported to have committed suicide. Elections in May gave the Communists the expected large majority. Next month the venerable President Eduard Beneš, who had led his country also in the prewar period, felt constrained to resign his position. He was succeeded by the Communist leader, Gottwald, and thus all of Eastern Europe, except Finland was now in Communist hands.

Even more dramatic than the Communist takeover in Prague was the pro-

* See "Marshall Plan," *EMM*, No. 173.
† See "Establishment of Communist Information Bureau," *EMM*, No. 174.

tracted Berlin Airlift crisis that began in June, 1948. Having failed to dissuade the British and Americans from setting up a separate West German government, the Russians retaliated by cutting off railway and road access to the three Western sectors of Berlin. The justification given was that with the end of four-power government in Berlin there was no further need for the Western powers to remain in the city. The Americans replied with an unprecedented airlift that supplied the food, coal, and other essentials needed by the two million people in the Western sectors. By the spring of 1949 the success of the airlift was apparent, and in May the Russians called off the blockade. In the same month a West German Parliamentary Council adopted the Basic Law of the future "Federal Republic of Germany," while the East German People's Congress completed a constitution for the "German Democratic Republic." In September, the Federal Republic was officially launched in West Germany, and in the next month the Democratic Republic was launched in the East. Thus the Cold War had split Germany in two.

These various manifestations of Communist aggressiveness—the coup in Czechoslovakia, the Berlin blockade, and the continuing civil war in Greece—persuaded the Western powers that some defensive alliance system was necessary. In March, 1947, Britain and France concluded a military alliance (Treaty of Dunkirk), which in March, 1948, was broadened to include the Benelux countries—Belgium, the Netherlands and Luxembourg (Treaty of Brussels). It was apparent, however, that Western Europe could not be defended without American assistance, and the New World became involved with the signing of the North Atlantic Treaty in Washington on April 4, 1949. The treaty included the United States and Canada, the five members of the Brussels Pact, and Italy, Portugal, Denmark, Iceland, and Norway. These twelve original powers were joined later by Greece and Turkey (1951) and by West Germany (1955). The treaty provided that "an armed attack against one or more" of the signatories, in Europe, North Africa, or North America, "shall be considered an attack against them all." Originally the treaty called only for the establishment of the North Atlantic Council, but the outbreak of the Korean War stimulated the creation of an integrated defense force under a single command. It was financed largely by the United States, and its supreme commander was an American, although various signatories contributed specified numbers of divisions. This force never was sufficiently strong to stop a major Soviet invasion, but could fight a costly delaying action and cause the Russians to think twice before advancing westward.*

Meanwhile, the Soviet Union had made corresponding political and military arrangements in Eastern Europe. Even before the end of the war Stalin had concluded mutual assistance pacts with Czechoslovakia, Yugoslavia, and Poland, and by 1948 similar pacts were signed with the former Axis satellites—Bulgaria, Rumania, and Hungary. In May, 1955, a more formal and comprehensive military alliance was concluded between Russia and the East European countries. This was known as the Warsaw Pact and constituted the Eastern response to the North Atlantic Treaty. Thus Europe as well as Germany was cut in two by the Cold War—the Western half armed and organized under the aegis of the United States and the Eastern under that of the Soviet Union.

* See "North Atlantic Treaty," *EMM*, No. 175.

VIII. COLD WAR IN THE FAR EAST

In 1950, the focus of the Cold War shifted from Europe to the Far East. By this time a balance had been reached in Europe between East and West. But in the Far East the balance was upset by a momentous development—the triumph of the Communists in China. Just as the Bolshevik Revolution was the outstanding by-product of World War I, so the Chinese Communist Revolution was the outstanding by-product of World War II.

Chiang Kai-shek had become the master of China in 1928, but from the outset his Kuomintang regime was threatened by two mortal enemies, the Communists within and the Japanese without. During World War II his position became particularly difficult. The country was divided into three sections: the east, controlled by the Japanese and administered through a puppet government at Nanking; the northwest, controlled by the Communists operating from their capital at Yenan; and the west and southwest, ruled by Chiang's Nationalist government from its capital in Chungking.

It was during the war years that Chiang's regime was irretrievably undermined. Chiang traditionally had depended on the support of the conservative landlord class and of the relatively enlightened big businessmen. The latter were largely eliminated when the Japanese overran the east coast, and Chiang was left with the self-centered and short-sighted landlords of the interior. His government became increasingly corrupt and unresponsive to the needs of a peasantry wracked and aroused by years of war. In contrast to the decaying Kuomintang, the Communists carried out land reforms in their territories, thereby winning the support of the peasant masses. They also had a disciplined and efficient organization that brought order out of political and economic chaos in the areas under their control. They were more successful than the Nationalists, moreover, in portraying themselves as patriots dedicated to ridding the country of foreign invaders and restoring China's unity, pride, and greatness.

Such was the situation when Japan's surrender in August, 1945, set off a wild scramble by the Nationalists and Communists to take over the Japanese-occupied parts of China. The Communists issued orders to their troops to take over the areas held by the Japanese. Chiang Kai-shek promptly cancelled these orders and insisted that the Communists make no move without instructions from him. He was ignored, and clashes occurred between Communist and Kuomintang forces. With civil war imminent, the United States sent a mission under General George Marshall to attempt to negotiate a settlement. But neither side could overcome its fear and suspicion of the other, and Marshall's mediation proved abortive. By 1947 the final showdown was at hand.

The Communists occupied the countryside around the major cities, being helped by the Russians, who turned over to them the arms the Japanese had surrendered in Manchuria. The Nationalists, aided by the transportation services of the United States Navy and Air Force, won all the main cities, including Nanking, and also rushed troops north to Manchuria. The latter move was a strategic blunder. The Kuomintang forces found themselves in indefensible positions and were forced in the fall of 1948 to surrender to the Chinese Red Army. A chain of comparable military disasters followed in quick succession. The Communist armies swept down from Manchuria through the major cities of North China. By April, 1949, they were crossing the Yangtze and fanning out over South China. The American ambassador in Nanking reported at the time to Washington: "The ridiculously easy Communist crossing of the Yangtze was made possible by defections at key points, disagreements in the High Command, and the failure of the Air Force to give effective support." [6]

The Communist steamroller advanced even more rapidly in the south than in the north. By the end of 1949 it had overrun all of mainland China. Chiang fled to the island of Taiwan (Formosa), while in Peking the Communist leader, Mao Tse-tung, proclaimed the People's Republic of China on October 1, 1949,* and brought about a turning point in the history of China, and indeed of the entire world.

In the few years since 1949 the Communists have transformed China at an unprecedented rate. In place of the flabby and decentralized political state of the past they imposed a monolithic and omniscient structure, extending into every city, every village, and every household. The Communists at the head of this structure were able to reach down to the individual citizen, moving him to new occupations and forcing him to live and think in new ways. They uprooted the traditional Confucian culture by weakening the old family system, ending the inferior position of women, and ignoring the old classics in favor of a new literature and art designed to help build the new society. This degree of regimentation and efficiency made possible the collectivization of agriculture and a massive speed-up in industrialization—all within a few years. And this in turn made China a major world power, viewed apprehensively as an aggressive nation to be feared, rather than eyed covetously as a helpless country to be partitioned.

The repercussions of this great transformation were felt throughout the world. Washington and other capitals are watching the new China closely, especially after her intervention in Korea, in Tibet, and in northern India. Moscow was equally concerned, particularly following the historic split between Khrushchev and Mao Tse-tung. The underdeveloped and uncommitted nations observed with interest the Communist techniques by which China was pulling herself up by her bootstraps. China's population is so tremendous— 582,603,417 in 1953, according to the National Bureau of Statistics in Peking —that she would have been a world force to be reckoned with had she remained an underdeveloped nation. When a quarter of the world's population enters an extraordinarily dynamic phase, as China did in 1949, then one is justified in asserting that a turning point has been reached in the history of the world.

The victory of communism in China was a serious setback for the United States. In Japan, however, the postwar occupation was dominated by the United States. Japan, in contrast to Germany, was governed by a single Supreme Command of the Allied powers, which included Allied representatives. The Supreme Commander (General Douglas MacArthur) and the bulk of the occupation forces were American.

* See "Communist Triumph in China," EMM, No. 176.

MacArthur's instructions were to disarm and demilitarize the country, develop democratic institutions, and create a viable economy. Accordingly, he disbanded the imperial army and navy, banned patriotic organizations, stripped Emperor Hirohito of the divinity attributed to him, and purged education of its militaristic elements. In 1947 he proclaimed a democratic constitution that transferred sovereignty from the emperor to the people, guaranteed individual rights, and granted women equal status with men. In the economic field the most important measure was wholesale redistribution of land. By 1952, 90 per cent of the arable acreage was owned by former tenants. Less successful was the attempt to break up the large family corporations, or *zaibatsu,* that had dominated the prewar industry, finance, and foreign trade. The initial measures against the *zaibatsu* were dropped because it was felt that they hampered economic recovery.

Although far less revolutionary than the Communist upheaval in China, the occupation of Japan nevertheless had a profound impact on that country. The Japanese always had been receptive to foreign ways, but never to the degree in which they were since World War II. The cataclysmic defeat suffered in that struggle discredited the old order. The younger generation in particular sought new models and leaders, and was persuasively encouraged to do so.

By 1951, when the occupation had accomplished most of its aims, a peace treaty was concluded and signed by the United States and most of the Allies, with the notable exception of China and the Soviet Union, who considered the terms overly generous. The treaty restored Japanese sovereignty, but only over the four main islands. There were no military or economic restrictions, except that the United States was permitted to maintain military bases in Japan. The United States also gained trusteeship over the Ryuku and Bonin islands and over Japan's former Pacific mandates. Japan relinquished the Kuril islands and southern Sakhalin (which had been allotted to Russia) as well as Formosa, but the future disposition of these islands was left open. In effect, this treaty made Japan the main bastion of the American position in the Far East. In support of this bastion the United States spent about $2 billion in the first six years after the war. Only with the demand for a wide variety of goods during the Korean War was the Japanese economy able to get back on its feet.

In the Far East, as in Europe, then, World War II was followed by Cold War. Russia backed Mao Tse-tung, albeit belatedly, while the United States vainly attempted to maintain Chiang Kai-shek as master of China. Conversely, in Japan the United States dominated the occupation and utilized it to further her interests, while the Soviet representatives impotently protested. Once the outcome had apparently been settled in both countries, there was hope, as expressed by Secretary of State Dean Acheson, for "the dust to settle" and for a balance to be reached, as had been done in Europe. The hope was shattered when in 1950 fighting broke out in Korea and the Cold War became hot.

IX. Hot War in Korea

The tragedy of Korea is that its location has made it a natural bridge between China and Japan. Repeatedly it has been fought over by the two countries, and occasionally by Russia also. Since 1895—and formally since

1910—Korea had passed under Japanese rule. Thereafter it was in effect a colony, though unique in that it was under Asian rather than European domination. During World War II, at the 1943 Cairo Conference, the United States, Britain, and China declared that, "in due course" Korea should once more be free and independent. But a generation of Japanese rule had left Korea without the necessary experience for self-government. The victorious Allies decided, therefore, that for a period of not more than five years Korea, though independent, should be under the trusteeship of the United States, Russia, Britain, and China.

With the surrender of Japan, American and Russian troops poured into Korea. For purposes of military convenience the 38th parallel was set as the dividing line in their operations. The coming of the Cold War froze this temporary division in Korea as it did in Germany. The Russians set up in their zone a regime dominated by the Communist New People's Party. In the south, the Americans leaned on English-speaking Koreans, who usually were members of the conservative upper class. In August, 1948, a Republic of Korea was proclaimed in the south, with Dr. Syngman Rhee as president. A month later the North Koreans formed their People's Democratic Republic under Kim Il-sung.

These two leaders symbolized in their persons the basic differences between the two zones. Kim Il-sung, still in his thirties, was Moscow-trained, secretary of the Korean Communist Party, and since 1931 an underground resistance fighter against the Japanese. Syngman Rhee, an elder statesman of over seventy, had fought the Japanese since the turn of the century. A graduate of Harvard and Princeton, a student and admirer of Woodrow Wilson, and a Methodist missionary, he had lived for decades in China and the United States as head of the Korean government-in-exile. A UN commission attempted without success to mediate between the regimes headed by these two men. So strong were the feelings that the commission warned in September, 1949, of the danger of civil war.

On June 24, 1950, civil war did begin, when North Korean troops suddenly crossed the 38th parallel in order to "liberate" South Korea. Within a few hours the UN commission reported that South Korea was the victim of aggression. The next day the UN Security Council adopted an American resolution calling for an immediate cease-fire and the withdrawal of the North Koreans to the 38th parallel. The same afternoon and on the following day President Truman conferred with his advisors and decided to give full military support to South Korea. On June 27 the Security Council asked UN members to "furnish such assistance to the Republic of Korea as may be necessary to repel the armed attack and to restore international peace and security in the area." Thus the United Nations for the first time in its brief history had decided to use force. The Security Council's decision was made possible only because of Russia's temporary boycott of its meetings in protest against the refusal to admit Communist China in place of Nationalist China.*

Forty UN member states responded to the Security Council's appeal and provided supplies, transport, hospital units, and, in some cases, combat forces. But the main contribution, aside from that of South Korea, came from the United States, and General MacArthur served as commander in chief. The course of the Korean War fell into two phases—the first before, and the second after, the Chinese intervention. The first phase began with the headlong rush

* See "War in Korea," *EMM*, No. 177.

594

of the North Korean forces down the length of the peninsula to within fifty miles of the port of Pusan at the southern tip. Then on September 14, 1950, an American army landed at Inchon, far up the coast near the 38th parallel, and in twelve days retook the South Korean capital, Seoul. The North Koreans, their communications severed, fell back as precipitously as they had advanced. By the end of September the UN forces had reached the 38th parallel.

The question now was whether to cross or not to cross. The issue was transferred to the General Assembly, because the Soviet Union, with its veto power, had returned to the Security Council. On October 7, 1950, the Assembly resolved that "all constituent acts be taken . . . for the establishment of a unified, independent, and democratic government in the sovereign state of Korea." The next day American forces crossed the 38th parallel and quickly occupied Pyongyang, the North Korean capital. By November 22 they reached the Yalu River, the boundary line between Korea and the Chinese province of Manchuria.

At this point the second phase of the Korean War began with a massive attack by Chinese "volunteers" supported by Russian-made jets. The Chinese drove southward rapidly in what looked like a repetition of the first phase of the war. Early in January, 1951, they retook Seoul, but the UN forces now recovered and held their ground. In March, Seoul once more changed hands, and by June the battleline ran roughly along the 38th parallel. The most significant feature of this second phase of the war is that it was kept strictly localized despite the involvement of both China and the United States. This occurred because neither regarded the future of Korea as a matter of really vital national interest. Hence the United States did not use the atomic bomb, and the Soviet Union sent no troops. The war was kept at the level of an "incident," despite the scale of the fighting.

By mid-1951 it was apparent that a stalemate prevailed at the front. Large-scale fighting petered out, and armistice negotiations started. After two years of stormy and often-interrupted negotiations, an armistice agreement was concluded on July 27, 1953. The terms reflected the military stalemate. The line of partition between North and South Korea remained roughly where it had been before the war. The Western powers had successfully contained communism in Korea and had vindicated the authority of the United Nations. The Chinese had secured North Korea as a Communist buffer-state between Manchuria and Western influences. And meanwhile, most of the Korean countryside had been laid waste and about 10 per cent of the Korean people had been killed.

SUGGESTED READING

For contrasting interpretations of the Cold War, see J. Lukacs, *A History of the Cold War* (Garden City, N. Y.: Doubleday, 1961), which is highly critical of Soviet policy, and the following two studies which are critical of Western as well as Soviet diplomacy: D. F. Fleming, *The Cold War and Its Origins, 1917–1960* (London: G. Allen, 1961) 2 vols. and F. L. Schuman, *The Cold War: Retrospect and Prospect* (Baton Rouge: Louisiana State Univ., 1963). See also the convenient collection of varying interpretations in N. A. Graebner, ed., *The Cold War: Ideological Conflict or Power Struggle* (Boston: Heath, 1964).

Excellent brief surveys of general post-World War II history are provided by G. Bruun and D. E. Lee, *The Second World War and After* (Boston: Houghton, 1964), and H. W. Gatzke, *The Present in Perspective,* 2nd ed. (Chicago: Rand McNally, 1961).

The diplomacy of World War II is analyzed competently and succinctly by J. L. Snell, *Illusion and Necessity: The Diplomacy of Global War, 1939–1945* (Boston: Houghton, 1963). For the satellite treaties, see T. V. Kalijarvi, ed., "Peace Settlements of World War II," *The Annals of the American Academy of Political and Social Science,* which includes contributions by twenty authors. Competent studies of the UN are provided by D. C. Coyle, *The United Nations and How It Works,* rev. ed. (New York: New Am. Lib., 1962; A Mentor Book); W. H. C. Laves and C. A. Thomson, *UNESCO: Purpose, Progress, Prospects* (Bloomington, Ind.: Indiana Univ., 1957); and G. N. Shuster, *UNESCO: Assessment and Promise* (New York: Harper, 1964). Specific aspects of postwar diplomacy are considered in the following: J. L. Snell, ed., *The Meaning of Yalta* (Baton Rouge: Louisiana State Univ., 1956), and *Wartime Origins of the East-West Dilemma over Germany* (New Orleans: Hauser, 1959); H. B. Price, *The Marshall Plan and Its Meaning* (Ithaca: Cornell Univ., 1955); and B. T. Moore, *NATO and the Future of Europe* (New York: Harper, 1958).

For developments in the Far East, see C. A. Johnson, *Peasant Nationalism and Communist Power: The Emergence of a Revolutionary China, 1937–1945* (Stanford: Stanford Univ., 1962); A. N. Young, *China and the Helping Hand, 1937– 1945* (Cambridge: Harvard Univ., 1963); Tang Tsou, *America's Failure in China: 1941–50* (Chicago: Univ. of Chicago, 1964); D. Rees, *Korea: The Limited War* (New York: St. Martins, 1964); L. M. Goodrich, *Korea: A Study of U. S. Policy in the United Nations* (New York: Council on Foreign Relations, 1956); and A. D. Barnett, ed., *Communist Strategies in Asia* (New York: Praeger, 1964).

*Hereafter, perhaps, the natives of those [overseas]
countries may grow stronger, or those of Europe may
grow weaker, and the inhabitants of all the different
quarters of the world may arrive at that equality of
courage and force which, by inspiring mutual fear, can
alone overawe the injustice of independent nations into
some sort of respect for the rights of one another. But
nothing seems more likely to establish this equality of
force than that mutual communication of knowledge
and of all sorts of improvements which an extensive
commerce from all countries to all countries naturally,
or rather necessarily, carries along with it.*

ADAM SMITH

*We prefer self-government with danger
to servitude in tranquillity.*

KWAME NKRUMAH

End of Empires

major difference between World War I and World War II
lay in their colonial aftermaths. Europe's hold over the colonial
empires was weakened but not broken by World War I; indeed, the
colonial holdings were expanded by the acquisition of Arab lands as
mandates. After World War II, by contrast, an irrepressible revolutionary wave swept the colonial empires and ended European
domination with dramatic dispatch. In 1939, the only independent
states in sub-Saharan Africa were Liberia and South Africa, and they
owed their independence to their atypical historical backgrounds. The
one had been settled in the early nineteenth century by freed slaves,
and the other was controlled by a resident European minority. Twenty-
five years later, the only significant colonies left in sub-Saharan Africa
were Portuguese Angola and Mozambique, and the cluster under
South Africa's shadow: Southern Rhodesia, South-West Africa,
Bechuanaland, Swaziland, and Basutoland. Just as most of Europe's
colonies had been swiftly acquired in the last two decades of the
nineteenth century, so most of them now were lost in an equally short
period of time in the two decades following World War II. Between
1944 and 1964, a total of 53 countries had won their independence.
These included in mid-1963 a little over one billion people, or 31
per cent of the world's 3.18 billion at that date (see Table 1). After
so many epoch-making triumphs and achievements overseas, the

TABLE 1. African-Asian March to Independence

	Became independent of	Year	Estimated population mid-1963 (millions)		Became independent of	Year	Estimated population mid-1963 (millions)
Syria	France	1944	5.0	Mali	France	1960	4.4
Lebanon	France	1944	1.8	Senegal	France	1960	3.0
Jordan	Britain	1946	1.8	Malagasy	France	1960	5.9
Philippines	United States	1946	30.6	Togo	France	1960	1.5
India	Britain	1947	461.3	Cyprus	Britain	1960	0.5
Pakistan	Britain	1947	98.6	Ivory Coast	France	1960	3.4
Burma	Britain	1948	22.8	Upper Volta	France	1960	4.5
N. Korea	Japan	1948	8.9	Niger	France	1960	3.1
S. Korea	Japan	1948	26.9	Dahomey	France	1960	2.2
Israel	Britain	1948	2.3	Congo Republic	France	1960	0.9
Ceylon	Britain	1948	10.8	Central African			
Indonesia	Netherlands	1949	100.1	Republic	France	1960	1.3
Libya	Italy	1952	1.3	Chad	France	1960	2.8
Cambodia	France	1954	5.9	Gabon	France	1960	0.5
Laos	France	1954	2.0	Mauritania	France	1960	0.8
N. Vietnam	France	1954	17.0	Sierra Leone	Britain	1961	2.6
S. Vietnam	France	1954	15.5	Tanganyika †	Britain	1961	9.7
Sudan	Britain-Egypt	1956	12.8	Algeria	France	1962	12.0
Morocco	France	1956	12.6	Burundi	Belgium	1962	2.6
Tunisia	France	1956	4.4	Rwanda	Belgium	1962	2.9
Ghana	Britain	1957	7.3	Uganda	Britain	1962	7.2
Malaya *	Britain	1957	7.6	Kenya	Britain	1963	8.8
Guinea	France	1958	3.3	Zanzibar †	Britain	1963	0.7
Republic of				Malta	Britain	1964	0.3
the Congo	Belgium	1960	15.2	Malawi	Britain	1964	3.0
Somalia	Italy	1960	2.0	Zambia	Britain	1964	2.5
Nigeria	Britain	1960	37.2	Gambia	Britain	1965	0.3
Cameroon	France	1960	4.4				
				TOTAL			1,006.8

* Combined in 1963 with Singapore, Sarawak, and Sabah (British North Borneo), to form the state of Malaysia with a population of 10 million.
† Tanganyika and Zanzibar combined in 1964 to form the United Republic of Tanganyika and Zanzibar, or Tanzania.

Europeans appeared in the mid-twentieth century to be retreating back to the small Eurasian peninsula whence they had set forth half a millennium earlier.

I. COLD WAR AND COLONIAL REVOLUTION

The Cold War between East and West was paralleled by the struggle between colonial subjects and imperial authorities. The two movements were interrelated, and they interacted one upon the other. The Soviet Union, and especially Communist China, supported colonial revolution as a means of undermining the prestige and strength of the West. Conversely, the Western countries supported one another over colonial issues, though they did so with grave reservations, because of Cold War considerations—hence the United States support of Britain in Cyprus and of France in Indochina and Algeria. Likewise, the exigencies of Cold War led to the curious East-West competition in courting colonial and ex-colonial peoples. The latter quickly exploited this situation to extract maximum assistance from Moscow and Peking as well as from Washington, London, and Paris.

598

Despite this interrelatedness, the colonial revolution was not a by-product of the Cold War. The colonial awakening antedated by far the Cold War, reaching back at least to the 1905 Russian Revolution and Russo-Japanese War (see Chapter 19, section V). Besides, the colonial revolution undoubtedly would have occurred even had there been no Cold War, though the latter did affect in certain cases the tempo and the form of the colonial uprisings.

During the course of World War II, the leaders of the imperial nations made clear their determination to hold on to their colonies. Winston Churchill made his oft-quoted pronouncement in 1942 that he had "not become the King's First Minister in order to preside over the liquidation of the British empire." Likewise, the Brazzaville Conference held in 1944 under the auspices of the Free French government, declared that "The attainment of self-government in the colonies even in the most distant future must be excluded." [1]

The actions of the British and the French during the war years corresponded with these pronouncements. Both powers paid little attention to the wishes or the interests of colonial peoples. In the Atlantic Charter they had committed themselves to "respect the right of all peoples to choose the form of government under which they will live; and . . . to see sovereign rights and self-government restored to those who have been forcibly deprived of them." Allied policies soon demonstrated that these principles were regarded as applicable to Europe but not to the overseas territories.

The British, for example, brought India into the war without consulting the Congress party leaders, Nehru and Gandhi, and they arranged with the Russians for a joint occupation of the nominally independent nation of Iran. In Egypt, another technically independent country, the British took advantage of their special treaty rights to set up at Cairo and Alexandria their main Middle Eastern bases. The French decided the fate of their "natives" in accord with military necessity; the allegiance of the various colonies to the Vichy government or to de Gaulle depended on the decisions of the French governors or military commanders rather than on the wishes of the local populations. Yet, despite these unilateral actions, virtually all the Asian colonies were free within a decade after the war, and virtually all the African colonies, within two decades after the war.*

II. Roots of Colonial Revolution

The United Nations Charter, adopted in June, 1945, created a system of colonial trusteeship to replace the mandate arrangement of the League of Nations. Article 76 of the Charter stipulated that the trustee countries "promote the political, economic, social, and educational advancement of the inhabitants of the trust territories, and their progressive development toward self-government or independence as may be appropriate to the particular circumstances of each territory and its peoples and the freely expressed wishes of the peoples concerned. . . ."

The prewar mandates were now converted into trusteeships, and provision was made for UN members to place their own colonies under trusteeship status. No country proved willing to do this—the Union of South Africa insisted on

* See "Colonial Revolution after World War I and World War II," *EMM*, No. 178.

administering South-West Africa as a "C" mandate. It is not surprising that although the UN did contribute appreciably to the winning of independence by some colonies, such as the Dutch East Indies, the dynamism behind the great colonial revolution did not emanate from the UN. Rather it was the product of the exceptionally favorable international situation at the end of World War II, and of certain historical forces within the colonial world that had been gathering momentum for several decades.

An unprecedented weakening of the foremost colonial powers took place during the Second World War: France and Holland were overrun and occupied, while Britain was debilitated economically and militarily. Equally important was the growth of democratic, anti-imperialist sentiment within the imperial countries themselves. Gone were the days when white men in the colonies confidently asserted, "We are here because we are superior." Now their presence was questioned, not only by their subjects but also by their own fellow countrymen. Mussolini's attack on Ethiopia in 1935 was widely regarded in Western Europe as a deplorable throwback, while the Anglo-French assault on the Suez in 1956 aroused vehement popular opposition in both Britain and France. The end of the West's global hegemony was due as much to the lack of will to rule as it was to lack of strength.

In addition, the colonial revolution was helped along by the fact that the two dominant postwar powers, the United States and the Soviet Union, were not interested in acquiring overseas possessions at the expense of their defeated enemies or their weakened allies. They did gain control, directly or indirectly, over strategic islands and satellite states in the Pacific Ocean and in Eastern Europe, but they did not follow the example of Britain and France who eagerly divided German and Turkish colonies following World War I. Instead, by a curious paradox, the opposite occurred: The colonials exploited the Cold War to play off the Soviet Union against the United States and to use both powers in winning their independence and in obtaining economic assistance.

The short-lived Japanese Empire in Asia also contributed substantially to the colonial revolution. Western military prestige was shattered by the ease with which the Japanese drove the British out of Malaya and Burma, the French out of Indochina, the Dutch out of Indonesia, and the Americans out of the Philippines. The political foundations of Western imperialism were undermined by Japanese propaganda based on the slogan "Asia for the Asians." When the Japanese were at last forced to surrender their conquests, they deliberately made the restoration of Western rule as difficult as possible by leaving arms with local nationalist organizations and by recognizing these organizations as independent governments—as in the case of Ho Chi Minh's Viet Minh in Indochina, and Sukarno's Putera in Indonesia.

It should be noted, however, that the Africans who escaped Japanese invasion also won freedom along with the Asians, thus pointing up the fact that, important as the Japanese impact was, it merely intensified the great unrest and awakening that had been gathering momentum since the beginning of the century. The series of colonial uprisings followed World War I reflected this burgeoning movement (see Chapter 21). In the intervening years it had gained strength and purpose, with the growth of a Western-educated native intelligentsia. It was not accidental that the successful nationalist leaders were

600

not unreconstructed Malayan sultans or Nigerian chiefs or Indian princes, but rather men who had studied in Western universities and observed Western institutions in operation—men like Gandhi, Nehru, Sukarno, Nkrumah, Azikwe, and Bourguiba.

This worldwide colonial awakening was further stimulated during World War II with the service of millions of colonials in both Allied and Japanese armies and labor battalions. Many Africans fought under the British, French, and Italian flags, while over two million Indians volunteered for the British forces, and an additional 40,000 Indian prisoners captured in Hong Kong, Singapore, and Burma signed up for the Japanese-sponsored Indian National army. When all these men returned to their homes, they inevitably regarded in a new light the local colonial officials and native leaders. The civilian populations were affected at this time, as during World War I, by the Allied propaganda regarding freedom and self-determination, as well as by the privation and suffering brought on by the war in certain regions.

III. India and Pakistan

By far the most important single event in the colonial revolution was the winning of independence by India and Pakistan. The Indian subcontinent, with its vast resources, human and material, had from the beginning been the keystone of the British Empire and the epitome of European imperial authority. More than a century of British rule had prepared India better than any other colony for self-rule. The Civil Service had been largely Indianized; the universities had turned out generations of Western-educated leaders; and the Congress party had voiced and directed into the proper channels nationalist aspirations (see Chapter 15, section IV–VI).

When Britain declared war on Germany on September 3, 1939, the viceroy, the Marquis of Linlithgow, on the same day proclaimed India also to be at war. The Congress leader, Nehru, observed bitterly, "One man, and he a foreigner and a representative of a hated system, could plunge four hundred millions of human beings into war, without the slightest reference to them. . . . In the dominions the decision was taken by popular representatives after full debate. . . . Not so in India, and it hurt." [2] Congress protestations were curtly rejected by London until the national emergency created by the fall of France and the beginning of the battle for Britain. The viceroy then announced that basic changes were not feasible during the war, but that afterward India would be granted dominion status. Congress promptly rejected this offer and the deadlock continued.

Japan's precipitous conquest of Southeast Asia in early 1942 fundamentally changed the Indian situation. With Japanese armies poised on Bengal's borders, India was transformed from a reluctant ally in a quiet byway to one positioned directly in the path of the rapidly advancing enemy. Churchill responded by sending to India on March 22 a cabinet member, Sir Stafford Cripps. Again major change was excluded for the duration of the war, but as soon as it was over, India could become fully autonomous, with the right to secede from the Commonwealth. Congress turned down Cripp's offer and on August 7, 1942, passed a "Quit India Resolution" demanding immediate

The last British troops leave India. (Wide World Photos)

freedom, "both for the sake of India and for the success of the cause of the UN." Congress further threatened, if its demand was not met, to wage "a mass struggle on non-violent lines." Britain's response was wholesale repression: Over 60,000 people were arrested, including all the Congress leaders; 14,000 were detained without trial; 940 were killed; and 1,630 were injured in clashes with the police and military.*

It was a most critical moment for the Allies as well as for India. The Germans had by then reached the Volga and were only thirty miles from Alexandria, while the Japanese had overrun Burma. The gigantic German and Japanese pincers were separated only by India, which was seething with disaffection, and by the Arab countries, which sided more with the Axis than with the Allies. Little effort would have been needed for the Germans and the Japanese to penetrate into these countries and to set fire to the smoldering tinder. Had they done so, they would have completely closed in the Eurasian landmass, with incalculable repercussions resulting.

This near catastrophe for the West was averted only because Hitler chose to squander his divisions on the Russian plains, and because the Japanese, despite their threats and maneuvers, never really planned to invade India. Even so, Britain's position in the subcontinent would have been precarious, if not impossible, had Congress made any preparations for armed revolt. Instead, under Gandhi's influence, only nonviolent resistance was offered. Despite this lack of militant leadership, however, the arrest of the Congress leaders precipitated strikes and riots in the cities and the countryside; but the resistance was unplanned and uncoordinated, so that the British were able to crush the centers of violence one after another.

During the remaining years of the war, the British stood firm in refusing to release the Congress leaders unless they modified their "Quit India" demand.

* See "Nationalist Riots in India," *EMM,* No. 181.

602

The leaders, in turn, refused to do so, and remained incarcerated for the duration. Meanwhile, Mohammed Jinnah, head of the Muslim League, took advantage of this hobbling of Congress to win India's Muslims to his organization and thus prepare the ground for an independent postwar Muslim state. Tirelessly and passionately he preached his gospel of a free Pakistan. "Muslim India cannot accept any constitution which must necessarily result in a Hindu majority government. . . . Mussulmans are not a minority as it is commonly known and understood. . . . Mussulmens are a nation according to any definition of a nation, and they must have their homelands, their territory, and their state." [3]

A new and decisive turn in Indian affairs was taken with the Labour party victory in the British elections of July, 1945. Labour traditionally had championed Indian freedom, and now Prime Minister Attlee acted swiftly for its materialization. Apart from his party's commitments and sympathies, the fact is that Attlee had little choice but to accept independence. Indian nationalism, inflamed by the wartime experiences, no longer could be repressed by sheer physical force, as became apparent when the government brought to trial at the end of 1945 some officers of the Japanese-sponsored Indian National army. These men immediately became national heroes, not because they had cooperated with the Japanese, but because their aim had been to oust the hated British. So strong was the feeling throughout the country that the trial had to be dropped. The truth was that Britain could no longer rule the country against the wishes of its people. Nor was there much inclination any longer to attempt to do so. The Indian Civil Service had become even more Indianized during the war, while British investments in India had shrunk drastically; and the British public had become weary of the never-ending Indian problem. Thus Attlee was now able to sever ties with the former jewel of the empire with relatively little opposition at home.

In March, 1946, a three-man cabinet mission went to India to make arrangements for self-government. Two months later a plan was made public, but it failed to win the support of the feuding Congress and League. The Labour government then sent out Admiral Lord Louis Mountbatten as the new viceroy. After hurried conferences, he concluded that no plan for preserving Indian political unity was feasible, and recommended partition, with the two governments each to have dominion status. By this time the Congress leaders had realized that partition was inevitable, so they accepted the plan. In July, 1947, the British Parliament passed the Indian Independence Act, and on August 15, both Pakistan and the Union of India became free nations in the British Commonwealth. The elasticity of the Commonwealth was stretched one degree further to permit the two newcomers to participate as republics in an institution that necessarily maintained a monarch as its symbolic head.

IV. SOUTHEAST ASIA

Southeast Asia, in contrast to India, was occupied by the Japanese during the war. A common pattern is discernible throughout the area during this brief occupation period between 1942 and 1945. In almost every country, widespread disaffection against Western rule had contributed substantially to the

A veiled woman votes in an Indian village. (Indian Information Service)

swift conquests of the Japanese (see Chapter 25, section II). The latter then proclaimed, like the Germans, that their conquests inaugurated the beginning of a "New Order." The watchwords of this "New Order" were "Asia for the Asians," "Greater East Asia Co-Prosperity Sphere," and "no conquests, no oppression and no exploitation."

If these principles had been applied, the Japanese could have mobilized solid popular support in most of Southeast Asia, especially since they had been welcomed generally by the local populations as liberators. The Japanese military, however, had other plans, so that the principles remained propagandist slogans which soon sounded hollow and unconvincing. These military leaders viewed Greater East Asia not as a "Co-Prosperity Sphere" but as a region consisting of satellite states held under varying degrees of control. The Japanese armed forces everywhere lived off the land as much as possible, frequently creating severe local shortages of food and supplies; and they expropriated ruthlessly whatever foodstuffs and industrial raw materials were needed for the home islands. In return, the Japanese were able to offer little, since their economy was not strong enough to produce both war materials and consumer goods.

It is understandable that after the initial honeymoon period, relations between the Japanese and the local nationalists rapidly deteriorated. If the occupation had been prolonged, the Japanese undoubtedly would have been faced with serious uprisings. Fortunately for them, they were forced to pull out during 1945. In doing so, they did everything possible to create obstacles in the way of a restoration of Western rule. In Indochina they overthrew the Vichy regime and recognized Ho Chi Minh's provisional government; in

604

Indonesia they handed over the administration to the nationalist leader Sukarno; and in many regions they distributed arms to local revolutionary groups.

It is not surprising that within ten years of the Japanese withdrawal, all Southeast Asia was independent. The manner in which the various countries won their freedom varied, depending upon the imperial rulers involved. The British, having been forced to face facts in India, were the most realistic in coping with Southeast Asian nationalism. In January, 1948, they recognized Burma as an independent republic outside the Commonwealth,* and in the next month they granted Ceylon full Dominion status within the Commonwealth. Malayan independence, however, was delayed until February, 1957, one reason being the country's mosaic-like ethnic composition, including Malayans and Chinese—each a little over 40 per cent of the total population—as well as Indians, Pakistanis, and a few Europeans. The Chinese were the prime movers behind a Communist uprising that began in 1948; the ensuing jungle warfare was very costly and dragged on until 1955. In 1963, Malaya combined with Singapore, Sarawak, and Sabah (British North Borneo) to constitute the new state of Malaysia.

The French and the Dutch, whose subjects also demanded independence, proved less adjustable and fared much worse. The Japanese continued to occupy Indonesia even after their surrender in September, 1945, because the Netherlands had no forces with which to replace them. The task of dealing with Sukarno's nationalist government, which had been proclaimed on August 17, fell to Admiral Mountbatten. When the Dutch returned the following year, they were willing to grant Indonesia some measure of self-government but not enough to satisfy the nationalists. The negotiations broke down and the Dutch resorted to armed force to reassert their authority. The war dragged on until 1947 when the Dutch finally recognized the independent United States of Indonesia. This legacy of armed conflict embittered the future relations between the two countries, and although a Dutch-Indonesian Union with a common crown existed for a few years, it ended when Sukarno withdrew in 1954. Relations became more strained in the following years because the Dutch refused to yield Netherlands New Guinea to the new republic. In 1957, in retaliation, Indonesia seized more than $1 billion worth of Dutch assets and in 1960, severed diplomatic relations with The Hague. Three years later Sukarno gained control over West Irian, thus liquidating the last remnant of an empire older than most of the British Empire.

The French in Indochina fought longer and more stubbornly to retain their colony, but in the end they, too, were forced out. Indochina consisted of three nations: Vietnam, Laos, and Cambodia. Resistance against the restoration of French rule was led by the Vietminh, or League for the Independence of Vietnam. Though comprising many elements, the Vietminh was led by a Communist, Ho Chi Minh, who had lived in Paris, Moscow, and China. As had happened in Indonesia, delay in evicting the Japanese after the war's end enabled Ho Chi Minh to proclaim in 1945 the provisional Republic of Vietnam.†

The French refused to recognize the new regime, and war ensued. Laos and

* See "Independence for Burma," *EMM*, No. 180.
† See "Declaration of Independence in Vietnam," *EMM*, No. 179.

Cambodia were easily reoccupied by the French, but an exhausting struggle dragged on in Vietnam. What chance there was for a French victory ended when China went Communist and lent support to Ho Chi Minh. With the advent of the Cold War, the United States backed up the French financially as a part of the policy of "containment." By 1954, most of northern Vietnam was in the hands of the Vietminh, and in the same year, the French suffered a major defeat at Dien Bien Phu. At this point an armistice was concluded by which Vietnam was divided at the 17th parallel. A plebiscite to decide the future of the whole country, scheduled for 1956, was not held. Instead, all of the new succession states of Indochina maintained a precarious existence, being subjected to the centrifugal forces of internal social conflict and external Cold War pressures.

V. Tropical Africa

In Africa the colonial revolution was even more dramatic than it was in Asia. The triumph of nationalism in the latter area was not altogether unexpected, given the ancient indigenous cultures and the local political organizations that had been agitating for some decades. In Africa, by contrast, the nationalist movements were much younger and weaker, besides which the continent had not been jarred and aroused by Japanese occupation. And yet, just as the first postwar decade witnessed the liberation of Asia, so the second witnessed the liberation of Africa. During that decade, no less than 31 African countries won their independence; the few remaining colonies stood out painfully as obsolete hang-overs from the past. The course of this nationalist awakening differed fundamentally from region to region because of the varying historical backgrounds and contemporary developments. Accordingly, the colonial revolution will be considered not on a continentwide basis, but individually in tropical Africa, South Africa, and North Africa.

Nationalist movements of any significance did not appear in tropical Africa until after World War I. The form they assumed depended on the policies and administrative institutions established by the colonial powers. In British West Africa, authority was vested in the hands of governors who were appointed from London and who were advised by executive and legislative councils. The executive councils consisted entirely of British officials, but the legislative councils included a few African nominees. The African leaders in these colonies sought to convert the legislative councils into African parliaments, and then to convert the executive councils into African ministries responsible to such parliaments. In the French colonies, by contrast, authority was wielded to a much greater degree from Paris, and the French Africans tried to affiliate with the metropolitan parties in order to be in a position to influence decisions in the capital.

These strategies had little impact prior to World War II. Only a few western-educated leaders were awake and active; the mass of the people were largely apathetic. The few nationalist organizations were more like debating societies than political parties, and they devoted more energy to sniping at the European administrators than to communicating with their own peoples. The Second World War drastically altered this traditional African pattern. In

606

the first place, a tremendous economic expansion occurred during the war years because of the pressing demand for African raw materials and foodstuffs. Between 1939 and 1953, the value of exports from the Congo increased fourteen times, while government revenue rose four times. In the same period, Northern Rhodesian exports multiplied ninefold, and government revenues, twentyfold. In British West Africa, government purchasing agencies were established for basic produce such as cocoa and palm oil. These agencies broke the stranglehold of European trading companies on the peasant economies and led to the creation after the war of marketing boards under local control. These guaranteed the farmers a stable price for their produce and also accumulated substantial reserves that were used to finance local economic and social projects.

This general economic upsurge led to a boom in the building of schools, the construction of roads, and the improvement of housing, sanitation, and medical services. At the same time, the Africans, observing a host of Asian peoples gaining their independence, naturally asked why they, too, should not be rid of the bonds of colonialism. The question became acute with the return of the war veterans, large numbers of whom had served for the French in Europe and for the British in Burma and the Middle East. All these factors combined to shake up and awaken tropical Africa out of her traditional lethargy. The new roads, schools, and economic opportunities meant new horizons, greater mobility, and higher aspirations. In innumerable ways, a new climate was developing that was incompatible with continued European domination.

The first outburst occurred on the Gold Coast in 1948, where the small farmers now had more income than ever before, but consumer goods were in short supply and very expensive. They suspected the European traders of profiteering, and organized a widespread boycott of their concerns. This was followed by rioting in the towns and general ferment in the countryside. A new leader now appeared who exploited this disaffection with startling success: Kwame Nkrumah had studied in American and English universities, where he had become converted to the Marxist socialism current among colonial students, and had met other African leaders, such as Jomo Kenyatta from Kenya. Nkrumah quickly overshadowed the older West African nationalists by demanding immediate independence and organizing in 1949 the Convention People's party on a genuine mass basis.

In a general election held in 1951 under a new constitution, this party won an overwhelming majority. Nkrumah was in prison on election day, charged with sedition, but the British governor, sensing the trend of events, released Nkrumah and gave him and his colleagues leading posts in the administration. In the next few years the cabinet became all-African and was entrusted with full authority except for defense and foreign affairs. With this apprenticeship in self-government, it proved possible to make the transition to full independence without violence or dislocation. By 1957, thanks to the initiative of Nkrumah and the statesmanship of the British, the Gold Coast became the independent Commonwealth country of Ghana.

Once the colonial dam had been broken in Ghana, it was impossible to keep it from breaking elsewhere. Most decisive was the course of events in Nigeria, the most populous country in Africa, with its 35 million people. The three regions of the country—the North, the West, and the South—differed basically from each other in ethnic composition, cultural traditions, and economic development; this diversity led to serious interregional conflicts that delayed the winning of independence to 1960. The other British West African colonies, Sierra Leone and Gambia, followed in 1961 and 1963 respectively, their delay being due primarily to poverty and small size.

The British did not foresee how quickly their new colonial policy would affect the rest of tropical Africa. Repercussions were felt first in the surrounding French holdings. Paradoxically enough, the Paris governments were as conciliatory south of the Sahara as they were stubborn to the north. In 1956, they enacted a "framework law" that granted representative institutions to their twelve West African territories and to the island of Madagascar. Two years later the new de Gaulle regime, brought into power by the crisis in Algeria (see section VII, this chapter) decided to avoid a similar ordeal in tropical Africa. The sub-Saharan colonies were given the option of voting either for full independence or for autonomy as separate republics in the French "Community" that was to replace the Empire. At first this strategy appeared to be successful; in the ensuing referendum, all the territories except Guinea, which was under the influence of the trade-union leader, Sékou

Accra, Ghana, with corrugated iron shanties amidst the modern buildings. (Photographic Department, Volta River Project, Accra)

Touré, voted for autonomy. The arrangement, however, proved transitory. In 1959, Senegal and the French Sudan asked for full independence within the Community as the Federation of Mali. When this was granted, four other territories—the Ivory Coast, Niger, Dahomey, and Upper Volta—went a step further and secured independence outside the Community. By the end of 1960, all the former colonies of both French West Africa and French Equatorial Africa had won their independence, and all but one had become members of the United Nations.

In contrast to the smooth transition to independence in French and British West Africa, the Belgian Congo endured a bitter and costly struggle involving the Great Powers as well as Belgium and assorted Congolese factions. One source of this trouble was the rigid paternalistic character of Belgian rule. Though they were often enlightened in their measures for economic advance and technical training, Belgian officials allowed no opportunity for political training to the Africans, or for that matter, to the resident Belgians. The educated native elite were few in number and inexperienced, while tribal alliances and rivalries remained prominent. Such was the situation when the French colonies across the Congo were given self-rule, thus stimulating latent hostility to European rule, and bringing to the fore Patrice Lumumba, the only Congolese leader with any pretence to more than a regional following. His radical and nationwide approach to the problem of Congo independence won him a substantial following within his country as well as among pan-Africanists everywhere.

Early in 1959, after the Congo capital had been shaken by nationalist riots, the Belgians hastily decided that they could best protect their vast economic interests by allowing free elections and immediate independence. The predictable outcome was conflict and chaos. Lumumba became the first Premier, but he found he could govern only with the help of Belgian army officers and Civil Service officials. Some of the soldiers mutinied against the remaining officers, and attacks upon whites occurred in various parts of the country. At the same time, fighting broke out between tribes taking advantage of the opportunity to repay old scores. Most serious was the virtual secession of the rich mining province of Katanga, owing to an unholy alliance of local African politicians and Belgian mining interests. The spreading anarchy moved the Belgian government to reconsider and to return its troops to key points and airfields.

The Cold War now intruded when the Soviet Union threatened unilateral intervention under the guise of supporting the Congolese against a restoration of imperialist rule. Faced with the prospect of a Korea-like situation in Africa, the United Nations assumed the responsibility of policing the Congo with an international force consisting largely of Africans. After months of confused violence some semblance of order was restored, though not without the sacrifice of Lumumba, who was murdered by Katanga secessionists, and of the UN Secretary-General, Dag Hammarskjöld, who died in an airplane crash during a mediatory mission in the Congo.

Meanwhile, across the continent in East Africa, the nationalist cause was encountering much stiffer resistance because of the presence of white settlers in the salubrious highlands. In Kenya, the conflict between African and settler was particularly acute because of the settler's appropriation of much of the best farming land. This contributed to the uprising of the Mau Mau, a secret terrorist society made up of members of the Kikuyu tribe. Settlers were killed on many a lonely farm, though a good number of Kikuyus who refused to join the revolt also were slaughtered. Before the fighting was over, nearly 7,000 Mau Mau had been killed, over 83,000 were in prison, and many more were held in temporary detention camps. The uprising, though it led to sickening excesses on both sides, did force the British to recognize the futility of attempting to follow a conciliatory policy in West Africa and a rigid one in the East. Accordingly, they released from prison the outstanding Kikuyu leader, Jomo Kenyatta. Educated in London, and author of an anthropological study of his people, Kenyatta had been imprisoned for suspected sympathies with the Mau Mau, though actual collaboration was never proven. Now he was released and, like Nkrumah, he won a majority vote in an election and was allowed in 1963 to become Premier. In the same year, Kenya became an independent state amidst wild rejoicing in Nairobi for the cherished *Uruhu,* or Freedom.

In neighboring Uganda, where the whites had not been allowed to take land, the issues were simpler and independence had been granted peaceably in 1962. Tanganyika, a German possession before World War I, had become a British mandate in 1922, with two segments, Ruanda and Urundi, becoming Belgian mandates. All three territories were granted independence in 1962, with Julius K. Nycrere of Tanganyika playing a key role in the transition.

The Central African Federation, comprising Southern Rhodesia, Northern Rhodesia, and Nyasaland, was organized to the south of Tanganyika in 1953. Though it was created with the declared objective of "racial partnership," the Federation was beset by crises and violence, the root cause being the political and economic domination of more than nine million Africans by 300,000 Europeans, most of whom were living in Southern Rhodesia, a self-governing territory on the northern border of the Republic of South Africa. The nationalist movement made strong gains in Northern Rhodesia and Nyasaland, and in 1962, both were given self-rule under African prime ministers. Since Southern Rhodesia refused to follow suit and to give Africans the vote, the Federation became impossible and was dissolved on January 1, 1964. Later in the year, Northern Rhodesia became fully independent as Zambia, and Nyasaland as Malawi. The center of strife then shifted to Southern Rhodesia, now known as Rhodesia, where the black majority was demanding the vote and the white minority was threatening, if pressed by London, to declare independence unilaterally and/or conclude an alliance with South Africa.

At the same time, there has been the problem of underlying economic ties being endangered by the political disintegration. (The old Central African Federation had been put together essentially for economic reasons.) The natural wealth lies in Zambia's great copper belt; the labor comes from Malawi; the administrative and technical skills and the marketing have been Rhodesia's contribution. Some form of economic association between the three territories is called for if the divisive race issue can be resolved.

Portugal has been attempting to stem the tide of colonial revolution in

Copper mining in Southern Rhodesia.

Angola and Mozambique, the remaining tropical African territories, with the obsolete fiction that there are no Portuguese colonies—only overseas provinces of Portugal herself. Lisbon has received strong support from South Africa, a country interested in preserving the *status quo* in Angola and Mozambique as a barrier against the spreading African nationalism. Yet in Angola, despite Portuguese attempts to isolate the colony from outside contamination, an insurrection began in March, 1961. The rebels lacked military training and an over-all strategy, but owing to the advantage of a surprise attack, they seized a considerable amount of territory in the north. When the Portuguese recovered, they were able to regain about half the lost ground. The fighting then settled down to a stalemate, since the rebels were supplied with arms from newly liberated Algeria and also were given military training in Algeria and across the river in the Congo.

By the end of 1963, some 7,500 troops of the Angolan Revolutionary army were waging increasingly effective guerrilla warfare against a Portuguese army of 40,000. The extent to which Angola was being affected by the "winds of change" sweeping the entire continent, was made clear by an American correspondent who was with the Angolan rebels in late 1963.* He cited as follows a 32-year-old commander who had been trained in Algeria: "The war here is like Algeria. We can't beat the Portuguese in the field but we can wear them down until the politicians are ready to talk. This is a war of the will. It took the Algerians seven years before the French gave in. We are just as determined." Equally revealing were the remarks of an army private who had been in the Congo: "I've seen freedom in the Congo. My boy is never going to have to do what I had to do." [4]

* See "Liberation Struggles in Algeria and Angola," *EMM*, No. 182.

VI. SOUTH AFRICA 611

The basic difference between tropical Africa on the one hand and North Africa and South Africa on the other is the relative absence of European settlers in the former region and their presence in large numbers in the latter two. This difference explains the brutal armed struggle that ravaged Algeria between 1954 and 1962, and the tense undercover conflict wracking South Africa in the mid-Sixties. South Africa became a self-governing dominion of the British Commonwealth in 1909, following the Boer War (see Chapter 18, section II). A little more than half a century later, in May, 1961, South Africa left the Commonwealth to become an independent republic. The main reason for the separation was the clash between South Africa and new African and Asian Commonwealth members, such as Nigeria and India, over the issue of apartheid.

Apartheid involves two basic policies: the exclusion of all non-whites from any share in political life; and the relegation of the Africans to separate areas (Bantustans or preserves for the "Bantu," as the Africans have been known), where it is vaguely theorized that they will some day form separate nations. Paradoxically, the whites comprised only three of the sixteen million total population of South Africa in 1960, and the Afrikaners (Boers), who have controlled South African politics and were responsible for apartheid, were

A shanty-town in Johannesburg, since demolished by the South African government. (Union of South Africa Government Information Office)

612

themselves a minority of two-fifths within the white minority. The Afrikaners were able to have their own way partly because parliamentary representation was weighed in favor of the predominantly Afrikaner rural areas, but also because many English-speaking whites supported apartheid for economic reasons. This was especially true of Labour, which feared competition in employment from non-whites in the event that the latter be given equal opportunities. In fact, the first Afrikaner (Nationalist) government was able to take office in 1924 because of support from the South African Labour party.

It has been generally agreed that apartheid is not a viable program, either economically or politically. If the Africans had in fact been segregated on the proposed Bantustans, the entire economy of South Africa would have collapsed. Their labor, as well as that of the 1,500,000 Coloreds and the 500,000 Indians, has been essential for the conduct of agriculture and commerce as well as mining and other industries. In addition, Bantustans have not been able to support even a third of the African population, and the government has been unwilling to spend the large sums needed to increase their absorptive capacity. Most important of all, the great majority of Africans have had no desire to be isolated as separate "tribal" entities. Instead, they have demanded a fair share in the united South Africa of which they are an integral part, and in this demand they have been backed by the growing power of African nationalism in the rest of the continent.

VII. NORTH AFRICA

The course of colonial revolution in North Africa was molded not only by the existence of large European settlements but also by two other factors that were not to be found in the rest of the continent: the military campaigns fought on North African soil during World War II; and more important, the upsurge of Arab nationalism over the whole area.

Between 1940 and 1943, British, French, and American armies had fought against Italian and German forces in the North African coastlands and in Northeast Africa. At the war's end, Ethiopia regained its status as an independent state, with the addition of former Italian Eritrea. By contrast, Italian Somaliland remained under the administration of Italy for ten years, and was then combined with British Somaliland to form the independent Somali Republic. The Italian colony of Libya remained under British military administration until December 24, 1951, when it became independent under King Idris el Senussi, spiritual leader of the Seniussi Muslim sect that had spearheaded the opposition to Italian rule (see Chapter 21, section III). The granting of self-rule to Libya undermined Anglo-French imperial authority in the rest of North Africa. Since Libya was the least developed region of North Africa, its independence made British influence in Egypt and the Sudan, and French rule in Tunis, Algeria, and Morocco, appear particularly anachronistic and intolerable to Arab nationalists. (For the nationalist struggle in Egypt and Sudan, see section VIII, this chapter.)

In North Africa, as in Indochina, the French fought long and stubbornly to retain their possessions, a principal reason being the substantial number of French settlers in this region—250,000 in Tunisia, 400,000 in Morocco, and

1,000,000 in Algeria. These colons, in league with powerful French economic interests in North Africa, bitterly opposed all proposals for self-rule, and sabotaged a number of provisional moves in this direction made by certain Paris cabinets.

Tunisia and Morocco had the legal status of protectorates, which France claimed to administer in behalf of their traditional rulers. Both territories were governed autocratically—not even the resident Europeans were allowed political rights. This foreign domination stimulated movements for national liberation: in Tunisia, the Neo-Destour party, established in 1934 and led by Habib Bourguiba; and in Morocco, the Istiqlal party, founded in 1944 and given some support by Sultan Mohamed Ben Youssef.

Tunisia and Morocco won their freedom relatively easily following World War II. The French were determined to hang on to Algeria, and were willing to accept losses elsewhere in order to concentrate on this prime objective. Accordingly, when armed resistance began in Tunisia in 1952, the French, after two years of guerrilla warfare, agreed to grant it autonomous status; and having made this concession in Tunisia, they were ready to do likewise in Morocco. Sultan Mohamed, who had been exiled for his pro-Istiqlal sympathies, was allowed to return to his throne; he then demanded complete independence, which the French conceded on March 2, 1956. In the same month, Tunisia also became fully independent, with Bourguiba as President of the new republic.

The French now were able to deal with the crucial Algerian problem without distractions. Legally, Algeria was not a colony but an integral part of France, with representatives in the National Assembly in Paris. In practice, a double standard of citizenship prevailed in Algeria, so that the country was dominated economically and politically by the Europeans who comprised only one-tenth of the ten million total population. On the other hand, the colons, like the Afrikaners at the other tip of the continent, did not regard themselves as mere colonists. Algeria was their homeland as much as that of the native Algerians. Their fathers and grandfathers had worked and died there, and they were resolved to defend their patrimony. This meant unalterable opposition to any concessions to the Algerian nationalists.

Armed revolt against French rule began in the fall of 1954. Having been ousted from Indochina only four months earlier, the French were in no mood for compromise. With the enthusiastic approval of the colons and of the army officers, who were still smarting from the Indochina humiliation, the Paris government resolved to crush the uprising. The result was an exhausting, brutalizing struggle that dragged on until 1962. At its height, the French were forced to send 500,000 men into Algeria, thus draining off almost all their divisions assigned to NATO in Europe, besides which the war was costing Paris nearly $1 billion annually. The Algerians paid much more heavily in human terms, including one million dead, or one-ninth of their total numbers. Another million were forcibly herded into "regroupment" camps in a vain effort to isolate the rebels, and 300,000 more fled as refugees to neighboring Morocco and Tunisia.

Although the French suffered little by comparison—apart from the financial drain—they also paid much more heavily than they had anticipated. The imponderable cost of the psychological trauma experienced by French soldiers

Veiled Moslem women cast ballots in the referendum of July 1, 1962, in which Algerians voted for independence. (Wide World Photos)

who were forced to participate in the bestialities of a repressive war of this type was very real; the clergy and many of the intellectuals in France spoke up with troubled consciences against the "dirty war." The government responded with arbitrary arrests and sporadic censorship of the press. Indeed, the heaviest price paid by the French was the steady erosion of their personal liberties, culminating in the overthrow of the Fourth Republic itself.

In May, 1958, a North African "Committee of Public Safety" seized power in Algeria in order to replace the Republic with an authoritarian regime that presumably would be more successful in holding the empire together. The demoralized National Assembly bowed to this show of force, especially since most of the armed forces were in Algeria. In June, 1958, the Assembly voted full power to de Gaulle to rule France in whatever manner he wished for six months, and to prepare a new constitution for the country. Before the end of the year the Fourth Republic had given way to the Fifth, and political power had been shifted decisively from the legislative to the executive branch—specifically to the President.

President de Gaulle now used his unprecedented popularity to end the Algerian bloodshed, despite the opposition of the colons and the military who had made possible his rise to power. In March, 1962, after a referendum in France had approved such a move, de Gaulle agreed to a cease-fire and to a plebiscite to determine Algeria's future. A "Secret Army Organization" immediately launched a terror campaign in both Algeria and France to upset this agreement, but with massive popular support, de Gaulle stuck to his course, and on July 3, 1962, he proclaimed the independence of Algeria after its people had voted overwhelmingly in favor of it.* All of North Africa was

* See "Liberation Struggles in Algeria and Angola," *EMM,* No. 182.

now free for the first time since French soldiers had landed in Algeria in 1830. The granting of independence to Algeria marked the end of a French African empire that once covered nearly 4,000,000 square miles and contained more than 41,000,000 people.

VIII. MIDDLE EAST

Meanwhile, Arab nationalism had been as militant in the Middle East as it had been in North Africa. During the interwar years the British had relinquished their hold on Egypt and Iraq, and both countries had entered the League of Nations. Arab nationalists, however, were far from appeased, since the British still exercised controlling authority over these countries. They had reserved various privileges, including the right to maintain a garrison along the Suez Canal, to maintain three air bases in Iraq, and to administer the Sudan together with Egypt. More galling had been the stiff-necked attitude of the French, who continued to hold Syria and Lebanon as mandates. Above all, Arab nationalism had been aroused by large-scale Jewish immigration into the British-held Palestine mandate during the 1930's (see Chapter 21, section II).

During World War II most politically conscious Arabs were either neutral or openly hostile to the Western powers. Referring to the unhappy experiences of the interwar years, an Arab scholar observed that ". . . there was nothing to choose between the oppression exercised in the name of democracy, and that exercised in the name of Fascism." [5] Many Arab leaders were convinced that Hitler would win and wanted to be on the side of the victor. These considerations explain the pro-Axis uprising in Iraq in May, 1941, and the extremely reluctant assistance that King Farouk I of Egypt gave to the British despite his treaty obligations.

Although the Arab nationalists had been unable to satisfy their aspirations during World War II, the new postwar balance of power offered them a unique opportunity which they promptly exploited. Britain and France, who had dominated the Middle East before the War, now emerged drastically weakened. A power vacuum was created, which the United States and the Soviet Union attempted to fill. The Arabs skillfully took advantage of the Anglo-French weakness and the American-Russian rivalry to play off one side against the other, thus enabling them to win concessions that would have seemed preposterous only a few years earlier. The Arabs were further aided by their control over vast Middle East oil reserves, which appeared particularly indispensable to the West during the immediate postwar years.

In October, 1944, the Arabs organized a League of Arab states to coordinate their policies and maximize their effectiveness. The Arab League won its first success against the French in Syria and Lebanon. In May, 1945, a French expeditionary force landed in Beirut and proceeded to bombard Damascus in an attempt to cow the local nationalists; such tactics had prevailed in the 1920's, but they did not work now. The Arab League Council promptly met and passed a resolution demanding the evacuation of all French forces. Churchill supported the Arabs, especially since the War was not yet over; and he had no desire to cope with an aroused Arab nationalism in the Middle

East. Under British pressure the French withdrew their troops, and in July, 1945, they accepted the end of their rule in the Middle East.

In Egypt, the aim of the nationalist leaders after the war was to end or modify the 1936 treaty, which was the legal basis for Britain's control of the Canal Zone and of the Sudan. Direct negotiations in 1946 ended without agreement. The following year Egypt submitted her case to the UN Security Council, but again received no satisfaction. In 1951, Egypt resorted to direct action and denounced the 1936 treaty. Farouk was proclaimed "King of Egypt and the Sudan," and voluntary battalions waged guerrilla warfare against the British garrison in the Canal Zone. Neither the proclamation nor the guerrilla action proved effective. The resulting frustration, together with the general resentment against the disastrous failure in the Palestine War, culminated in an army revolt in July, 1952. General Muhammad Naguib assumed power and forced King Farouk to abdicate.

Naguib removed one of the sources of friction between Egypt and Britain when he concluded an agreement with Britain on February 12, 1953, by which the Sudanese were to be given a choice of independence, union with Egypt, or some other course. The decision was for independence, and in 1956, the Sudan joined the ranks of free nations. The remaining Egyptian grievance —the British presence at the Suez—was ended by Gamal Abdel Nasser, who displaced Naguib as head of the new Egyptian regime. After prolonged negotiations, Nasser signed an agreement with Britain on October 19, 1954, by which under certain stipulated conditions, the British garrison was to be removed and the British installations transferred to Egypt.*

Arab nationalism was successful in Syria and Lebanon, and in Egypt and the Sudan, but it failed disastrously in Palestine. The mass extermination of Jews in Hitler-controlled Europe engendered strong pressures for opening up Palestine to the desperate survivors. In August, 1945, President Truman proposed that 100,000 Jews be allowed to enter the mandate; in April, 1946, an Anglo-American investigating committee reported in favor of the President's proposal. The Arab League responded by warning that it was unalterably opposed to such an influx, and that it was prepared, if necessary, to use force to stop it. The United Nations then sent a fact-finding commission to Palestine, and the General Assembly, after receiving the commission's report, voted on November 29, 1947 in favor of partitioning the mandate. On May 14 of the following year, the Jews invoked the partition resolution and proclaimed the establishment of a Jewish state to be called Israel; on the same day, President Truman extended recognition to the new state. On the following day, the Arabs carried out their long-standing threat and sent their armies across the Israeli border.

The course of the war went contrary to expectations. The Arab armies lacked discipline, unity, and effective leadership; the Israelis, fighting literally with their backs to the sea, possessed all three qualities to a high degree. They not only repulsed the Arab attacks from all sides, but advanced and occupied more territory than had been awarded to them by the UN Assembly's resolution. After two abortive truces, the Israelis finally signed armistice agreements with the various Arab states between February and July, 1949.

* See "British Departure and Egyptian Rejoicing," EMM, No. 183.

A peace settlement did not follow the cessation of fighting. Two big issues have continued to divide Israel from the surrounding Arab states, one being the question of what to do with the almost one million Arab refugees who fled from Israel in the course of the fighting and who have been living miserably in camps near the Israeli borders. The Arab states have insisted that the refugees be allowed to return to their former homes; Israel has rejected this, partly because the refugees, being violently anti-Israel, would destroy the state if they were allowed to return, but also because Jewish refugees, some from Arab countries, have in the meantime occupied the areas vacated by the Arabs. In addition to the refugee question, there has existed the problem of the frontiers: The armistice agreements left Israel with more territory than had been allotted by the UN; the Arabs have been demanding that this extra territory be surrendered, while Israel has maintained that it was won in a war that the Arabs themselves started, and that the extra land has been needed for the Jewish immigrants constantly pouring in from all parts of the world.

IX. LAST STAND OF IMPERIALISM

Since the establishment of the state of Israel, Middle Eastern affairs have been dominated largely by two factors: the unresolved Israeli-Arab conflict, and the intrusion of the Cold War. The United States, for example, sought to strengthen its position in the Middle East by sponsoring the Bagdad Pact, signed on November 1, 1955 by Britain, Turkey, Iraq, and Pakistan, which provided that the signatories should cooperate to "defend their territories against aggression or subversion and to promote the welfare and prosperity of the peoples in that region." The aim of the United States was to implement the "northern tier" defense strategy popular at the time in Washington, a plan designed to overcome the Arab fixation against Israel which was diverting attention from the Russian danger to the north. American policy makers conceived the strategy of bringing together the "northern tier" of Middle Eastern countries to form a barrier against any Soviet push southward. This would divert Iran's attention northward against Russia, and hopefully, would isolate Egypt and encourage her to turn toward Africa rather than Israel and the Middle East.

In practice, this strategy boomeranged; both Nasser and the Soviets were naturally strongly opposed, and they retaliated by concluding an arms pact that exchanged Egyptian cotton for Soviet war materials. This deal gave the Soviet Union a toehold in the Middle East that it had never had before. The next major development in the Middle East was Nasser's nationalization of the Suez Canal on July 26, 1956, an unexpected and daring move made in retaliation against Secretary of State John Foster Dulles' sudden retraction of a provisional offer to finance the building of the High Dam at Aswan.* Outraged cries of protest were raised by the numerous and influential holders of Suez Canal Company shares. Also, many in the British Conservative government, who had opposed the earlier withdrawal of troops from the Canal Zone, now demanded that strong measures be taken against Nasser. The French, too,

* See "Nasser Nationalizes the Canal," *EMM*, No. 184.

618

had been thinking along these lines because of Nasser's propaganda and material aid to the Algerian rebels. Israel had been independently planning a preventive war against Egypt to put a stop to unceasing border raids. When the British and French got wind of Israel's plans, they decided to join forces for a combined operation—hence the attack by Israel on the Sinai Peninsula on October 29, 1956, and by Britain and France on the Canal Zone two days later.

From the beginning this undertaking was hopelessly bungled. The Israelis cut swiftly through the Egyptian lines in the Sinai Peninsula, but the British and the French were inadequately prepared and did not begin actual landings until November 5. The resistance was feeble, and a British colonel remarked, "It's all like a bloody good exercise." But by this time it was too late. Overwhelming criticism and opposition were mounting on all sides. The Soviet Union, as might be expected, was vehemently opposed, and sent a virtual ultimatum demanding that Britain and France stop the attack. The United States, which had received no word of the attack, also reacted strongly against its allies, though not in concert with the Russians. The UN passed with a crushing majority a resolution demanding that all foreign troops be withdrawn from Egypt "forthwith." The demand was at first rejected by the aggressors, but eventually they were forced to yield by irresistible pressures from without and bitter dissension from within. The UN sent an emergency force to the Sinai Peninsula to keep peace between Israel and Egypt, and by the end of December, the last of the Anglo-French units had sailed for home.

The immediate outcome of the Suez crisis was a major defeat for the West and a resounding triumph for Nasser and his Soviet backers. Relations between the United States and her European allies were seriously, albeit temporarily, compromised. Nasser, whose army had been easily scattered by the Israelites, emerged as the hero of the entire Arab world because he had seized and retained the Suez Canal.

Viewed from a longer perspective, the Suez expedition can be seen as the last stand of old-fashioned imperialism. Given Nasser's provocation in aiding the Algerian rebels, in drawing close to the Soviet Union, in conducting an unremitting anti-West radio campaign, and finally, in seizing the Suez Canal, it is not surprising that Britain and France acted as they did. Judged from the attitudes and practices of the past, the Suez expedition appears perfectly explicable and justified, and was so regarded by its sponsors.

What is significant, however, is that it was not accepted on these terms by the world of the mid-twentieth century. Instead, it was greeted by a solid wall of opposition among the Asian and African nations. One reason for the British decision to back down was a blunt warning from India and Pakistan that if she did not do so they would quit the Commonwealth. Even within Britain and France there were bitter differences of opinion. The great majority of the British newspapers, for example, supported the innumerable meetings and demonstrations at which the expedition was denounced as "Eden's War." The significance of the Suez crisis is that, like a flash of lightning, it revealed the extent to which the world of Nasser and Nehru differed from that of Rhodes and Kipling, even though a mere half-century separated the two. The age of imperialism had given way to the age of colonial revolution.

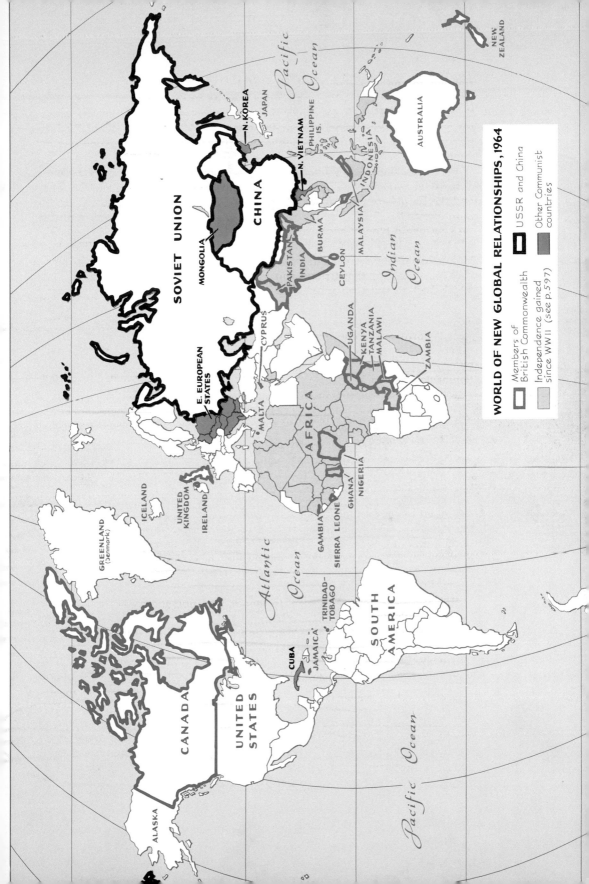

WORLD OF NEW GLOBAL RELATIONSHIPS, 1964

Members of British Commonwealth

USSR and China

Other Communist countries

Independence gained since WWII (see p.597)

SOVIET UNION

CHINA

MONGOLIA

N. KOREA

JAPAN

N. VIETNAM

PHILIPPINE IS.

INDONESIA

MALAYSIA

BURMA

INDIA

PAKISTAN

CEYLON

CYPRUS

E. EUROPEAN STATES

MALTA

AFRICA

UGANDA

KENYA

TANZANIA

MALAWI

ZAMBIA

NIGERIA

GHANA

SIERRA LEONE

GAMBIA

Indian Ocean

Pacific Ocean

NEW ZEALAND

AUSTRALIA

Atlantic Ocean

GREENLAND (Denmark)

ICELAND

UNITED KINGDOM

IRELAND

CUBA

JAMAICA

TRINIDAD-TOBAGO

SOUTH AMERICA

CANADA

UNITED STATES

ALASKA

Pacific Ocean

Within a period of two decades, some 53 countries, with almost one-third of the total world population, have won their independence. A movement of such unprecedented magnitude inevitably had profound international repercussions. Paradoxically, one of the most significant of these has been negative in nature—namely, that the loss of colonies did not ruin the colonial powers. For many decades Marxists had preached that the prosperity of capitalist Europe depended on the exploitation of her huge overseas empires, and that the loss of these empires would undermine capitalism, a doctrine that was firmly believed by the imperialists themselves. In 1895, Cecil Rhodes stated,

> In order to save the forty million inhabitants of the United Kingdom from a bloody civil war, our colonial statesmen must acquire new lands for settling the surplus population of this country, to provide new markets for the goods produced in the factories and mines. The Empire as I have always said is a bread and butter question. If you want to avoid civil war, you must become imperialists.[6]

Today, with the British Empire almost completely relinquished, Britain is enjoying unprecedented prosperity. The masses of the people are not revolting in desperation as Rhodes prophesied, but rather are cared for by the welfare state to a degree unimaginable in the nineteenth century. Likewise, Holland without Indonesia, Belgium without the Congo, and France without Indochina and Algeria, all have living standards that are higher than at any other time in their histories. Nor is it altogether fortuitous that West Germany, the country with no colonial wars to finance, is also the country that has made the most economic progress. Conversely, Portugal has refused to give up its colonies and has been wallowing in endemic poverty. It may be concluded, then, that the prosperity of the developed countries is not dependent upon the subjugation of overseas underdeveloped territories—in fact, just the opposite is true. One of the pressing problems of this postimperialist era has been how to utilize the human and material resources of the developed world to reverse the current trend of the rich countries becoming richer and the poor becoming poorer.

Although the colonial revolution did not affect adversely the prosperity of the imperialist powers, it naturally did affect their systems of imperial organization. Some of the constitutional changes introduced were obvious propaganda devices of little real significance. Such was the case with Portugal's hurried grant of full citizenship to all Africans following the outbreak of revolution in Angola. In a different category was de Gaulle's proposal to the French colonies, offering a choice of either full independence or autonomy within the French "Community"; as noted earlier, they all eventually chose independence. Consequently, all that has remained of France's imperial domain are a few minuscule outposts such as Martinique, Guadeloupe, Réunion, Guiana, and French Somaliland. On the other hand, the bonds between Paris

620

and the former colonies have by no means disappeared entirely; past associations leave imprints that cannot be wiped out. The newly independent states continue looking to France for guidance and assistance in such areas as education, commerce, finance, and technology.

The most important carry-over from the prewar empires is the Commonwealth, successor to the former British Empire and Commonwealth, which consists, as of mid-1964, of 20 independent member states and 28 dependencies. The latter are, for the most part, possessions that are too small to afford the cost of separate existence. The classic definition of the relations between the United Kingdom and the prewar Dominions (see Chapter 18, section IV) was set forth as follows in the 1926 Balfour Declaration: "autonomous communities within the British Empire, equal in status, in no way subordinate one to another in any aspect of their domestic or external affairs, though united by a common allegiance to the Crown and freely associated as members of the British Commonwealth of Nations." Legal effect was given to this definition in the United Kingdom by the Westminster Statute of 1931.

Following World War II, the Commonwealth was enlarged by the admission of numerous Asian and African ex-colonies that had won independence. The entry of these states raised basic new issues concerning the future of the Commonwealth. Its membership hitherto had been confined to countries populated by people of predominantly United Kingdom origin, people who had strong, natural bonds with the "mother country," whereas the new member states were Afro-Asian, with political traditions of hostility to British rule. Would the subtle bonds of the Commonwealth, which had withstood the strain of two world wars, prove capable of holding together such diverse elements? Or would the Commonwealth dissolve as swiftly as had the French Community? The outcome is a gratifying tribute to the foresight of the British in relinquishing imperial authority gracefully and expeditiously. Indeed, the paradox is that the two states that have left the Commonwealth are both former dominions—Eire and South Africa.

Today the Commonwealth may be defined as a free association of completely independent states having a broad community of interests that stem partly from the fact that each at one time was associated with the British Empire. Some Commonwealth states are republics while others are monarchies owing allegiance to Queen Elizabeth II. But all, without exception, accept the Queen as the symbolic head of the Commonwealth. The ties holding the Commonwealth together are partly intangible and partly concrete: The intangibles include a common heritage, common use of the English language, and common traditions in politics, law, justice, and education; the tangibles include membership in the sterling currency bloc (except for Canada), a network of trade agreements providing tariff preferences, and a continuous exchange of views on foreign affairs through numerous standing committees and periodic meetings of prime ministers. All discussion is based on the principle of voluntary cooperation, which Nehru described as "the silken bond around the Commonwealth."

The colonial revolution has led not only to the reorganization of old imperial structures but also to the creation of new international alignments of former colonial countries. These new states have held several conferences in the belief that by working together they will be better able to cope with common problems and to exert influence where desired.

The first of these conferences, held in Bandung, Indonesia in April, 1955, was attended by 29 Afro-Asian countries representing about half the world's population. The states represented included such recently emancipated colonial nations as Libya and Ceylon, partially self-governing colonies like the Gold Coast and the Sudan, Communist powers such as China, and NATO members such as Turkey. With a large and diverse gathering like this, there was little chance for agreement on specific issues. Rather, the delegates expressed unanimous agreement on certain basic matters such as their condemnation of colonialism and racial discrimination, advocacy of general disarmament and economic cooperation, and a general "plague-on-both-houses" attitude concerning the Cold War.

The African counterpart of the Bandung meeting was the May, 1963 Addis Ababa Conference of all African states. Before this gathering took place, a split had been developing between the so-called Casablanca group (Ghana, Guinea, Mali, Morocco, Libya, Algeria, and the United Arab Republic), which tended to be more militant and aggressively neutral, and the Monrovia group (including Nigeria and most of the former French colonies), which was generally more moderate. This threatening split was patched over at Addis Ababa. Most of the delegates wanted to set up some sort of a permanent, continentwide organization, though some preferred a strong centralized structure; still others wanted varying degrees of loose autonomy. In the end, the Organization of African Unity was created, with provisions for a Secretary-General, a Secretariat, and periodic meetings of Heads of State. The Organization adopted a charter based on principles such as sovereign equality of all member states, peaceful settlement of disputes, commitment to the emancipation of all remaining African colonies, and nonalignment in the Cold War.

This desire of the Afro-Asian states to cooperate in order to exert maximum influence was soon evident in the United Nations also. In contrast to the mere 13 Afro-Asian states out of a total of 51 members when the UN was first established, by the end of 1964 there were 59 out of 115, or a full majority. This flood of new members altered basically the balance of power in the UN. It was noticeable as early as 1961 when the post of Secretary-General, previously held by Scandinavians, went to the Burmese U Thant. At the same time, an Indian replaced an American as Thant's executive assistant, and two Africans were made under-secretaries.

Even more striking evidence of the new power of the Afro-Asian block was the proposal in late 1963 of certain amendments to the Charter—the first since it was signed in 1945. These amendments would increase the 11-member Security Council to 15, and the 18-member Economic and Social Council to 27. In the Security Council, as expanded, the Afro-Asians would have 5 of the 10 elected seats, with the remainder divided as follows: Eastern Europe, 1; Western Europe and "other states" (meaning Canada, Australia, and New Zealand), 2; Latin America, 2. This would supersede the "gentlemen's agreement" of 1946, which awarded 2 of the 6 elected seats to Latin America and one each to Western Europe, Eastern Europe, the Middle East,

621

622

and the British Commonwealth. The difference between the original and the revised representation would reflect the basic shift in the balance of power within the UN, a shift that will have obviously important consequences as the Afro-Asian bloc proceeds with its campaign to bring about the independence of Portugal's African territories and the elimination of apartheid in South Africa. Indeed, there has been growing concern in some quarters about what is considered to be the unrealistic, small-nation domination of the Assembly. In early 1964, the American Secretary of State, Dean Rusk, expressed this concern as follows: "A two-thirds majority of the General Assembly could now be formed by nations with only 10 per cent of the world's population, or who contribute, altogether, 5 per cent of the assessed budget. . . . The United Nations simply cannot take significant action without the support of the members who supply it with resources and have the capacity to act."

Although Afro-Asian countries have cooperated to attain common objectives, they have had many differences within their own ranks. In 1965, for example, among the African states, Somalia had territorial claims against Ethiopia and Kenya, Morocco had claims against Algeria, while some African leaders believed that Nkrumah was advocating pan-Africanism as a means for extending his authority beyond Ghana. At the Addis Ababa conference, Prime Minister Balewa of Nigeria declared bluntly, "I want to tell you the bitter truth. To my mind we cannot achieve this unity as long as some African countries continue to carry on subversive activities in other African countries." [7] Similarly, among the Asian states, Cambodia had frontier disputes with both Thailand and South Vietnam, Ceylon and India had not resolved their long-standing differences over the rights of Indians living in Ceylon, India and Pakistan feuded bitterly over Kashmir, and most dramatic, the border war between India and China made a travesty of the "five principles of coexistence" formulated by Nehru and Chou En-lai at Bandung.

It is paradoxical that newly independent states find it necessary to call back troops of their former imperial rulers in order to protect frontiers and to maintain domestic order. At the beginning of 1964, Britain had, by invitation, 10,000 soldiers in Malaysia to resist feared aggression by Indonesia, 6,000 in Cyprus to keep the peace between the island's Greek- and Turkish-speaking citizens, as well as several battalions in Kenya, Uganda, and Tanganyika to maintain order against mutinous local soldiery. It is indeed ironical that Prime Minister Jomo Kenyatta, imprisoned for nine years, until 1961, for alleged Mau Mau connections, should in 1963 be asking back British troops to help keep his government in office. The spectacle recalls an incident that occurred during the official ceremonies held in Nairobi when Kenya become independent in 1963. Just when the British flag was about to be lowered and the new flag raised, Prince Philip, who was representing Britain, turned to Kenyatta and said: "Sure you don't want to change your mind?" *

SUGGESTED READING

The best over-all studies of the colonial revolution are by R. Emerson, *From Empire to Nation: The Rise to Self-Assertion of Asian and African Peoples* (Cambridge: Harvard Univ. 1960); J. Strachey, *The End of Empire* (London: Gol-

* See "Colonialism in Retrospect," *EMM,* No. 185.

lancz, 1959); and S. C. Easton, *The Rise and Fall of Western Colonialism* (New York: Praeger, 1964). General surveys of the awakening of Asia are given in M. Edwardes, *Asia in the European Age, 1498–1955* (London: Thames, 1961) and J. Romein, *The Asian Century: A History of Modern Nationalism in Asia* (Berkeley: Univ. of California, 1962).

623

The winning of independence by India is analyzed by M. Edwardes, *The Last Years of the British in India* (London: Cassell, 1963) and V. P. Menon, *The Transfer of Power in India* (Princeton: Princeton Univ., 1957). The transfer of power in Southeast Asia is described in W. H. Elsbree, *Japan's Role in Southeast Asian Nationalist Movements, 1940–1945* (Cambridge: Harvard Univ., 1953); F. C. Jones, *Japan's New Order in East Asia: Its Rise and Fall* (New York: Oxford Univ., 1954); E. J. Hammer, *Struggle for Indochina* (Stanford: Stanford Univ., 1954); and A. M. Taylor, *Indonesian Independence and the United Nations* (Ithaca: Cornell Univ., 1960).

For general surveys of Africa's awakening, see I. Wallerstein, *Africa: The Politics of Independence* (New York: Random, 1963; a Vintage Book); M. Perham, *The Colonial Reckoning* (New York: Knopf, 1963); and T. Hodgkin, *Nationalism in Colonial Africa* (New York: New York Univ., 1956). On regional developments there are B. Timothy, *Kwame Nkrumah* (London: G. Allen, 1963); D. Apter, *Ghana in Transition*, rev. ed. (New York: Atheneum, 1963); H. Franklin, *Unholy Wedlock: The Failure of the Central African Federation* (London: G. Allen, 1963); P. Keatley, *The Politics of Partnership* (Baltimore: Penguin, 1963) concerning the Federation of Rhodesia and Nyasaland; V. Thompson and R. Adloff, *The Emerging States of French Equatorial Africa* (Stanford: Stanford Univ., 1960); T. Okum, *Angola in Ferment* (Boston: Beacon, 1963); A. Moreira, *Portugal's Stand in Africa* (New York: University Pub., 1963); J. Kenyatta, *Facing Mount Kenya* (London: Secker, 1938); J. C. Taylor, *The Political Development of Tanganyika* (Stanford: Stanford Univ., 1963); C. Legum, *Congo Disaster* (Baltimore: Penguin, 1961); R. and J. Brace, *Ordeal in Algeria* (Princeton: Van Nostrand, 1960); R. and J. Brace, *Algerian Voices* (Princeton: Van Nostrand, 1964); and C. F. Gallagher, *The United States and North Africa: Morocco, Algeria and Tunisia* (Cambridge: Harvard Univ., 1964). For differing views of the South African situation, see E. H. Louw, *The Case for South Africa* (New York: Macfadden, 1963); B. Sachs, *The Road from Sharpeville* (New York: Margani, 1961); and A. Luthuli, *Let My People Go* (New York: McGraw, 1962), the latter being the testimony of the South African chief who won the Nobel Peace Prize.

For the rise of nationalism in the Middle East, see Gamal Abdel Nasser, *Egypt's Liberation: The Philosophy of the Revolution* (Washington, D.C., Public Affairs Press, 1955); K. Wheelock, *Nasser's New Egypt* (New York: Praeger, 1960); and W. Z. Laqueur, *Communism and Nationalism in the Middle East* (London: Routledge, 1956). Differing interpretations of the Arab-Israeli conflict are given in E. B. Childers, *The Road to Suez* (London: MacGibbon, 1962); R. H. S. Crossman, *A Nation Reborn* (New York: Atheneum, 1960); the two works of the Israeli leader David Ben-Gurion, *Rebirth and Destiny of Israel* (New York: Philosophical Lib., 1953) and *Israel: Years of Challenge* (New York: Holt, 1963); and N. Safran, *The United States and Israel* (Cambridge: Harvard Univ., 1963). The diplomacy of the Great Powers is analyzed by G. Lenczowski, *The Middle East in World Affairs* (Ithaca: Cornell Univ., 1952); the documentary collection in J. C. Hurewitz, *A Diplomatic History of the Near and*

624

Middle East (Princeton: Van Nostrand, 1956), 2 vols.; E. Monroe, *Britain's Moment in the Middle East, 1914–1956* (Baltimore: Hopkins, 1963); I. Spector, *The Soviet Union and the Moslem World, 1917–1958* (Seattle: Univ. of Washington, 1959); F. C. Mattison, ed., *Survey of American Interests in the Middle East* (Washington: Middle East Institute, 1953); and H. Finer, *Dulles over Suez* (Chicago: Quadrangle, 1964).

For the international repercussions of the colonial revolution, see K. London, ed., *New Nations in a Divided World: The International Relations of the Afro-Asian States* (New York: Praeger, 1964); L. W. Martin, ed., *Neutralism and Nonalignment: The New States in World Affairs* (New York: Praeger, 1962); and the invaluable materials in the two volumes by N. Mansergh, *Documents and Speeches on British Commonwealth Affairs, 1931–1952,* and *Documents and Speeches on Commonwealth Affairs, 1952–1962,* published by Oxford University Press in 1953 and 1963, respectively.

*We have no perpetual allies
and we have no perpetual enemies.
Our interests are perpetual.*

LORD PALMERSTON

End of Bipolarism

At the very time when the European colonial empires were falling apart, the continent of Europe paradoxically was regaining its economic health and political independence. The losses endured during World War II, together with the pressures of the ensuing Cold War, had combined to make Western Europe dependent upon the United States, and Eastern Europe upon the Soviet Union. The future of the Continent that only a few decades earlier had ruled the entire globe now appeared bleak and precarious. But the 1950's witnessed a remarkable comeback by the European states, both of the East and the West. This revival, together with the growing strength and assertiveness of China, produced an entirely new configuration of world politics. The short-lived American-Russian primacy gave way to a new pluralism. This represented essentially a return, at least in a political sense, to the global regionalism that had characterized world affairs during the millennia before 1500.

I. AMERICAN-RUSSIAN GLOBAL HEGEMONY

"What is Europe now?" Winston Churchill asked in 1947. "It is a rubble heap, a charnel house, a breeding-ground of pestilence and hate." This was a valid portrayal of the whole Continent, East as well as West. Both parts had been left devastated and exhausted by World War II. Both were forced after the war to turn for support to the two new superpowers, the United States and the Soviet Union. In military affairs Western Europe depended on the American-organized NATO, while Eastern Europe depended on the Russian-organized Warsaw Pact. In economic matters Western Europe relied on the Marshall Plan financed by the United States, while Eastern Europe depended on the Council for Mutual Economic Assistance, which theoretically funneled Soviet aid, though in practice it did the opposite.

This situation was a startling reversal of the familiar pattern of European global hegemony that had prevailed during the nineteenth and early twentieth centuries. The world had become accustomed to European powers dividing whole continents amongst themselves and had come to regard this almost as a part of the natural order of things. But now the precise opposite was happening. Now Europe herself was being divided by two outside colossi into what amounted to spheres of influence. At the same time, Europe's colonial possessions were breaking away en masse, with or without the consent of the imperial capitals. It is not surprising that obituaries for Europe appeared during those immediate postwar years. Europe was compared to Greece in the Hellenistic Age, and was written off in treatises bearing such titles as *Inquest on Europe, The Political Collapse of Europe,* and *The Passing of the European Age.* Just as the German historian Oswald Spengler wrote *The Decline of the West* following the trauma of World War I, so the German sociologist Alfred Weber wrote *Farewell to European History* following the greater trauma of World War II.

II. Relaxation of the Cold War

The primacy of Washington and Moscow was accepted, albeit reluctantly, partly because their support was needed in the face of the pressures and tensions engendered by the Cold War. But after building up for several years (see Chapter 26, section VII), this Cold War began to subside in 1953. One reason was the death in April, 1953, of Joseph Stalin, who had become increasingly paranoid and inflexible in his later years. The younger men who succeeded him were ready for a relaxation of both the Cold War abroad and the dictatorship at home. At the same time, the new Eisenhower administration was replacing that of Truman in the United States. This also contributed to the international "thaw," for Eisenhower was able to make a compromise peace in Korea, whereas Truman would have found this extremely difficult because of domestic political considerations. Thus the Korean War was ended in July, 1953, eliminating the most serious single source of international tension.

The following month the Soviet government announced that it also possessed the secret of the hydrogen bomb. Paradoxically, this strengthened the movement for a settlement by underscoring the fact that war had become an impossible way of dealing with international disputes. It was known that the hydrogen bomb exploded by the United States at Bikini was equal to 15 million tons of TNT. This was 750 times more powerful than the Hiroshima atomic bomb, which had killed 78,000 people. Winston Churchill, in a speech to the House of Commons on March 1, 1955, pointed out that the new weapon transformed international relations as well as warfare. It threatened the existence not only of little countries like England but also of the American and Russian superpowers themselves. "It may well be," declared Churchill, "that we shall, by a process of sublime irony, have reached a stage in this story where safety will be the sturdy child of terror."

A dramatic display of the new international atmosphere was the July, 1955, Geneva "summit" meeting of President Eisenhower, Premier Bulganin, Prime Minister Eden, and Premier Faure. This was the first meeting of the "Big Four" since the Potsdam Conference ten years earlier. No tangible decisions were reached, but the atmosphere was cordial. The mere fact that the leaders of the United States and the Soviet Union could meet and hold amicable discussions was a significant gain after the deepfreeze of the preceding years.*

The military stalemate, together with the slackening of the Cold War, had immediate repercussions all over the globe. The growing conviction that a world war was improbable eased the international tension and lessened the rigidity of the opposing blocs. The Western European states, no longer so apprehensive of the danger of Russian invasion, did not feel so dependent upon Washington and were more ready to formulate and pursue their own policies. To a lesser extent this was true also in Eastern Europe, which explains in part the Polish and Hungarian outbreaks in 1956. Even in the colonial world there were repercussions. Britain and France failed in their Suez expedition not because they were weaker than Nasser but because they dared not risk an international conflagration in an age of hydrogen bomb warfare. The same consideration held back the Western powers from going to the aid of the revolutionaries in Hungary, and deterred the Russians from armed action against the nationalistic Communists in Poland.

The most spectacular example of Great Power restraint was displayed during the 1962 Cuba crisis, precipitated when American air reconaissance revealed that Russian missile bases were under construction in Cuba and that a large part of the United States soon would be within range. In a dramatic broadcast on October 22, 1962, President Kennedy announced decisive measures to remove the threat to the United States, but not humiliate Khrushchev to the point of provoking him to dangerous reaction. Kennedy proclaimed a "quarantine" to halt ships carrying offensive weapons to Cuba, and demanded the removal of the Russian strategic missiles. But he did not demand the removal of the Castro regime or even of the Cuban defensive missiles. It became clear that neither country wanted war when Soviet vessels bound for Cuba altered course and the United States permitted a Soviet tanker to proceed when satisfied that it carried no offensive weapons. Finally, on October 28, Khrushchev announced that he had ordered Soviet missiles withdrawn and all Soviet bases in Cuba dismantled under U.N. inspection, in return for the ending of the United States blockade and a pledge not to invade Cuba.

The Cuban crisis demonstrated once more that neither of the great nuclear powers dared to follow the traditional practice of using war as an instrument of national policy. Although the confrontation ended peaceably, it was a very near thing—so near that it stimulated renewed efforts to alleviate world

* See "Cold War Thaw—Peaceful Coexistence," *EMM,* No. 186.

628

tensions. One result was the test ban treaty signed in Moscow on August 5, 1963, by the United States, Britain, and Russia. The pact was limited in scope, banning only nuclear explosions in the atmosphere, in outer space, and under water. Nevertheless it did represent a step forward and was hailed enthusiastically by most countries, which promptly adhered to the pact along with the original signatories. The only holdouts, significantly, were the two powers currently challenging American-Russian primacy—France and China.

III. WESTERN EUROPE ITS OWN MASTER

During the 1950's the Western European states were able to dispense with the economic crutches provided by the United States, and thereby to gain more maneuverability in political matters. The economic independence was made possible by a remarkable increase in productivity and general prosperity, and also by the organization of the Common Market, which made Western Europe an economic power comparable to the United States.

The roots of the Common Market go back very far in European history. Since medieval times philosophers and statesmen had propounded schemes for the unification of Western Europe. Nothing of a practical nature was done until the trauma of World War I aroused doubts concerning an international order based on completely sovereign states. In the late 1920's the French and German foreign ministers considered plans for the organization of a United States of Europe. But the coming of the Depression and the aggressions of Nazi Germany and Fascist Italy ended any possibility of European integration.

World War II, with its unprecedented destruction of material and human resources, again highlighted the need to find some way out of the international anarchy. The breakthrough came on May 9, 1950, when the French foreign minister, Robert Schuman, proposed a Coal and Steel Community as a pilot plant for the development of United Europe. The proposal was designed to integrate the coal and iron resources of the Rhine Basin which were divided among four states: France, Germany, Belgium, and Luxembourg, and to allay French fears of an industrially resurgent West Germany, by making war, in Schuman's words, "not only unthinkable but impossible."

The response to Schuman's proposal was immediate and enthusiastic. The European Coal and Steel Community (ECSC), as the organization set up was called, was established by treaty on April 18, 1951, and was formally launched in 1952. Its members came to be known as the Six: France, Germany, Italy, Belgium, Netherlands, and Luxembourg. The member states gave ECSC full power in fixing prices, setting export and import duties, and allocating materials. A governing body, the High Authority, was established, with headquarters in the city of Luxembourg. Major policy decisions were made the province of the ECSC Common Assembly, elected by the parliaments of the member states; and disputes among members were to be settled by the Community's own Court of Justice. ECSC achieved surprising success in short order. It eliminated not only all customs duties on coal and steel products among members of the Community, but all restrictions of any sort, such as quotas, export and import licenses, discriminatory freight rates or price differentials. By mid-1954 roughly 40 per cent more coal and steel was being shipped across the national boundaries within the Community than prior to the appearance of ECSC.

But this was only the beginning of Western Europe's integration. The next step was taken on March 25, 1957, when the Six signed two additional treaties, establishing the European Atomic Energy Community (Euratom) and the European Economic Community (EEC), or Common Market. The purpose of Euratom was to make the necessary preparations for meeting the energy gap of the future with nuclear power. This involved joint research, sharing of atomic information, and a common market for fissionable equipment and materials. Euratom paralleled the United States' Atomic Energy Commission, except that it was to be concerned exclusively with the use of atomic power for peaceful purposes. The establishment of the Common Market was even more important, for its purpose was to extend the work of ECSC to all goods and services, by reducing all internal tariffs in specified stages until by December 31, 1969, they would be completely eliminated, and the Six would constitute one vast free trade area.

Partly because of this integration and partly because of other developments, such as the introduction of American production and managerial techniques, Europe now experienced remarkable economic growth. Between 1950 and 1959 the growth rate of the national product per worker was 4.7 per cent for Italy, 4.5 per cent for Germany, 3.6 per cent for France, 2.2 per cent for the United States, and 1.2 per cent for the United Kingdom. This disparity in the rate of economic growth gradually reversed the economic positions of the United States and Western Europe. At the end of 1948 the United States held 71 per cent of the free world's gold and Western Europe only 15 per cent. By 1962 the American share had fallen to 40 per cent and Western Europe's had risen to 44 per cent. Another indication of the same trend was that by 1962 the six countries of the Common Market between them had surpassed the United States in volume of exports and imports combined. The Common Market had become the largest single trading bloc in the world.*

The change in economic relationships between Western Europe and the United States was paralleled by a corresponding change in political relationships. This was particularly true of France under de Gaulle, who pursued his own independent policies in every field. This was demonstrated dramatically when in 1963 he vetoed Britain's application for entry into the Common Market. Britain had refused to join at the outset, both because it would have meant giving up her preferential trade arrangements with her Commonwealth and because she had traditionally preferred to remain aloof from Continental involvement. "We are with them but not of them," Winston Churchill had stated in the House of Commons. Accordingly, in 1960 Britain had organized the more limited European Free Trade Association (Britain, Sweden, Norway, Denmark, Austria, Switzerland, and Portugal), known as the "Outer Seven" as against the "Inner Six." This provided for gradual elimination of internal tariffs but, unlike the Common Market, did not establish supranational devices for control and coordination, and did not require a single common tariff to the outside world.

* See "Affluence in Europe," *EMM,* No. 187.

630

The "Outer Seven" did not function effectively, as was reflected in Britain's low rate of economic growth. In 1962 Britain began negotiations for entry into the "Inner Six," but difficulties arose over the question of Commonwealth economic relations. There were political complications, too, as de Gaulle made clear when he vetoed Britain's application in January, 1963. The inclusion of Britain and her "Outer Seven" partners, he explained, would mean, ultimately, "a colossal Atlantic Community under American dependence and leadership." This was unacceptable; he wanted instead "a strictly European construction" in which he would play the leading role.

Equally decisive was de Gaulle's independent course concerning NATO strategy and nuclear power. American policy makers preferred that NATO forces be equipped with conventional weapons, while the United States remained ready to intervene when needed with its great nuclear striking force. De Gaulle rejected this strategy because it left the decisive power in foreign hands, and Washington alone would decide when it should be used. He proceeded, therefore, to develop his own atomic weapons and aerial striking force, to be bolstered in time by nuclear submarines and hydrogen bombs, which de Gaulle considered to be the essential power basis for his independent diplomacy. In December, 1962, for example, he rejected an agreement by Prime Minister Macmillan and President Kennedy for establishing a NATO nuclear force armed with United States Polaris missiles equipped with British warheads. To de Gaulle, this smacked of domination by what he called the Anglo-Saxon powers, for which he bore little love, especially because of his unfortunate wartime relations with Roosevelt and Churchill. Likewise, de Gaulle refused to adhere to the test ban treaty concluded in Moscow in July, 1963, by the United States, Britain, and Russia. The treaty, which banned further nuclear explosions in the water, in the atmosphere, and in outer space, was unacceptable to France, for it would hamper further development of her nuclear force.

Even more spectacular was de Gaulle's free-wheeling diplomacy. On January 27, 1964, he extended full diplomatic recognition to Communist China despite repeated remonstrances from Washington. Three days later he explained that he was simply "recognizing the world as it is." "On this [Asian] continent," he added, "there is no imaginable peace or war without her [China] being implicated and it is inconceivable to suppose that it is possible ever to conclude a neutrality treaty concerning the states of Southeast Asia, to which we French show a very special and cordial attention, without China's being a party to it." [1] Thus the general was laying down the gauntlet also in Southeast Asia where the United States was then backing, with money, arms, and military missions, the existing Vietnam government against the Viet Cong communist rebels. De Gaulle was convinced that these efforts were doomed to failure and that the Americans would be forcibly expelled, as the French themselves had been a decade earlier. Instead, he urged neutralization for the whole area, which would "exclude various forms of foreign intervention."

Such was de Gaulle's challenge to American policies and American leadership. Furthermore, it was a challenge of global proportions, as he demonstrated by despatching French diplomatic and trade missions to Latin America, and himself visiting Mexico (March, 1964) where he stressed the common heritage of the Latin peoples and "independence" of big power blocs.* Nor was de Gaulle speaking only for himself and for France. His assertiveness struck responsive chords in a fully recuperated Europe that was now able and eager to cast aside crutches and apron strings. This was reflected in the following comments of responsible European leaders at the beginning of 1964:

631

> BRITISH M.P.: One lesson of 1963 is that it will no longer be possible for the U.S. to impose policies on her allies as if she were handing down the tablets from Mount Sinai. Washington will now have to pay some sort of price for its allies' support.
>
> SENIOR ITALIAN OFFICIAL: Gaullism is now a trans-European philosophy. We may not like the man, but his ideas have taken hold and will certainly outlive him. There isn't a European who isn't proud when de Gaulle tells the big powers off.
>
> DUTCH AVIATION EXECUTIVE: The U.S. should understand we are not being anti-American in hoping de Gaulle succeeds. A special protectorate relationship with the U.S. was necessary because of the cold war. But Europe must now organize itself and think of the future, of opening up new markets—which, of course, implies new relations.[2]

IV. EASTERN EUROPE WINS AUTONOMY

While Western Europe was becoming independent of the United States, Eastern Europe was gaining a measure of autonomy from the Soviet Union. Here also the change was made possible by the American-Russian military stalemate and by the easing of the Cold War. An additional important factor in Eastern Europe was the change in leadership in the Soviet Union. The death of Stalin marked the beginning of a new era not only in Soviet domestic affairs but also in the relations between the Soviet Union and its East European satellites.

Some time elapsed before a stable new leadership emerged in Moscow. At first an informal five-man directory ruled the country—Georgi Malenkov for the bureaucracy, Vyacheslav Molotov for the old-line Stalinists, Marshal Bulganin for the military, Lavrenti Beria for the secret police, and the relatively obscure Nikita Khrushchev for the party apparatus. Within three months this group was reduced by one with the fall of Beria. His position as head of the secret police had made him the most hated and feared man in the country, especially in the later paranoid years of Stalin's dictatorship. Now his colleagues first stripped him of authority, and then executed him in December, 1953. This proved to be a significant turning point in the evolution of Soviet society. Though still far from enjoying full personal freedom, the average Russian citizen gradually became less fearful of the knock on the door in the dead of night, and the attendant execution or exile to a prison camp. Soviet leaders also breathed easier. Henceforth they did not pay with their lives when they lost power during the frequent reshuffles and purges; rather they were forced to obscurity by demotion or by exile to the provinces.

* See "President de Gaulle's Independent Course," EMM, No. 188.

Malenkov, who assumed leadership of the remaining four, shifted from Stalin's emphasis on military preparedness and heavy industrial production to providing more consumer goods for the long-neglected public. He encouraged the peasantry by relaxing government control of collective farms, reducing delivery quotas, and increasing payments for farm produce. In foreign affairs, Malenkov allowed more autonomy for the satellite states and even made friendly overtures to the Western powers. "There is not one disputed and undecided question," he declared in his inaugural address to the Supreme Soviet, "that cannot be decided by peaceful means. . . . This is our attitude toward all states, among them the United States of America."

This program of relaxation at home and abroad did not sit well with the military and the orthodox Stalinists. They combined forces to engineer the downfall of Malenkov in February, 1955. From the power struggle that followed, the military at first emerged with the commanding posts. Marshal Bulganin became prime minister, and Marshal Zhukov, the conquerer of Berlin, came out of the retirement forced by Stalin to head the defense ministry. Again there was renewed emphasis on armaments and heavy industry, while in mid-May, 1955, the satellite states for the first time were bound together in a formal military alliance with the Soviet Union. The Warsaw Pact, as the alliance was called, was essentially a reaction to NATO, and more particularly to the current rearming of West Germany.

This preponderance of the Soviet military soon gave way before the steady rise to power of the master politician, Khrushchev. Using his power base in the Communist Party rank and file, he pushed aside one after another of his colleagues. By March, 1958, he was able to replace Bulganin as premier, thus becoming the boss of both the party and the government. This marked the end of the transition period of "collective leadership"; Khrushchev now was the undisputed successor to Stalin.

Two years earlier, on February 25, 1956, Khrushchev had already exploded a bombshell that rocked the entire Communist world. Addressing the Twentieth Congress of the Communist Party of the USSR, he excoriated the dead Stalin for excessive self-glorification and for unspeakable acts of treachery and terrorism. Reportedly weeping at times, he portrayed the former dictator as "a very distrustful man, sickly suspicious," who was responsible for the official murder of "many thousands of honest and innocent Communists." In the course of this incredible four-hour tirade, Khrushchev also attacked Stalin for rewriting and distorting official Communist history, and even criticized his conduct of the war, which, he charged, was responsible for the disastrous defeats and the appalling loss of lives.

The ebullient Khrushchev, perhaps carried away by his own eloquence and long suppressed emotions, may have divulged more than he intended. Certainly the repercussions were more drastic and far-reaching than he could have desired or foreseen. Stalin's body was removed from the mausoleum in Red Square where it had rested beside Lenin's; his statues were smashed; and his name was erased from the literally thousands of Russian and East European cities and streets that had been named after him. A new ideological "thaw" allowed artists and writers more freedom in criticizing Soviet society. Foreign Communist parties, hitherto tightly controlled by Stalin's henchmen, experienced a painful soul-searching that undermined their ideological and organizational discipline. "Liberal," nationalist-minded Communist leaders now began to assert themselves against the old Kremlin-oriented party bosses. Such was the "fallout" from Khrushchev's bombshell, and, together with the catalytic effect of the military stalemate and the Cold War relaxation, it transformed the relations between the Soviet Union and its satellites.

The first anti-Soviet outbreak in Eastern Europe had occurred almost a decade earlier in Yugoslavia. The issue basically was whether Communist party leaders who had become heads of states should remain subject to Kremlin discipline. Even during the war years Josip Broz, or Tito, had insisted on the independence of the individual national parties and had acted accordingly. He continued to do so, and was able to get away with it partly because of Yugoslavia's accessibility to Western naval power. More important was the fact that Tito, unlike most other East European Communist chiefs, had stayed in his country and built up a powerful resistance army with which he successfully defied Stalin in the postwar years. He felt, for example, that the Soviets did not support his claim to Trieste strongly, and attributed this to their desire to strengthen the Communist party in Italy. "It is said," declared Tito, "that this is a just war, and we have considered it such. However, we also seek a just end. We demand that everyone shall be master in his own house. We do not want to pay for others. We do not want to be used as a bribe in international bargaining."

Moscow reacted quickly to this heretical notion of the independence of Communist parties and states. "Tell Comrade Tito," the Soviet ambassador warned, "that if he should once again permit such an attack on the Soviet Union we shall be forced to reply with open criticism in the press and disavow him." [3] The heretic refused to recant. Instead, he committed more sins. He criticized the behavior of Soviet officers and officials in Yugoslavia. He tried to form a Yugoslav-Bulgarian federation which Moscow forestalled by ordering the Bulgars to withdraw. And when Tito found that he was being spied upon, he had his own secret-servicemen shadow Russian diplomats and technicians in Yugoslavia. Finally, in June, 1948, the Cominform expelled the Yugoslav party in an angry proclamation. But Tito did not succumb, thanks to his strong position at home and to generous economic and military support from the Western powers. A popular saying in Eastern Europe at the end of 1949 was, "Karl Marx is God, Lenin is Jesus, Stalin is St. Paul, and Tito the first Protestant."

The new heresy spread, but had to remain underground because Soviet authority was effective in the other East European states. Yet "Titoism," a new word in the Marxist lexicon, remained endemic, waiting for an opportunity to burst out. It did so in 1956, thanks to the favorable combination of circumstances that developed that year. The most violent explosions occurred in two countries with long anti-Russian traditions—Poland and Hungary. In both, Khrushchev's February speech encouraged literary discussion groups to appear. The next step was the establishment of contacts between the intellectuals and the more articulate urban workers. In the spring and summer of 1956, events in Hungary and Poland ran a parallel course. But by the autumn they began to diverge, the one to end in armed revolt and repression; the other to win a measure of individual and national freedom.

Poland's leading "national" Communist, Wladyslaw Gomulka, who had

634

been purged on charges of Titoism in 1948, was rehabilitated in the spring of 1956. His ideas soon began to spread in the intermediate echelons of the Communist party. A workers' uprising at Poznan (the former Prussian city of Posen) reflected the weakening influence of the Polish Stalinists. The latter were ousted one by one from the leading party positions until a crisis developed over the Polish-born marshal of the Soviet army, Konstantin Rokossovsky, who was also Polish defense minister and a member of Poland's Politburo. In an unprecedented move in support of Rokossovsky, Khrushchev hurried to Warsaw on October 19, 1956, with all but two members of the Soviet Politbureau, while at the same time the Red Army made menacing troop movements. But in the end it was Khrushchev who backed down and accepted Rokossovsky's dismissal and Gomulka's election on October 21 as First Secretary of the Polish Communist party. Khrushchev was willing to suffer this serious setback because he was convinced that Gomulka was a devoted though independent Communist who would never turn to the West. This assumption proved correct, and in the following years a mutually satisfactory relationship developed, with Poland becoming increasingly autonomous of the Kremlin yet remaining definitely a Communist state and a dependable adherent to the Warsaw Pact.

In Hungary, the situation was more complicated. The party boss, Matyas Rakosi, was a Jew, which aggravated matters in a country with a tradition of anti-Semitism. He was also an old-line Stalinist who had spent sixteen years in Hungarian jails in the interwar period, and who was now unwilling to share authority with the "nationalist" Hungarian Communists. Thus change from above, as in Poland, was blocked. Instead, there was revolution from below, and since this was unpredictable, Khrushchev sent in the Red Army.

The trouble began in Budapest on October 23, 1956, when a large crowd of demonstrators—inspired by the events in Poland—demanded that Rakosi resign in favor of the nationalist-minded Communist Imre Nagy. The secret police responded by opening fire, thereby transforming a protest demonstration into an open revolution, which swept Nagy into the premiership and led him to make promises and to take actions that were intolerable to the Russians. To appease the demonstrators, who soon were active in the provinces as well as the capital, Nagy invited two non-Communists into his government, abolished collectivization, declared a general amnesty for the rebels, promised free elections, and persuaded the Russians to withdraw their tanks from Budapest.

This did not suffice for the revolutionaries, who now attacked Communist party headquarters and even harried the withdrawing Soviet forces. In doing so they revealed their all-out anti-Communism and anti-Sovietism. They were not content with autonomy within the Soviet orbit, as were the Poles. Instead, they wanted a Western-type democracy, completely free of commitments to Moscow or to the Warsaw Pact. These developments constituted an intolerable threat to the Russians' security system in Eastern Europe. On November 1, they turned their tanks around and sent them back to Budapest. Premier Nagy thereupon declared Hungary a neutral country, repudiated the Warsaw Pact, and sent an appeal to the United Nations. No help was forthcoming from the outside, for the United States was occupied with its Presidential election, and France and Britain were in the midst of their Suez expedition. The revolutionists were crushed by overwhelming force, and a new Communist dictatorship was installed under Janos Kadar.

The Russians had their way, but the price was a great moral and psychological defeat. The spectacle of Hungarian workers and students throwing Molotov cocktails against Soviet tanks disillusioned many devoted Communists and fellow-travellers. This was a far cry from the original Communist dream of international proletarian brotherhood. The shock was particularly great in Western European intellectual circles, where many distinguished writers and artists now turned in their party cards.

The Russians were quite aware of this negative reaction and hastened to make amends. At the height of the Hungarian crisis they had proclaimed their readiness to revise their relations with the satellite states. They had declared their aim to be a "Commonwealth of Socialist States," based on the principles of "national sovereignty, mutual advantage, and equality," and they had offered to revise the Warsaw Pact with the view to withdrawing Russian troops from Eastern Europe. This was neither philanthropy nor cynical deception on the part of the Russians. Rather, they realized that they could not remain encamped indefinitely as blatant interventionists and occupationists. The nineteenth century Tsars perhaps could afford the opprobrium of being universally branded as "the hangmen of liberty" in Eastern Europe. It was a very different matter for a professedly Socialist country to face this charge in an era of mass communication media when the minds of men everywhere were accessible and receptive. Accordingly, Khrushchev gradually modified his policies toward the neighboring countries until substantially new relationships were established.

Heretofore all the satellite states had been deliberately isolated by Stalin, not only from the West but also from one another. Moreover, they had been ruthlessly exploited by a variety of unequal trade treaties and development arrangements that operated in favor of the Soviet Union. The Kremlin commandment to "industrialize, industrialize, and again industrialize" was enforced in Eastern Europe without discrimination or economic sense. The region was studded with Stalin's "white elephants"—enormous plants for which the necessary raw materials were not easily available, and whose output could compete in the world markets only by paying substandard wages to the workers. The burden on the general public was aggravated by the fact that many of the new plants, on orders from Moscow, were devoted to arms production. Even agriculture had been disrupted by forced collectivization and by pressure to raise industrial crops such as cotton and flax. The net result throughout the region was food shortages, scarcity of consumer goods, substantial unemployment, miserably low wages, and correspondingly low living standards. All this, it should be noted, had contributed decisively to the general unrest that culminated in the explosions of 1956. It is not accidental that the least turbulent country, Czechoslovakia, was also the most developed economically; hence it was able to meet Stalin's demands for heavy industry and armaments at lighter cost for its people than were less developed countries such as Poland and Hungary.

After 1956, this pattern changed quickly and significantly. Trade treaties and development aggreements were renegotiated and made more equitable. Each country was allowed gradually to make its own decisions regarding the

636

pace and course of economic development. Industries no longer had to be integrated with those of Russia or the other Communist countries. Instead, the trend was toward more independent national development, more leeway to both industry and agriculture, and more trade with the West.* For example, Rumania's trade with the West between 1960 and 1964 rose from 20 to 33 pcr ccnt of her total trade. Khrushchev likewise found it necessary to modify his ambitious plans for the Council for Mutual Economic Assistance (Comecon) which he had hoped would become the medium for comprehensive integration of the Soviet Union, its Eastern European allies, and Mongolia. When the integration did not occur, because of the objections of the East European countries against having their economic plans directed by Moscow through Comecon, a series of bilateral agreements was negotiated in 1963 and 1964 between the Soviet Union and the East European states. Khrushchev found it necessary to settle for the half-loaf of bilateral integration when he could not get the full loaf of Comecon-wide integration. The United States encouraged Rumania in her independent course by signing an agreement for substantial increase in trade between the two countries, and providing credit to finance the new commercial ties.

This economic relaxation and broadening had its counterpart in the cultural field. Symptomatic were the cultural agreements concluded with Western countries, less frequent jamming of foreign broadcasts, increase in tourism, greater freedom to foreign correspondents, and freer circulation of Western films, books, and periodicals. So pronounced was this general trend that on May 23, 1964, President Lyndon Johnson declared: † "There is no longer a single Iron Curtain. There are many. Each differs in strength and thickness, in the light that can pass through it and the hopes that can prosper behind it. . . . We will continue to build bridges across the gulf which has divided us from Eastern Europe. They will be bridges of increased trade, of ideas, of visitors and of humanitarian aid." [4]

V. China Challenges Russia

When the victorious Chinese Communists established their People's Republic in 1949, they were promptly recognized by the Soviet Union. A score of other countries, including Britain and India, did likewise. The United States, however, continued to treat Chiang Kai-shek's exiled regime in Taiwan as the legal government of China. Also largely because of American diplomatic initiative, the Taiwan regime represented the Chinese people at the United Nations and on the Security Council, where it enjoyed a permanent seat and the power to veto resolutions. Under these circumstances, relations between Washington and Peking were strained even before the open break over Korea. By contrast, Moscow and Peking signed a thirty-year treaty of "friendship, alliance, and mutual assistance" in 1950. Under its terms, the Soviet Union helped China to build a large modern army and to undertake a sweeping program of industrialization. Although the Russians provided loans on generous terms, they still were loans and not grants. China shipped more

* See " 'Polycentrism' in the Communist World," EMM, No. 189.
† See "The United States and the New Eastern Europe," EMM, No. 190.

than half her exports to the Soviet Union to pay for the flow of capital goods, technical aid, and military supplies.

This Russo-Chinese alliance began to show signs of disruption in 1960. Peking criticized Khrushchev indirectly with thinly veiled barbs against "Yugoslav revisionists," while Moscow spokesmen retaliated with attacks against "dogmatists" and "left infantilists." During the Twenty-second Soviet Party Congress in October, 1961, Khrushchev and Chou En-lai clashed openly, and the latter left the Congress and flew back to Peking. About this time the Russians recalled from China nearly all their technical experts; in February, 1964, the Chinese charged specifically that the Russians had withdrawn 1,390 experts and cancelled 257 projects of scientific and technical cooperation. Worst of all, from the Chinese viewpoint, the Soviets refused to share their atomic weapons or the technical information and the resources necessary for their manufacture. Thus the quarrel between the two Communist giants grew to the proportion of an outright schism, including unseemly name calling, ideological vituperation, and open rivalry all over the globe. In the beginning of 1964 Mao Tse-tung stated to a French Parliamentary group that Khrushchev was destined to fall from office, and that the Soviet-Chinese alliance of 1950 was null and void because of "repeated Soviet violations, ideological and otherwise."

The roots of this dramatic and fateful rift in the Communist world appear to be partly a conflict of national interests and partly a conflict of ideologies. The national issues arose from traditional material considerations such as *Lebensraum,* frontier demarcation, and different economic interests because of different levels of development. The Soviet Union has a land area two and a half times that of China, and a population density of 24 per square mile as against China's 190. The 2,000 mile frontier separating the two countries has been drawn in precise detail in Soviet maps, whereas on Chinese maps certain sections have been depicted as "undemarcated": the eastern margins of the Pamir highlands, some islands at the confluence of the Amur and Ussuri Rivers, and almost the entire frontier with Mongolia. More significant and ominous was the following passage in an editorial of the Peking *People's Daily* of March 8, 1963:

> During the hundred or so years preceding the victorious Chinese [Communist] Revolution, the colonial and imperialistic powers—the USA, Great Britain, France, Czarist Russia, Germany, Japan, Italy, Austria, Belgium, the Netherlands, Spain and Portugal—became unreservedly engaged in a campaign of aggression against China. They imposed on the various regimes of the old China numerous unequal treaties: the Treaty of Nanking in 1842; the Treaty of Aigun in 1858; the Treaty of Tientsin in 1858; the Treaty of Peking in 1860; the Treaty of Ili in 1881; the Convention for the Extension of Hong Kong in 1898; the Treaty of 1901; etc. . . . . By virtue of these unequal treaties, they annexed Chinese territory in the North, South, East and West; or they caused territories to be ceded to them on lease along the coast of China and even in the Chinese hinterland. . . . . When the People's Republic of China was founded in 1949, our Government clearly stated its intention of eventually re-examining all the treaties concluded by

637

previous Chinese regimes with foreign governments and, according to their respective texts, either recognizing, denouncing, revising or re-negotiating them at the appropriate time.[5]

Of the above-mentioned pacts, the Ili Treaty gave Russia certain territory adjacent to Sinkiang, the Aigun Treaty ceded to Russia the entire Amur basin, and the Peking Treaty gave her the large Maritime Province. Suffice it to add that the importance attached to this editorial was underscored when it was broadcast worldwide by Radio Peking.

Another aspect of the conflict of national interests arose from the time difference in Russian and Chinese economic development, resulting in a disparity in living standards. The harsh but understandable fact is that neither Khrushchev nor his people were prepared to share their hard-won rewards with their Chinese comrades. This attitude was vigorously expressed as follows by a Soviet historian in conversation with an American correspondent:

> Yes, we are two large, socialist countries, both opposed to imperialism; on this matter we are united. But we have had independent national experiences and are at different levels of revolutionary development. China is going through some stages we passed thirty years ago. We wish she could learn from our mistakes but it can't always be so. We have a higher standard of living, our people need and demand more, and we can't get them to make the sacrifices the Chinese make. Not any more. We said, relax a bit; *the socialist world is secure.* But the Chinese won't have it so; they want three shifts a day and complain if our machines break down under the strain. They are very proud. They want equality in the world. We have won it; they are still struggling for it. They are going to get it their own way and by their own efforts—and their way may be best for them. We have a Russian proverb that sums up the situation. "You can't fit one man's head on another man's shoulders." [6]

What will probably prove more significant in the long run than this clash of national interests is the clash in ideology that has paralleled it. This is more subtle and sophisticated than the common assumption that the lean and hungry Chinese are ready to risk thermonuclear war in order to further the socialist cause, whereas the fat Russians prefer to play it safe with their strategy of peaceful coexistence. Rather, the Russians and the Chinese have differed fundamentally in their interpretations of the nature of the historical period through which the world is passing, and the appropriate strategy for manipulating current historical forces to expedite the triumph of socialism.

The Russians have begun with the basic thesis that the all-important world issue is war or peace. If thermonuclear war comes, they have argued, both capitalist and socialist societies will be destroyed or set back for centuries. But if war can be avoided, the superiority of socialism over capitalism will be clearly demonstrated after a few decades of peaceful competition, and this example will persuade the entire world to embrace socialism. Such has been the theoretical analysis upon which the Russians have based their political strategy and their hopes for disarmament, peaceful coexistence, and peaceful transition from capitalism to socialism.

The Chinese have asserted that they also favor these objectives, but they are doubtful of their attainability. The great obstacle is the imperialism of the Western powers, for imperialism by its very nature is expansionist and war-provoking. Therefore the proper strategy is not to strive directly for peace and disarmament, as does the Soviet Union, but to struggle against imperialism which stands in the way of peace and disarmament. The most effective way of combatting imperialism, the Chinese have maintained, is to support the rapidly growing revolutionary movement in the underdeveloped world. This revolutionary spirit amongst the majority of mankind living in the underdeveloped countries constitutes the Achilles' heel of imperialism.

639

> To achieve world peace it is necessary to rely mainly on the strength of the masses of the people of the world and on their struggles. In the course of the struggle to defend world peace it is necessary to enter into negotiations on one issue or another with the governments of the imperialist countries, including the government of the U.S. for the purpose of easing international tensions, reaching some kind of compromise and arriving at certain agreements. . . . However, world peace can never be achieved by negotiations alone, and in no circumstances must we pin our hopes on imperialism and divorce ourselves from the struggles of the masses. . . . The more the national liberation movements and the revolutionary struggles develop, the better for the defense of world peace.[7]

In short, the Chinese have believed that peace will be preserved by the disruption of imperialism through revolutionary movements in the underdeveloped world. The Russians, by contrast, have held that the growing prosperity and strength of the socialist world (meaning essentially the Soviet Union) will neutralize the war propensity of Western imperialism, will speed its decline by the sheer force of example, and thus will ease the way for successful revolution in the underdeveloped countries.

These Marxist disputations may seem unreal and abstract; in fact, they have had a very real and practical bearing on contemporary world politics. In accordance with their contention that agreements with "imperialist" countries are necessary under certain circumstances, the Chinese reached an agreement with de Gaulle on January 27, 1964, for the establishment of diplomatic relations between the two countries (see section III, this chapter). The effect was to alter substantially the pattern of global power relationships. Mao, like de Gaulle, challenged vigorously the test ban treaty concluded in Moscow in July, 1963, by the United States, Russia, and Britain. "Two great countries," charged Mao, "the Soviet Union and the United States, want to lead the world without consulting anyone. Did they consult General de Gaulle . . .? The treaty of Moscow is a swindle." Mao also championed the de Gaulle concept of a third great bloc to counterbalance the United States and the Soviet Union. "France herself, Germany, Italy, England, on the condition that she ceases to be the courtier of America, Japan and we, ourselves—there is your third world." [8]

Equally independent and aggressive has been the Chinese policy regarding the underdeveloped countries. For example, Peking officially recognized the Algerian rebels at an early date, to the embarrassment of Khrushchev, who

Two examples of Chinese art—"Lotus Gathering," from the sixteenth century, and "Increase Steel Production to Speed Socialist Industrialization," from the twentieth—point up the drive for modernization that is occurring in China.

was then anxious to avoid offending de Gaulle in the hope of broadening the General's differences with the United States. Likewise, China was the first country to give a financial grant and also a number of tractors to the new revolutionary regime established in Zanzibar in January, 1964. Most impressive was Chou En-lai's visit to several African countries in January, 1964, during which he met local political leaders and delivered public speeches that were as much anti-Soviet as anti-West. The gist of his speeches was that emerging China was a more relevant and practical model for the underdeveloped world than industrialized Russia or the affluent West. Chou also appealed subtly to Afro-Asian racial affinities, and identified the Russians with the "white" Western imperialists. More concrete were his proposals for financial and technical aid, including an offer to construct a highway from Algeria's Mediterranean coast to Mali and Chad. The Algerian leader, Ben Bella, was much taken by this prospect of reviving the old North-South routes across the Sahara as a channel for revolutionary ideas as well as for trade. On the completion of his tour, Chou characteristically stated that the prospects for revolution in Africa were highly promising.

Most spectacular has been the militant anti-Soviet campaign of the Chinese amongst the Communist parties of the world. They have challenged the Russians not only in matters of doctrine but also for the allegiance of the approxi-

mately ninety national Communist parties. They have been particularly
successful in Asia because of their geographic proximity, their racial appeal,
and their emphasis on militant revolutionary tactics. At the beginning of 1964   641
Moscow claimed the allegiance of at least 65 of the 90 parties, but the Chinese
counterclaimed that half of the 42.5 million Communist party members in
the world were on their side. In February, 1964, Peking issued a major
declaration accusing the Communist Party of the Soviet Union (CPSU) of
"splittism"—another new term in the Marxist lexicon. Under "splittism" they
enumerated a list of horrendous crimes which they charged to the CPSU.

> The events of recent years show that the leaders of the CPSU
> headed by Khrushchev have become . . . the greatest splitters in the
> international Communist movement. . . . Far from working to con-
> solidate and expand the Socialist camp, the leaders of the CPSU have
> endeavored to split and disintegrate it. They have thus made a mess of
> the splendid Socialist camp. . . . They have arbitrarily infringed the
> sovereignty of fraternal countries, interfered in their internal affairs,
> carried on subversive activities and striven in every way to control
> fraternal countries. . . . The leaders of the CPSU are bent on seeking
> Soviet-United States cooperation for the domination of the world . . .
> and they treat their fraternal partners and countries adhering to
> Marxism-Leninism as their enemy. . . . The leaders of the CPSU ob-
> struct and oppose the revolutionary struggles of other peoples and act
> as apologists for imperialism and neo-colonialism. . . . If the CPSU
> leaders insist on marking off the "majority" from the "minority," then
> we would like to tell them quite frankly that we do not recognize their
> majority. The majority you bank on is a false one. The genuine majority
> is not on your side. Today, more than 90 per cent of the world's popula-
> tion desire revolution, including those who are not yet but will even-
> tually become politically conscious. . . . We would like to advise the
> leaders of the CPSU to think matters over calmly: what will your
> clinging to revisionism and splittism lead to? [9]

The content and the tone of this extraordinary statement implied strongly
that Peking was preparing the way for a formal break with Moscow and for
the establishment of a new international Communist organization. Thus China,
the pawn of international diplomacy for over a century, was now challenging
simultaneously the two greatest powers of the world. The Middle Kingdom
of past millennia was reappearing on the center of the world stage.

VI. End of Bipolarism

By 1965—only two decades after the end of World War II—a drastically
new configuration of world politics was beginning to emerge. The bipolariza-
tion of world power that prevailed in the immediate postwar years had already evaporated. Europe no longer was a pawn, or two pawns, on the global
chessboard, nor was China a satellite nor even a junior partner of the Soviet
Union.

France's recognition of Communist China dramatically symbolized the new global balance. For France, this was a bold and calculated challenge to the United States, marking the beginning of the end of the American-sponsored trade embargo against Communist China and the beginning of the end of the American-sponsored effort to keep Peking out of the United Nations. For mainland China, the new tie with France marked the beginning of the end of Soviet economic constraint, and a major step forward in Peking's campaign to unite, in its own words, with all nations of "different social systems" who are eager to escape "United States aggression, control, interference, and bullying," and who oppose "the Soviet leaders' hopes for U.S.-Soviet cooperation to dominate the world."

If these dramatic developments are viewed in the light of the foregoing analysis of world history during the past five centuries, they suggest a new phase in the evolution of global relationships. It will be recalled that prior to Europe's fateful transformation and expansion, several regions had coexisted either autonomously or in complete isolation—the autonomous European, Moslem, and Confucian regions; the largely isolated sub-Saharan Africa, and the completely isolated Americas and Australia. After Columbus and da Gama and Magellan, this compartmentalization gave way to ever increasing interaction and integration directed and exploited by Europe. By the nineteenth century this trend had culminated in the unprecedented hegemony over the entire globe by a few great powers of Europe. The two world wars shattered this European dominance and replaced it with only a decade or two of bipolar predominance by Moscow and Washington—the brevity of this phase reflecting the constantly accelerating tempo of world events.

If the passing of bipolarism has now become self-evident, the same cannot be said about what will take its place. China appears to be well on the way to attaining a status comparable to that of the United States and the Soviet Union, thanks to her growing influence in East Asia and in the underdeveloped world as a whole. But beyond that, the shape of the future as regards regional interrelationships remains blurred and unpredictable. It might be projected that as the process of modernization proceeds apace, other non-Western regions will follow the examples of China and form new centers of power. Certainly there are "pan-" movements, such as Nasser's pan-Arabism and Nkrumah's pan-Africanism, that seek to unify and modernize their respective regions in order to achieve full political and economic independence. If these movements prove successful, then a new global pluralism would gradually evolve. Alongside the United States, the Soviet Union, and China, would emerge, under a variety of political and social forms, new centers of power in regions such as the Middle East, sub-Saharan Africa, India, Latin America, and, if de Gaulle has his way, a European bloc stretching from the Atlantic to the Urals. Such an outcome would represent, in the political sphere, a return to the traditional pre-1500 regional autonomy, while at the same time, in all other spheres, the process of modernization would be pulling the regions together into unprecedented unity.

Interregional relations might conceivably develop along these lines, though it is improbable, at least for the foreseeable future. The fact is that in most regions the centrifugal forces now seem stronger than the centripetal. Africa is torn by religious conflicts such as the Moslem-Christian in Nigeria and the Moslem-pagan in the Sudan, and by meaningless frontiers drawn by nineteenth century European diplomats and now defended by each independent state as a sacred national heritage. In the Middle East there are corresponding religious conflicts such as those between Moslem and Christian Arabs and amongst rival Moslem sects, in addition to dynastic feuds and the perennial antagonism of the haves and have-nots over oil royalties. The two fragments into which the Indian peninsula has been divided are far from solid, as indicated by the language riots in India and the tensions between West and East Pakistan. Likewise, de Gaulle's vision of a united Europe, despite the progress in economic integration, remains a vision in the realm of practical politics.

In addition to these divisive forces within regions, there are the equally divisive policies of the Great Powers. Testimony to their potency is to be found all over the globe—in divided Germany, in divided Korea, in divided Vietnam, and in the anarchical Congo. This fragmentive role of the Great Powers may well be accentuated in the future as Chinese-Russian and Chinese-Western rivalries are added to the Soviet-Western of the past two decades.

The range of possibilities in such a fluid situation is so wide that any conclusions are bound to be highly speculative and hypothetical. The end of empires may conceivably lead to regional unification and regional blocs. Burgeoning technology may force mankind to world government as the only viable alternative to nuclear holocaust. But for the present it can only be said that bipolarism is giving way in the 1960's just as European hegemony crumbled in the first half of the century.

Suggested Reading

Considerable literature has appeared recently on the changing relationships between the United States and Western Europe. Noteworthy are J. Freymond, *Western Europe Since the War* (New York: Praeger, 1964); R. Steel, *The End of the Alliance: America and the Future of Europe* (New York: Viking, 1964); R. Kleiman, *Atlantic Crisis* (New York, Norton, 1964); G. Lichtheim, *The New Europe* (New York: Praeger, 1963); and V. W. Kitzinger, *The Politics and Economics of European Integration: Britain, Europe and the United States* (New York: Praeger, 1964).

The loosening of the ties in the Communist world as a whole is described by A. Dallin, ed., *Diversity in International Communism: A Documentary Record, 1961–1963* (New York: Columbia Univ., 1963) and by W. Laqueur and L. Labedz, *Polycentrism: The New Factor in International Communism* (New York: Praeger, 1962). The significance of the new polycentrism for Western policymakers is analyzed by G. F. Kennan, "Polycentrism and Western Policy," *Foreign Affairs* (January, 1964) pp. 171–83.

For the effects of polycentrism in Eastern Europe, see P. E. Zinner, ed., *National Communism and Popular Revolt in Eastern Europe: A Selection of Documents on Events in Poland and Hungary, February–November 1956* (New York: Columbia Univ., 1956); R. Hiscocks, *Poland: Bridge for the Abyss? An Interpretation of Developments in Post-War Poland* (New York: Oxford Univ., 1963); and G. W. Hoffman and F. W. Neal, *Yugoslavia and the New Communism* (New York: Twentieth Century Fund, 1962).

644

For the historical background of the Soviet-Chinese split, see the brief, stimulating essay by C. P. Fitzgerald, *The Chinese View of Their Place in the World* (New York: Oxford Univ., 1964) and the authoritative analysis by K. Mehnert, *Peking and Moscow* (London: Weidenfeld, 1964). On the split itself there are several studies: G. F. Hudson, R. Lowenthal and R. MacFarquhar, *The Sino-Soviet Dispute* (New York: Praeger, 1961); H. Schwartz, *Tsars, Mandarins and Commissars: A History of Chinese-Russian Relations* (Philadelphia: Lippincott, 1964); D. Floyd, *Mao Against Khrushchev: A Short History of the Sino-Soviet Conflict* (New York: Praeger, 1964); and the collection of articles in K. Mehnert, *et al.* "Communist China and the Soviet Bloc: A History and Tradition," *Annals of the American Academy of Political and Social Science,* September, 1963.

*In World War II, which was decided by the
participation of the Soviet Union and the United
States, the collapse of the traditional European
system became an irrevocable fact. What is
commonly called the "historic Europe" is dead
and beyond redemption.*

HAJO HOLBORN, *1951*

*The western world is today the arbiter of man-
kind's fate. It is paradoxical but true that the
reaction against Western physical domination
has gone far to complete the conquest of the
world by Western culture. To ensure its own
survival the rest of the world has been obliged
to imitate the West. It is Western methods,
beliefs and goals that have been accepted and
utilized to combat Western control.*

F. L. K. HSU, *1953*

Decline and Triumph of the West

In one sense, the course of twentieth century history represented the decline of Europe. London, Paris, and Berlin no longer
dominated world news. No longer did they control world empires.
Their armies and navies and alliance systems had ceased to dominate
the globe. In 1860, for example, Western Europe was responsible
for 72 per cent of the world's total industrial output; by 1913
the percentage had dropped to 42; by the eve of World War II, to
30; and by 1960, to 25. It was self-evident that Europe's nineteenth
century global hegemony had ended, and ended forever: there is no
possibility of Europe's regaining her colonial empires or re-establish-
ing her former military and political predominance. On the other hand,
Europe had not fallen from primacy to subservience, as had appeared
likely to happen immediately following World War II. To the contrary,
although Europe was suffering relative decline in her military, economic, and political power, her culture was sweeping the world as
never before.

Europe was entering a period of triumph as well as decline: her
ideas, techniques, and institutions were spreading throughout the
globe more rapidly than at any time in the past. Fundamentally, this
represented the diffusion of Europe's three great revolutions—the
Industrial, the scientific, and the political—which earlier had given
her the power, the drive, and the knowledge to expand all over the

world and to conquer the great colonial empires (see Chapters 10, 11, and 12). But Europe's epochal success had boomeranged: for the colonial empires, by their very existence, facilitated the diffusion of the three revolutions. The subject peoples, profoundly affected by these revolutions, had reacted by selectively adopting some of their features in order better to resist the intruding West.

The Industrial Revolution spread in the nineteenth century from England to Europe and the United States, and in the first half of the twentieth century to Japan and the British Dominions. Following World War II, this diffusion accelerated rapidly. As each new country became independent, its first and foremost task was to promote economic development. All over the world a wide assortment of economic plans was being formulated and implemented, with varying degrees of success.* Typical was Ghana's Seven Year Plan (1963–1970), designed to increase national income 5.5 per cent annually for a total of 42 per cent over the seven years. Ghana's President Kwame Nkrumah described the rationale and objectives of the Plan in terms that reflect clearly the influence of Europe's economic revolution:

> The Seven-Year Development Plan provides the blueprint for the future progress and development of Ghana as a nation. It is a program of social and economic development based on the use of science and technology to revolutionize our agriculture and industry. Our aim is to establish in Ghana a strong and progressive society . . . where poverty and illiteracy no longer exist and disease is brought under control; and where our educational facilities provide all the children of Ghana with the best possible opportunities for the development of their potentialities.[1]

Science also spread rapidly from Europe, and, indeed, has become the one body of knowledge that all peoples have been anxious to acquire. Its objective methodology has made it acceptable to non-Western peoples who, by contrast, may not be interested in European art or religion or philosophy. Science has been eagerly sought after also because it constitutes the basis for advance in technology and general economic development. Thus, Europe has lost its monopoly on science; in the mid-sixties, more scientific work was being done in the United States and the Soviet Union than in any Western European country. By 1964, the United States had won 64 Nobel Prizes in science, as against 5 each for the closest competitors, Germany and Britain. The scientific revolution also has begun to make itself felt in non-Western countries, though the obstacles here have been formidable because of the interrelatedness of science and industry. While it is true that research in pure science can be undertaken independently of industry, the *development* of scientific discoveries depends upon a considerable industrial base. Even if a scientist has mastered the theory of breaking up the atom and has evolved a technical process for doing so, the production of atomic energy could only be undertaken by a society with large financial and industrial resources. Consequently, advanced scientific work is possible only in an advanced industrial country.

* See "Triumph of Europe: Economic," *EMM*, No. 192.

Many of the new Afro-Asian states have been trapped in this vicious circle, so that even the most modest scientific progress has been virtually impossible in the poorer and least developed of the new countries. Others of them, however, have had the requisite material and human resources, and have utilized them to the utmost. This is especially true of the two giant states, India and China, which by 1964 had won one and two Nobel Prizes respectively in science. India began with the strongest base in science, for the British had established certain technical institutes, and, more important, the industrial magnate Jamshedji Tata had founded the Indian Institute of Science in 1905. The scale of operations has been expanded since the winning of independence, so that Indian science has begun to make significant contributions in various fields. This is also true of China, where the government, like most Communist regimes, has allocated an extraordinary percentage of the national income to scientific research. In 1955 it adopted a Twelve Year Science Plan, calling for the graduation by 1967 of two million engineers and 10,500 scientists with doctoral degrees. The stated objective of China's Plan was to catch up with the world "in those branches of science and technology which are essential to our national economy."

Even in Africa and the Middle East there have been modest beginnings in scientific work. Ghana, for example, established in 1959 an Academy of Learning "to promote the study and the extension and dissemination of all the sciences and learning . . . relating not only to Ghana but to the whole of Africa." More ambitious was the Five Year Plan for the Promotion of Science

The common aspiration of two countries to modernize, following the example of the West. (left) An Indian artist's vision of the ideal village. (right) A Nigerian woman cooking on a kerosene stove.

A vision of China's future, as depicted in a modern poster.

adopted by the United Arab Republic in 1962.* The Plan involved work in six main areas: (1) mathematical and physical sciences; (2) chemical sciences and industries; (3) geological and metallurgical sciences; (4) engineering and auxiliary industries; (5) agricultural and biological sciences; and (6) medical sciences. Typical of the importance attached to science by non-Western leaders was the following injunction by President Nasser to the Supreme Science Council directing the Five Year Plan:

> We have to keep up with the new world and new discoveries. We suffered so much in the past because we were left behind by the ages of steam and electricity. What suffering awaits those who fail to keep up with the new dawn will certainly be much greater than whatever we have experienced in the past. . . . In this world of breathtaking discoveries, to be left behind is to forfeit one's right to existence.[2]

As significant as the formal plans and institutes for the advancement of science has been the gradual diffusion of scientific knowledge and practices among the masses of people in non-Western areas. In China, for example, the Association for the Dissemination of Scientific and Technical Knowledge by 1964 had a membership of 300,000 professors, engineers, and technicians, and was publishing several mass-circulation popular science magazines. In a single year its members gave 160 lectures on space satellites to the public in Shanghai. Likewise, in Malaya the backwoods medicinemen, or "bomohs," had

* See "Triumph of Europe: Scientific," *EMM,* No. 193.

begun to rely on modern medicine as well as traditional incantations to cure disease. Having received instruction by government agencies concerning anti-malarial drugs, vitamin pills, antiseptic lotions, and the rudiments of hygiene, they were returning to their villages with graduation badges marking their new status as "medical assistants." They were making effective use of their new knowledge and first-aid kits, even though they were still accompanying their treatments with the age-old incantations to give science a gloss of magic.

Europe's third revolution, the political, also has been sweeping the entire globe. The most obvious manifestation of this political awakening has been the burgeoning nationalism expressed in the colonial revolutions and the end of empires (see Chapter 27). But nationalism has by no means been the only wind blowing from the West. A variety of other isms have been enveloping the globe, including constitutionalism, communism, socialism, and military authoritarianism. The first of these enjoyed a brief vogue with the wave of democratic enthusiasm immediately after World War II. In country after country, however, the parliamentary regimes succumbed to military dictator-ships or to Marxist, one-party rule. This trend, it should be noted, also had ample precedent in Europe. With the exception of Czechoslovakia, every country in Central and Eastern Europe was by 1939 under one form or another of authoritarian government. Nasser, Sukarno, and General Ne Win had their counterparts in Stojadinović, Metaxas, and Marshal Pilsudski. In both cases, corrupt and ineffective parliamentary systems together with the lack of the necessary economic and social foundations led to the imposition of dictatorial rule.

Despite the variety of institutional forms, all the new countries have had one common political characteristic: the gradual awakening and activization of the masses regardless of whether they were participating formally in their governments.* This is the essence of the political revolution—the passing of the age-old concept of a divinely ordained division of humanity into rulers and ruled. In more general terms, it means replacing the isolation, ignorance, and acquiescence of traditionalism with the participation, knowledge, and initiative of modernism. This political revolution is illustrated vividly and unmistakably in the following report by an American correspondent concerning an Egyptian laborer who doubtless had little voice in the government of his country.

> On a height overlooking the site of the future High Dam at Aswan, in the Nile Valley of southern Egypt, this correspondent asked a ragged laborer to pose for a picture with his arm outstretched, pointing to the site.
>
> He posed and the writer held out a coin for baksheesh. Baksheesh—a tip—has been for so long so much a part of daily life in Egypt that old-timers begin the day by acquiring a pocketful of coins.
>
> But the laborer at Aswan turned on his heel when offered baksheesh, and he was restored to good humor only by a hearty handshake and pro-fuse thanks. The guide explained that Mahmoud knew what he was point-ing at and its meaning, and was insulted to be offered a tip for such a gesture. . . . many Egyptians feel, for the first time in their lives, a

---

* See "Triumph of Europe: Political," *EMM,* No. 194.

The political awakening of colonial peoples is reflected in the statues here and on page 651. At left is the statue at the entrance of a park in Kampala, Uganda, commemorating the winning of independence.

sense of national dignity, a sense that nationally they are doing something and going somewhere.[3]

Nationalism is not the only form that the awakening and activization of the masses has taken, as is evident in the following description of an incident during a general strike that paralyzed Nigeria in June, 1964:

"Do you drive a Mercedes?" a union leader shouts.
"No!" roars the crowd.
"Do you live in a big house?"
"No!"
"Who goes dancing? Who drinks whisky and gin? Who takes money under the table, builds another house, buys another car?"
There is silence.
"So what do we say?" the leader cries.
"Strike!"
"Louder!"
"Strike!" the crowd roars again.[4]

We may conclude that behind Europe's decline has been Europe's triumph. The one led naturally and inevitably to the other. If Europe has lost its place

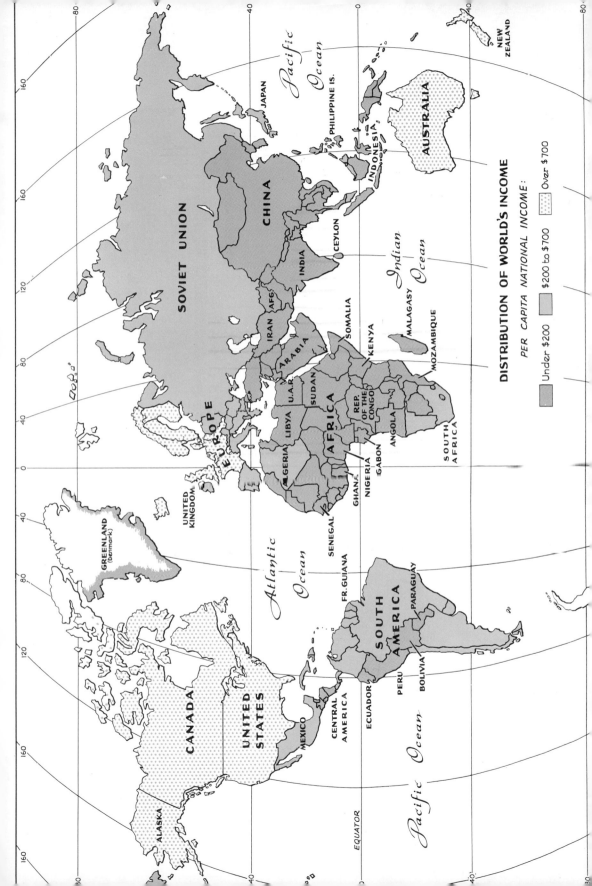

DISTRIBUTION OF WORLD'S INCOME

PER CAPITA NATIONAL INCOME:

Under $200 $200 to $700   Over $700

The statue of Kwame Nkrumah before the Parliament building in Accra, Ghana. One of the inscriptions below the statue is quoted on page 659.

as the dominant force in the world, the basic reason has been the diffusion throughout the world of Europe's three great revolutions. Furthermore, this diffusion has continually been gaining in momentum, because for the first time it has affected the masses of the people. Until the twentieth century only an insignificant leisure class was participating in the process of westernization. Only this handful comprehended the meaning of the West from their knowledge of European languages and literatures, and their travels in European lands. In the postwar years, by contrast, a growing proportion of the masses were being involved actively and consciously.

The explanation is to be found partly in the factories where they have found employment and the highways that have been ending their isolation. But equally important have been the new mass media of tabloids, radio, and movies which have overshadowed the old class media of books and travel. Westernization has gained its tremendous impetus by becoming dependent not on Oxford colleges and Paris salons, but on loudspeakers blaring out on illiterate yet responsive multitudes in village squares. New regimes and leaders have begun purposefully to exploit the mass media to the utmost in order to mobilize popular support for their revolutionary programs. "It is true," stated President Nasser, "that most of our people are still illiterate. But politically that counts far less than it did twenty years ago. . . . Radio has changed everything. . . . Today people in the most remote villages hear of what is happening everywhere and form their opinions. Leaders cannot govern as they once did. We live in a new world." [5]

652

Nasser's "new world" now has been taking form all over the globe. This is evident in the following headlines from *The New York Times*—which could be multiplied indefinitely, for they appear daily in the world's press:

Life in Baku Fits the Soviet Mold. Azerbajan's Capital Shows Impact of Standardization—Old Order Vanishing. (Oct. 16, 1960)

Students to Brush Up. Egypt to Give Toothbrush and Paste Free to Schools. (April 22, 1960)

Indonesia Fights Cha-Cha Culture. "Crazy" Music and Dances Assailed by Sukarno as "Subversive" Influence. (Feb. 7, 1960)

Seoul Revising Family System. Feudal Customs in Korea are Called Outmoded. (Sept. 16, 1962)

Nudity Forbidden by Guinea Regime. Dresses of Young Women Now Cover Torso, as do Those of Ghanaians. (May 18, 1959)

Folk Music is Fading in Kenya. Official's Research Shows Art Losing to Western Ways. (Nov. 8, 1959)

China's Folk Art Toes Party Line. Culture Becomes a Weapon as Craftsmen Shape the New Out of the Old. (Sept. 25, 1960)

Cairo TV Invaded by Cowboys and the Children Just Love It. But Parents Fret at Programs' Effect. (Nov. 25, 1962)

Papuans Moving From Stone Age. Highlanders in Netherlands New Guinea Adopt Steel Tools and Halt Fights. (July 1, 1960)

Rhodesia Girls Fighting Lobola, Ancient Marriage-Fee Custom. Urban Foes of Males' Dominance Rebel at "Humiliating" Customs of Price Once Set in Cattle, Now Cash. (Sept. 25, 1960)

Young Love vs. Japan's Old Code. Boy Now Has the Constitutional Right to Meet (and Get) Girl. (March 9, 1958)

Ghana Spurring New Five-Year Plan. Exhibit Traces Gains Under First Project and Outlines Future Development. (Nov. 29, 1959)

Industry Denting India's Folkways. Weakening Family and Caste Systems. (Jan. 12, 1955)

Africans Evolve New Middle Class. Sons of Rural Tribesmen Run Businesses in Rhodesia—Some Achieve Wealth. (Aug. 28, 1959)

Expense-Accountitis Draws a Pravda Blast. Denounces Not-Too-Busy "Business" Trip on a Fat Expense Account. (Sept. 15, 1958)

Education Gains in Peiping Drive. Massive Effort to Extend Schooling Reaches Most Children and Adults. (Dec. 9, 1959)

Outer Mongolia Seeks to Catch Up With 20th Century. Teachers Leading in Drive to Change Nomads. (Aug. 3, 1959)

The significance of these headlines becomes apparent if it is recalled that only a century ago virtually all Moslems looked down with contempt upon the infidel Christian world, convinced that nothing in that world could be worthy of their attention. In 1793, likewise, the emperor of China flatly refused to consider closer relations with England because "there is nothing we lack . . . we have never set much store on strange or ingenious objects. . . ." Today, by contrast, all people everywhere hanker not only for

A father and son learn to read and write in Iran.

such "strange or ingenious objects," but also, as the headlines quoted above indicate, for the other attributes of what is now commonly referred to as "civilization." This is indicative of the scope and depth of Europe's triumph, or, of what is commonly called the process of modernization. The latter term is preferable to *Europeanization* or *westernization* because the impulse for change, despite its ultimate European origins, may come today from the United States, or the Soviet Union, or even China, as well as from Europe.

Whatever term is used, the essential point is that societies everywhere are now being affected to a greater or lesser degree by this inexorable march of change. The question naturally arises whether the regional autonomy now developing in the political sphere will be nullified by a global homogenization process, as indicated by the headlines quoted above. Some maintain that homogenization will never become complete and all-embracing because of the residual effect of very different indigenous civilizations. It is pointed out that although industrialization is spreading rapidly, the social organization of a Japanese factory today differs basically from that of a Soviet or American factory. Likewise, modernization is proceeding apace in agriculture, but the organizational forms differ drastically from an American family farm to an Israeli kibbutz and to a Soviet state farm. Reference has also been made to "the durable qualities of one-party government in Russia, the alternation of multi-party instability and charismatic political unity in France, and the hardy survival of parliamentary government in England." [6]

654

Relevant in this connection is the observation of an eminent sinologist, Dr. Jaroslav Prusek of the Oriental Institute at Prague, that "all new Asian literatures have closer affinities with world literature of today than with their own literatures [of the past]."[7] The same basic point can be made about developments in other fields. Modern American and Russian farmers operate their lands in very different ways, yet their practices and ways of living have more in common between them than either have with their forefathers on their respective frontiers. In political matters the institutional forms vary widely, and yet, as noted above, all countries share the awakening and activization of the masses, regardless of whether they are actually participating in their governments. Likewise, the spread of industrialization has led to varying forms of factory organization, but at the same time certain basic aspects of life have been uniformly affected, including acceptance of labor discipline, gearing of life to the clock, discarding of traditional costume, and living in large urban concentrations.

It may be concluded that homogeneity indeed is taking place, though with regional variations reflecting the hetrogeneity of cultural backgrounds. The global diffusion of Europe's three revolutions, though proceeding today under varying auspices, seems nevertheless to be creating at accelerating speed a world culture that will be uniform in basic characteristics, though diverse in detail.*

SUGGESTED READING

Studies of the contemporary impact of the West on the world as a whole are available in Margaret Mead, ed., *Cultural Patterns and Technical Change* (New Am. Lib., 1955; a Mentor paperback); Margaret Mead, *Continuities in Cultural Evolution* (New Haven: Yale Univ., 1964); G. M. Foster, *Traditional Cultures and the Impact of Technological Change* (New York: Harper, 1963); C. Geertz, ed., *Old Societies and New States* (New York: Free Press, 1963); E. Stillman and W. Pfaff, *The Politics of Hysteria: The Sources of Twentieth-Century Conflict* (New York: Harper, 1964); and W. Schramm, *Mass Media and National Development: The Role of Information in the Developing Countries* (Stanford: Stanford Univ., 1964). For the impact of the West on specific areas, see D. Lerner, *The Passing of Traditional Society: Modernizing the Middle East* (New York: Free Press, 1958); L. S. S. O'Malley, *Modern India and the West: A Study of the Interaction of their Civilizations* (London: Oxford Univ., 1941); J. Numata, "Acceptance and Rejection of Elements of European Culture in Japan," *Journal of World History,* III (1956), 231–53; J. K. Fairbank, "China's Response to the West: Problems and Suggestions," *Journal of World History,* III (1956), 381–406; and K. Little, "African Culture and the Western Intrusion," *Journal of World History,* III (1957), 941–64. Perceptive and stimulating analyses of the dynamics of the contemporary world are provided by G. Barraclough, *An Introduction to Contemporary History* (New York: Basic Books, 1965); R. L. Heilbroner, *The Future as History* (New York: Harper, 1959); and K. Boulding, *The Meaning of the Twentieth Century: The Great Transition* (New York: Harper, 1964).

* See "Global Homogenization," *EMM,* No. 195.

*What a piece of work is a man! How noble in
reason! how infinite in faculty! in form and
moving, how express and admirable! in action
how like an angel! in apprehension, how
like a god!*

SHAKESPEARE, *Hamlet*

*Sometimes, in moments of horror, I have been
tempted to doubt whether there is any reason
to wish that such a creature as man should
continue to exist.*

BERTRAND RUSSELL

Chapter
30

Epilogue:
Our Golden Age?

The world of today is essentially the product of Europe's expansion and global hegemony, and the reaction provoked by that expansion and hegemony. The impact and the response have resulted in a great variety of conditions, and have produced a multitude of problems and also of promises. All this means a contemporary world in a state of flux, undergoing change in virtually all fields of human endeavor. Every age, by definition, is an age of transition. But the process of change today is unprecedented in tempo, in scope, and in depth. Inevitably this creates dislocation and distress, but it also opens up new vistas and new opportunities. In this chapter problems will be considered first, then the promises, and finally the balance sheet—the prospects for the future in the light of the perspective afforded by this survey of man's history in the past half millennium.

I. PROBLEMS OF THE TWENTIETH CENTURY

Racial Conflict

An obvious, yet frequently overlooked, result of Europe's expansion is the mixing of the races of mankind (see the map "Racial Distribution in the World"). Prior to 1500, the Negroids were concen-

655

trated in Africa; the Mongoloids, in Central, North, and East Asia and in the Americas; and the Caucasoids, in Europe, North Africa, the Middle East, and India. After 1500 this racial segregation was gradually modified by mass migrations, both free and forced. Today there is a high degree of racial intermixture in the Americas, and a lesser amount in Africa, Central Asia, and Siberia (see Chapter 9, section II).

Where there is such intermixture there is naturally much more likelihood of conflict than where there is little contact amongst the races. A good example is the case of England since World War II. Before the war, England had experienced almost no race troubles. But after the war, a considerable number of Indians, Pakistanis, and Arabs, as well as Negroes from the British West Indies, emigrated to England. For the first time England had sizable colored settlements in certain urban centers. And for the first time England experienced outbreaks of racial violence.

It does not follow that the change in the racial map of the world made racial conflict inevitable. What did promote conflict was the circumstance of Europe's expansion—the fact that technological and military superiority enabled Europeans to occupy the relatively empty lands of Siberia, Australia, and the Americas; to transport millions of Africans to slave plantations in the New World; to conquer vast colonial possessions in Africa and Asia; and then to concoct a racial superiority myth in order to rationalize their overlordship. "I contend that we are the first race in the world," proclaimed Cecil Rhodes, "and that the more of the world we inhabit, the better it is for the human race." [1] This attitude of superiority perhaps aroused more resentment among colored peoples than did the economic exploitation—and particularly so in recent decades, when scientists in various fields are almost unanimously agreed that no race is superior in intelligence to any other.

Race relations at present vary greatly from country to country. At one extreme are Hawaii and Brazil, where racial intermixture is extensive and continuing, and where racial discrimination is relatively minor. At the other extreme is South Africa with its rigid policy of apartheid or "separateness"— a policy that is rapidly alienating not only black Africa to the north, but also public opinion throughout the world. Between these two is the United States, where the position of the Negro has improved substantially in recent decades, but where a combination of factors now has stimulated a civil rights campaign of unprecedented magnitude. So dramatic is this Negro upsurgence that it has shattered the traditional complacence of American society and attracted widespread international attention.

A new feature of racial conflict is that it has now become a global problem with global repercussions. Prior to World War II racial troubles were regarded as purely the business of the country involved, but today this is no longer the case. Worldwide attention is now instantly focused on all incidents, whether in a South African mine, an American schoolyard, or an English industrial town. Reports of discrimination or violence arouse strong feelings among all colored peoples, who comprise two-thirds of all mankind. This situation is being exploited currently by the Communist Chinese who are seeking to arouse the colored peoples against the "white exploiters," with the Russians being included in the latter category. And the Russians, after years of propagandizing against the "racist imperialists" of the West, are now themselves experiencing demonstrations in their own cities by Afro-Asian students protesting against Soviet racism and carry signs with inscriptions such as "Moscow is a Second Alabama." The danger is that the worldwide anti-colonialism will assume an increasingly antiwhite character, with unforeseeable repercussions.* In the words of the distinguished British authority, Barbara Ward:

> At present, most Westerners think of the race problem as being primarily one of whether men and women of African stock—in Africa or the United States—can achieve full equality of status. But this definition is probably already outdated. The question is no longer whether Africans can achieve equality. It is becoming the wider query whether men and women of white color shall lose it. There is no certainty that mankind will, after three hundred years of white dominance, move safely to race equality.[2]

Rich Lands and Poor

Prior to modern times, Western Europe was an underdeveloped rather than a developed region. In the eleventh century China was producing two and a half times as much iron as did England and Wales together in 1640. By the twelfth century several Chinese cities each had a population equal to that of the whole of contemporary England—about 1.3 million people. When the Westerners began their siege of Constantinople in 1203, they were awestruck by "those high walls and those mighty towers . . . and those rich palaces and lofty churches, of which there were so many that no man could believe it unless he had seen it with his own eyes." [3]

In modern times this situation was reversed, thanks in large part to the stimulus and profits from overseas trade and colonies, and to the settlement and exploitation of entire continents. Thus 90 per cent of the world's total industrial output derives today from Europe and regions inhabited by peoples of European origin. Our map "Distribution of World's Income" shows that in 1960, 64.5 per cent of the world's people were earning under $200 per capita; 22.6 per cent were earning $200 to $700, and 12.9 per cent, over $700. The map also shows that this economic division of the globe is latitudinal, with the poor majority living mostly south of the 30th parallel of north latitude. This north-south division of the globe on economic lines is in many respects more meaningful than the traditional division by national frontiers or ideological blocs.

Not only is the world divided into a rich north and poor south, but the gap between the two is becoming greater. During the decade between 1950 and 1960, countries with an annual per capita income below $200 had a growth rate of only 2 per cent a year; countries with an income of over $700 showed an increase of about 3 per cent a year; while the middle-range countries, with incomes between $200 and $700 per person enjoyed the greatest increase— more than 4 per cent a year.

One reason for the disparity in the global distribution of income is the disparity in birth rates (see Table 1). Almost the entire world is currently

* See "Race Conflict," *EMM*, No. 196.

experiencing a population explosion, but, generally speaking, regions with lower incomes have rising birth rates while those with higher incomes have falling birth rates. This is particularly serious for the underdeveloped countries, because rapid population growth hinders their economic progress. The population figures in Table 1 make it clear how much more the underdeveloped countries must increase their aggregate product to maintain current standards of living.

TABLE 1. Population Growth (in millions)

	1960	2000 (projected)	% increase
The "haves"			
Europe	424	568	33.9
Soviet Union	215	379	76.2
U.S. and Canada	197	312	58.4
The "have-nots"			
Asia	1,524	3,717	143.9
Africa	237	517	118.4
Latin America	206	592	187.4

Source: Population Reference Bureau, Inc., 1755 Massachusetts Avenue, N.W., Washington, D. C.

Another reason for the global disparity in income distribution is the shortage of trained manpower in the underdeveloped countries. Sixty percent of their people at, or over, school age cannot read or write. But even the achievement of literacy will not suffice, for economic growth requires both widespread vocational training to produce skilled workers and advanced education for top executives and professional people. The training of such human resources is more difficult and time-consuming than the erection of factories or the building of roads.

The increasing gap between rich lands and poor arises also from the terms of international trade, which discriminate against the underdeveloped countries. The prices of the foodstuffs and raw materials produced by these countries tend to fall, while the prices of the manufactured goods they purchase tend to rise. In the decade 1950 to 1960, the prices of industrial goods in international trade increased 24 per cent, while the prices of raw materials fell 5 per cent. In other words, by the end of that decade the underdeveloped countries were able to purchase one-third less industrial goods for a set quantity of their raw materials than they were ten years earlier. This dilemma of the poorer countries was expressed bluntly at a meeting of the United Nations Conference on Trade and Development in March, 1964, by the Nigerian delegate, Zana Dipcharima: "In 1952 Nigeria sold 140,000 tons of peanuts for $120 a ton. In 1963 Nigeria produced 850,000 tons of nuts and still received $120 a ton. . . . Why is it that in the United States Chevrolets cost a lot more money than they did 10 years ago, even though far more Chevrolets are being produced? . . . You in the west tell us to work harder and we will get rich. Well, we are working hard and we are getting poorer." [4]

These unfavorable terms of international trade erode the purchasing power of the underdeveloped countries, in some cases to a greater amount than the extensive grants and loans received from the Western powers and the Soviet Union since World War II. Hence the growing demand by these countries for trade rather than aid, but trade on more equitable terms. Various proposals have been made to ensure equity. One is international commodity agreements to support and even raise the prices of key commodities. Another is compensatory financing, by which the wealthier nations would tax themselves to make up for any worsening in the trade terms for the poorer countries. The money would go into a pool on which these countries could draw to finance development projects.

Despite this discouraging array of formidable problems, the people of the underdeveloped countries are generally optimistic in their outlook. Samplings made about 1960 of public opinion in Brazil, Cuba, and the Philippines revealed that the peoples of those countries "are more buoyant about their recent progress and more hopeful of the future." [5] than are the Americans. The basic reason is the growing realization that, thanks to modern technology, man is not predestined to a life of poverty, disease, and early death. There is an awareness that certain countries provide a decent livelihood for the mass of their citizens, and the hope that this will be extended to benefit the whole of mankind. The crucial question is how this "revolution of rising expectations" will be fulfilled, for fulfilled it will be in one manner or another. The answer to this question—which will depend on many imponderables such as the course of Russo-Chinese relations, the policies of the affluent Western countries, and the relative progress of China's and India's economic plans—will affect profoundly the course of world history in the future. Furthermore, this is a question that is inextricably related to the problem of race relations, for the rich nations are white and the poor are black, yellow, or brown. Hence the warning of the London *Economist* that if the present gap between the rich North and the poor South persists, the world may soon witness the "white man's 1789." *

Nationalism in a One-World

Before the government buildings in Accra stands a statue of Kwame Nkrumah with the following inscription: "We prefer self-government with danger to servitude in tranquility." This slogan points up a paradox and a problem of the contemporary era—the burgeoning of nationalism in an otherwise increasingly unified world. This problem also is traceable directly to Europe's influence, for nationalism originated in Europe and was diffused throughout the world with the expansion of that continent.

In fact, national cohesion and aggressiveness explain to a large degree the success of the Europeans in establishing their domination over the globe. The victories of the conquistadors in the New World were greatly facilitated by their single-minded drive and ruthlessness, in contrast to the ruinous dissension and flabby resistance of the Aztecs and Incas. A handful of Englishmen were able to conquer the Indian subcontinent not so much because of technological superiority as because India then lacked the cement of nationalism and was

* See "Rich Lands and Poor," *EMM*, No. 197.

660

unable to present a united front against the Western intruder. How different the story would have been if the Indians at that time had been animated by a sense of national consciousness, or conversely, how different the response would have been if a few Indian adventurers had appeared in England rather than the opposite. In China, the story was very much the same, as Sun Yat-sen realized when he complained that his compatriots "have only family and clan solidarity; do not have national spirit," and therefore they are "just a heap of loose sand," and their country is "the poorest and weakest nation in the world."

Just as Napoleon's conquests stimulated nationalism in Europe, however, so Europe's conquests have stimulated nationalism overseas. Hence the colonial uprisings following World War I, and the historic upheavals following World War II. The ending of imperial rule, however, does not mean that the new overseas nationalisms are satiated or that political stability is ensured. Rather, nationalism appears to breed nationalism. The ending of British rule led to conflict between Moslems and Hindus in India, between Greeks and Turks in Cyprus, and between Sinhalese and Tamils in Ceylon. Likewise, Prime Minister Jomo Kenyatta of Kenya proclaimed in 1964 that his government "will not entertain any secession or handing over of one inch of territory" to neighboring Somalia. Emperor Haile Selassie of Ethiopia made a similar reply to Somali claims on his Ogaden province. Thus, the new African states are ready to defend to the last man the inviolability of artificial frontiers drawn by nineteenth century European imperialists with little regard to local peoples or resources.

At the same time the older nation-states are clinging tenaciously to their respective national sovereignties. It is true that, with their nationalist growing pains far behind them, they now can afford to decry and to adopt a superior attitude toward perfervid manifestations of nationalist sentiment. It is also true that in Europe the Common Market has involved the yielding of certain national prerogatives in restricted areas. But the Common Market has by no means proven itself where vital national interests are in conflict. And the Suez and Cuban crises both revealed the readiness of the major powers, when issues involving national security were at stake, to act unilateraly without consulting either allies or the United Nations. The course of these crises pointed up the implications of such unrestricted national sovereignty in an atomic age.

Pandora's Box of Science

On the night of July 9, 1962, on Johnston Island in the mid-Pacific, the United States detonated a hydrogen bomb with the explosive force of two million tons of TNT. The entire heavens lighted up and remained bright for fifteen minutes in a dazzling kaleidoscope of interweaving reds, purples, yellow-oranges, and whites. Natives on American Samoa, 2,000 miles away, rushed panic-stricken into their homes or into churches to pray. When informed of the source of the terrifying celestial display, they commented, "Crazy white man." [6]

Other observers, more sophisticated than these Samoans, reacted in essentially the same way. This explosion, together with others that preceded and followed, raised fundamental questions concerning science and the prospects for the future. Science admittedly is one of the great achievements of the human mind. But has it become a Pandora's box, and does it now represent an uncontrollable menace for mankind?

The implications of this question involve much more than mere nuclear explosions. Throughout history, changes in technology have profoundly affected man's culture—his ways of living and thinking and doing things. The agricultural revolution, for example, made it possible for man to increase dramatically in numbers, and also compelled him to adjust to a sedentary existence, and eventually to worship new gods and to evolve new forms of social and political organizations. Likewise, the Industrial Revolution brought with it not only greatly increased productivity but also the manifold problems associated with the factories and the new industrial towns. Today we are experiencing what is in effect a second Industrial Revolution, with ultimate repercussions at least as far-reaching as those of the first.

It should be noted, furthermore, how rapidly the tempo of technological advance is accelerating. It took man roughly a million years to arrive at the agricultural revolution, but he needed only another 10,000 to come to the first Industrial Revolution, and less than two centuries to attain the second. We do not know where we shall go from here, but we do know that we shall get there fast. And we know this because of the great investment of material and human resources for the furtherance of science. Ninety per cent of all scientists ever born are alive and working today. The United States spent more on scientific research in the year 1965 than in the entire period from the American Revolution to 1945. Certainly science is the hallmark of the contemporary age. If the pyramids symbolize ancient Egypt, and if Notre Dame symbolizes the Western Middle Ages, then the corresponding symbols of our era are the high-energy accelerators and the high-flux research reactors, together with attendant technological symbols such as the automated factory and the space ships.

This headlong advance of science and technology raises for the first time the question of whether man as a species is sufficiently pliable to adjust to an environment that he is so rapidly transforming. Is he capable of modifying his traditional habits and institutions to cope with the formidable array of problems that have sprouted as unwanted by-products of science and technology? Here are some examples:

UNBALANCING OF NATURE. Modern technology is creating countless products that combine within human organisms as well as in the physical environment to cause reactions about which little is known. Radiation has been a principal cause of concern, but it is only one of many. Within cities there are the fumes from both industry and automobiles, while in the countryside there are the herbicides and pesticides that are applied to the land and then leach into the streams.*

THE POPULATION EXPLOSION. Throughout history man's problem has been to keep his numbers from declining. Today, thanks to medical science and to increased productivity, the problem is precisely the opposite—how to bring under control the population explosion that is braking the progress of the underdeveloped countries and creating serious problems for those that are affluent.

* See "The Good Non-Life," *EMM*, No. 200.

PROBLEMS OF URBANIZATION. Throughout the world, in developed and underdeveloped states alike, people are leaving the countryside and crowding into cities. This great exodus far overshadows the overseas migrations of the nineteenth century. The resulting dislocations and tensions are correspondingly staggering—unemployment, brutalizing slums, traffic jams, disruption of traditional habits of life, and mounting social tensions arising from the disparity between rising expectations and static economies.*

INCREASING PRODUCTIVITY AND INCREASED UNEMPLOYMENT. The first Industrial Revolution provided power-driven machinery that aided man with certain types of labor: the second Industrial Revolution is replacing man himself, thanks to automation or cybernation—a combination of the computer that does man's planning and of the machine that does man's work. In other words, the first Industrial Revolution combined *human* skill and machine power: the second combines *machine* skill and machine power, thereby eliminating man from the production process. Despite increased productivity, the unemployment rate in the United States has held at 5 to 6 per cent, with double and triple these percentages in the case of Negroes and teenagers. Hence President Kennedy's statement that unemployment is "the major domestic challenge of the Sixties," and hence President Johnson's "War on Poverty." †

AWESOME THRESHOLDS. Scientists are on the threshold of creating artificial life, and expect eventually to breed intelligent animals artificially. Scientists also now understand the general principles underlying the construction of self-repairing and self-reproducing machines, and some believe they will be able eventually to construct such machines that will be more intelligent and more versatile than man. Aside from such artificial creations, man increasingly is able to control the hereditary traits in his own species by manipulating the DNA molecule as well as by deep-frozen sperm banks. The latter open up the possibility of offspring from parents separated in time as well as in space, while the former raises disturbing questions such as whether human heredity control should be systematically practiced, and if so, for what ends?

MUSHROOM CLOUDS. Since Hiroshima and Nagasaki, the world has been living in dread of all-out nuclear war, made all the more unthinkable by the dwarfing of the original atomic bombs by hydrogen bombs. Nuclear weapons have been stockpiled to such an extent that it was estimated in the early Sixties that the United States could overkill the Soviet Union 1,250 times, and the Soviet Union overkill the United States 145 times. As harrowing as the specter of nuclear war is the appalling investment of material and human resources for war purposes. In the United States in 1964, 10 per cent of the gross national product, 9 per cent of the total labor force, 50 per cent of the federal budget, and 60 per cent of the scientists and engineers were engaged directly or indirectly in defense work. In the same year, the combined American and Soviet military expenditures were equal to the total annual

* See "Problems of Urbanization," *EMM*, No. 199.
† See "Increasing Production and Increasing Unemployment," *EMM*, No. 198.

income of the people of all the underdeveloped countries with an average income of $100 a year or less. An observer on the moon viewing the earth might well conclude that this is a strange planet with full arsenals, empty larders, and pervasive terror.*

663

It may be concluded from the above that the diffusion of science and technology has created for man a new environment and a new set of problems. Early man had to face the environment of nature, but he could cope with nature primarily as an individual—as a farmer or hunter or fisherman. Today the new environment and the new problems preclude individual action and solutions; they require organized and collective action. In contrast to earlier periods, the present needs *social* regulation and *social* control. This at once raises the issue of freedom versus regimentation; the problem of personal liberty and initiative on the one hand and of social organization and discipline on the other. This issue has been a primary source of tension in modern society, and is likely to cause more tension in the future.

II. Promise of the Twentieth Century

Global Responsibility

The perilous condition of man today is reflected in this analysis of contemporary problems, and their number could have been extended substantially. Yet for every one of these problems there is also a promise—a promise that could leave its imprint on the future if recognized and fostered. Arnold Toynbee, for example, has stated that "our age will be remembered chiefly neither for its horrifying crimes nor for its astonishing inventions, but for its having been the first age since the dawn of civilization, some five or six thousand years back, in which people dared to think it practicable to make the benefits of civilization available for the whole human race." [7]

This sense of global consciousness and global responsibility does exist, and should be recognized, along with such trends as race conflict and divisive nationalism. It began with the acceptance of responsibility for the welfare of the less fortunate citizens of one's own country. As late as 1839 the English Parliament appropriated $150,000 for the schools of the entire country, and $350,000 for the care of Queen Victoria's horses. Reformers who favored a popular system of education were branded as visionaries who endangered the foundations of society. Yet this same Britain is today a welfare state, assuming responsibility for the care of its citizens "from the cradle to the grave."

In recent decades this concept of social responsibility has been extended to embrace not only fellow citizens but all humanity.† This universal obligation has been reiterated and acted upon so frequently that it is now taken for granted, and its novelty and significance are overlooked. Yet few could have foreseen at the beginning of this century that billions of dollars would be contributed each year by the developed countries for foreign aid. Granted that this is by no means entirely altruistic giving; still, neither is it entirely devoid

* See "Threat of Nuclear War," *EMM*, No. 201.
† See "Global Responsibility," *EMM*, No. 204.

664

of altruism. Witness the United Nations Universal Declaration of Human Rights, with its call for liberty and security of person, freedom of movement and residence, right to own property, freedom of thought and religion, right to education, and right to work and to an adequate standard of life. Witness also the following eloquent definition of goals by President Lyndon Johnson —goals that admittedly are far from realization, but that a few decades ago scarcely would have been considered, let alone enunciated, by the responsible head of a great nation:

> . . . people in the rest of the world want for themselves the same things that you and I want. . . . They intend that their families shall live a decent life and that they have a job that gives them survival and dignity. They intend that their children shall be taught to read and write. They intend that the hungry shall be fed and the sick shall be treated. They intend to take their place in the great movement of modern society, to take their share in the benefits of that society. These just desires, once unleashed, can never be stifled. The people of the developing world are on the march, and we want to be beside them on that march. . . .
>
> Every night when I go to bed I ask myself, "What did we do today that we can point to for future generations to come, to say that we laid the foundation for a better and more peaceful and more prosperous world?" [8]

End to Want

Today there exists not only a growing sense of global responsibility, but, equally important, the means for acting upon this responsibility. As noted above, a central problem of the present world is the widening gap between the rich nations and poor. Yet this problem, too, holds a promise: the means for eliminating the gap do exist and await utilization. This is why a responsible world statesman such as President Johnson can proclaim publicly his quest for "a better and more peaceful and more prosperous world." Thanks to the advances of sciences and to the second Industrial Revolution, such a goal for the first time can be pursued without sacrificing the living standards of the advanced nations. Walter Lippmann has pointed out, apropos of President Johnson's domestic War on Poverty, that "in an advanced economy like ours we are now living in a time when the technological and fiscal revolution can liberate us from the ancient quarrel between the haves and the have-nots. . . . Here in the United States, as in most of Western Europe, this is the post-Marxian age. That is why President Johnson is able to wage a war against poverty and at the same time win so much confidence among the well-to-do." [9] This observation holds true for the world as a whole as well.

This is not to deny that half the people of the world still are illiterate and still go to bed hungry every night. But even that is very different from the mid-fourteenth century, when a third to a half of Europe's total population was wiped out by the Black Death. It is different also from 1846, when a million Irish died of hunger, and from 1876, when five million Indians starved to death. These victims of plague and famine could not possibly have been saved, because man simply lacked the necessary medical and agronomic knowledge. Today there still are a tragic number of victims, but because of political and organizational obstacles rather than ignorance. The enormous and constantly accelerating increase in productive capacity is making it at least possible for man to free himself in the foreseeable future from the scourges that have afflicted him throughout history. This surely is a momentous achievement, comparable to the development of agriculture or to the attainment of civilization.*

665

Awakening of Mankind

Of equal significance is the current awakening of peoples all over the globe, for this awakening is prerequisite for the effective utilization of the technological potential. This mass stirring has many roots in the past, including the shock of two World Wars, the diffusion of Western ideologies, the impact of modern transportation facilities and mass communication media, and the influence of affluent societies that suggest privation and misery are not the divinely ordained fate of man. Hence the revolution of rising expectations, or, more correctly, the revolution of rising demands. This revolution explains the extraordinary spectacle of over fifty countries winning their independence in the two decades since World War II. The "winds of change" have indeed blown with a force and a scope unprecedented in history. They still are blowing with almost undiminished vigor, as is indicated by the daily headline reports of riots and revolutions.

All this agitation and unrest is deplored by some who yearn for the good old days of the bwana and the sahib. It is deplored by others who are apprehensive of the divisiveness and intolerance of the proliferating new nationalisms. But this awakening represents more than simply excessive nationalist manifestations. It represents a new way of thinking and acting and looking at life. It is the acceptance of social change as desirable and inevitable. It is the belief that the individual can and should participate in, and contribute to, this change. It is the desire for new material goods and comforts, and the persuasion that misery is not an act of God. It is, finally, the conviction that all citizens should have the opportunity to learn and to advance themselves, depending on their ability and efforts rather than on their money or class.

Aladdin's Lamp of Science

This is an age of promise also because of man's burgeoning knowledge—knowledge of himself and his past, and knowledge of the physical world about him. During the past century, thanks to the advances of anthropology, archeology, physiology, and many other sciences, reliable information has been made available concerning the species *Homo sapiens*. Likewise during the past century a substantial body of data has been amassed concerning the historical past of this species. Our age, in fact, is unique in the extent of its historical knowledge and in the degree of its historical mindedness. The classical civilizations of Asia and of Greece and Rome were basically unhistorical in their outlook. Their writers were, on the whole, as little interested in the past as in the future: Thucydides, the most objective of ancient his-

* See "Second Industrial Revolution," *EMM*, No. 203.

torians, began his account of the Peloponnesian War by stating that nothing of great importance had occurred before his time. It is astonishing, yet undeniable, that we are far better informed of the early history of the Greeks, Romans, Egyptians, Chinese, and Indians than were these peoples themselves.

More spectacular than the new knowledge of the past is the new knowledge and mastery of the physical world. Less than four hundred years, or about six average life spans, separate the work of Copernicus from that of Einstein. Yet in that short space of time science has grown from an esoteric avocation of a handful of devotees to the dominant force of civilization. Furthermore, science and science-based technology now are making important contributions to humanistic studies and the arts. Carbon-14 dating has aided significantly the work of archeologists; X-ray flourescence spectometry established the skull and jawbone of Piltdown man as a fraud; and computers have made possible the deciphering of the Maya hieroglyphs and are now beginning to be used for translation from foreign languages.

Despite these achievements, science is frequently regarded as a menacing and uncontrollable Pandora's box. This is understandable, for science has led mankind to the awesome thresholds noted above. But again there is promise: the thresholds are awe-inspiring for the new vistas they open as well as for the new dangers they create. Atomic power can destroy man, but it can also transform living conditions throughout the globe. Rockets can be used for intercontinental warfare but also for transporting man around the globe and to other planets. Heredity control raises frightening questions but also exciting possibilities. More specifically, scientists now look forward to the materialization of the following within the next few decades:

Self-guiding automobiles and atomic trains
Motor energy transmitted to airplanes via radio
Weather dams across the arctic seas to change world climate
Volcanoes harnessed to provide power for cities
Shallow seas turned into marine farms
Robot mining vehicles exploring deep under the earth's crust
Desalination process producing fresh water at competitive price
Nuclear fusion producing unlimited power
Landings on the moon

Science, then, can be Aladdin's Lamp as well as Pandora's box. 1984 can be a good year as well as bad. The choice is man's, for science is neutral.*

III. OUR GOLDEN AGE?

It may be concluded that this is an age of great problems and great opportunities, of great peril and great potential. This is not a soothing or cozy situation; it is uncomfortable and unsettling. But it has been characteristic of all great ages of the past. In fact, our age is remarkably similar to bygone "golden" ages that are glorified and looked back to with nostalgia. Every golden age has had elements of tension, peril, and apprehension. This is true of Periclean Athens, of Renaissance Italy, and of Elizabethan England.

* See "Promise of Science," *EMM*, No. 202.

Elizabethan England, for example, was confronted with a host of dangers that are quite comparable to those facing us today. There was, in the first place, the constant threat or actuality of war. Englishmen had to face up to a threatening Spain, the first military power of Europe, and were forced to wage both a cold war and a hot war in defense of their liberties.

This was also a period of economic and social dislocation produced by the shift from traditional subsistence farming to large-scale pasturage and wool production. The resulting enclosures forced thousands of yeomen onto the highways where they were picked up as vagrants. The plight of these "beggars" is evident in the nursery rhyme:

> Hark! hark! the dogs do bark; the beggars are coming to town.
> Some give them white bread, and some give them brown,
> And some gave them a good horsewhip, and sent them out of town.

The Elizabethan Golden Age also had its "space exploration" comparable to that of today. Columbus and da Gama had opened up new continents and new oceans, while Copernicus and Galileo removed the earth from the center of the universe. This broadening of horizons required a familiarly uncomfortable revising of traditional dogmas and assumptions. John Donne expressed anxiety, as do modern poets, when he wrote:

> T'is all in peeces, all cohaerence gone;
> All just supply, and all relation.

Finally, the Elizabethans lived under the shadow of the plague which regularly devastated London and the other cities. Poets and preachers constantly dwelt on the imminence of death, which would transform in an instant "thy beautiful face, thy fair nose, thy clear eyes, thy white hands, thy goodly body," into "earth, ashes, dust, and worm's meat." The contemporary world indeed lives in dread of a thermonuclear holocaust. But this is perhaps comparable to Tudor England where, in the words of an authority, "almost every imagination was touched with a form of necrophilia." [10]

The Elizabethans, then, lived in a period not too dissimilar from the present. They experienced cold and hot war, economic and social dislocation, unsettling intellectual challenge, and recurring visitations of the plague. It would have been understandable if they had given up hope and yielded to despair. It is clear in retrospect that such a reaction would have been unnecessary and disastrous.

So it is with this period in the second half of the twentieth century.* This also may well be judged by future historians as having been another golden age, though far surpassing any in the past. For the future now holds infinitely greater promise, and the stage today is not a peninsula in the Mediterranean or an island in the North Sea, but the entire globe itself—and before long, more. When man leaves the surface of this earth on which his ancestors have crawled for countless generations, and sets foot on heavenly bodies other than his own, a new stage in his career will have been reached. Just as the discoveries of Columbus, da Gama, and the other explorers deeply affected man's

* See "One Vote for This Age of Anxiety," EMM, No. 205.

thinking and world outlook, so the current space exploration is bound to have a corresponding impact. What might be found, and the repercussions of the findings, cannot now be foreseen, just as no one foresaw the consequences of Columbus' sailing from Palos, Spain, on August 3, 1492. But surely there can be no doubt that what man is achieving now is beyond compare, and what he could achieve in the forthcoming decades is almost beyond imagination.

Whether he will in fact realize this dazzling promise is quite another matter. For this is an age of unprecedented peril as well as promise. The question mark following this chapter's title is all too justified. The father of this atomic age, Albert Einstein, has left this sobering observation: "The unleashed power of the atom has changed everything save our modes of thinking, and thus we drift to unparalleled catastrophe."

SUGGESTED READING

A general discussion of the myths of race is available in A. Montagu, *Man's Most Dangerous Myth: The Fallacy of Race,* 3rd ed. (New York: Harper, 1952). Aspects of world race relations and attitudes are discussed in P. Mason, ed., *Man, Race and Darwin* (New York: Oxford Univ., 1960), which is a symposium discussion of man's thought about race since Darwin's time, and in P. D. Curtin, *The Image of Africa: British Ideas and Action, 1780–1850* (Madison: Univ. of Wisconsin, 1964). The Institute of Race Relations in England prepares numerous studies of race relations in various parts of the world, and these are published by the Oxford University Press.

A voluminous literature has appeared on the problem of global economic inequality. Authoritative yet brief analyses are provided by R. Theobald, *The Rich and the Poor: A Study of the Economic of Rising Expectations* (New Am. Lib., 1961; a Mentor paperback); Gunnar Myrdal, *Rich Lands and Poor: The Road to World Prosperity* (New York: Harper, 1957) and his *Challenge to Affluence* (New York: Random, 1963); Barbara Ward, *Rich Nations and Poor Nations* (New York: Norton paperback, 1962); and R. Heilbroner, *The Great Ascent: The Struggle for Economic Development in Our Time* (New York: Harper, 1963).

For the historical evolution of global nationalism, see H. Kohn, *The Age of Nationalism: The First Era of Global History* (New York: Harper, 1962). More current are the studies by K. W. Deutsch and W. J. Foltz, *Nation-Building* (New York: Atherton, 1964); B. Crozier, *The Morning After* (New York: Oxford Univ., 1963); and R. Harris, *Independence and After: Revolution in Underdeveloped Countries* (New York: Oxford Univ., 1962).

For the perils and promise of science and technology, see *Science and Technology for Development. Report on the United Nations Conference on the Application of Science and Technology for the Benefit of the Less Developed Areas,* Vol. 1, *World of Opportunity* (New York: United Nations, 1963); Ruth Gruber, ed., *Science and the New Nations: The Proceedings of the International Conference on Science in the Advancement of New States at Rehovath, Israel* (New York: Basic Books, 1961); A. C. Clarke, *Profiles of the Future: An Inquiry into the Limits of the Possible* (New York: Bantam, 1964); N. Lansdell, *The Atom and the Energy Revolution* (Baltimore: Penguin, 1958). L. Herber, *Our Synthetic*

Environment (New York: Knopf, 1962); D. N. Michael, *Cybernation: The Silent Conquest* (Santa Barbara: Center for the Study of Democratic Institutions, 1962); J. Diebold, *Automation: Its Impact on Business and Labor,* National Planning   669 Association, Planning Pamphlet No. 106 (Washington, 1959); B. H. Bagdikian, *In The Midst of Plenty: The Poor in America* (Boston: Beacon, 1964); H. P. Miller, *Rich Man, Poor Man* (New York: Crowell, 1963); and J. Henry, *Culture Against Man* (New York: Random, 1964), the last-mentioned being an analysis of the position of the individual in affluent society. The problem of nuclear war and armaments is analyzed from varying viewpoints in H. Kahn, *On Thermonuclear War* (Princeton: Princeton Univ., 1960); C. A. Barker, ed., *Problems of World Disarmament* (Boston: Houghton, 1963); S. Melman, *The Peace Race* (New York: Ballentine, 1961); and Norman Cousins, *In Place of Folly* (New York: Harper, 1961; paperback).

NOTES
AND INDEX

Notes

CHAPTER 1

[1] F. Boas, "Racial Purity," *Asia,* XL (May, 1940), 231.
[2] Cited by R. W. Southern, *The Making of the Middle Ages* (New Haven: Yale Univ., 1959), p. 71.

CHAPTER 2

[1] Cited by J. H. Parry, *The Age of Reconnaissance* (Cleveland: World, 1963), p. 19.
[2] Cited by W. Clark, "New Europe and the New Nations," *Daedalus* (Winter, 1964), p. 136.
[3] H. Yule and H. Cordier, *Cathay and the Way Thither,* III, rev. ed. (London: Hakluyt Soc., 1913–1916), p. 74; 4 vols.
[4] *China in the Sixteenth Century: The Journals of Matthew Ricci: 1583–1610,* tr. by Louis J. Gallagher, S. J. (New York: Random, 1953), pp. 105, 55.
[5] Bishop Marvin A. Franklin, "We Must be Ready with Christ's Word," *Together,* II (May 15, 1958), 13.
[6] "On the Education of Children," in F. L. Van Baumer, ed., *Main Currents of Western Thought* (New York: Knopf, 1952), p. 129.
[7] Parry, *op. cit.,* p. 36.
[8] Cited in manuscript by L. V. Thomas on *Ottoman Awareness of Europe, 1650–1800.*
[9] L. White, "Technology and Invention in the Middle Ages," *Speculum,* XV (April, 1940), 157.
[10] A. G. Keller, "A Byzantine Admirer of 'Western' Progress: Cardinal Bessarion," *Cambridge Historical Journal,* XI (1955), 343–48.
[11] Cited by G. Bruun, *Europe in Evolution, 1415–1815* (Boston: Houghton, 1945), p. 92.
[12] A. E. Monroe, ed., *Early Economic Thought* (Cambridge: Harvard Univ., 1924), pp. 113–14.
[13] Cited by L. C. Goodrich, *A Short History of the Chinese People* (New York: Harper, 1943), p. 194.
[14] R. H. Tawney, *Religion and the Growth of Capitalism* (London: Murray, 1925), p. 68.

674

CHAPTER 3

[1] Cited by T. W. Arnold, *The Preaching of Islam,* 2nd ed. (London: Constable, 1913), p. 238.
[2] *Ibid.,* p. 353.
[3] Mehmed Pasha, *Ottoman Statecraft: The Book of Counsel for Vezirs and Governors,* ed. and tr. by W. L. Wright (Princeton: Princeton Univ., 1935), p. 21.
[4] Cited by E. D. Ross, ed., *Sir Anthony Sherley and His Persian Adventure* (London: Routledge, 1933), p. 21.
[5] P. Spear, *The Nabobs,* rev. ed. (New York: Oxford Univ., 1963), p. xiv. Paperback.
[6] C. T. Forster and F. H. B. Daniell, eds., *The Life and Letters of Ogier Ghiselin de Busbecq* (London, 1881), pp. 221, 222.
[7] Cited by Ross, *op. cit.,* p. 217.
[8] Forster and Daniell, *op. cit.,* pp. 154, 155.
[9] Cited by H. Pfeffermann, *Die Zusammenarbeit der Renaissancepäpste mit den Türken* (Winterthur, Switzerland, 1946), p. 14.
[10] Cited by W. H. Moreland, *India at the Death of Akbar: An Economic Study* (London: Macmillan, 1920), p. 286.
[11] Letter from Colonel Clive to his father, August 8, 1757. In R. Muir, *The Making of British India, 1756–1858* (London: Longmans, 1923), pp. 59, 60.
[12] *The Letters and Works of Lady Mary Whortley Montagu. . . ,* I (London, 1893), p. 322.
[13] *Voyages du Sr A. de la Motraye en Europe, Asie et Afrique. . . ,* I (Le Havre, 1727), p. 462.
[14] Evliya Effendi, *Narrative of Travels in Europe, Asia and Africa in the Seventeenth Century,* tr. by R. J. von Hammer, Vol. I, Pt. II (London, 1850), p. 12.
[15] E. D. Clarke, *Travels in Various Countries of Europe, Asia and Africa,* I (Cambridge, England, 1810), pp. 689, 690.
[16] F. Bernier, *Travels in the Mogul Empire,* A.D. *1656–1668,* tr. by A. Constable and V. A. Smith (New York: Oxford Univ., 1916), pp. 225–27.
[17] Cited by G. K. Kordatos, *Rhigas Pheraios and Balkan Federation;* in Greek (Athens, 1945), p. 28.
[18] Cited by W. Eton, *A Survey of the Turkish Empire. . .* (London, 1808), p. 109.
[19] Bernier, *op. cit.,* pp. 229, 240.

CHAPTER 5

[1] H. W. Johnston, *The Negro in the New World* (London, 1910), pp. 14–15.
[2] P. Bohannan, *Africa and Africans* (New York: Amer. Mus. Science, 1964), pp. 67–68.
[3] Cited by T. Hodgkin, "Islam in West Africa," *Africa South,* II (April–June, 1958), p. 93.
[4] Leo Africanus, *A History and Description of Africa,* ed. R. Brown, III (London: Hakluyt Soc., 1896), p. 825.
[5] Cited by J. C. de Graft-Johnson, *African Glory* (London: Watts, 1954), p. 106.
[6] Africanus, *op. cit.,* III, 827.
[7] Cited by R. Oliver and D. Fage, *A Short History of Africa* (Baltimore: Penguin, 1962), pp. 106, 107.
[8] Cited by K. O. Dike, *Trade and Politics in the Niger Delta, 1830–1885* (New York: Oxford Univ., 1956), p. 7.
[9] Adam Smith, *Wealth of Nations* (Edinburgh, 1838), p. 286.
[10] *The Memoirs of the Conquistador Bernal Díaz Del Castillo . . .* translated by John Ingram Lockhart, I (London: J. Hatchard & Son, 1844), pp. 231–32.
[11] Cited by A. G. Price, *White Settlers and Native Peoples* (Victoria: Melbourne Univ., 1949), p. 121.
[12] Cited by C. Turnbull, *Black War: The Extermination of the Tasmanian Aborigines* (Victoria: Melbourne Univ., 1948), pp. 2–3.

CHAPTER 6

[1] *The Commentaries of the Great Afonso Dalboquerque,* ed. and tr. by W. de G. Birch, III (London: Hakluyt Soc., 1888), p. 116.

[2] *The Memoirs of the Conquistador Bernal Díaz del Castillo.* . . , tr. by John Ingram Lockhart, II (London: J. Hatchard & Son, 1844), p. 390.

[3] Cited by G. F. Hudson, *Europe and China: A Survey of Their Relations from the Earliest Times to 1800* (London: Longmans 1931), p. 183.

[4] Cited by E. W. Bovill, *Caravans of the Old Sahara* (New York: Oxford Univ., 1933), p. 143.

[5] *The Commentaries of . . . Dalboquerque,* III, 116–17.

[6] *The Memoirs of . . . del Castillo.* . . , I, 236.

[7] *A Journal of the First Voyage of Vasco da Gama, 1497–1499,* ed. and tr. by E. G. Ravenstein (London: Hakluyt Soc., 1898), pp. 69–70.

[8] Cited by K. M. Panikkar, *Asia and Western Dominance* (London: G. Allen; New York: Day, 1953), p. 42.

[9] *Ibid.*

[10] *A Journal of the First Voyage of Vasco da Gama,* p. 75.

[11] E. J. Hamilton, "American Treasure and the Rise of Capitalism (1500–1700)," *Economica,* No. 27 (November, 1929), pp. 347–48.

[12] Cited by G. B. Sansom, *The Western World and Japan* (New York: Knopf, 1950), p. 57

[13] *Ibid.,* p. 91.

[14] Cited by Panikkar, *op. cit.,* pp. 30–31.

[15] "Pigafetta's Voyage Around the World," in J. Pinkerton, *Voyages and Travels in All Parts of the World,* XI (London, 1812), p. 322.

[16] Cited by *The New Cambridge Modern History,* I (New York: Cambridge Univ., 1957), p. 458.

[17] Cited by J. Lynch, *Spain Under the Habsburgs. Vol. I, Empire and Absolutism, 1516–1598* (Oxford: Blackwell, 1964), p. 114.

[18] Cited *ibid.,* pp. 217–18.

[19] Cited by *The New Cambridge Modern History,* I, 454.

[20] Cited by R. Trevor Davies, *Spain in Decline, 1621–1700* (London: Macmillan; New York: St. Martins, 1957), pp. 148–150.

[21] Cited by C. R. Boxer, *Four Centuries of Portuguese Expansion, 1415–1825* (Johannesburg: Witwatersrand Univ., 1961), p. 75.

CHAPTER 7

[1] *The Complete English Tradesman.* Cited by *The New Cambridge Modern History,* VII (New York: Cambridge Univ., 1957), p. 59.

[2] Cited by L. Huberman, *Man's Worldly Goods* (New York: Harper, 1936), p. 103.

[3] E. J. Hamilton, "American Treasure and the Rise of Capitalism (1500–1700)," *Economica* (November, 1929), p. 356.

[4] J. M. Keynes, *A Treatise on Money,* II (New York: Harcourt, 1930), p. 159.

[5] R. Hakluyt, *The Principal Navigations, Voyages, Traffiques & Discoveries of the English Nation* (Glasgow: MacLehose, 1903), p. 223.

[6] *The Three Voyages of Martin Frobisher . . .,* ed. by R. Collinson (London: Hakluyt Soc., 1867), p. 70.

[7] Cited by C. Wilson, *Profit and Power* (London: Longmans, 1957), p. 134.

[8] Cited by J. H. Parry, *Europe and a Wider World, 1415–1715* (London: Hutchinson, 1949), p. 145.

[9] Cited by E. Wingfield-Stratford, *History of British Civilization,* 2nd ed. (London: Routledge, 1930), pp. 313–14.

[10] Cited by W. L. Dorn, *Competition for Empire, 1740–1763* (New York: Harper, 1940), p. 114.

[11] J. R. Green, *A Short History of England,* rev. ed. (London: American, 1916), p. 758.

CHAPTER 8

[1] M. Gorki, *In the World* (London: Laurie, 1917), p. 57. Reprinted by permission of The Bodley Head, Ltd.

[2] S. Aksakov, *A Russian Gentleman* (London: Oxford Univ., 1923), pp. 2–4.

[3] N. V. Gogol, *Taras Bulba* (New York: Crowell, 1886), pp. 18–20.

[4] L. Wiener, ed., *Anthology of Russian Literature,* I (New York: Putnam's, 1902), pp. 173–74.

[5] R. J. Kerner, *The Urge to the Sea* (Berkeley: Univ. of Calif., 1942), p. 86.
[6] Cited by G. V. Lantzeff, *Siberia in the Seventeenth Century* (Berkeley: Univ. of Calif., 1940), p. 105.
[7] D. W. Treadgold, *The Great Siberian Migration* (Princeton: Princeton Univ., 1957), p. 32.
[8] B. Pares, *A History of Russia*, rev. ed. (New York: Knopf, 1953), p. 121.

CHAPTER 9

[1] B. H. M. Vlekke, *Nusantara, A History of the East Indian Archipelago* (Cambridge: Harvard Univ., 1943), p. 198.
[2] Cited by A. Reichwein, *China and Europe: Intellectual and Artistic Contacts in the Eighteenth Century* (New York: Knopf, 1925), p. 17.
[3] Cited by F. Whyte, *China and Foreign Powers* (London: Oxford Univ., 1927), p. 38.
[4] Cited by R. Pearson, *Eastern Interlude: A Social History of the European Community in Calcutta* (Calcutta: Thacker, 1954), p. 64.
[5] Cited by A. I. Hallowell, "The Backwash of the Frontier: The Impact of the Indian on American Culture," in W. D. Wyman and C. B. Kroeber, *The Frontier in Perspective* (Madison: Univ. of Wisconsin, 1957), p. 235.
[6] Cited *ibid.*, p. 232.
[7] Cited by J. C. de Graft-Johnson, *African Glory: The Story of Vanished Negro Civilizations* (London: Watts, 1954), p. 129.
[8] Cited by A. C. Wood, *A History of the Levant Company* (London: Oxford Univ., 1935), p. 230.
[9] Cited by W. G. East and O. H. K. Spate, *Changing Map of Asia* (New York: Dutton, 1957), p. 14.
[10] Cited by L. S. S. O'Malley, ed., *Modern India and the West* (New York: Oxford Univ., 1941), p. 51.
[11] Cited by S. Teng and J. K. Fairbank, *China's Response to the West: A Documentary Survey, 1839–1923* (Cambridge: Harvard Univ., 1954), p. 12. Reprinted by permission of the publishers. Copyright 1954 by the President and Fellows of Harvard College.
[12] Cited by G. B. Sansom, *The Western World and Japan* (New York: Knopf, 1951), p. 14.
[13] H. Blount, "A Voyage into the Levant," in J. Pinkerton, ed., *A General Collection of the Best and Most Interesting Voyages. . .*, X (London: 1808–1814), p. 222.
[14] Cited by D. Lach, "Leibniz and China," *Journal of the History of Ideas*, VI (October, 1945), 440.
[15] Cited by Reichwein, *op. cit.*, p. 152.
[16] F. Bernier, *Travels in the Mogul Empire*, tr. by A. Constable and V. A. Smith (London: Oxford Univ., 1916), pp. 472–73.
[17] Cited by O'Malley, *op. cit.*, p. 546.
[18] Cited by Reichwein, *op. cit.*, p. 151.

CHAPTER 10

[1] J. B. Conant, *Science and Common Sense* (New Haven: Yale Univ., 1951), p. 25.
[2] Cited by J. U. Nef, "The Genesis of Industrialism and of Modern Science (1560–1640)," in N. Downs, ed., *Essays in Honor of Conyers Read* (Chicago: Univ. of Chicago, 1953), p. 225.
[3] Cited by F. L. V. Baumer, ed., *Main Currents of Western Thought* (New York: Knopf, 1954), p. 251.
[4] Cited by J. D. Bernal, *Science in History* (London: Watts, 1954), pp. 277–78.
[5] Joseph Glanvill, *Vanity of Dogmatizing*. Cited by M. H. Carré, "The Old Order and the New: The Intellectual Revolution of the Seventeenth Century," *History Today*, V (April, 1955), 261.
[6] T. Sprat, *The History of the Royal Society of London, for the Improving of General Knowledge* (London, 1734), p. 72.
[7] *De revolutionibus orbium coelestium*, Lib. 1, Cap. X, tr. by W. C. D. and M. D. Whetham, *Readings in the Literature of Science* (Cambridge: Cambridge Univ., 1924), p. 13.
[8] *Sidereus nuncius*, tr. by E. S. Carlos (1880). Cited by M. Nicolson, *Science and Imagination* (Ithica: Cornell Univ., 1956), p. 15.

9 A complimentary poem of Johannes Faber. Cited by Nicolson, *op. cit.,* p. 19.

10 Cited *ibid.,* p. 30.

11 P. Rousseau, *Histoire de la science* (Paris, 1945), p. 249. Cited by J. B. Wolf, *The Emergence of the Great Powers, 1685–1715* (New York: Harper, 1951), pp. 212–13.

12 *Novum Organum,* Aphorism 81.

13 William Stukeley, *Memoirs of Sir Isaac Newton's Life,* ed. by A. Hastings White (London: Oxford Univ., 1936), pp. 19–20. Cited by A. R. Hall, *The Scientific Revolution, 1500–1800* (Boston: Beacon, 1954), pp. 248–49.

14 In *Ignorant Philosopher.* Cited by W. C. Dampier, *A History of Science and its Relations with Philosophy and Religion* (New York: Macmillan, 1944), p. 214.

15 Cited by W. C. Dampier, *A Shorter History of Science* (New York: Meridian, 1957), p. 87.

16 *Elements of Chemistry,* trans. Robert Kerr (Edinburgh, 1790). Cited by Hall, *op. cit.,* p. 332.

17 H. Spencer, *Illustrations of Universal Progress* (New York, 1865), p. 3.

18 Cited by Dampier, *A History of Science,* p. 295.

19 *Life and Letters of Charles Darwin,* ed. by Francis Darwin, Vol. I (New York: Appleton, 1897, 1898, 1919), p. 384.

20 *Ibid.,* p. 473.

21 Charles Darwin, *Origin of Species,* Vol. I (New York: 1872), p. 3.

22 Charles Russell and Alfred Russell Wallace, *Evolution by Natural Selection* (Cambridge: Cambridge Univ., 1958), p. 22.

23 Charles Darwin, *The Descent of Man and Selection in Relation to Sex* (New York: Appleton, 1888), pp. 630–31.

24 Cited by H. S. Dinerstein, "The Sovietization of Uzbekistan," p. 503 in Hugh McLean, Martin E. Malia, and George Fischer, editors, *Russian Thought and Politics,* Harvard Slavic Studies, Vol. IV. Reprinted by permission of the publishers. Copyright 1957 by the President and Fellows of Harvard College.

25 H. Butterfield, *The Origins of Modern Science, 1300–1800* (London: Bell, 1957), p. 179.

CHAPTER 11

1 Cited by E. Williams, *Capitalism and Slavery* (Chapel Hill: Univ. of North Carolina, 1944), p. 83.

2 Cited by S. B. Clough and C. W. Cole, *Economic History of Europe,* 3rd ed. (Boston: Heath, 1952), p. 271.

3 In E. Lipson, *The History of the Woollen and Worsted Industries* (London: Black, 1921), pp. 46–47.

4 John Maynard Keynes, *A Treatise on Money,* Vol. II (New York: Harcourt, 1930), p. 156.

5 Cited by Williams, *op. cit.,* p. 61.

6 Clough and Cole, *op. cit.,* p. 66.

7 Cited by J. U. Nef, *War and Human Progress* (Cambridge: Harvard Univ., 1952), p. 10.

8 Voltaire to Abbé d' Olivet. *Ibid.,* p. 277.

9 Cited by H. Heaton, *Economic History of Europe,* rev. ed. (New York: Harper, 1948), p. 484.

10 *Ibid.,* p. 541.

11 W. Lippmann, *Preface to Morals* (New York: Macmillan, 1929), p. 235.

12 Cited by J. Mirsky and Allan Nevins, *The World of Eli Whitney* (New York: Macmillan, 1952), p. 216.

13 C. Merz, *And Then Came Ford* (New York: Doubleday, 1929), pp. 198–99. Copyright 1929 by Doubleday & Company, Inc. Reprinted by permission of the publisher.

14 E. C. Kirkland, *History of American Economic Life* (New York: Crofts, 1932), pp. 453–54.

15 Cited by L. Huberman, *We, the People,* rev. ed. (New York: Harper, 1947), p. 218.

16 *Parliamentary Papers,* 1842, vols. XV–XVII, Appendix I, p. 252.

17 T. S. Ashton, cited by E. E. Lampard, *Industrial Revolution: Interpretations and Perspectives* (Washington: Service Center for Teachers of History, 1957), p. 31.

18 B. Disraeli, *Sybil, or the Two Nations* (London: Macmillan, 1895), p. 74.

19 Cited by S. Zavala, "The Frontiers of Hispanic America," in *The Frontier in Perspective,* ed. by W. D. Wyman and C. B. Kroeber (Madison: Univ. of Wisconsin, 1957), p. 40.

20 Cited by Huberman, *op. cit.,* p. 259.

[21] *Ibid.*, p. 263.
[22] W. L. Langer, *Diplomacy of Imperialism 1890–1902*, 2nd ed. (New York: Knopf, 1935), p. 67.
[23] Phyllis Deane, *Colonial Social Accounting* (Cambridge: Cambridge Univ., 1953), p. 37.

CHAPTER 12

[1] Cited by G. Wint, *The British in Asia* (New York: Institute of Pacific Relations, 1954), p. 18.
[2] Sir Edwin Sandys, in a speech in Parliament. Cited by H. J. Laski, *The Rise of Liberalism* (New York: Harper, 1936), p. 117.
[3] C. V. Wedgewood, *The Common Man in the Great Civil War* (Leicester: Leicester University Press, 1957), p. 22.
[4] *Ibid.*, p. 7.
[5] P. Zagorin, "The English Revolution, 1640–1660," *Journal of World History*, II (1955), 907.
[6] *Ibid.*, 908.
[7] A. S. P. Woodhouse, *Puritanism and Liberty* (London: Dent, 1938), p. 55.
[8] Adam Smith, *An Inquiry into the Nature and Causes of the Wealth of Nations*, ed. J. E. T. Rogers, Vol. II (Oxford: Clarendon, 1869), p. 272.
[9] G. P. Noyes, ed., *The Life and Adventures of Dimitrije Obradović* (Berkeley: Univ. of California, 1953), p. 243.
[10] A. P. Whitaker, *Latin America and the Enlightenment* (New York: Appleton, 1942), p. 48.
[11] K. M. Khalid, *From Here We Start* (Washington: American Council of Learned Societies, 1953), p. 30.
[12] E. C. Channing and A. C. Coolidge, eds., *The Barrington-Bernard Correspondence* (Cambridge: Harvard Univ., 1912), pp. 96–98. Cited by E. Robson, "The American Revolution Reconsidered," *History Today*, II (February, 1952), 127–28.
[18] D. E. Wheller, ed., *Life and Writings of Thomas Paine*, Vol. II (New York: Vincent Perke, 1908), pp. 43, 58, 92.
[14] Cited by H. Koht, *The American Spirit in Europe* (Philadelphia: Univ. of Pennsylvania, 1949), p. 18.
[15] Cited by M. Kraus, *The North Atlantic Civilization* (Princeton: Van Nostrand, 1957), p. 34.
[16] *Ibid.*, p. 35.
[17] *Ibid.*, pp. 36–37.
[18] Cited by Koht, *op. cit.*, p. 7.
[19] Cited by G. Lefebvre, *The Coming of the French Revolution* (New York: Vintage, 1957), p. 157.
[20] Cited by B. C. Shafer, *Nationalism: Myth and Reality* (New York: Harcourt, 1955), pp. 120–21.
[21] Cited by T. C. Mendenhall *et al.*, *The Quest for a Principle of Authority in Europe, 1715–Present* (New York: Holt, 1948), p. 83.
[22] Cited by I. Deutscher, "The French Revolution and the Russian Revolution: Some Suggestive Analogies," *World Politics* IV (April, 1952), 376.
[23] T. Kolokotrones and E. M. Edmonds, *Kolokotrones, Klepht and Warrior* (London: 1892), pp. 127–28.
[24] Shafer, *op. cit.*, p. 105.
[25] Cited *ibid.*, p. 147.
[26] H. Kohn, *Nationalism: Its Meaning and History* (Princeton: Van Nostrand, Anvil Book, 1955), p. 89.
[27] Cited by H. J. Laski, *The Rise of Liberalism* (New York: Harper, 1936), p. 262.
[28] Cited by D. W. Morris, *The Christian Origins of Social Revolt* (London: Allen, 1949), p. 34.
[29] Cited by G. L. Mosse *et al.*, *Europe in Review* (Chicago: Rand McNally, 1957), p. 300.
[30] Karl Marx and Friedrich Engels, *Communist Manifesto* (New York: League for Industrial Democracy, 1933), p. 56.
[31] *Ibid.*, pp. 59–60.

CHAPTER 13

[1] Cited by B. Pares, *A History of Russia* (New York: Knopf, 1953), p. 117.
[2] Cited by H. Lamb, *March of Muscovy* (New York: Doubleday, 1948), p. 177.
[3] From pp. 18–24 of *Potemkin* (New York: Norton, 1947) by George Soloveytchik, whose permission to reprint this selection is gratefully acknowledged.
[4] Cited by F. Nowak, *Medieval Slavdom and the Rise of Russia* (New York: Holt, 1930), p. 91.
[5] Cited by A. G. Mazour, *The First Russian Revolution, 1825* (Berkeley: Univ. of Calif., 1937), pp. 55–56.
[6] Cited in H. Kohn, *The Mind of Modern Russia* (New Brunswick: Rutgers Univ., 1955), p. 64.
[7] *Ibid.*, pp. 51–52.
[8] Cited by D. M. Wallace, *Russia*, rev. ed. (London: Cassell, 1912), p. 442.
[9] G. T. Robinson, *Rural Russia under the Old Regime* (New York: Macmillan, 1932), p. 64.
[10] Cited by J. Mavor, *An Economic History of Russia*, Vol. II (New York: Dutton, 1925), p. 41.
[11] *Ibid.*, p. 402.
[12] E. J. Dillon, cited in M. Hindus, *The Russian Peasant and the Revolution* (New York: Holt, 1920), p. 214.
[13] Cited by F. A. Golden, *Russian Expansion on the Pacific, 1641–1850* (Cleveland: Clark, 1914), p. 134.
[14] Lord Curzon, *Russia in Central Asia* (London, 1859), p. 318.
[15] Cited by I. Spector, *The First Russian Revolution* (Englewood Cliffs: Prentice-Hall, Spectrum, 1962), p. 1.
[16] Cited by T. H. Von Laue, *Why Lenin? Why Stalin? A Reappraisal of the Russian Revolution, 1900–1930* (Philadelphia: Lippincott, 1964), p. 53.
[17] *Ibid.*, p. 79.

CHAPTER 14

[1] Cited by G. K. Kordatos, *Regas Pheraios kai he Balkaniki homospondia* [*Rhigas Pheraios and Balkan Federation*] (Athens, 1945), p. 28.
[2] S. S. Wilson, *A Narrative of the Greek Mission* (London, 1839), p. 206.
[3] Ch. Photios, *Apomnemoneumata peri tes Hellenikes Epanastaseos* [*Memoirs on the Greek Revolution*], Vol. I (Athens, 1899), p. 1.
[4] W. Eton, *A Survey of the Turkish Empire*, 4th ed. (London, 1809), p. 192.
[5] E. F. Knight, *Turkey: The Awakening of Turkey: The Turkish Revolution of 1908* (Boston, 1910), pp. 109–13.
[6] Lowther to Grey, Aug. 4, 1908. *British Documents on the Origins of the War 1898–1914*, V, 265.
[7] Cited by H. Temperley, "British Policy Towards Parliamentary Rule and Constitutionalism in Turkey," *Cambridge Historical Journal*, IV (1932), 186.
[8] Cited by Abdel-Aziz Abdel-Meguid, "The Impact of Western Culture and Civilization on the Arab World," *Islamic Quarterly*, II (December, 1955), 289.
[9] Cited by G. Antonius, *The Arab Awakening* (New York: Lippincott, 1939), p. 31.
[10] Cited by W. L. Langer, *European Alliances and Alignments 1871–1890*, 2nd ed. (New York: Knopf, 1956), p. 281.
[11] Cited by Z. N. Zeine, *Arab-Turkish Relations and the Emergence of Arab Nationalism* (Beirut: Khayat's, 1958), p. 64.
[12] Cited by T. C. Young, ed., *Near Eastern Culture and Society* (Princeton: Princeton Univ., 1951), pp. 136, 137.
[13] E. G. Browne, *The Persian Revolution of 1905–1909* (London: Cambridge Univ., 1910), pp. xix–xx.

CHAPTER 15

[1] Cited by L. S. S. O'Malley, ed., *Modern India and the West* (New York: Oxford Univ., 1941), p. 14.

[2] Cited by P. Spear, *India, Pakistan, and the West* (London: Home Univ. Lib., 1958), pp. 132–133.

[3] E. J. Thompson and G. T. Garratt, *Rise and Fulfillment of British Rule in India* (London: Macmillan, 1934), pp. 91–92.

[4] Cited by K. M. Panikkar, *Asia and Western Dominance* (London: G. Allen; New York: Day, 1953), p. 101.

[5] *Ibid.*, p. 106.

[6] Cited by G. Wint, *The British in Asia* (New York: Inst. of Pacific Relations, 1954), p. 23.

[7] Cited by K. Goshal, *The People of India* (New York: Sheridan, 1944), p. 129.

[8] *Ibid.*, p. 130.

[9] Cited in A. B. Keith, ed., *Speeches & Documents on Indian Policy 1750–1921* (London: Oxford Univ., 1922), I, 209.

[10] Cited by W. T. de Bary *et al.*, *Sources of Indian Tradition* (New York: Columbia Univ., 1958), p. 590.

[11] *Ibid.*, p. 593.

[12] *Ibid.*, p. 601.

[13] John Strachey, *The End of Empire* (New York: Praeger, 1964), p. 55.

[14] Cited by O'Malley, *op. cit.*, p. 740.

[15] *Ibid.*, p. 741.

[16] D. Naoroji, *Speeches and Writings* (Madras: Natesan, N. D.), p. 2.

[17] Cited by Goshal, *op. cit.*, pp. 168–169.

CHAPTER 16

[1] Cited by K. M. Panikkar, *Asia and Western Dominance* (London: G. Allen; New York: Day, 1953), p. 133.

[2] S. Teng and J. K. Fairbank, *China's Response to the West: A Documentary Survey, 1839–1923* (Cambridge: Harvard Univ., 1954), p. 26. Reprinted by permission of the publishers. Copyright 1954 by the President and Fellows of Harvard College.

[3] *Ibid.*, p. 28.

[4] Cited by E. Swisher, "Chinese Intellectuals and the Western Impact, 1838–1900," *Comparative Studies in Science and History,* I (October, 1958), 35.

[5] Cited by Panikkar, *op. cit.*, p. 183.

[6] Teng and Fairbank, *op. cit.*, pp. 163–64.

[7] Cited by J. R. Levenson, *Confucian China and Its Modern Fate* (Berkeley: Univ. of Calif., 1958), p. 105.

[8] Cited by J. K. Fairbank, "China's Response to the West: Problems and Suggestions," *Journal of World History,* III (1956), 403.

[9] Cited by J. K. Fairbank, *The United States and China* (Cambridge: Harvard Univ., 1958), p. 150.

[10] Cited by N. Peffer, *The Far East* (Ann Arbor: Univ. of Mich., 1958), p. 236.

[11] *Ibid.*, pp. 240–41.

[12] Cited by C. R. Boxer, "Sakoku, or the Closed Country, 1640–1854," *History Today,* VII (February, 1957), 85.

[13] Cited by Panikkar, *op. cit.*, pp. 205–6.

[14] In R. Tsunoda *et al.*, *Sources of the Japanese Tradition* (New York: Columbia Univ., 1958), p. 644.

[15] G. B. Sansom, *The Western World and Japan* (New York: Knopf, 1951), p. 383.

[16] *The Japan Year Book, 1939–1940* (Tokyo: Foreign Affairs Assoc. of Japan, 1939), p. 633.

[17] Cited by R. F. Hackett, "Nishi Aurane—A Tokugawa—Meiji Bureaucrat," *Journal of Asian Studies,* XVIII (February, 1959), 224.

[18] Teng and Fairbank, *op. cit.*, pp. 126–27.

CHAPTER 17

[1] G. A. de Azurara, *The Chronicle of the Discovery and Conquest of Guinea,* tr. by C. Beazley and E. Prestage, Vol. I (London: Hakluyt Soc., 1896), pp. 84–85.

[2] Cited by H. Russell, *Human Cargoes* (London: Longmans, 1948), p. 36.

[3] Cited *ibid.*, p. 36.

4 Cited *ibid.*, p. 40.
5 Cited by T. W. Wallbank, *Contemporary Africa* (Princeton: Van Nostrand, 1956) p. 25.
6 Cited by J. H. Plumb, "The Niger Quest," *History Today*, II (April, 1952), 247.
7 Cited by W. L. Langer, *European Alliances and Alignments, 1871–1890*, 2nd ed. (New York: Knopf, 1956), p. 286.
8 Cited by J. Holland Rose, *The Development of the European Nations*, Part II (New York: Putnam, 1916), p. 268.
9 Cited by L. Bauer, *Leopold the Unloved* (Boston: Little, 1935), p. 264.
10 Cited by P. Mitchell, "Africa and the West in Historical Perspective," *Africa Today*, ed. by C. G. Haines (Baltimore: Hopkins, 1955), p. 11.
11 Cited by T. Hodgkin, *Nationalism in Colonial Africa* (New York: New York Univ., 1957), p. 98.

CHAPTER 18

1 William Knox, Under-Secretary for the American Department, cited in C. Martin, *Empire and Commonwealth* (Oxford: Clarendon, 1929), p. 108.
2 Earl of Durham, *Report on the Affairs of British North America* (Ordered by the House of Commons to be Printed, February 11, 1839), p. 100.
3 G. I. Blanksten, *Ecuador: Constitutions and Caudillos* (Berkeley: Univ. of California, 1951), p. 36.
4 Russell to Poulett Thomson, Oct. 14, 1839. W. P. M. Kennedy, ed., *Statutes, Treaties and Documents of the Canadian Constitution 1713–1929* (London: Oxford Univ., 1930), pp. 421–22.
5 Earl Grey to Sir John Harvey, Nov. 3, 1846. *Ibid.*, pp. 494–95.
6 Elgin to Bruce, September, 1852. *Ibid.*, p. 514.
7 Cited by J. A. Williamson, *A Short History of British Expansion*, Vol. II (London: Macmillan, 1930), p. 76.
8 Instructions to Governor Murray, Dec. 7, 1763, in Kennedy, *op. cit.*, p. 49.
9 H. G. Ward, *Mexico in 1827*, Vol. II (London, 1828), pp. 481–82.
10 From Mackenzie's paper, *Constitution* (Mar. 1, 1837).
11 H. L. Stoddard, *It Costs to be President* (New York: Harper, 1938), p. 164.
12 T. L. Nichols, *Forty Years of American Life, 1821–1861* (Harrisburg: Stackpole, 1937, first published in 1864), p. 63.
13 *Ibid.*, p. 46.
14 *The Education of Henry Adams: An Autobiography* (London: Constable, 1919), pp. 319–20.
15 V. L. Parrington, *Main Currents in American Thought*, Vol. III (New York: Harcourt, 1930), p. 86.
16 H. C. Lodge, *Studies of History* (Boston, 1884), p. 352. Cited by H. L. Mencken, *The American Language: An Inquiry into the Development of English in the United States*, 4th ed. (New York: Knopf, 1946), pp. 20–21.
17 J. MacCormac, *Canada: America's Problem* (New York: Viking, 1940), p. 199.
18 *Report, Royal Commission on National Development in the Arts, Letters and Sciences, 1949–1951* (Ottawa: 1951), p. 18.
19 *New York Times* (Nov. 16, 1959).

CHAPTER 19

1 O. M. Utieshenovich, *Die Hauskommunionen der Südslaven* (Vienna, 1859), p. 128.
2 Surendranath Banerjea, cited in L. S. S. O'Malley, *Modern India and the West* (New York: Oxford Univ., 1941), p. 766.
3 From "The White Man's Burden" in *Rudyard Kipling's Verse: Definitive Edition.* Reprinted by permission of Mrs. George Bambridge and Doubleday & Company, Inc.
4 Arnold Toynbee, *Civilization on Trial* (New York: World, 1958), p. 27. Meridian Books.
5 Cited by R. Emerson, *From Empire to Nation* (Cambridge: Harvard Univ., 1960), p. 403.
6 W. T. Stead, *The Last Will and Testament of Cecil John Rhodes* (London: 1902), p. 190.
7 E. G. Browne, *The Persian Revolution of 1905–1909* (Cambridge, at the University Press, 1910), pp. 120, 122, 123.

[8] G. H. Fitzmaurice to Mr. Tyrell, Aug. 25, 1908, in G. P. Gooch and Harold Temperley, eds., *British Documents on the Origins of the War 1898–1914*, X, No. 210 (London:H.M.S.O., 1936), p. 268.
[9] Cited by I. Spector, *The First Russian Revolution: Its Impact on Asia* (Englewood Cliffs: Prentice-Hall, 1962), pp. 70–71. A Spectrum Book.
[10] Cited *ibid.*, p. 81.
[11] *Ibid.*, p. 89.
[12] *Ibid.*, p. 94.

CHAPTER 20

[1] Cited by L. Albertini, *The Origins of the War of 1914*, Vol. II tr. and ed. by I. H. Massey (London: Oxford, 1953), p. 49.
[2] Cited by S. B. Fay, *The Origins of the World War*, Vol. II 2nd rev. ed. (New York: Macmillan, 1930), p. 87.
[3] Cited by Albertini, *op. cit.*, p. 21.
[4] Cited by J. C. Adams, *Flight in Winter* (Princeton: Princeton Univ., 1942), p. 29.
[5] H. Morgenthau, *Ambassador Morgenthau's Story* (New York: Doubleday, 1918), p. 225.
[6] Cited in F. A. Golder, *Documents of Russian History, 1914–1917* (New York: Appleton, 1927), p. 36.
[7] Cited *ibid.*, p. 37.
[8] M. Paleologue, *An Ambassador's Memoirs* (New York: Doubleday, 1925), I, 222; II, 34.
[9] Cited by M. T. Florinsky, *The End of the Russian Empire* (New Haven: Yale Univ., 1931), p. 208.
[10] Cited *ibid.*, p. 247.
[11] Winston Churchill, *The Second World War: The Gathering Storm* (Boston: Houghton, 1948), p. 10.
[12] Cited by R. S. Baker, *Woodrow Wilson and World Settlement*, Vol. III (New York: Doubleday, 1922), p. 451.
[13] Charles Seymour, ed., *The Intimate Papers of Colonel House*, Vol. IV (Boston: Houghton, 1928), p. 389.
[14] R. Delavignette, *Freedom and Authority in French West Africa* (New York: Oxford Univ., 1950), p. 149.
[15] Cited by K. M. Panikkar, *Asia and Western Dominance* (New York: Day, 1953), p. 262.
[16] Cited *ibid.*, p. 364.

CHAPTER 21

[1] Cited by H. Kohn, *A History of Nationalism in the East* (New York: Harcourt, 1929), p. 257.
[2] H. Ammar, *Growing up in an Egyptian Village* (London: Routledge, 1954), pp. 72, 73.
[3] Cited by M. Burrows, *Palestine Is Our Business* (Philadelphia: Westminster, 1949), p. 44.
[4] Cited by W. R. Polk, "What the Arabs Think," *Headline Series*, No. 96, p. 38.
[5] Cited by A. J. Toynbee, *Survey of International Affairs, 1925. Vol. I: The Islamic World Since the Peace Settlement* (London: Oxford Univ., Royal Institute of International Affairs, 1927), p. 134.
[6] J. M. Balfour, *Recent Happenings in Persia* (London: Blackwood, 1922), p. 145.
[7] M. K. Gandhi, *An Autobiography* (Boston: Beacon, 1957), p. 448.
[8] *Toward Freedom: The Autobiography of Jawaharlal Nehru* (New York: Day, 1941), p. 232.
[9] *Ibid.*, p. 314.

CHAPTER 22

[1] G. F. Kennan, *Russia and the West under Lenin and Stalin* (Boston: Little, 1960), p. 117.
[2] E. A. Mowrer, *Germany Puts the Clock Back* (New York: Morrow, 1933), pp. 17, 18.

CHAPTER 23

1 Cited by S. and B. Webb, *Soviet Communism: A New Civilization,* Vol. II (London: Gollancz, 1937), p. 605.
2 Cited by J. Maynard, *Russia in Flux* (New York: Macmillan, 1949), p. 218.
3 Harrison E. Salisbury in *The New York Times* (Sept. 29, 1953). © 1953 by The New York Times Company. Reprinted by permission.
4 Cited by J. K. Galbraith, *The Great Crash, 1929* (Boston: Houghton, 1955), pp. 75, 20.
5 F. Sternberg, *Capitalism and Socialism on Trial* (New York: Day, 1951), p. 281.
6 J. P. Goebbels, *My Part in Germany's Flight* (London: Hurst, 1935), pp. 180–82.
7 *Ibid.,* p. 248.
8 London *Times* (Feb. 4, 1932).

CHAPTER 24

1 The *China Critic* (Shanghai), IV (1931), 924.
2 Cited by H. Gannes, *When China Unites* (New York: Knopf, 1937), p. 142.
3 Adolf Hitler, *Mein Kampf,* tr. by R. Manheim (Boston: Houghton, 1943), pp. 611, 649, 654, 140.
4 Cited by V. Yakhontoff, *USSR Foreign Policy* (New York: Coward, 1945), p. 109.
5 Cited by Anthony Eden, *Facing the Dictators* (Boston: Houghton, 1962), p. 425.
6 *Ibid.,* p. 136.
7 Cited by *Bulletin of International News,* XII (July 27, 1935), 7.
8 Cited by Eden, *op. cit.,* p. 293.
9 *Ibid.,* p. 368.
10 Paul Schmidt, *Hitler's Interpreter* (London: Heinemann, 1951), p. 60.
11 Winston S. Churchill, *The Second World War: The Gathering Storm* (Boston: Houghton, 1948), p. 197.
12 *Ibid.,* pp. 221–22.
13 Schmidt, *op. cit.,* p. 110.
14 Churchill, *op. cit.,* p. 251.
15 Eden, *op. cit.,* p. 636.
16 K. von Schuschnigg, *Austrian Requiem* (New York: Putnam, 1946), pp. 16–17.
17 *Ibid.,* p. 36.
18 *Bulletin of International News,* XV (Mar. 5, 1938), 9.
19 K. Feiling, *The Life of Neville Chamberlain* (London: Macmillan, 1946), p. 403.
20 Churchill, *op. cit.,* p. 376.
21 W. L. Langer and S. E. Gleason, *The Challenge to Isolation, 1937–1940* (New York: Harper, 1952), p. 181.
22 A. J. P. Taylor, *The Origins of the Second World War* (London: Hamilton, 1961), p. 263.
23 *New York Times* (Aug. 27, 1939).

CHAPTER 25

1 Cited by A. Dallin, "The Fateful Pact: Prelude to World War II," *New York Times Magazine* (Aug. 21, 1949), p. 40.
2 Cited by G. L. Weinberg, *Germany and the Soviet Union, 1939–1941* (Leiden: Brill, 1954), p. 115.
3 *Ciano's Diary 1939–1943,* ed. by Malcom Muggeridge (London: Heinemann, 1947), p. 297.
4 R. J. Sontag and J. S. Beddie, *Nazi-Soviet Relations, 1939–1941* (New York: Didier, 1948), pp. 260–61.
5 Ernest von Weizäcker, cited by Weinberg, *op. cit.,* p. 163.
6 Cited by Dallin, *op. cit.,* p. 40.
7 Winston S. Churchill, *The Second World War: The Grand Alliance* (Boston: Houghton, 1950), p. 620.
8 Winston S. Churchill, *The Second World War: The Hinge of Fate* (Boston: Houghton, 1950), p. 92.

CHAPTER 26

[1] Winston S. Churchill, *The Second World War: The Grand Alliance* (Boston: Houghton, 1950), p. 373.
[2] Winston S. Churchill, *The Second World War: Triumph and Tragedy* (Boston: Houghton, 1953), p. 286.
[3] J. F. Byrnes, *Speaking Frankly* (New York: Harper, 1947), p. 73.
[4] P. E. Mosely, "Face to Face with Russia," *Headline Series,* No. 70 (July–August, 1948), p. 23.
[5] Byrnes, *op. cit.,* pp. 73–74.
[6] April 23, 1949. *United States Relations with China. . . . Department of State Publication 3573, Far Eastern Series 30* (Washington, D.C., 1949), p. 305.

CHAPTER 27

[1] Cited by H. Luethy, *France Against Herself* (New York: World, 1955; a Meridan paperback), p. 218.
[2] J. Nehru, *The Discovery of India* (New York: Day, 1946), p. 432.
[3] Jamil-ud-Din Ahmad, ed., *Some Recent Speeches . . . of Mr. Jinnah,* Vol. I (Lahore: Sh. Muhammad Ashraf, 1943), p. 180.
[4] Lloyd Garrison in *The New York Times* (Dec. 16, 1963).
[5] A. H. Hourani, *Syria and Lebanon* (London: Oxford Univ., Royal Institute of International Affairs, 1946), pp. 230–31.
[6] Cited by J. Strachey, *The End of Empire* (London: Gollancz, 1959), p. 146.
[7] Cited by *Toward Freedom,* XII, No. 7 (July–August, 1963).

CHAPTER 28

[1] *The New York Times* (Feb. 1, 1964).
[2] "Pax Atomica: Looking to '64," *Newsweek* (Jan. 6, 1964), p. 11. Copyright Newsweek, Inc., January, 1964. "France: A Return to Greatness," *Newsweek* (Feb. 2, 1964), p. 40. Copyright Newsweek, Inc., February, 1964.
[3] *The Soviet-Yugoslav Dispute: Text of the Published Correspondence* (New York: Oxford Univ., Royal Institute of International Affairs, 1948), pp. 35, 36.
[4] *The New York Times* (May 24, 1964).
[5] Cited by J. Jacquet-Francillon, "The Borders of China: Mao's Bold Challenge to Khrushchev," *New Republic* (Apr. 20, 1963), p. 18. © 1963, Harrison-Blaine of New Jersey, Inc.
[6] Edgar Snow, *The Other Side of the River: Red China Today* (New York: Random, 1961), p. 662.
[7] *Chicago Sun-Times* (Jan. 20, 1963).
[8] *The New York Times* (Jan. 21, 1964).
[9] *The New York Times* (Feb. 7, 1964). © 1964 by The New York Times Company. Reprinted by permission.

CHAPTER 29

[1] *The New York Times* (Jan. 20, 1964).
[2] "UAR Plans Growth Through Science," *Arab World* (July–August, 1963), p. 15.
[3] Dana Adams Schmidt in *The New York Times* (Dec. 29, 1959).
[4] Dana Adams Schmidt in *The New York Times* (June 8, 1964). © 1964 by The New York Times Company. Reprinted by permission.
[5] Cited by D. Lerner, *The Passing of Traditional Society: Modernizing the Middle East* (New York: Free Press, 1958), p. 214.
[6] A. S. Feldman and W. E. Moore, "Industrialization and Industrialism: Convergence

and Differentiation" *Transactions of the Fifth World Congress of Sociology,* Vol. II
(Washington, D.C., International Sociological Association, 1962), p. 155.
[7] Cited by *The Times Literary Supplement* (Sept. 27, 1963), p. 745.

CHAPTER 30

[1] Cited by J. G. Lockhardt and C. M. Woodhouse, *Rhodes* (London: Hodder, 1963), pp. 36–37.
[2] Barbara Ward, "Race Relations as a World Issue," *The New York Times Magazine* (Nov. 11, 1956), p. 12.
[3] Mailhard de la Couture, ed., *Chroniques de Villehardouin et de Henri de Valenciennes, De la Conquête de Constantinople* (Paris, 1889), pp. 63–64.
[4] *The New York Times* (Mar. 25, 1964).
[5] H. Cantril, "A Study of Aspirations," *Scientific American* (February, 1963), p. 41.
[6] *The New York Times* (July 11, 1962).
[7] Arnold J. Toynbee, "Not the Age of Atoms But of Welfare for All," *The New York Times Magazine* (Oct. 21, 1951), p. 15.
[8] *The New York Times* (Apr. 22, 1964).
[9] Walter Lippmann in *Chicago Sun-Times* (May 26, 1964).
[10] Lacey Baldwin Smith, *A Tudor Tragedy* (London: Cape, 1961), p. 84.

Index

8, 13, 21-30